Dodge Caravan & Plymouth Voyager Automotive Repair Manual

by Curt Choate, Mike Stubblefield and John H Haynes
Member of the Guild of Motoring Writers

Models covered:
Dodge Caravan/Mini Ram Van, Plymouth Voyager, and Chrysler Town and Country
1984 through 1995
Does not include four-wheel drive information

(3Z11 - 30010)
(1231)

ABCDE
FGHIJ
KLMNO
P   2

Haynes Publishing Group
Sparkford Nr Yeovil
Somerset BA22 7JJ England

Haynes North America, Inc
861 Lawrence Drive
Newbury Park
California 91320 USA

Acknowledgements

We are grateful to the Chrysler Corporation for assistance with technical information, certain illustrations and vehicle photos. Technical writers who contributed to this project include Robert Maddox, Larry Warren and Doug Nelson.

A book in the **Haynes Automotive Repair Manual Series**

Printed in the U.S.A.

ISBN 1 56392 132 4

Library of Congress Catalog Card Number 94-79927

While every attempt is made to ensure that the information in this manual is correct, no liability can be accepted by the authors or publishers for loss, damage or injury caused by any errors in, or omissions from, the information given.

Contents

1989 Plymouth Grand Voyager LE

About this manual

Its purpose

The purpose of this manual is to help you get the best value from your vehicle. It can do so in several ways. It can help you decide what work must be done, even if you choose to have it done by a dealer service department or a repair shop; it provides information and procedures for routine maintenance and servicing; and it offers diagnostic and repair procedures to follow when trouble occurs.

We hope you use the manual to tackle the work yourself. For many simpler jobs, doing it yourself may be quicker than arranging an appointment to get the vehicle into a shop and making the trips to leave it and pick it up. More importantly, a lot of money can be saved by avoiding the expense the shop must pass on to you to cover its labor and overhead costs. An added benefit is the sense of satisfaction and accomplishment that you feel after doing the job yourself.

Using the manual

The manual is divided into Chapters. Each Chapter is divided into numbered Sections, which are headed in bold type between horizontal lines. Each Section consists of consecutively numbered paragraphs.

At the beginning of each numbered Section you will be referred to any illustrations which apply to the procedures in that Section. The reference numbers used in illustration captions pinpoint the pertinent Section and the Step within that Section. That is, illustration 3.2 means the illustration refers to Section 3 and Step (or paragraph) 2 within that Section.

Procedures, once described in the text, are not normally repeated. When it's necessary to refer to another Chapter, the reference will be given as Chapter and Section number. Cross references given without use of the word "Chapter" apply to Sections and/or paragraphs in the same Chapter. For example, "see Section 8" means in the same Chapter.

References to the left or right side of the vehicle assume you are sitting in the driver's seat, facing forward.

Even though we have prepared this manual with extreme care, neither the publisher nor the author can accept responsibility for any errors in, or omissions from, the information given.

NOTE

A Note provides information necessary to properly complete a procedure or information which will make the procedure easier to understand.

CAUTION

A Caution provides a special procedure or special steps which must be taken while completing the procedure where the Caution is found. Not heeding a Caution can result in damage to the assembly being worked on.

WARNING

A Warning provides a special procedure or special steps which must be taken while completing the procedure where the Warning is found. Not heeding a Warning can result in personal injury.

Introduction to the Dodge Caravan, Plymouth Voyager and Chrysler Town and Country

Dodge Caravan, Plymouth Voyager and Chrysler Town and Country models are front engine, front-wheel drive mini-vans.

The transverse-mounted, inline four-cylinder and V6 engines used in these models are equipped with a carburetor or fuel- injection system (both single-point and multi-point fuel injection systems are available). The engine drives the front wheels through either a four- or five-speed manual or three- or four-speed automatic transaxle via independent driveaxles.

Independent suspension, featuring coil springs and struts, is used at the front wheels. A beam-type axle, with struts and leaf springs, is used at the rear wheels. The rack and pinion steering unit is mounted behind the engine.

The brakes are disc at the front and drums at the rear, with power assist available on most models.

Vehicle identification numbers

Modifications are a continuing and unpublicized process in vehicle manufacturing. Since spare parts lists are compiled on a numerical basis, the individual vehicle numbers are essential to correctly identify the component required.

Vehicle Identification Number (VIN)

This very important identification number is stamped on a plate attached to the left side of the dashboard, just inside the windshield on the driver's side of the vehicle (see illustration). The VIN also appears on the Vehicle Certificate of Title and Registration. It contains information such as where and when the vehicle was manufactured, the model year and the body style.

Body code plate

This metal plate is located in the engine compartment, on top of the radiator support (see illustration). Like the VIN, it contains valuable information concerning the production of the vehicle as well as information about the way in which the vehicle is equipped. This plate is especially useful for matching the color and type of paint during repair work.

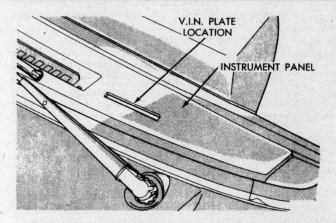

The Vehicle Identification Number is visible from outside the vehicle through the driver's side of the windshield

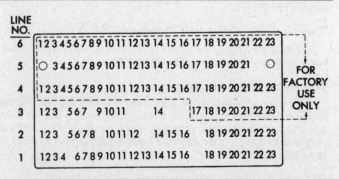

Typical body code plate

The body code plate is located in the engine compartment, on top of the radiator support

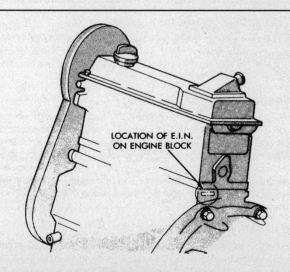

Location of the engine identification number on 2.2L and 2.5L engines

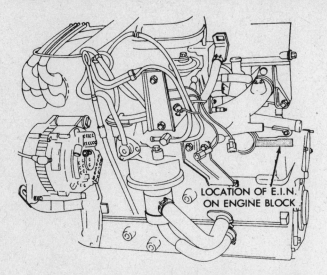

Location of the engine identification number on 2.6L and 3.0L engines

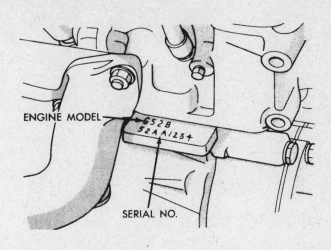

Location of the engine serial number on 2.6L and 3.0L engines

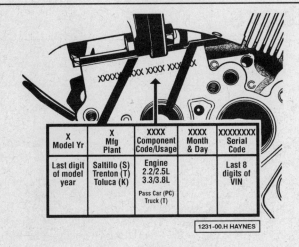

X Model Yr	X Mfg Plant	XXXX Component Code/Usage	XXXX Month & Day	XXXXXXXX Serial Code
Last digit of model year	Saltillo (S) Trenton (T) Toluca (K)	Engine 2.2/2.5L 3.3/3.8L Pass Car (PC) Truck (T)		Last 8 digits of VIN

1231-00.H HAYNES

Location of the engine identification and serial number on the 3.3L and 3.8L engines

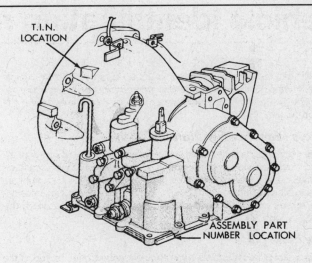

Transaxle number locations

Vehicle safety certification label

This label is affixed to the rear face of the driver's door. The plate contains the name of the manufacturer, the month and year of production, the Gross Vehicle Weight Rating (GVWR) and the certification statement.

Engine Identification Number

The Engine Identification Number (EIN) is stamped into a machined boss on the engine block. On 2.2L and 2.5L engines, it is stamped into the left end of the engine block, just above the transaxle bellhousing (see illustration). On 2.6L and 3.0L engines, it is on the radiator side of the block, between the core plug and the rear of the block (see illustration). The 3.3L and 3.8L engine identification number is located on the rear of the cylinder block just below the cylinder head (see illustration).

Engine serial numbers

In addition to the EIN, a serial number, which is required when buying replacement parts, is also stamped into the block. On 2.2L and 2.5L engines, it is located just below the EIN on the block. On 2.6L and 3.0L engines, it is located on the right-rear side of the engine block, adjacent to the exhaust manifold stud (dashboard side of the vehicle) (see illustration). On 3.0L and 3.8L engines the serial number is incorporated into the EIN.

Transaxle Identification Number (TIN)

The transaxle identification number is stamped into the boss on the upper surface of the housing (see illustration).

Transaxle serial number

The transaxle serial number, also called the assembly part number, is required when buying parts. On manual transaxles, it is located on a metal tag attached to the front side of the transaxle. On automatic transaxle models, it is located on a pad just above the oil pan at the rear of the transaxle.

Vehicle Emissions Control Information label

This label is located under the hood, usually attached to the front edge of the hood, on the underside (see Chapter 6 for more information on this label).

Buying parts

Replacement parts are available from many sources, which generally fall into one of two categories - authorized dealer parts departments and independent retail auto parts stores. Our advice concerning these parts is as follows:

Retail auto parts stores: Good auto parts stores will stock frequently needed components which wear out relatively fast, such as clutch components, exhaust systems, brake parts, tune-up parts, etc. These stores often supply new or reconditioned parts on an exchange basis, which can save a considerable amount of money. Discount auto parts stores are often very good places to buy materials and parts needed for general vehicle maintenance such as oil, grease, filters, spark plugs, belts, touch-up paint, bulbs, etc. They also usually sell tools and general accessories, have convenient hours, charge lower prices and can often be found not far from home.

Authorized dealer parts department: This is the best source for parts which are unique to the vehicle and not generally available elsewhere (such as major engine parts, transmission parts, trim pieces, etc.).

Warranty information: If the vehicle is still covered under warranty, be sure that any replacement parts purchased - regardless of the source - do not invalidate the warranty!

To be sure of obtaining the correct parts, have engine and chassis numbers available and, if possible, take the old parts along for positive identification.

Maintenance techniques, tools and working facilities

Maintenance techniques

There are a number of techniques involved in maintenance and repair that will be referred to throughout this manual. Application of these techniques will enable the home mechanic to be more efficient, better organized and capable o;f performing the various tasks properly, which will ensure that the repair job is thorough and complete.

Fasteners

Fasteners are nuts, bolts, studs and screws used to hold two or more parts together. There are a few things to keep in mind when working with fasteners. Almost all of them use a locking device of some type, either a lockwasher, locknut, locking tab or thread adhesive. All threaded fasteners should be clean and straight, with undamaged threads and undamaged corners on the hex head where the wrench fits. Develop the habit of replacing all damaged nuts and bolts with new ones. Special locknuts with nylon or fiber inserts can only be used once. If they are removed, they lose their locking ability and must be replaced with new ones.

Rusted nuts and bolts should be treated with a penetrating fluid to ease removal and prevent breakage. Some mechanics use turpentine in a spout-type oil can, which works quite well. After applying the rust penetrant, let it work for a few minutes before trying to loosen the nut or bolt. Badly rusted fasteners may have to be chiseled or sawed off or removed with a special nut breaker, available at tool stores.

If a bolt or stud breaks off in an assembly, it can be drilled and removed with a special tool commonly available for this purpose. Most automotive machine shops can perform this task, as well as other repair procedures, such as the repair of threaded holes that have been stripped out.

Flat washers and lockwashers, when removed from an assembly, should always be replaced exactly as removed. Replace any damaged washers with new ones. Never use a lockwasher on any soft metal surface (such as aluminum), thin sheet metal or plastic.

Fastener sizes

For a number of reasons, automobile manufacturers are making wider and wider use of metric fasteners. Therefore, it is important to be able to tell the difference between standard (sometimes called U.S. or SAE) and metric hardware, since they cannot be interchanged.

All bolts, whether standard or metric, are sized according to diameter, thread pitch and length. For example, a standard 1/2 - 13 x 1 bolt is 1/2 inch in diameter, has 13 threads per inch and is 1 inch long. An M12 - 1.75 x 25 metric bolt is 12 mm in diameter, has a thread pitch of 1.75 mm (the distance between threads) and is 25 mm long. The two bolts are nearly identical, and easily confused, but they are not interchangeable.

In addition to the differences in diameter, thread pitch and length, metric and standard bolts can also be distinguished by examining the bolt heads. To begin with, the distance across the flats on a standard bolt head is measured in inches, while the same dimension on a metric bolt is sized in millimeters (the same is true for nuts). As a result, a standard wrench should not be used on a metric bolt and a metric wrench should not be used on a standard bolt. Also, most standard bolts have slashes radiating out from the center of the head to denote the grade or strength of the bolt, which is an indication of the amount of torque that can be applied to it. The greater the number of slashes, the greater the strength of the bolt. Grades 0 through 5 are commonly used on automobiles. Metric bolts have a property class (grade) number, rather than a slash, molded into their heads to indicate bolt strength. In this case, the higher the number, the stronger the bolt. Property class numbers 8.8, 9.8 and 10.9 are commonly used on automobiles.

Strength markings can also be used to distinguish standard hex nuts from metric hex nuts. Many standard nuts have dots stamped into one side, while metric nuts are marked with a number. The greater the number of dots, or the higher the number, the greater the strength of the nut.

Metric studs are also marked on their ends according to property class (grade). Larger studs are numbered (the same as metric bolts), while smaller studs carry a geometric code to denote grade.

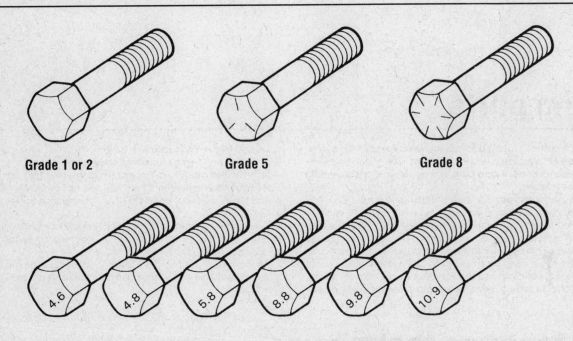

Grade 1 or 2   Grade 5   Grade 8

4.6   4.8   5.8   8.8   9.8   10.9

Bolt strength markings (top - standard/SAE/USS; bottom - metric

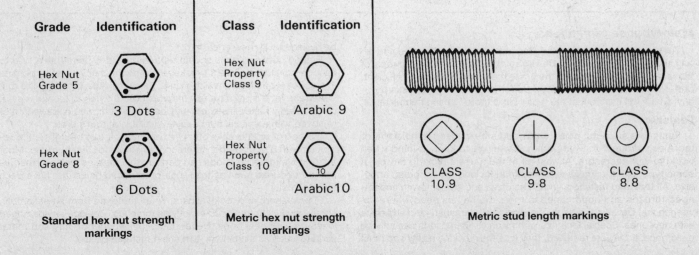

Grade	Identification	Class	Identification
Hex Nut Grade 5	3 Dots	Hex Nut Property Class 9	Arabic 9
Hex Nut Grade 8	6 Dots	Hex Nut Property Class 10	Arabic 10

CLASS 10.9   CLASS 9.8   CLASS 8.8

Standard hex nut strength markings   **Metric hex nut strength markings**   **Metric stud length markings**

It should be noted that many fasteners, especially Grades 0 through 2, have no distinguishing marks on them. When such is the case, the only way to determine whether it is standard or metric is to measure the thread pitch or compare it to a known fastener of the same size.

Standard fasteners are often referred to as SAE, as opposed to metric. However, it should be noted that SAE technically refers to a non-metric fine thread fastener only. Coarse thread non-metric fasteners are referred to as USS sizes.

Since fasteners of the same size (both standard and metric) may have different strength ratings, be sure to reinstall any bolts, studs or nuts removed from your vehicle in their original locations. Also, when replacing a fastener with a new one, make sure that the new one has a strength rating equal to or greater than the original.

Tightening sequences and procedures

Most threaded fasteners should be tightened to a specific torque value (torque is the twisting force applied to a threaded component such as a nut or bolt). Overtightening the fastener can weaken it and cause it to break, while undertightening can cause it to eventually come loose. Bolts, screws and studs, depending on the material they are made of and their thread diameters, have specific torque values, many of which are noted in the Specifications at the beginning of each Chapter. Be sure to follow the torque recommendations closely. For fasteners not assigned a specific torque, a general torque value chart is presented here as a guide. These torque values are for dry (unlubricated) fasteners threaded into steel or cast iron (not aluminum). As was previously mentioned, the size and grade of a fastener determine

Metric thread sizes	Ft–lbs	Nm
M–6	6 to 9	9 to 12
M–8	14 to 21	19 to 28
M–10	28 to 40	38 to 54
M–12	50 to 71	68 to 96
M–14	80 to 140	109 to 154
Pipe thread sizes		
1/8	5 to 8	7 to 10
1/4	12 to 18	17 to 24
3/8	22 to 33	30 to 44
1/2	25 to 35	34 to 47
U.S. thread sizes		
1/4 - 20	6 to 9	9 to 12
5/16 - 18	12 to 18	17 to 24
5/16 - 24	14 to 20	19 to 27
3/8 - 16	22 to 32	30 to 43
3/8 - 24	27 to 38	37 to 51
7/16 - 14	40 to 55	55 to 74
7/16 - 20	40 to 60	55 to 81
1/2 - 13	55 to 80	75 to 108

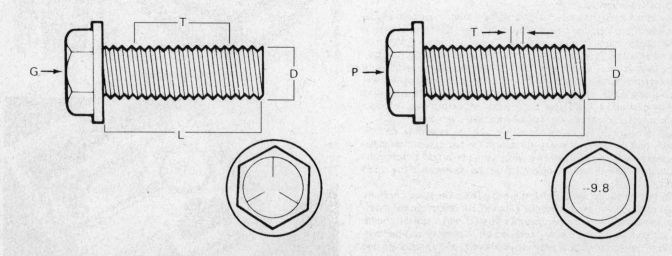

Standard (SAE and USS) bolt dimensions/grade marks

G   Grade marks (bolt length)
L   Length (in inches)
T   Thread pitch (number of threads per inch)
D   Nominal diameter (in inches)

Metric bolt dimensions/grade marks

P   Property class (bolt strength)
L   Length (in millimeters)
T   Thread pitch (distance between threads in millimeters)
D   Diameter

the amount of torque that can safely be applied to it. The figures listed here are approximate for Grade 2 and Grade 3 fasteners. Higher grades can tolerate higher torque values.

Fasteners laid out in a pattern, such as cylinder head bolts, oil pan bolts, differential cover bolts, etc., must be loosened or tightened in sequence to avoid warping the component. This sequence will normally be shown in the appropriate Chapter. If a specific pattern is not given, the following procedures can be used to prevent warping.

Initially, the bolts or nuts should be assembled finger-tight only. Next, they should be tightened one full turn each, in a criss-cross or diagonal pattern. After each one has been tightened one full turn, return to the first one and tighten them all one-half turn, following the same pattern. Finally, tighten each of them one-quarter turn at a time until each fastener has been tightened to the proper torque. To loosen and remove the fasteners, the procedure would be reversed.

Component disassembly

Component disassembly should be done with care and purpose to help ensure that the parts go back together properly. Always keep track of the sequence in which parts are removed. Make note of special characteristics or marks on parts that can be installed more than one way, such as a grooved thrust washer on a shaft. It is a good idea to lay the disassembled parts out on a clean surface in the order that they were removed. It may also be helpful to make sketches or take instant photos of components before removal.

When removing fasteners from a component, keep track of their locations. Sometimes threading a bolt back in a part, or putting the washers and nut back on a stud, can prevent mix-ups later. If nuts and bolts cannot be returned to their original locations, they should be kept in a compartmented box or a series of small boxes. A cupcake or muffin tin is ideal for this purpose, since each cavity can hold the bolts and nuts from a particular area (i.e. oil pan bolts, valve cover bolts, engine mount bolts, etc.). A pan of this type is especially helpful when working on assemblies with very small parts, such as the carburetor, alternator, valve train or interior dash and trim pieces. The cavities can be marked with paint or tape to identify the contents.

Whenever wiring looms, harnesses or connectors are separated, it is a good idea to identify the two halves with numbered pieces of masking tape so they can be easily reconnected.

Gasket sealing surfaces

Throughout any vehicle, gaskets are used to seal the mating surfaces between two parts and keep lubricants, fluids, vacuum or pressure contained in an assembly.

Many times these gaskets are coated with a liquid or paste-type gasket sealing compound before assembly. Age, heat and pressure can sometimes cause the two parts to stick together so tightly that they are very difficult to separate. Often, the assembly can be loosened by striking it with a soft-face hammer near the mating surfaces. A regular hammer can be used if a block of wood is placed between the hammer and the part. Do not hammer on cast parts or parts that could be easily damaged. With any particularly stubborn part, always recheck to make sure that every fastener has been removed.

Avoid using a screwdriver or bar to pry apart an assembly, as they can easily mar the gasket sealing surfaces of the parts, which must remain smooth. If prying is absolutely necessary, use an old broom handle, but keep in mind that extra clean up will be necessary if the wood splinters.

After the parts are separated, the old gasket must be carefully scraped off and the gasket surfaces cleaned. Stubborn gasket material can be soaked with rust penetrant or treated with a special chemical to soften it so it can be easily scraped off. A scraper can be fashioned from a piece of copper tubing by flattening and sharpening one end. Copper is recommended because it is usually softer than the surfaces to be scraped, which reduces the chance of gouging the part. Some gaskets can be removed with a wire brush, but regardless of the method used, the mating surfaces must be left clean and smooth. If for some reason the gasket surface is gouged, then a gasket sealer thick enough to fill scratches will have to be used during reassembly of the components. For most applications, a non-drying (or semi-drying) gasket sealer should be used.

Hose removal tips

Warning: *If the vehicle is equipped with air conditioning, do not disconnect any of the A/C hoses without first having the system depressurized by a dealer service department or a service station.*

Hose removal precautions closely parallel gasket removal precautions. Avoid scratching or gouging the surface that the hose mates against or the connection may leak. This is especially true for radiator hoses. Because of various chemical reactions, the rubber in hoses can bond itself to the metal spigot that the hose fits over. To remove a hose, first loosen the hose clamps that secure it to the spigot. Then, with slip-joint pliers, grab the hose at the clamp and rotate it around the spigot. Work it back and forth until it is completely free, then pull it off. Silicone or other lubricants will ease removal if they can be applied between the hose and the outside of the spigot. Apply the same lubricant to the inside of the hose and the outside of the spigot to simplify installation.

As a last resort (and if the hose is to be replaced with a new one anyway), the rubber can be slit with a knife and the hose peeled from the spigot. If this must be done, be careful that the metal connection is not damaged.

If a hose clamp is broken or damaged, do not reuse it. Wire-type clamps usually weaken with age, so it is a good idea to replace them with screw-type clamps whenever a hose is removed.

Tools

A selection of good tools is a basic requirement for anyone who plans to maintain and repair his or her own vehicle. For the owner who has few tools, the initial investment might seem high, but when compared to the spiraling costs of professional auto maintenance and repair, it is a wise one.

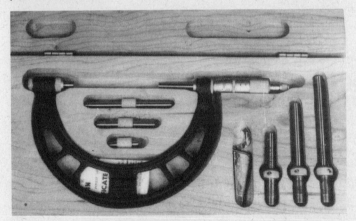

Micrometer set

Dial indicator set

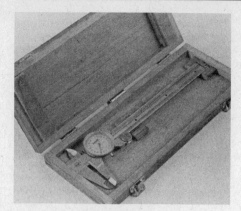

Dial caliper

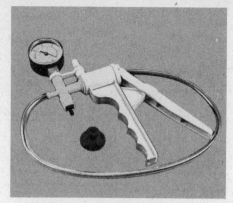

Hand-operated vacuum pump

Timing light

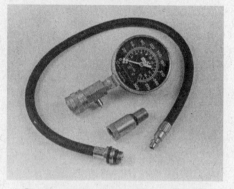

Compression gauge with spark plug hole adapter

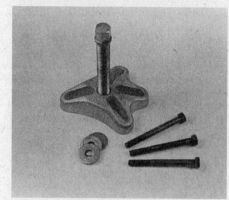

Damper/steering wheel puller

General purpose puller

Hydraulic lifter removal tool

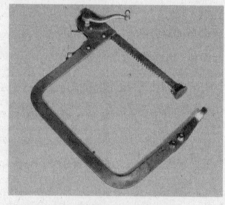

Valve spring compressor

Valve spring compressor

Ridge reamer

Piston ring groove cleaning tool

Ring removal/installation tool

Ring compressor

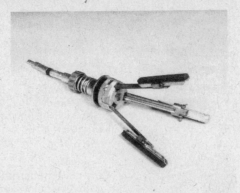

Cylinder hone

Brake hold-down spring tool

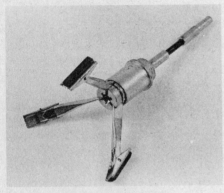

Brake cylinder hone

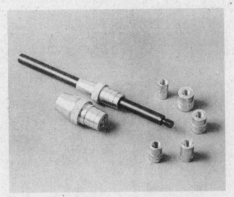

Clutch plate alignment tool

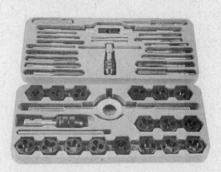

Tap and die set

To help the owner decide which tools are needed to perform the tasks detailed in this manual, the following tool lists are offered: Maintenance and minor repair, Repair/overhaul and Special.

The newcomer to practical mechanics should start off with the maintenance and minor repair tool kit, which is adequate for the simpler jobs performed on a vehicle. Then, as confidence and experience grow, the owner can tackle more difficult tasks, buying additional tools as they are needed. Eventually the basic kit will be expanded into the repair and overhaul tool set. Over a period of time, the experienced do-it-yourselfer will assemble a tool set complete enough for most repair and overhaul procedures and will add tools from the special category when it is felt that the expense is justified by the frequency of use.

Maintenance and minor repair tool kit

The tools in this list should be considered the minimum required for performance of routine maintenance, servicing and minor repair work. We recommend the purchase of combination wrenches (box-end and open-end combined in one wrench). While more expensive than open end wrenches, they offer the advantages of both types of wrench.

Combination wrench set (1/4-inch to 1 inch or 6 mm to 19 mm)
Adjustable wrench, 8 inch
Spark plug wrench with rubber insert
Spark plug gap adjusting tool
Feeler gauge set
Brake bleeder wrench
Standard screwdriver (5/16-inch x 6 inch)
Phillips screwdriver (No. 2 x 6 inch)
Combination pliers - 6 inch
Hacksaw and assortment of blades
Tire pressure gauge
Grease gun
Oil can
Fine emery cloth
Wire brush
Battery post and cable cleaning tool

Oil filter wrench
Funnel (medium size)
Safety goggles
Jackstands(2)
Drain pan

Note: *If basic tune-ups are going to be part of routine maintenance, it will be necessary to purchase a good quality stroboscopic timing light and combination tachometer/dwell meter. Although they are included in the list of special tools, it is mentioned here because they are absolutely necessary for tuning most vehicles properly.*

Repair and overhaul tool set

These tools are essential for anyone who plans to perform major repairs and are in addition to those in the maintenance and minor repair tool kit. Included is a comprehensive set of sockets which, though expensive, are invaluable because of their versatility, especially when various extensions and drives are available. We recommend the 1/2-inch drive over the 3/8-inch drive. Although the larger drive is bulky and more expensive, it has the capacity of accepting a very wide range of large sockets. Ideally, however, the mechanic should have a 3/8-inch drive set and a 1/2-inch drive set.

Socket set(s)
Reversible ratchet
Extension - 10 inch
Universal joint
Torque wrench (same size drive as sockets)
Ball peen hammer - 8 ounce
Soft-face hammer (plastic/rubber)
Standard screwdriver (1/4-inch x 6 inch)
Standard screwdriver (stubby - 5/16-inch)
Phillips screwdriver (No. 3 x 8 inch)
Phillips screwdriver (stubby - No. 2)
Pliers - vise grip
Pliers - lineman's

Pliers - needle nose
Pliers - snap-ring (internal and external)
Cold chisel - 1/2-inch
Scribe
Scraper (made from flattened copper tubing)
Centerpunch
Pin punches (1/16, 1/8, 3/16-inch)
Steel rule/straightedge - 12 inch
Allen wrench set (1/8 to 3/8-inch or 4 mm to 10 mm)
A selection of files
Wire brush (large)
Jackstands (second set)
Jack (scissor or hydraulic type)

Note: *Another tool which is often useful is an electric drill with a chuck capacity of 3/8-inch and a set of good quality drill bits*

Special tools

The tools in this list include those which are not used regularly, are expensive to buy, or which need to be used in accordance with their manufacturer's instructions. Unless these tools will be used frequently, it is not very economical to purchase many of them. A consideration would be to split the cost and use between yourself and a friend or friends. In addition, most of these tools can be obtained from a tool rental shop on a temporary basis.

This list primarily contains only those tools and instruments widely available to the public, and not those special tools produced by the vehicle manufacturer for distribution to dealer service departments. Occasionally, references to the manufacturer's special tools are included in the text of this manual. Generally, an alternative method of doing the job without the special tool is offered. However, sometimes there is no alternative to their use. Where this is the case, and the tool cannot be purchased or borrowed, the work should be turned over to the dealer service department or an automotive repair shop.

Valve spring compressor
Piston ring groove cleaning tool
Piston ring compressor
Piston ring installation tool
Cylinder compression gauge
Cylinder ridge reamer
Cylinder surfacing hone
Cylinder bore gauge
Micrometers and/or dial calipers
Hydraulic lifter removal tool
Balljoint separator
Universal-type puller
Impact screwdriver
Dial indicator set
Stroboscopic timing light (inductive pick-up)
Hand operated vacuum/pressure pump
Tachometer/dwell meter
Universal electrical multimeter
Cable hoist
Brake spring removal and installation tools
Floor jack

Buying tools

For the do-it-yourselfer who is just starting to get involved in vehicle maintenance and repair, there are a number of options available when purchasing tools. If maintenance and minor repair is the extent of the work to be done, the purchase of individual tools is satisfactory. If, on the other hand, extensive work is planned, it would be a good idea to purchase a modest tool set from one of the large retail chain stores. A set can usually be bought at a substantial savings over the individual tool prices, and they often come with a tool box. As additional tools are needed, add-on sets, individual tools and a larger tool box can be purchased to expand the tool selection. Building a tool set gradually allows the cost of the tools to be spread over a longer period of time and gives the mechanic the freedom to choose only those tools that will actually be used.

Tool stores will often be the only source of some of the special tools that are needed, but regardless of where tools are bought, try to avoid cheap ones, especially when buying screwdrivers and sockets, because they won't last very long. The expense involved in replacing cheap tools will eventually be greater than the initial cost of quality tools.

Care and maintenance of tools

Good tools are expensive, so it makes sense to treat them with respect. Keep them clean and in usable condition and store them properly when not in use. Always wipe off any dirt, grease or metal chips before putting them away. Never leave tools lying around in the work area. Upon completion of a job, always check closely under the hood for tools that may have been left there so they won't get lost during a test drive.

Some tools, such as screwdrivers, pliers, wrenches and sockets, can be hung on a panel mounted on the garage or workshop wall, while others should be kept in a tool box or tray. Measuring instruments, gauges, meters, etc. must be carefully stored where they cannot be damaged by weather or impact from other tools.

When tools are used with care and stored properly, they will last a very long time. Even with the best of care, though, tools will wear out if used frequently. When a tool is damaged or worn out, replace it. Subsequent jobs will be safer and more enjoyable if you do.

Working facilities

Not to be overlooked when discussing tools is the workshop. If anything more than routine maintenance is to be carried out, some sort of suitable work area is essential.

It is understood, and appreciated, that many home mechanics do not have a good workshop or garage available, and end up removing an engine or doing major repairs outside. It is recommended, however, that the overhaul or repair be completed under the cover of a roof.

A clean, flat workbench or table of comfortable working height is an absolute necessity. The workbench should be equipped with a vise that has a jaw opening of at least four inches.

As mentioned previously, some clean, dry storage space is also required for tools, as well as the lubricants, fluids, cleaning solvents, etc. which soon become necessary.

Sometimes waste oil and fluids, drained from the engine or cooling system during normal maintenance or repairs, present a disposal problem. To avoid pouring them on the ground or into a sewage system, pour the used fluids into large containers, seal them with caps and take them to an authorized disposal site or recycling center. Plastic jugs, such as old antifreeze containers, are ideal for this purpose.

Always keep a supply of old newspapers and clean rags available. Old towels are excellent for mopping up spills. Many mechanics use rolls of paper towels for most work because they are readily available and disposable. To help keep the area under the vehicle clean, a large cardboard box can be cut open and flattened to protect the garage or shop floor.

Whenever working over a painted surface, such as when leaning over a fender to service something under the hood, always cover it with an old blanket or bedspread to protect the finish. Vinyl covered pads, made especially for this purpose, are available at auto parts stores.

Booster battery (jump) starting

Observe these precautions when using a booster battery to start a vehicle:

a) Before connecting the booster battery, make sure the ignition switch is in the Off position.
b) Turn off the lights, heater and other electrical loads.
c) Your eyes should be shielded. Safety goggles are a good idea.
d) Make sure the booster battery is the same voltage as the dead one in the vehicle.
e) The two vehicles MUST NOT TOUCH each other!
f) Make sure the transaxle is in Neutral (manual) or Park (automatic).
g) If the booster battery is not a maintenance-free type, remove the vent caps and lay a cloth over the vent holes.

Connect the red jumper cable to the positive (+) terminals of each battery (see illustration).

Connect one end of the black jumper cable to the negative (-) terminal of the booster battery. The other end of this cable should be connected to a good ground on the vehicle to be started, such as a bolt or bracket on the body.

Start the engine using the booster battery, then, with the engine running at idle speed, disconnect the jumper cables in the reverse order of connection.

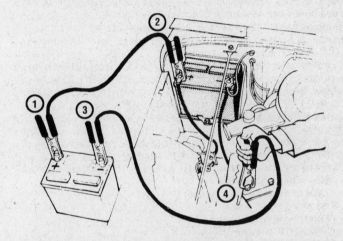

Make the booster battery cable connections in the numerical order shown (note that the negative cable of the booster battery is NOT attached to the negative terminal of the dead battery)

Jacking and towing

Jacking

Warning: *The jack supplied with the vehicle should only be used for raising the vehicle when changing a tire or placing jackstands under the frame. Never work under the vehicle or start the engine while the jack is being used as the only means of support.*

The vehicle must be on a level surface with the wheels blocked, the hazard flashers on and the transaxle in Park (automatic) or Reverse (manual). Apply the parking brake if the front of the vehicle must be raised. Make sure no one is in the vehicle when using the jack to lift it.

Remove the jack, lug nut wrench and spare tire (if needed) from the vehicle. If a tire is being changed, use the lug wrench to remove the wheel cover. **Warning:** *Wheel covers may have sharp edges - be very careful not to cut yourself.* Loosen the lug nuts one-half turn, but leave them in place until the tire is off the ground.

Position the jack under the vehicle at the indicated jacking point. There's a jack locator pin near each wheel **(see illustrations)**. Turn the jack handle clockwise until the tire clears the ground. Remove the lug nuts, pull the tire off and install the spare. Thread the lug nuts back on with the beveled edges facing in and tighten them snugly. Don't attempt to tighten them completely until the vehicle is lowered to the ground.

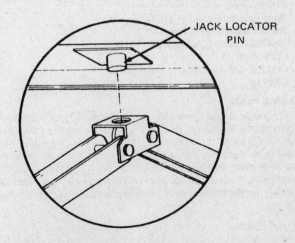

JACK LOCATOR PIN

The jack supplied with the vehicle fits over a pin on the underside of the vehicle - there's one near each wheel

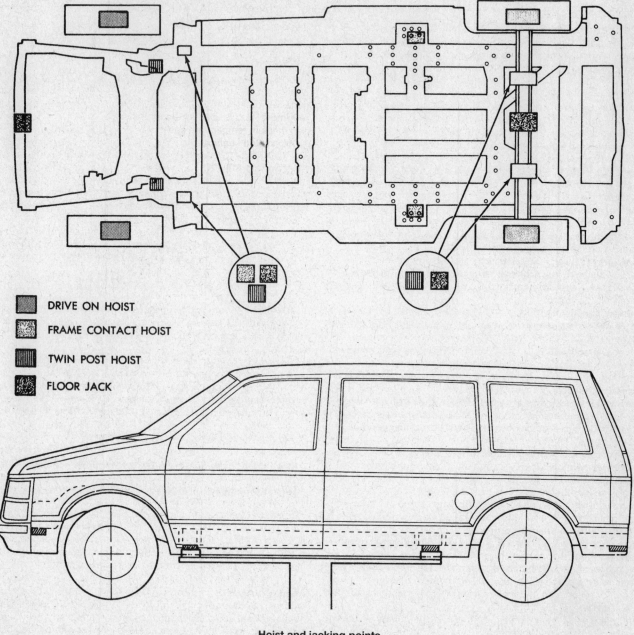

- ▮ DRIVE ON HOIST
- ▨ FRAME CONTACT HOIST
- ▥ TWIN POST HOIST
- ▦ FLOOR JACK

Hoist and jacking points

Turn the jack handle counterclockwise to lower the vehicle. Remove the jack and tighten the lug nuts (if loosened or removed) in a criss-cross pattern. If possible, use a torque wrench to tighten them (see Chapter 1 for the torque figures). If you don't have a torque wrench, have the nuts checked by a service station or repair shop as soon as possible.

Stow the tire, jack and wrench and unblock the wheels.

Towing

Vehicles with an automatic transaxle can be towed with all four wheels on the ground, provided that speeds do not exceed 25 mph and the distance is not over 15 miles. Otherwise, transmission damage can result. If the transmission is damaged or the distance will exceed 15 miles, the vehicle must be towed with the front wheels off the ground.

Vehicles with a manual transaxle can be towed at any legal highway speed for any distance. If the vehicle has a damaged transaxle, tow it only with the front wheels off the ground.

Towing equipment specifically designed for this purpose should be used and should be attached to the main structural members of the vehicle and not the bumper or brackets.

Safety is a major consideration when towing and all applicable state and local laws must be obeyed. A safety chain system must be used for all towing.

While towing, the parking brake should be released and the transmission must be in Neutral. The steering must be unlocked (ignition switch in the Off position). Remember that power steering and power brakes will not work with the engine off.

Automotive chemicals and lubricants

A number of automotive chemicals and lubricants are available for use during vehicle maintenance and repair. They include a wide variety of products ranging from cleaning solvents and degreasers to lubricants and protective sprays for rubber, plastic and vinyl.

Cleaners

Carburetor cleaner and choke cleaner is a strong solvent for gum, varnish and carbon. Most carburetor cleaners leave a dry-type lubricant film which will not harden or gum up. Because of this film it is not recommended for use on electrical components

Brake system cleaner is used to remove grease and brake fluid from the brake system, where clean surfaces are absolutely necessary. It leaves no residue and often eliminates brake squeal caused by contaminants.

Electrical cleaner removes oxidation, corrosion and carbon deposits from electrical contacts, restoring full current flow. It can also be used to clean spark plugs, carburetor jets, voltage regulators and other parts where an oil-free surface is desired.

Demoisturants remove water and moisture from electrical components such as alternators, voltage regulators, electrical connectors and fuse blocks. They are non-conductive, non-corrosive and non-flammable.

Degreasers are heavy-duty solvents used to remove grease from the outside of the engine and from chassis components. They can be sprayed or brushed on and, depending on the type, are rinsed off either with water or solvent.

Lubricants

Motor oil is the lubricant formulated for use in engines. It normally contains a wide variety of additives to prevent corrosion and reduce foaming and wear. Motor oil comes in various weights (viscosity ratings) from 5 to 80. The recommended weight of the oil depends on the season, temperature and the demands on the engine. Light oil is used in cold climates and under light load conditions. Heavy oil is used in hot climates and where high loads are encountered. Multi-viscosity oils are designed to have characteristics of both light and heavy oils and are available in a number of weights from 5W-20 to 20W-50.

Gear oil is designed to be used in differentials, manual transmissions and other areas where high-temperature lubrication is required.

Chassis and wheel bearing grease is a heavy grease used where increased loads and friction are encountered, such as for wheel bearings, balljoints, tie-rod ends and universal joints.

High-temperature wheel bearing grease is designed to withstand the extreme temperatures encountered by wheel bearings in disc brake equipped vehicles. It usually contains molybdenum disulfide (moly), which is a dry-type lubricant.

White grease is a heavy grease for metal-to-metal applications where water is a problem. White grease stays soft under both low and high temperatures (usually from -100 to +190-degrees F), and will not wash off or dilute in the presence of water.

Assembly lube is a special extreme pressure lubricant, usually containing moly, used to lubricate high-load parts (such as main and rod bearings and cam lobes) for initial start-up of a new engine. The assembly lube lubricates the parts without being squeezed out or washed away until the engine oiling system begins to function.

Silicone lubricants are used to protect rubber, plastic, vinyl and nylon parts.

Graphite lubricants are used where oils cannot be used due to contamination problems, such as in locks. The dry graphite will lubricate metal parts while remaining uncontaminated by dirt, water, oil or acids. It is electrically conductive and will not foul electrical contacts in locks such as the ignition switch.

Moly penetrants loosen and lubricate frozen, rusted and corroded fasteners and prevent future rusting or freezing.

Heat-sink grease is a special electrically non-conductive grease that is used for mounting electronic ignition modules where it is essential that heat is transferred away from the module.

Sealants

RTV sealant is one of the most widely used gasket compounds. Made from silicone, RTV is air curing, it seals, bonds, waterproofs, fills surface irregularities, remains flexible, doesn't shrink, is relatively easy to remove, and is used as a supplementary sealer with almost all low and medium temperature gaskets.

Anaerobic sealant is much like RTV in that it can be used either to seal gaskets or to form gaskets by itself. It remains flexible, is solvent resistant and fills surface imperfections. The difference between an anaerobic sealant and an RTV-type sealant is in the curing. RTV cures when exposed to air, while an anaerobic sealant cures only in the absence of air. This means that an anaerobic sealant cures only after the assembly of parts, sealing them together.

Thread and pipe sealant is used for sealing hydraulic and pneumatic fittings and vacuum lines. It is usually made from a Teflon compound, and comes in a spray, a paint-on liquid and as a wrap-around tape.

Chemicals

Anti-seize compound prevents seizing, galling, cold welding, rust and corrosion in fasteners. High-temperature ant-seize, usually made with copper and graphite lubricants, is used for exhaust system and exhaust manifold bolts.

Anaerobic locking compounds are used to keep fasteners from vibrating or working loose and cure only after installation, in the absence of air. Medium strength locking compound is used for small nuts, bolts and screws that may be removed later. High-strength locking compound is for large nuts, bolts and studs which aren't removed on a regular basis.

Oil additives range from viscosity index improvers to chemical treatments that claim to reduce internal engine friction. It should be noted that most oil manufacturers caution against using additives with their oils.

Gas additives perform several functions, depending on their chemical makeup. They usually contain solvents that help dissolve gum and varnish that build up on carburetor, fuel injection and intake parts. They also serve to break down carbon deposits that form on the inside surfaces of the combustion chambers. Some additives contain upper cylinder lubricants for valves and piston rings, and others contain chemicals to remove condensation from the gas tank.

Miscellaneous

Brake fluid is specially formulated hydraulic fluid that can withstand the heat and pressure encountered in brake systems. Care must be taken so this fluid does not come in contact with painted surfaces or plastics. An opened container should always be resealed to prevent contamination by water or dirt.

Weatherstrip adhesive is used to bond weatherstripping around doors, windows and trunk lids. It is sometimes used to attach trim pieces.

Undercoating is a petroleum-based, tar-like substance that is designed to protect metal surfaces on the underside of the vehicle from corrosion. It also acts as a sound-deadening agent by insulating the bottom of the vehicle.

Waxes and polishes are used to help protect painted and plated surfaces from the weather. Different types of paint may require the use of different types of wax and polish. Some polishes utilize a chemical or abrasive cleaner to help remove the top layer of oxidized (dull) paint on older vehicles. In recent years many non-wax polishes that contain a wide variety of chemicals such as polymers and silicones have been introduced. These non-wax polishes are usually easier to apply and last longer than conventional waxes and polishes.

Safety first

Regardless of how enthusiastic you may be about getting on with the job at hand, take the time to ensure that your safety is not jeopardized. A moment's lack of attention can result in an accident, as can failure to observe certain simple safety precautions. The possibility of an accident will always exist, and the following points should not be considered a comprehensive list of all dangers. Rather, they are intended to make you aware of the risks and to encourage a safety conscious approach to all work you carry out on your vehicle.

Essential DOs and DON'Ts

DON'T rely on a jack when working under the vehicle. Always use approved jackstands to support the weight of the vehicle and place them under the recommended lift or support points.

DON'T attempt to loosen extremely tight fasteners (i.e. wheel lug nuts) while the vehicle is on a jack - it may fall.

DON'T start the engine without first making sure that the transmission is in Neutral (or Park where applicable) and the parking brake is set.

DON'T remove the radiator cap from a hot cooling system - let it cool or cover it with a cloth and release the pressure gradually.

DON'T attempt to drain the engine oil until you are sure it has cooled to the point that it will not burn you.

DON'T touch any part of the engine or exhaust system until it has cooled sufficiently to avoid burns.

DON'T siphon toxic liquids such as gasoline, antifreeze and brake fluid by mouth, or allow them to remain on your skin.

DON'T inhale brake lining dust - it is potentially hazardous (see Asbestos below)

DON'T allow spilled oil or grease to remain on the floor - wipe it up before someone slips on it.

DON'T use loose fitting wrenches or other tools which may slip and cause injury.

DON'T push on wrenches when loosening or tightening nuts or bolts. Always try to pull the wrench toward you. If the situation calls for pushing the wrench away, push with an open hand to avoid scraped knuckles if the wrench should slip.

DON'T attempt to lift a heavy component alone - get someone to help you.

DON'T rush or take unsafe shortcuts to finish a job.

DON'T allow children or animals in or around the vehicle while you are working on it.

DO wear eye protection when using power tools such as a drill, sander, bench grinder, etc. and when working under a vehicle.

DO keep loose clothing and long hair well out of the way of moving parts.

DO make sure that any hoist used has a safe working load rating adequate for the job.

DO get someone to check on you periodically when working alone on a vehicle.

DO carry out work in a logical sequence and make sure that everything is correctly assembled and tightened.

DO keep chemicals and fluids tightly capped and out of the reach of children and pets.

DO remember that your vehicle's safety affects that of yourself and others. If in doubt on any point, get professional advice.

Asbestos

Certain friction, insulating, sealing, and other products - such as brake linings, brake bands, clutch linings, torque converters, gaskets, etc. - contain asbestos. Extreme care must be taken to avoid inhalation of dust from such products, since it is hazardous to health. If in doubt, assume that they do contain asbestos.

Fire

Remember at all times that gasoline is highly flammable. Never smoke or have any kind of open flame around when working on a vehicle. But the risk does not end there. A spark caused by an electrical short circuit, by two metal surfaces contacting each other, or even by static electricity built up in your body under certain conditions, can ignite gasoline vapors, which in a confined space are highly explosive. Do not, under any circumstances, use gasoline for cleaning parts. Use an approved safety solvent.

Always disconnect the battery ground (-) cable at the battery before working on any part of the fuel system or electrical system. Never risk spilling fuel on a hot engine or exhaust component. It is strongly recommended that a fire extinguisher suitable for use on fuel and electrical fires be kept handy in the garage or workshop at all times. Never try to extinguish a fuel or electrical fire with water.

Fumes

Certain fumes are highly toxic and can quickly cause unconsciousness and even death if inhaled to any extent. Gasoline vapor falls into this category, as do the vapors from some cleaning solvents. Any draining or pouring of such volatile fluids should be done in a well ventilated area.

When using cleaning fluids and solvents, read the instructions on the container carefully. Never use materials from unmarked containers.

Never run the engine in an enclosed space, such as a garage. Exhaust fumes contain carbon monoxide, which is extremely poisonous. If you need to run the engine, always do so in the open air, or at least have the rear of the vehicle outside the work area.

If you are fortunate enough to have the use of an inspection pit, never drain or pour gasoline and never run the engine while the vehicle is over the pit. The fumes, being heavier than air, will concentrate in the pit with possibly lethal results.

The battery

Never create a spark or allow a bare light bulb near a battery. They normally give off a certain amount of hydrogen gas, which is highly explosive.

Always disconnect the battery ground (-) cable at the battery before working on the fuel or electrical systems.

If possible, loosen the filler caps or cover when charging the battery from an external source (this does not apply to sealed or maintenance-free batteries). Do not charge at an excessive rate or the battery may burst.

Take care when adding water to a non maintenance-free battery and when carrying a battery. The electrolyte, even when diluted, is very corrosive and should not be allowed to contact clothing or skin.

Always wear eye protection when cleaning the battery to prevent the caustic deposits from entering your eyes.

Household current

When using an electric power tool, inspection light, etc., which operates on household current, always make sure that the tool is correctly connected to its plug and that, where necessary, it is properly grounded. Do not use such items in damp conditions and, again, do not create a spark or apply excessive heat in the vicinity of fuel or fuel vapor.

Secondary ignition system voltage

A severe electric shock can result from touching certain parts of the ignition system (such as the spark plug wires) when the engine is running or being cranked, particularly if components are damp or the insulation is defective. In the case of an electronic ignition system, the secondary system voltage is much higher and could prove fatal.

Conversion factors

Length (distance)
Inches (in)	X 25.4	= Millimetres (mm)	X 0.0394	= Inches (in)
Feet (ft)	X 0.305	= Metres (m)	X 3.281	= Feet (ft)
Miles	X 1.609	= Kilometres (km)	X 0.621	= Miles

Volume (capacity)
Cubic inches (cu in; in³)	X 16.387	= Cubic centimetres (cc; cm³)	X 0.061	= Cubic inches (cu in; in³)
Imperial pints (Imp pt)	X 0.568	= Litres (l)	X 1.76	= Imperial pints (Imp pt)
Imperial quarts (Imp qt)	X 1.137	= Litres (l)	X 0.88	= Imperial quarts (Imp qt)
Imperial quarts (Imp qt)	X 1.201	= US quarts (US qt)	X 0.833	= Imperial quarts (Imp qt)
US quarts (US qt)	X 0.946	= Litres (l)	X 1.057	= US quarts (US qt)
Imperial gallons (Imp gal)	X 4.546	= Litres (l)	X 0.22	= Imperial gallons (Imp gal)
Imperial gallons (Imp gal)	X 1.201	= US gallons (US gal)	X 0.833	= Imperial gallons (Imp gal)
US gallons (US gal)	X 3.785	= Litres (l)	X 0.264	= US gallons (US gal)

Mass (weight)
Ounces (oz)	X 28.35	= Grams (g)	X 0.035	= Ounces (oz)
Pounds (lb)	X 0.454	= Kilograms (kg)	X 2.205	= Pounds (lb)

Force
Ounces-force (ozf; oz)	X 0.278	= Newtons (N)	X 3.6	= Ounces-force (ozf; oz)
Pounds-force (lbf; lb)	X 4.448	= Newtons (N)	X 0.225	= Pounds-force (lbf; lb)
Newtons (N)	X 0.1	= Kilograms-force (kgf; kg)	X 9.81	= Newtons (N)

Pressure
Pounds-force per square inch (psi; lbf/in²; lb/in²)	X 0.070	= Kilograms-force per square centimetre (kgf/cm²; kg/cm²)	X 14.223	= Pounds-force per square inch (psi; lbf/in²; lb/in²)
Pounds-force per square inch (psi; lbf/in²; lb/in²)	X 0.068	= Atmospheres (atm)	X 14.696	= Pounds-force per square inch (psi; lbf/in²; lb/in²)
Pounds-force per square inch (psi; lbf/in²; lb/in²)	X 0.069	= Bars	X 14.5	= Pounds-force per square inch (psi; lbf/in²; lb/in²)
Pounds-force per square inch (psi; lbf/in²; lb/in²)	X 6.895	= Kilopascals (kPa)	X 0.145	= Pounds-force per square inch (psi; lbf/in²; lb/in²)
Kilopascals (kPa)	X 0.01	= Kilograms-force per square centimetre (kgf/cm²; kg/cm²)	X 98.1	= Kilopascals (kPa)

Torque (moment of force)
Pounds-force inches (lbf in; lb in)	X 1.152	= Kilograms-force centimetre (kgf cm; kg cm)	X 0.868	= Pounds-force inches (lbf in; lb in)
Pounds-force inches (lbf in; lb in)	X 0.113	= Newton metres (Nm)	X 8.85	= Pounds-force inches (lbf in; lb in)
Pounds-force inches (lbf in; lb in)	X 0.083	= Pounds-force feet (lbf ft; lb ft)	X 12	= Pounds-force inches (lbf in; lb in)
Pounds-force feet (lbf ft; lb ft)	X 0.138	= Kilograms-force metres (kgf m; kg m)	X 7.233	= Pounds-force feet (lbf ft; lb ft)
Pounds-force feet (lbf ft; lb ft)	X 1.356	= Newton metres (Nm)	X 0.738	= Pounds-force feet (lbf ft; lb ft)
Newton metres (Nm)	X 0.102	= Kilograms-force metres (kgf m; kg m)	X 9.804	= Newton metres (Nm)

Power
Horsepower (hp)	X 745.7	= Watts (W)	X 0.0013	= Horsepower (hp)

Velocity (speed)
Miles per hour (miles/hr; mph)	X 1.609	= Kilometres per hour (km/hr; kph)	X 0.621	= Miles per hour (miles/hr; mph)

Fuel consumption*
Miles per gallon, Imperial (mpg)	X 0.354	= Kilometres per litre (km/l)	X 2.825	= Miles per gallon, Imperial (mpg)
Miles per gallon, US (mpg)	X 0.425	= Kilometres per litre (km/l)	X 2.352	= Miles per gallon, US (mpg)

Temperature
Degrees Fahrenheit = ($°C \times 1.8$) + 32

Degrees Celsius (Degrees Centigrade; °C) = ($°F - 32$) x 0.56

*It is common practice to convert from miles per gallon (mpg) to litres/100 kilometres (l/100km), where mpg (Imperial) x l/100 km = 282 and mpg (US) x l/100 km = 235

Troubleshooting

Contents

This section provides an easy reference guide to the more common problems which may occur during the operation of a vehicle. The problems and their possible causes are grouped under headings denoting various components or systems, such as Engine, Cooling System, etc. They also refer you to the Chapter and/or Section which deals with the problem.

Remember, successful troubleshooting isn't a mysterious black art practiced only by professional mechanics. It's simply the result of the right knowledge combined with an intelligent, systematic approach to a problem. Always use the process of elimination, starting with the simplest solution and working through to the most complex - and never overlook the obvious. Anyone can run the gas tank dry or leave the lights on overnight, so don't assume that it can't happen to you.

Finally, always try to establish a clear idea why a problem has occurred and take steps to ensure that it doesn't happen again. If the electrical system fails because of a poor connection, check all other connections in the system to make sure they don't fail as well. If a particular fuse continues to blow, find out why - don't just replace one fuse after another. Remember, failure of a small component can often be indicative of potential failure or incorrect functioning of a more important component or system.

Engine

1   Engine will not rotate when attempting to start

1   Battery terminal connections loose or corroded. Check the cable terminals at the battery. Tighten the cable or remove corrosion as necessary.
2   Battery discharged or faulty. If the cable connections are clean and tight on the battery posts, turn the key to the On position and switch on the headlights and/or windshield wipers. If they fail to function, the battery is discharged.
3   Automatic transaxle not completely engaged in Park or Neutral or clutch pedal not completely depressed.
4   Broken, loose or disconnected wiring in the starting circuit. Inspect all wiring and connectors at the battery, starter solenoid and ignition switch.
5   Starter motor pinion jammed in flywheel ring gear. If manual transaxle, place transaxle in gear and rock the vehicle to manually turn the engine. Remove starter and inspect pinion and flywheel at earliest convenience (Chapter 5).
6   Starter solenoid faulty (Chapter 5).
7   Starter motor faulty (Chapter 5).
8   Ignition switch faulty (Chapter 12).

2   Engine rotates but will not start

1   Fuel tank empty.
2   Faulty carburetor or fuel injection system (Chapter 4).
3   Battery discharged (engine rotates slowly). Check the operation of electrical components as described in the previous Section.
4   Battery terminal connections loose or corroded (see previous Section).
5   Fuel pump faulty (Chapter 4).
6   Excessive moisture on, or damage to, ignition components (Chapter 5).
7   Worn, faulty or incorrectly gapped spark plugs (Chapter 1).
8   Broken, loose or disconnected wiring in the starting circuit (see previous Section).
9   Distributor loose (engines so equipped), causing ignition timing to change. Turn the distributor as necessary to start the engine, then set the ignition timing as soon as possible (Chapter 1).
10   Broken, loose or disconnected wires at the ignition coil or faulty coil (Chapter 5).

3   Starter motor operates without rotating engine

1   Starter pinion sticking. Remove the starter (Chapter 5) and inspect.
2   Starter pinion or flywheel teeth worn or broken. Remove the flywheel/driveplate access cover and inspect.

4   Engine hard to start when cold

1   Battery discharged or low. Check as described in Section 1.
2   Fault in the fuel or electrical systems (Chapters 4 and 5).
3   Carburetor needs overhaul (Chapter 4).
4   Distributor rotor carbon tracked and/or damaged (Chapters 1 and 5).
5   Choke control stuck or inoperative (Chapters 1 and 4).

5   Engine hard to start when hot

1   Air filter clogged (Chapter 1).
2   Fault in the fuel or electrical systems (Chapters 4 and 5).
3   Fuel not reaching the carburetor or fuel injection system (see Section 2).

6   Starter motor noisy or excessively rough in engagement

1   Pinion or flywheel gear teeth worn or broken. Remove the cover at the rear of the engine (if so equipped) and inspect.
2   Starter motor mounting bolts loose or missing.

7   Engine starts but stops immediately

1   Loose or faulty electrical connections at distributor, coil or alternator.
2   Fault in the fuel or electrical systems (Chapters 4 and 5).
3   Insufficient fuel reaching the carburetor or fuel injection system. Check the fuel pump (Chapter 4).
4   Vacuum leak at the gasket surfaces of the intake manifold, or carburetor/throttle body. Make sure all mounting bolts/nuts are tightened securely and all vacuum hoses connected to the carburetor/throttle body and manifold are positioned properly and in good condition.

8   Engine lopes while idling or idles erratically

1   Vacuum leaks. Check the mounting bolts/nuts at the carburetor/throttle body and intake manifold for tightness. Make sure all vacuum hoses are connected and in good condition. Use a stethoscope or a length of fuel hose held against your ear to listen for vacuum leaks while the engine is running. A hissing sound will be heard. A soapy water solution will also detect leaks.
2   Faulty fuel or electrical systems (Chapters 4 and 5).
3   Leaking EGR valve or plugged PCV valve (see Chapters 1 and 6).
4   Air filter clogged (Chapter 1).
5   Fuel pump not delivering sufficient fuel to the carburetor or fuel injection system (see Chapter 4).
6   Carburetor/throttle body out of adjustment (Chapter 4).
7   Leaking head gasket. Perform a compression check (Chapter 2).
8   Camshaft lobes worn (Chapter 2).

9   Engine misses at idle speed

1   Spark plugs worn or gap too wide (Chapter 1).
2   Faulty fuel or electrical systems (Chapters 4 and 5).
3   Faulty spark plug wires (Chapter 1).

10   Engine misses throughout driving speed range

1   Fuel filter clogged and/or impurities in the fuel system (Chapter 1).
2   Faulty or incorrectly gapped spark plugs (Chapter 1).
3   Faulty fuel or electrical systems (Chapters 4 and 5).
4   Incorrect ignition timing (Chapter 1).
5   Check for cracked distributor cap, disconnected distributor wires and damaged distributor components (Chapter 1).
6   Defective spark plug wires (Chapter 1).
7   Faulty emissions system components (Chapter 6).
8   Low or uneven cylinder compression pressures. Remove the spark plugs and test the compression with a gauge (Chapter 2).
9   Weak or faulty ignition system (Chapter 5).
10   Vacuum leaks at the carburetor/throttle body, intake manifold or vacuum hoses (see Section 8).

11   Engine stalls

1   Idle speed incorrect. Refer to the VECI label and Chapter 1.
2   Fuel filter clogged and/or water and impurities in the fuel system (Chapter 1).
3   Distributor components damp or damaged (Chapter 5).
4   Faulty fuel system or emission control system information sensors (Chapters 4 and 6).
5   Faulty emissions system components (Chapter 6).
6   Faulty or incorrectly gapped spark plugs (Chapter 1). Also check the spark plug wires (Chapter 1).
7   Vacuum leak at the carburetor/throttle body, intake manifold or vacuum hoses. Check as described in Section 8.

12   Engine lacks power

1   Incorrect ignition timing (Chapter 1).
2   Faulty fuel or electrical systems (Chapters 4 and 5).
3   Excessive play in the distributor shaft (except DIS systems). At the same time, check for a damaged rotor, faulty distributor cap, wires, etc. (Chapters 1 and 5).
4   Faulty or incorrectly gapped spark plugs (Chapter 1).
5   Carburetor/throttle body not adjusted properly or excessively worn (Chapter 4).
6   Defective coil (Chapter 5).
7   Brakes binding (Chapter 1).
8   Automatic transaxle fluid level incorrect (Chapter 1).
9   Clutch slipping (Chapter 8).
10   Fuel filter clogged and/or impurities in the fuel system (Chapter 1).
11   Emissions control system not functioning properly (Chapter 6).
12   Use of substandard fuel. Fill the tank with the proper octane fuel.
13   Low or uneven cylinder compression pressures. Test with a compression tester, which will detect leaking valves and/or a blown head gasket (Chapter 2).

13   Engine backfires

1   Emissions system not functioning properly (Chapter 6).
2   Faulty fuel or electrical systems (Chapters 4 and 5).
3   Ignition timing incorrect (Chapter 1).
4   Faulty secondary ignition system (cracked spark plug insulator, faulty plug wires, distributor cap and/or rotor) (Chapters 1 and 5).
5   Carburetor in need of adjustment or worn excessively (Chapter 4).
6   Vacuum leak at the carburetor/throttle body, intake manifold or vacuum hoses. Check as described in Section 8.
7   Valves sticking (Chapter 2).

14   Pinging or knocking engine sounds during acceleration or uphill

1   Incorrect grade of fuel. Fill the tank with fuel of the proper octane rating.
2   Faulty fuel or electrical systems (Chapters 4 and 5).
3   Ignition timing incorrect (Chapter 1).
4   Carburetor out of adjustment (Chapter 4).
5   Incorrect spark plugs. Check the plug type against the VECI label located in the engine compartment. Also check the plugs and wires for damage (Chapter 1).
6   Worn or damaged distributor components (Chapter 5).
7   Faulty emissions system (Chapter 6).
8   Vacuum leak. Check as described in Section 9.

15   Engine diesels (continues to run) after switching off

1   Idle speed too high. Refer to Chapter 1.
2   Faulty fuel or electrical systems (Chapters 4 and 5).
3   Ignition timing incorrect (Chapter 1).
4   Thermo-controlled air cleaner heat valve not operating properly (Chapters 1 and 6).
5   Excessive engine operating temperature. Probable causes of this are a malfunctioning thermostat, clogged radiator, faulty water pump (Chapter 3).

Engine electrical system

16   Battery will not hold a charge

1   Alternator drivebelt defective or loose (Chapter 1).
2   Electrolyte level low or battery discharged (Chapter 1).
3   Battery terminals loose or corroded (Chapter 1).
4   Alternator not charging properly (Chapter 5).
5   Loose, broken or faulty wiring in the charging circuit (Chapter 5).
6   Short in the vehicle wiring causing a continual drain on battery (refer to Chapter 12 and the Wiring Diagrams).
7   Battery defective internally.

17   Ignition light fails to go out

1   Defective alternator or charging circuit (Chapter 5).
2   Alternator drivebelt defective or loose (Chapter 1).

18   Ignition light fails to come on when key is turned on

1   Instrument cluster warning light bulb defective (Chapter 12).
2   Alternator faulty (Chapter 5).
3   Fault in the instrument cluster printed circuit, dashboard wiring or bulb holder (Chapter 12).

Fuel system

19   Excessive fuel consumption

1   Dirty or clogged air filter element (Chapter 1).
2   Incorrect ignition timing (Chapter 1).
3   Choke sticking or incorrectly adjusted (Chapter 1).
4   Emissions system not functioning properly (Chapter 6).
5   Faulty fuel or electrical systems (Chapters 4 and 5).
6   Carburetor internal parts excessively worn or damaged (Chapter 4).
7   Low tire pressure or incorrect tire size (Chapter 1).

20 Fuel leakage and/or fuel odor

1 Leak in a fuel feed or vent line (Chapter 4).
2 Tank overfilled. Fill only to automatic shut-off.
3 Evaporative emissions system canister clogged (Chapter 6).
4 Vapor leaks from system lines (Chapter 4).
5 Carburetor internal parts excessively worn or out of adjustment (Chapter 4).
6 Leaking fuel injector(s) (Chapter 4).
7 Leaking fuel pressure regulator (Chapter 4).

Cooling system

21 Overheating

1 Low coolant level (Chapter 1).
2 Water pump drivebelt defective or loose (Chapter 1).
3 Radiator core blocked or radiator grille restricted (Chapter 3).
4 Thermostat faulty (Chapter 3).
5 Fan blades broken or cracked (Chapter 3).
6 Radiator cap not maintaining proper pressure. Have the cap pressure tested by gas station or repair shop.
7 Ignition timing incorrect (Chapter 1).

22 Overcooling

Thermostat faulty (Chapter 3).

23 External coolant leakage

1 Deteriorated or damaged hoses or loose clamps. Replace hoses and/or tighten the clamps at the hose connections (Chapter 1).
2 Water pump seals defective. If this is the case, coolant will drip from the weep hole in the water pump body (Chapter 3).
3 Leakage from radiator core or header tank. This will require the radiator to be professionally repaired (see Chapter 3 for removal procedures).
4 Engine drain plug leaking (Chapter 1) or water jacket core plugs leaking (see Chapter 2).

24 Internal coolant leakage

Note: *Internal coolant leaks can usually be detected by examining the oil. Check the dipstick and inside of the cylinder head cover for water deposits and an oil consistency resembling a milkshake.*

1 Leaking cylinder head gasket. Have the cooling system pressure tested.
2 Cracked cylinder bore or cylinder head. Dismantle the engine and inspect (Chapter 2).

25 Coolant loss

1 Too much coolant in the system (Chapter 1).
2 Coolant loss caused by overheating (see Section 15).
3 External or internal leakage (see Sections 23 and 24).
4 Faulty radiator cap. Have the cap pressure tested.

26 Poor coolant circulation

1 Inoperative water pump. A quick test is to pinch the top radiator

hose closed with your hand while the engine is idling, then let it loose. You should feel a surge of coolant if the pump is working properly (Chapter 1).
2 Restriction in the cooling system. Drain, flush and refill the system (Chapter 1). If necessary, remove the radiator (Chapter 3) and have it reverse flushed.
3 Water pump drivebelt defective or loose (Chapter 1).
4 Thermostat sticking (Chapter 3).

Clutch

27 Fails to release (pedal pressed to the floor - shift lever does not move freely in and out of Reverse)

1 Worn cable (Chapter 8).
2 Clutch plate warped or damaged (Chapter 8).
3 Worn or dry clutch release shaft bushing (Chapter 8).

28 Clutch slips (engine speed increaseswith no increase in vehicle speed)

1 Cable out of adjustment (Chapter 1).
2 Clutch plate oil soaked or lining worn. Remove clutch (Chapter 8) and inspect.
3 Clutch plate not seated. It may take 30 or 40 normal starts for a new one to seat.

29 Grabbing (chattering) as clutch is engaged

1 Oil on clutch plate lining. Remove (Chapter 8) and inspect. Correct any leakage source.
2 Worn or loose engine or transaxle mounts. The mounts move slightly when the clutch is released. Inspect the mounts and bolts (Chapter 2).
3 Worn splines on clutch plate hub. Remove the clutch components (Chapter 8) and inspect.
4 Warped pressure plate or flywheel. Remove the clutch components and inspect.

30 Squeal or rumble with clutch fully disengaged (pedal depressed)

1 Worn or damaged release bearing (Chapter 8).
2 Worn or broken pressure plate diaphragm fingers (Chapter 8).

31 Clutch pedal stays on floor when disengaged

Linkage or release bearing binding. Inspect the linkage or remove the clutch components as necessary.

Manual transaxle

32 Noisy in Neutral with engine running

1 Worn or damaged mainshaft bearing.
2 Worn countershaft bearings.
3 Countershaft endplay incorrect.

33 Noisy in all gears

1 Any of the above causes, and/or:
2 Insufficient lubricant (see the checking procedures in Chapter 1).

34 Noisy in one particular gear

1   Worn, damaged or chipped gear teeth for that particular gear.
2   Worn or damaged synchronizer for that particular gear.

35 Slips out of high gear

1   Transaxle loose on clutch housing (Chapter 7).
2   Shift rods interfering with the engine mounts or clutch lever (Chapter 7).
3   Shift rods not working freely (Chapter 7).
4   Dirt between the transaxle case and engine or misalignment of the transaxle (Chapter 7).
5   Worn or improperly adjusted linkage (Chapter 7).

36 Difficulty in engaging gears

1   Clutch not releasing completely (see clutch adjustment in Chapter 1).
2   Loose, damaged or out-of-adjustment shift linkage. Make a thorough inspection, replacing parts as necessary (Chapter 7).

37 Oil leakage

1   Excessive amount of lubricant in the transaxle (see Chapter 1 for correct checking procedure). Drain lubricant as required.
2   Defective driveaxle oil seal or speedometer oil seal (Chapter 7).

Automatic transaxle

Note: *Due to the complexity of the automatic transaxle, it's difficult for the home mechanic to properly diagnose and service. For problems other than the following, the vehicle should be taken to a dealer service department or a transmission shop.*

38 General shift mechanism problems

1   Chapter 7 deals with checking and adjusting the shift linkage on automatic transaxles. Common problems which may be attributed to poorly adjusted linkage are:
   Engine starting in gears other than Park or Neutral.
   Indicator on shifter pointing to a gear other than the one actually being selected.
   Vehicle moves when in Park.
2   Refer to Chapter 7 to adjust the linkage.

39 Transaxle will not downshift with accelerator pedal pressed to the floor

   Chapter 7 deals with adjusting the throttle cable to enable the transaxle to downshift properly.

40 Transaxle slips, shifts rough, is noisy or has no drive in forward or reverse gears

1   There are many probable causes for the above problems, but the home mechanic should be concerned with only one possibility - fluid level.
2   Before taking the vehicle to a repair shop, check the level and condition of the fluid as described in Chapter 1. Correct fluid level as necessary or change the fluid and filter if needed. If the problem persists, have a professional diagnose the probable cause.

41 Fluid leakage

1   Automatic transaxle fluid is a deep red color. Fluid leaks shouldn't be confused with engine oil, which can easily be blown by air flow to the transaxle.
2   To pinpoint a leak, first remove all built-up dirt and grime from around the transaxle. Degreasing agents and/or steam cleaning will achieve this. With the underside clean, drive the vehicle at low speeds so air flow will not blow the leak far from its source. Raise the vehicle and determine where the leak is coming from. Common areas of leakage are:
   a) **Pan:** Tighten the mounting bolts and/or replace the pan gasket as necessary (see Chapter 7).
   b) **Filler pipe:** Replace the rubber seal where the pipe enters the transaxle case.
   c) **Transaxle oil lines:** Tighten the connectors where the lines enter the transaxle case and/or replace the lines.
   d) **Speedometer connector:** Replace the O-ring where the speedometer cable enters the transaxle case (Chapter 7).

Driveaxles

42 Clicking noise in turns

   Worn or damaged outer joint. Check for cut or damaged boots. Repair as necessary (Chapter 8).

43 Knock or clunk when accelerating after coasting

   Worn or damaged inner joint. Check for cut or damaged boots. Repair as necessary (Chapter 8)

44 Shudder or vibration during acceleration

1   Excessive joint angle. Check and correct as necessary (Chapter 8).
2   Worn or damaged CV joints. Repair or replace as necessary (Chapter 8).
3   Sticking CV joint assembly. Service or replace as necessary (Chapter 8).

Rear axle

45 Noise

1   Road noise. No corrective action available.
2   Tire noise. Inspect tires and check tire pressures (Chapter 1).
3   Rear wheel bearings loose, worn or damaged (Chapter 1).

Brakes

Note: *Before assuming a brake problem exists, make sure the tires are in good condition and inflated properly (see Chapter 1), the front end alignment is correct and the vehicle isn't loaded with weight in an unequal manner.*

46 Vehicle pulls to one side during braking

1   Defective, damaged or oil contaminated disc brake pads on one side. Inspect as described in Chapter 1.

2 Excessive pad or disc wear on one side. Inspect and correct as necessary.

3 Loose or disconnected front suspension components. Inspect and tighten all bolts to the specified torque (Chapter 10).

4 Defective caliper assembly. Remove the caliper and inspect for a stuck piston or other damage (Chapter 9).

47 Noise (high-pitched squeal with the brakes applied)

Disc brake pads worn out. The noise comes from the wear sensor rubbing against the disc (does not apply to all vehicles) or the actual pad backing plate itself if the lining material is completely worn away. Replace the pads with new ones immediately (Chapter 9). If the pad material has worn completely away, the brake discs should be inspected for damage as well.

48 Excessive brake pedal travel

1 Partial brake system failure. Inspect the entire system (Chapter 9) and correct as required.

2 Insufficient fluid in the master cylinder. Check (Chapter 1), add fluid and bleed the system if necessary (Chapter 9).

3 Rear brakes not adjusting properly. Make a series of starts and stops while the transaxle is in Reverse. If this doesn't correct the situation, remove the drums and inspect the self-adjusters (Chapter 9).

49 Brake pedal feels spongy when depressed

1 Air in the hydraulic lines. Bleed the brake system (Chapter 9).

2 Defective brake hoses. Inspect all system hoses and lines. Replace parts as necessary.

3 Master cylinder mounting bolts/nuts loose.

4 Master cylinder defective (Chapter 9).

50 Excessive effort required to stop vehicle

1 Power brake booster not operating properly (Chapter 9).

2 Excessively worn linings or pads. Inspect and replace if necessary (Chapter 9).

3 One or more caliper pistons or wheel cylinder cups seized or sticking. Inspect and rebuild as required (Chapter 9).

4 Brake linings or pads contaminated with oil or grease. Inspect and replace as required (Chapter 9).

5 New pads or shoes installed and not yet seated. It will take a while for the new material to seat against the drum (or rotor).

51 Pedal travels to the floor with little resistance

Little or no fluid in the master cylinder reservoir caused by leaking wheel cylinder(s), leaking caliper piston(s), loose, damaged or disconnected brake lines. Inspect the entire system and correct as necessary.

52 Brake pedal pulsates during brake application

1 Caliper improperly installed. Remove and inspect (Chapter 9).

2 Disc or drum defective. Remove (Chapter 9) and check for excessive lateral runout and parallelism. Have the disc or drum resurfaced or replace it with a new one.

Suspension and steering systems

53 Vehicle pulls to one side

1 Tire pressures uneven (Chapter 1).

2 Defective tire (Chapter 1).

3 Excessive wear in suspension or steering components (Chapter 10).

4 Front end alignment incorrect.

5 Front brakes dragging. Inspect the brakes as described in Chapter 9.

54 Shimmy, shake or vibration

1 Tire or wheel out-of-balance or out-of-round.

2 Loose, worn or out-of-adjustment rear wheel bearings (Chapter 1).

3 Shock absorbers and/or suspension components worn or damaged (Chapter 10).

55 Excessive pitching and/or rolling around corners or during braking

1 Defective shock absorbers. Replace as a set (Chapter 10).

2 Broken or weak springs and/or suspension components. Inspect as described in Chapters 1 and 10.

56 Excessively stiff steering

1 Lack of fluid in power steering fluid reservoir (Chapter 1).

2 Incorrect tire pressures (Chapter 1).

3 Front end out of alignment.

57 Excessive play in steering

1 Excessively worn suspension or steering components (Chapter 10).

2 Steering gear damaged (Chapter 10).

58 Lack of power assistance

1 Steering pump drivebelt loose or defective (Chapter 1).

2 Fluid level low (Chapter 1).

3 Hoses or lines restricted. Inspect and replace parts as necessary.

4 Air in power steering system. Bleed the system (Chapter 10).

59 Excessive tire wear (not specific to one area)

1 Incorrect tire pressures (Chapter 1).

2 Tires out-of-balance.

3 Wheels damaged. Inspect and replace as necessary.

4 Suspension or steering components excessively worn (Chapter 10).

60 Excessive tire wear on outside edge

1 Incorrect tire pressures (Chapter 1).

2 Excessive speed in turns.

3 Front end alignment incorrect (excessive toe-in).

4 Suspension arm bent or twisted (Chapter 10).

61   Excessive tire wear on inside edge

1   Incorrect tire pressures (Chapter 1).
2   Front end alignment incorrect.
3   Loose or damaged steering components (Chapter 10).

62   Tire tread worn in one place

1   Tires out-of-balance.
2   Damaged or buckled wheel. Inspect and replace if necessary.
3   Defective tire (Chapter 1).

Chapter 1 Tune-up and routine maintenance

Contents

Specifications

Recommended lubricants and fluids

Engine oil	
Type	API SG or SG/CD
Viscosity	See accompanying chart
Manual transaxle lubricant	
1986 and earlier	MOPAR ATF Plus Type 7176 or DEXRON II
1987-on	SAE 5W30 engine oil
Automatic transaxle fluid	MOPAR ATF Plus Type 7176 or DEXRON II
Power steering fluid	Mopar 4-253 power steering fluid or equivalent
Brake fluid	DOT 3 brake fluid
Combustion chamber conditioner (Canadian leaded fuel models)	Autopar combustion chamber conditioner (no. VU788 or equivalent)
Engine coolant	50/50 mixture of ethylene glycol-based antifreeze and water
Transaxle shift linkage grease	NLGI no. 2 chassis grease
Clutch linkage grease	NLGI no. 2 chassis grease
Parking brake mechanism grease	White lithium-based grease NLGI no. 2
Chassis lubrication grease	NLGI no. 2 EP grease
Rear wheel bearing grease	NLGI no. 2 EP high-temperature wheel bearing grease
Manual steering gear lubricant	API GL-4 SAE 90W gear oil
Hood, door and trunk/liftgate hinge lubricant	Engine oil
Door hinge half and check spring grease	NLGI no. 2 multi-purpose grease
Key lock cylinder lubricant	Graphite spray
Hood latch assembly lubricant	Mopar Lubriplate or equivalent
Door latch striker lubricant	Mopar Door Ease (no. 3744859 or equivalent)

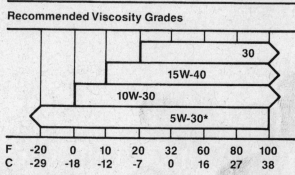

Recommended Viscosity Grades

F	-20 0 10 20 32 60 80 100
C	-29 -18 -12 -7 0 16 27 38

Temperature range anticipated before next oil change

For best fuel economy and cold starting, select the lowest SAE viscosity grade for the expected temperature range

Note: *SAE 10W-30 is recommended for use in turbo engines*

*SAE 5W-30 engine oil is not recommended for use in 2.5L engines above 32°F (0° C)

Capacities

Engine oil (including filter)	
Four-cylinder engine	
2.2L	4.0 qts
2.6L	5.0 qts
2.5L	
1990 and earlier	4.0 qts
1991 and later	4.5 qts.
V6 engine	
3.0L	4.0 qts
3.3L and 3.8L	4.5 qts.
Fuel tank	15 gal
Automatic transaxle (approximate)	4.0 qts
Manual transaxle (approximate)	2.3 qts
Cooling system (approximate)	
2.2L and 2.5L four-cylinder	8.5 qts (8.0 liters)
2.6L four-cylinder	9.0 qts (8.5 liters)
3.0 V6	10.0 qts (9.5 liters)
3.3L or 3.8L V6	8.5 qts (8.0 liters)

Radiator cap pressure rating .... 14 to 17 psi

Brakes
Disc brake pad wear limit .... 5/16 in (7.94 mm)
Drum brake shoe wear limit .... 1/8 in (3.17 mm)

Cylinder numbering on
four-cylinder engines

Valve clearances (2.6L engine only)
Intake .... 0.006 inch
Exhaust... 0.010 inch
Jet valve .... 0.006 inch

Ignition system
Spark plug type
  Four-cylinder... Champion RN12YC
  3.0L V6 .... Champion RN11YC4
  3.3L and 3.8L V6
    1993 and earlier .... Champion RN16YC5
    1994 and later.. Champion RN14MC5
Spark plug gap
  Four-cylinder
    2.2L and 2.5L... 0.035 in (0.9 mm)
    2.6L... 0.040 in (1.0 mm)
  V6 engine
    3.0L... 0.040 in (1.0 mm)
    3.3L and 3.8L... 0.050 in (1.3 mm)
Spark plug wire resistance
  Minimum .... 3000 ohms per foot
  Maximum .... 7200 ohms per foot
Ignition timing .... See the *Vehicle Emission Control Information* label in the engine compartment
Firing order
  Four-cylinder engine 1-3-4-2
  V6 engine 1-2-3-4-5-6

Cylinder numbering on
3.0L V6 engines

Drivebelt deflection
Note: *A used drivebelt is one that's been in operation for ten minutes or more.*
Alternator
  New .... 1/8 in (3 mm)
  Used .... 1/4 in (6 mm)
Power steering pump
  New .... 1/4 in (6 mm)
  Used .... 7/16 in (11 mm)
Water Pump
  New .... 1/8 in (3 mm)
  Used .... 1/4 in (6 mm)
Air conditioning compressor
  New .... 5/16 in (8 mm)
  Used .... 7/16 in (11 mm)
Air pump
  New .... 3/16 in (5 mm)
  Used .... 1/4 in (6 mm)

Distributor cap terminal routing for
3.0L V6 engines

Automatic transaxle band adjustment
Kickdown (front) .... Tighten to 72 in-lbs, then back off 2-1/2 turns
Low-Reverse .... Tighten to 41 in-lbs, then back off 3-1/2 turns

Torque specifications
Carburetor/throttle body mounting bolt/nut 20
Spark plugs 26
Wheel lug nuts 95
Automatic transaxle
  Pan bolts .... 170 in-lbs
  Filter-to-valve body screws .... 40 in-lbs

Ft-lbs (unless otherwise indicated)

Cylinder numbering on
3.3L and 3.8L V6 engines

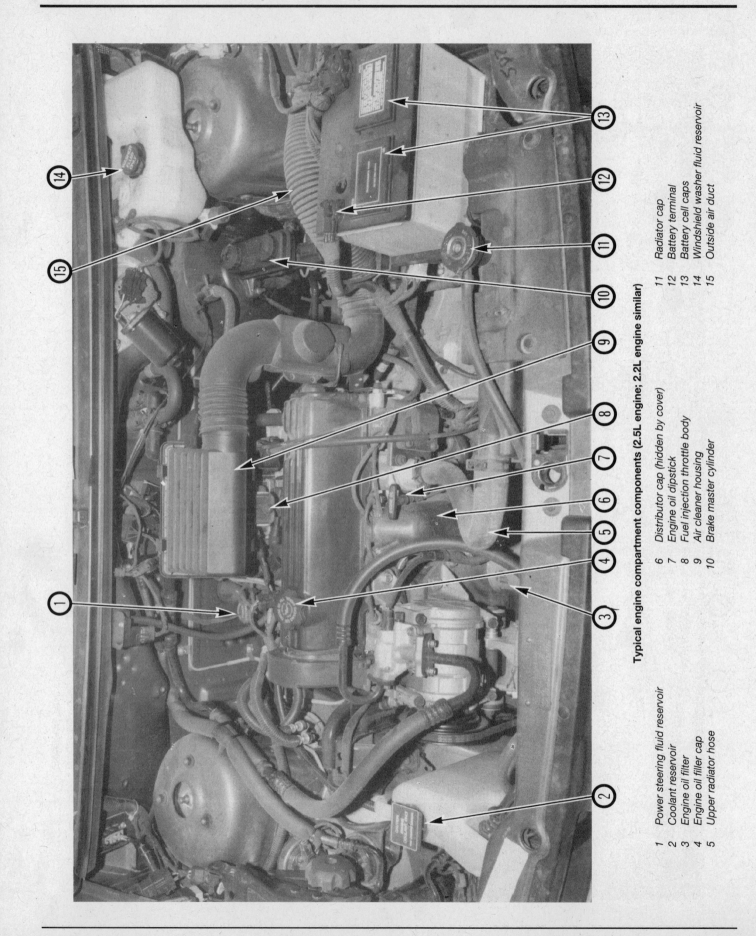

Typical engine compartment components (2.5L engine; 2.2L engine similar)

1   Power steering fluid reservoir
2   Coolant reservoir
3   Engine oil filter
4   Engine oil filler cap
5   Upper radiator hose

6   Distributor cap (hidden by cover)
7   Engine oil dipstick
8   Fuel injection throttle body
9   Air cleaner housing
10 Brake master cylinder

11 Radiator cap
12 Battery terminal
13 Battery cell caps
14 Windshield washer fluid reservoir
15 Outside air duct

Typical engine compartment components (2.6L engine)

1	Power steering fluid reservoir	8	Battery cell caps
2	Engine oil filler cap	9	Battery terminal
3	Valve cover	10	Coolant reservoir
4	Air cleaner housing	11	Battery cables
5	Heater hoses	12	Radiator cap
6	Windshield washer reservoir	13	Outside air duct
7	Brake fluid reservoir		

14	Upper radiator hose
15	Carburetor
16	Fuel hose
17	Fuel filter
18	Distributor
19	PCV valve

1

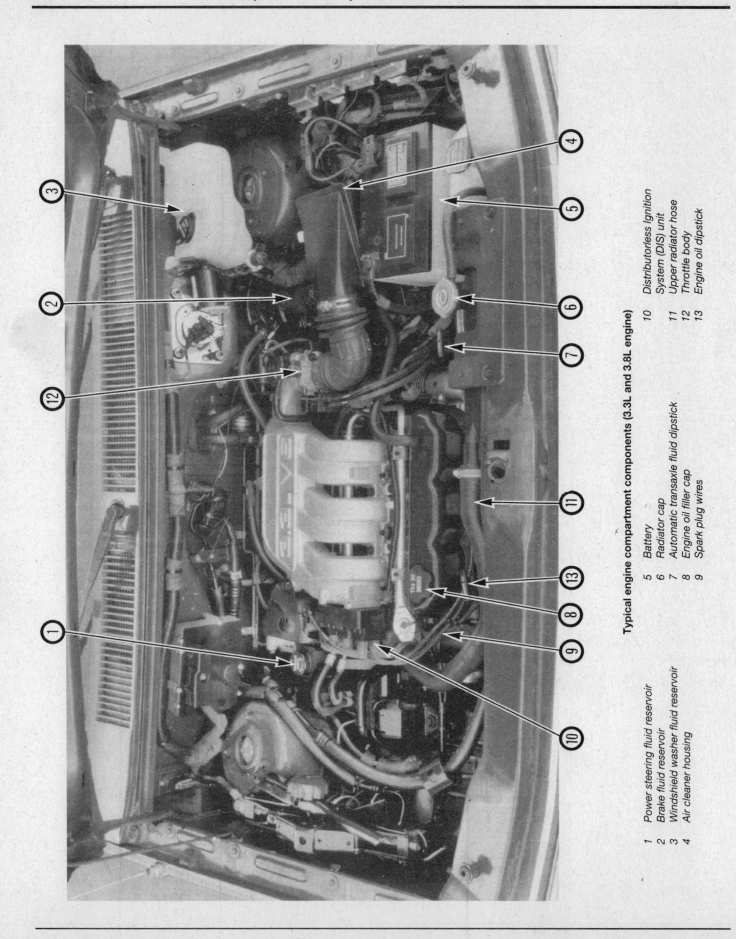

Typical engine compartment components (3.3L and 3.8L engine)

1   Power steering fluid reservoir
2   Brake fluid reservoir
3   Windshield washer fluid reservoir
4   Air cleaner housing
5   Battery
6   Radiator cap
7   Automatic transaxle fluid dipstick
8   Engine oil filler cap
9   Spark plug wires
10 Distributorless Ignition System (DIS) unit
11 Upper radiator hose
12 Throttle body
13 Engine oil dipstick

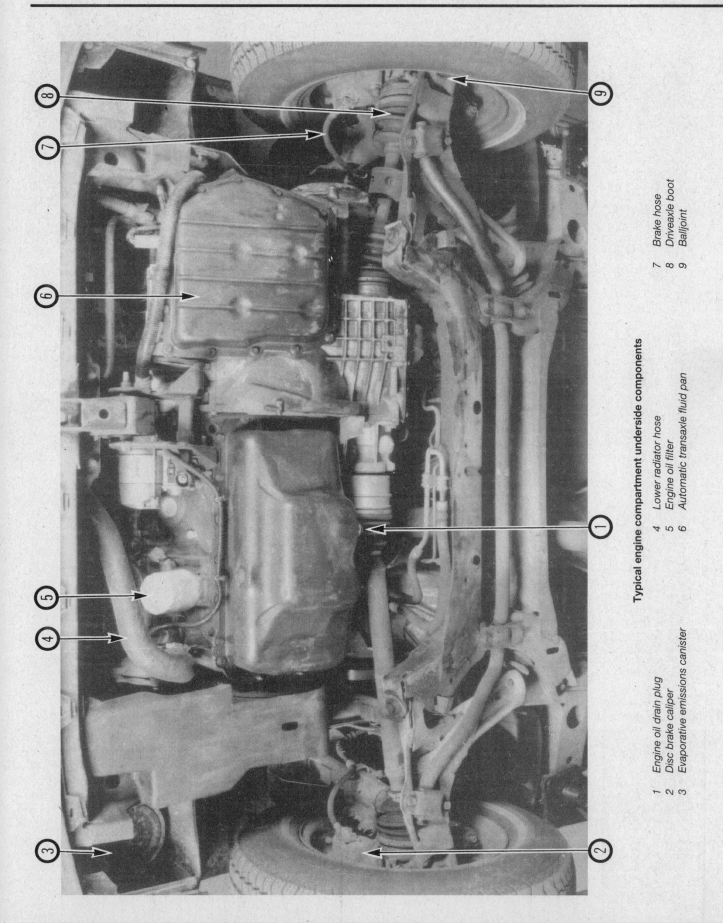

Typical engine compartment underside components

1 Engine oil drain plug
2 Disc brake caliper
3 Evaporative emissions canister
4 Lower radiator hose
5 Engine oil filter
6 Automatic transaxle fluid pan
7 Brake hose
8 Driveaxle boot
9 Balljoint

1

Typical rear underside components

1   Exhaust system expansion chamber
2   Fuel hoses
3   Fuel tank
4   Parking brake cable adjuster
5   Shock absorber
6   Brake hose
7   Brake assembly

1 Chrysler mini-van maintenance schedule

The following maintenance intervals are based on the assumption that the vehicle owner will be doing the maintenance or service work, as opposed to having a dealer service department do the work. Although the time/mileage intervals are loosely based on factory recommendations, most have been shortened to ensure, for example, that such items as lubricants and fluids are checked/changed at intervals that promote maximum engine/driveline service life. Also, subject to the preference of the individual owner interested in keeping his or her vehicle in peak condition at all times, and with the vehicle's ultimate resale in mind, many of the maintenance procedures may be performed more often than recommended in the following schedule. We encourage such owner initiative.

When the vehicle is new it should be serviced initially by a factory authorized dealer service department to protect the factory warranty. In many cases the initial maintenance check is done at no cost to the owner (check with your dealer service department for more information).

Every 250 miles or weekly, whichever comes first

Check the engine oil level; add oil as necessary (see Section 4)
Check the engine coolant level; add coolant as necessary (see Section 4)
Check the windshield washer fluid level (see Section 4)
Check the battery electrolyte level (see Section 4)
Check the brake fluid level (see Section 4)
Check the tires and tire pressures (see Section 5)
Check the automatic transaxle fluid level (see Section 6)
Check the power steering fluid level (see Section 7)
Check the wiper blade condition (see Section 8)
Check the operation of all lights
Check the horn operation

Every 3000 miles or 3 months, whichever comes first

Change the engine oil and filter (all models) (see Section 9)*

Every 7500 miles or 6 months, whichever comes first

Check the fuel system hoses, lines and connections for leaks and damage (see Section 26)
Add combustion chamber conditioner (Canadian models only) (see Section 34)
Check the brake hoses and lines for leaks and damage (see Section 31)
Check the suspension balljoint and steering linkage boots for damage and lubricant leaks (see Section 29)*

Check the driveaxle boots for damage and lubricant leaks (see Section 39)*
Check the manual transaxle lubricant level (see Section 12)
Check and clean the battery (see Section 10)
Rotate the tires (see Section 11)

Every 15,000 miles or 12 months, whichever comes first

Check and adjust, if necessary, the valve clearances (2.6L engine only)(Section 17)
Check the drivebelts (see Section 18)
Check the cooling system hoses and connections for leaks and damage (see Section 27)
Check the carburetor/fuel injection throttle body mounting nut torque (see Section 24)

Every 22,500 miles or 18 months, whichever comes first

Check the EGR system components for proper operation (see Section 22)
Check the condition of all vacuum hoses and connections (see Section 23)
Check the condition of the primary ignition wires and spark plug wires (see Section 16)
Check the distributor cap and rotor (see Section 16)
Check the exhaust pipes and hangers (see Section 28)
Check for freeplay in the steering linkage and balljoints (see Section 29)
Check the fuel evaporative emission system hoses and connections (see Section 40)
Replace the fuel filter (see Section 13)
Check the brakes (see Section 31)*

Every 30,000 miles or 24 months, whichever comes first

Check and service the rear wheel bearings (see Section 30)*
Replace the air filter element (see Section 19)*
Check the PCV valve (see Section 20)
Check the operation of the carburetor choke (Section 21)
Replace the spark plugs (see Section 15)
Check the parking brake operation (see Section 31)
Lubricate the front suspension balljoints and tie-rod ends (see Section 14)*
Drain and replace the engine coolant (see Section 32)
Change the manual transaxle lubricant (see Section 36)*
Change the automatic transaxle fluid and filter (see Section 37)*
Adjust the automatic transaxle bands (three-speed models only) (see Section 38)*

Every 50,000 miles or 60 months, whichever comes first

Replace the PCV valve (see Section 20)
Replace the oxygen sensor (1988 and earlier models)
  (see Chapter 6)

Every 60,000 miles or 68 months, whichever comes first

Inspect the timing belt (3.0 V6 engine only) (see Chapter 2)

Every 80,000 miles or 72 months, whichever comes first

Replace the oxygen sensor (1989 and later models)
  (see Chapter 6)

* This item is affected by "severe" operating conditions as described below. If the vehicle in question is operated under "severe" conditions, perform all maintenance procedures marked with an asterisk (*) at the following intervals:

Every 1,000 miles
Change the engine oil and filter (turbo models only)

Every 2,000 miles
Change the engine oil and filter (non-turbo models only)
Check the driveaxle, suspension and steering boots

Every 9,000 miles
Check the brakes
Service the rear wheel bearings

Every 15,000 miles
Replace the air filter element
Lubricate the tie-rod ends
Change the automatic transaxle fluid and filter
Adjust the automatic transaxle bands (three-speed models)
Change the manual transaxle lubricant and clean the pan
  magnet

Consider the conditions "severe" if most driving is done . . .
  In dusty areas
  Towing a trailer
  Idling for extended periods and/or low-speed operation
  When outside temperatures remain below freezing and
    most trips are less than four miles
  In heavy city traffic where outside temperatures regularly
    reach 90-degrees F or higher

2 Introduction

This Chapter is designed to help the home mechanic maintain the Chrysler minivan with the goals of maximum performance, economy, safety and reliability in mind.

Included is a master maintenance schedule, followed by procedures dealing specifically with each item on the schedule. Visual checks, adjustments, component replacement and other helpful items are included. Refer to the accompanying illustrations of the engine compartment and the underside of the vehicle for the locations of various components.

Adhering to the mileage/time maintenance schedule and following the step-by-step procedures, which is simply a preventive maintenance program, will result in maximum reliability and vehicle service life. Keep in mind that it's a comprehensive program - maintaining some items but not others at the specified intervals will not produce the same results.

As you service the vehicle, you'll discover that many of the procedures can - and should - be grouped together because of the nature of the particular procedure you're performing or because of the close proximity of two otherwise unrelated components to one another.

For example, if the vehicle is raised, you should inspect the exhaust, suspension, steering and fuel systems while you're under the vehicle. When you're rotating the tires, it makes good sense to check the brakes, since the wheels are already removed. Finally, let's suppose you have to borrow or rent a torque wrench. Even if you only need it to tighten the spark plugs, you might as well check the torque of as many critical fasteners as time allows.

The first step in this maintenance program is to prepare yourself before the actual work begins. Read through all the procedures you're planning to do, then gather up all the parts and tools needed. If it looks like you might run into problems during a particular job, seek advice from a mechanic or an experienced do-it-yourselfer.

3 Tune-up general information

The term "tune-up" is used in this manual to represent a combina-

tion of individual operations rather than one specific procedure.

If, from the time the vehicle is new, the routine maintenance schedule is followed closely and frequent checks are made of fluid levels and high wear items, as suggested throughout this manual, the engine will be kept in relatively good running condition and the need for additional work will be minimized.

More likely than not, however, there will be times when the engine is running poorly due to lack of regular maintenance. This is even more likely if a used vehicle, which hasn't received regular and frequent maintenance checks, is purchased. In such cases, an engine tune-up will be needed outside of the regular routine maintenance intervals.

The first step in any tune-up or diagnostic procedure to help correct a poor running engine is a cylinder compression check. A compression check (see Chapter 2, Part E) will help determine the condition of internal engine components and should be used as a guide for tune-up and repair procedures. For instance, if a compression check indicates serious internal engine wear, a conventional tune-up will not improve the performance of the engine and would be a waste of time and money. Because of its importance, the compression check should be done by someone with the right equipment and the knowledge to use it properly.

The following procedures are those most often needed to bring a generally poor running engine back into a proper state of tune:

Minor tune-up
Check all engine related fluids (see Section 4)
Clean, inspect and test the battery (see Section 10)
Replace the spark plugs (see Section 15)
Inspect the distributor cap and rotor (see Section 16)
Inspect the spark plug and coil wires (see Section 16)
Check and adjust the drivebelts (see Section 18)
Check the air filter (see Section 19)
Check the PCV valve (see Section 20)
Check all underhood hoses (see Section 23)
Check and adjust the engine idle speed (carbureted models)
  (see Section 33)
Check and adjust the ignition timing (see Section 34)
Check the cooling system (see Section 27)

4.4a The engine oil dipstick is located on the front (radiator side) of the engine

4.4b On 2.6L engines, the oil level should be between the ADD and FULL marks on the dipstick - if it isn't, add enough oil to bring the level up to or near the FULL mark (it takes one quart to raise the level from the ADD to the FULL mark)

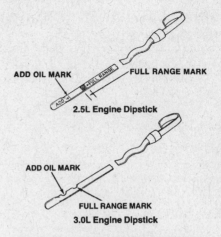

4.4c 2.5L four-cylinder (2.2L similar) and 3.0L V6 engine oil dipstick details

Major tune-up

All items listed under Minor tune-up plus . . .

Replace the air filter (see Section 19)
Replace the distributor cap and rotor (see Section 16)
Replace the spark plug wires (see Section 16)
Check the EGR system (see Section 22)
Check the fuel system (see Section 26)
Check the ignition system (Chapter 5)
Check the charging system (Chapter 5)

---

4   Fluid level checks

Note: *The following are fluid level checks to be done on a 250 mile or weekly basis. Additional fluid level checks can be found in specific maintenance procedures which follow. Regardless of the intervals, develop the habit of checking under the vehicle periodically for evidence of fluid leaks.*

1   Fluids are an essential part of the lubrication, cooling, brake and window washer systems. Because the fluids gradually become depleted and/or contaminated during normal operation of the vehicle, they must be replenished periodically. See Recommended lubricants and fluids at the beginning of this Chapter before adding fluid to any of the following components. **Note:** *The vehicle must be on level ground when fluid levels are checked.*

Engine oil

Refer to illustrations 4.4a, 4.4b, 4.4c, 4.4d and 4.5

2   The engine oil level is checked with a dipstick which is located on the front (radiator) side of the engine block. The dipstick extends through a tube and into the oil pan at the bottom of the engine.

3   The oil level should be checked before the vehicle has been driven, or about 15 minutes after the engine has been shut off. If the oil is checked immediately after driving the vehicle, some of the oil will remain in the upper engine components, resulting in an inaccurate reading on the dipstick.

4   Pull the dipstick out of the tube **(see illustration)** and wipe all the oil off the end with a clean rag or paper towel. Insert the clean dipstick all the way back into the tube, then pull it out again. Note the oil level at the end of the dipstick. Add oil as necessary to keep the level at the Full or MAX mark **(see illustrations)**.

5   Oil is added to the engine after removing a twist-off cap located on the valve cover **(see illustration)**. The cap will be marked "Engine oil" or something similar. A funnel may help reduce spills as the oil is poured in.

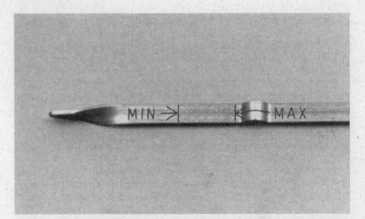

4.4d On the 3.3L V6 engine, the oil level should be kept within the cross-hatched area on the dipstick

4.5 The oil filler cap is located on the valve cover - turn it counterclockwise to remove it

6   Don't allow the level to drop below the Add mark or engine damage may occur. On the other hand, don't overfill the engine by adding too much oil - it may result in oil fouled spark plugs, oil leaks or seal failures.

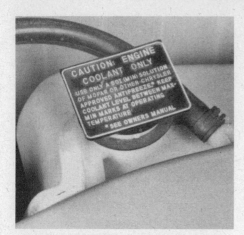

4.12   The coolant reservoir is located next to the radiator - flip up the cap to add more coolant

4.15a   The windshield washer reservoir is mounted on the firewall in the engine compartment

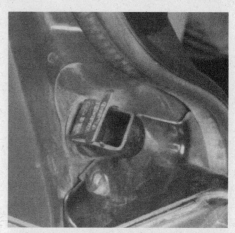

4.15b   Open the liftgate for access to the rear window washer fluid reservoir - flip up the cap to add more fluid and fill it to the base of the neck

7   Checking the oil level is an important preventive maintenance step. A consistently low oil level indicates oil leakage through damaged seals, defective gaskets or past worn rings or valve guides. If the oil looks milky in color or has water droplets in it, the block may be cracked. The engine should be checked immediately. The condition of the oil should also be checked. Each time you check the oil level, slide your thumb and index finger up the dipstick before wiping off the oil. If you see small dirt or metal particles clinging to the dipstick, the oil should be changed (see Section 9).

Engine coolant
Refer to illustration 4.12

Warning: *Do not allow antifreeze to come in contact with your skin or painted surfaces of the vehicle. Flush contaminated areas immediately with plenty of water. Don't store new coolant or leave old coolant lying around where it's accessible to children or pets - they're attracted by its sweet smell. Ingestion of even a small amount of coolant can be fatal! Wipe up garage floor and drip pan spills immediately. Keep antifreeze containers covered and repair cooling system leaks as soon as they're noticed.*

8   All vehicles covered by this manual are equipped with a pressurized coolant recovery system, which makes coolant level checks very easy. A coolant reservoir attached to the inner fender panel or the radiator itself is connected by a hose to the radiator filler neck. As the engine warms up, some coolant escapes through a valve in the radiator cap and travels through the hose into the reservoir. As the engine cools, the coolant is automatically drawn back into the cooling system to maintain the correct level.

9   The coolant level should be checked when the engine is at normal operating temperature. Simply note the fluid level in the reservoir - it should be at or near the Max mark.

10   The coolant level can also be checked by removing the radiator cap. **Warning:** *Don't remove the cap to check the coolant level when the engine is warm! Wait until the engine has cooled (at least five hours after operation), then wrap a thick cloth around the cap and turn it to the first stop. If any steam escapes from the cap, allow the engine to cool further, then remove the cap and check the level in the radiator.*

11   If only a small amount of coolant is required to bring the system up to the proper level, regular water can be used. However, to maintain the proper antifreeze/water mixture in the system, both should be mixed together to replenish a low level. High-quality antifreeze/coolant should be mixed with water in the proportion specified on the antifreeze container.

12   Coolant should be added to the reservoir after removing the cap **(see illustration)**.

13   As the coolant level is checked, note the condition of the coolant as well. It should be relatively clear. If it's brown or rust colored, the system should be drained, flushed and refilled (see Section 32).

14   If the coolant level drops consistently, there may be a leak in the system. Check the radiator, hoses, filler cap, drain plugs and water pump (see Section 27). If no leaks are noted, have the radiator filler cap pressure tested by a service station.

Windshield and rear window washer fluid
Refer to illustrations 4.15a and 4.15b

15   The fluid for the windshield and rear washer systems is stored in a plastic reservoirs in the engine compartment and at the rear of the vehicle. The level inside each reservoir should be maintained about one inch below the filler cap. The reservoirs are accessible after opening the hood and liftgate **(see illustrations)**.

16   In milder climates, plain water can be used in the reservoir, but it should be kept no more than two-thirds full to allow for expansion if the water freezes. In colder climates, use windshield washer system antifreeze, available at any auto parts store, to lower the freezing point of the fluid. Mix the antifreeze with water in accordance with the manufacturer's directions on the container. **Caution:** *Don't use cooling system antifreeze - it'll damage the vehicle's paint. To help prevent icing in cold weather, warm the windshield with the defroster before using the washer.*

Battery electrolyte
Refer to illustration 4.19

Warning: *Certain precautions must be followed when checking or servicing a battery. Hydrogen gas, which is highly flammable, is produced in the cells, so keep lighted tobacco, open flames, bare light bulbs and sparks away from the battery. The electrolyte inside the battery is dilute sulfuric acid, which can burn skin and cause serious injury if splashed in your eyes (wear safety glasses). It'll also ruin clothes and painted surfaces. Remove all metal jewelry which could contact the positive battery terminal and a grounded metal source, causing a direct short.*

17   Vehicles equipped with a maintenance-free battery require no maintenance - the battery case is sealed and has no removable caps for adding water.

18   If a maintenance-type battery is installed, the caps on top of the battery should be removed periodically to check for a low electrolyte level. This check is more critical during warm summer months.

19   Remove each of the caps and add distilled water to bring the level in each cell to the split ring in the filler opening **(see illustration)**.

20   At the same time the battery water level is checked, the overall condition of the battery and related components should be noted. See Section 10 for complete battery check and maintenance procedures.

Brake fluid
Refer to illustration 4.22

21   The brake master cylinder is located on the driver's side of the engine compartment firewall.

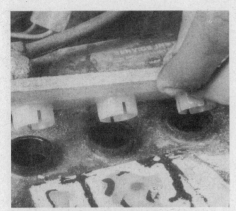

4.19 Remove the cell caps to check the water level in the battery - if the level is low, add distilled water only

4.22 The brake fluid level on non-ABS models should be kept at or near the bottom of the rings inside the reservoir filler neck

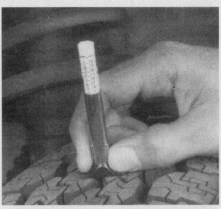

5.2 Use a tire tread depth indicator to monitor tire wear - they are available at auto parts stores and service stations and cost very little

1

5.3 This chart will help you determine the condition of the tires, the probable cause(s) of abnormal wear and the corrective action necessary

Condition	Probable cause	Corrective action	Condition	Probable cause	Corrective action
Shoulder wear	• Underinflation (both sides wear) • Incorrect wheel camber (one side wear) • Hard cornering • Lack of rotation	• Measure and adjust pressure. • Repair or replace axle and suspension parts. • Reduce speed. • Rotate tires.	Feathered edge Toe wear	• Incorrect toe	• Adjust toe-in.
Center wear	• Overinflation • Lack of rotation	• Measure and adjust pressure. • Rotate tires.	Uneven wear	• Incorrect camber or caster • Malfunctioning suspension • Unbalanced wheel • Out-of-round brake drum • Lack of rotation	• Repair or replace axle and suspension parts. • Repair or replace suspension parts. • Balance or replace. • Turn or replace. • Rotate tires.

22 Before removing the cap(s) to check the fluid, use a rag to clean all dirt off the top of the reservoir. If any foreign matter enters the master cylinder when the caps are removed, blockage in the brake system lines can occur. Also, make sure all painted surfaces around the master cylinder are covered, since brake fluid will ruin paint. On non-ABS models, the level should be maintained at the bottom of the rings in the neck of the reservoir (there are actually two separate reservoirs, so be sure to check both of them) **(see illustration)**. On ABS-equipped models, it is necessary to depressurize the hydraulic accumulator before checking the fluid level to get an accurate reading. With the ignition off, apply hard pressure (approximately 50 lbs) to the brake pedal 40 or 50 times to deplete the pressure (you'll feel the change in the pedal). Remove the caps and make sure the fluid level is even with the top of the white screen in the front filter/strainer.

23 If additional fluid is necessary to bring the level up, carefully pour new, clean brake fluid into the master cylinder. Be careful not to spill the fluid on painted surfaces. Be sure the specified fluid is used; mixing different types of brake fluid can cause damage to the system. See Recommended lubricants and fluids at the beginning of this Chapter or your owner's manual.

24 At this time the fluid and the master cylinder can be inspected for contamination. Normally the brake hydraulic system won't need periodic draining and refilling, but if rust deposits, dirt particles or water droplets are seen in the fluid, the system should be dismantled, cleaned and refilled with fresh fluid.

25 Reinstall the master cylinder caps.

26 The brake fluid in the master cylinder will drop slightly as the brake shoes or pads at each wheel wear down during normal operation. If the master cylinder requires repeated replenishing to keep the level up, it's an indication of leaks in the brake system which should be corrected immediately. Check all brake lines and connections, along with the wheel cylinders and booster (see Chapter 9 for more information).

27 If you discover one or both reservoirs empty or nearly empty, the brake system should be bled (see Chapter 9).

---

5 Tire and tire pressure checks

Refer to illustrations 5.2, 5.3, 5.4a, 5.4b and 5.8

1 Periodic inspection of the tires may spare you the inconvenience of being stranded with a flat tire. It can also provide you with vital information regarding possible problems in the steering and suspension systems before major damage occurs.

2 The original tires on this vehicle are equipped with 1/2-inch wide bands that will appear when tread depth reaches 1/16-inch, but they don't appear until the tires are worn out. Tread wear can be monitored with a simple, inexpensive device known as a tread depth indicator **(see illustration)**.

3 Note any abnormal tread wear **(see illustration)**. Tread pattern irregularities such as cupping, flat spots and more wear on one side than the other are indications of front end alignment and/or balance

5.4a   If a tire loses air on a steady basis, check the valve core first to make sure it's snug (special inexpensive wrenches are commonly available at auto parts stores)

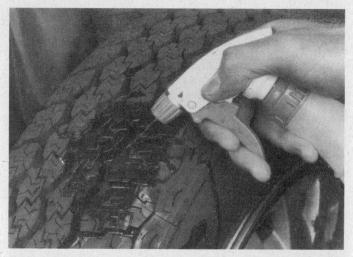

5.4b   If the valve core is tight, raise the corner of the vehicle with the low tire and spray a soapy water solution onto the tread as the tire is turned slowly – leaks will cause small bubbles to appear

5.8 To extend the life of the tires, check the air pressure at least once a week with an accurate gauge (don't forget the spare!)

6.3   The fluid is checked by removing the dipstick on the transaxle case - don't confuse it with the engine oil dipstick

problems. If any of these conditions are noted, take the vehicle to a tire shop or service station to correct the problem.

4   Look closely for cuts, punctures and embedded nails or tacks. Sometimes a tire will hold air pressure for a short time or leak down very slowly after a nail has embedded itself in the tread. If a slow leak persists, check the valve stem core to make sure it's tight **(see illustration)**. Examine the tread for an object that may have embedded itself in the tire or for a "plug" that may have begun to leak (radial tire punctures are repaired with a plug that's installed in a puncture). If a puncture is suspected, it can be easily verified by spraying a solution of soapy water onto the puncture area **(see illustration)**. he soapy solution will bubble if there's a leak. Unless the puncture is unusually large, a tire shop or service station can usually repair the tire.

5   Carefully inspect the inner sidewall of each tire for evidence of brake fluid leakage. If you see any, inspect the brakes immediately.

6   Correct air pressure adds miles to the lifespan of the tires, improves mileage and enhances overall ride quality. Tire pressure cannot be accurately estimated by looking at a tire, especially if it's a radial. A tire pressure gauge is essential. Keep an accurate gauge in the vehicle. The pressure gauges attached to the nozzles of air hoses at gas stations are often inaccurate.

7   Always check tire pressure when the tires are cold. Cold, in this case, means the vehicle has not been driven over a mile in the three

hours preceding a tire pressure check. A pressure rise of four to eight pounds is not uncommon once the tires are warm.

8   Unscrew the valve cap protruding from the wheel or hubcap and push the gauge firmly onto the valve stem **(see illustration)**. Note the reading on the gauge and compare the figure to the recommended tire pressure shown on the placard on the driver's side door pillar. Be sure to reinstall the valve cap to keep dirt and moisture out of the valve stem mechanism. Check all four tires and, if necessary, add enough air to bring them up to the recommended pressure.

9   Don't forget to keep the spare tire inflated to the specified pressure (refer to your owner's manual or the tire sidewall). Note that the pressure recommended for the compact spare is higher than for the tires on the vehicle.

---

6   Automatic transaxle fluid level check

Refer to illustrations 6.3 and 6.4

1   The fluid inside the transaxle should be at normal operating temperature to get an accurate reading on the dipstick. This is done by driving the vehicle for several miles, making frequent starts and stops to allow the transaxle to shift through all gears.

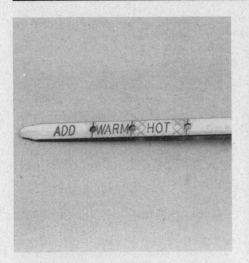

6.4 Check the fluid with the transaxle at normal operating temperature - the level should be kept in the HOT range (between the two upper holes)

7.2 The power steering fluid reservoir is located at the right end of the engine, towards the rear of the engine compartment

7.5 The power steering fluid dipstick on most models is marked so the fluid can be checked both cold and hot

2   Park the vehicle on a level surface, place the gear selector lever in Park and leave the engine running.
3   Remove the transaxle dipstick **(see illustration)** and wipe all the fluid from the end with a clean rag.
4   Push the dipstick back into the transaxle until the cap seats completely. Remove the dipstick again and note the fluid on the end. The level should be in the area marked Hot (between the two upper holes in the dipstick) **(see illustration)**. If the fluid isn't hot (temperature about 100-degrees F), the level should be in the area marked Warm (between the two lower holes).
5   If the fluid level is at or below the Add mark on the dipstick, add enough fluid to raise the level to within the marks indicated for the appropriate temperature. Fluid should be added directly into the dipstick hole, using a funnel to prevent spills.
6   Do not overfill the transaxle. Never allow the fluid level to go above the upper hole on the dipstick - it could cause internal transaxle damage. The best way to prevent overfilling is to add fluid a little at a time, driving the vehicle and checking the level between additions.
7   Use only the transaxle fluid specified by the manufacturer. This information can be found in the Recommended lubricants and fluids Section at the beginning of this Chapter.
8   The condition of the fluid should also be checked along with the level. If it's a dark reddish-brown color, or if it smells burned, it should be changed. If you're in doubt about the condition of the fluid, purchase some new fluid and compare the two for color and smell.

7   Power steering fluid level check

Refer to illustrations 7.2 and 7.5

1   Unlike manual steering, the power steering system relies on fluid which may, over a period of time, require replenishing.
2   The reservoir for the power steering pump is located on the rear side of the engine on the passenger's side of the engine compartment **(see illustration)**.
3   The power steering fluid level can be checked with the engine cold.
4   With the engine off, use a rag to clean the reservoir cap and the area around the cap. This will help prevent foreign material from falling into the reservoir when the cap is removed.
5   Turn and pull out the reservoir cap, which has a dipstick attached to it. Remove the fluid at the bottom of the dipstick with a clean rag. Reinstall the cap to get a fluid level reading. Remove the cap again and note the fluid level. It should be at the top of the Cold range on the dipstick **(see illustration)**. If the engine is warm, the level should be at

the top of the Hot range.
6   If additional fluid is required, pour the specified type directly into the reservoir using a funnel to prevent spills.
7   If the reservoir requires frequent fluid additions, all power steering hoses, hose connections, the power steering pump and the steering box should be carefully checked for leaks.

8   Wiper blade inspection and replacement

1   The windshield and rear wiper blade elements should be checked periodically for cracks and deterioration.
2   To gain access to the wiper blades, turn on the ignition switch and cycle the wipers to a position on the where the work can be performed, then turn off the ignition.
3   Lift the wiper blade assembly away from the glass.

Windshield wipers
Refer to illustrations 8.4a, 8.4b, 8.5a and 8.5b
4   Use a small screwdriver to press the release button and slide blade off the wiper arm pin **(see illustrations)**.
5   Squeeze the metal tabs on the together with needle-nose pliers and slide the element out of wiper bridge **(see illustrations)**.
6   Slide the new element into the bridge until it locks in place.
7   Installation is the reverse of removal.

Rear wiper
Early models
Refer to illustration 8.8
8   Use a pair of needle-nose pliers to pinch the release lock on the end, slide the end of the element back through the bridge claw, then remove it from the claw **(see illustration)**.
9   Installation is the reverse of removal.

Later models
Refer to illustrations 8.10, 8.11a, 8.11b and 8.12
10   Lift the release tab and remove the wiper blade assembly from the arm **(see illustration)**.
11   Use a small screwdriver to pry up the lock levers, squeeze the bridges and rotate them to detach them from the frame **(see illustrations)**.
12   Slide the bridges off the element **(see illustration)**.
13   Slide the bridges onto the new element, snap the frame on the bridges, then secure them with the lock levers.
14   Installation is reverse of removal

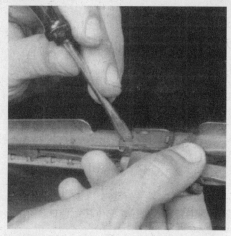

8.4a   Press the release button in with a
small screwdriver

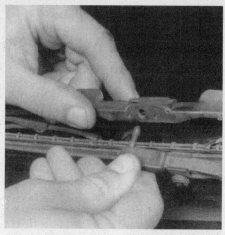

8.4b   then slide the wiper blade assembly
off the pin on the arm

8.5a   Use needle-nose pliers to squeeze
the end of the element . . .

8.5b   . . . then slide it out of the bridge

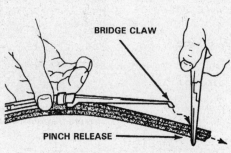

8.8   Pinch the release tab with needle-
nose pliers, then push the element back
through the end of the claw and
slide it out

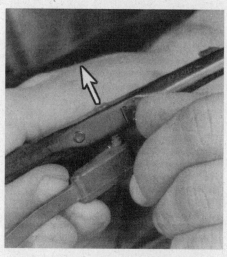

8.10   Lift the release tab and slide the
rear wiper off the pin

8.11a   Pry the lock levers to the
Up position

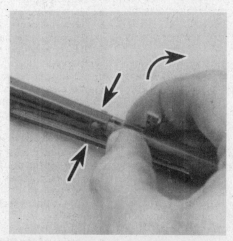

8.11b   then squeeze the bridges together
while rotating them

8.12   Slide the bridges off the element

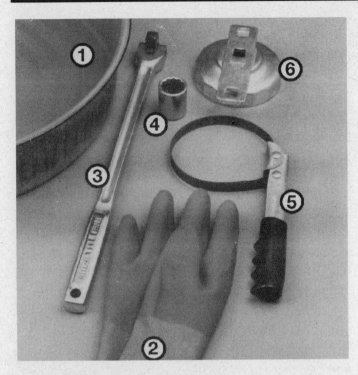

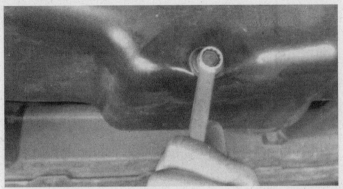

9.9   To avoid rounding off the corners, use the correct size box-end wrench or a six-point socket to remove the engine oil drain plug

9.3   These tools are required when changing the engine oil and filter

1   *Drain pan – It should be fairly shallow in depth, but wide to prevent spills*
2   *Rubber gloves – When removing the drain plug and filter, you will get oil on your hands (the gloves will prevent burns)*
3   *Breaker bar – Sometimes the oil drain plug is tight and a long breaker bar is needed to loosen it*
4   *Socket – To be used with the breaker bar or a ratchet (must be the correct size to fit the drain plug – six- point preferred)*
5   *Filter wrench – This is a metal band-type wrench, which requires clearance around the filter to be effective*
6   *Filter wrench – This type fits on the bottom of the filter and can be turned with a ratchet or breaker bar (different size wrenches are available for different types of filters)*

9.14   The oil filter is usually on very tight and normally will require a special wrench for removal - DO NOT use the wrench to tighten the new filter!

9   Engine oil and filter change

Refer to illustrations 9.3, 9.9, 9.14 and 9.19

1   Frequent oil changes are the most important preventive maintenance procedures that can be done by the home mechanic. When engine oil ages, it gets diluted and contaminated, which ultimately leads to premature engine wear.
2   Although some sources recommend oil filter changes every other oil change, a new filter should be installed every time the oil is changed.
3   Gather together all necessary tools and materials before beginning this procedure **(see illustration)**. **Note:** *To avoid rounding off the corners of the drain plug, use a six-point socket.*
4   In addition, you should have plenty of clean rags and newspapers handy to mop up any spills. Access to the underside of the vehicle is greatly improved if it can be lifted on a hoist, driven onto ramps or supported by jackstands. Warning: Don't work under a vehicle that is supported only by a jack!
5   If this is your first oil change on the vehicle, crawl underneath it and familiarize yourself with the locations of the oil drain plug and the oil filter. Since the engine and exhaust components will be warm during the actual work, it's a good idea to figure out any potential prob-

lems beforehand.
6   Allow the engine to warm up to normal operating temperature. If oil or tools are needed, use the warm-up time to gather everything necessary for the job. The correct type of oil to buy for your application can be found in the Recommended lubricants and fluids Section at the beginning of this Chapter.
7   With the engine oil warm (warm oil will drain better and more built-up sludge will be removed with it), raise the vehicle and support it securely on jackstands. They should be placed under the portions of the body designated as hoisting and jacking points (see Jacking and towing at the front of this manual).
8   Move all necessary tools, rags and newspapers under the vehicle. Place the drain pan under the drain plug. Keep in mind that the oil will initially flow from the engine with some force, so position the pan accordingly.
9   Being careful not to touch any of the hot exhaust components, use the breaker bar and socket to remove the drain plug near the bottom of the oil pan **(see illustration)**. Depending on how hot the oil is, you may want to wear gloves while unscrewing the plug the final few turns.
10   Allow the oil to drain into the pan. It may be necessary to move the pan further under the engine as the oil flow reduces to a trickle.
11   After all the oil has drained, clean the plug thoroughly with a rag. Small metal particles may cling to it and would immediately contaminate the new oil.
12   Clean the area around the oil pan opening and reinstall the plug. Tighten it securely.
13   Move the drain pan into position under the oil filter.
14   Now use the filter wrench to loosen the oil filter **(see illustration)**. Chain or metal band-type filter wrenches may distort the filter canister, but don't worry about it - the filter will be discarded anyway.
15   Sometimes the oil filter is on so tight it cannot be loosened, or it's positioned in an area inaccessible with a conventional filter wrench.

9.19   Lubricate the oil filter gasket with clean engine oil before installing the filter on the engine

Other type of tools, which fit over the end of the filter and turned with a ratchet/breaker bar, are available and may be better suited for removing the filter. If the filter is extremely tight, position the filter wrench near the threaded end of the filter, close to the engine.

16   Completely unscrew the old filter. Be careful, it's full of oil. Empty the old oil inside the filter into the drain pan.

17   Compare the old filter with the new one to make sure they're identical.

18   Use a clean rag to remove all oil, dirt and sludge from the area where the oil filter mounts on the engine. Check the old filter to make sure the rubber gasket isn't stuck to the engine mounting surface.

19   Apply a light coat of oil to the rubber gasket on the new oil filter **(see illustration)**.

20   Attach the new filter to the engine following the tightening directions printed on the filter canister or packing box. Most filter manufacturers recommend against using a filter wrench due to the possibility of overtightening and damaging the canister.

21   Remove all tools and materials from under the vehicle, being careful not to spill the oil in the drain pan. Lower the vehicle off the jackstands.

22   Move to the engine compartment and locate the oil filler cap on the engine.

23   If the filler opening is obstructed, use a funnel when adding oil.

24   Pour the specified amount of new oil into the engine. Wait a few minutes to allow the oil to drain to the pan, then check the level on the dipstick (see Section 4 if necessary). If the oil level is at or above the Add mark, start the engine and allow the new oil to circulate.

25   Run the engine for only about a minute, then shut it off. Immediately look under the vehicle and check for leaks at the oil pan drain plug and around the oil filter. If either one is leaking, tighten with a bit more force.

26   With the new oil circulated and the filter now completely full, recheck the level on the dipstick. If necessary, add enough oil to bring the level to the Full mark on the dipstick.

27   During the first few trips after an oil change, make it a point to check for leaks and keep a close watch on the oil level.

28   The old oil drained from the engine cannot be reused in its present state and should be disposed of. Oil reclamation centers, auto repair shops and gas stations will normally accept the oil. After the oil has cooled, it should be drained into containers (plastic bottles with screw-on tops are preferred) for transport to a disposal site.

---

10   Battery check, maintenance and charging

Check and maintenance
Refer to illustrations 10.1, 10.6a, 10.6b, 10.7a and 10.7b

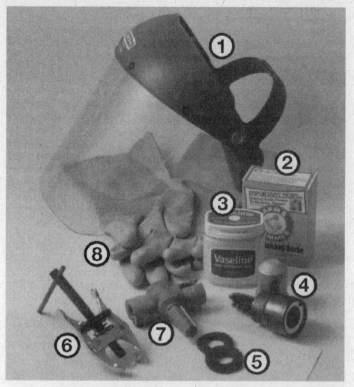

10.1   Tools and materials required for battery maintenance

1   ***Face shield/safety goggles*** – *When removing corrosion with a brush, the acidic particles can easily fly up into your eyes*

2   ***Baking soda*** – *A solution of baking soda and water can be used to neutralize corrosion*

3   ***Petroleum jelly*** – *A layer of this on the battery posts will help prevent corrosion*

4   ***Battery post/cable cleaner*** – *This wire brush cleaning tool will remove all traces of corrosion from the battery posts and cable clamps*

5   ***Treated felt washers*** – *Placing one of these on each post, directly under the cable clamps, will help prevent corrosion*

6   ***Puller*** – *Sometimes the cable clamps are very difficult to pull off the posts, even after the nut/bolt has been completely loosened. This tool pulls the clamp straight up and off the post without damage*

7   ***Battery post/cable cleaner*** – *Her is another cleaning tool which is a slightly different version of number 4 above, but it does the same thing*

8   ***Rubber gloves*** – *Another safety item to consider when servicing the battery; remember, that's acid inside the battery!*

1   A routine preventive maintenance program for the battery in your vehicle is the only way to ensure quick and reliable starts. But before performing any battery maintenance, make sure that you have the proper equipment necessary to work safely around the battery **(see illustration)**.

2   There are also several precautions that should be taken whenever battery maintenance is performed. Before servicing the battery, always turn the engine and all accessories off and disconnect the cable from the negative terminal of the battery.

3   The battery produces hydrogen gas, which is both flammable and explosive. Never create a spark, smoke or light a match around the battery. Always charge the battery in a ventilated area.

4   Electrolyte contains poisonous and corrosive sulfuric acid. Do not allow it to get in your eyes, on your skin on on your clothes. Never in-

10.6a   Battery terminal corrosion usually appears as light, fluffy powder

10.6b   Removing the cable from a battery post with a wrench - sometimes a special battery pliers is required for this procedure if corrosion has caused deterioration of the nut hex (always remove the ground cable first and hook it up last!)

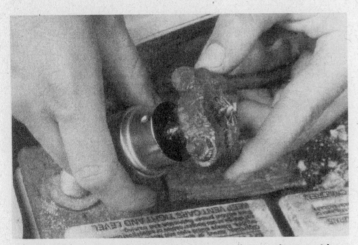

10.7a   When cleaning the cable clamps, all corrosion must be removed (the inside of the clamp is tapered to match the taper on the post, so don't remove too much material)

10.7b   Regardless of the type of tool used on the battery posts, a clean, shiny surface should be the result

gest it. Wear protective safety glasses when working near the battery. Keep children away from the battery.

5   Note the external condition of the battery. If the positive terminal and cable clamp on your vehicle's battery is equipped with a rubber protector, make sure that it's not torn or damaged. It should completely cover the terminal. Look for any corroded or loose connections, cracks in the case or cover or loose hold-down clamps. Also check the entire length of each cable for cracks and frayed conductors.

6   If corrosion, which looks like white, fluffy deposits **(see illustration)** is evident, particularly around the terminals, the battery should be removed for cleaning. Loosen the cable clamp nuts with a wrench, being careful to remove the negative cable first, and slide them off the terminals **(see illustration)**. Then disconnect the hold-down clamp nuts, remove the clamp and lift the battery from the engine compartment.

7   Clean the cable clamps thoroughly with a battery brush or a terminal cleaner and a solution of warm water and baking soda **(see illustration)**. Wash the terminals and the top of the battery case with the same solution but make sure that the solution doesn't get into the battery. When cleaning the cables, terminals and battery top, wear safety goggles and rubber gloves to prevent any solution from coming in contact with your eyes or hands. Wear old clothes too - even diluted, sulfuric acid splashed onto clothes will burn holes in them. If the terminals have been extensively corroded, clean them up with a terminal cleaner **(see illustration)**. Thoroughly wash all cleaned areas with plain water.

8   Before reinstalling the battery in the engine compartment, inspect the plastic battery carrier. If it's dirty or covered with corrosion, remove it and clean it in the same solution of warm water and baking soda. Inspect the metal brackets which support the carrier to make sure that they are not covered with corrosion. If they are, wash them off. If corrosion is extensive, sand the brackets down to bare metal and spray them with a zinc-based primer (available in spray cans at auto paint and body supply stores).

9   Reinstall the battery carrier and the battery back into the engine compartment. Make sure that no parts or wires are laying on the carrier during installation of the battery.

10   Install a pair of specially treated felt washers around the terminals (available at auto parts stores), then coat the terminals and the cable clamps with petroleum jelly or grease to prevent further corrosion. Install the cable clamps and tighten the nuts, being careful to install the negative cable last.

11   Install the hold-down clamp and nuts. Tighten the nuts only enough to hold the battery firmly in place. Overtightening these nuts can crack the battery case.

Charging

12   Remove all of the cell caps (if equipped) and cover the holes with a clean cloth to prevent spattering electrolyte. Disconnect the negative battery cable and hook the battery charger leads to the battery posts (positive to positive, negative to negative), then plug in the charger. Make sure it is set at 12 volts if it has a selector switch.

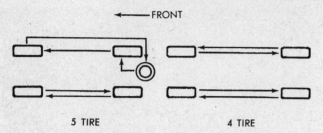

11.2   The recommended tire rotation pattern for these models

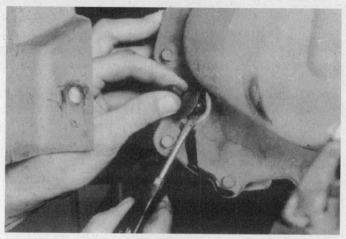

12.3   Use a screwdriver to pry the rubber fill plug out of the transaxle

13   If you're using a charger with a rate higher than two amps, check the battery regularly during charging to make sure it doesn't overheat. If you're using a trickle charger, you can safely let the battery charge overnight after you've checked it regularly for the first couple of hours.

14   If the battery has removeable cell caps, measure the specific gravity with a hydrometer every hour during the last few hours of the charging cycle. Hydrometers are available inexpensively from auto parts stores - follow the instructions that come with the hydrometer. Consider the battery charged when there's no change in the specific gravity reading for two hours and the electrolyte in the cells is gassing (bubbling) freely. The specific gravity reading from each cell should be very close to the others. If not, the battery probably has a bad cell(s).

15   Some batteries with sealed tops have built-in hydrometers on the top that indicate the state of charge by the color displayed in the hydrometer window. Normally, a bright-colored hydrometer indicates a full charge and a dark hydrometer indicates the battery still needs charging. Check the battery manufacturer's instructions to be sure you know what the colors mean.

16   If the battery has a sealed top and no built-in hydrometer, you can hook up a digital voltmeter across the battery terminals to check the charge. A fully charged battery should read 12.6 volts or higher.

17   Further information on the battery and jump starting can be found in Chapter 5 and at the front of this manual.

11   Tire rotation

Refer to illustration 11.2

1   The tires should be rotated at the specified intervals and whenever uneven wear is noticed. Since the vehicle will be raised and the tires removed anyway, this is a good time to check the brakes (see Section 31) and/or repack the rear wheel bearings (see Section 30). Read over the appropriate Section if other work will be done at the same time.

2   The rotation pattern depends on whether or not the spare is included in the rotation **(see illustration)**.

3   See the information in Jacking and towing at the front of this manual for the proper procedures to follow when raising the vehicle and changing a tire; however, if the brakes are to be checked, don't apply the parking brake as stated. Make sure the tires are blocked to prevent the vehicle from rolling.

4   Preferably, the entire vehicle should be raised at the same time. This can be done on a hoist or by jacking up each corner of the vehicle and lowering it onto jackstands. Always use four jackstands and make sure the vehicle is safely supported.

5   After the tire rotation, check and adjust the tire pressures as necessary and be sure to check wheel lug nut tightness.

12   Manual transaxle lubricant level check

Refer to illustration 12.3

1   Manual transaxles don't have a dipstick. The lubricant level is checked by removing a rubber or screw-type plug from the side of the transaxle case. Check the lubricant level with the engine cold.

2   Locate the plug and use a rag to clean it and the surrounding area. It may be necessary to remove the left inner fenderwell cover for access to the plug.

3   Unscrew the fill plug with a wrench. On models with a rubber plug, pry it out with a small screwdriver **(see illustration)**. If lubricant immediately starts leaking out, insert the plug back into the transaxle - the lubricant level is alright. If lubricant doesn't leak out, completely remove the plug and use a finger to feel the lubricant level. The lubricant level should be even with the bottom of the plug hole.

4   If the transaxle requires additional lubricant, use a funnel with a rubber tube or a syringe to pour or squeeze the recommended lubricant into the plug hole to restore the level. **Caution:** *Use only the specified transaxle lubricant - see Recommended lubricants and fluids at the beginning of this Chapter.*

5   Push or screw the plug securely back into the transaxle. Drive the vehicle and check for leaks around the plug.

13   Fuel filter replacement

Warning: *Gasoline is extremely flammable, so take extra precautions when you work on any part of the fuel system. Don't smoke or allow open flames or bare light bulbs near the work area, and don't work in a garage where a natural gas-type appliance (such as a water heater or clothes dryer) with a pilot light is present. If you spill any fuel on your skin, rinse it off immediately with soap and water. When you perform any kind of work on the fuel system, wear safety glasses and have a Class B type fire extinguisher on hand.*

Carbureted models

Refer to illustrations 13.1a and 13.1b

1   The fuel filter is a disposable unit and is located in the fuel line between the fuel pump and the carburetor **(see illustrations)**.

2   This job is best done with the engine cold (after sitting at least three hours) and the cooling fan or negative battery cable disconnected. You will need pliers to loosen and slide back the fuel line clamps, the correct replacement filter and some clean rags.

3   Place the rags under the filter to catch any fuel that is spilled as the fuel line is disconnected.

4   Slide back the clamps, pull the hoses off and remove the filter. On 2.6L engines it will be necessary to disengage the mounting bracket.

5   Push the hoses onto the new filter and install the clamps.

6   Connect the battery and/or fan, start the engine, check for leaks and make sure the filter is securely mounted.

Fuel-injected models

Refer to illustration 13.10

7   Depressurized the fuel system (see Chapter 4).

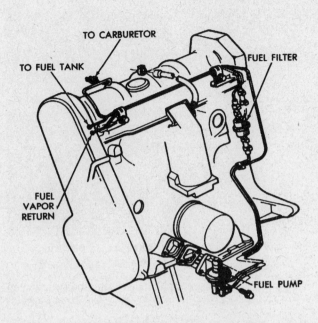

13.1a   2.2L engine fuel filter details

13.1b On 2.6L engines, the fuel filter is mounted near the carburetor

1

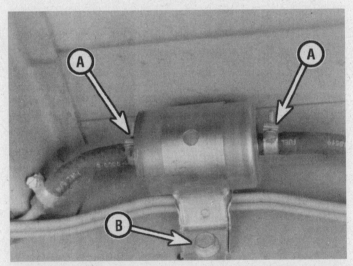

13.10   On fuel-injected models, the fuel filter is located under the right rear of the vehicle and is secured by two hose clamps (A) and a bolt (B)

8   The fuel filter is a disposable canister type and is located in the fuel line under the right rear of the vehicle, adjacent to the fuel tank.
9   Raise the rear of the vehicle and support it securely on jackstands.
10   Loosen the filter hose clamps (see illustration).
11   Wrap a cloth around the fuel filter to catch the residual fuel (which may still be under slight pressure) and disconnect the hoses. It's a good idea to tie rags around your wrists to keep fuel from running down your arms.
12   Remove the bracket mounting bolt and detach the filter from the vehicle; hold your finger over the outlet to keep the residual fuel from running out.
13   Place the new filter in position, install the mounting bolt and tighten it securely. If the hoses are damaged or deteriorated, install new ones along with the new filter.
14   Install new clamps and attach the hoses to the filter. Tighten the clamps securely.
15   Start the engine and check carefully for leaks at the hose connections.

14.1 Materials required for chassis and body lubrication

1   *Engine oil* – *Light engine oil in a can like this can be used for door and hood hinges*
2   *Graphite spray* – *Used to lubricate lock cylinders*
3   *Grease* – *Grease, in a variety of types and weights, is available for use in a grease gun. Check the Specifications for your requirements.*
4   *Grease gun* – *A common grease gun, shown here with a detachable hose and nozzle, is needed for chassis lubrication. After use, clean it thoroughly!*

14   Chassis lubrication

Refer to illustrations 14.1 and 14.6

1   A grease gun and a cartridge filled with the proper grease (see *Recommended lubricants and fluids*), graphite spray and an oil can filled with engine oil will be required to lubricate the chassis components (see illustration). Occasionally, on later model vehicles, plugs will be installed rather than grease fittings. If so, grease fittings will

14.6   Pump the grease into the balljoint fitting until the rubber seal is firm

have to be purchased and installed.

2   Look under the vehicle and see if grease fittings or plugs are installed. If there are plugs, remove them with a wrench and buy grease fittings which will thread into the component. A dealer parts department or auto parts store will be able to supply the correct fittings. Straight and angled fittings are available.

3   For easier access under the vehicle, raise it with a jack and place jackstands under the portions of the body designated as hoisting and jacking points front and rear (see Jacking and towing at the front of this manual). Make sure it's securely supported by the stands.

4   Before beginning, force a little grease out of the nozzle to remove any dirt from the end of the gun. Wipe the nozzle clean with a rag.

5   With the grease gun and plenty of clean rags, crawl under the vehicle and begin lubricating the components.

6   Wipe the suspension balljoint grease fitting clean and push the nozzle firmly over it **(see illustration)**. Operate the lever on the grease gun to force grease into the component. The balljoints should be lubricated until the rubber seal is firm to the touch. Don't pump too much grease into the fitting as it could rupture the seal. For all other suspension and steering components, continue pumping grease into the fitting until it oozes out of the joint between the two components. If grease escapes around the grease gun nozzle, the fitting is clogged or the nozzle is not completely seated on the fitting. Resecure the gun nozzle to the fitting and try again. If necessary, replace the fitting with a new one.

7   Wipe the excess grease from the components and the grease fitting. Repeat the procedure for the remaining fittings.

8   Lubricate the sliding contact and pivot points of the manual transaxle shift linkage with the specified grease. While you're under the vehicle, clean and lubricate the parking brake cable along with the cable guides and levers. This can be done by smearing some of the chassis grease onto the cable and related parts with your fingers. Lubricate the clutch adjuster and cable, as well as the cable positioner, with a thin film of multi-purpose grease.

9   Lower the vehicle to the ground.

10   Open the hood and smear a little chassis grease on the hood latch mechanism. Have an assistant pull the hood release lever from inside the vehicle as you lubricate the cable at the latch.

11   Lubricate all the hinges (door, hood, etc.) with the recommended lubricant to keep them in proper working order.

12   The key lock cylinders can be lubricated with spray-on graphite or silicone lubricant which is available at auto parts stores.

13   Lubricate the door weatherstripping with silicone spray. This will reduce chafing and retard wear

---

15   Spark plug replacement

Refer to illustrations 15.2, 15.5a, 15.5b, 15.7, 15.9a, 15.9b and 15.11

1   *The spark plugs are located on the front side of the engine, facing*

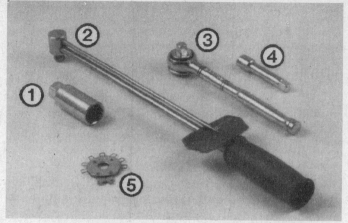

15.2   Tools required for changing spark plugs

1   *Spark plug socket – This will have special padding inside to protect the spark plug's porcelain insulator*

2   *Torque wrench – Although not mandatory, using this tool is the best way to ensure the plugs are tightened properly*

3   *Ratchet – Standard hand tool to fit the spark plug socket*

4   *Extension – Depending on model and accessories, you may need special extensions and universal joints to reach one or more of the plugs*

5   *Spark plug gap gauge – This gauge for checking the gap comes in a variety of styles. Make sure the gap for your engine is included.*

the radiator on four-cylinder models and on both the front and rear sides on V6 models. **Caution:** *Before beginning work, disconnect the negative battery cable to prevent the electric cooling fan from coming on.*

2   In most cases the tools necessary for spark plug replacement include a spark plug socket which fits onto a ratchet (this special socket will be padded inside to protect the porcelain insulators on the new plugs), various extensions and a feeler gauge to check and adjust the spark plug gap **(see illustration)**. A special plug wire removal tool is available for separating the wire boot from the spark plug, but it isn't absolutely necessary. Since these engines are equipped with an aluminum cylinder head, a torque wrench should be used for tightening the spark plugs.

3   The best approach when replacing the spark plugs is to purchase the new spark plugs beforehand, adjust them to the proper gap and then replace each plug one at a time. When buying the new spark plugs, be sure to obtain the correct plug for your specific engine. This information can be found on the Emission Control Information label located under the hood, in the factory owner's manual or in the Specifications at the front of this Chapter. If differences exist between the sources, purchase the spark plug type specified on the VECI label as it was printed for your specific engine.

4   Allow the engine to cool completely before attempting to remove any of the plugs. During this cooling off time, each of the new spark plugs can be inspected for defects and the gaps can be checked.

5   The gap is checked by inserting the proper thickness gauge between the electrodes at the tip of the plug **(see illustration)**. The gap between the electrodes should be as specified on the VECI label in the engine compartment. The wire should touch each of the electrodes. If the gap is incorrect, use the adjuster on the thickness gauge body to bend the curved side electrode slightly until the proper gap is obtained **(see illustration)**. Also, at this time check for cracks in the spark plug body (if any are found, the plug should not be used). If the side electrode is not exactly over the center one, use the adjuster to align the two.

6   Cover the front of the vehicle to prevent damage to the paint.

7   With the engine cool, remove the spark plug wire from one spark

15.5a Spark plug manufacturers recommend using a wire type gauge when checking the gap - if the wire does not slide between the electrodes with a slight drag, adjustment is required

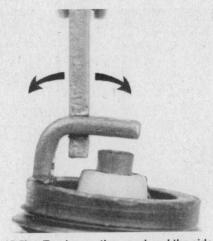

15.5b To change the gap, bend the side electrode only, as indicated by the arrows, and be very careful not to crack or chip the porcelain insulator surrounding the center electrode

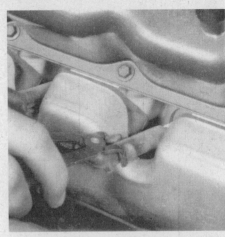

15.7 Pull on the spark plug wire boot and twist it back-and-forth while pulling it - a plug wire removal tool makes this job easier

1

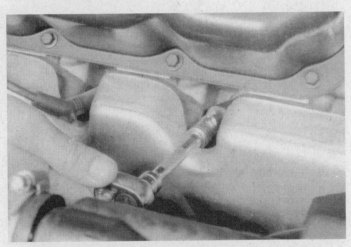

15.9a Use a ratchet and short extension to remove the spark plugs

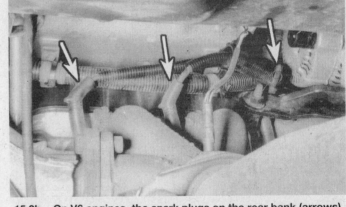

15.9b On V6 engines, the spark plugs on the rear bank (arrows) are accessible from below the vehicle

plug. Pull only on the boot at the end of the wire; don't pull on the wire. Use a twisting motion to free the boot and wire from the plug. A plug wire removal tool (mentioned earlier) should be used if available **(see illustration)**.

8   If compressed air is available, use it to blow any dirt or foreign material away from the spark plug area. A common bicycle pump will also work. The idea here is to eliminate the possibility of material falling into the cylinder through the plug hole as the spark plug is removed.

9   Now place the spark plug socket over the plug and remove it from the engine by turning it in a counterclockwise direction **(see illustration)**. On V6 models, it will be necessary to raise the vehicle and support it on jackstands for access to the rear bank spark plugs **(see illustration)**.

10   Compare the spark plug with those shown in the accompanying photos to get an indication of the overall running condition of the engine.

11   Thread one of the new plugs into the hole, tightening it as much as possible by hand. **Caution:** *Be extremely careful - these engines have aluminum cylinder heads, which means the spark plug hole threads can be stripped easily. It may be a good idea to slip a short length of rubber hose over the end of the plug to use as a tool to thread it into place. The hose will grip the plug well enough to turn it, but will start to slip on the plug if the plug begins to cross-thread in the*

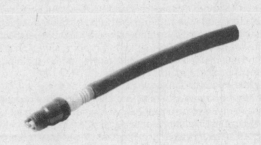

15.11 A length of 3/16-inch ID rubber hose will save time and prevent damaged threads when installing the spark plugs

hole - this will prevent damaged threads and the accompanying costs involved in repairing them **(see illustration)**.

12   Attach the plug wire to the new spark plug, again using a twisting motion on the boot until it's seated on the spark plug.

13   Repeat the above procedure for the remaining spark plugs, replacing them one at a time to prevent mixing up the spark plug wires.

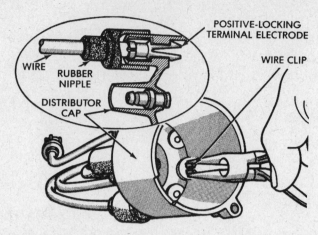

16.7　When replacing the spark plug wires, use a pair of pliers to compress the wire retaining clips inside the distributor cap before pulling the wires out

16　Spark plug wire, distributor cap and rotor check and replacement

Refer to illustrations 16.7, 16.9, 16.10a and 16.10b

Note: *3.3L engines use a Distributorless Ignition System (DIS), so on these models only the spark plug wires can be replaced.*

1　The spark plug wires should be checked at the recommended intervals or whenever new spark plugs are installed.

2　The wires should be inspected one at a time to prevent mixing up the order which is essential for proper engine operation.

3　Disconnect the plug wire from the spark plug. A removal tool can be used for this, or you can grab the rubber boot, twist slightly and then pull the wire free. Don't pull on the wire itself, only on the rubber boot.

4　Check inside the boot for corrosion, which will look like a white, crusty powder (don't mistake the white dielectric grease used on some plug wire boots for corrosion).

5　Now push the wire and boot back onto the end of the spark plug. It should be a tight fit on the plug end. If not, remove the wire and use a pair of pliers to carefully crimp the metal connector inside the wire boot until the fit is snug.

6　Now, using a cloth, clean each wire along its entire length. Remove all built-up dirt and grease. As this is done, inspect for burned areas, cracks and any other form of damage. Bend the wires in several places to ensure that the conductive material inside hasn't hardened. Repeat the procedure for the remaining wires (don't forget the distributor cap-to-coil wire).

7　Remove the distributor cap splash shield and check the wires at the cap, making sure they aren't loose and that the wires and boots aren't cracked or damaged. **Note:** *Don't attempt to pull the wires off the cap - they're retained on the inside by wire clips.* The manufacturer doesn't recommend removing the wires from the cap for inspection because this could damage the integrity of the boot seal. If the wires appear to be damaged, replace them with new ones. Remove the distributor cap, release the wire clips with a pair of pliers and remove the wires **(see illustration)**. Insert the new wires into the cap while squeezing the boots to release any trapped air as you push them into place. Continue pushing until you feel the wire clips snap into position.

8　A visual check of the spark plug wires can also be made. In a darkened garage (make sure there is ventilation), start the engine and look at each plug wire. Be careful not to come into contact with any moving engine parts. If there's a crack in the insulation, you'll see arcing or a small spark at the damaged area.

9　Remove the distributor cap with the wires attached and check the cap for cracks, carbon tracks and other damage. Examine the terminals inside the cap for corrosion (slight corrosion can be removed

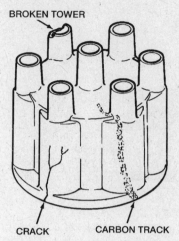

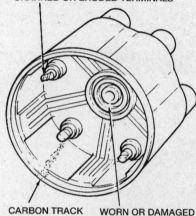

16.9　Shown here are some of the common defects to look for when inspecting the distributor cap (if in doubt about its condition, install a new one)

with a pocket knife) **(see illustration)**.

10　Check the rotor (now visible on the end of the distributor shaft) for cracks and a secure fit on the shaft. Make sure the terminals aren't burned, corroded or pitted excessively. A small fine file can be used to restore the rotor terminals **(see illustration)**. To replace the rotor, remove the rotor locking screw (models so equipped) and pull the rotor straight off the distributor shaft **(see illustration)**.

11　If new spark plug wires are needed, purchase a complete pre-cut set for your particular engine. The terminals and rubber boots should already be installed on the wires. Replace the wires one at a time to avoid mixing up the firing order and make sure the terminals are securely seated in the distributor cap and on the spark plugs.

17　Valve clearance check and adjustment (2.6L engine only)

Refer to illustrations 17.7 and 17.12

Warning: *The electric cooling fan can activate at any time, even when the ignition is in the Off position. Disconnect the fan motor or negative battery cable when working in the vicinity of the fan.*

1　The valve clearances must be checked and adjusted at the specified intervals with the engine at normal operating temperature.

2　Remove the air cleaner assembly (see Chapter 4).

3　Remove the valve cover (see Chapter 2).

4　Place the number one piston at Top Dead Center (TDC) on the

Common spark plug conditions

NORMAL
Symptoms: Brown to grayish-tan color and slight electrode wear. Correct heat range for engine and operating conditions.
Recommendation: When new spark plugs are installed, replace with plugs of the same heat range.

WORN

Symptoms: Rounded electrodes with a small amount of deposits on the firing end. Normal color. Causes hard starting in damp or cold weather and poor fuel economy.
Recommendation: Plugs have been left in the engine too long. Replace with new plugs of the same heat range. Follow the recommended maintenance schedule.

CARBON DEPOSITS

Symptoms: Dry sooty deposits indicate a rich mixture or weak ignition. Causes misfiring, hard starting and hesitation.
Recommendation: Make sure the plug has the correct heat range. Check for a clogged air filter or problem in the fuel system or engine management system. Also check for ignition system problems.

ASH DEPOSITS

Symptoms: Light brown deposits encrusted on the side or center electrodes or both. Derived from oil and/or fuel additives. Excessive amounts may mask the spark, causing misfiring and hesitation during acceleration.
Recommendation: If excessive deposits accumulate over a short time or low mileage, install new valve guide seals to prevent seepage of oil into the combustion chambers. Also try changing gasoline brands.

OIL DEPOSITS

Symptoms: Oily coating caused by poor oil control. Oil is leaking past worn valve guides or piston rings into the combustion chamber. Causes hard starting, misfiring and hesitation.
Recommendation: Correct the mechanical condition with necessary repairs and install new plugs.

GAP BRIDGING

Symptoms: Combustion deposits lodge between the electrodes. Heavy deposits accumulate and bridge the electrode gap. The plug ceases to fire, resulting in a dead cylinder.
Recommendation: Locate the faulty plug and remove the deposits from between the electrodes.

TOO HOT

Symptoms: Blistered, white insulator, eroded electrode and absence of deposits. Results in shortened plug life.
Recommendation: Check for the correct plug heat range, over-advanced ignition timing, lean fuel mixture, intake manifold vacuum leaks, sticking valves and insufficient engine cooling.

PREIGNITION

Symptoms: Melted electrodes. Insulators are white, but may be dirty due to misfiring or flying debris in the combustion chamber. Can lead to engine damage.
Recommendation: Check for the correct plug heat range, over-advanced ignition timing, lean fuel mixture, insufficient engine cooling and lack of lubrication.

HIGH SPEED GLAZING

Symptoms: Insulator has yellowish, glazed appearance. Indicates that combustion chamber temperatures have risen suddenly during hard acceleration. Normal deposits melt to form a conductive coating. Causes misfiring at high speeds.
Recommendation: Install new plugs. Consider using a colder plug if driving habits warrant.

DETONATION

Symptoms: Insulators may be cracked or chipped. Improper gap setting techniques can also result in a fractured insulator tip. Can lead to piston damage.
Recommendation: Make sure the fuel anti-knock values meet engine requirements. Use care when setting the gaps on new plugs. Avoid lugging the engine.

MECHANICAL DAMAGE

Symptoms: May be caused by a foreign object in the combustion chamber or the piston striking an incorrect reach (too long) plug. Causes a dead cylinder and could result in piston damage.
Recommendation: Repair the mechanical damage. Remove the foreign object from the engine and/or install the correct reach plug.

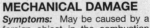

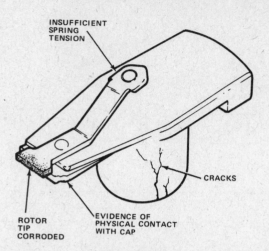

16.10a   The ignition rotor should be checked for wear and corrosion as indicated here (if in doubt about its condition, buy a new one)

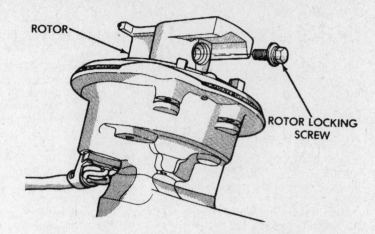

16.10b   Some models have a rotor locking screw that must be removed before the rotor can be pulled off

17.7   There should be a slight drag as the feeler gauge is pulled between the jet valve adjusting screw and the valve stem

17.12   To make sure the adjusting screw doesn't move when the locknut is tightened, use a box-end wrench and have a good grip on the screwdriver

compression stroke (see Chapter 2). The number one cylinder rocker arms (closest to the timing chain end of the engine) should be loose (able to move up and down slightly) and the camshaft lobes should be facing away from the rocker arms.

5   With the crankshaft in this position, the number one cylinder jet valve (if equipped), intake valve and exhaust valve clearances can be checked and adjusted. **Note:** *Some engines are not equipped with jet valves (small valves next to the intake valves which are actuated by extensions of the intake valve rocker arms). If you're not sure whether or not the engine is equipped with jet valves, see illustration 17.7*

6   First, adjust the jet valve - if equipped - (if the engine is not equipped with jet valves, loosen the intake valve adjusting screw two turns and proceed to Step 9). Make sure the intake valve adjusting screw has been backed off two full turns, then loosen the locknut on the jet valve adjusting screw.

7   Turn the jet valve adjusting screw counterclockwise and insert the appropriate size feeler gauge (see this Chapter's Specifications) between the valve stem and the adjusting screw. Carefully tighten the adjusting screw until you can feel a slight drag on the feeler gauge as you withdraw it from between the stem and adjusting screw **(see illustration)**.

8   Since the jet valve spring is relatively weak, use special care not

to force the jet valve open. Be particularly careful if the adjusting screw is hard to turn. Hold the adjusting screw with a screwdriver (to keep it from turning) and tighten the locknut. Recheck the clearance to make sure it hasn't changed.

9   Next, check and adjust the intake valve clearance. Insert the appropriate size feeler gauge between the intake valve stem and the adjusting screw. Carefully tighten the adjusting screw until you can feel a slight drag on the feeler gauge as you withdraw it from between the stem and adjusting screw.

10   Hold the adjusting screw with a screwdriver (to keep it from turning) and tighten the locknut. Recheck the clearance to make sure it hasn't changed.

11   Loosen the locknut on the exhaust valve adjusting screw. Turn the adjusting screw counterclockwise and insert the appropriate size feeler gauge between the valve stem and the adjusting screw. Carefully tighten the adjusting screw until you can feel a slight drag on the feeler gauge as you withdraw it from between the stem and adjusting screw.

12   Hold the adjusting screw with a screwdriver (to keep it from turning) and tighten the locknut **(see illustration)**. Recheck the clearance to make sure it hasn't changed.

13   Rotate the crankshaft to position each of the remaining pistons at

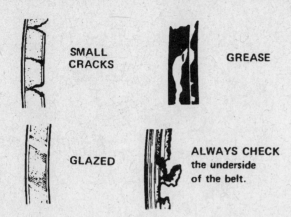

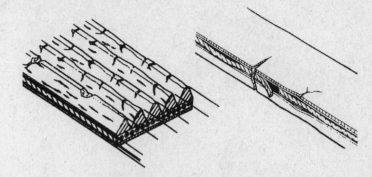

18.3b   Check V-ribbed belts for signs of wear like these - if the belt looks worn, replace it

18.3a   Here are some of the more common problems associated with drivebelts (check the belts very carefully to prevent an untimely breakdown)

TDC on the compression stroke (see Chapter 2) and adjust the valves for each cylinder. Only adjust the valves for the cylinder that's at TDC. Always adjust the jet valve first.

14   Install the valve cover and the air cleaner assembly.

18   Drivebelt check, adjustment and replacement

Refer to illustrations 18.3a, 18.3b, 18.4, 18.6a, 18.6b, 18.6c, 18.6d, 18.6e, 18.6f, 18.6g, 16.6h and 18.10

Warning: *The electric cooling fan on some models can activate at any time, even when the ignition switch is in the Off position. Disconnect the negative battery cable when working in the vicinity of the fan.*

Note: *Later models are equipped with one serpentine drivebelt that turns all engine accessories. The belt tension is automatically controlled - so no adjustment is required. The serpentine drivebelt should be inspected for wear or damage, however.*

Check

1   The drivebelts are either V-belts or V-ribbed belts. Sometimes referred to as "fan" belts, the drivebelts are located at the left end of the engine. The good condition and proper adjustment of the belts is critical to the operation of the engine. Because of their composition and the high stresses to which they are subjected, drivebelts stretch and deteriorate as they get older. They must therefore be periodically inspected.

2   The number of belts used on a particular vehicle depends on the accessories installed. One belt transmits power from the crankshaft to the alternator and water pump. The air conditioning compressor and power steering pumps are driven by other belts.

3   With the engine off, open the hood and locate the drivebelts at the right end of the engine. With a flashlight, check each belt: On V-belts, check for cracks and separation of the belt plies **(see illustration)**. On V-ribbed belts, check for separation of the adhesive rubber on both sides of the core, core separation from the belt side and a severed core **(see illustration)**. Also on V-ribbed belts, check for separation of the ribs from the adhesive rubber, cracking or separation of the ribs, and torn or worn ribs or cracks in the inner ridges of the ribs. On both belt types, check for fraying and glazing, which gives the belt a shiny appearance. Both sides of the belt should be inspected, which means you will have to twist the belt to check the underside. Use your fingers to feel the belt where you can't see it. If any of the above conditions are evident, replace the belt (go to Step 8).

4   The tightness of each belt is checked by pushing on it at a distance halfway between the pulleys **(see illustration)**. Apply about 10 pounds of force with your thumb and see how much the belt moves

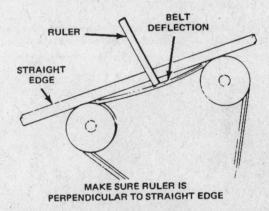

18.4   Measuring drivebelt deflection with a straightedge and ruler

down (deflects). Refer to the Specifications listed in this Chapter for the amount of deflection allowed in each belt.

Adjustment

5   If adjustment is necessary, it is done by moving the belt-driven accessory on the bracket.

6   On some components, if a belt must be adjusted, loosen the locking screw or nut and the adjustment bolt or screw that secures the component to the slotted bracket. Pivot the component (away from the engine block to tighten the belt, toward the block to loosen the belt) **(see illustrations)**. Many accessories are equipped with a square hole designed to accept a 3/8-inch or 1/2-inch square drive breaker bar. The bar enables you to precisely position the component until the adjuster bolt or screw is tightened. Be very careful not to damage the housing of the component, particularly the aluminum housing of the alternator. Recheck the belt tension using the above method.

7   On some components, loosen the locking screw or nut. Turn the adjusting screw to tension the belt, then retighten the locking screw or nut.

Replacement

8   To replace a belt, follow the above procedures for drivebelt adjustment, but slip the belt off the crankshaft pulley and remove it. To replace some belts, you'll have to remove other belts to get at the one you're replacing because of the way the belts are arranged on the crankshaft pulley. Because of this and because belts tend to wear out more or less together, it is a good idea to replace all belts at the same time. Mark each belt and its appropriate pulley groove so the replacement belts can be installed in their proper positions.

9   Take the old belts to the parts store in order to make a direct comparison for length, width and design.

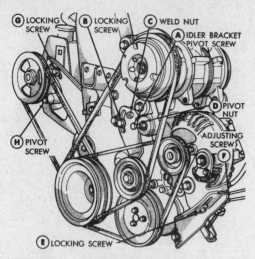

18.6a   2.2L engine drivebelt adjustment details (Chrysler alternator)

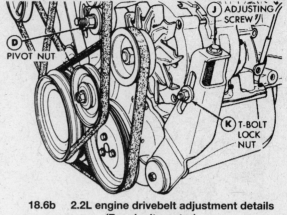

18.6b   2.2L engine drivebelt adjustment details (Bosch alternator)

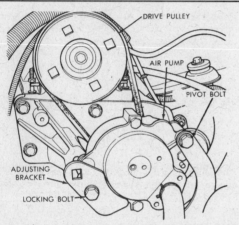

18.6c   2.2L engine air pump drivebelt adjustment details

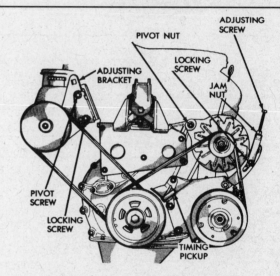

18.6d   2.6L engine drivebelt details

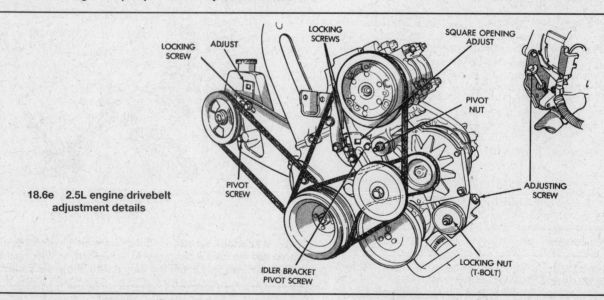

18.6e   2.5L engine drivebelt adjustment details

10   After replacing a V-ribbed drivebelt, make sure it fits properly in the ribbed grooves in the pulleys (**see illustration**). It is essential that the belt be properly centered.

11   Adjust the belt(s) in accordance with the procedure outlined above.

12   When replacing a serpentine drivebelt (used on later models), insert a 1/2-inch drive breaker bar into the tensioner and rotate it to release the tension. Make sure the belt is routed as shown in the accompanying illustrations and that it completely engages in the grooves in the pulleys (**see illustration 18.10**).

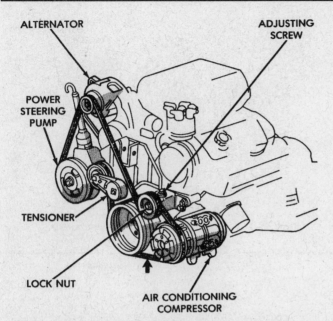

18.6f 3.0L V6 engines have self-adjusting serpentine drivebelts, but on some models the air conditioning compressor has a separate drivebelt that has to be adjusted - check the deflection at the arrow

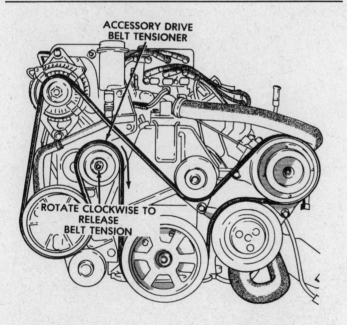

18.6h Rotate the tensioner clockwise to release the serpentine belt tension on 3.3L and 3.8L engines

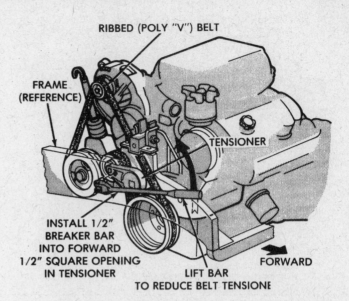

18.6g Release the serpentine drivebelt tension on the 3.0L V6 engine by rotating the tensioner counterclockwise

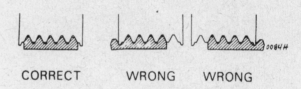

18.10 When installing a V-ribbed belt, make sure it is centered on the pulley - it must not overlap either edge of the pulley

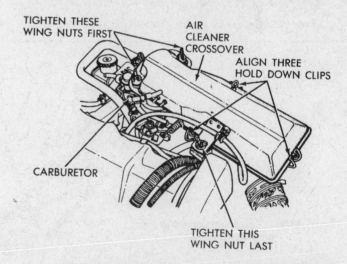

19.3a 2.2L engine air cleaner details - the wing nuts must be removed and the clips disengaged to access the air filter element - when reinstalling, tighten the wing nuts in the order shown

19   Air filter replacement

Refer to illustrations 19.3a, 19.3b, 19.3c, 19.3d, 19.3e, 19.3f, 19.3g, 19.3h, 19.3i, 19.3j, 19.3k and 19.3l

1   At the specified intervals, the air filter element should be replaced and the PCV system crankcase ventilation filter cleaned.
2   The air filter element is located in a housing adjacent to the engine.
3   Referring to the accompanying illustrations, remove the nuts (if equipped), detach the clips, remove the cover, then lift the element out **(see illustrations)**.

4   Be careful not to drop anything down into the air cleaner assembly. Clean the inside of the housing with a rag.
5   Pull the crankcase ventilation filter out of the housing. Wash the crankcase filter in solvent and oil it lightly before reinstalling.
6   Place the new filter element in position and install the cover. Be sure to tighten any hose clamps which were loosened or removed.

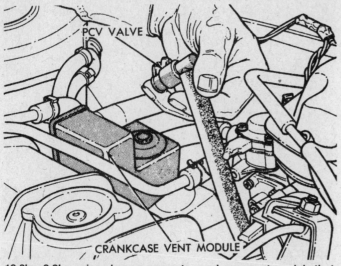

19.3b 2.2L engines have a separate crankcase vent module that houses the crankcase ventilation filter - service it as described in Section 20

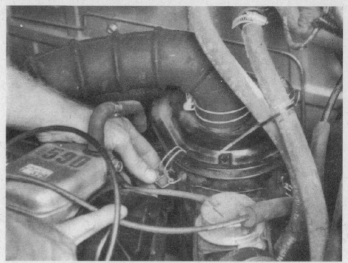

19.3c On 2.6L engines, release the clips, lift off the cover . . .

19.3d . . . and lift the element out of the housing

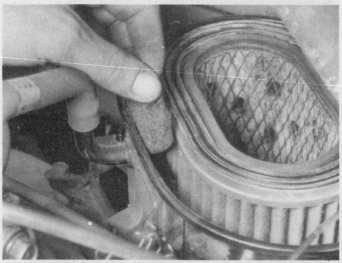

19.3e Removing the 2.6L engine crankcase ventilation filter

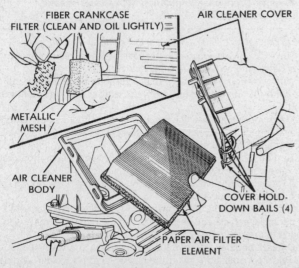

19.3f 2.5L engine air cleaner details

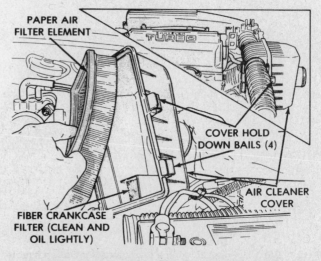

19.3g Turbocharged engine air cleaner details

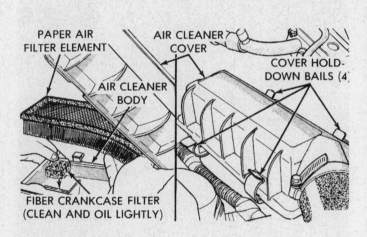

PAPER AIR
FILTER ELEMENT

AIR CLEANER
COVER

COVER HOLD-
DOWN BAILS (4)

AIR CLEANER
BODY

FIBER CRANKCASE FILTER
(CLEAN AND OIL LIGHTLY)

19.3h   3.0L V6 engine air cleaner details

19.3i   On 3.3L and 3.8L V6 engines, detach the clips . . .

19.3j   . . . raise the cover . . .

19.3k   . . . and lift the filter out of the housing

19.3l   The 3.3L and 3.8L engine crankcase ventilation filter is
located in the corner of the housing

20   Positive Crankcase Ventilation (PCV) valve check and replacement

Refer to illustrations 20.2a, 20.2b, 20.2c, 20.2d and 20.2e

1   The PCV valve is located in the valve (cylinder head) cover or, on 2.2L engines, in a vent module adjacent to it.

2   With the engine idling at normal operating temperature, pull the valve (with the hose attached) from the rubber fitting **(see illustrations)**.

3   Place your finger over the valve opening. If there's no vacuum at the valve, check for a plugged hose, manifold port or valve. Replace any plugged or deteriorated hoses.

4   Turn off the engine and shake the PCV valve, listening for a rattle. If the valve doesn't rattle, replace it with a new one.

5   To replace the valve, pull it from the end of the hose, noting its installed position and direction.

6   When purchasing a replacement PCV valve, make sure it's for your particular vehicle and engine size. Compare the old valve with the new one to make sure they're the same.

7   On 2.2L engines, remove the vent module and wash it with solvent. Prior to installation, invert the module and pour clean engine oil into it, then allow the oil to drain through the vent in the top into a container. With the interior of the module now wet with oil, reinstall it.

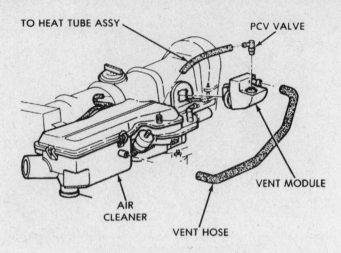

20.2a   2.2L engine PCV system details

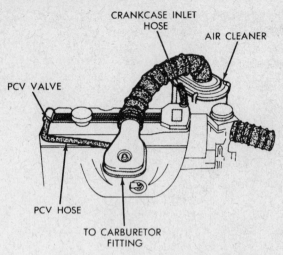

20.2b   2.6L engine PCV system details

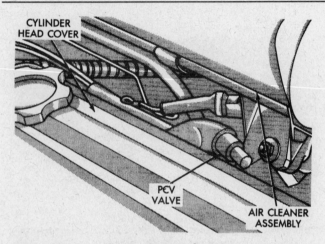

20.2c   The 2.5L engine PCV valve is connected to the cylinder head cover

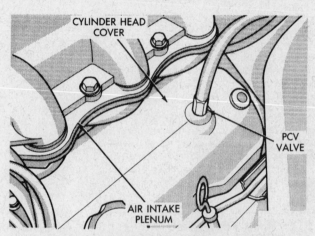

20.2d   The 3.0L engine PCV valve is located in the cylinder head cover

8   On all models, push the valve into the end of the hose until it's seated.
9   Inspect the rubber fitting for damage and replace it with a new one if necessary.
10   Push the PCV valve and hose securely into position.

20.2e   Pulling the PCV valve out of the fitting on the valve cover (3.3L and 3.8L engine)

21   Carburetor choke check and cleaning

Refer to illustrations 21.3, 21.8a and 21.8b

Warning: *The electric cooling fan can activate at any time, even when the ignition is in the Off position. Disconnect the fan motor or negative battery cable when working in the vicinity of the fan.*

Check

1   The choke operates only when the engine is cold, so this check should be performed before the engine has been started for the day.
2   Expose the top of the carburetor by taking off the top of the air cleaner assembly or the air inlet duct (see Section 19). If any vacuum hoses must be disconnected, make sure you tag the hoses for reinstallation in their original positions. Place the top plate and wing nut aside, out of the way of moving engine components.
3   Look at the center of the air cleaner housing. You will notice a flat plate at the carburetor opening **(see illustration)**.
4   Press the accelerator pedal to the floor. The plate should close completely. Start the engine while you watch the plate at the carburetor. Don't position your face near the carburetor, as the engine could backfire, causing serious burns. When the engine starts, the choke plate should open slightly.
5   Allow the engine to continue running at an idle speed. As the engine warms up to operating temperature, the plate should slowly open, allowing more air to enter through the top of the carburetor.
6   After a few minutes, the choke plate should be fully open to the

21.3 The choke plate is located in the carburetor throat and should be closed when the engine is cold

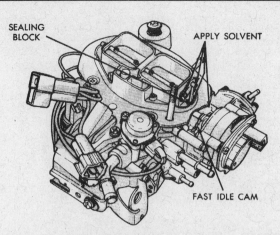

21.8a On 2.2L engines, apply solvent to the choke shaft linkage, fast idle cam and sealing block

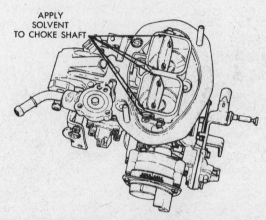

21.8b Spray the solvent on the areas shown to prevent the choke shaft from binding

vertical position. Tap the accelerator to make sure the fast idle cam disengages.

7   You'll notice that the engine speed corresponds with the plate opening. With the plate fully closed, the engine should run at a fast idle speed. As the plate opens and the throttle is moved to disengage the fast idle cam, the engine speed will decrease.

Cleaning

8   With the engine off, use aerosol carburetor solvent (available at auto parts stores) to clean the contact surfaces of the choke plate shaft where it passes through the carburetor body. Also clean the fast idle cam and link mechanism **(see illustrations)**.

9   Refer to Chapter 4 for specific information on adjusting and servicing the choke components

---

22   Exhaust Gas Recirculation (EGR) system check

2.2L, 2.5L, 3.0L, 3.3L and 3.8L engines

1   The EGR valve is located on the intake manifold or in a pipe connected to it.

2   Check the EGR valve hose and pipe for damage and leaks.

3   With the engine idling at normal operating temperature, watch the stem under the valve for movement and increase the engine speed to approximately 2500 rpm.

4   The stem should move up and down as the engine speed changes, indicating that the EGR system is operating properly.

2.6L engines

5   These models use two EGR valves. The sub EGR valve is located at the base of the carburetor and is operated by the carburetor linkage. The dual EGR valve bolts to the intake manifold and is controlled by engine vacuum.

6   Check the sub EGR valve linkage to make sure it is securely connected and inspect the dual EGR valve vacuum hoses for damage.

7   See Chapter 6 for more information on the EGR system.

---

23   Underhood hose check and replacement

Caution: *Replacement of air conditioning hoses must be left to a dealer service department or air conditioning shop equipped to depressurize the system safely. Never remove air conditioning components or hoses until the system has been depressurized.*

General

1   High temperatures under the hood can cause the deterioration of the rubber and plastic hoses used for engine, accessory and emission systems operation. Periodic inspection should be made for cracks, loose clamps, material hardening and leaks.

2   Information specific to the cooling system hoses can be found in Section 27.

3   Some, but not all, hoses use clamps to secure the hoses to fittings. Where clamps are used, check to be sure they haven't lost their tension, allowing the hose to leak. Where clamps are not used, make sure the hose hasn't expanded and/or hardened where it slips over the fitting, allowing it to leak.

Vacuum hoses

4   It's quite common for vacuum hoses, especially those in the emissions system, to be color coded or identified by colored stripes molded into the hose. Various systems require hoses with different wall thicknesses, collapse resistance and temperature resistance. When replacing hoses, make sure the new ones are made of the same material.

5   Often the only effective way to check a hose is to remove it completely from the vehicle. Where more than one hose is removed, be sure to label the hoses and their attaching points to insure proper reattachment.

6   When checking vacuum hoses, be sure to include any plastic T-fittings in the check. Check the fittings for cracks and the hose where it fits over the fitting for enlargement, which could cause leakage.

7   A small piece of vacuum hose (1/4-inch inside diameter) can be used as a stethoscope to detect vacuum leaks. Hold one end of the hose to your ear and probe around vacuum hoses and fittings, listening for the "hissing" sound characteristic of a vacuum leak.

24.4   Typical throttle body-to-manifold bolt details (2.5L engine shown) - the upper arrows point to the rear bolts, which are not visible

25.5   The vacuum air control valve (2.6L model shown) is located in the air cleaner duct fitting (in this case it is in the Down or Heat off position)

Warning: *When probing with the vacuum hose stethoscope, be careful not to allow your body or the hose to come into contact with moving engine components such as the drivebelt, cooling fan, etc.*

Fuel hose

Warning: *Gasoline is extremely flammable, so take extra precautions when you work on any part of the fuel system. Don't smoke or allow open flames or bare light bulbs near the work area, and don't work in a garage where a natural gas-type appliance (such as a water heater or clothes dryer) with a pilot light is present. If you spill any fuel on your skin, rinse it off immediately with soap and water. When you perform any kind of work on the fuel system, wear safety glasses and have a Class B type fire extinguisher on hand. On fuel-injected models, the fuel system must be depressurized before any hoses are replaced (see Chapter 4).*

8   Check all rubber fuel hoses for damage and deterioration. Check especially for cracks in areas where the hose bends and just before clamping points, such as where a hose attaches to the carburetor or fuel injection unit.

9   High quality fuel line, specifically designed for fuel systems, should be used for fuel line replacement. **Warning:** *Never use vacuum line, clear plastic tubing or water hose for fuel lines.*

10   Spring-type clamps are commonly used on fuel lines. These clamps often lose their tension over a period of time, and can be "sprung" during the removal process. Therefore it is recommended that all spring-type clamps be replaced with screw clamps whenever a hose is replaced.

Metal lines

11   Sections of metal line are often used for fuel line between the fuel pump and carburetor or fuel injection unit. Check carefully to be sure the line has not been bent and crimped and that cracks have not started in the line.

12   If a section of metal fuel line must be replaced, only seamless steel tubing should be used, since copper and aluminum tubing do not have the strength necessary to withstand normal engine operating vibration.

13   Check the metal brake lines where they enter the master cylinder and brake proportioning unit (if used) for cracks in the lines or loose fittings. Any sign of brake fluid leakage calls for an immediate thorough inspection of the brake system.

24   Carburetor/fuel injection throttle body mounting bolt/nut torque check

Refer to illustration 24.4

1   The carburetor or fuel injection throttle body is attached to the intake manifold by bolts or nuts. The bolts or nuts can sometimes work

loose during normal engine operation and cause a vacuum leak.

2   To properly tighten the mounting bolts or nuts, a torque wrench is necessary. If you do not own one, they can usually be rented on a daily basis.

3   Remove the air cleaner and/or hose assembly.

4   Locate the mounting bolts/nuts at the base of the carburetor or throttle body **(see illustration)**. Decide what special tools or adaptors will be be necessary, if any, to tighten the bolts/nuts with a socket and the torque wrench.

5   Tighten the bolts/nuts to the torque listed in this Chapter's Specifications. Do not overtighten the bolts/nuts, as the threads may strip. On turbo models, check the hoses and clamps between the throttle body and the turbocharger and the turbocharger and the intake manifold to make sure there are no leaks.

6   If you suspect a vacuum leak exists at the bottom of the carburetor or throttle body, obtain a short length of rubber hose. Start the engine and place one end of the hose next to your ear as you probe around the base of the throttle body with the other end. You should hear a hissing sound if a leak exists. **Warning:** *Stay clear of rotating engine components when probing with the hose.*

7   If, after the bolts/nuts are properly tightened, a vacuum leak still exists, the carburetor or throttle body must be removed and a new gasket installed. See Chapter 4 for more information.

8   After tightening the bolts/nuts, reinstall the air cleaner housing or hoses.

25   Heated inlet air system check

Refer to illustration 25.5

1   All carbureted and non-turbo TBI models are equipped with a heated inlet air cleaner which draws air to the fuel injection throttle body from different locations, depending on engine temperature.

2   This is a simple visual check; however, the outside air duct must be removed.

3   Locate the vacuum air control valve in the air cleaner assembly. It's located inside the air cleaner duct fitting, where you removed the outside air duct from. Make sure the flexible heat duct under the air cleaner is securely attached and undamaged.

4   The check should be done when the engine and outside air are cold (less than 65-degrees F). Start the engine and look through the duct fitting at the valve (which should move up to the "heat on" position). With the valve up, air cannot enter through the end of the duct fitting, but instead enters the air cleaner through the heat duct attached to the exhaust manifold. If you can't see into the duct fitting, a mirror may be helpful.

5   As the engine warms up to operating temperature, the valve should move down to the "heat off" position to allow air through the

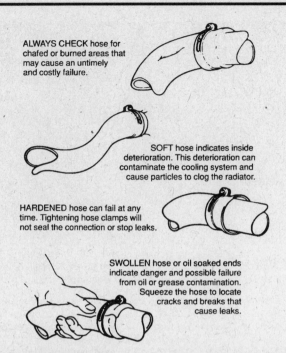

ALWAYS CHECK hose for chafed or burned areas that may cause an untimely and costly failure.

SOFT hose indicates inside deterioration. This deterioration can contaminate the cooling system and cause particles to clog the radiator.

HARDENED hose can fail at any time. Tightening hose clamps will not seal the connection or stop leaks.

SWOLLEN hose or oil soaked ends indicate danger and possible failure from oil or grease contamination. Squeeze the hose to locate cracks and breaks that cause leaks.

27.4   Hoses, like drivebelts, have a habit of failing at the worst possible time - to prevent the inconvenience of a blown radiator or heater hose, inspect them carefully as shown here

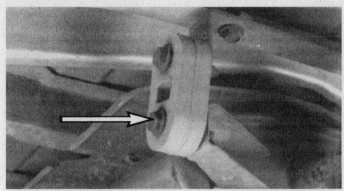

28.2   Check the rubber exhaust system hangers for cracks and deterioration, because they are prone to damage

duct fitting **(see illustration)**. Depending on outside air temperature, this may take 10 to 15 minutes. To speed up the check you can reconnect the outside air duct, drive the vehicle and then check to see if the valve has moved down.

6   If the air cleaner isn't operating properly, see Chapter 6 for more information.

26   Fuel system check

Warning: *Gasoline is extremely flammable, so take extra precautions when you work on any part of the fuel system. Don't smoke or allow open flames or bare light bulbs near the work area, and don't work in a garage where a natural gas-type appliance (such as a water heater or clothes dryer) with a pilot light is present. If you spill any fuel on your skin, rinse it off immediately with soap and water. When you perform any kind of work on the fuel system, wear safety glasses and have a Class B type fire extinguisher on hand.*

1   On models equipped with fuel injection, the fuel system is under pressure even when the engine is off. Consequently, the fuel system must be depressurized (see Chapter 4) whenever it is worked on. Even after depressurization, if any fuel lines are disconnected for servicing, be prepared to catch some fuel as it spurts out. Plug all disconnected fuel lines immediately to prevent the tank from emptying itself.

2   The fuel system is most easily checked with the vehicle raised on a hoist where the components on the underside are readily visible and accessible.

3   If the smell of gasoline is noticed while driving, or after the vehicle has been parked in the sun, the fuel system should be thoroughly inspected immediately.

4   Remove the gas tank cap and check for damage, corrosion and a proper sealing imprint on the gasket. Replace the cap with a new one if necessary.

5   Inspect the gas tank and filler neck for punctures, cracks and other damage. The connection between the filler neck and the tank is especially critical. Sometimes a rubber filler neck will leak due to loose clamps or deteriorated rubber; problems a home mechanic can usually rectify. **Warning:** *Do not, under any circumstances, try to repair a fuel tank yourself (except to replace rubber components) unless you have*

considerable experience. *A welding torch or any open flame can easily cause the fuel vapors to explode if the proper precautions are not taken.*

6   Carefully check all rubber hoses and metal lines leading away from the fuel tank. Check for loose connections, deteriorated hoses, crimped lines and damage of any kind. Follow the lines up to the front of the vehicle, carefully inspecting them all the way. Repair or replace damaged sections as necessary (see Chapter 4).

27   Cooling system check

Refer to illustration 27.4

Warning: *The electric cooling fan on these models can activate at any time, even when the ignition switch is in the Off position. Disconnect the fan motor or the negative battery cable when working in the vicinity of the fan.*

1   Many major engine failures can be attributed to a faulty cooling system. If the vehicle is equipped with an automatic transaxle, the cooling system is also used to cool the transaxle fluid.

2   The cooling system should be checked with the engine cold. Do this before the vehicle is driven for the day or after it has been shut off for three or four hours.

3   Remove the radiator cap and thoroughly clean the cap (inside and out) with water. Also clean the filler neck on the radiator. All traces of corrosion should be removed.

4   Carefully check the upper and lower radiator hoses along with the smaller diameter heater hoses. Inspect the entire length of each hose, replacing any that are cracked, swollen or deteriorated. Cracks may become more apparent when a hose is squeezed **(see illustration)**.

5   Also check that all hose connections are tight. A leak in the cooling system will usually show up as white or rust-colored deposits on the areas adjoining the leak.

6   Use compressed air or a soft brush to remove bugs, leaves, and other debris from the front of the radiator or air conditioning condenser. Be careful not to damage the delicate cooling fins, or cut yourself on them.

7   Finally, have the cap and system pressure tested. If you do not have a pressure tester, most gas stations and repair shops will do this for a minimal charge.

28   Exhaust system check

Refer to illustration 28.2

1   With the engine cold (at least three hours after the vehicle has been driven), check the complete exhaust system from its starting point at the engine to the end of the tailpipe. This should be done on a hoist where unrestricted access is available.

2   Check the pipes and connections for signs of leakage and/or corrosion indicating a potential failure. Make sure that all brackets and hangers are in good condition and tight **(see illustration)**.

29.4 With the vehicle weight resting on the suspension, try to move the balljoint grease fittings with your fingers - if the fittings can be moved easily, the balljoints are worn and must be replaced

3   At the same time, inspect the underside of the body for holes, corrosion and open seams which may allow exhaust gases to enter the passenger compartment. Seal all body openings with silicone sealant or body putty.

4   Rattles and other noises can often be traced to the exhaust system, especially the mounts and hangers. Try to move the pipes, muffler and catalytic converter. If the components can come into contact with the body, secure the exhaust system with new mounts.

5   This is also an ideal time to check the running condition of the engine by inspecting the very end of the tailpipe. The exhaust deposits here are an indication of engine state-of-tune. If the pipe is black and sooty or coated with white deposits, the engine may be in need of a tune-up (including a thorough carburetor or fuel injection system inspection and adjustment).

29   Steering and suspension check

Refer to illustration 29.4

1   Whenever the front of the vehicle is raised for service it is a good idea to visually check the suspension and steering components for wear and damage.

2   Indications of wear and damage include excessive play in the steering wheel before the front wheels react, excessive lean around corners, body movement over rough roads or binding at some point as the steering wheel is turned.

3   Before the vehicle is raised for inspection, test the shock absorbers by pushing down to rock the vehicle at each corner. If it does not come back to a level position within one or two bounces, the shocks are worn and should be replaced. As this is done, check for squeaks and unusual noises from the suspension components. Check the shock absorbers for fluid leakage. Information on shock absorbers and suspension components can be found in Chapter 10.

4   Check the balljoints for wear by grasping the grease fittings securely and attempting to move them **(see illustration)**. If the grease fittings move easily, the balljoints are worn and must be replaced with new ones.

5   Now raise the front end of the vehicle and support it securely with jackstands placed under the jacking and hoisting points (see Jacking and towing at the front of this manual). Because of the work to be done, the vehicle must be stable and safely supported.

6   Check the front wheel hub nuts (in the center of each wheel after the cover is removed) for correct tightness and make sure they're properly crimped in place.

7   Crawl under the vehicle and check for loose bolts, broken or disconnected parts and deteriorated rubber bushings on all suspension and steering components. Look for grease or fluid leaking from around the steering gear boots. Check the power steering hoses and connec-

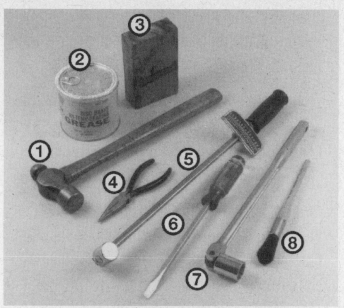

30.1   Tools and materials needed for front wheel bearing maintenance

1   *Hammer – A common hammer will do just fine*
2   *Grease – High temperature grease that is formulated specially for front wheel bearings should be used*
3   *Wood block – If you have a scrap piece of 2x4, it can be used to drive the new seal into the hub*
4   *Needle nose pliers – Used to straighten and remove the cotter pin in the spindle*
5   *Torque wrench – This is very important in this procedure; if the bearing is too tight, the wheel won't turn freely - if it's too loose, the wheel will "wobble" on the spindle. Either way, it could mean extensive damage.*
6   *Screwdriver – Used to remove the seal from the hub (a long screwdriver would be preferred)*
7   *Socket/breaker bar – Needed to loosen the nut on the spindle if it's extremely tight*
8   *Brush – Together with some clean solvent, this will be used to remove old grease from the hub and spindle*

tions for leaks. Check the steering joints for wear.

8   Have an assistant turn the steering wheel from side-to-side and check the steering components for free movement, chafing and binding. If the wheels don't respond immediately to the movement of the steering wheel, try to determine where the slack is located.

30   Rear wheel bearing check, repack and adjustment

Check
Refer to illustration 30.1

1   In most cases the rear wheel bearings won't need servicing until the brake shoes are changed. However, the bearings should be checked whenever the rear of the vehicle is raised for any reason. Several items, including a torque wrench and special grease, are required for this procedure **(see illustration)**.

2   With the vehicle securely supported on jackstands, spin each wheel and check for noise, rolling resistance and freeplay.

3   Grasp the top of each tire with one hand and the bottom with the other. Move the wheel in-and-out on the spindle. If there's any noticeable movement, the bearings should be checked and then repacked with grease or replaced if necessary.

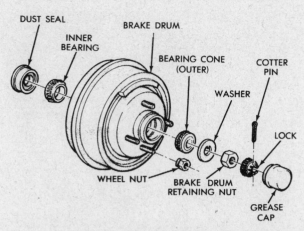

30.7   An exploded view of the rear brake drum/hub and bearing components

30.8   Pull the drum/hub out slightly and push it back in to unseat the outer bearing

30.10   Use a large screwdriver to pry dust seal out of the drum/hub, working around the edge

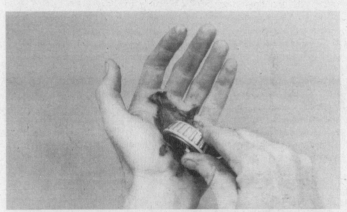

30.14   Put grease in the palm of one hand and use the other hand to force the large-diameter-end edge of each bearing onto the grease - this will force grease up through the bearing, along the rollers (you should see grease come out the other end) - work all the way around the bearing edge, completely packing the bearing with grease

Repack

Refer to illustrations 30.7, 30.8, 30.10 and 30.14

4   Remove the wheel.

5   Pry the grease cap out of the hub with a screwdriver or hammer and chisel.

6   Straighten the bent ends of the cotter pin, then pull the cotter pin out of the lock. Discard the cotter pin and use a new one during re-assembly.

7   Remove the lock and brake drum retaining nut from the end of the spindle **(see illustration)**.

8   Pull the brake drum/hub assembly out slightly, then push it back into its original position **(see illustration)**. This should force the outer bearing and washer off the spindle enough so they can be removed.

9   Pull the brake drum/hub assembly off the spindle. If it does not come off easily, back off the adjuster as described in the drum brake shoe replacement procedure in Chapter 9.

10   Use a screwdriver to pry the dust seal out of the rear of the hub. As this is done, note how the seal is installed **(see illustration)**.

11   Remove the inner wheel bearing from the hub.

12   Use solvent to remove all traces of old grease from the bearings, hub and spindle. A small brush may prove helpful; however, make sure no bristles from the brush embed themselves inside the bearing rollers. Allow the parts to air dry.

13   Carefully inspect the bearings for cracks, heat discoloration, worn rollers, etc. check the bearing races inside the hub for wear and damage. If the bearing races are defective, the hubs should be taken to a machine shop with the facilities to remove the old races and press new ones in. Note that the bearings and races come as matched sets - old bearings should never be installed on new races and vice-versa.

14   Use high-temperature wheel bearing grease to pack the bearings. Work the grease completely into the bearings, forcing it between the

rollers, cone and cage from the back side **(see illustration)**.

15   Apply a thin coat of grease to the spindle at the outer bearing seat, inner bearing seat, shoulder and seal seat.

16   Put a small quantity of grease inboard of each bearing race inside the hub. Using your finger, form a dam at these points to provide extra grease availability and to keep thinned grease from flowing out of the bearing.

17   Place the grease-packed inner bearing into the rear of the hub and put a little more grease outboard of the bearing.

18   Place a new dust seal over the inner bearing and tap the seal evenly into place with a hammer and block of wood until it's flush with the hub.

19   Carefully place the drum/hub assembly on the spindle and push the grease-packed outer bearing into position.

20   Install the washer and nut. Tighten the nut only slightly (no more than 12 ft-lbs of torque).

Adjustment

Refer to illustration 30.26

21   Spin the drum/hub in a forward direction to seat the bearings and remove any grease or burrs which could cause excessive bearing play later.

22   Check to see that the tightness of the nut is still approximately 12 ft-lbs.

23   Loosen the nut until it's just loose, no more.

30.26   Use a hammer and punch to seat the grease cap - tap all around the circumference, seating it evenly

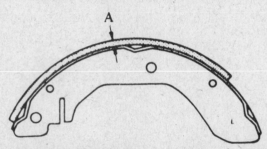

31.14   If the lining is bonded to the brake shoe, measure the lining thickness from the outer surface to the metal shoe, as shown here; if the lining is riveted to the shoe, measure from the lining outer surface to the rivet head

24   Using your hand (not a wrench of any kind), tighten the nut until it's snug. Install the lock and a new cotter pin through the hole in the spindle and lock. If the lock slots don't line up, take it off and rotate it to another position.

25   Bend the ends of the cotter pin until they're flat against the nut. Cut off any extra length which could interfere with the grease cap.

26   Install the grease cap, tapping it into place with a hammer and punch **(see illustration)**.

27   Install the tire/wheel assembly on the drum/hub and tighten the lug nuts.

28   Grasp the top and bottom of the tire and check the bearings in the manner described earlier in this Section.

29   Lower the vehicle.

31   Brake system check

Refer to illustrations 31.5, 31.14 and 31.16

1   The brakes should be inspected every time the wheels are removed or whenever a defect is suspected. Indications of a potential brake system problem include the vehicle pulling to one side when the brake pedal is depressed, noises coming from the brakes when they are applied, excessive brake pedal travel, pulsating pedal and leakage of fluid, usually seen on the inside of the tire or wheel.

Disc brakes (front)

2   Disc brakes can be visually checked without removing any parts except the wheels.

3   Raise the vehicle and place it securely on jackstands. Remove the front wheels (see Jacking and towing at the front of this manual if necessary).

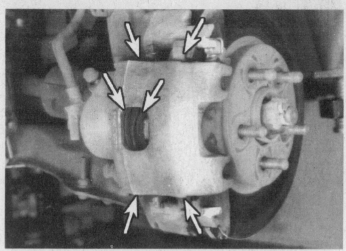

31.5   There's an inspection hole like this in each caliper - by looking through the hole and at the pads where they extend below the caliper, you can determine the thickness of the remaining friction material on both the inner and outer pads (arrows)

4   Now visible is the disc brake caliper which contains the pads. There is an outer brake pad and an inner pad. Both should be checked for wear.

5   Note the pad thickness by looking at each end of the caliper and through the inspection hole in the caliper body **(see illustration)**. If the combined thickness of the pad lining and metal shoe is 5/16-inch or less, the pads should be replaced.

6   Since it'll be difficult, if not impossible, to measure the exact thickness of the pad, if you're in doubt as to the pad quality, remove them for further inspection or replacement. See Chapter 9 for disc brake pad replacement.

7   Before installing the wheels, check for leakage around the brake hose connections leading to the caliper and for damaged brake hoses (cracks, leaks, chafed areas, etc.). Replace the hoses or fittings as necessary (see Chapter 9).

8   Also check the disc for score marks, wear and burned spots. If these conditions exist, the hub/disc assembly should be removed for servicing (see Chapter 9).

Drum brakes (rear)

9   Raise the vehicle and support it securely on jackstands. Block the front tires to prevent the vehicle from rolling; however, don't apply the parking brake or it will lock the drums in place.

10   Remove the wheels, referring to Jacking and towing at the front of this manual if necessary.

11   Mark the hub so it can be reinstalled in the same position. Use a scribe, chalk, etc. on the drum, hub and backing plate.

12   Remove the brake drum as described in Section 30.

13   With the drum removed, carefully brush away any accumulations of dirt and dust. **Warning:** *Don't blow the dust out with compressed air and don't inhale any of it (it may contain asbestos, which is harmful to your health).*

14   Note the thickness of the lining material on both front and rear brake shoes. If the material has worn away to within 1/8-inch of the recessed rivets or metal backing, the shoes should be replaced **(see illustration)**. The shoes should also be replaced if they're cracked, glazed (shiny areas), or covered with brake fluid.

15   Make sure all the brake assembly springs are connected and in good condition.

16   Check the brake components for signs of fluid leakage. With your finger or a small screwdriver, carefully pry back the rubber cups on the wheel cylinder located at the top of the brake shoes **(see illustration)**. Any leakage here is an indication that the wheel cylinders should be overhauled immediately (see Chapter 9). Also, check all hoses and connections for signs of leakage.

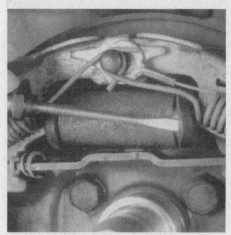

31.16 Pry the wheel cylinder cup back carefully to check for signs of fluid leakage

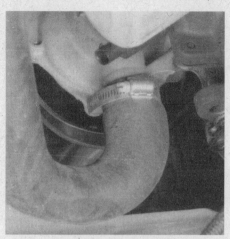

32.5a If the drain fitting located at the bottom of the radiator is not easily accessible, detach the lower radiator hose

32.5b To allow the system to drain on 2.2L/2.5L engines, remove the vacuum switch or bleeder plug (shown here) on top of the thermostat housing

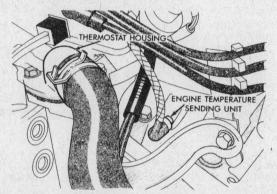

32.5c Remove the temperature sending unit from the cylinder head on 3.3L models

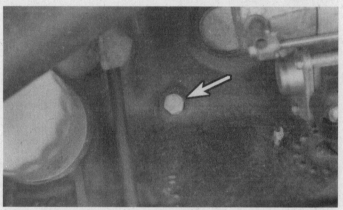

32.7 On some models, a drain plug (arrow) can be removed so the engine block can be drained - V6 models have plugs on both sides of the engine

17 Wipe the inside of the drum with a clean rag and denatured alcohol or brake cleaner. Again, be careful not to breathe the dangerous asbestos dust.

18 Check the inside of the drum for cracks, score marks, deep scratches and "hard spots" which will appear as small discolored areas. If imperfections cannot be removed with fine emery cloth, the drum must be taken to an automotive machine shop for resurfacing.

19 Repeat the procedure for the remaining wheel. If the inspection reveals that all parts are in good condition, reinstall the brake drums. Install the wheels and lower the vehicle to the ground.

32 Cooling system servicing (draining, flushing and refilling)

Refer to illustrations 32.5a, 32.5b, 32.5c and 32.7

Warning: *Do not allow engine coolant (antifreeze) to come in contact with your skin or painted surfaces of the vehicle. Rinse off spills immediately with plenty of water. Antifreeze is highly toxic if ingested. Never leave antifreeze lying around in an open container or in puddles on the floor; children and pets are attracted by it's sweet smell and may drink it. Check with local authorities about disposing of used antifreeze. Many communities have collection centers which will see that antifreeze is disposed of safely.*

1 Periodically, the cooling system should be drained, flushed and refilled to replenish the antifreeze mixture and prevent formation of rust and corrosion, which can impair the performance of the cooling system and cause engine damage. When the cooling system is serviced, all hoses and the radiator cap should be checked and replaced, if necessary.

Draining

2 At the same time the cooling system is serviced, all hoses and the radiator cap should be inspected and replaced if faulty (see Section 27).

3 With the engine cold, set the heater control to Heat (Max).

4 Move a large container under the radiator to catch the coolant mixture as it's drained.

5 Open the drain fitting at the bottom of the radiator or detach the lower radiator hose **(see illustration)**. On 2.2L, 2.5L and 3.3L engines it is necessary to vent the system to allow draining. Remove the vacuum switch or bleeder plug from the top of the thermostat housing (2.2L and 2.5L) or the temperature sending unit on the cylinder head (3.3L) **(see illustrations)**.

6 Disconnect the coolant reservoir hose, remove the reservoir and flush it with clean water.

7 After coolant stops draining out of the radiator, move the container under the engine block drain plug(s) **(see illustration)** and remove the plug(s)

Flushing

8 Place a hose (a common garden hose is fine) in the radiator filler neck at the top of the radiator and flush the system until the water runs clear at all drain points.

9 In severe cases of contamination or clogging of the radiator, remove it (see Chapter 3) and reverse flush it. This involves inserting the hose in the bottom radiator outlet to allow the clean water to run against the normal flow, draining through the top. A radiator repair shop should be consulted if further cleaning or repair is necessary.

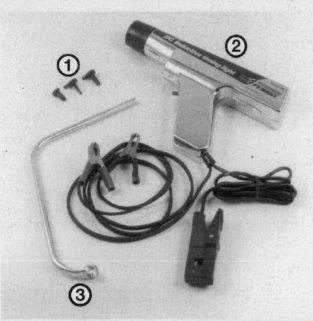

34.2 Tools needed to check and adjust the ignition timing

1   **Vacuum plugs** – *Vacuum hoses will, in most cases, have to be disconnected and plugged. Molded plugs in various shapes and sizes are available for this.*

2   **Inductive pick up timing light** – *Flashes a bright concentrated beam of light when the number one spark plug fires. Connect the leads according to the instructions supplied with the light.*

3   **Distributor wrench** – *On some models, the hold-down bolt for the distributor is difficult to reach and turn with conventional wrenches or sockets. A special wrench like this must be used.*

10   Where the coolant is regularly drained and the system refilled with the correct antifreeze mixture there should be no need to employ chemical cleaners or descalers.

Refilling

11   Install the coolant reservoir, reconnect the hoses, install the block drain plug(s) and close the drain fitting.

12   Add coolant to the radiator. Fill until the coolant reaches the bottom of the threaded bleeder plug/vacuum switch hole in the thermostat housing (2.2L/2.5L) or sending unit hole in the cylinder head (3.3L). Reinstall the switch, plug or sending unit and tighten it securely. On all models, continue adding coolant to the radiator until it reaches the radiator cap seat.

13   Add coolant to the reservoir until the level is between the Min and Max marks.

14   Run the engine until normal operating temperature is reached and, with the engine idling, add coolant up the the correct level.

15   Always refill the system with a mixture of antifreeze and water in the proportion called for on the antifreeze container or in your owner's manual.

16   Keep a close watch on the coolant level and the various cooling system hoses during the first few miles of driving. Tighten the hose clamps and add more coolant mixture as necessary. On 2.6L engines, it may be necessary to add coolant to the reservoir the first few times the vehicle is driven as the system expels air.

33 Engine idle speed check and adjustment (carbureted models only)

1   Engine idle speed is the speed at which the engine operates when no accelerator pedal pressure is applied, as when stopped at a traffic light. This speed is critical to the performance of the engine itself, as well as many engine subsystems.

2   Set the parking brake firmly set and block the wheels to prevent the vehicle from rolling. Put the transaxle in Neutral.

3   Hook up a hand-held tachometer in accordance with the tachometer manufacturer's instructions.

4   The manufacturer has used several different throttle linkages and positioners on these vehicles in the time period covered by this book, so it would be impractical to cover every type. Chapter 4 contains information on each individual carburetor used. Also, each vehicle has an Emission Control information label in the engine compartment that contains instructions for setting your particular vehicle's idle speed.

5   Basically, on most models, the idle speed is set by turning an adjustment screw located on the side of the carburetor. The screw opens or closes the throttle plate, depending on how much it is turned and in which direction. The screw may be on the linkage itself or may be part of the idle stop solenoid. Refer to the emissions label and Chapter 4.

6   Once you have found the idle speed screw, experiment with different length screwdrivers until the adjustments can be made easily, without coming into contact with hot or moving engine components.

7   Check and adjust if necessary, the ignition timing (Section 34).

8   Check the engine idle speed on the tachometer and compare it to the Emission Control Information label in the engine compartment.

9   If the idle speed is too low or too high, turn the speed adjusting screw until the specified idle speed is obtained.

34 Ignition timing check and adjustment

Note: *Ignition timing on 3.3L V6 models is computer-controlled and therefore not adjustable.*

Refer to illustrations 34.2, 34.6a, 34.6b, 34.11a, 34.11b, and 34.13

1   All vehicles are equipped with an Emissions Control Information label inside the engine compartment. The label contains important ignition timing specifications and the proper timing procedure for your specific vehicle. If the information on the emissions label is different from the information included in this Section, follow the procedure on the label.

2   At the specified intervals, or when the distributor has been removed, the ignition timing must be checked and adjusted if necessary. Tools required for this procedure include an inductive pick-up timing light, a tachometer and a distributor wrench **(see illustration)**.

3   Before you check the timing, make sure the engine is at normal operating temperature.

4   On carbureted models, make sure the idle speed is correct (Section 33). On models with a carburetor switch, connect a jumper wire between the switch and a good ground. Disconnect and plug the vacuum hose at the Spark Control Computer (2.2L engine) or at the distributor (2.6L engine). If the engine is already idling at or below the specified speed, proceed with the next Step. If the idle is too high, turn the idle speed adjusting screw until the specified idle is attained.

5   Connect a timing light in accordance with the manufacturer's instructions. Usually, the light must be connected to the battery and the number one spark plug is some fashion. The number one spark plug wire or terminal should be marked at the distributor; trace it back to the spark plug and attach the timing light lead near the plug. **Caution:** *If an inductive pick-up timing light isn't available, don't puncture the spark plug wire to attach the timing light pick-up lead. Instead, use an adapter between the spark plug and plug wire. If the insulation on the plug wire is damaged, the secondary voltage will jump to ground at the damaged point and the engine will misfire.*

6   Locate the timing marks at the window in the transaxle bellhousing or at the front of the engine **(see illustrations)**.

7   Locate the notched groove across the flywheel/driveplate or the pulley. It may be necessary to have an assistant temporarily turn the ignition on and off in short bursts without starting the engine in order to bring the groove into a position where it can easily be cleaned and marked. **Warning:** *Stay clear of all moving engine components when the engine is turned over in this manner.*

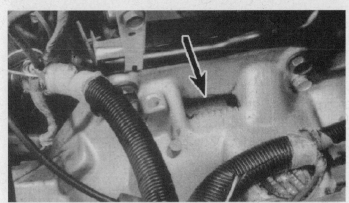

34.6a On 2.2L/2.5L engines, the bellhousing window allows you to view the flywheel/driveplate notch (arrow) - mark this notch and the mark along the side of the window that corresponds to the number of degrees specified on the Vehicle Emission Control Information label in the engine compartment

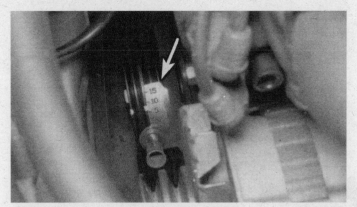

34.6b On 2.6L and 3.0L engines, the timing marks are attached to the front of the engine and the crankshaft pulley has a groove in it for reference

34.11a On 2.5L engines, unplug the coolant sensor connector located in the thermostat housing (arrow)

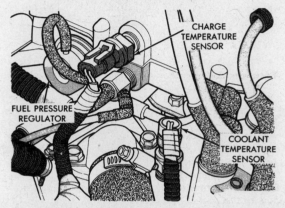

34.11b Unplug the coolant temperature sensor connector on 3.0L engines, located next to the thermostat housing

12 Aim the timing light at the marks, again being careful not to come into contact with moving parts. The marks you made should appear stationary. If the marks are in alignment, the timing is correct. If the marks are not aligned, turn off the engine.

13 Loosen the hold-down bolt/nut at the base of the distributor **(see illustration)**. Loosen the bolt only slightly, just enough to turn the distributor (see Chapter 5).

14 Now restart the engine and turn the distributor very slowly until the timing marks are aligned.

15 Shut off the engine and tighten the distributor bolt, being careful not to move the distributor.

16 Start the engine and recheck the timing to make sure the marks are still in alignment. Reconnect all hoses and wires.

34.13 Loosen the nut or bolt so you can turn the distributor if the timing is not as specified

8 Use white chalk or paint to mark the groove in the flywheel or pulley (see illustrations 34.6a and 34.6b). Also, mark the number corresponding to the number of degrees specified on the Emission Control Information label in the engine compartment.

9 Connect a tachometer to the engine, setting the selector to the correct cylinder position.

10 Make sure the wiring for the timing light is clear of all moving engine components, then start the engine.

11 On fuel-injected models, disconnect the coolant temperature sensor connector **(see illustrations)**.

35 Combustion chamber conditioner application (Canadian leaded fuel models only)

1 At the intervals specified in the Maintenance schedule at the beginning of this Chapter, combustion chamber conditioner *(see Recommended lubricants and fluids)* must be sprayed into the carburetor or fuel injection throttle body to help prevent the buildup of deposits in the combustion chamber and on the valves.

2 Remove the air cleaner or throttle body air inlet hose.

3 With the engine idling at normal operating temperature, the transaxle in Park (automatic) or Neutral (manual) and the parking brake applied, spray a can of the specified conditioner into the throttle body opening.

4 Reattach the hose to the air inlet.

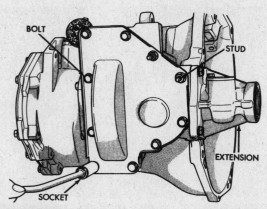

36.2   Remove the bolts and nuts, then separate the differential cover from the transaxle case to drain the lubricant (1984 through 1986 models only)

37.3   Pry at the rear corner of the transaxle pan to break the seal and allow the fluid to drain - be careful, the fluid will gush out under considerable force

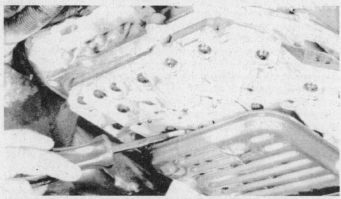

37.4   On four-speed models, the fluid filter can be detached by prying carefully with a small screwdriver

36   Manual transaxle lubricant change

1984 through 1986 models

Refer to illustrations 36.2 and 36.4

1   Raise the front of the vehicle and support it securely on jackstands. Apply the parking brake.

2   Unbolt the cover from the side of the differential and allow the lubricant to drain into a container **(see illustration)**.

3   Attached to the inside of the cover is a small magnet, installed to trap metal particles before they can damage the transaxle bearings. Clean the magnet and the inside surface of the cover thoroughly.

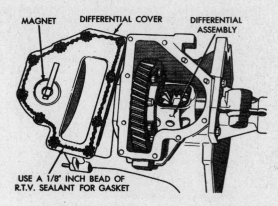

36.4   Apply a bead of RTV sealant to the differential cover contact surface (1984 through 1986 models only)

4   Clean the gasket surfaces on the differential and cover thoroughly with a gasket scraper, then wipe them with a rag soaked in lacquer thinner or acetone. Use RTV sealant to form a new gasket for the cover and install the cover on the differential **(see illustration)**. Tighten the bolts evenly and securely in a criss-cross pattern.

5   Fill the transaxle with the recommended lubricant (see Recommended lubricants and fluids at the beginning of this Chapter) until the level is at the bottom edge of the filler plug. Drive the vehicle and check the cover for leaks.

1987 and later models

6   Do not remove the differential cover on models produced after 1986. Check for a drain plug. If no drain plug is present draw fluid out through the fill plug with a suction syringe.

7   Refill the transaxle with the specified lubricant, test drive and check for leaks.

37   Automatic transaxle fluid and filter change

Refer to illustrations 37.3, 37.4 and 37.7

1   The automatic transaxle fluid and filter should be changed, the magnet cleaned and the bands adjusted at the recommended intervals.

2   Raise the front of the vehicle and support it securely on jackstands. Apply the parking brake.

3   Position a container under the transaxle fluid pan. Loosen the pan bolts. Completely remove the bolts along the rear of the pan. Tap the corner of the pan or pry carefully to break the seal and allow the fluid to drain into the container (the remaining bolts will prevent the pan from separating from the transaxle) **(see illustration).** Remove the remaining bolts and detach the pan.

4   On three-speed models, remove the filter screws and detach the filter (a special Torx bit may be required for the screws). On four-speed models, the filter is a press fit and can be detached by prying carefully with a screwdriver **(see illustration)**.

5   On three-speed models, refer to Section 38 and adjust the bands before proceeding with the fluid change.

6   On three-speed models, install the new gasket and filter. Tighten the filter screws securely. On four-speed models, press the new filter securely into place.

7   Using a scraper, carefully remove all traces of old sealant from the pan and transaxle body (don't nick or gouge the sealing surfaces). After scraping, wipe the gasket surfaces with a rag soaked in lacquer thinner or acetone. Clean the magnet in the pan with a clean, lint-free cloth **(see illustration)**.

8   Apply a 1/8-inch bead of RTV sealant to the pan sealing surface and position it on the transaxle. Install the bolts and tighten them to the torque listed in this Chapter's Specifications, following a criss-cross pattern. Work up to the final torque in three or four steps.

9   Lower the vehicle and add three quarts of the specified fluid (see Recommended lubricants and fluids at the beginning of this Chapter)

37.7   Wash the pan and clean the magnet, then place the magnet back in it's original position

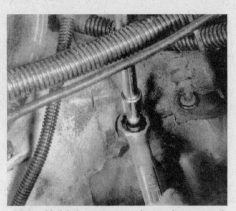

38.7   Hold the screw so it won't turn and tighten the locknut with a box-end wrench

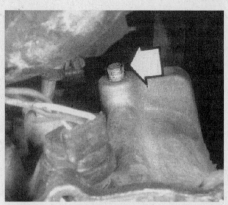

38.9   Low-Reverse band pressure plug location (arrow)

1

38.10   Insert feeler gauges between the Low-Reverse band ends to measure wear - if the gap is less than 0.080-inch, a new band is needed

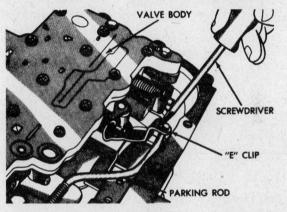

38.11a   Use a screwdriver to pry off the parking rod E-clip, . . .

to the transaxle. Start the engine and allow it to idle for at least two minutes, then move the shift lever through each of the gear positions, ending in Park or Neutral. Check for fluid leakage around the pan.
10   Add more fluid until the level is between the Add and Full marks on the dipstick. Add fluid a little at a time until it is full (be careful not to overfill it).
11   Make sure the dipstick is seated completely or dirt could get into the transaxle.

38   Automatic transaxle band adjustment (three-speed models only)

Refer to illustrations 38.7, 38.9, 38.10, 38.11a, 38.11b, 38.12a, 38.12b and 38.15
1   The transaxle bands should be adjusted when specified in the maintenance schedule or at the time of a fluid and filter change (Section 37).

Kickdown band
2   The kickdown band adjustment screw is located at the top left side of the transaxle case.
3   On some models the throttle cable may interfere with band adjustment. If so, mark its position and then remove the throttle cable adjustment bolt. Move the cable away from the band adjustment screw.
4   Loosen the locknut approximately five turns and make sure the adjusting screw turns freely.
5   Tighten the adjusting screw to the torque listed in this Chapter's Specifications.
6   Back the adjusting screw off the specified number of turns (see the Specifications section at the beginning of this Chapter).

7   Hold the screw in position and tighten the locknut securely **(see illustration)**.

Low-Reverse band
8   To gain access to the low-Reverse band, the transaxle pan must be removed (Section 37).
9   To determine if the band is worn excessively, remove the Low-Reverse pressure plug from the transaxle case **(see illustration)** and apply 30 psi of air pressure to the port.
10   Measure the gap between the band ends **(see illustration)**. It should be 0.080-inch minimum. If it's less than that, the band should be replaced with a new one
11   To proceed with adjustment, pry off the parking rod E-clip and remove the rod **(see illustrations)**.
12   Loosen the locknut approximately five turns **(see illustration)**. Use an in-lb torque wrench to tighten the adjusting screw to the torque listed in this Chapter's Specifications **(see illustration)**.
13   Back the screw off the specified number of turns (see the specifications section at the beginning of this Chapter).
14   Hold the adjusting screw in position and tighten the locknut securely.
15   Push the shift pawl in the transaxle case to the rear and reinstall the parking rod **(see illustration)**.
16   Install the pan and refill the transaxle (see Section 37).

39   Driveaxle boot check

Refer to illustrations 39.3 and 39.4
1   If the driveaxle boots are damaged or deteriorated, serious and costly damage can occur to the CV joints the boots are designed to

protect. The boots should be inspected very carefully at the recommended intervals.

2   Raise the front of the vehicle and support it securely on jackstands (see *Jacking and towing* at the front of this manual if necessary).

3   Crawl under the vehicle and check the four driveaxle boots (two on each driveaxle) very carefully for cracks, tears, holes, deteriorated rubber and loose or missing clamps **(see illustration)**. If the boots are dirty, wipe them clean before beginning the inspection.

4   If damage or deterioration is evident, replace the boots with new ones and check the CV joints for damage (see Chapter 8) **(see illustration)**.

40   Evaporative emissions control system check

Refer to illustration 40.2

1   The function of the evaporative emissions control system is to draw fuel vapors from the gas tank and fuel system, store them in a charcoal canister and route them to the intake manifold during normal engine operation.

2   The most common symptom of a fault in the evaporative emissions system is a strong fuel odor in the engine compartment. If a fuel odor is detected, inspect the charcoal canister, located in the engine compartment on the passenger's side, behind the headlight or under-

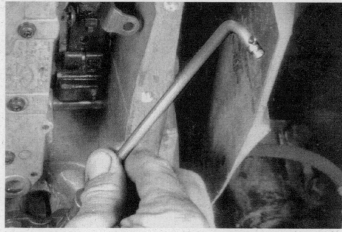

38.11b   . . . then lower the rod from the transaxle

neath the vehicle. Check the canister and all hoses for damage and deterioration **(see illustration)**.

3   The evaporative emissions control system is explained in more detail in Chapter 6.

38.12a   Loosen the locknut five turns

38.12b   It may be necessary to use a universal joint between the socket and extension when tightening the Low-Reverse band adjusting screw

38.15   Push the shift pawl back with your finger before inserting the parking rod

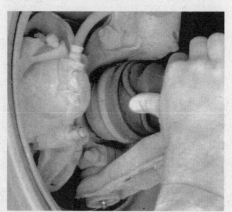

39.3   Flex the driveaxle boots by hand to check for damage and deterioration

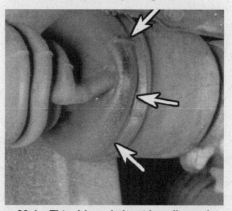

39.4   This driveaxle boot is collapsed because all the grease has leaked out through cracks at the inner end (arrows) - it should be replaced immediately or the CV joint will fail for lack of lubrication

40.2   Check all of the hoses (arrows) connected to the evaporative emissions canister for cracks and damage

Chapter 2 Part A
2.2L and 2.5L four-cylinder engines

Contents

Contents

General

Firing order	1-3-4-2
Cylinder numbers (drivebelt end-to-transaxle end)........................	1–2–3–4
Bore and stroke	
2.2L	3.44 x 3.62 inches
2.5L	3.44 x 4.09 inches
Displacement	
2.2L	135 cubic inches
2.5L	153 cubic inches

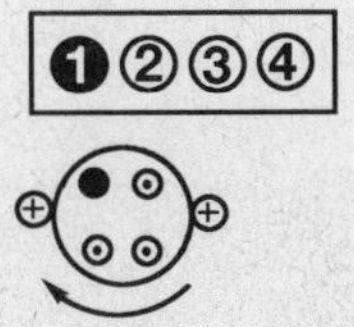

Camshaft

Endplay	0.005 to 0.013 inch
Runout	0.0004 inch
Journal diameter	
Standard	1.375 to 1.376 inch
Oversize	1.395 to 1.396 inch
Lobe wear (maximum)	
1984 2.2L engine	0.005 inch
All others	0.010 inch

Cylinder location chart

Front

Cylinder head

Warpage limit	0.004 inch

Intake/exhaust manifolds

Warpage limit	0.008 inch per foot of manifold length

Oil pump

Outer rotor-to-housing clearance	
Standard	0.010 inch
Service limit	0.014 inch

Oil pump (continued)

Outer rotor thickness
    1984 and 1985 2.2L engines
        Standard.. 0.826 to 0.827 inch
        Service limit .... 0.825 inch
    All others
        Standard.. 0.944 to 0.945 inch
        Service limit .... 0.9435 inch
Inner rotor-to-outer rotor tip clearance
    1984 and 1985 2.2L engines
        Standard.. 0.010 inch
        Service limit .... 0.010 inch
    All others
        Standard.. 0.004 inch
        Service limit .... 0.008 inch
Inner and outer rotor-to-housing clearance
    Standard .... 0.001 to 0.003 inch
    Service limit .... 0.0035 inch
Pump cover flatness
    1984 and 1985 2.2L engines
        Standard.. 0.010 inch maximum
        Service limit .... 0.015 inch
    All others
        Standard.. 0.002 inch maximum
        Service limit .... 0.003 inch
Relief spring free length .... 1.95 inch

Torque specifications

Ft-lbs (unless otherwise indicated)

Camshaft bearing cap bolts
    1987 and earlier .... 165 in-lbs
    1988 on .... 215 in-lbs
Valve cover bolts/nuts .... 105 in-lbs
Timing belt tensioner bolt 45
Camshaft sprocket bolt 65
Crankshaft pulley Torx head bolts
    1992 and earlier .... 250 in-lbs
    1993 .... 280 in-lbs
Crankshaft pulley center bolt 50
Cylinder head bolts — engine cold *(use the tightening sequence shown in Section 12)*
    1984 and 1985
        First step 30
        Second step 45
        Third step 45
        Fourth step 1/4-turn
    1986 on
        First step 45
        Second step 65
        Third step 65
        Fourth step. 1/4-turn
Driveplate-to-crankshaft bolts
    M10 70
    M12 100
Flywheel-to-crankshaft bolts
    1984 and 1985 65
    1986 on 70
Crankshaft front oil seal housing bolts .... 105 in-lbs
Intake/exhaust manifold nuts/bolts 16
Intermediate shaft oil seal housing bolts .... 105 in-lbs
Intermediate shaft sprocket bolt 65
Oil pan-to-engine block fasteners
    M8 16
    M6 .... 105 in-lbs
Oil pick-up tube-to-oil pump housing bolt 16
Oil pump mounting bolts.. 21
Oil pump cover bolts .... 105 in-lbs
Oil pan drain plug 20
Rear main oil seal housing bolts .... 105 in-lbs
Timing belt cover bolts .... 40 in-lbs
Water pump hub bolt 21

1   General information

This Part of Chapter 2 is devoted to in-vehicle repair procedures for the 2.2L and 2.5L engines. All information concerning engine removal and installation and engine block and cylinder head overhaul can be found in Part E of this Chapter.

The following repair procedures are based on the assumption that the engine is installed in the vehicle. If the engine has been removed from the vehicle and mounted on a stand, many of the steps outlined in this Part of Chapter 2 will not apply.

The Specifications included in this Part of Chapter 2 apply only to the procedures contained in this Part. Part E of Chapter 2 contains the Specifications necessary for cylinder head and engine block rebuilding.

2   Repair operations possible with the engine in the vehicle

Many major repair operations can be accomplished without removing the engine from the vehicle.

Clean the engine compartment and the exterior of the engine with some type of degreaser before any work is done. It will make the job easier and help keep dirt out of the internal areas of the engine.

Depending on the components involved, it may be helpful to remove the hood to improve access to the engine as repairs are performed (refer to Chapter 11 if necessary). Cover the fenders to prevent damage to the paint. Special pads are available, but an old bedspread or blanket will also work.

If vacuum, exhaust, oil or coolant leaks develop, indicating a need for gasket or seal replacement, the repairs can generally be made with the engine in the vehicle. The intake and exhaust manifold gaskets, oil pan gasket, crankshaft oil seals and cylinder head gasket are all accessible with the engine in place.

Exterior engine components, such as the intake and exhaust manifolds, the oil pan (and the oil pump), the water pump, the starter motor, the alternator, the distributor and the fuel system components can be removed for repair with the engine in place.

Since the cylinder head can be removed without pulling the engine, camshaft and valve component servicing can also be accomplished with the engine in the vehicle. Replacement of the timing belt and sprockets is also possible with the engine in the vehicle.

In extreme cases caused by a lack of necessary equipment, repair or replacement of piston rings, pistons, connecting rods and rod bearings is possible with the engine in the vehicle. However, this practice is not recommended because of the cleaning and preparation work that must be done to the components involved.

3   Top Dead Center (TDC) for number one piston — locating

Refer to illustrations 3.6 and 3.8
Note: *The following procedure is based on the assumption that the spark plug wires and distributor are correctly installed. If you are trying to locate TDC to install the distributor correctly, piston position must be determined by feeling for compression at the number one spark plug hole, then aligning the ignition timing marks as described in Step 8. In the event of timing belt breakage, remove the timing belt cover and align the marks on the camshaft sprocket as shown in illustration 6.19, then align the mark on the flywheel with the correct mark on the timing scale as directed in Step 4.*

1   Top Dead Center (TDC) is the highest point in the cylinder that each piston reaches as it travels up-and-down when the crankshaft turns. Each piston reaches TDC on the compression stroke and again on the exhaust stroke, but TDC generally refers to piston position on the compression stroke.

2   Positioning the piston(s) at TDC is an essential part of many procedures such as camshaft and timing belt/sprocket removal and distributor removal.

3   Before beginning this procedure, be sure to place the transmission in Neutral and apply the parking brake or block the rear wheels.

Also, disable the ignition system by detaching the coil wire from the center terminal of the distributor cap and grounding it on the block with a jumper wire. Remove the spark plugs (see Chapter 1).

4   In order to bring any piston to TDC, the crankshaft must be turned using one of the methods outlined below. When looking at the front of the engine, normal crankshaft rotation is clockwise.

   a) The preferred method is to turn the crankshaft with a socket and ratchet attached to the bolt threaded into the front of the crankshaft.

   b) A remote starter switch, which may save some time, can also be used. Follow the instructions included with the switch. Once the piston is close to TDC, use a socket and ratchet as described in the previous paragraph.

   c) If an assistant is available to turn the ignition switch to the Start position in short bursts, you can get the piston close to TDC without a remote starter switch. Make sure your assistant is out of the vehicle, away from the ignition switch, then use a socket and ratchet as described in Paragraph a) to complete the procedure.

5   Note the position of the terminal for the number one spark plug wire on the distributor cap. If the terminal isn't marked, follow the plug wire from the number one cylinder spark plug to the cap.

6   Use a felt-tip pen or chalk to make a mark on the distributor body directly under the terminal **(see illustration)**.

7   Detach the cap from the distributor and set it aside (see Chapter 1 if necessary).

8   Locate the round window in the bellhousing. You'll see the timing increments on the edge of the window. Turn the crankshaft (see Paragraph 3 above) until the TDC mark (zero) on the edge of the bellhousing is aligned with the groove in the flywheel **(see illustration)**.

2A

3.6 Use a felt-tip marker or chalk to mark the distributor housing directly beneath the number one spark plug wire terminal

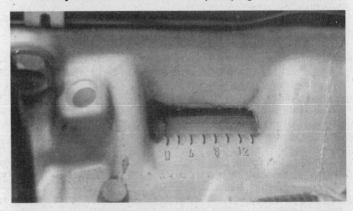

3.8 When you're bringing the number one piston to TDC, look at the timing mark on the edge of the flywheel/driveplate through the opening in the bellhousing, and align the mark with the 0-degree mark on the bellhousing — you may have to remove a plug from the bellhousing to see the flywheel

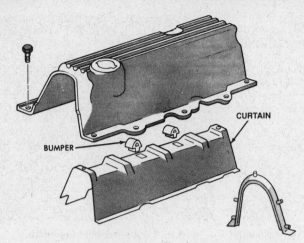

4.4a Typical valve cover and related components

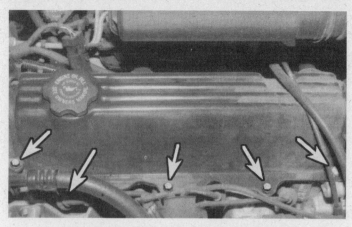

4.4b Remove the valve cover bolts (arrows)

9   Look at the distributor rotor — it should be pointing directly at the mark you made on the distributor body. If the rotor is pointing at the mark, go to Step 12. If it isn't, go to Step 10.

10   If the rotor is 180-degrees off, the number one piston is at TDC on the exhaust stroke.

11   To get the piston to TDC on the compression stroke, turn the crankshaft one complete turn (360-degrees) clockwise. The rotor should now be pointing at the mark on the distributor. When the rotor is pointing at the number one spark plug wire terminal in the distributor cap and the ignition timing marks are aligned, the number one piston is at TDC on the compression stroke.

12   After the number one piston has been positioned at TDC on the compression stroke, TDC for any of the remaining pistons can be located by turning the crankshaft and following the firing order. Mark the remaining spark plug wire terminal locations on the distributor body just like you did for the number one terminal, then number the marks to correspond with the cylinder numbers. As you turn the crankshaft, the rotor will also turn. When it's pointing directly at one of the marks on the distributor, the piston for that particular cylinder is at TDC on the compression stroke.

4   Valve cover — removal and installation

Removal

Refer to illustrations 4.4a, 4.4b, 4.5 and 4.6

1   Detach the cable from the negative battery terminal.
2   Detach the accelerator cable from the cable bracket.
3   Wipe off the valve cover thoroughly to prevent debris from falling

onto the exposed cylinder head or camshaft/valve train assembly.

4   Remove the upper half of the timing belt cover (see Section 6). Remove the valve cover bolts **(see illustrations)**.

5   Carefully lift off the valve cover and gasket. If the gasket is stuck to the cylinder head, use a putty knife or flat-bladed screwdriver to remove it **(see illustration)**. Set the cover aside.

6   If the vehicle is fuel-injected or turbocharged, you'll note a "curtain" (baffle for enhancing air/oil separation) under the valve cover. If you're simply replacing a leaking valve cover gasket, you don't need to remove the curtain. If you want to adjust the valves or service the camshaft assembly or cylinder head, remove the curtain **(see illustration)**. Don't lose the two small rubber "bumpers" which act as cushions between the curtain and the valve cover.

Installation

Refer to illustrations 4.9a and 4.9b

7   Make sure the gasket mating surfaces of the cylinder head and the valve cover are clean. **Note:** *Chrysler Corporation states that all 1989 and 1990 vehicles equipped with a 2.2L or 2.5L engine must have the valve cover changed if it continues to leak oil. The updated valve cover uses RTV sealant instead of a gasket. The new cover also includes all new bolts (shorter length) and washers. The parts are only available at a dealer parts department.*

8   If the engine is equipped with a curtain (and it has been removed), install it now, manifold side first, with the cutouts over the cam towers and contacting the cylinder head floor, then press the opposite (distributor) side into position below the gasket mating surface. Be sure to install the rubber bumpers on top of the curtain.

9   Install new gaskets on the valve cover **(see illustration 12.8a)**. Install the molded rubber gaskets to the ends of the cover by pushing the tabs through the slots in the cover **(see illustration)**. Apply a 1/8-

4.5 Carefully pry the valve cover off the cylinder head — be careful not to bend the rails, which could cause oil leaks later on

4.6 Lift the curtain off the cylinder head

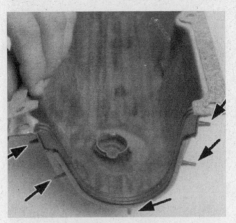

4.9a Use a small pair of pliers to pull the tabs (arrows) through the housing, insuring the seal is flush against the valve

4.9b Apply a small amount of RTV sealant to the corners of the cylinder head to prevent oil leaks

5.15 Intake manifold fasteners (2.2L engine shown)

inch wide bead of RTV sealant to the cylinder head rail in the area indicated **(see illustration)**. Install the cover and bolts and tighten the bolts to the torque listed in this Chapter's Specifications.

10   Turbocharged versions of the newer 2.5L engine also use a molded one-piece rubber gasket, but the gasket is attached differently. A continuous slot molded into the valve cover retains the gasket **(see illustration 12.8a)**. Install the gasket by pressing the gasket rail section into the slot. Install the cover and bolts and tighten the bolts to the torque listed in this Chapter's Specifications.

11   The remainder of installation is the reverse of removal.

5   Intake/exhaust manifold — removal and installation

Warning: *Gasoline is extremely flammable, so take extra precautions when you work on any part of the fuel system. Don't smoke or allow open flames or bare light bulbs near the work area, and don't work in a garage where a natural gas-type appliance (such as a water heater or clothes dryer) with a pilot light is present. If you spill any fuel on your skin, rinse it off immediately with soap and water. When you perform any kind of work on the fuel system, wear safety glasses and have a Class B type fire extinguisher on hand.*

TBI and carbureted engines

Refer to illustrations 5.15 and 5.18

Note: *On these models the throttle body assembly and intake manifold must be removed as a unit before the exhaust manifold can be removed.*

Removal

1   Relieve the fuel system pressure (see Chapter 4).
2   Detach the cable from the negative battery terminal.
3   Drain the cooling system (see Chapter 1).
4   Remove the air cleaner (see Chapter 4).
5   Clearly label and detach all vacuum lines, electrical wiring and fuel lines.
6   Detach the accelerator cable from the throttle linkage (see Chapter 4).
7   Loosen the power steering pump (if equipped) and remove the drivebelt (see Chapter 1).
8   Detach the power brake vacuum hose from the intake manifold.
9   If you're working on a Canadian model engine, remove the coupling hose from the air injection tube.
10   Remove the water hoses from the coolant crossover lines.
11   Raise the front of the vehicle and support it securely on jackstands. Detach the exhaust pipe from the exhaust manifold.
12   Remove the power steering pump (if equipped) and set it aside (see Chapter 10).

13   Remove the intake manifold support bracket and detach the EGR tube from the exhaust manifold.
14   If you're working on a Canadian model with a 2.2L engine, remove the air injection tube assembly.
15   Remove the intake manifold fasteners **(see illustration)**.
16   Lower the vehicle.
17   If you're working on a TBI engine:
   a) Remove the throttle body and the intake manifold as a single assembly.
   b) Detach the throttle body and gasket from the intake manifold (see Chapter 4) after the unit is on the bench.
18   Remove the exhaust manifold nuts **(see illustration)** and detach the exhaust manifold. Discard the old gaskets and clean all gasket mating surfaces.
19   Clean the manifolds with solvent and dry them with compressed air.
20   Check the mating surfaces of the manifolds for flatness with a precision straightedge and feeler gauges. Refer to this Chapter's Specifications for the warpage limit.
21   Inspect the manifolds for cracks and distortion.
22   If the manifolds are cracked or warped, replace them or see if they can be resurfaced/repaired at an automotive machine shop.

Installation

23   If you're replacing either manifold, transfer the studs from the old manifold to the new one.
24   When working on a TBI engine:
   a) Apply a thin coat of gasket sealant to the manifold sides of the new gaskets and place them in position on the manifolds.
   b) Place the exhaust manifold in position on the cylinder head and install the nuts. Starting at the center, tighten the nuts in a criss-

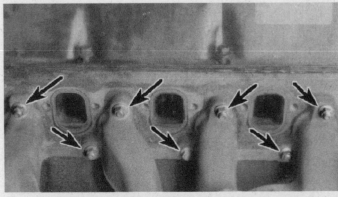

5.18 Exhaust manifold fasteners (2.2L engine shown)

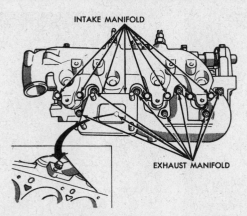

5.36 Intake/exhaust manifold fasteners on a turbocharged model

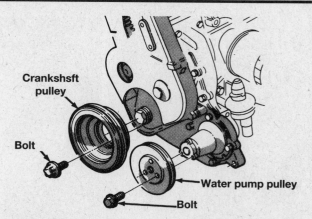

6.3 Crankshaft and water pump pulleys — exploded view

cross pattern until the torque listed in this Chapter's Specifications is reached.

  c) Position the intake manifold on the head.

  d) Raise the vehicle and support it securely on jackstands.

  e) Working under the vehicle, install the intake manifold bolts finger tight. Starting at the center and working out in both directions, tighten the bolts in a criss-cross pattern until the torque listed in this Chapter's Specifications is reached.

25   The remainder of the installation procedure is the reverse of removal.

Turbocharged engines

Refer to illustration 5.36

Removal

26   Disconnect the negative cable from the battery.

27   Drain the cooling system (see Chapter 1).

28   Raise the front of the vehicle and support it securely on jackstands.

29   Remove the front engine mount through bolt and rotate the engine away from the cowl.

30   Working under the vehicle, remove the turbocharger (see Chapter 4).

31   Lower the vehicle.

32   Working in the engine compartment, remove the air cleaner assembly along with the throttle body, hose and air cleaner box and bracket (see Chapter 4).

33   Disconnect the throttle linkage and throttle body electrical connector and vacuum hoses.

34   Position the fuel rail out of the way (complete with injectors, wiring harness and fuel line) by removing the hose retainer bracket screw, the four bracket screws from the intake manifold and the two retaining clips (see Chapter 4).

35   Disconnect the upper radiator hose from the thermostat housing.

36   Remove the bolts and nuts securing the intake and exhaust manifolds **(see illustration)**.

37   Remove the manifolds as an assembly.

38   Place the manifolds on a clean working surface. Discard the old gaskets and clean both surfaces (manifolds and cylinder head).

39   Check the gasket mating surfaces of the manifolds for flatness with a precision straightedge and feeler gauges. Refer to this Chapter's Specifications for the warpage limit.

40   Inspect the manifolds for cracks, corrosion and damage. If they're warped or cracked, an automotive machine shop may be able to resurface/repair them.

Installation

41   Install a new gasket. **Note:** *Don't use sealant on the manifold gasket.*

42   Place the exhaust manifold in position. Apply anti-seize compound to the threads and install the mounting nuts. Working from the center out in both directions, tighten the nuts in 1/4-turn increments to

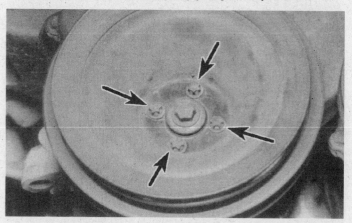

6.4 Remove the four Torx head bolts (arrows) from the crankshaft pulley

the torque listed in this Chapter's Specifications.

43   Place the intake manifold in position and install the bolts and washers. Working from the center out in both directions, tighten the bolts in 1/4-turn increments until all bolts are at the torque listed in this Chapter's Specifications.

44   Place the turbocharger in position on the exhaust manifold (see Chapter 4). Apply anti-seize compound to the threads and install the retaining nuts. Tighten the nuts to the torque listed in the Chapter 4 Specifications. Tighten the connector tube clamps securely.

45   Install the coolant return tube in the water box connector, tighten the tube nut and install the tube support bracket on the cylinder head.

46   Connect the turbocharger oil feed line.

47   Install the air cleaner assembly and reconnect the throttle linkage, wires and vacuum hoses.

48   Install the fuel rail (see Chapter 4).

49   Reconnect the exhaust pipe.

50   Connect the upper radiator hose to the thermostat housing.

51   Fill the cooling system (see Chapter 1).

52   Connect the negative battery cable.

---

6   Timing belt and sprockets — removal, inspection and installation

Timing belt removal

Refer to illustrations 6.3, 6.4, 6.5, 6.6a, 6.6b, 6.6c, 6.6d, 6.7, 6.8a, 6.8b and 6.8c

1   Detach the cable from the negative battery terminal.

2   Remove all accessory drivebelts (see Chapter 1).

3   Remove the bolts and detach the water pump pulley **(see illustration)**.

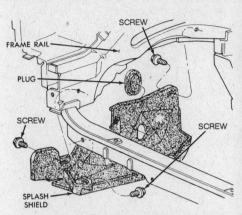

6.5 Raise the vehicle and detach the right inner splash shield to remove the crankshaft pulley

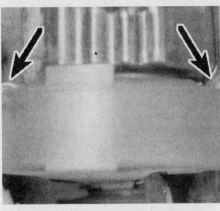

6.6a Remove the two bolts (arrows) that secure the timing belt upper cover to the valve cover

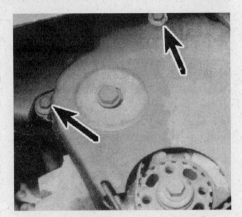

6.6b Remove the bolts from the timing belt lower cover (arrows) — the third bolt is located behind the water pump

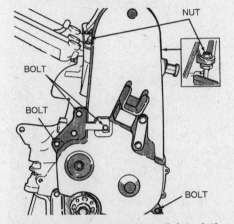

6.6c Remove the fasteners and detach the two timing cover halves

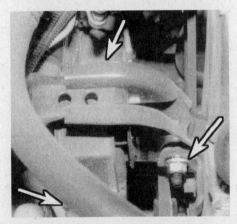

6.6d Remove the bolts (arrows) and separate the engine mount from the chassis (the rear bolt is hidden from view)

6.7 If you have correctly positioned the number one piston at TDC, the marks on the crankshaft and intermediate shaft sprockets will be aligned

6.8a Loosen the tensioner locking bolt and remove the tensioner

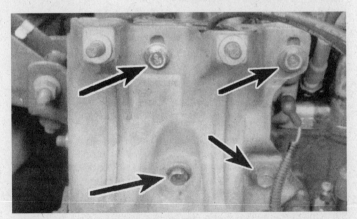

6.8b Remove the bolts (arrows) and the air conditioning compressor bracket from the engine

4   Remove the crankshaft pulley bolts (see illustration).

5   Raise the vehicle, support it securely on jackstands and remove the right inner splash shield (see illustration). Remove the crankshaft pulley.

6   Remove the screws and nuts holding the timing belt cover to the cylinder head and block (see illustrations). Remove both halves of the timing belt cover. Also remove the engine mount closest to the cover (see illustration). Use a block of wood and a floor jack positioned under the transaxle to keep the engine level while the engine mount is removed.

7   Position the number one piston at Top Dead Center on the compression stroke (see Section 3). The marks on the crankshaft and intermediate shaft sprocket will be aligned (see illustration) and the arrows on the camshaft sprocket will line up with the bearing cap parting line (see illustration 6.19).

8   Use a wrench to loosen the center bolt of the belt tensioner, releasing the tension from the timing belt. Remove the belt and the tensioner (see illustrations). Note: If the engine is equipped with air conditioning, remove the air conditioning compressor (see Chapter 3) and the bracket (see illustration).

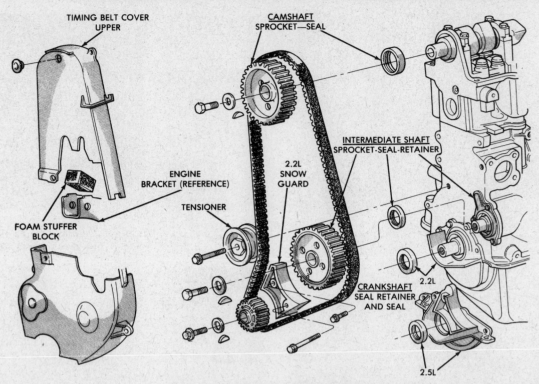

6.8c Timing belt and related components

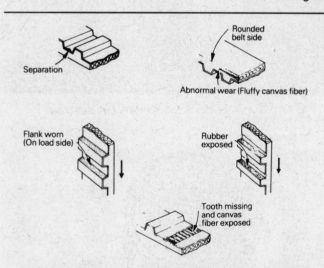

6.10 Carefully inspect the timing belt for the conditions shown here

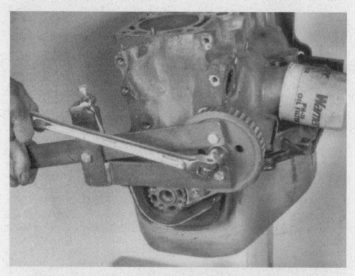

6.13 A pin spanner (or homemade substitute like the one shown here) will hold the intermediate shaft sprocket while the bolt is loosened

Timing belt, tensioner and sprocket inspection

Refer to illustration 6.10

9   Rotate the tensioner pulley by hand and move it side-to-side to detect roughness and excessive play. Replace it if it doesn't turn smoothly or if play is noted.

10   Inspect the timing belt for cracks, wear, signs of stretching, ply separation and damaged or missing teeth. Look for contamination by oil, gasoline, coolant and other liquids, which could damage the belt **(see illustration)**. Replace the belt if it's worn or damaged. **Note:** *Unless the engine has very low mileage, it's common practice to replace the timing belt with a new one every time it's removed. Don't reinstall the original belt unless it's in like-new condition. Never reinstall a belt in questionable condition.*

11   Visually inspect the sprockets for wear and damage. If any of the sprockets are damaged or worn, replace them.

12   Inspect the area directly below each sprocket for leaking engine oil. If there is oil below a sprocket, the seal behind that sprocket is leaking and must be replaced (see Sections 7, 8 and 9).

Sprocket removal and installation

Refer to illustrations 6.13, 6.14, 6.16 and 6.19

13   Remove the intermediate shaft sprocket bolt while holding the sprocket with a pin spanner or a homemade substitute **(see illustration)**. Pull the sprocket off the shaft.

14   Remove the bolt and use a puller to remove the crankshaft sprocket **(see illustration)**.

15   Hold the camshaft sprocket as described in Step 13 and remove the bolt, then detach the sprocket from the cam.

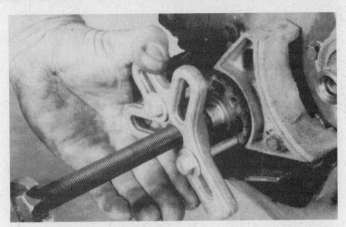

6.14 Use a puller to get the crankshaft sprocket off

6.16 Use a straightedge to make sure the marks (dimples) line up with the centers of the sprocket bolt holes

2A

6.19 The small hole must be at the top (arrow) and the triangles on the camshaft sprocket must be aligned with the bearing cap parting line (arrows)

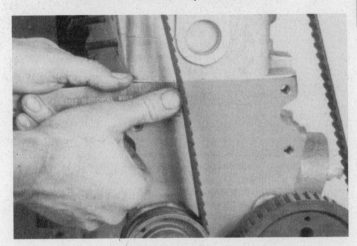

6.23 Use a ruler to measure timing belt deflection

16   Make sure the Woodruff keys are in place, then install the crankshaft and intermediate shaft sprockets. Turn the shafts until the marks are aligned **(see illustration)**.

17   Install the crankshaft sprocket bolt, lock the crankshaft to keep it from rotating and tighten the bolt to the torque listed in this Chapter's Specifications.

18   Install the intermediate shaft sprocket bolt and tighten it to the torque listed in this Chapter's Specifications. Double-check to make sure the marks are aligned as shown in illustration 6.16.

19   Install the camshaft sprocket and bolt. Tighten the bolt to the torque listed in this Chapter's Specifications. The triangles on the sprocket hub must align with the camshaft bearing cap parting line **(see illustration)**.

Timing belt installation

Refer to illustrations 6.23 and 6.25

20   When installing the timing belt, the marks on the sprockets MUST BE ALIGNED as described in Steps 16 and 19.

21   Install the timing belt without turning any of the sprockets.

22   Install the tensioner pulley with the bolt finger tight.

23   With the help of an assistant, apply tension to the timing belt and temporarily tighten the tensioner bolt. Measure the deflection of the belt half-way between the camshaft sprocket and tensioner pulley. Adjust the tensioner until belt deflection is approximately 5/16-inch **(see illustration)**.

24   Turn the crankshaft two complete revolutions in a clockwise direction (viewed from the front). This will align the belt on the pulleys. Recheck the belt deflection and tighten the tensioner pulley. **Note:** *When tightening the tensioner, use two wrenches. One wrench must*

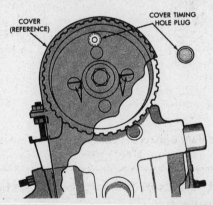

6.25 To check the camshaft timing when the timing belt cover is installed, bring the number one piston to TDC on the compression stroke and verify the small hole in the camshaft sprocket is aligned with the hole in the cover

keep the large hex surface in a stationary position (adjusted position) while the other wrench tightens the smaller bolt (locking bolt).

25   Recheck the camshaft timing mark with the timing belt cover installed and the number one piston at TDC on the compression stroke. The small hole in the camshaft sprocket must be centered in the timing belt cover hole **(see illustration)**.

26   The remainder of installation is the reverse of removal.

7.2 Wrap tape around the end of a small screwdriver and pry the seal out of the housing

7.5 If you don't have a socket large enough to drive in the new seal, tap around the outer edge with the large end of a punch

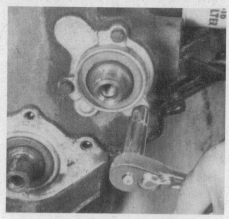

8.3 Remove the bolts and detach the seal housing

8.7 Using a soft-face hammer, carefully tap the new seal into the housing

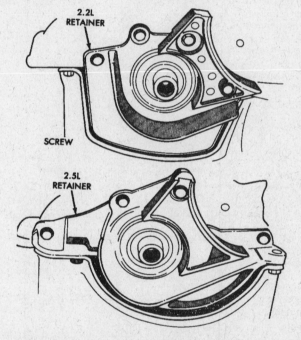

9.5 Remove the bolts and detach the housing/seal assembly

7   Camshaft oil seal — replacement

Refer to illustrations 7.2 and 7.5
Note: *The following procedure applies to the camshaft oil seal on both 2.2L and 2.5L engines.*

1   Remove the timing belt and camshaft sprocket (see Section 6).
2   Wrap the tip of a small screwdriver with tape and use it to careful-ly pry out the seal. Don't nick or scratch the camshaft journal or the new seal will leak **(see illustration)**.
3   Thoroughly clean and inspect the seal bore and the seal journal on the camshaft. Both must be clean and smooth. Use emery cloth or 400-grit sandpaper to remove small burrs.
4   If a groove has been worn into the journal on the camshaft (from contact with the seal lip), installing a new seal probably won't stop the leak. Such wear normally indicates the camshaft or the bearing sur-faces in the caps are worn. It's probably time to overhaul the cylinder head (see Chapter 2, Part E) or replace the head or camshaft.
5   Coat the lip of the new seal with clean engine oil or multi-purpose grease and carefully tap the seal into place with a large socket or piece of pipe and a hammer. If you don't have a socket as large in di-ameter as the seal, tap around the outer edge of the seal with the large end of a punch **(see illustration)**.
6   Install the camshaft sprocket and timing belt (see Section 6).
7   Start the engine and check for oil leaks.

8   Intermediate shaft oil seal — replacement

Refer to illustrations 8.3 and 8.7
1   Drain the engine oil (see Chapter 1).
2   Remove the timing belt and intermediate shaft sprocket (see Sec-tion 6).
3   Remove the oil seal housing **(see illustration)**.
4   Pry the old seal out of the housing with a screwdriver (wrap the tip of the screwdriver with tape). Make sure you don't scratch the seal bore.
5   Thoroughly clean and inspect the seal bore and the seal journal on the intermediate shaft. Both must be clean and smooth. Remove small burrs with emery cloth or 400-grit sandpaper.
6   If a groove has been worn in the seal journal (from contact with the seal lip), installing a new seal probably won't stop the leak. Such wear normally indicates the intermediate shaft or shaft bearing sur-faces in the engine block are worn. It's probably time to overhaul the engine (see Chapter 2, Part E).
7   Using a soft-face hammer, carefully tap the new seal into the

9.9 Tap the new crankshaft oil seal into the housing with a soft-face hammer

10.3 The camshaft bearing caps are numbered from 1 to 5 (arrow) so they don't get mixed up — if the caps aren't numbered, mark them (they must be reinstalled in their original locations)

housing **(see illustration)**.

8   Coat the lip of the seal with clean engine oil or multi-purpose grease and install the housing and seal on the front of the engine block. Make sure you don't damage the seal lip. Install the housing bolts and tighten them to the torque listed in this Chapter's Specifications.

9   Install the intermediate shaft sprocket and the timing belt (see Section 6).

10   Check the engine oil level and add oil, if necessary (see Chapter 1).

11   Start the engine and check for oil leaks.

9   Crankshaft front oil seal — replacement

Refer to illustrations 9.5 and 9.9

1   Drain the engine oil (see Chapter 1).

2   Remove the timing belt and crankshaft sprocket (see Section 6).

3   Raise the front of the vehicle and support it securely on jackstands.

4   Remove the oil pan (see Section 13). **Note:** *It is possible to remove the seal without removing the oil pan, if a special seal puller tool is used.*

5   Working underneath the vehicle, remove the bolts and detach the oil seal housing **(see illustration)**.

6   Use a punch and hammer to drive the old seal out of the housing. Make sure you don't damage the seal bore. To prevent this, wrap the tip of the punch with tape.

7   Thoroughly clean the seal bore in the housing and the seal journal on the end of the crankshaft. Remove small burrs with emery cloth or 400-grit sandpaper.

8   If a groove has been worn in the seal journal on the crankshaft (from contact with the seal lip), installing a new seal probably won't stop the leak. Such wear normally indicates the crankshaft and/or the main bearings are excessively worn. It's probably time to overhaul the engine (see Chapter 2, Part E).

9   Apply a thin coat of RTV sealant to the surface of the seal bore, lay the housing on a clean, flat work surface, position the new seal in the bore and tap it into place with a soft-face hammer **(see illustration)**. Make sure the seal lip faces the proper direction (towards the engine).

10   Lubricate the seal lip with multi-purpose grease and apply a 1 mm wide bead of anaerobic gasket sealant to the engine block mating surface of the seal housing. Position the housing on the engine. Install the retaining bolts and tighten them to the torque listed in this Chapter's Specifications.

11   Reinstall the crankshaft sprocket, timing belt and related components.

12   Install the oil pan (see Section 13).

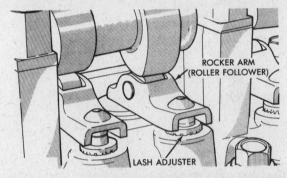

10.5 Mark the rocker arms and lash adjusters before removing them

13   Check the engine oil level and add oil, if necessary (see Chapter 1).

14   Start the engine, let it warm up and check for leaks.

10   Camshaft and hydraulic lash adjusters/rocker arms — removal, inspection and installation

Note: *It is possible to remove the rocker arms and lash adjusters without removing the camshaft (see Section 11 for details)*

Removal

Refer to illustrations 10.3, 10.5, 10.6 and 10.8

1   Remove the valve cover (see Section 4).

2   Remove the timing belt cover, timing belt and camshaft sprocket (see Section 6). **Note:** *If you want to save time by not removing and installing the timing belt, you can unfasten the camshaft sprocket and suspend it out of the way — with the belt still attached — on a piece of wire. Be sure the wire maintains tension on the belt so it won't disengage any of the sprockets.*

3   The camshaft rides on five bearings. Each bearing cap is held by two fasteners. On some engines, the bearing caps are numbered from 1 to 5, beginning at the drivebelt end of the engine (see illustration). **Note:** *All numbers face either the spark plug or manifold side of the engine. This is to ensure you install the caps facing the right direction.*

4   On some engines, the bearing caps aren't numbered. If this is the case, you must mark them before removal. Be sure to put the marks on the same ends of all the caps to prevent incorrect orientation of the caps during installation.

5   Also mark the rocker arms **(see illustration)** to ensure they're installed in the same position during reassembly.

10.6 Remove the bolts (arrows) from the camshaft bearing caps

10.8 The lash adjusters should slide out easily if they aren't coated with varnish

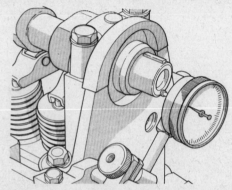

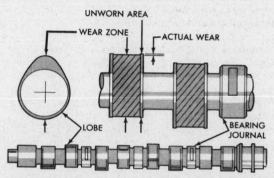

10.9 To check camshaft endplay, set up a dial indicator like this, with the gauge plunger touching the nose of the camshaft — pry the camshaft back-and-forth and note the reading on the dial indicator

10.12 Measure the height of the camshaft lobes at the wear zone and unworn area, then subtract the wear zone measurement from the unworn area measurement to get the actual wear — compare the wear to the limit listed in this Chapter's Specifications

6   Remove the bolts from all the bearing caps **(see illustration)** ex-cept cap numbers 2 and 4. Next, loosen each of the four fasteners on 2 and 4 a little at a time to relieve valve spring tension evenly until the caps are loose. If any of the caps stick, gently tap them with a soft-face hammer. **Caution:** *Failure to follow this procedure exactly as de-scribed could tilt the camshaft in the housing, which could damage the housing or bend the camshaft.*

7   Lift out the camshaft, wipe it off with a clean shop towel and set it aside.

8   Lift out each rocker arm and lash adjuster **(see illustration)**, wipe them off and set them aside in labelled plastic bags or an egg carton.

Inspection

Refer to illustrations 10.9 and 10.12

9   To check camshaft endplay:
   a) Install the camshaft and secure it with caps 1 and 5.
   b) Mount a dial indicator on the head **(see illustration)**.
   c) Using a large screwdriver as a lever at the opposite end, move the camshaft forward-and-backward and note the dial indicator reading.
   d) Compare the reading with the endplay listed in this Chapter's Specifications.
   e) If the indicated reading is higher, either the camshaft or the head is worn. Replace parts as necessary.

10   To check camshaft runout:
   a) Support the camshaft with a pair of V-blocks and attach a dial indicator with the stem resting against the center bearing jour-nal on the camshaft.
   b) Rotate the camshaft and note the indicated runout.
   c) Compare the results to the camshaft runout listed in this Chap-

ter's Specifications.
   d) If the indicated runout exceeds the specified runout, replace the camshaft.

11   Check the camshaft bearing journals and caps for scoring and signs of wear. If they are worn, replace the cylinder head with a new or rebuilt unit. Measure the journals on the camshaft with a micrometer, comparing your readings with this Chapter's Specifications. If the di-ameter of any of the journals is out of specification, replace the camshaft. **Note:** *When servicing the camshaft or cylinder head, it is necessary to be certain that oversized camshafts are used only with oversized journals. Cylinder heads with oversized journals can be iden-tified by green paint on the tops of the camshaft bearing caps and OS/J stamped to the rear of the oil gallery plug on the air pump end of the cylinder head. Camshafts with oversized journals are identified by green paint on the barrel of the shaft and OS/J stamped on the end of the shaft.*

12   Check the cam lobes for wear:
   a) Check the toe and ramp areas of each cam lobe for score marks and uneven wear. Also check for flaking and pitting.
   b) If there's wear on the toe or the ramp, replace the camshaft, but first try to find the cause of the wear. Check the lash adjusters, look for abrasive substances in the oil and inspect the oil pump and oil passages for blockage. Lobe wear is usually caused by inadequate lubrication or dirty oil.
   c) Using a micrometer, calculate the lobe wear **(see illustration)**. If the lobe wear is greater than listed in this Chapter's Specifica-tions, replace the camshaft.

13   Inspect the rocker arms and hydraulic lash adjusters for wear, galling and pitting of the contact surfaces.

14   If any of the conditions described above are noted, the cylinder head is probably getting insufficient lubrication or dirty oil, so make

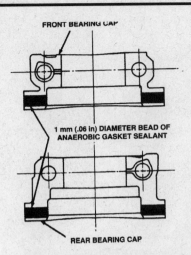

10.17 Install the camshaft with the lobes pointing away from the number one cylinder intake and exhaust valves

10.20 Apply anaerobic-type gasket sealant to the dark areas only on the front and rear camshaft bearing caps

10.21 Apply RTV sealant to the outer circumference of the camshaft rear plug before installing the number 5 cap

2A

sure you track down the cause of this problem (low oil level, low oil pump capacity, clogged oil passage, etc.) before installing a new head, camshaft or followers.

Installation

Refer to illustrations 10.17, 10.20 and 10.21

15   Thoroughly clean the camshaft, the bearing surfaces in the head and caps, the rocker arms and hydraulic lash adjusters. Remove all sludge and dirt. Wipe off all components with a clean, lint-free cloth.
16   Lubricate the lash adjuster and the contact surfaces on the top of the rocker arms with assembly lube or moly-base grease. Install the lash adjusters and rocker arms, making sure you put them in their original locations.
17   Lubricate the camshaft bearing surfaces in the head and the bearing journals and lobes on the camshaft with assembly lube or moly-base grease. Carefully lower the camshaft into position with the lobes for the number one cylinder pointing away from the cam followers or rocker arms **(see illustration)**. **Caution:** *Failure to adequately lubricate the camshaft and related components can cause serious damage to bearing and friction surfaces during the first few seconds after engine start-up, when the oil pressure is low or nonexistent.*
18   Apply a thin coat of assembly lube or moly-base grease to the bearing surfaces of the camshaft bearing caps and install the caps in their original locations.
19   Install the bolts for bearing caps 2 and 4. Gradually tighten all four fasteners — 1/4-turn at a time — until the camshaft is drawn down and seated in the bearing saddles. Don't tighten the fasteners completely at this time.
20   Apply anaerobic-type sealant to the contact surfaces of bearing caps 1 and 5 **(see illustration)**.
21   Install bearing caps 3 and 5 **(see illustration)** and tighten the fasteners the same way you did for caps 2 and 4.
22   Install a new oil seal on the front of the camshaft, then install bearing cap 1. Don't tighten the fasteners completely at this time.
23   Remove any excess sealant from the two end bearing caps.
24   Working in a criss-cross pattern, tighten the fasteners for bearing caps 2 and 4 to the torque listed in this Chapter's Specifications. Then torque the fasteners for bearing caps 3 and 5 the same way. Finally, tighten the fasteners for bearing cap 1.
25   Install the camshaft sprocket, timing belt, timing belt cover and related components (see Section 6). If you suspended the camshaft sprocket out of the way and didn't disturb the timing belt or sprockets, the valve timing should still be correct. Rotate the camshaft as necessary to reattach the sprocket to the camshaft. If the valve timing was disturbed, align the sprockets and install the belt as described in Section 6.
26   Remove the spark plugs and rotate the crankshaft by hand to

11.4   This is what the air hose adapter that threads into the spark plug hole looks like - they're commonly available from auto parts stores

make sure the valve timing is correct. After two revolutions, the timing marks on the sprockets should still be aligned. If they're not, reindex the timing belt to the sprockets (see Section 6). **Note:** *If you feel resistance while rotating the crankshaft, stop immediately and check the valve timing by referring to Section 6.*

11   Valve springs, retainers and seals — replacement

Refer to illustrations 11.4, 11.5, 11.9, 11.15 and 11.17

Note: *Broken valve springs and defective valve stem seals can be replaced without removing the cylinder heads. Two special tools and a compressed air source are normally required to perform this operation, so read through this Section carefully and rent or buy the tools before beginning the job. If compressed air isn't available, a length of nylon rope can be used to keep the valves from falling into the cylinder during this procedure.*

1   Refer to Section 4 and remove the valve cover.
2   Remove the spark plug from the cylinder which has the defective component. If all of the valve stem seals are being replaced, all of the spark plugs should be removed.
3   Turn the crankshaft until the piston in the affected cylinder is at top dead center on the compression stroke (see Section 3 for instructions). If you're replacing all of the valve stem seals, begin with cylinder number one and work on the valves for one cylinder at a time. Move from cylinder-to-cylinder following the firing order sequence (see the Specifications).
4   Thread an adapter into the spark plug hole and connect an air

11.5 Using this tool, the valve springs can be depressed and the rocker arms removed without removing the camshaft — this is also the preferred type of spring compressor to use when removing the valve keepers

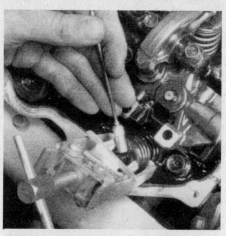

11.9 If the special tool isn't available, use a screw-type spring compressor — remove the keepers with a magnet or needle-nose pliers

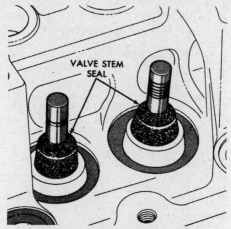

11.15 Be sure to note if there are differences in the intake and exhaust valve stem seals. Use a special valve stem seal or a deep socket to install the new seal(s).

hose from a compressed air source to it **(see illustration)**. Most auto parts stores can supply the air hose adapter. **Note:** *Many cylinder compression gauges utilize a screw-in fitting that may work with your air hose quick-disconnect fitting.*

5   Depress the valve spring with a valve spring compressor (Chrysler tool no. 4682, or equivalent) **(see illustration)** and remove the rocker arm for the valve with the defective part. If all of the valve stem seals are being replaced, all of the rocker arms should be removed.

6   Apply compressed air to the cylinder. **Warning:** *The piston may be forced down by compressed air, causing the crankshaft to turn suddenly. If the wrench used when positioning the number one piston at TDC is still attached to the bolt in the crankshaft nose, it could cause damage or injury when the crankshaft moves.*

7   The valves should be held in place by the air pressure. If the valve faces or seats are in poor condition, leaks may prevent air pressure from retaining the valves — refer to the alternative procedure below.

8   If you don't have access to compressed air, an alternative method can be used. Position the piston at a point approximately 45-degrees before TDC on the compression stroke, then feed a long piece of nylon rope through the spark plug hole until it fills the combustion chamber. Be sure to leave the end of the rope hanging out of the engine so it can be removed easily. Use a large ratchet and socket to rotate the crankshaft in the normal direction of rotation until slight resistance is felt.

9   Stuff shop rags into the cylinder head holes above and below the valves to prevent parts and tools from falling into the engine, then use a valve spring compressor to compress the spring. Remove the keepers with small needle-nose pliers or a magnet. **Note:** *A couple of different types of tools are available for compressing the valve springs with the head in place. One type, shown here, grips the lower spring coils and presses on the retainer as the knob is turned, while the other type utilizes the rocker arm assembly for leverage. Both types work very well, although the lever type is usually less expensive* **(see accompanying illustration and illustration 11.5).**

10   Remove the spring retainer, shield and valve spring, then remove the umbrella type guide seal. **Note:** *If air pressure fails to hold the valve in the closed position during this operation, the valve face or seat is probably damaged. If so, the cylinder head will have to be removed for additional repair operations.*

11   Wrap a rubber band or tape around the top of the valve stem so the valve won't fall into the combustion chamber, then release the air pressure. **Note:** *If a rope was used instead of air pressure, turn the crankshaft slightly in the direction opposite normal rotation.*

12   Inspect the valve stem for damage. Rotate the valve in the guide

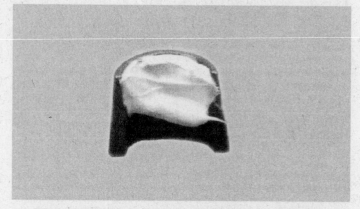

11.17   Apply a small dab of grease to each keeper before installation to hold it in place on the valve stem unil the spring compressor is released

and check the end for eccentric movement, which would indicate that the valve is bent.

13   Move the valve up-and-down in the guide and make sure it doesn't bind. If the valve stem binds, either the valve is bent or the guide is damaged. In either case, the head will have to be removed for repair.

14   Reapply air pressure to the cylinder to retain the valve in the closed position, then remove the tape or rubber band from the valve stem. If a rope was used instead of air pressure, rotate the crankshaft in the normal direction of rotation until slight resistance is felt.

15   Lubricate the valve stem with engine oil and install a new guide seal **(see illustration)**.

16   Install the spring(s) in position over the valve.

17   Install the valve spring retainer. Compress the valve spring and carefully position the keepers in the groove. Apply a small dab of grease to the inside of each keeper to hold it in place **(see illustration)**.

18   Remove the pressure from the spring tool and make sure the keepers are seated.

19   Disconnect the air hose and remove the adapter from the spark plug hole. If a rope was used in place of air pressure, pull it out of the cylinder.

20   Refer to Section 10 and install the rocker arm(s).

21   Install the spark plug(s) and hook up the wire(s).

22   Refer to Section 4 and install the valve cover.

23   Start and run the engine, then check for oil leaks and unusual

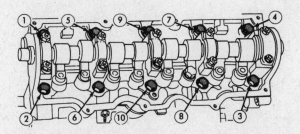

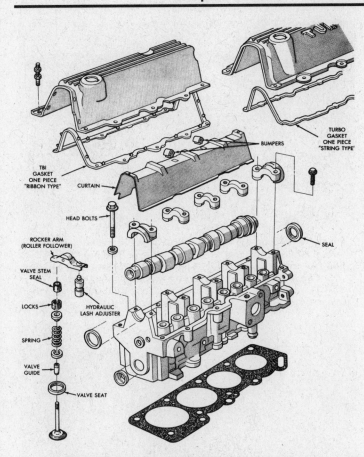

12.8a Exploded view of the cylinder head and related components — 2.2L engine shown, 2.5L similar

sounds coming from the valve cover area.

12   Cylinder head — removal and installation

Caution: *Allow the engine to cool completely before beginning this procedure.*

Removal

Refer to illustrations 12.8a, 12.8b and 12.9

1   Position the number one piston at Top Dead Center (see Sec-

12.8b Loosen the head bolts 1/4-turn at a time, in the sequence shown, until they can be removed by hand

tion 3).

2   Disconnect the negative cable from the battery.

3   Drain the cooling system and remove the spark plugs (see Chapter 1).

4   Remove the intake/exhaust manifold (see Section 5). **Note:** *If you're only replacing the cylinder head gasket, it isn't necessary to remove the manifolds. If you leave the manifold attached, you may need an assistant to help lift the head off the engine.*

5   Remove the distributor (see Chapter 5), including the cap and wires.

6   Remove the timing belt (see Section 6).

7   Remove the valve cover (see Section 4).

8   Loosen the head bolts in 1/4-turn increments until they can be removed by hand. Follow the recommended sequence to avoid warping the head **(see illustrations)**.

9   Lift the head off the engine. If resistance is felt, don't pry between the head and block gasket mating surfaces — damage to the mating surfaces will result. Instead, pry against the casting protrusions on the sides of the cylinder head **(see illustration)**. Set the head on blocks of wood to prevent damage to the gasket sealing surfaces.

10   Cylinder head disassembly and inspection procedures are covered in detail in Chapter 2, Part E. It's a good idea to have the head checked for warpage, even if you're just replacing the gasket.

Installation

Refer to illustrations 12.12, 12.14, 12.15 and 12.16

11   The mating surfaces of the cylinder head and block must be perfectly clean when the head is installed.

12   Use a gasket scraper to remove all traces of carbon and old gasket material **(see illustration)**, then clean the mating surfaces with lacquer thinner or acetone. If there's oil on the mating surfaces when the head is installed, the gasket may not seal correctly and leaks may develop. When working on the block, stuff the cylinders with clean shop

12.9 If the cylinder head is difficult to remove, pry only on the protrusions located on the side of the cylinder head as this will not damage the cylinder head surface

12.12 Use a gasket scraper to remove the old head gasket

2A

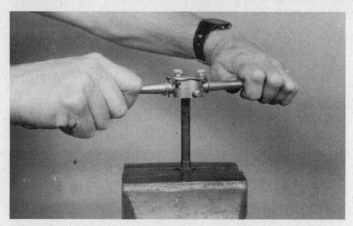

12.14 A die should be used to remove sealant and corrosion from the head bolt threads prior to installation

12.15 When you put the new head gasket in position on the engine block, be sure it's right side up and facing the right direction — the holes in the gasket must match the passages in the block for coolant and oil to circulate properly

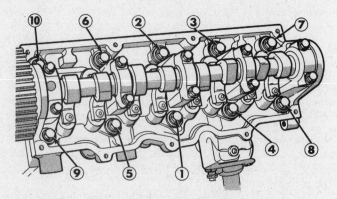

12.16 Cylinder head bolt TIGHTENING sequence

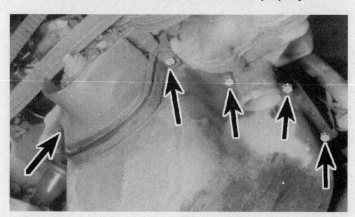

13.4 Remove the bolts (arrows) from the oil pan

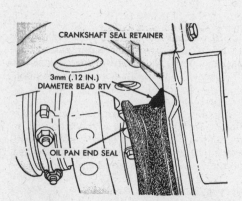

13.8a Install new oil pan end seals and hold them in place with a bead of RTV sealant as shown here

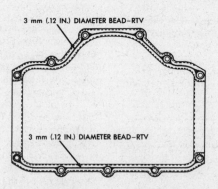

13.8b Apply a continuous 1/8-inch wide bead of RTV sealant to the oil pan, then install the pan

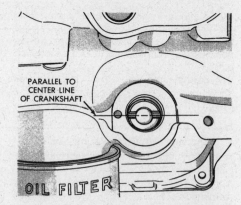

14.3 Oil pump drive shaft alignment

rags to keep out debris. Use a vacuum cleaner to remove material that falls into the cylinders. Since the head is made of aluminum, aggressive scraping can cause damage. Be extra careful not to nick or gouge the mating surfaces with the scraper.

13   Check the block and head mating surfaces for nicks, deep scratches and other damage. If damage is slight, it can be removed with a file; if it's excessive, machining may be the only alternative.

14   Use a tap of the correct size to chase the threads in the head bolt holes. Mount each head bolt in a vise and run a die down the threads to remove corrosion and restore the threads **(see illustration)**. Dirt, corrosion, sealant and damaged threads will affect torque readings.

15   Place a new gasket on the block **(see illustration)** and set the cylinder head in position.

16   Install the bolts. They must be tightened in four steps, following a specific sequence **(see illustration)**, to the torque listed in this Chapter's Specifications.

17   Reinstall the timing belt (see Section 6).

18   Reinstall the remaining parts in the reverse order of removal.

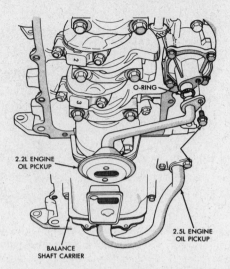

14.5a Engine oil pump pick-up mounting details

14.5c Oil pump mounting bolts (arrows)

19   Be sure to refill the cooling system and check all fluid levels.
20   Rotate the crankshaft clockwise slowly by hand through two complete revolutions. Recheck the camshaft timing marks (see Section 6).
21   Start the engine and check the ignition timing (see Chapter 1).
22   Run the engine until normal operating temperature is reached. Check for leaks and proper operation.

13   Oil pan — removal and installation

Refer to illustrations 13.4, 13.8a and 13.8b

Note: *The following procedure is based on the assumption that the engine is in the vehicle.*

Removal

1   Warm up the engine, then drain the oil and replace the oil filter (see Chapter 1).
2   Detach the cable from the negative battery terminal.
3   Raise the vehicle and support it securely on jackstands.
4   Remove the bolts securing the oil pan to the engine block **(see illustration)**.
5   Tap on the pan with a soft-face hammer to break the gasket seal, then detach the oil pan from the engine. Don't pry between the block and oil pan mating surfaces.
6   Using a gasket scraper, remove all traces of old gasket and/or sealant from the engine block and oil pan. Remove the seals from each end of the engine block or oil pan. Clean the mating surfaces

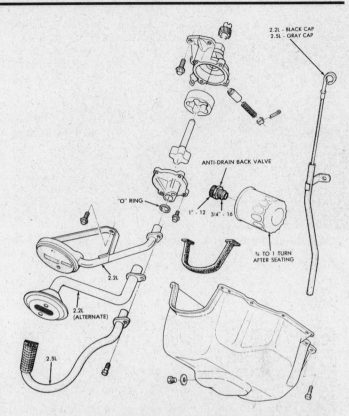

14.5b Oil pump and related components — exploded view

with lacquer thinner or acetone. Make sure the threaded bolt holes in the block are clean.
7   Clean the oil pan with solvent and dry it thoroughly. Check the gasket flanges for distortion, particularly around the bolt holes. If necessary, place the pan on a block of wood and use a hammer to flatten and restore the gasket surfaces.

Installation

8   Install new seals in the retainers at the front and rear of the engine block **(see illustration)**. Apply a 1/8-inch wide bead of RTV sealant to the oil pan gasket surfaces. Continue the bead across the end seals. Make sure the sealant is applied to the inside of the bolt holes **(see illustration)**.
9   Carefully place the oil pan in position.
10   Install the bolts and tighten them in 1/4-turn increments to the torque listed in this Chapter's Specifications. Start with the bolts closest to the center of the pan and work out in a spiral pattern. Don't overtighten them or leakage may occur. Note that some 2.2L engines have bolts with different diameters, which require different torque values.
11   Add oil, run the engine and check for oil leaks.

14   Oil pump — removal, inspection and installation

Removal

Refer to illustrations 14.3, 14.5a, 14.5b and 14.5c

1   Position the number one piston at Top Dead Center on the compression stroke (see Section 3).
2   Remove the distributor (see Chapter 5).
3   Check to see that the oil pump shaft slot is parallel to the center line of the crankshaft **(see illustration)**.
4   Remove the oil pan (see Section 13).
5   Remove the oil pump mounting bolts. If equipped, also remove the brace bolt **(see illustrations)**.
6   Remove the oil pump assembly.

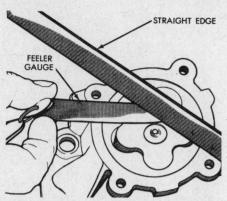

14.8 Check the rotor endplay by placing a precision straightedge across the pump housing like this and inserting feeler gauges between the rotor face and the straightedge

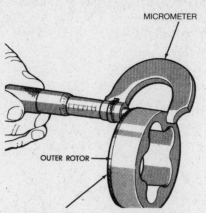

14.9 Measure the thickness of the oil pump rotor with a micrometer

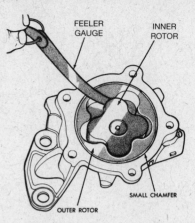

14.10 Check the inner rotor-to-outer rotor tip clearance with feeler gauges

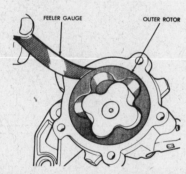

14.11 Check the outer rotor-to-pump body clearance with feeler gauge

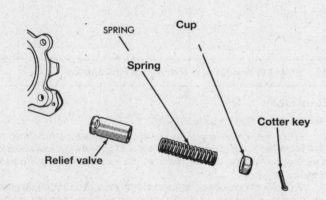

14.12 Check the oil pump cover for warpage with a straightedge and feeler gauges

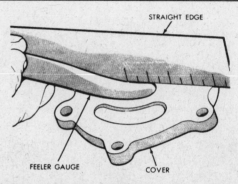

14.13 Oil pressure relief valve components — exploded view

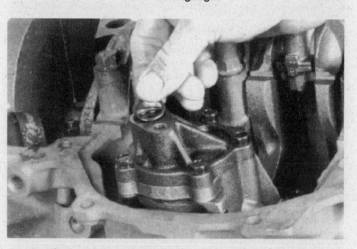

14.18 Before attaching the oil pick-up tube assembly, lubricate the new O-ring and install it in the oil pump

Inspection

Refer to illustrations 14.8, 14.9, 14.10, 14.11, 14.12 and 14.13

7   Remove the bolts and lift off the oil pump cover.

8   Check the rotor endplay with feeler gauges and a straightedge **(see illustration)**.

9   Remove the outer rotor and measure its thickness **(see illustration)**.

10   Check the clearance between the inner and outer rotor tips with feeler gauges **(see illustration)**.

11   Measure the outer rotor-to-pump body clearance **(see illustration)**.

12   Check the oil pump cover for warpage with feeler gauges and a straightedge **(see illustration)**.

13   Remove the cotter pin and cup, then extract the spring and oil pump relief valve from the pump housing **(see illustration)**. Measure the free length of the oil pressure relief valve spring.

14   Compare the measurements to the oil pump Specifications at the beginning of this Chapter. If any of them are outside the limits, replace the pump.

15   Install the rotor with the large chamfered edge facing toward the

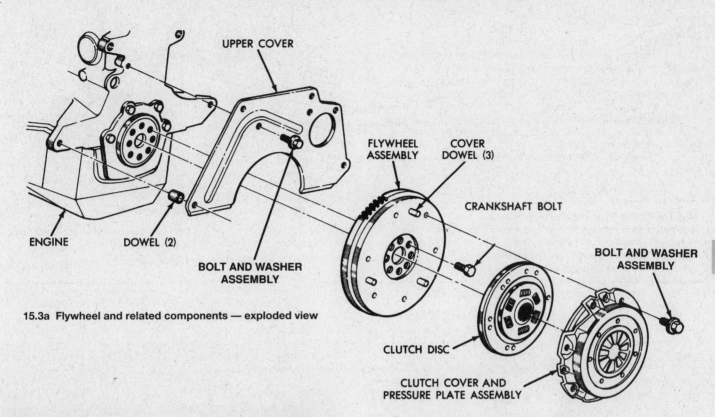

UPPER COVER

FLYWHEEL ASSEMBLY

COVER DOWEL (3)

CRANKSHAFT BOLT

ENGINE

DOWEL (2)

BOLT AND WASHER ASSEMBLY

BOLT AND WASHER ASSEMBLY

CLUTCH DISC

CLUTCH COVER AND PRESSURE PLATE ASSEMBLY

15.3a Flywheel and related components — exploded view

2A

15.3b If the bolts are arranged in a staggered pattern, it isn't necessary to mark the crankshaft and flywheel (note the two bolts [arrows] are spaced much farther apart than the others) — if they aren't spaced like this, be sure to mark the relationship of the flywheel to the crankshaft

pump body. Install the oil pressure relief valve and spring assembly. Install the pump cover and tighten the bolts to the torque listed in this Chapter's Specifications.

Installation

Refer to illustration 14.18

16   Apply a thin coat of RTV sealant to the mating surface of the pump and place the pump in position. Rotate it back-and-forth a little to ensure there's positive contact between the pump and the engine block.

17   Coat the threads of the mounting bolts with sealant and, while holding the pump securely in place, install the bolts. Tighten them to

the torque listed in this Chapter's Specifications.

18   Install a new O-ring in the oil pump pick-up opening **(see illustration)**.

19   Carefully work the pick-up tube into the pump, install the retaining bolt and tighten it to the torque listed in this Chapter's Specifications.

20   Install the brace bolt and tighten it securely.

21   Install the oil pan (see Section 13).

---

15   Flywheel/driveplate — removal and installation

Removal

Refer to illustrations 15.3a and 15.3b

1   Raise the vehicle and support it securely on jackstands, then refer to Chapter 7 and remove the transaxle. If it's leaking, now would be a very good time to replace the front pump seal/O-ring (automatic transaxle only).

2   Remove the pressure plate and clutch disc (see Chapter 8) (manual transaxle equipped vehicles). Now is a good time to check/replace the clutch components and pilot bearing.

3   Remove the bolts that secure the flywheel/driveplate to the crankshaft **(see illustrations)**. If the crankshaft turns, wedge a screwdriver in the ring gear teeth to jam the flywheel.

4   Remove the flywheel/driveplate from the crankshaft. Since the flywheel is fairly heavy, be sure to support it while removing the last bolt.

5   Clean the flywheel to remove grease and oil. Inspect the surface for cracks, rivet grooves, burned areas and score marks. Light scoring can be removed with emery cloth. Check for cracked and broken ring gear teeth. Lay the flywheel on a flat surface and use a straightedge to check for warpage.

6   Clean and inspect the mating surfaces of the flywheel/driveplate and the crankshaft. If the crankshaft rear seal is leaking, replace it be-

fore reinstalling the flywheel/driveplate.

Installation

7　Position the flywheel/driveplate against the crankshaft. Be sure to align the marks made during removal. Note that some engines have an alignment dowel or staggered bolt holes to ensure correct installation. Before installing the bolts, apply thread locking compound to the threads.

8　Wedge a screwdriver through in the ring gear teeth to keep the flywheel/driveplate from turning as you tighten the bolts to the torque listed in this Chapter's Specifications.

9　The remainder of installation is the reverse of the removal procedure.

16　Rear main oil seal — replacement

Refer to illustration 16.4

1　Remove the transaxle (see Chapter 7).

2　If the vehicle has a manual transaxle, remove the clutch and flywheel (see Chapter 8 and Section 15 of this Chapter).

3　If the vehicle has an automatic transaxle, remove the driveplate (see Section 15).

4　Pry the oil seal from the retainer with a screwdriver **(see illustration)**. Be careful not to nick or scratch the crankshaft or the seal retainer bore. Thoroughly clean the seal bore in the seal housing with a shop towel. Remove all traces of oil and dirt.

5　Lubricate the lips of the new seal with engine oil or multi–purpose grease. Install the seal over the end of the crankshaft (make sure the lips of the seal point toward the engine) and carefully tap it into place with a plastic hammer.

6　Install the driveplate or flywheel (see Section 15) and clutch (see Chapter 8).

7　Install the transaxle (see Chapter 7).

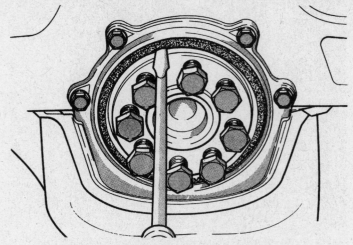

16.4 Carefully pry the seal from the retainer

17　Engine mounts — check, replacement and adjustment

Refer to illustrations 17.4a, 17.4b, 17.4c, 17.4d, 17.4e and 17.15

1　Engine mounts seldom require attention, but broken or deteriorated mounts should be replaced immediately or the added strain placed on the driveline components may cause damage or wear.

Check

2　During the check, the engine must be raised slightly to remove the weight from the mounts.

3　Raise the vehicle and support it securely on jackstands, then position a jack under the engine oil pan. Place a large block of wood between the jack head and the oil pan, then carefully raise the engine just enough to take the weight off the mounts. **Warning:** *DO NOT place*

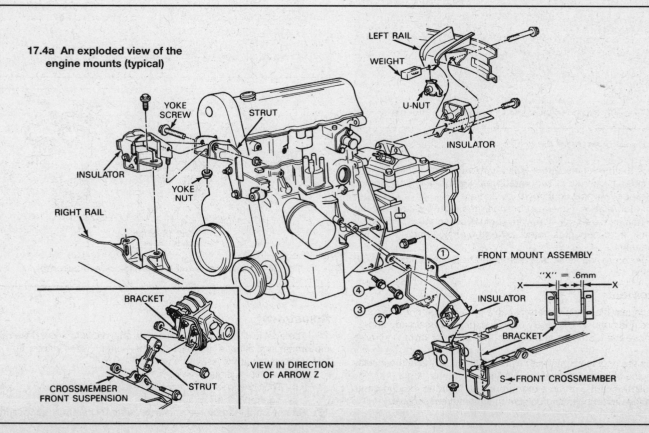

17.4a An exploded view of the engine mounts (typical)

YOKE SCREW
STRUT
LEFT RAIL
WEIGHT
U-NUT
INSULATOR
INSULATOR
YOKE NUT
RIGHT RAIL
FRONT MOUNT ASSEMBLY
"X" = .6mm
X — X
INSULATOR
BRACKET
BRACKET
STRUT
CROSSMEMBER FRONT SUSPENSION
VIEW IN DIRECTION OF ARROW Z
S←FRONT CROSSMEMBER

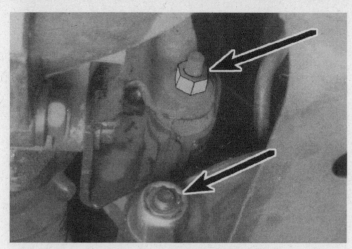

17.4b Remove the bolts and nuts (arrows) that hold the rear strut onto the crossmember and the engine

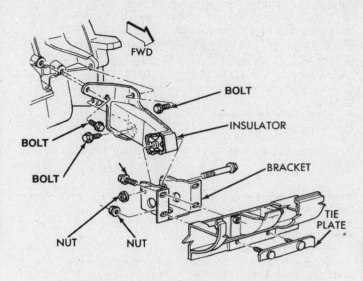

17.4c An exploded view of the front engine mount

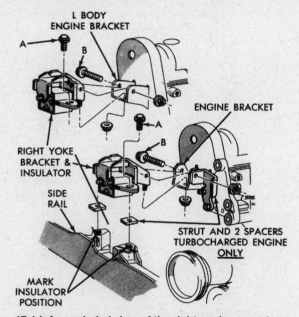

17.4d An exploded view of the right engine mount

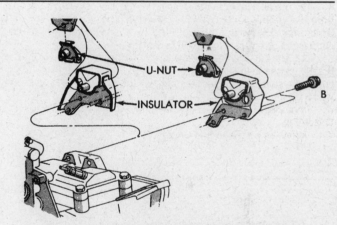

17.4e An exploded view of the left engine mount

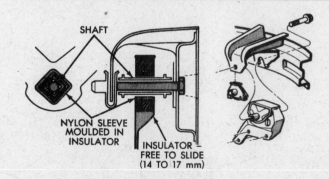

17.15 Cutaway of the left insulator sleeve assembly

any part of your body under the engine when it's supported only by a jack!

4   Check the mount insulators **(see illustrations)** to see if the rubber is cracked, hardened or separated from the metal plates. Sometimes the rubber will split right down the center.

5   Check for relative movement between the mount plates and the engine or frame (use a large screwdriver or prybar to attempt to move the mounts). If movement is noted, lower the engine and tighten the mount fasteners.

6   Rubber preservative should be applied to the insulators to slow deterioration.

Replacement

7   Disconnect the negative battery cable from the battery, then raise the vehicle and support it securely on jackstands (if not already done).

8   Remove the fasteners and detach the insulator from the frame bracket.

9   Raise the engine slightly with a jack or hoist. Remove the insulator–to–engine bolts and detach the insulator.

10   Installation is the reverse of removal. Use thread locking compound on the mount bolts and be sure to tighten them securely.

Adjustment

11   The right and left engine mounts are adjustable to allow drivetrain movement in relation to driveaxle assembly length (see Chapter 8).

12   Always adjust the insulators when:
   a) You service the driveaxles.
   b) The vehicle sustains front end structural damage.
   c) You replace an insulator.

13   Remove the load on the engine mounts by carefully supporting

the engine and transaxle assembly with a floor jack.

14   Loosen the right insulator vertical fasteners and the front engine mount bracket-to-front crossmember bolts and nuts.

15   The left engine mount insulator is sleeved over the shaft and long support bolt **(see illustration)** to provide lateral movement adjustment.

16   Pry the engine right or left as required to achieve the proper driveaxle length (see Chapter 8).

17   Tighten the right engine mount insulator vertical bolts securely, tighten the front engine mount bolts and nuts securely and center the left engine mount insulator.

18   Recheck the driveaxle length.

Chapter 2 Part B 2.6L four-cylinder engine

Contents

Specifications

General

Firing order	1-3-4-2
Cylinder numbers (drivebelt end-to-transaxle end)	1–2–3–4
Bore and stroke	3.59 X 3.86 inches
Displacement	156 cubic inches

Camshaft

Endplay	0.004 to 0.008 inch
Runout	0.03 inch
Lobe wear (maximum)	0.020 inch

Cylinder head warpage limit .... 0.002 inch

Intake/exhaust manifold warpage limit .... 0.006 inch per foot of manifold length

Oil pump
Drive gear-to-bearing clearance .... 0.0008 to 0.0020 inch
Driven gear-to-bearing clearance .... 0.0008 to 0.0020 inch
Drive gear-to-housing clearance .... 0.0043 to 0.0059 inch
Driven gear-to-housing clearance .... 0.0043 to 0.0059 inch
Drive gear endplay .... 0.0020 to 0.0043 inch
Driven gear endplay .... 0.0016 to 0.0039 inch
Relief spring free length .... 1.85 inch

Torque specifications   Ft-lbs (unless otherwise indicated)
Camshaft bearing cap bolts .... 160 in-lbs
Valve cover bolts/nuts .... 53 in-lbs
Silent shaft chain guides **(see illustration 9.8)**
    Chain guide A bolts .... 156 in-lbs
    Chain guide B bolts
        Bolt A .... 12 in-lbs
        Bolt B... 14
    Chain guide C bolts .... 156 in-lbs
Timing chain guides bolts .... 156 in-lbs
Carburetor air heater mounting bolts **(see illustration 8.9)**
    A .... 100 in-lbs
    B .... 80 in-lbs
Exhaust manifold heat cowl screws **(A in illustration 8.10)**. .... 80 in-lbs
Engine mount - right **(see illustration 19.1)**
    A .... 250 in-lbs
    B and C .... 75 in-lbs
Engine mount - front **(see illustration 19.2)**
    A 40
    B 45
Camshaft sprocket bolt 40
Crankshaft sprocket bolt 87
Cylinder head bolts (use the tightening sequence shown in Section 14)
    First step (engine cold).. 34
    Second step (engine cold) 69
    Third step (engine hot) 75
Driveplate-to-crankshaft bolts 50
Flywheel-to-crankshaft bolts 60
Intake manifold bolts .... 150 in-lbs
Exhaust manifold nuts **(B in illustration 8.10)**.................................. 150 in-lbs
Silent shaft sprocket bolt 25
Oil pan-to-engine block fasteners .... 60 in-lbs
Oil pick-up tube bolt(s) .... 50 in-lbs
Oil pump sprocket bolt 25
Oil pump mounting bolts .... 71 in-lbs
Oil pump cover bolts .... 71 in-lbs
Rear main oil seal housing bolts .... 105 in-lbs
Timing chain cover bolts .... 160 in-lbs

1   General information

This Part of Chapter 2 is devoted to in-vehicle repair procedures for the 2.6L engine. All information concerning engine removal and installation and engine block and cylinder head overhaul can be found in Part E of this Chapter.

The following repair procedures are based on the assumption that the engine is installed in the vehicle. If the engine has been removed from the vehicle and mounted on a stand, many of the steps outlined in this Part of Chapter 2 will not apply.

The Specifications included in this Part of Chapter 2 apply only to the procedures contained in this Part. Part E of Chapter 2 contains the Specifications necessary for cylinder head and engine block rebuilding.

The 2.6 liter engine is an inline vertical four, with a chain-driven overhead camshaft and a silent shaft counterbalancing system which cancels the engine's power pulses and produces relatively vibration-free operation. The crankshaft rides in five renewable insert-type main bearings, with the center bearing (the thrust bearing) assigned the additional task of controlling crankshaft endplay.

The pistons have two compression rings and one oil control ring. The semi-floating piston pins are press fitted into the small end of the connecting rod. The connecting rod big ends are also equipped with renewable insert-type plain bearings.

The engine is liquid-cooled, utilizing a centrifugal impeller-type

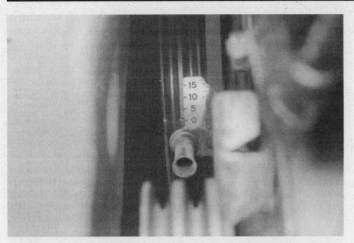

3.1   Align the notch in the pulley with the 0 on the timing plate, then check to see if the distributor rotor is pointing to number 1 cylinder; if not, the camshaft is 180-degrees out of time (number 4 is at TDC) – the crankshaft will have to be rotated 360-degrees

4.4   Remove the carburetor brace bolts (arrows) and lift the brace from the engine

2B

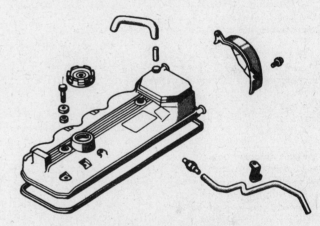

4.9a   An exploded view of the valve cover and related components

pump, driven by a belt from the camshaft, to circulate coolant around the cylinders and combustion chambers and through the intake mani-fold.

Lubrication is handled by a gear-type oil pump mounted on the front of the engine under the timing chain cover. It is driven by the silent shaft chain. The oil is filtered continuously by a cartridge-type fil-ter mounted on the radiator side of the engine.

2   Repair operations possible with the engine in the vehicle

Many major repair operations can be accomplished without removing the engine from the vehicle.

Clean the engine compartment and the exterior of the engine with some type of degreaser before any work is done. It will make the job easier and help keep dirt out of the internal areas of the engine.

Depending on the components involved, it may be helpful to remove the hood to improve access to the engine as repairs are per-formed (refer to Chapter 11 if necessary). Cover the fenders to prevent damage to the paint. Special pads are available, but an old bedspread or blanket will also work.

If vacuum, exhaust, oil or coolant leaks develop, indicating a need for gasket or seal replacement, the repairs can generally be made with the engine in the vehicle. The intake and exhaust manifold gaskets, oil pan gasket, crankshaft oil seals and cylinder head gasket are all accessible with the engine in place.

Exterior engine components, such as the intake and exhaust manifolds, the oil pan, the water pump, the starter motor, the alterna-tor, the distributor and the fuel system components can be removed for repair with the engine in place.

Since the cylinder head can be removed without pulling the engine, camshaft and valve component servicing can also be accom-plished with the engine in the vehicle. Replacement of the timing chain and sprockets is also possible with the engine in the vehicle.

In extreme cases caused by a lack of necessary equipment, repair or replacement of piston rings, pistons, connecting rods and rod bearings is possible with the engine in the vehicle. However, this prac-tice is not recommended because of the cleaning and preparation work that must be done to the components involved.

3   Top Dead Center (TDC) for number one piston - locating

Refer to illustration 3.1

This procedure is essentially the same as for the 2.2L/2.5L

engine. Refer to Part A, Section 3 and follow the procedure outlined there, except use the accompanying illustration.

4   Valve cover - removal and installation

Removal

Refer to illustrations 4.4, 4.9a and 4.9b

1   Detach the cable from the negative battery terminal.
2   Remove the water pump pulley cover from the valve cover (see Chapter 3).
3   Remove the air cleaner inlet hose and housing assembly from the carburetor and the top of the valve cover (see Chapter 4).
4   Remove the bolts from the carburetor/valve cover brace **(see illustration)** and lift the brace from the engine.
5   Remove the distributor cap and wires from the cylinder head (see Chapter 1). Be sure to mark each wire for correct installation.
6   Remove any fuel lines or vent lines from the carburetor or fuel fil-ter that will interfere with the removal of the valve cover.
7   Disconnect any electrical connections from the carburetor that will interfere with the removal of the valve cover.
8   Wipe off the valve cover thoroughly to prevent debris from falling onto the exposed cylinder head or camshaft/valve train assembly.
9   Remove the valve cover bolts **(see illustrations)**.

4.9b   Remove the two bolts (arrows) from the valve cover and lift the cover off the engine

10   Carefully lift off the valve cover and gasket. If the gasket is stuck to the cylinder head, tap it with a rubber mallet to break the seal. Do not pry between the cover and cylinder head or you'll damage the gasket mating surfaces.

Installation

Refer to illustration 4.13

11   Use a gasket scraper to remove all traces of old gasket material from the gasket mating surfaces of the cylinder head and the valve cover. Clean the surfaces with a rag soaked in lacquer thinner or acetone.

12   Be sure to install the semi-circular seal (camshaft plug) on top of the cylinder head near the camshaft sprocket. Apply beads of RTV sealant to the points where the seal meets the valve cover mating surfaces.

13   Install a new gasket onto the valve cover. Install the molded rubber gasket onto the cover by pushing the new gasket into the slot that circles the valve cover perimeter. Apply beads of RTV sealant where the cylinder head and camshaft bearing cap meet **(see illustration)**. Wait five minutes or so and let the RTV "set-up" (slightly harden) and then install the cover and bolts and tighten them to the torque listed in this Chapter's Specifications.

14   The remainder of installation is the reverse of removal.

---

5   **Rocker arm assembly - removal, inspection and installation**

Note 1: *The camshaft bearing caps are removed together with the rocker arm assembly. To prevent the water-pump end of the camshaft from popping up (from timing-chain tension) after the assembly is removed, have an assistant hold the water-pump end of the camshaft down, then reinstall the main bearing cap on that end to hold it in place until reassembly.*

Note 2: *While the camshaft bearing caps are off, inspect them, as well as the camshaft bearing journals, as described in Section 13.*

Removal

Refer to illustration 5.3

1   Remove the valve cover (see Section 4).

2   Position the number one piston at Top Dead Center (see Section 3).

3   Have an assistant hold down the water-pump end of the camshaft, then loosen the camshaft bearing cap bolts 1/4-turn at a time each until the spring pressure is relieved **(see illustration)**. Do not remove the bolts.

4   Lift the rocker arms and shaft assembly from the cylinder head. Reinstall the bearing cap at the water-pump end to hold the camshaft in place.

4.13   Apply a small amount of RTV sealant to the corners of the cylinder head next to the camshaft bearing cap

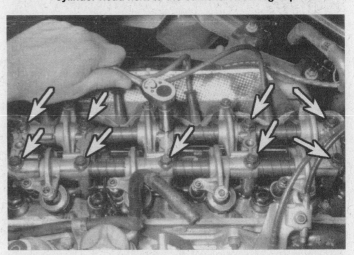

5.3   Remove the rocker arm assembly bolts   (arrows)

Inspection

Refer to illustrations 5.5 and 5.6

5   If you wish to disassemble and inspect the rocker arm assemblies (a good idea as long as you have them off), remove the retaining bolts and slip the rocker arms, springs and bearing caps off the shafts **(see illustration)**. Keep the parts in order so you can reassemble them in the same positions.

6   Thoroughly clean the parts and inspect them for wear and damage. Check the rocker arm faces that contact the camshaft and the adjusting screw tips **(see illustration)**. Check the surfaces of the shafts that the rocker arms ride on, as well as the bearing surfaces inside the rocker arms, for scoring and excessive wear. Replace any parts that are damaged or excessively worn. Also, make sure the oil holes in the shafts are not plugged.

Installation

Refer to illustrations 5.7, 5.8a and 5.8b

7   Loosen the locknuts and back off the adjusters until they only protrude 1 mm (0.040-inch) **(see illustration)**.

8   Lubricate all components with assembly lube or engine oil and reassemble the shafts. When installing the rocker arms, shafts and springs, note the markings and the difference between the left and right side parts **(see illustration)**. Place the marks in the end of the shaft directly in line with the marks on the caps **(see illustration)** to keep them aligned until they are ready to be installed onto the cylinder head.

9   Position the rocker arm assemblies on the cylinder head and

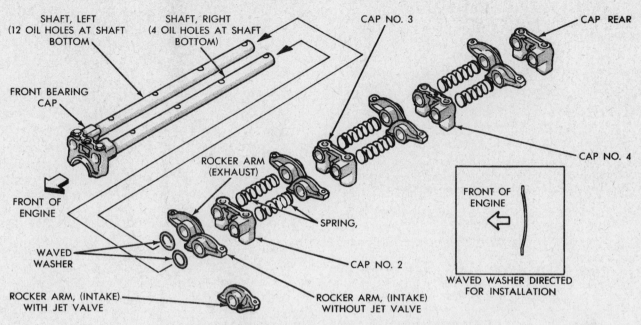

5.5   An exploded view of the rocker arms and shafts (typical)

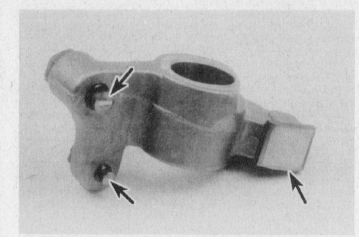

5.6   Check the contact faces and adjusting screw tips (arrows)

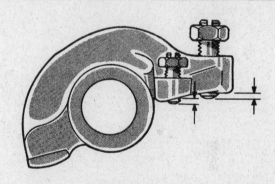

5.7   Back off the adjusters until they only protrude 1 mm (0.040 in)

install the mounting bolts finger tight. **Note:** *Check the numbered markings on the caps to make sure the caps are in the correct numerical sequence.*

10   Tighten the camshaft bearing cap bolts as described in Section 13.

11   Adjust the valve clearances (cold) as described in Chapter 1.

12   Temporarily install the valve cover and run the engine until it is fully warmed up.

13   Readjust the valves while the engine is still warm (see Chapter 1).

14   Reinstall the remaining parts in the reverse order of removal.

15   Run the engine and check for oil leaks and proper operation.

---

6   Valve springs, retainers and seals - replacement

Note: *The jet valve is mounted directly beside each exhaust valve. Refer to Chapter 2, Part E for the jet valve servicing procedure.*

This procedure is essentially the same as for the 2.2L/2.5L engine. Refer to Part A Section 11 and follow the procedure outlined there.

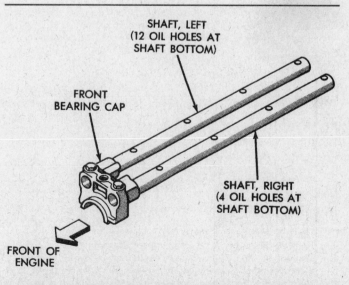

5.8a   Install the rocker shafts into the front bearing cap

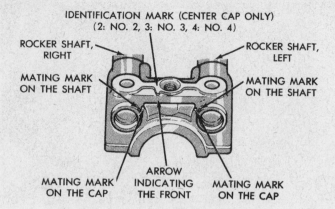

IDENTIFICATION MARK (CENTER CAP ONLY)
(2: NO. 2, 3: NO. 3, 4: NO. 4)

ROCKER SHAFT,
RIGHT

ROCKER SHAFT,
LEFT

MATING MARK
ON THE SHAFT

MATING MARK
ON THE SHAFT

MATING MARK
ON THE CAP

ARROW
INDICATING
THE FRONT

MATING MARK
ON THE CAP

5.8b   Be sure the mating mark on the cap is aligned with the mating mark on the shaft

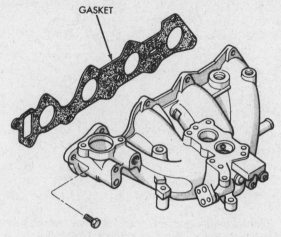

GASKET

7.11   An exploded view of the intake manifold

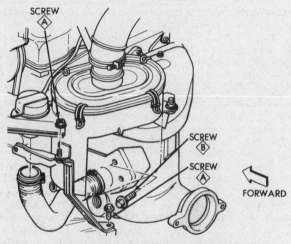

SCREW
A

SCREW
B

SCREW
A

FORWARD

8.9   Remove the carburetor air heater from the exhaust manifold

---

7   Intake manifold - removal and installation

Refer to illustration 7.11

Warning: *Gasoline is extremely flammable, so take extra precautions when you work on any part of the fuel system. Don't smoke or allow open flames or bare light bulbs near the work area, and don't work in a garage where a natural gas-type appliance (such as a water heater or clothes dryer) with a pilot light is present. If you spill any fuel on your skin, rinse it off immediately with soap and water. When you perform any kind of work on the fuel system, wear safety glasses and have a Class B type fire extinguisher on hand.*

Removal

1   Detach the cable from the negative battery terminal.
2   Drain the cooling system (see Chapter 1).
3   Remove the air cleaner (see Chapter 4).
4   Clearly label, then detach all vacuum lines, electrical wiring and fuel lines.
5   Detach the accelerator cable from the throttle linkage (see Chapter 4).
6   Remove the drivebelts (see Chapter 1).
7   Remove the carburetor from the intake manifold (see Chapter 4).
8   Remove the coolant hoses from the intake manifold.
9   Disconnect the fuel inlet line at the fuel filter (see Chapter 4).
10   Remove the fuel pump and fuel filter and lay them aside (see Chapter 4).

11   Remove the intake manifold bolts **(see illustration)** and remove the manifold from the engine.

Installation

12   Clean the manifold with solvent and dry them with compressed air. **Warning:** *Wear eye protection!*
13   Check the mating surfaces of the manifold for flatness with a precision straightedge and feeler gauges. Refer to this Chapter's Specifications for the warpage limit.
14   Inspect the manifold for cracks and distortion.
15   If the manifold is cracked or warped, replace it or see if it can be resurfaced/repaired at an automotive machine shop.
16   Check carefully for any stripped or broken intake manifold bolts. Replace any defective bolts with new parts.
17   Using a scraper, remove all traces of old gasket material from the cylinder head and manifold mating surfaces. Clean the surfaces with lacquer thinner or acetone.
18   Install the intake manifold with a new gasket and tighten the bolts finger-tight. Starting at the center and working out in both directions, tighten the bolts in a criss-cross pattern until the torque listed in this Chapter's Specifications is reached.
18   The remainder of the installation procedure is the reverse of removal.

---

8   Exhaust manifold - removal and installation

Removal

Refer to illustrations 8.9 and 8.10

1   Disconnect the negative battery cable from the battery.
2   Drain the cooling system (see Chapter 1).
3   Remove the air cleaner (see Chapter 4).
4   Loosen the power steering pump and remove the belt (see Chapter 1).
5   Raise the front of the vehicle and support it securely on jackstands. Detach the exhaust pipe from the exhaust manifold (see Chapter 4). Apply penetrating oil to the fastener threads if they are difficult to remove.
6   Disconnect the air injection tube assembly from the air pump and move the tube assembly to one side.
7   Remove the power steering pump (if equipped) and set it aside (see Chapter 10).
8   Remove the heat cowl from the exhaust manifold. Be sure to soak the bolts and nuts with penetrating oil before attempting to remove them from the manifold.
9   Remove the carburetor air heater from the exhaust manifold

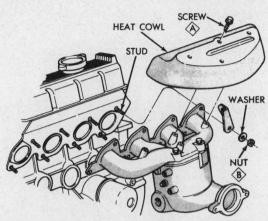

8.10 Remove the exhaust manifold nuts from the exhaust manifold. Be sure to soak the nuts with penetrating oil before attempting to remove them.

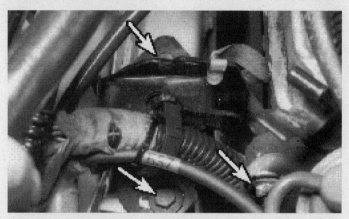

9.5a Remove the bolts (arrows) and separate the engine mount from the chassis

assembly (see illustration).

10 Remove the exhaust manifold nuts (see illustration) and detach the exhaust manifold.

11 Separate the front catalytic converter from the exhaust manifold.

Installation

12 Discard the old gaskets and use a scraper to clean the gasket mating surfaces on the manifold and head, then clean the surfaces with a rag soaked in lacquer thinner or acetone.

13 Place the exhaust manifold and converter assembly in position on the cylinder head and install the nuts. Starting at the center, tighten the nuts in a criss-cross pattern until the torque listed in this Chapter's Specifications is reached.

14 The remainder of installation is the reverse of removal.

15 Start the engine and check for exhaust leaks between the manifold and the cylinder head and between the manifold and the exhaust pipe.

9 Silent shaft chain/sprockets - removal, inspection and installation

Removal

Refer to illustrations 9.5a, 9.5b, 9.7 and 9.8

1 Disconnect the cable from the negative terminal of the battery. Remove the air cleaner assembly.

2 Remove the drivebelts. Remove the alternator, power steering pump and air conditioning compressor, if equipped, and lay them aside. **Warning:** *The air conditioning system is under high pressure - don't disconnect the hoses!*

3 Remove the valve cover (see Section 4). Remove the two front cylinder head-to-timing chain cover bolts. **Caution:** *Do not loosen any other cylinder head bolts.*

4 Raise the vehicle and support it securely on jackstands. Remove the right-side splash guard. Remove the large bolt at the front of the crankshaft and slide the pulley off. **Note:** *To keep the crankshaft from turning while you're removing this bolt, remove the starter (see Chapter 5) and wedge a large screwdriver or prybar into the flywheel/driveplate ring gear. If the pulley does not come off easily, puller sets are available at auto parts stores that will make removal easier.*

5 Position a floor jack with a block of wood on the jack head under the engine. Jack the engine up slightly to relieve the pressure and remove the right-side engine mount **(see illustration)**. Remove the engine mounting plate and the timing indicator from the timing cover **(see illustration)**.

6 Drain the engine oil and remove the oil pan (see Section 15).

7 Remove the bolts attaching the timing chain cover to the engine block **(see illustration)**. Draw a simple diagram showing the location of each bolt so they can be returned to the same holes from which they were removed. Tap the timing chain cover with a soft-faced hammer to break the gasket seal, then remove the cover from the engine block. **Caution:** *Prying between the cover and the engine block can*

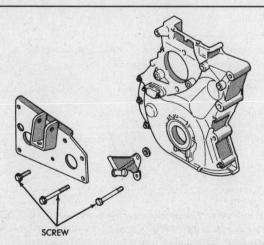

9.5b Engine mounting plate installation details

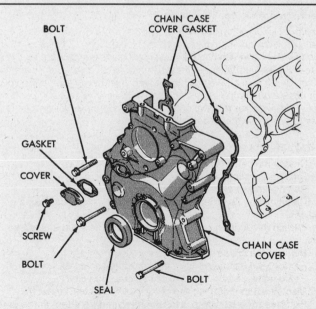

9.7 Timing chain cover installation details

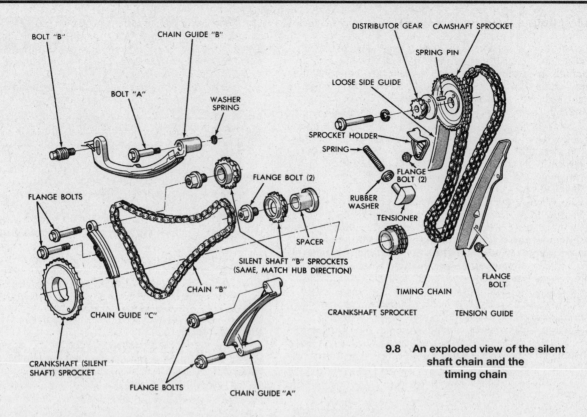

BOLT "B"

CHAIN GUIDE "B"

BOLT "A"

WASHER
SPRING

FLANGE BOLTS

FLANGE BOLT (2)

SILENT SHAFT "B" SPROCKETS
(SAME, MATCH HUB DIRECTION)

CHAIN "B"

CHAIN GUIDE "C"

SPACER

CRANKSHAFT (SILENT
SHAFT) SPROCKET

FLANGE BOLTS

CHAIN GUIDE "A"

DISTRIBUTOR GEAR   CAMSHAFT SPROCKET

SPRING PIN

LOOSE SIDE GUIDE

SPROCKET HOLDER

SPRING

FLANGE
BOLT (2)

RUBBER
WASHER

TENSIONER

TIMING CHAIN

CRANKSHAFT SPROCKET

FLANGE
BOLT

TENSION GUIDE

**9.8   An exploded view of the silent
shaft chain and the
timing chain**

damage the gasket sealing surface.

8   Remove the chain guides labeled A, B and C **(see illustration)**. Each guide is held in place by two bolts. Again, draw a simple diagram showing the location of each bolt so that it can be returned to the same hole from which it was removed.

9   Reinstall the large bolt in the end of the crankshaft. Hold it in place with a wrench to prevent the crankshaft from turning while loosening the bolt on the end of the rear (firewall side) silent shaft, the bolt attaching the rear silent shaft drive sprocket to the oil pump shaft and the bolt in the end of the front (radiator side) silent shaft.

10   Slide the crankshaft sprocket, the silent shaft sprockets and the chain off the engine as an assembly. Leave the bolt in the end of the crankshaft in place. Do not lose the keys that index the sprockets to the shafts.

Inspection

11   Check the sprocket teeth for wear and damage. Check the sprocket cushion rings and ring guides (silent shaft sprockets only) for wear and damage. Rotate the cushion rings and check for smooth operation. Inspect the chain for cracked side plates and pitted or worn rollers. Replace any defective or worn parts with new ones.

Installation

Refer to illustrations 9.16a, 9.16b and 9.16c

12   Before installing the silent shaft chain and sprockets, the timing chain must be properly installed and the number one piston must be at TDC on the compression stroke. Both silent shafts and the oil pump must also be in place.

13   Slide the crankshaft sprocket part way onto the front of the

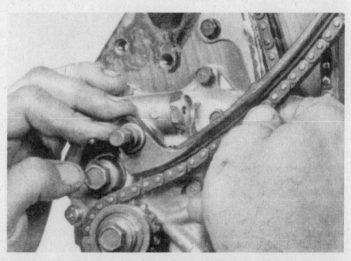

9.16a   Installing the silent shaft chain guide C

9.16b   Installing the silent shaft chain guide B

crankshaft by lining up the keyway in the sprocket with the key on the shaft.

14 Install the front silent shaft sprocket part way. The dished or recessed side of the front silent shaft sprocket must face out. Install the silent shaft chain onto the crankshaft sprocket and the front silent shaft sprocket. Line up the plated links on the chain with the mating marks stamped into the sprockets **(see illustration 9.16c)**.

15 With the dished or recessed side facing in, slide rear silent shaft sprocket part way onto the lower oil pump gear shaft. Line up the plated link on the chain with the mating mark on the sprocket. Push the silent shaft sprockets all the way onto their respective shafts, lining up the keyways in the sprockets with the keys on the shafts. Simultaneously, push the crankshaft sprocket back until it bottoms on the crankshaft timing chain sprocket. Recheck the position of the mating marks on the chain and sprockets, then install the silent shaft sprocket bolts and tighten them to the torque listed in **illustration 9.8**.

16 Install the chain guides labeled A, B and C **(see illustrations)** and tighten the mounting bolts for chain guides A and C securely (leave the mounting bolts for chain guide B finger-tight). Note the difference between the upper and lower chain guide B mounting bolts. Make sure they are installed in the proper location.

17 Adjust the chain slack as follows: rotate the rear silent shaft clockwise and the front silent shaft counterclockwise so the chain slack is collected at point F **(see illustration 9.16c)**. Pull the chain with your finger tips in the direction of arrow F, then move the lower end of the chain guide B up or down, as required, until the clearance between the chain and the guide (chain slack) is as specified **(see illustration 9.16c)**. Tighten the chain guide B mounting bolts securely, then recheck the slack to make sure it has not changed. If the chain is not tensioned properly, engine noise will result.

18 Apply a coat of clean moly-based grease to the chain and chain guides.

19 Using a hammer and punch, drive the oil seal out of the timing chain case (see Section 12).

20 Lay a new seal in place - make sure the lip faces inward - and tap around its circumference with a block of wood and a hammer until it is properly seated.

21 Using a new gasket and RTV-type gasket sealant, fit the timing chain cover onto the engine **(see illustration 9.6)**. Install the bolts in a crisscross pattern and tighten them to the torque listed in this Chapter's Specifications. If the gasket protrudes beyond the top or bottom of the case and engine block, trim off the excess with a razor blade.

22 Install the engine mounting plate onto the face of the timing chain cover **(see illustration 9.5)**. Tighten to the torque listed in this Chapter's Specifications.

23 Apply a thin layer of clean moly-based grease to the seal contact surface of the crankshaft pulley, then slide it onto the crankshaft. Install the bolt and tighten it finger-tight only. **Note:** *The bolt should be tightened to the specified torque only after the cylinder head and camshaft have been installed.*

24 The remainder of installation is the reverse of removal.

---

10 Timing chain/sprockets - removal, inspection and installation

Refer to illustrations 10.6, 10.7, 10.8, 10.9a and 10.9b

Removal

1 The silent shaft chain and sprockets must be removed to gain access to the timing chain assembly (see Section 9).

2 Remove the camshaft sprocket holder and the right and left timing chain guides from the front of the engine block **(see illustration 9.8)**.

3 Depress the timing chain tensioner plunger on the oil pump and slide the camshaft sprocket, the crankshaft sprocket and the timing chain off the engine as an assembly. Do not lose the key that indexes the crankshaft sprocket in the proper place. Remove the timing chain tensioner plunger and spring from the oil pump.

Inspection

4 Inspect the sprocket teeth for wear and damage. Check the chain for cracked plates and pitted or worn rollers. Check the chain tensioner rubber shoe for wear and the tensioner spring for cracks and deterioration. Check the chain guides for wear and damage. Replace any defective parts with new ones.

Installation

5 Install the sprocket holder and the right and left timing chain guides onto the engine block. Tighten the bolts securely. The upper bolt in the left timing chain guide should be installed finger-tight only. Then coat the entire length of the chain contact surfaces of the guides with clean, high-quality moly-based grease.

6 Turn the crankshaft bolt with a large wrench until the number one piston is at Top Dead Center (TDC) (refer to Section 3 for TDC locating). Apply a layer of clean moly-based grease or engine assembly lube to the timing chain tensioner plunger and install the tensioner spring and plunger loosely into the oil pump body **(see illustration)**. **Note:** *Chrysler Corporation officially recognizes a problem with the timing chain at start-up. Because of insufficient oil pressure, the timing chain will make a knocking noise when the engine is first started. This will not harm the engine, but it is necessary to update the tensioner. Purchase from a dealership parts department a rubber spacer and insert it into the tensioner spring. This spacer will prevent the oil from flowing out of the tensioner and back into the oil pump.*

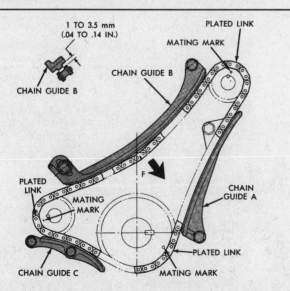

9.16c Push in the direction of arrow F to remove the slack from the silent shaft chain

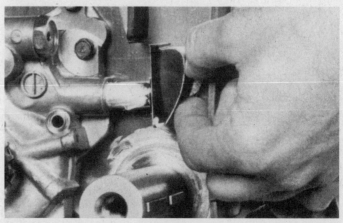

10.6 Lubricate the timing chain tensioner plunger and install it in the oil pump bore

10.7   Install the timing chain sprocket on the end of the crankshaft with the wide shoulder facing out

10.8   Mesh the camshaft sprocket and the timing chain with the mark on the sprocket directly opposite the plated link on the chain

10.9a   Installing the timing chain on the crankshaft sprocket (note that the sprocket mark and the plated link are opposite each other)

7   Position the timing chain sprocket on the end of the crankshaft with the wide shoulder facing out (see illustration). Line up the key-way in the sprocket with the key on the crankshaft.

8   Install the camshaft sprocket onto the chain, lining up the plated link on the chain with the marked tooth on the sprocket (see illustration).

9   Slip the chain over the crankshaft sprocket, lining up the plated link on the chain with the marked tooth on the sprocket (see illustration). Slide the crankshaft sprocket all the way onto the crankshaft while depressing the chain tensioner so the chain fits into place in the guides. Rest the camshaft sprocket on the sprocket holder (see illustration) and make sure the plated links and mating marks are aligned properly. Caution: Do not rotate the crankshaft for any reason until the cylinder head and camshaft have been properly installed.

10   The remainder of installation is the reverse of removal.

11   Camshaft (water pump pulley) oil seal - replacement

Refer to illustrations 11.2 and 11.5

1   Remove the water pump pulley from the camshaft (see Chapter 3).

2   Use a special tool (C-4847-1) and remove the seal from the cylinder head (see illustration). If the special tool is not available, wrap the tip of a small screwdriver with tape and use it to carefully pry out the seal. Don't nick or scratch the camshaft journal or the new seal will leak.

3   Thoroughly clean and inspect the seal bore and the seal journal on the camshaft. Both must be clean and smooth. Use emery cloth or 400-grit sandpaper to remove small burrs.

4   If a groove has been worn into the journal on the camshaft (from contact with the seal lip), installing a new seal probably won't stop the leak. Such wear normally indicates the camshaft or the bearing sur-

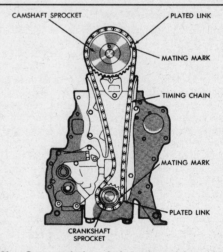

10.9b   Correct timing chain and sprocket relationship

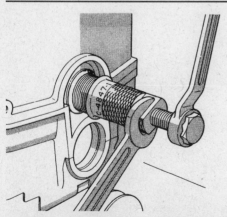

11.2   Use a special tool (C-4847-1) to remove the seal from the cylinder head

11.5   Tap the seal into place with a special tool (C-4848)

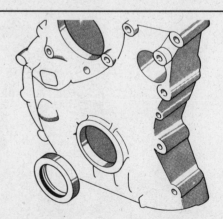

12.3   Crankshaft front oil seal

faces in the caps are worn. It's probably time to overhaul the cylinder head (see Chapter 2, Part E) or replace the head or camshaft.

5   Coat the lip of the new seal with clean engine oil or moly-base grease and carefully tap the seal into place with a special tool (C-4848) **(see illustration)**. If a special tool is not available, use a large socket or piece of pipe and a hammer. If you don't have a socket as large in diameter as the seal, tap around the outer edge of the seal with the large end of a punch.

6   Install the water pump pulley and belt (see Chapter 3).

7   Start the engine and check for oil leaks.

12   Crankshaft front oil seal - replacement

Refer to illustration 12.3

1   Remove the drivebelts (see Chapter 1).

2   Remove the crankshaft pulley.

3   Carefully pry the seal out of the front cover **(see illustration)** with a seal removal tool or a screwdriver. Don't scratch the seal bore or damage the crankshaft in the process (if the crankshaft is damaged, the new seal will end up leaking).

4   Clean the bore in the timing chain cover and coat the outer edge of the new seal with engine oil or multi-purpose grease. Using a socket with an outside diameter slightly smaller than the outside diameter of the seal, carefully drive the seal into place with a hammer. If a socket is not available, a short section of a large diameter pipe will work. Check the seal after installation to be sure the spring did not pop out.

5   Installation is the reverse of removal.

6   Run the engine and check for leaks.

13   Camshaft - removal, inspection and installation

Removal

Refer to illustration 13.6

1   Remove the valve cover (see Section 4).

2   Remove the distributor (see Chapter 5).

3   Remove the rocker arm assembly (see Section 5). If the camshaft bearing caps do not have numbers on them, number them before removal. Be sure to put the marks on the same ends of all the caps to prevent incorrect orientation of the caps during installation.

4   In order to keep the tensioner from collapsing once the sprocket has been removed, install a special retaining tool between the timing chain, near the tensioner **(see illustration 14.7)**. The tool will extend down into the timing chain cover, so be sure the strap or wire hanger on the tool does not fall into the cover or it will be very difficult to remove the tool when the camshaft has been installed.

5   If a tensioner retaining tool is not available, try using a block of wood with some mechanics wire tied through it as an alternative.

6   Remove the camshaft sprocket bolt and distributor drive gear. **Note:** *Lock the camshaft using a large pair of Vise-grips or Channel-locks. Fasten the tool onto the camshaft without contacting the camshaft lobes. Position the tool only on the spaces between the lobes that are equipped with a notched relief specifically designed for retaining the camshaft. Remove the timing chain and camshaft sprocket as a single unit from the camshaft* **(see illustration)**. *Suspend the camshaft sprocket, with the chain still attached, out of the way.*

7   Lift out the camshaft, wipe it off with a clean shop towel and set it aside.

2B

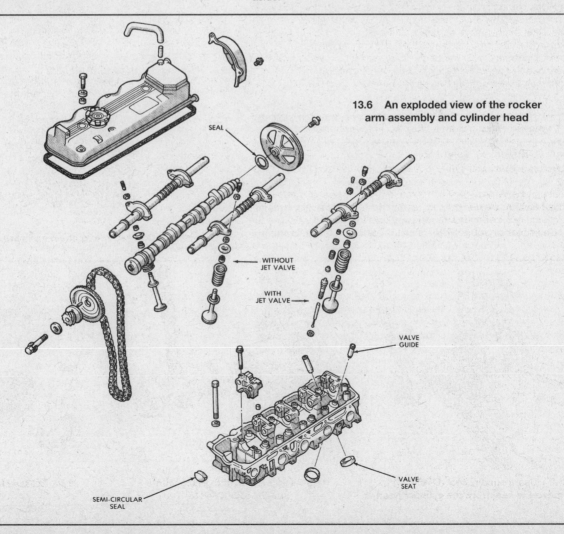

13.6   An exploded view of the rocker arm assembly and cylinder head

SEAL

WITHOUT JET VALVE

WITH JET VALVE

VALVE GUIDE

VALVE SEAT

SEMI-CIRCULAR SEAL

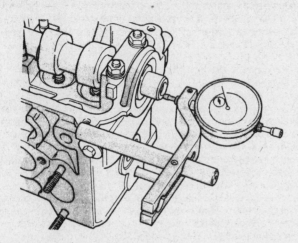

13.8   To check camshaft endplay, set up a dial indicator like this, with the gauge plunger touching the nose of the camshaft

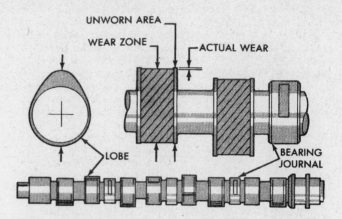

13.11   Measure the height of the camshaft lobes at the wear zone and unworn area, then subtract the wear zone measurement from the unworn area measurement to get the actual wear – compare the wear to the limit listed in this Chapter's Specifications

Inspection

Refer to illustrations 13.8 and 13.11

8   To check camshaft endplay:

a)   Install the camshaft and secure it with caps 1 and 5.

b)   Mount a dial indicator on the head **(see illustration)**.

c)   Using a large screwdriver as a lever at the opposite end, move the camshaft forward-and-backward and note the dial indicator reading.

d)   Compare the reading with the endplay listed in this Chapter's Specifications.

e)   If the indicated reading is higher, either the camshaft or the head is worn. Replace parts as necessary.

9   To check camshaft runout:

a)   Support the camshaft with a pair of V-blocks and attach a dial indicator with the stem resting against the center bearing journal on the camshaft.

b)   Rotate the camshaft and note the indicated runout.

c)   Compare the results to the camshaft runout listed in this Chapter's Specifications.

d)   If the indicated runout exceeds the specified runout, replace the camshaft.

10   Check the camshaft bearing journals and caps for scoring and signs of wear. If they are worn, replace the cylinder head with a new or rebuilt unit. Measure the journals on the camshaft with a micrometer, comparing your readings with this Chapter's Specifications. If the diameter of any of the journals is out of specification, replace the camshaft.

11   Check the cam lobes for wear:

a)   Check the toe and ramp areas of each cam lobe for score marks and uneven wear. Also check for flaking and pitting.

b)   If there's wear on the toe or the ramp, replace the camshaft, but first try to find the cause of the wear. Look for abrasive substances in the oil and inspect the oil pump and oil passages for blockage. Lobe wear is usually caused by inadequate lubrication or dirty oil.

c)   Using a micrometer, calculate the lobe wear **(see illustration)**. If the lobe wear is greater than listed in this Chapter's Specifications, replace the camshaft.

12   Inspect the rocker arms for wear, galling and pitting of the contact surfaces.

13   If any of the conditions described above are noted, the cylinder head is probably getting insufficient lubrication or dirty oil, so make sure you track down the cause of this problem (low oil level, low oil pump capacity, clogged oil passage, etc.) before installing a new head, camshaft or followers.

Installation

Refer to illustration 13.16

14   Thoroughly clean the camshaft, the bearing surfaces in the head and caps and the rocker arms. Remove all sludge and dirt. Wipe off all components with a clean, lint-free cloth.

15   Lubricate the contact surfaces on the top of the rocker arms with assembly lube or moly-base grease. Install the rocker arms, making sure you put them in their original locations.

16   Lubricate the camshaft bearing surfaces in the head and the bearing journals and lobes on the camshaft with assembly lube or moly-base grease. Carefully lower the camshaft into position with the dowel pin pointing up **(see illustration)**. **Caution:** *Failure to adequately lubricate the camshaft and related components can cause serious damage to bearing and friction surfaces during the first few seconds after engine start-up, when the oil pressure is low or nonexistent.*

17   Apply a thin coat of assembly lube or moly-base grease to the bearing surfaces of the camshaft bearing caps.

18   Apply anaerobic-type sealant to the cylinder head contact surfaces of bearing caps 1 and 5 and install the rocker arm assembly.

19   Install the bolts for bearing caps 2 and 4. Gradually tighten all four fasteners - 1/4-turn at a time - until the camshaft is drawn down and seated in the bearing saddles. Don't tighten the fasteners completely at this time.

20   Install the bolts into bearing caps 3 and 5 and tighten the fasteners the same way you did for caps 2 and 4.

21   Install a new oil seal on the camshaft, then install bearing cap 1.

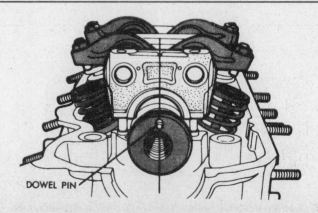

13.16   Install the camshaft with the dowel pin pointing up

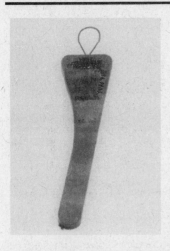

14.7   Before removing the camshaft sprocket, position the tensioner locking tool between the chain, at the tensioner - be sure the tool has a long rope or wire attached to the end of it so it can be easily removed after the job - if the tool is not available, a block of wood and a length of mechanic's wire may also work

Don't tighten the fasteners completely at this time.

22   Remove any excess sealant from the two end bearing caps.

23   Working in a criss-cross pattern, tighten the fasteners for bearing caps 2 and 4 to the torque listed in this Chapter's Specifications. Then torque the fasteners for bearing caps 3 and 5 the same way. Finally, tighten the fasteners for bearing cap 1.

24   Install the camshaft sprocket and timing chain and related components (see Section 10). If you suspended the camshaft sprocket out of the way and didn't disturb the timing chain or sprockets, the valve timing should still be correct. Rotate the camshaft as necessary to reattach the sprocket to the camshaft. If the valve timing was disturbed, align the sprockets and install the chain as described in Section 10.

25   Remove the spark plugs and rotate the crankshaft by hand to make sure the valve timing is correct. After two revolutions, the timing marks on the sprockets should still be aligned. If they're not, reindex the timing chain to the sprockets (see Section 10). **Note:** *If you feel resistance while rotating the crankshaft, stop immediately and check the valve timing by referring to Section 10.*

26   The remainder of installation is the reverse of removal.

---

14   Cylinder head - removal and installation

Caution: *Allow the engine to cool completely before beginning this procedure.*

Removal

Refer to illustrations 14.7 and 14.8

1   Position the number one piston at Top Dead Center (see Section 3).

2   Disconnect the negative cable from the battery.

3   Drain the cooling system and remove the spark plugs (see Chapter 1).

4   Remove the intake and exhaust manifold (see Sections 7 and 8). **Note:** *If you're only replacing the cylinder head gasket, it isn't necessary to remove the manifolds. If you leave the manifolds attached, you may need an assistant to help lift the head off the engine, since it will be quite heavy.*

5   Remove the valve cover (see Section 4).

6   Remove the distributor (see Chapter 5), including the cap and wires.

7   Remove the silent shaft chain and sprockets (see Section 9) and the timing chain and sprocket (see Section 10). **Note:** *It is possible to use a tensioner locking tool* **(see illustration)** *to hold the chain and tensioner in place while the cylinder head is off the engine. This will save time you by not having to remove the timing chain and silent shaft chain assemblies. Be sure to install the tool very tight to prevent it from popping out when the engine is shaken or jarred.*

8   Loosen the head bolts in 1/4-turn increments until they can be removed by hand. Follow the recommended sequence to avoid warping the head **(see illustration)**. Note where each bolt goes so it can be returned to the same location on installation.

9   Lift the head off the engine. If resistance is felt, don't pry between the head and block gasket mating surfaces - damage to the mating surfaces will result. Instead, pry against the casting protrusions on the sides of the cylinder head. Set the head on blocks of wood to prevent damage to the gasket sealing surfaces.

10   Cylinder head disassembly and inspection procedures are covered in detail in Chapter 2, Part E. It's a good idea to have the head checked for warpage, even if you're just replacing the gasket.

Installation

Refer to illustration 14.16

11   The mating surfaces of the cylinder head and block must be perfectly clean when the head is installed.

12   Use a gasket scraper to remove all traces of carbon and old gasket material, then clean the mating surfaces with lacquer thinner or acetone. If there's oil on the mating surfaces when the head is installed, the gasket may not seal correctly and leaks may develop. When working on the block, stuff the cylinders with clean shop rags to keep out debris. Use a vacuum cleaner to remove material that falls into the cylinders. Since the head is made of aluminum, aggressive scraping can cause damage. Be extra careful not to nick or gouge the mating surfaces with the scraper.

13   Check the block and head mating surfaces for nicks, deep scratches and other damage. If damage is slight, it can be removed with a file; if it's excessive, machining may be the only alternative.

14   Use a tap of the correct size to chase the threads in the head bolt holes. Mount each head bolt in a vise and run a die down the threads to remove corrosion and restore the threads. Dirt, corrosion, sealant and damaged threads will affect torque readings.

15   Place a new gasket on the block. Check to see if there are any markings (such as "TOP") on the gasket that say how it is to be installed. Set the cylinder head in position.

16   Install the bolts. They must be tightened in a specific sequence **(see illustration)**, in the stages and to the torques listed in this Chap-

---

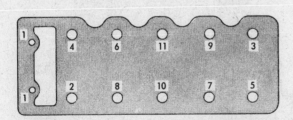

14.8   Loosen the head bolts 1/4-turn at a time, in the sequence shown, until they can be removed by hand

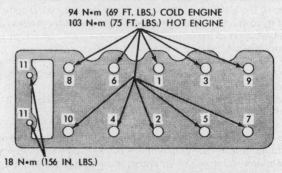

94 N•m (69 FT. LBS.) COLD ENGINE
103 N•m (75 FT. LBS.) HOT ENGINE

18 N•m (156 IN. LBS.)

14.16   Cylinder head bolt TIGHTENING sequence

2B

ter's Specifications. **Note:** *Use the first and second ("engine cold") steps in the Specifications.*

17   Reinstall the timing chain and silent shaft chain, if removed. If a tensioner locking tool was used, attach the camshaft sprocket and remove the tool.

18   Reinstall the remaining parts in the reverse order of removal.

19   Be sure to refill the cooling system and check all fluid levels.

20   Rotate the crankshaft clockwise slowly by hand through two complete revolutions. Recheck the camshaft timing marks (see Section 10). **Caution:** *If you feel any resistance while turning the engine over, stop and recheck the camshaft timing. The valves may be hitting the pistons.*

21   Start the engine and check the ignition timing (see Chapter 1).

22   Run the engine until normal operating temperature is reached. Check for leaks and proper operation.

23   Remove the valve cover and re-torque the cylinder head bolts while the engine is hot (use Step 3 in the Specifications), then re-install the valve cover.

15   Oil pan - removal and installation

Refer to illustration 15.4

Note: *The following procedure is based on the assumption that the engine is in the vehicle.*

1   Warm up the engine, then drain the oil and replace the oil filter (see Chapter 1).

2   Detach the cable from the negative battery terminal.

3   Raise the vehicle and support it securely on jackstands.

4   Remove the bolts securing the oil pan to the engine block **(see illustration)**.

5   Tap on the pan with a soft-face hammer to break the gasket seal,

then detach the oil pan from the engine. Don't pry between the block and oil pan mating surfaces.

6   Using a gasket scraper, remove all traces of old gasket and/or sealant from the engine block and oil pan. Remove the seals from each end of the engine block or oil pan. Clean the mating surfaces with lacquer thinner or acetone. Make sure the threaded bolt holes in the block are clean.

7   Clean the oil pan with solvent and dry it thoroughly. Check the gasket flanges for distortion, particularly around the bolt holes. If necessary, place the pan on a block of wood and use a hammer to flatten and restore the gasket surfaces.

8   Install the oil pan end seals, then apply a 1/8-inch wide bead of RTV sealant to the oil pan gasket surfaces. Continue the bead across the end seals. Make sure the sealant is applied to the inside edge of the bolt holes.

9   Carefully place the oil pan in position.

10   Install the bolts and tighten them in 1/4-turn increments to the

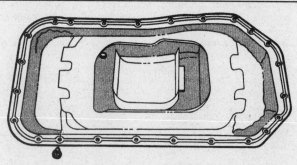

15.4   Remove the bolts from the oil pan

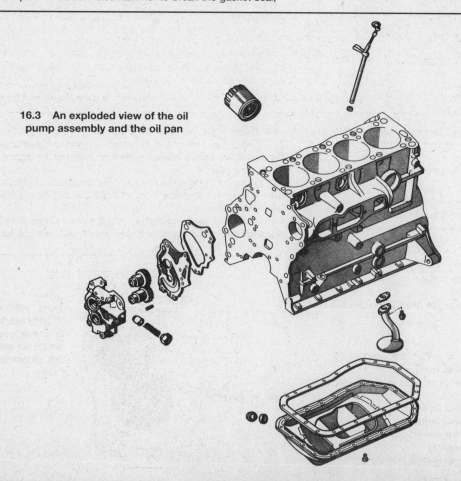

16.3   An exploded view of the oil pump assembly and the oil pan

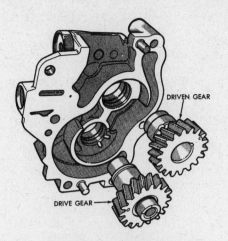

16.5 Check oil pump bearing clearance on each gear

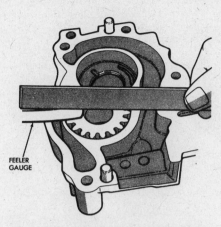

16.6a Use a straightedge and a feeler gauge to check the endplay on the driven gear

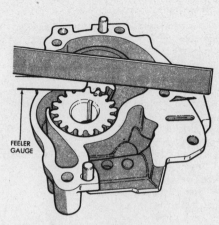

16.6b Use a straightedge and a feeler gauge to check the endplay on the drive gear

2B

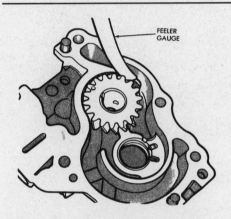

16.7 Check the driven gear-to-housing clearance

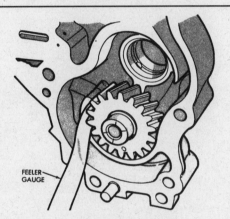

16.8 Check the drive gear-to-housing clearance

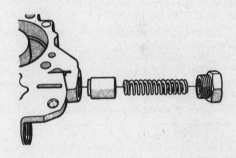

16.9 Remove the oil pressure relief valve spring and measure its free length

torque listed in this Chapter's Specifications. Start with the bolts closest to the center of the pan and work out in a spiral pattern. Don't overtighten them or leakage may occur.

11 Add oil, run the engine and check for oil leaks.

16 Oil pump - removal, inspection and installation

Removal

Refer to illustration 16.3

1 Remove the timing chain (see Section 10).
2 Remove the oil pan (see Section 15).
3 Remove the oil pump mounting bolts **(see illustration)** and remove the oil pump assembly.

Inspection

Refer to illustrations 16.5, 16.6a 16.6b, 16.7, 16.8, 16.9 and 16.11

4 Remove the bolts and lift off the oil pump cover.
5 Check the oil pump bearing clearance on each gear **(see illustration)**.
6 Using feeler gauges and a straightedge, check the endplay of the driven gear and the drive gear **(see illustrations)**.
7 Check the clearance between the driven gear and the pump housing with feeler gauges **(see illustration)**.
8 Check the clearance between the drive gear and the pump hous-

ing with feeler gauges **(see illustration)**.
9 Extract the spring and oil pump relief valve from the pump housing **(see illustration)**. Measure the free length of the oil pressure relief valve spring.
10 Compare the measurements to the oil pump Specifications at the beginning of this Chapter. If any of them are outside the limits, replace the pump.
11 Install the gears with the mating marks aligned together **(see illustration)**. Install the oil pressure relief valve and spring assembly.

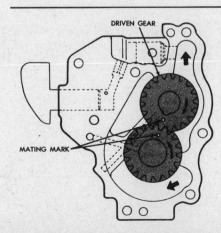

16.11 Be sure the mating marks on the oil pump gears are set when assembling the oil pump

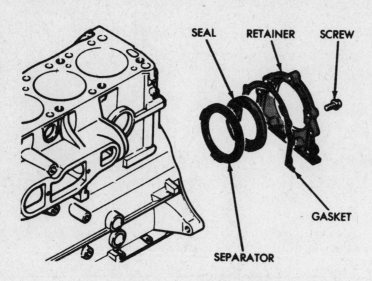

18.1   An exploded view of the rear main oil seal assembly

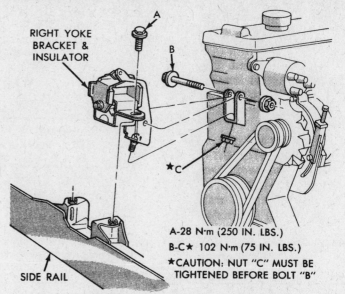

A-28 N·m (250 IN. LBS.)
B-C★ 102 N·m (75 IN. LBS.)
★CAUTION: NUT "C" MUST BE
TIGHTENED BEFORE BOLT "B"

19.1a   An exploded view of the right engine mount on the 2.6L engine

Install the pump cover and tighten the bolts to the torque listed in this Chapter's Specifications.

Installation

12   Apply a thin coat of RTV sealant to the mating surface of the pump and place the pump in position. Rotate it back-and-forth a little to ensure there's positive contact between the pump and the engine block.

13   Coat the threads of the mounting bolts with RTV sealant and, while holding the pump securely in place, install the bolts. Tighten them to the torque listed in this Chapter's Specifications.

14   Install a new gasket on the oil pick-up tube - if removed - **(see illustration 16.3)** and Install the oil pick-up tube and screen. Tighten the bolts to the torque listed in this Chapter's Specifications.

15   Install the oil pan (see Section 15).

17   Flywheel/driveplate - removal and installation

This procedure is essentially the same for all engines. Refer to Part A and follow the procedure outlined there. However, use the bolt torque listed in this Chapter.

18   Rear main oil seal - replacement

Refer to illustration 18.1

This procedure is essentially the same for all engines. Refer to Part A and follow the procedure outlined there. However, use the bolt torque listed in this Chapter **(see illustration)**.

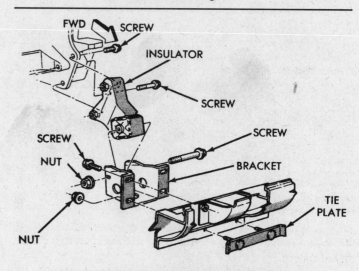

19.1b   An exploded view of the front engine mount on the 2.6L engine

19   Engine mounts - check, replacement and adjustment

Refer to illustrations 19.1a and 19.1b

This procedure is essentially the same for all engines. Refer to Part A and follow the procedure outlined there **(see illustrations)**.

Chapter 2 Part C 3.0L V6 engine

Contents

Specifications

General

Displacement	181 cubic inches
Compression ratio	8.85:1
Firing order	1-2-3-4-5-6
Cylinder numbers (drivebelt end-to-transaxle end)	
Rear (firewall side)	1–3–5
Front (radiator side)	2–4–6

Cylinder location diagram

Camshaft and related components

Camshaft runout limit	0.004 inch
Lobe height..	1.624 inch
Lobe wear limit	0.02 inch

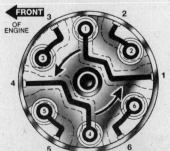

Distributor cap terminal routing for 3.0L V6

Oil pump

Case-to-outer rotor clearance	0.004 to 0.007 inch
Rotor end clearance	0.0015 to 0.0035 inch
Case-to-inner rotor clearance	0.0010 to 0.0028 inch

1231-01.spcs HAYNES

Torque specifications

		Ft-lbs (unless otherwise indicated)
Rocker arm shaft bolts	......	180 in-lbs
Intake manifold nuts/bolts	......	174 in-lbs
Distributor drive adaptor bolts	......	130 in-lbs
Engine mounts **(see illustration 21.1)**		
A	......	125
B	......	100
C	......	75
D	......	50
E	......	40
F	......	16
G	......	200 in-lbs
Exhaust manifold nuts	......	175 in-lbs
Exhaust manifold heat shield bolts	......	130 in-lbs
Exhaust pipe-to-manifold bolts	......	250 in-lbs
Exhaust crossover pipe bolts	......	51
Crankshaft pulley-to-crankshaft bolt	......	112
Camshaft sprocket bolt	......	70
Timing belt cover **(see illustration 10.13b)**		
A (M6 X 20)	......	115 in-lbs
B (M6 X 55)	......	115 in-lbs
C (M6 X 25)	......	115 in-lbs
D (M6 X 10)	......	115 in-lbs
Timing belt tensioner locking bolt	......	250 in-lbs
Cylinder head bolts	......	70
Flywheel/driveplate mounting bolts*	......	72 to 80
Oil pan mounting bolts	......	50 in-lbs
Oil pump assembly mounting bolts	......	130 in-lbs
Oil pump relief plug	......	36
Oil pick–up tube-to-pump bolts	......	191 in-lbs
Oil pump cover bolts	......	104 in-lbs
Valve cover bolts	......	88 in-lbs

* Apply a thread locking compound to the threads prior to installation

1 General information

This Part of Chapter 2 is devoted to in-vehicle repair procedures for the 3.0L V6 engine. All information concerning engine removal and installation and engine block and cylinder head overhaul can be found in Part E of this Chapter.

The following repair procedures are based on the assumption that the engine is installed in the vehicle. If the engine has been removed from the vehicle and mounted on a stand, many of the steps outlined in this Part of Chapter 2 will not apply.

The Specifications included in this Part of Chapter 2 apply only to the procedures contained in this Part. Part E of Chapter 2 contains the Specifications necessary for cylinder head and engine block rebuilding.

The 60-degree V6 has a cast iron block and aluminum heads with a camshaft in each head. The block has thin walled sections for light weight. A "cradle frame" main bearing casting – the main bearing caps are cast as a unit, with a bridge, or truss, connecting them – supports the cast ductile iron crankshaft.

Both camshafts are driven off the crankshaft by a cog belt. A spring loaded tensioner, adjusted by an eccentric type locknut, maintains belt tension. Each camshaft actuates two valves per cylinder through hydraulic lash adjusters and shaft–mounted forged aluminum rocker arms.

Each cast aluminum three-ring piston has two compression rings and a three-piece oil control ring. The piston pins are pressed into forged steel connecting rods. The flat-topped pistons produce a 8.85:1 compression ratio.

The distributor, which is mounted on the drivebelt end of the front cylinder head, is driven by a helical gear on the camshaft. The water pump, which is bolted to the timing belt end of the block, is driven off the crankshaft by a drivebelt and pulley. The gear type oil pump is mounted in the oil pump case and attached to the timing belt cover. It is driven by the crankshaft.

From the oil pump, oil travels through the filter to the main oil gallery, from which it is routed either directly to the main bearings, crankshaft, connecting rod bearings and pistons and cylinder walls or to the cylinder heads.

2 Repair operations possible with the engine in the vehicle

Many major repair operations can be accomplished without removing the engine from the vehicle.

Clean the engine compartment and the exterior of the engine with some type of degreaser before any work is done. It will make the job easier and help keep dirt out of the internal areas of the engine.

Depending on the components involved, it may be helpful to remove the hood to improve access to the engine as repairs are performed (refer to Chapter 11 if necessary). Cover the fenders to prevent damage to the paint. Special pads are available, but an old bedspread or blanket will also work.

If vacuum, exhaust, oil or coolant leaks develop, indicating a need for gasket or seal replacement, the repairs can generally be made with the engine in the vehicle. The intake and exhaust manifold gaskets, oil pan gasket, camshaft and crankshaft oil seals and cylinder head gaskets are all accessible with the engine in place.

Exterior engine components, such as the intake and exhaust manifolds, the oil pan (and the oil pump), the water pump, the starter motor, the alternator, the distributor and the fuel system components can be removed for repair with the engine in place.

Since the cylinder heads can be removed without pulling the engine, camshaft and valve component servicing can also be accomplished with the engine in the vehicle. Replacement of the timing belt and sprockets is also possible with the engine in the vehicle.

In extreme cases caused by a lack of necessary equipment, repair or replacement of piston rings, pistons, connecting rods and rod bearings is possible with the engine in the vehicle. However, this practice is not recommended because of the cleaning and preparation work that must be done to the components involved.

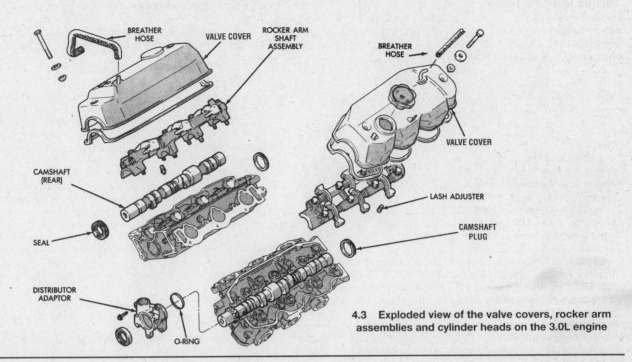

4.3   **Exploded view of the valve covers, rocker arm assemblies and cylinder heads on the 3.0L engine**

---

3   Top Dead Center (TDC) for number one piston – locating

Note: The following procedure is based on the assumption that the spark plug wires and distributor are correctly installed. If you are trying to locate TDC to install the distributor correctly, piston position must be determined by feeling for compression at the number one spark plug hole as the crankshaft is slowly turned clockwise, then aligning the ignition timing marks as described in Step 8.

1   Top Dead Center (TDC) is the highest point in the cylinder that each piston reaches as it travels up-and-down when the crankshaft turns. Each piston reaches TDC on the compression stroke and again on the exhaust stroke, but TDC generally refers to piston position on the compression stroke.

2   Positioning the piston(s) at TDC is an essential part of many procedures such as camshaft and timing belt/sprocket removal and distributor removal.

3   Before beginning this procedure, be sure to place the transmission in Neutral and apply the parking brake or block the rear wheels. Also, disable the ignition system by detaching the coil wire from the terminal marked "C" on the distributor cap and grounding it on the block with a jumper wire. Remove the spark plugs (see Chapter 1).

4   In order to bring any piston to TDC, the crankshaft must be turned using one of the methods outlined below. When looking at the drivebelt end of the engine, normal crankshaft rotation is clockwise.

  a)   The preferred method is to turn the crankshaft with a socket and ratchet attached to the bolt threaded into the front of the crankshaft.

  b)   A remote starter switch, which may save some time, can also be used. Follow the instructions included with the switch. Once the piston is close to TDC, use a socket and ratchet as described in the previous paragraph.

  c)   If an assistant is available to turn the ignition switch to the Start position in short bursts, you can get the piston close to TDC without a remote starter switch. Make sure your assistant is out of the vehicle, away from the ignition switch, then use a socket and ratchet as described in Paragraph a) to complete the procedure.

5   Note the position of the terminal for the number one spark plug wire on the distributor cap **(see illustration)**. If the terminal isn't

marked, follow the plug wire from the number one cylinder spark plug to the cap.

6   Use a felt-tip pen or chalk to make a mark on the distributor body directly under the terminal.

7   Detach the cap from the distributor and set it aside (see Chapter 1 if necessary).

8   Turn the crankshaft (see Paragraph 3 above) until the "0" notch in the crankshaft pulley is aligned with the timing indicator (located at the front of the engine).

9   Look at the distributor rotor – it should be pointing directly at the mark you made on the distributor body. If it is, go to Step 12.

10   If the rotor is 180-degrees off, the number one piston is at TDC on the exhaust stroke – proceed to the next Step.

11   To get the piston to TDC on the compression stroke, turn the crankshaft one complete turn (360-degrees) clockwise. The rotor should now be pointing at the mark on the distributor. When the rotor is pointing at the number one spark plug wire terminal inside the distributor cap and the ignition timing marks are aligned, the number one piston is at TDC on the compression stroke.

12   After the number one piston has been positioned at TDC on the compression stroke, TDC for any of the remaining pistons can be located by turning the crankshaft and following the firing order.

13   Mark the remaining spark plug wire terminal locations on the distributor body just like you did for the number one terminal, then number the marks to correspond with the cylinder numbers. As you turn the crankshaft, the rotor will also turn. When it's pointing directly at one of the marks on the distributor, the piston for that particular cylinder is at TDC on the compression stroke.

---

4   Valve covers – removal and installation

Refer to illustrations 4.3 and 4.16

1   Relieve the fuel system pressure (see Chapter 4).

2   Disconnect the negative cable from the battery.

Removal

Front (radiator side) cover

3   Remove the breather hose by sliding the hose clamp back and pulling the hose off the fitting on the valve cover **(see illustration)**.

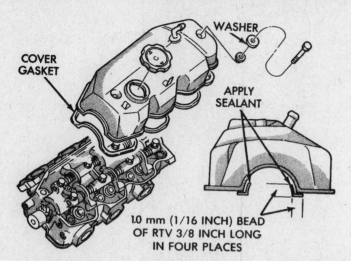

4.16   It's not necessary to use RTV gasket sealer on the inside of the gasket if the gasket is a tight fit and does not budge once it is installed inside the valve cover - it IS necessary to apply RTV to the edges (arrows) on the outside of the gasket where it mates with the camshaft seal

4   Remove the spark plug wires from the spark plugs. Mark them clearly with pieces of masking tape to prevent confusion during installation.

5   Remove the wires and hoses attached to the valve cover.

6   Remove the valve cover bolts and washers.

7   Detach the valve cover. **Caution:** *If the cover is stuck to the head, bump one end with a block of wood and a hammer to jar it loose. If that doesn't work, try to slip a flexible putty knife between the head and cover to break the gasket seal. Don't pry at the cover-to-head joint or damage to the sealing surfaces may occur (leading to oil leaks in the future).*

Rear (firewall side) cover

8   Remove the breather hose from the cover **(see illustration 4.3)**.

9   Tag and detach the spark plug wires.

10   Release the wiring retainers. Label and move the wiring and hoses aside.

11   Remove the air cleaner and the air cleaner assembly (see Chapter 4).

12   Remove the air intake plenum (see Chapter 4).

13   Remove the valve cover bolts and washers and lift off the valve cover. Read the Caution in Step 7.

Installation

14   The mating surfaces of each cylinder head and valve cover must be perfectly clean when the covers are installed. Use a gasket scraper to remove all traces of sealant and old gasket material, then clean the mating surfaces with lacquer thinner or acetone. If there's sealant or oil on the mating surfaces when the cover is installed, oil leaks may develop.

15   If necessary, clean the mounting screw threads with a die to remove any corrosion and restore damaged threads. Make sure the threaded holes in the head are clean – run a tap into them to remove corrosion and restore damaged threads.

16   The gaskets should be mated to the covers before the covers are installed. Apply a bead of RTV sealant to the cover in the areas indicated **(see illustration)**, then position the gasket inside the cover and allow the sealant to set up so the gasket adheres to the cover. If the sealant isn't allowed to set, the gasket may fall out of the cover as it's installed on the engine.

17   Carefully position the cover on the head and install the bolts.

18   Tighten the bolts in three or four steps to the torque listed in this Chapter's Specifications.

19   The remaining installation steps are the reverse of removal.

20   Start the engine and check carefully for oil leaks as the engine warms up.

---

5   Rocker arm components – removal and installation

Refer to illustrations 5.2, 5.4 and 5.5

1   Position the engine at TDC compression for the number 1 cylinder (see Section 3). Remove the valve cover (see Section 4).

2   Loosen the rocker arm shaft bolts **(see illustration)** in two or three stages, working your way from the ends toward the middle of the shafts. **Caution:** *Some of the valves will be open when you loosen the rocker arm shaft bolts and the rocker arm shafts will be under a certain amount of valve spring pressure. Therefore, the bolts must be loosened gradually. Loosening a bolt all at once near a rocker arm under*

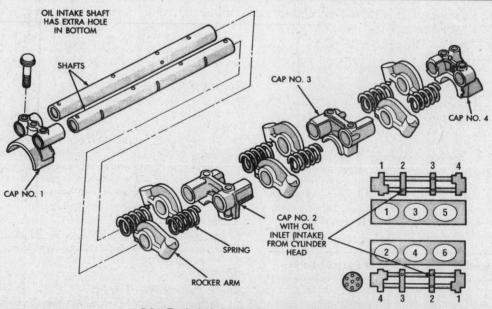

5.2   Exploded view of the rocker arm assembly

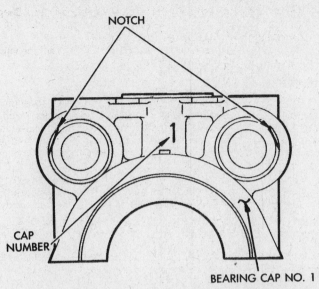

5.4 **Check each bearing cap stamped numeral and the position of the notches to aid in the correct assembly**

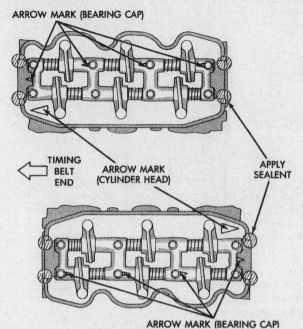

5.5 **The arrows on the bearing caps should point in the same direction as the arrows on the cylinder heads**

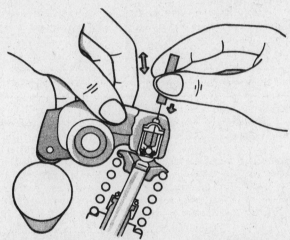

6.1 **When performing the freeplay test, make sure the adjuster that is being tested has the corresponding camshaft lobe pointing away from the rocker arm (closed valve)**

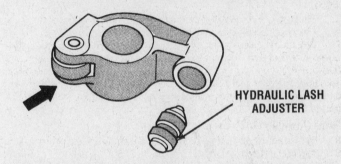

6.4 **The hydraulic lash adjusters are precision units installed in the machined openings in the rocker arm assemblies**

spring pressure could bend or break the rocker arm shaft.

3   Prior to removal, scribe or paint identifying marks on the rockers to ensure they will be installed in their original locations.

4   Remove the bolts and lift off the rocker arm shaft assemblies one at a time. Lay them down on a nearby workbench in the same relationship to each other that they're in when installed. They must be reinstalled on the same cylinder head. Note the location of the stamped bearing cap number and the position of the notches **(see illustration)**.

5   Installation is the reverse of the removal procedure. **Note:** Be sure the arrows stamped into the cylinder head and the bearing caps **(see illustration)** are pointing in the same direction. Tighten the rocker arm shaft bolts, in several steps, to the torque listed in this Chapter's Specifications. Work from the ends of the shafts toward the middle.

6   **Hydraulic lash adjusters – check, removal and installation**

Refer to illustration 6.1

Check

1   Check the hydraulic lash adjusters for freeplay by inserting a

small wire through the air bleed hole in the rocker arm while lightly pushing the check ball down **(see illustration)**.

2   While lightly holding the check ball down, move the rocker arm up and down to check for freeplay. There should be a small amount of movement. If there is no freeplay, replace the adjuster with a new unit.

Removal and installation

Refer to illustration 6.4

3   Remove the valve cover(s) (see Section 4) and the rocker arm shaft components (see Section 5).

4   Pull the hydraulic lash adjuster(s) out of the rocker arm(s) **(see illustration)**. **Note:** Be sure to label each rocker arm and adjuster and place them in a partitioned box or something suitable to keep them from getting mixed with each other.

5   Installation is the reverse of removal.

7   **Intake manifold – removal and installation**

Removal

Refer to illustrations 7.6 and 7.8

1   Relieve the fuel system pressure (see Chapter 4).

2   Disconnect the cable from the negative terminal of the battery.

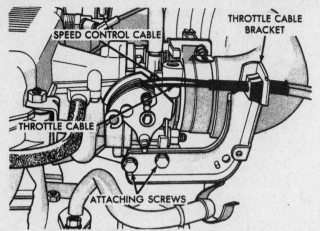

7.6   Remove the attaching screws and lift the throttle cable bracket from the air intake plenum

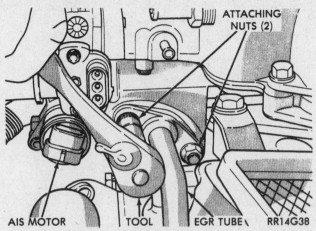

7.8   Remove the bolts and separate the EGR tube from the air intake plenum

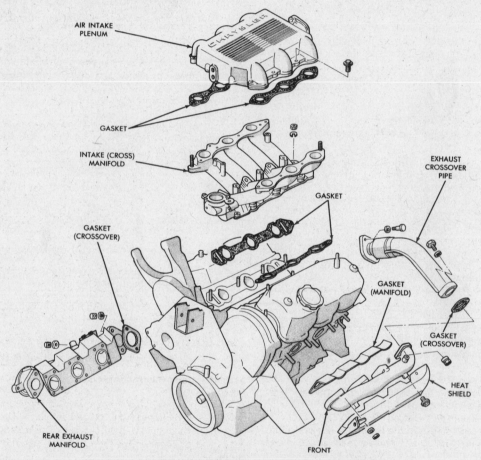

7.17   Details of the intake manifold and related components

3   Drain the cooling system (don't forget to drain the cylinder block) (see Chapter 1).

4   Remove the air cleaner-to-throttle body inlet hose (see Chapter 4).

5   Remove the spark plug wires and distributor cap. Be sure to mark the spark plug wires for proper reinstallation (see Chapter 1).

6   Remove the throttle cable and transaxle kickdown linkage (see Chapters 4 and 7B). Also, remove the throttle cable bracket from the air collector **(see illustration).**

7   Remove the Automatic Idle Speed (AIS) motor and throttle posi-

tion sensor (TPS) electrical connectors from the throttle body.

8   Remove the EGR tube flange from the air intake plenum **(see illustration).**

9   Label and detach any vacuum lines from the throttle body.

10   Detach the fuel lines from the fuel rail (see Chapter 4).

11   Remove the throttle body, air intake plenum and the fuel injectors (see Chapter 4).

12   Label and remove any remaining hoses, wires or cables attached to the intake manifold or its components.

13   Loosen the manifold mounting bolts/nuts in 1/4-turn increments

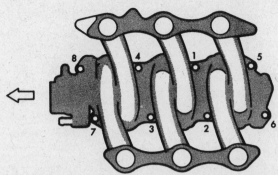

7.20 Intake manifold bolt tightening sequence

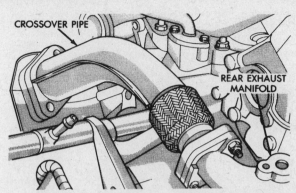

8.3 Remove the crossover pipe from the engine (located over the transmission bellhousing)

2C

until they can be removed by hand. Loosen the outer bolts first, then the inner bolts.

14 The manifold will probably be stuck to the cylinder heads and force may be required to break the gasket seal. **Caution:** *Don't pry between the manifold and the heads or damage to the gasket sealing surfaces may occur, leading to vacuum leaks.*

Installation

Refer to illustration 7.17 and 7.20

Note: *The mating surfaces of the cylinder heads and manifold must be perfectly clean when the manifold is installed. Gasket removal solvents in aerosol cans are available at most auto parts stores and may be helpful when removing old gasket material that's stuck to the heads and manifold (since they're made of aluminum, aggressive scraping can cause damage). Be sure to follow the directions printed on the container.*

15 Use a gasket scraper to remove all traces of sealant and old gasket material, then clean the mating surfaces with lacquer thinner or acetone. If there's old sealant or oil on the mating surfaces when the manifold is installed, oil or vacuum leaks may develop. Use a vacuum cleaner to remove any material that falls into the intake ports in the heads.

16 Use a tap of the correct size to chase the threads in the bolt holes, then use compressed air (if available) to remove the debris from the holes. **Warning:** *Wear safety glasses or a face shield to protect your eyes when using compressed air!*

17 Position the gaskets on the cylinder heads **(see illustration)**. No sealant is required; however, follow the instructions included with the new gaskets.

18 Make sure all intake port openings, coolant passage holes and bolt holes are aligned correctly.

19 Carefully set the manifold in place. Be careful not to disturb the gaskets.

20 Install the nuts/bolts and tighten them to the torque listed in this Chapter's Specifications following the recommended sequence **(see illustration)**. Work up to the final torque in two steps.

21 Install the air intake plenum (see Chapter 4).

22 The remaining installation steps are the reverse of removal. Start the engine and check carefully for oil and coolant leaks at the intake manifold joints.

8 Exhaust manifolds – removal and installation

Refer to illustrations 8.3, 8.4 and 8.9

Note: *The engine must be completely cool when this procedure is done.*

1 Disconnect the negative cable from the battery. Raise the vehicle and support it securely on jackstands.

2 Spray penetrating oil on the exhaust manifold fasteners and allow it to soak in.

3 Remove the bolts and nuts that retain the cross-over pipe to the

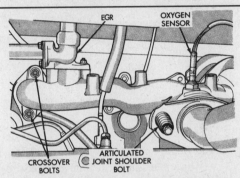

8.4 If you're removing the rear exhaust manifold, remove the bolts that retain the EGR tube to the manifold and detach the tube

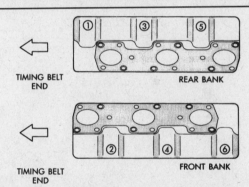

8.9 Be sure to install the correct exhaust manifold gasket onto the corresponding cylinder head

manifolds **(see illustration)** and lift the pipe from the engine compartment.

4 If you're removing the rear (firewall side) manifold, unplug the electrical connector to the oxygen sensor. Disconnect the exhaust pipe from the exhaust manifold **(see illustration 8.3)**. Remove the bolts and detach the EGR tube from the rear manifold **(see illustration)**.

5 If you're working on the front manifold, remove the nuts retaining the heat shield to the manifold near the cylinder head and slip it off the mounting studs **(see illustration 7.17)**.

6 Remove the nuts that retain the manifold to the cylinder head and lift the exhaust manifold off.

7 Carefully inspect the manifolds and fasteners for cracks and damage.

8 Use a scraper to remove all traces of old gasket material and carbon deposits from the manifold and cylinder head mating surfaces. If the gasket was leaking, have the manifold checked for warpage at an automotive machine shop and resurfaced if necessary.

9 Position new gaskets over the cylinder head studs. **Note:** *Install the gasket with the numbers 1-3-5 on the top onto the rear bank (cylin-*

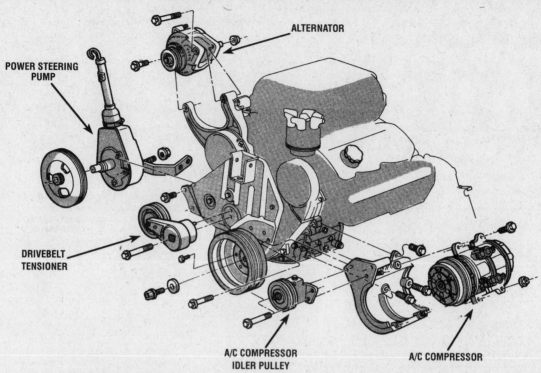

ALTERNATOR

POWER STEERING
PUMP

DRIVEBELT
TENSIONER

A/C COMPRESSOR
IDLER PULLEY

A/C COMPRESSOR

10.9a   Details of the engine accessories, drivebelt tensioner and idler pulley (1990 and earlier models)

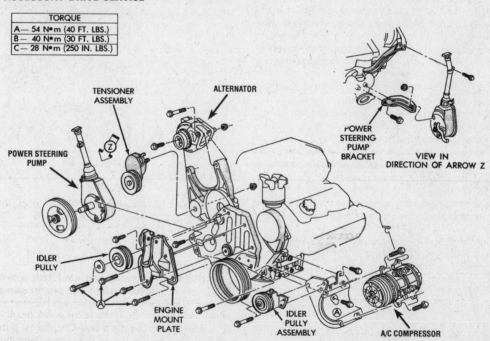

ACCESSORY DRIVE SERVICE

TORQUE
A— 54 N•m (40 FT. LBS.)
B — 40 N•m (30 FT. LBS.)
C — 28 N•m (250 IN. LBS.)

TENSIONER
ASSEMBLY

ALTERNATOR

POWER STEERING
PUMP

POWER
STEERING
PUMP
BRACKET

VIEW IN
DIRECTION OF ARROW Z

IDLER
PULLY

ENGINE
MOUNT
PLATE

IDLER
PULLY
ASSEMBLY

A/C COMPRESSOR

10.9b   Details of the engine accessories, drivebelt tensioner and idler pulleys (1991 models)

der head) and install the gasket with the numbers 2-4-6 onto the front bank (cylinder head) **(see illustration)**.

10   Install the manifold and thread the mounting nuts into place.
11   Working from the center out, tighten the nuts to the torque listed in this Chapter's Specifications in three or four equal steps.
12   Reinstall the remaining parts in the reverse order of removal. Use new gaskets when connecting the exhaust pipes.
13   Run the engine and check for exhaust leaks.

9   Crankshaft pulley/vibration damper – removal and installation

Removal

1   Disconnect the negative cable from the battery.
2   Loosen the lug nuts of the right front wheel, raise the front of the vehicle and support it securely on jackstands. Remove the wheel.

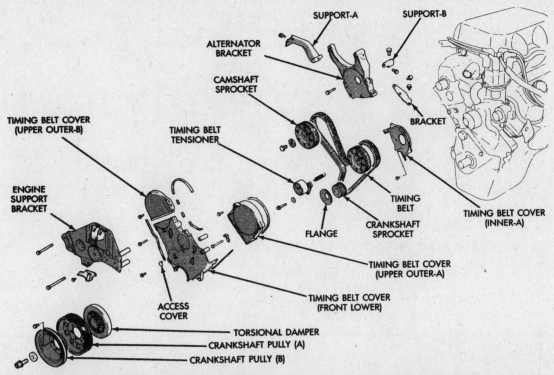

10.13a   Exploded view of the timing belt, covers and related components

3   Remove the drivebelts (see Chapter 1).

4   Remove the bolts that retain the pulley to the vibration damper. Remove the pulley from the engine. **Note:** *The crankshaft pulley is separated into two sections.*

5   Wrap a cloth around the vibration damper to protect the belt surface and attach a chain wrench to the pulley. Hold the crankshaft from turning and use a socket wrench to loosen the bolt.

6   Install a special tool (vibration damper/steering wheel puller) to the damper and slowly draw the vibration damper off.

Installation

7   Lightly lubricate the seal contact surface with engine oil and position it on the nose of the crankshaft. Align the keyway in the pulley with the key in the crankshaft and push the pulley into place by hand. If necessary, tap lightly on the damper using a block of wood and a hammer.

8   Prevent the crankshaft from turning as described in Step 5, then install the bolt and tighten it to the torque listed in this Chapter's Specifications.

9   Reinstall the remaining parts in the reverse order of removal.

---

10   Timing belt – removal, installation and adjustment

Removal

Refer to illustrations 10.9a, 10.9b, 10.13a, 10.13b and 10.14

1   Disconnect the cable from the negative terminal of the battery.

2   If equipped, unbolt the cruise control servo and set it aside, without disconnecting the wires or cables.

3   Remove the coolant reservoir (see Chapter 3).

4   Loosen the lug nuts on the right front wheel.

5   Raise the front of the vehicle and support it securely on jackstands.

6   Remove the right front wheel and detach the splash shield from the inner fenderwell (see Chapter 11).

7   Remove the splash pan and drain the cooling system (see Chapter 1).

8   Position the number one piston at TDC on the compression

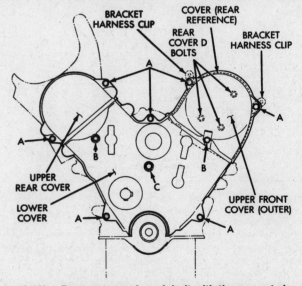

10.13b   Be sure to mark each bolt with the correct size and location for the proper reassembly

stroke (see Section 3). Remove the spark plugs (see Chapter 1).

9   Remove the drivebelts (see Chapter 1). Unbolt the serpentine belt tensioner and detach it from the engine **(see illustration)**.

10   Disconnect the radiator hose from the thermostat.

11   Position a floor jack and a block of wood under the transaxle for support. Separate the engine mount from the engine support bracket to the timing belt. Remove the air conditioning compressor idler pulley and bracket **(see illustration 10.9)**.

12   Remove the crankshaft pulley (see Section 9) and the vibration damper. **Note:** *Don't allow the crankshaft to rotate during removal of the pulley. If the crankshaft moves, the number one piston will no longer be at TDC.*

13   Remove the bolts securing the engine support bracket and the timing belt upper and lower covers **(see illustrations)**. Note the vari-

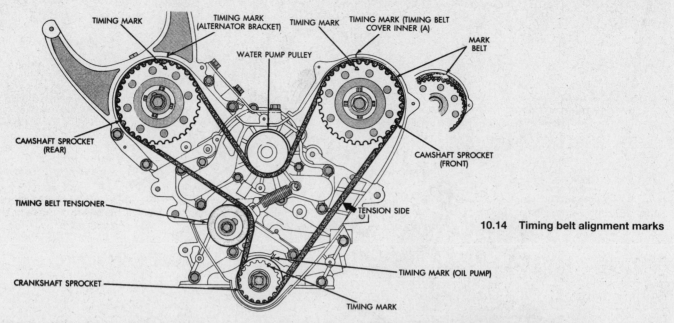

10.14   Timing belt alignment marks

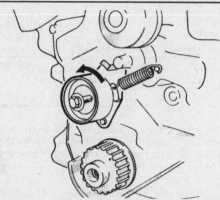

10.17a   Temporarily tighten the tensioner after moving it to the end of the slot

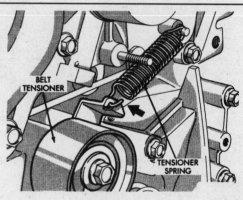

10.17b   Correct spring position on the tensioner

ous type and sizes of bolts by recording a diagram or making specific notes while the timing belt cover is being removed. The bolts must be reinstalled in their original locations.

14   Confirm that the number one piston is still at TDC on the compression stroke by verifying that the timing marks on all three timing belt sprockets are aligned with their respective stationary alignment marks **(see illustration).**

15   Relieve tension on the timing belt by loosening the nut on the timing belt tensioner **(see illustration 10.14).**

16   Check to see that the timing belt is marked with an arrow as to which side faces out. If there isn't a mark, paint one on (only if the same belt will be reinstalled). Slide the timing belt off the sprockets. Check the condition of the tensioner.

Installation

Refer to illustrations 10.17a and 10.17b

17   Prepare to install the timing belt by prying the tensioner away from the spring to the end of the adjustment slot **(see illustration),** then temporarily tightening the locking bolt. Make sure the tensioner spring is positioned properly **(see illustration).**

18   Install the belt on the crankshaft sprocket first, and simultaneously keep the belt tight on the tension side **(see illustration 10.14).**

19   Install the belt on the front (radiator side) camshaft sprocket and

then onto the water pump pulley and finally the rear camshaft sprocket and timing belt tensioner. Be careful not to nudge the camshaft sprocket(s) or crankshaft gear off the timing marks. Install the timing belt with the directional arrow pointing away from the engine.

20   Align the factory-made white lines on the timing belt with the punch mark on each of the camshaft sprockets and the crankshaft sprocket. Make sure all three sets of timing marks are properly aligned **(see illustration 10.14).** Note: *Be sure to install the crankshaft sprocket flange onto the crankshaft gear* **(see illustration 10.13a).**

Adjustment

21   Loosen the tensioner nut and let the tensioner assembly spring toward the belt – the spring tension will automatically apply the proper amount of tension to the belt.

22   Slowly turn the crankshaft clockwise two full revolutions, returning the number one piston to TDC on the compression stroke. **Caution:** *If excessive resistance is felt while turning the crankshaft, it's an indication that the pistons are coming into contact with the valves. Go back over the procedure to correct the situation before proceeding.*

23   Make sure the timing marks are still aligned properly **(see illustration 10.14).** Tighten the tensioner bolt to the torque listed in this Chapter's Specifications while keeping the tensioner steady with your hand.

24   Check the deflection of the timing belt by observing the force the

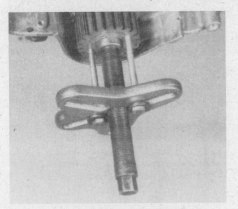

11.4   If the sprocket is stuck, drill and tap two holes and remove it with a bolt-type puller

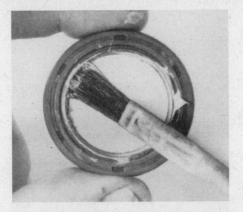

11.7   Apply a film of grease to the lips of the new seal before installing it (if you apply a small amount of grease to the outer edge, it will be easier to push into the bore)

11.8a   Fabricate a seal installation tool from a piece of pipe and a large washer . . .

11.8b   . . . to push the seal into the bore - the pipe must bear against the outer edge of the seal as the bolt is tightened

tensioner pulley applies to the timing belt. If the belt seems loose, re-place the tensioner spring.

25   Install the various components removed during disassembly, re-ferring to the appropriate sections as necessary.

11   Crankshaft front oil seal – replacement

Refer to illustrations 11.4, 11.7, 11.8a and 11.8b

1   Disconnect the negative cable from the battery.
2   Remove the drivebelts (see Chapter 1), crankshaft pulley and tim-ing belt (see Sections 9 and 10).
3   Wedge two screwdrivers behind the crankshaft sprocket. Care-fully pry the sprocket off the crankshaft. Some timing belt sprockets can be pried off easily with screwdrivers. Others are more difficult to remove because corrosion fuses them onto the nose of the crankshaft. If the pulley on your engine is difficult to pry off, don't damage the oil pump with the screwdrivers.
4   If the sprocket won't come loose, drill and tap two holes into the face of the sprocket and use a bolt-type puller to slip it off the crankshaft **(see illustration). Caution:** *Do not reuse a drilled sprocket – replace it.*
5   Turn the bolt of the puller until the pulley comes off. Remove the timing belt plate.
6   Carefully pry the oil seal out with a screwdriver or seal removal tool. Don't scratch or nick the crankshaft in the process!
7   Before installation, apply a coat of multi-purpose grease to the in-side of the seal **(see illustration)**.
8   Fabricate a seal installation tool with a short length of pipe of equal or slightly smaller outside diameter than the seal itself. File the end of the pipe that will bear down on the seal until it's free of sharp

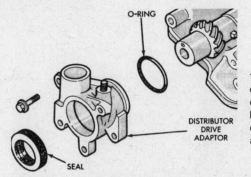

12.5   The oil seal on the rear camshaft is located inside the distributor drive adaptor

edges. You'll also need a large washer, slightly larger in diameter than the pipe, on which the bolt head can seat **(see illustration)**. Install the oil seal by pressing it into position with the seal installation tool **(see illustration)**. When you see and feel the seal stop moving, don't turn the bolt any more or you'll damage the seal.

9   Slide the timing belt plate onto the nose of the crankshaft.
10   Make sure the Woodruff key is in place in the crankshaft.
11   Apply a thin coat of assembly lube to the inside of the timing belt sprocket and slide it onto the crankshaft.
12   Installation of the remaining components is the reverse of re-moval. Be sure to refer to Section 10 for the timing belt installation and adjustment procedure. Tighten all bolts to the torque values listed in this Chapter's Specifications.

12   Camshaft oil seal – replacement

Refer to illustration 12.5

Note: *The 3.0L engine is equipped with two camshaft oil seals on the front (timing belt side) as well as two camshaft oil plugs on the rear (transaxle side) of the engine.*

1   Disconnect the negative battery cable from the battery.
2   Remove the drivebelts (see Chapter 1), crankshaft pulley (see Section 9) and timing belt (see Section 10).
3   Insert a screwdriver through a hole in the camshaft sprocket to lock it in place while loosening the mounting bolt.
4   Once the bolt is out, the pulley can be removed by hand. **Note:** *Mark each pulley with either an R or F. If you're removing both camshaft pulleys, don't mix them up. They must be installed on the same cam they were removed from; R on the rear (firewall side) and F on the front (radiator side).*
5   Carefully remove the old oil seal with a screwdriver **(see illustra-tion)**. Don't nick or scratch the camshaft in the process. Refer to Steps six, seven and eight in Section 11. The same seal installation tool used

2C

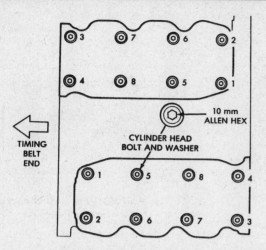

14.12   Cylinder head bolt REMOVAL sequence

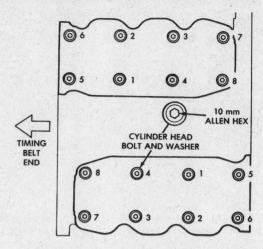

14.23   Cylinder head bolt TIGHTENING sequence

for the crankshaft seal can be used for both camshaft seals.

6   Install the sprocket. Make sure the R or F mark faces out! The side of the pulley with the deep recess must face the engine, which means the shallow recess must face out.

7   Insert a screwdriver through the top hole in the camshaft pulley to lock it in place while you tighten the bolt to the torque listed in this Chapter's Specifications.

8   Installation of the remaining components is the reverse of removal.

---

13   Valve spring, retainer and seals – replacement

This procedure is essentially the same as for the 2.2/2.5 liter four-cylinder engines. Refer to Part A, Section 11 and follow the procedure outlined there.

---

14   Cylinder head(s) – removal and installation

Note: Allow the engine to cool completely before beginning this procedure.

Removal

1   Position the engine at TDC on the compression stroke for the number 1 cylinder (see Section 3). Drain the engine coolant (see Chapter 1).

2   Remove the timing belt cover, timing belt and the camshaft sprockets see Sections 10 and 12).

3   Remove the intake manifold (see Section 7).

4   Remove the rocker arm components (see Section 5) and hydraulic lash adjusters (see Section 6).

5   Remove the exhaust manifold(s) as described in Section 8. **Note:** *If desired, each manifold may remain attached to the cylinder head until after the head is removed from the engine. However, the manifold must still be disconnected from the exhaust system and/or crossover pipe.*

Front (radiator side) cylinder head

6   Remove the distributor (crank angle sensor) (see Chapter 5).

7   Remove the air conditioning compressor from the bracket without disconnecting any hoses (see Chapter 3) and set it aside. It may be helpful to secure the compressor to the vehicle with rope or wire to make sure it doesn't hang by its hoses.

8   Remove the air conditioning compressor bracket (see Chapter 3).

Rear (firewall side) cylinder head

9   Detach the heater hoses and brackets from the transaxle end of

the head.

10   Remove the air cleaner housing from the engine compartment (see Chapter 4).

11   Remove the alternator and bracket from the cylinder head (see Chapter 5).

Both sides

Refer to illustration 14.12

12   Loosen the cylinder head bolts with a 10 mm hex drive tool in 1/4-turn increments until they can be removed by hand. Be sure to follow the proper numerical sequence **(see illustration)**.

13   Head bolts must be reinstalled in their original locations. To keep them from getting mixed up, store them in cardboard holders marked to indicate the bolt pattern. Mark the holders F (front) and R (rear) and indicate the timing belt end of the engine.

14   Lift the head off the block. If resistance is felt, dislodge the head by striking it with a wood block and hammer. If prying is required, pry only on a casting protrusion – be very careful not to damage the head or block!

15   If necessary, remove the camshaft(s) as described in Section 15.

Installation

Refer to illustrations 14.23

16   Remove all traces of old gasket material from the cylinder heads and the engine block. The mating surfaces of the cylinder heads and block must be perfectly clean when the heads are installed.

17   Use a gasket scraper to remove all traces of carbon and old gasket material, then clean the mating surfaces with lacquer thinner or acetone. If there's oil on the mating surfaces when the heads are installed, the gaskets may not seal correctly and leaks may develop. Use a vacuum cleaner to remove any debris that falls into the cylinders.

18   Check the block and head mating surfaces for nicks, deep scratches and other damage. If damage is slight, it can be removed with a file – if it's excessive, machining may be the only alternative.

19   Use a tap of the correct size to chase the threads in the head bolt holes. Mount each bolt in a vise and run a die down the threads to remove corrosion and restore the threads. Dirt, corrosion, sealant and damaged threads will affect torque readings. Ensure that the threaded holes in the block are clean and dry.

20   Position the new gaskets over the dowel pins on the block.

21   Carefully position the heads on the block without disturbing the gaskets.

22   Lightly oil the threads and install the bolts in their original locations. Tighten them finger tight.

23   Follow the recommended sequence and tighten the bolts in three steps to the torque listed in this Chapter's Specifications **(see illustration)**.

24   The remaining installation steps are the reverse of removal.

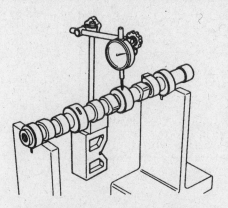

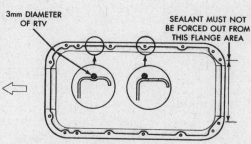

17.14   The bead of RTV sealant should not interfere with the holes for the oil pan bolts

16.2   A dial indicator and V-blocks are needed to check camshaft runout

16.3   Measuring cam lobe height with a micrometer

2C

25   Add coolant and change the engine oil and filter (see Chapter 1), then start the engine and check carefully for oil and coolant leaks.

---

15   Camshaft(s) – removal and installation

Removal

1   Position the engine at TDC on the compression stroke for the number 1 cylinder (see Section 3).
2   If you're removing the front (radiator side) cylinder head, remove the bolts and gently pry off the distributor drive adaptor **(see illustration 12.5).**
3   Remove the rocker arm assembly (see Section 5).
4   Carefully pry the camshaft plugs from the rear section (transaxle end) of the cylinder head **(see illustration 4.3)**. Don't scratch or nick the camshaft in the process!
5   Carefully lift the camshaft from the cylinder head. Inspect the camshaft as described in Section 16.

Installation

6   Lubricate the camshaft bearing journals and lobes with moly-base grease or engine assembly lube, then install it carefully in the head. Don't scratch the bearing surfaces with the cam lobes!
7   Install the distributor drive adaptor retaining bolts and tighten it to the torque listed in this Chapter's Specifications.
8   Check to make sure the mark on the crankshaft sprocket is still aligned with its mark on the oil pump. Slide the camshaft sprockets onto the camshafts and align the marks on the sprockets with their corresponding marks on the cylinder heads.
9   The remaining steps are the reverse of the removal procedure.

---

16   Camshaft and bearing surfaces – inspection

Refer to illustrations 16.2 and 16.3
1   Visually check the camshaft bearing surfaces for pitting, score marks, galling and abnormal wear. If the bearing surfaces are damaged, the head will have to be replaced.
2   Check camshaft runout by placing the camshaft between two V-blocks and set up a dial indicator on the center journal **(see illustration)**. Zero the dial indicator. Turn the camshaft slowly and note the total indicator reading. Record your readings and compare them with the specified runout in this Chapter. If the measured runout exceeds the runout specified in this Chapter, replace the camshaft.
3   Check the camshaft lobe height by measuring each lobe with a micrometer **(see illustration)**. Compare the measurement to the cam lobe height specified in this Chapter. Then subtract the measured cam lobe height from the specified height to compute wear on the cam

lobes. Compare it to the specified wear limit. If it's greater than the specified wear limit, replace the camshaft.
4   Inspect the contact and sliding surfaces of each hydraulic lash adjuster for scoring or damage (see Section 6). Replace any defective parts.
5   Check the rocker arms and shafts for abnormal wear, pits, galling, score marks and rough spots. Don't attempt to restore rocker arms by grinding the pad surfaces. Replace any defective parts.

---

17   Oil pan – removal and installation

Removal

1   Disconnect the negative cable from the battery.
2   Raise the vehicle and support it securely on jackstands.
3   Remove the under-vehicle splash pan.
4   Drain the engine oil and install a new oil filter (see Chapter 1).
5   Unbolt the exhaust pipe from the rear manifold (see Section 8).
6   Support the engine/transaxle securely with a hoist from above or a jack under the bellhousing. Protect the bellhousing by placing a wood block on the jack pad. **Warning:** *Be absolutely certain the engine/transaxle is securely supported! DO NOT place any part of your body under the engine/transaxle – it could crush you if the jack or hoist fails!*
7   Unbolt the engine mounts (see Section 21). Raise the engine/transaxle assembly to provide clearance for oil pan removal.
8   Remove the oil pan bolts.
9   Detach the oil pan. Don't pry between the pan and block or damage to the sealing surfaces may result and oil leaks could develop. If the pan is stuck, dislodge it with a hammer and a block of wood.
10   Use a gasket scraper to remove all traces of old gasket material and sealant from the block and pan. Clean the mating surfaces with lacquer thinner or acetone.
11   Unbolt the oil pick-up tube and screen assembly.

Installation

Refer to illustrations 17.14 and 17.15
12   Replace the gasket on the flange of the oil pick-up tube and reinstall the tube. Tighten the pick-up tube bolts to the torque listed in this Chapter's Specifications.
13   Ensure that the threaded holes in the block are clean (use a tap to remove any sealant or corrosion from the threads).
14   Apply a small amount of RTV sealant (or equivalent) to the oil pump-to-block and rear seal retainer-to-block junctions **(see illustration)** and apply a thin continuous bead along the circumference of the oil pan flange. **Note:** *Allow the sealant to "set-up" (slightly harden) before installing the gasket.*
15   Install the oil pan and tighten the bolts in three or four steps fol-

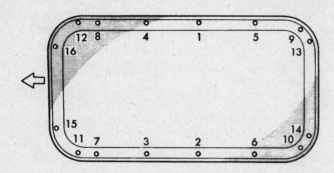

17.15   Oil pan bolt tightening sequence

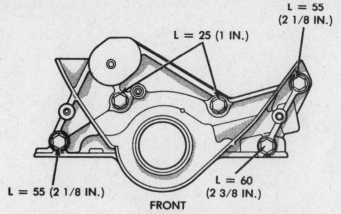

18.3   Be sure to mark the position of each bolt to aid in installation

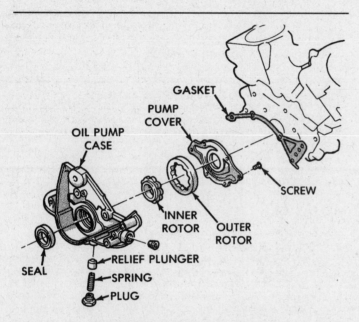

18.7   Exploded view of the oil pump

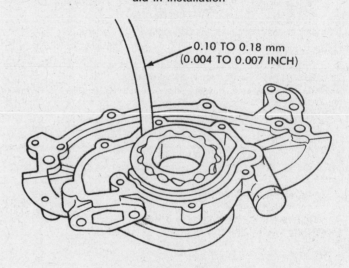

18.10a   Checking case-to-outer rotor clearance with a feeler gauge

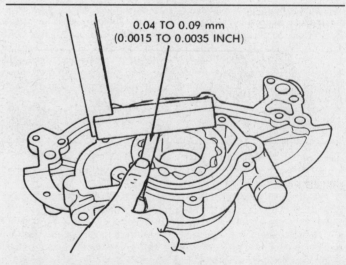

18.10b   Checking rotor end clearance with a straightedge and a feeler gauge

lowing the sequence shown **(see illustration)** to the torque listed in this Chapter's Specifications.

16   The remaining installation steps are the reverse of removal.

17   Allow at least 30 minutes for the sealant to dry. Fill the crankcase with oil (see Chapter 1), start the engine and check for oil pressure and leaks.

18   Oil pump – removal, inspection and installation

Removal

Refer to illustration 18.3

1   Remove the timing belt and the crankshaft sprocket (see Sections 10 and 11). Remove the oil pan and pick-up tube (see Section 17).

2   Unbolt the power steering pump (see Chapter 10) without disconnecting the hoses. Remove the power steering pump bracket.

3   Remove the oil pump-to-engine block bolts from the front of the engine **(see illustration)**.

4   Use a block of wood and a hammer to break the oil pump loose.

5   Pull out on the oil pump to remove it from the engine block.

6   Use a scraper to remove old gasket material and sealant from the oil pump and engine block mating surfaces. Clean the mating surfaces with lacquer thinner or acetone.

Inspection

Refer to illustrations 18.7, 18.10a, 18.10b and 18.10c

7   Remove the screws holding the rear cover to the oil pump **(see**

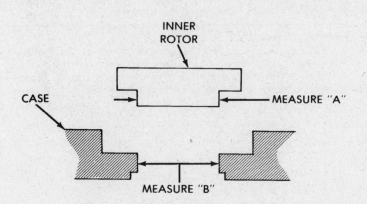

18.10c   Check for excessive clearance between the case and inner rotor

illustration).

8   Clean all components with solvent, then inspect them for wear and damage.

9   Remove the oil pressure relief valve plug, washer, spring and valve (plunger). Check the oil pressure relief valve sliding surface and valve spring. If either the spring or the valve is damaged, they must be replaced as a set.

10   Check the following clearances with a feeler gauge **(see illustrations)** and compare the measurements to the clearances listed in this Chapter's Specifications:

Case-to-outer rotor
Rotor end clearance
Case-to-inner rotor

If any of the clearances are excessive, replace the entire oil pump assembly.

11   Pack the cavities of the oil pump with petroleum jelly to prime it. Assemble the oil pump and tighten the screws to the torque listed in this Chapter's Specifications. Install the oil pressure relief valve, spring and washer, then tighten the oil pressure relief valve plug to the torque listed in this Chapter's Specifications.

Installation

12   Apply a thin film of RTV sealant to the new oil pump gasket.

13   Installation is the reverse of the removal procedure. Align the flats on the crankshaft with the flats in the inner rotor of the oil pump. Tighten all fasteners to the torque values listed in this Chapter's Specifications.

---

19   Flywheel/driveplate – removal and installation

This procedure is essentially the same for all engines. Refer to Part A and follow the procedure outlined there, but use the bolt torque listed in this Chapter's Specifications.

2C

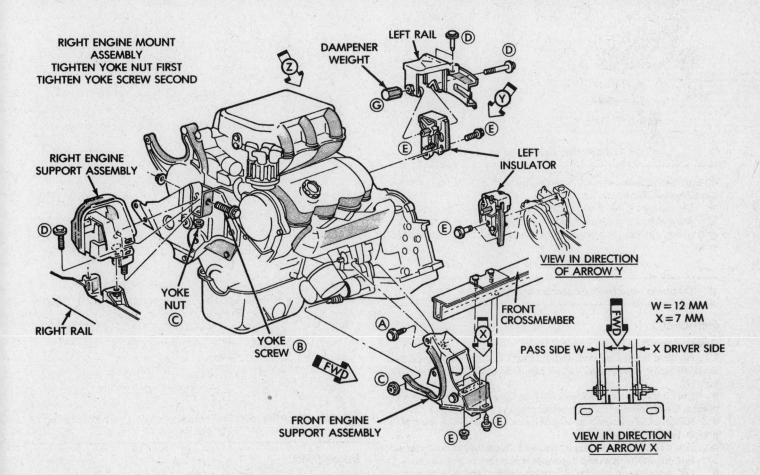

21.1   Exploded view of the engine mounts on the 3.0L engine

20   Rear main oil seal – replacement

This procedure is essentially the same for all engines. Refer to Part A and follow the procedure outlined there.

21   Engine mounts – check and replacement

Refer to illustration 21.1

This procedure is essentially the same for all engines. See Part A of this Chapter and follow the procedure outlined there, but use the torque values listed in this Chapter's Specifications. Use the accompanying exploded view for reference **(see illustration)**.

Chapter 2 Part D 3.3L and 3.8L V6 engines

Contents

Specifications

General

Cylinder numbers (drivebelt end-to-transaxle end)
Front bank (radiator side)	2–4–6
Rear bank	1–3–5
Firing order	1-2-3-4-5-6

Oil pump

Cover warpage limit	0.003 inch
Outer rotor thickness (min)	0.3005 inch
Inner rotor thickness (min)	0.301 inch
Rotor-to-pump cover clearance	0.004 inch
Outer rotor-to-housing clearance	
1992 and earlier	0.022 inch
1993 and later	0.015 inch
Inner rotor-to-outer rotor lobe clearance	0.008 inch

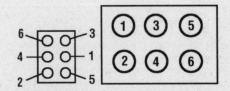

Cylinder and coil terminal locations

Torque specifications

Ft-lbs (unless otherwise indicated)

Camshaft sprocket bolt	40
Crankshaft pulley/vibration damper bolt	40
Cylinder head bolts **(see illustration 9.8 for the tightening sequence)**	
Bolts 1 through 8	
First step	45
Second step	65
Third step	65
Fourth step 1/4 turn clockwise (do not use a torque wrench for this step)	
Bolt 9 (fifth step)	25
Engine mount plate bolts	40
Engine mount bolts **(see illustration 19.1c)**	
A	50
B	100
C	75
D	200 in-lbs
E	40
Exhaust manifold-to-cylinder head bolts	200 in-lbs
Exhaust crossover bolts	25
Flywheel/driveplate-to-crankshaft bolts	50
Hydraulic lifter retaining plate bolts	105 in-lbs
Intake manifold-to-cylinder head bolts/nuts	200 in-lbs
Intake manifold gasket retaining bolts	105 in-lbs
Oil pan drain plug	
1984 through 1993	20
1994 and later	25
Oil pan bolts/nuts	105 in-lbs
Oil pump pick-up tube mounting bolts	250 in-lbs
Oil pump cover (plate) bolts (Torx no. 30)	105 in-lbs
Valve cover-to-cylinder head bolts	105 in-lbs
Rocker arm shaft bolts	250 in-lbs
Timing chain cover bolts	20
Timing chain snubber (guide)	105 in-lbs
Timing chain sprocket-to-camshaft bolt	35
Rear main oil seal retainer bolts	105 in-lbs

1   General information

This Part of Chapter 2 is devoted to in-vehicle repair procedures for the 3.3L and 3.8L V6 engine. This engine utilizes a cast-iron block with six cylinders arranged in a "V" shape at a 60-degree angle between the two banks. The overhead valve aluminum cylinder heads are equipped with replaceable valve guides and seats. Hydraulic roller lifters actuate the valves through tubular pushrods.

All information concerning engine removal and installation and engine block and cylinder head overhaul can be found in Part E of this Chapter. The following repair procedures are based on the assumption the engine is installed in the vehicle. If the engine has been removed from the vehicle and mounted on a stand, many of the steps outlined in this Part of Chapter 2 will not apply.

The Specifications included in this Part of Chapter 2 apply only to the procedures contained in this Part. Part E of Chapter 2 contains the Specifications necessary for cylinder head and engine block rebuilding.

2   Repair operations possible with the engine in the vehicle

Many major repair operations can be accomplished without removing the engine from the vehicle.

Clean the engine compartment and the exterior of the engine with some type of degreaser before any work is done. It'll make the job easier and help keep dirt out of the internal areas of the engine.

Depending on the components involved, it may be helpful to remove the hood to improve access to the engine as repairs are performed (refer to Chapter 11 if necessary). Cover the fenders to prevent damage to the paint. Special pads are available, but an old bedspread or blanket will also work.

If vacuum, exhaust, oil or coolant leaks develop, indicating a need for gasket or seal replacement, the repairs can generally be done with the engine in the vehicle. The intake and exhaust manifold gaskets, timing chain cover gasket, oil pan gasket, crankshaft oil seals and cylinder head gaskets are all accessible with the engine in place.

Exterior engine components, such as the intake and exhaust manifolds, the oil pan, timing chain cover (and the oil pump), the water pump, the starter motor, the alternator and the fuel system components can be removed for repair with the engine in place.

Since the cylinder heads can be removed without pulling the engine, valve component servicing can also be accomplished with the engine in the vehicle. Replacement of the timing chain and sprockets is also possible with the engine in the vehicle.

In extreme cases caused by a lack of necessary equipment, repair or replacement of piston rings, pistons, connecting rods and rod bearings is possible with the engine in the vehicle. However, this practice is not recommended because of the cleaning and preparation work that must be done to the components involved.

3   Top Dead Center (TDC) for number 1 piston – locating

1   Disconnect the cable from the negative terminal of the battery.

2   Remove the valve cover closest to the radiator (see Section 4).

3   Remove the spark plugs (see Chapter 1).

4   Using a socket and ratchet on the crankshaft pulley bolt, turn the crankshaft clockwise until there is play in both of the rocker arms for the number 2 cylinder (the cylinder closest to the right fender). With the engine set at this position, approximate TDC for cylinder number 2 has been found. To bring the engine to TDC (approximate) for cylinder number 1, make a mark on the crankshaft pulley and a corresponding mark on the engine, then turn the crankshaft 120-degrees counterclockwise.

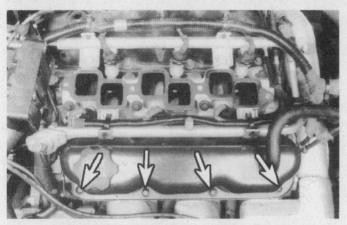

4.3 Remove the front valve cover mounting bolts (arrows) – the air intake plenum has been removed to expose the rear valve cover.

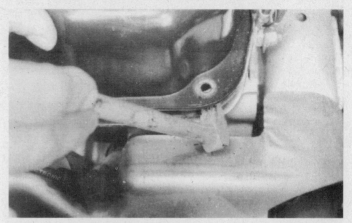

4.4 Be careful not to bend or damage the valve cover or cylinder head when prying

5   This position will be adequate for most operations requiring the engine to be set at TDC, but if exact TDC must be found, a degree wheel and a dial indicator (with the proper spark plug hole adapter) must be obtained.

6   Install the degree wheel on the crankshaft pulley. These can be found at most auto parts stores.

7   Position the engine at TDC (approximate for cylinder number 2 as described in Step 4. Using the proper adapter, install the dial indicator in the number 2 spark plug hole.

8   Slowly turn the crankshaft in a clockwise direction until the dial indicator shows the piston has reached its highest point.

9   Align the zero mark on the degree wheel with the mark made on the engine.

10   Rotate the crankshaft 120-degrees counterclockwise. The engine is now positioned at TDC for cylinder number 1.

11   TDC for any of the remaining cylinders can be located by turning the crankshaft clockwise 120-degrees at a time and following the firing order (see the Specifications at the beginning of this Chapter).

2D

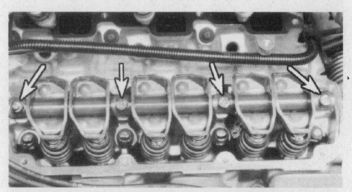

5.2 Remove the rocker arm mounting bolts from the cylinder head – be sure to start with the outer ones first

still won't come loose, pry on it carefully, but don't distort the sealing flange **(see illustration 4.4)**.

Installation

15   The mating surfaces of each cylinder head and valve cover must be perfectly clean when the covers are installed. Use a gasket scraper to remove all traces of sealant or old gasket material, then clean the mating surfaces with lacquer thinner or acetone (if there's sealant or oil on the mating surfaces when the cover is installed, oil leaks may develop). Be extra careful not to nick or gouge the mating surfaces with the scraper.

16   Clean the mounting bolt threads with a die if necessary to remove any corrosion and restore damaged threads. Use a tap to clean the threaded holes in the heads.

17   Place the valve cover and new gasket in position, then install the bolts. Tighten the bolts in several steps to the torque listed in this Chapter's Specifications.

18   Complete the installation by reversing the removal procedure. Start the engine and check carefully for oil leaks.

---

4   Valve covers – removal and installation

Refer to illustrations 4.3 and 4.4

Removal

Front (radiator side) cover

1   Disconnect the negative battery cable from the battery.

2   Remove the ignition wires from the spark plugs (see Chapter 1). Be sure each wire is labeled before removal to ensure correct reinstallation.

3   Remove the valve cover bolts **(see illustration)**.

4   Detach the valve cover. **Note:** *If the cover sticks to the cylinder head, use a block of wood and a hammer to dislodge it. If the cover still won't come loose, pry on it carefully, but don't distort the sealing flange* **(see illustration)**.

Rear (firewall side) cover

5   Disconnect the negative battery cable from the battery.

6   Label and detach the vacuum lines from the throttle body.

7   Remove the serpentine drivebelt (see Chapter 1).

8   Remove the alternator (see Chapter 5).

9   Remove the coil pack (see Chapter 5).

10   Remove the air intake plenum (see Chapter 4).

11   Remove the breather hose from the PCV valve.

12   Remove the ignition wires from the spark plugs (see Chapter 1). Be sure each wire is labeled before removal to ensure correct reinstallation.

13   Remove the valve cover bolts **(see illustration 4.3)**.

14   Detach the valve cover. **Note:** *If the cover sticks to the cylinder head, use a block of wood and a hammer to dislodge it. If the cover*

---

5   Rocker arms and pushrods – removal, inspection and installation

Refer to illustrations 5.2 and 5.3

Removal

1   Refer to Section 4 and remove the valve cover(s).

2   Loosen each rocker arm shaft bolt a little at a time until they are all loose enough to be removed by hand **(see illustration)**. If the

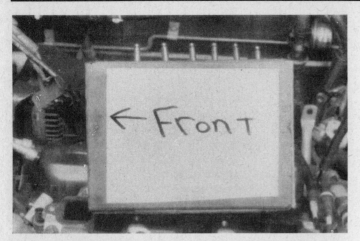

5.3   Place the pushrods in a box that will hold them in order

rocker arms are removed from the shaft, be sure to note how they are positioned.

3   Remove the pushrods and store them in order to make sure they don't get mixed up during installation **(see illustration)**.

Inspection

4   Inspect each rocker arm for wear, cracks and other damage, especially where the pushrods and valve stems make contact.
5   Check each rocker arm pivot area and shaft for wear, cracks and galling. If the rocker arms or shafts are worn or damaged, replace them with new ones.
6   Make sure the hole at the pushrod end of each rocker arm is open.
7   Inspect the pushrods for cracks and excessive wear at the ends. Roll each pushrod across a piece of plate glass to see if it's bent (if it wobbles, it's bent).

Installation

8   Lubricate the lower end of each pushrod with clean engine oil or moly-base grease and install them in their original locations. Make sure each pushrod seats completely in the lifter socket.
9   Apply moly-base grease to the ends of the valve stems and the upper ends of the pushrods.
10   Apply moly-base grease to the rocker arm shaft. Install the rocker arms on the shaft and lower the assembly onto the cylinder head. Tighten the bolts, a little at a time (working from the center out), to the torque listed in this Chapter's Specifications. As the bolts are tightened, make sure the pushrods engage properly in the rocker arms. **Caution:** *Allow the engine to set for 20 minutes before starting.*
11   Install the valve cover(s).

---

6   Valve springs, retainers and seals – replacement

This procedure is essentially the same as the one for the four-cylinder engines. Refer to Chapter 2 Part A, Section 11 and follow the procedure outlined there.

---

7   Intake manifold – removal and installation

Removal

Refer to illustrations 7.6, 7.8a, 7.8b, 7.11a, 7.11b and 7.12
1   Relieve the fuel system pressure (see Chapter 4).
2   Disconnect the negative battery cable from the battery.
3   Remove the air intake plenum, fuel rail and injectors (see Chapter 4). When disconnecting fuel line fittings, be prepared to catch some fuel with a rag, then cap the fittings to prevent contamination.

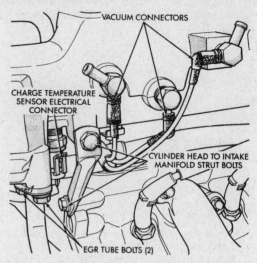

7.6   Remove the cylinder head-to-intake manifold strut

4   Remove the serpentine drivebelt and drain the cooling system (see Chapter 1).
5   Remove the alternator and loosen the bracket (see Chapter 5).
6   Remove the cylinder head-to-intake manifold strut **(see illustration)**.
7   Remove the upper radiator hose (see Chapter 3).
8   Disconnect the heater circulation tube **(see illustration)** and any other coolant hoses attached to the intake manifold **(see illustration)**.
9   Label and disconnect any remaining vacuum lines and wires from the manifold.
10   Remove the coolant temperature sensor with a deep socket in order to gain access to one of the upper intake manifold bolts (see Chapter 4).
11   Remove the intake manifold mounting bolts and separate the manifold from the engine **(see illustration)**. If the manifold is stuck, carefully pry on a casting protrusion – don't pry between the manifold and heads, as damage to the gasket sealing surfaces may result **(see illustration)**. If you're installing a new manifold, transfer all fittings and sensors to the new manifold.
12   Remove the intake manifold gasket retaining bolts **(see illustration)** and clamps and lift the gasket from the engine.

Installation

Refer to illustration 7.15
Note: *The mating surfaces of the cylinder heads, block and manifold must be perfectly clean when the manifold is installed. Gasket removal solvents in aerosol cans are available at most auto parts stores and may be helpful when removing old gasket material that's stuck to the heads and manifold (since the manifold is made of aluminum, aggressive scraping can cause damage). Be sure to follow the directions printed on the container.*

13   Lift the old gasket off. Use a gasket scraper to remove all traces of sealant and old gasket material, then clean the mating surfaces with lacquer thinner or acetone. If there's old sealant or oil on the mating surfaces when the manifold is installed, oil or vacuum leaks may develop. Use a vacuum cleaner to remove any gasket material that falls into the intake ports or the lifter valley.
14   Use a tap of the correct size to chase the threads in the bolt holes, if necessary, then use compressed air (if available) to remove the debris from the holes. **Warning:** *Wear safety glasses or a face shield to protect your eyes when using compressed air!*
15   Apply a 3/16-inch (5 mm) bead of RTV sealant or equivalent to the front and rear ridges of the engine block between the heads **(see illustration)**.
16   Install the intake manifold gasket.
17   Carefully lower the manifold into place and install the mounting bolts/nuts finger tight.

7.8a   Unscrew the heater circulation tube from the intake manifold

7.8b   Disconnect the coolant bypass hose from the intake manifold near the thermostat housing

2D

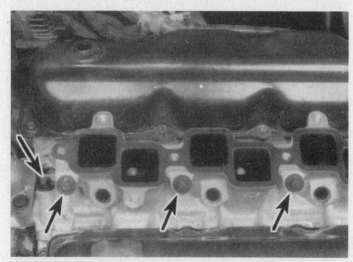

7.11a   Remove the intake manifold bolts using a circular pattern starting with the outer bolts first

7.11b   Pry on the intake manifold only in the areas where the gasket mating surface will not get damaged

7.12   Remove the intake manifold retaining bolts (arrows)

7.15   Apply RTV sealant to the corners of the cylinder head/block and let the sealant "set-up" (slightly harden) before installing the manifold

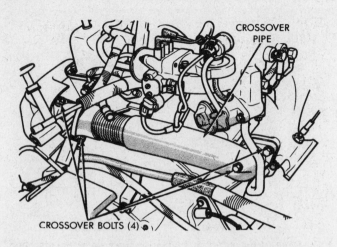

8.4a   Remove the bolts from the crossover pipe

8.4b   The lower bolt for the crossover pipe can be reached from under the engine compartment with an extension and swivel socket

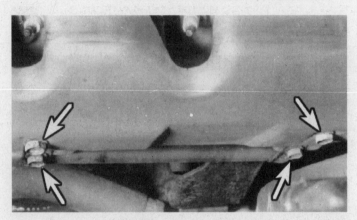

8.5   Remove the four bolts (arrows) to separate the heat shield from the exhaust manifold

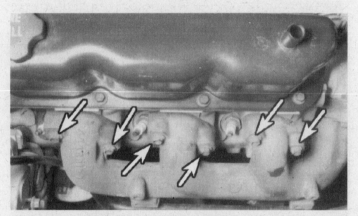

8.6   Remove the exhaust manifold bolts (arrows)

18   Tighten the mounting bolts/nuts in three steps, working from the center out, in a criss-cross pattern, until they're all at the torque listed in this Chapter's Specifications.
19   Install the remaining components in the reverse order of removal.
20   Change the oil and filter and refill the cooling system (see Chapter 1). Start the engine and check for leaks.

8   Exhaust manifold(s) – removal and installation

Front manifold

Refer to illustrations 8.4a, 8.4b, 8.5 and 8.6

1   Disconnect the negative battery cable from the battery.
2   Remove the air cleaner assembly (see Chapter 4).
3   Allow the engine to cool completely, then drain the coolant (see Chapter 1) and disconnect the coolant bypass tube, if necessary.
4   Unbolt the exhaust crossover pipe **(see illustration)** where it joins the front manifold. **Note:** *The lower bolt must be accessed from under the engine compartment* **(see illustration)**.
5   Remove the exhaust manifold heat shield mounting bolts **(see illustration)** and lift the heat shield from the engine.
6   Remove the mounting bolts and detach the manifold from the cylinder head **(see illustration)**. Be sure to spray penetrating lubricant onto the bolts and threads before attempting to remove them.
7   Clean the mating surfaces to remove all traces of old gasket material, then inspect the manifold for distortion and cracks. Warpage can be checked with a precision straightedge held against the mating flange. If a feeler gauge thicker than 0.030-inch can be inserted

between the straightedge and flange surface, take the manifold to an automotive machine shop for resurfacing.
8   Place the exhaust manifold in position with a new gasket and install the mounting bolts finger tight. **Note:** *Be sure to identify the exhaust manifold gaskets by the correct cylinder designation and the position of the exhaust ports on the gasket.*
9   Starting in the middle and working out toward the ends, tighten the mounting bolts a little at a time until all of them are at the torque listed in this Chapter's Specifications.
10   Install the remaining components in the reverse order of removal.
11   Start the engine and check for exhaust leaks between the manifold and cylinder head and between the manifold and exhaust pipe.

Rear manifold

Refer to illustrations 8.13 and 8.14

12   Disconnect the negative battery cable from the battery.
13   Allow the engine to cool completely, then disconnect the EGR tube from the exhaust manifold **(see illustration)**.
14   Remove the heat shield **(see illustration)**.
15   Unbolt the crossover pipe (or front manifold extension pipe) where it joins the rear manifold **(see illustration 8.4a)**.
16   Disconnect the oxygen sensor wire. If you intend to replace the manifold, transfer the sensor to the replacement manifold.
17   Set the parking brake, block the rear wheels and raise the front of the vehicle, supporting it securely on jackstands.
18   Working under the vehicle, remove the two exhaust pipe-to-manifold bolts. You may have to apply penetrating oil to the fastener threads – they're usually corroded.
19   Unbolt and remove the exhaust manifold.
20   Clean the mating surfaces of the cylinder head and manifold,

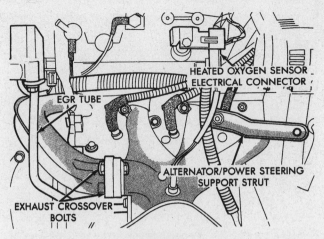

8.13   Disconnect the EGR tube from the exhaust manifold

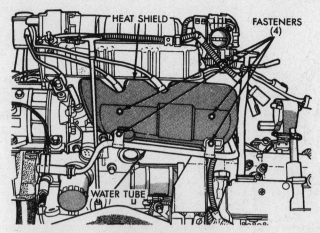

8.14   Remove the mounting bolts from the heat shield attached to the rear manifold

2D

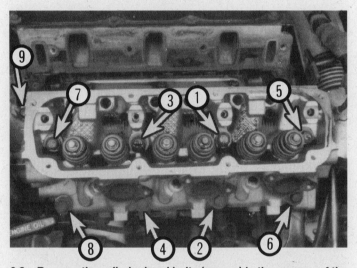

9.8   Remove the cylinder head bolts (arrows) in the reverse of the sequence shown (this is the TIGHTENING sequence)

9.9   Do not pry on the cylinder head near the gasket mating surface – use the corners under the casting protrusions

then check for warpage and cracks. Warpage can be checked with a precision straightedge held against the mating flange. If a feeler gauge thicker than 0.030-inch can be inserted between the straightedge and flange surface, take the manifold to an automotive machine shop for resurfacing.

21   Place the exhaust manifold in position with a new gasket and install the bolts finger tight.

22   Starting in the middle and working out toward the ends, tighten the mounting bolts a little at a time until all of them are at the torque listed in this Chapter's Specifications.

23   Install the remaining components in the reverse order of removal.

24   Start the engine and check for exhaust leaks between the manifold and cylinder head and between the manifold and exhaust pipe.

---

9   Cylinder head(s) – removal and installation

Refer to illustrations 9.8, 9.9, 9.12, 9.15 and 9.17

Caution: *Allow the engine to cool completely before loosening the cylinder head bolts.*

Removal

1   Disconnect the negative battery cable from the battery.

2   Remove the intake manifold as described in Section 7.

3   Disconnect all wires and vacuum hoses from the cylinder head(s). Be sure to label them to simplify reinstallation.

4   Disconnect the ignition wires and remove the spark plugs (see Chapter 1). Be sure the plug wires are labelled to simplify reinstallation.

5   Detach the exhaust manifold from the cylinder head being removed (see Section 8).

6   Remove the valve cover(s) (see Section 4).

7   Remove the rocker arms and pushrods (see Section 5).

8   Using the new head gasket, outline the cylinders and bolt pattern on a piece of cardboard (see Chapter 2A). Be sure to indicate the front (timing chain end) of the engine for reference. Punch holes at the bolt locations. Loosen each of the cylinder head mounting bolts 1/4-turn at a time **(see illustration)** until they can be removed by hand – work from bolt-to-bolt in a pattern that's the reverse of the tightening sequence. Store the bolts in the cardboard holder as they're removed – this will ensure they are reinstalled in their original locations, which is absolutely essential.

9   Lift the head(s) off the engine. If resistance is felt, don't pry between the head and block as damage to the mating surfaces will result. Recheck for head bolts that may have been overlooked, then use a hammer and block of wood to tap up on the head and break the gasket seal **(see illustration)**. Be careful because there are locating dowels in the block which position each head. As a last resort, pry each head up at the rear corner only and be careful not to damage anything. After removal, place the head on blocks of wood to prevent damage to the gasket surfaces.

10   Refer to Chapter 2, Part E, for cylinder head disassembly, inspection and valve service procedures.

9.12   Use a putty knife or gasket scraper to remove the gasket from the cylinder head

9.15   Be sure the stamped designations are facing up and forward

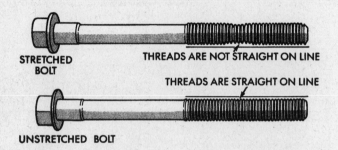

STRETCHED BOLT   THREADS ARE NOT STRAIGHT ON LINE

THREADS ARE STRAIGHT ON LINE

UNSTRETCHED BOLT

9.17   To check a cylinder head bolt for stretching, lay it against a straightedge – if any threads don't contact the straightedge, replace the bolt

10.6   Remove the bolts (arrows) that attach the lifter retaining plate

Installation

11   The mating surfaces of each cylinder head and block must be perfectly clean when the head is installed.

12   Use a gasket scraper to remove all traces of carbon and old gasket material **(see illustration)**, then clean the mating surfaces with lacquer thinner or acetone. If there's oil on the mating surfaces when the head is installed, the gasket may not seal correctly and leaks may develop. When working on the block, it's a good idea to cover the lifter valley with shop rags to keep debris out of the engine. Use a shop rag or vacuum cleaner to remove any debris that falls into the cylinders.

13   Check the block and head mating surfaces for nicks, deep scratches and other damage. If damage is slight, it can be removed with a file; if it's excessive, machining may be the only alternative.

14   Use a tap of the correct size to chase the threads in the head bolt holes. Dirt, corrosion, sealant and damaged threads will affect torque readings.

15   Position the new gasket over the dowel pins in the block. Some gaskets are marked TOP or FRONT to ensure correct installation **(see illustration)**.

16   Carefully position the head on the block without disturbing the gasket.

17   Check the threads of the cylinder head bolts for stretching **(see illustration)**. Replace any bolts that have stretched.

18   Tighten the bolts (numbers 1 through 8) to 45 ft-lbs in the recommended sequence **(see illustration 9.8)**. Next, tighten the bolts to 65 ft-lbs following the same recommended sequence. Tighten the same bolts to the same torque again as a double check. Tighten each bolt (except for number 9) an additional 90-degrees (1/4-turn) following the same sequence. Do not use a torque wrench for this step. **Note:** *After all the head bolts (numbers 1 through 8) have been torqued, tighten head bolt number 9 to 25 ft-lbs.*

19   The remaining installation steps are the reverse of removal.

20   Change the oil and filter (see Chapter 1).

---

10   Hydraulic roller lifters – removal, inspection and installation

---

Refer to illustrations 10.6, 10.7, 10.8, 10.9 and 10.11

1   A noisy valve lifter can be isolated when the engine is idling. Hold a mechanic's stethoscope or a length of hose near the location of each valve while listening at the other end. Another method is to remove the valve cover and, with the engine idling, touch each of the valve spring retainers, one at a time. If a valve lifter is defective, it'll be evident from the shock felt at the retainer each time the valve seats.

2   The most likely causes of noisy valve lifters are dirt trapped inside the lifter and lack of oil flow, viscosity or pressure. Before condemning the lifters, check the oil for fuel contamination, correct level, cleanliness and correct viscosity.

Removal

3   Remove the intake manifold and valve cover(s) as described in Sections 7 and 4.

4   Remove the rocker arms and pushrods (see Section 5).

5   Remove the cylinder heads from the engine block (see Section 9).

6   Remove the retaining plate bolts **(see illustration)** and lift the plate to gain access to the hydraulic roller lifters.

7   Each pair of lifters is retained with an alignment yoke. Lift the yoke from the lifters **(see illustration)**.

8   There are several ways to extract the lifters from the bores. A special tool designed to grip and remove lifters is manufactured by many tool companies and is widely available, but it may not be required in every case. On newer engines without a lot of varnish buildup, the lifters can often be removed with a small magnet or even with your fingers **(see illustration)**. A machinist's scribe with a bent

10.7   Lift off the alignment yokes

10.8   On engines with low mileage, the roller lifters can easily be removed by hand – if the lifters are coated with varnish, a special lifter removal tool may be required

10.9   Store the lifters in a box so each one will be reinstalled in its original bore

10.11   Check the roller for pitting or excessive looseness and the lifter surfaces for gouges, scoring wear or damage (arrows)

11.7a   Use a large screwdriver or prybar wedged into the corner of the bellhousing to lock the driveplate in place

11.7b   Remove the vibration damper bolt (arrow) with a breaker bar and a socket

2D

end can be used to pull the lifters out by positioning the point under the retainer ring in the top of each lifter. **Caution:** *Don't use pliers to remove the lifters unless you intend to replace them with new ones. The pliers may damage the precision machined and hardened lifters, rendering them useless.*

9   Store the lifters in a clearly labelled box to ensure they're reinstalled in their original locations **(see illustration)**.

Inspection

10   Clean the lifters with solvent and dry them thoroughly without mixing them up.

11   Check each lifter wall and pushrod seat for scuffing, score marks and uneven wear. If the lifter walls are damaged or worn inspect the lifter bores in the block **(see illustration)**.

12   Check the roller of each lifter for freedom of movement, excessive looseness, flat spots or pitting. The camshaft must also be inspected if any signs of abnormal wear are indicated. **Note:** *Used roller lifters can be reinstalled with a new camshaft or the original camshaft can be used if new roller lifters are installed, provided the used components are in good condition.*

Installation

13   When reinstalling used lifters, make sure they're replaced in their original bores. Soak new lifters in oil to remove trapped air. Coat all

lifters with moly-base grease or engine assembly lube prior to installation.

14   The remaining installation steps are the reverse of removal. Be sure to tighten the retaining plate bolts to the torque listed in this Chapter's Specifications.

15   Run the engine and check for oil leaks.

11   Crankshaft pulley/vibration damper – removal and installation

Refer to illustrations 11.7a, 11.7b and 11.8

1   Disconnect the negative battery cable from the battery.

2   Loosen the lug nuts on the right front wheel.

3   Raise the vehicle and support it securely on jackstands.

4   Remove the wheel.

5   Remove the right front inner fender splash shield (see Chapter 11).

6   Remove the serpentine drivebelt (see Chapter 1).

7   Remove the driveplate cover and position a large screwdriver in the ring gear teeth to keep the crankshaft from turning **(see illustration)** while an assistant removes the vibration damper-to-crankshaft bolt **(see illustration)**.

8   Pull the damper off the crankshaft with a two-jaw puller **(see**

11.8   Remove the vibration damper with a two-jaw puller

12.2   Be very careful not to damage the crankshaft surface when removing the front seal

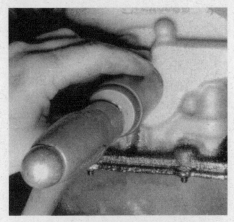

12.3   Use a large deep socket and gently tap the seal into place

illustration).

9   Installation is the reverse of removal. Be sure to apply clean engine oil or multi-purpose grease to the seal contact surface of the damper hub (if it isn't lubricated, the seal lip could be damaged and oil leakage would result).

10   Tighten the vibration damper-to-crankshaft bolt to the torque listed in this Chapter's Specifications.

11   Reinstall the remaining parts in the reverse order of removal.

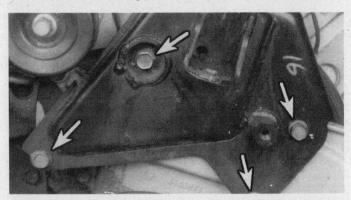

13.8   Remove the bolts (arrows) that retain the engine mounting plate to the engine

13.13   Remove the timing chain cover bolts from the engine (be sure to mark the location of each bolt to aid in proper installation)

12   Crankshaft front oil seal – replacement

Refer to illustrations 12.2 and 12.3

1   Remove the crankshaft pulley/vibration damper (see Section 11).

2   Note how the seal is installed – the new one must be installed to the same depth and facing the same way. Carefully pry the oil seal out of the cover with a seal puller or a large screwdriver **(see illustration)**. Be very careful not to distort the cover or scratch the crankshaft! Wrap tape around the tip of the screwdriver to avoid damage to the crankshaft.

3   Apply clean engine oil or multi-purpose grease to the outer edge of the new seal, then install it in the cover with the lip (spring side) facing IN. Drive the seal into place **(see illustration)** with a large socket and a hammer (if a large socket isn't available, a piece of pipe of the proper diameter will also work). Make sure the seal enters the bore squarely and stop when the front face is at the proper depth.

4   Reinstall the vibration damper.

13   Timing chain cover – removal and installation

Refer to illustrations 13.8 and 13.13

Removal

1   Disconnect the negative battery cable from the battery.

2   Remove the serpentine drivebelt (see Chapter 1).

3   Drain the coolant and remove the water pump pulley (see Chapter 3).

4   Raise the vehicle and support it on jackstands. Drain the engine oil (see Chapter 1).

5   Support the transaxle with a floor jack and a block of wood and remove the engine mount closest to the timing chain (right side) of the engine (see Section 19).

6   Remove the oil pan and the oil pump pick-up tube (see Section 15).

7   Remove the right wheel and inner splash shield (see Chapter 11).

8   Unbolt the idler pulley and remove the engine mounting plate **(see illustration)**.

9   Unbolt the air conditioning compressor from its bracket and set it off to the side. Use some mechanics wire to tie the assembly to the fender to keep it away from the work area (see Chapter 3). **Warning:** *The refrigerant hoses are under pressure – don't disconnect them.*

10   Remove the drivebelt tensioner from the engine.

11   Remove the cam sensor from the timing chain cover (see Chapter 4).

12   Disconnect the canister purge hose from the fenderwell area.

13   Remove the timing chain cover-to-engine block bolts **(see illustration)**. **Note:** *Draw a diagram showing the locations and sizes of the*

14.4 Timing chain details

A Crankshaft TDC mark
B Camshaft TDC mark

C Camshaft
   sprocket bolt

14.11 Be sure the timing chain reference links align with the marks on the sprockets (arrows)

2D

timing cover bolts to aid in installation.

14   Use a gasket scraper to remove all traces of old gasket material and sealant from the cover and engine block. The cover is made of aluminum, so be careful not to nick or gouge it. Clean the gasket sealing surfaces with lacquer thinner or acetone.

Installation

15   Apply a thin film of RTV sealant to both sides of the new gasket, then position the gasket on the engine block. Attach the cover to the block, making sure the flats of the oil pump gear are aligned with the flats on the crankshaft. Install the bolts and tighten them in a crisscross pattern, in three steps, to the torque listed in this Chapter's Specifications.

16   The remainder of installation is the reverse of removal.

17   Add oil and coolant (see Chapter 1), start the engine and check for leaks.

---

14 Timing chain and sprockets – inspection, removal and installation

---

Inspection

1   Remove the timing chain cover (see Section 13).

2   The timing chain should be replaced with a new one if the engine has high mileage, the chain has visible damage, or total freeplay midway between the sprockets exceeds one-inch. Failure to replace a worn timing chain may result in erratic engine performance, loss of power and decreased fuel mileage. Loose chains can "jump" timing. In the worst case, chain "jumping" or breakage will result in severe engine damage.

Removal

Refer to illustration 14.4

3   Remove the timing chain cover (see Section 13).

4   Temporarily install the vibration damper bolt and turn the crankshaft with the bolt to align the timing marks on the crankshaft and camshaft sprockets. The crankshaft arrow should be at the top (12 o'clock position) and the camshaft sprocket arrow should be in the 6 o'clock position **(see illustration)**.

5   Remove the camshaft sprocket bolt. Do not turn the camshaft in the process (if you do, realign the timing marks before the sprocket is removed).

6   Use two large screwdrivers to carefully pry the camshaft sprocket off the camshaft dowel pin.

7   Timing chains and sprockets should be replaced in sets. If you intend to install a new timing chain, remove the crankshaft sprocket with a puller and install a new one. Be sure to align the key in the crankshaft with the keyway in the sprocket during installation.

8   Inspect the timing chain dampener (guide) for cracks and wear and replace it if necessary.

9   Clean the timing chain and sprockets with solvent and dry them with compressed air (if available). **Warning:** *Wear eye protection when using compressed air.*

10   Inspect the components for wear and damage. Look for teeth that are deformed, chipped, pitted and cracked.

Installation

Refer to illustration 14.11

11   Turn the camshaft to position the dowel pin at 6 o'clock, if necessary **(see illustration 14.3)**. Mesh the timing chain with the camshaft sprocket, then engage it with the crankshaft sprocket. The timing marks should be aligned as shown in illustration 14.3. **Note:** *If the crankshaft has been disturbed, turn it until the arrow stamped on the crankshaft sprocket is exactly at the top. If the camshaft was turned, install the sprocket temporarily and turn the camshaft until the sprocket timing mark is at the bottom, opposite the mark on the crankshaft sprocket. The arrows should point to each other. The timing chain reference links should align with the camshaft and crankshaft timing marks that are in the 3 o'clock position* **(see illustration)**. *If you are using factory parts, check this alignment.*

12   Install the camshaft sprocket bolt and tighten it to the torque listed in this Chapter's Specifications.

13   Lubricate the chain and sprocket with clean engine oil. Install the timing chain cover (see Section 13).

14   The remaining installation steps are the reverse of removal.

---

15 Oil pan – removal and installation

Refer to illustrations 15.5a and 15.5b

1   Disconnect the cable from the negative battery terminal.

2   Raise the front of the vehicle and place it securely on jackstands. Apply the parking brake and block the rear wheels to keep it from rolling off the stands. Remove the lower splash pan and drain the engine oil (refer to Chapter 1 if necessary).

3   Remove the lower flywheel/driveplate cover.

4   Remove the starter (see Chapter 5).

5   Remove the bolts and nuts, then carefully separate the oil pan

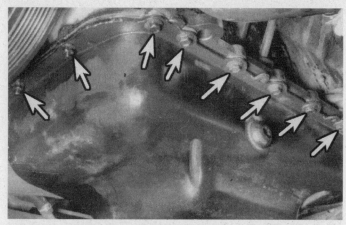

15.5a   Remove the bolts from the oil pan

15.5b   Use a soft faced hammer to loosen the oil pan – be careful
not to dent the pan

16.2   Remove the oil pump cover bolts (arrows) with a
Torx drive socket

16.4   Place a straightedge across the oil pump cover and check
it for warpage with a feeler gauge

from the block **(see illustration)**. Don't pry between the block and the pan or damage to the sealing surfaces could occur and oil leaks may develop. Instead, tap the pan with a soft-face hammer to break the gasket seal **(see illustration)**.

6   Clean the pan with solvent and remove all old sealant and gasket material from the block and pan mating surfaces. Clean the mating surfaces with lacquer thinner or acetone and make sure the bolt holes in the block are clear. Check the oil pan flange for distortion, particularly around the bolt holes. If necessary, place the pan on a block of wood and use a hammer to flatten and restore the gasket surface.

7   Apply a bead of RTV sealant to the bottom surface of the timing chain cover and to the bottom of the rear main oil seal retainer. Install a new gasket on the oil pan flange.

8   Place the oil pan in position on the block and install the nuts/bolts.

9   After the fasteners are installed, tighten them to the torque listed in this Chapter's Specifications. Starting at the center, follow a crisscross pattern and work up to the final torque in three steps.

10   The remaining steps are the reverse of the removal procedure.

11   Refill the engine with oil (see Chapter 1), run it until normal operating temperature is reached and check for leaks.

---

16   Oil pump – removal, check and installation

Refer to illustration 16.2

1   Remove the oil pan (see Section 15).

2   Remove the timing chain cover (see Section 13). Remove the oil pump cover (plate) from the timing chain cover **(see illustration)**.

Check

Refer to illustrations 16.4, 16.6, 16.7, 16.8 and 16.9

3   Clean all parts thoroughly in solvent and carefully inspect the rotors, pump cover and timing chain cover for nicks, scratches or burrs. Replace the assembly if it is damaged.

4   Use a straightedge and measure the oil pump cover for warpage with a feeler gauge **(see illustration)**. If it's warped more than the limit listed in this Chapter's Specifications, the pump should be replaced.

5   Measure the thickness of the outer rotor. If the thickness is less than the value listed in this Chapter's Specifications, the pump should be replaced.

6   Measure the thickness of the inner rotor **(see illustration)**. If the diameter is less than the value listed in this Chapter's Specifications, the pump should be replaced.

7   Insert the outer rotor into the timing chain cover/oil pump housing and measure the clearance between the rotor and housing **(see illustration)**. If the measurement is more than the maximum allowable clearance listed in this Chapter's Specifications, the pump should be replaced.

8   Install the inner rotor in the oil pump assembly and measure the clearance between the lobes on the inner and outer rotors **(see illustration)**. If the clearance is more than the value listed in this Chapter's Specifications, the pump should be replaced. **Note:** *Install the inner rotor with the mark facing up.*

9   Position a straightedge across the face of the oil pump assembly. If the clearance between the pump surface and the rotors is greater than the limit listed in this Chapter's Specifications, the pump should be replaced.

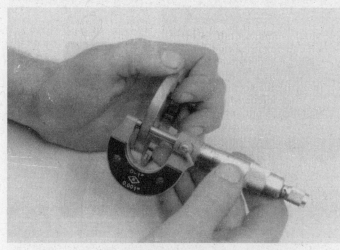

16.6 Use a micrometer to check the thickness of the inner rotor

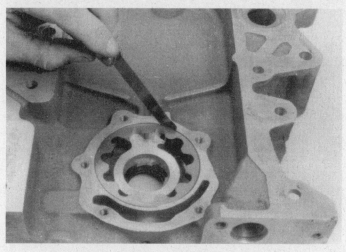

16.7 Check the outer rotor-to-housing clearance

16.8 Check the clearance between the lobes of the inner and outer rotor (arrow)

Installation

10 Install the pump cover and tighten the bolts to the torque listed in this Chapter's Specifications.

11 To install the pump, turn the flats in the rotor so they align with the flats on the crankshaft.

12 Install the timing chain cover (see Section 13) and tighten the bolts to the torque listed in this Chapter's specifications.

13 The remainder of installation is the reverse of removal.

2D

17 Flywheel/driveplate – removal and installation

This procedure is essentially the same for all engines. Refer to Part A and follow the procedure outlined there, but use the bolt torque listed in this Chapter's Specifications.

18 Rear main oil seal – replacement

This procedure is essentially the same for all engines. Refer to Part A and follow the procedure outlined there.

16.9 Using a straightedge and feeler gauges, check the clearance between the surface of the oil pump and the rotors

19.1a Remove the bolt (arrow) to separate the transmission mount from the chassis (the nut can be accessed through a hole behind the wheel assembly)

19.1b Remove the bolt (arrow) to separate the front engine mount from the block – the starter (see Chapter 5) must be removed for access.

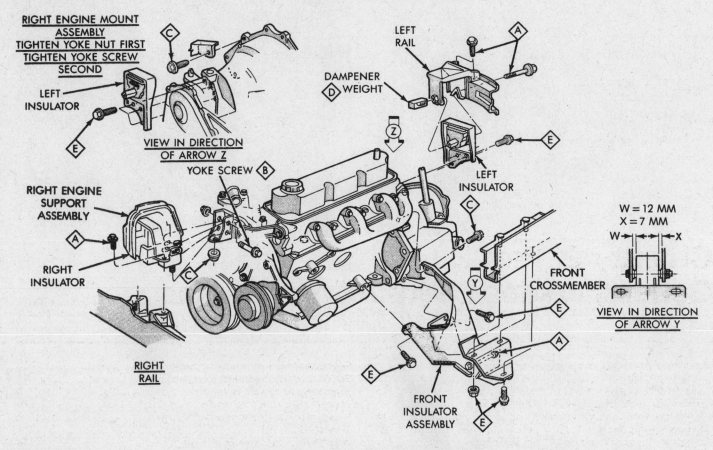

19.1c   Exploded view of the engine mounts

19   Engine mounts – check and replacement

Refer to illustrations 19.1a, 19.1b and 19.1c

This procedure is essentially the same for all engines. Refer to Part A and follow the procedure outlined there, but use the torque values listed in this Chapter's Specifications. Use the accompanying illustrations for reference **(see illustrations)**.

Chapter 2 Part E
General engine overhaul procedures

Contents

Specifications

2.2L and 2.5L engines
General
Displacement
2.2L	135 cubic inches
2.5L	153 cubic inches
Cylinder compression pressure	130 to 150 psi at 250 rpm
Oil pressure (at 3000 rpm)	25 to 80 psi

Engine block
Cylinder taper limit	0.005 inch
Cylinder out-of-round limit	0.002 inch

Pistons and rings
Piston diameter
2.2L engine	3.443 to 3.445 inches
2.5L engine	3.442 to 3.445 inches
2.5L Turbo engine	3.443 to 3.444 inches
Piston-to-bore clearance	0.001 to 0.003 inch

2.2L and 2.5L engines (continued)

Piston ring side clearance
  Non-turbo
    Top compression ring
      Standard .... 0.0015 to 0.0031 inch
      Service limit... 0.004 inch
    Second compression ring
      Standard .... 0.0015 to 0.0037 inch
      Service limit... 0.004 inch
    Oil ring .... 0.008 inch
  Turbo
    Top compression ring
      Standard .... 0.0016 to 0.0030 inch
      Service limit .... 0.004 inch
    Second compression ring
      Standard .... 0.0016 to 0.0035 inch
      Service limit .... 0.004 inch
    Oil ring ... . 0.008 inch
Piston ring end gap
  Non-turbo
    Top compression ring .... 0.010 to 0.020 inch
    Second compression ring .... 0.011 to 0.021 inch
    Oil ring
      Standard .... 0.015 to 0.055 inch
      Service limit .... 0.074 inch
  Turbo
    Top compression ring .... 0.010 to 0.020 inch
    Second compression ring .... 0.009 to 0.019 inch
    Oil ring
      Standard .... 0.015 to 0.055 inch
      Service limit... 0.074 inch

Crankshaft and connecting rods

Endplay
  Standard .... 0.002 to 0.007 inch
  Service limit... 0.014 inch
Main bearing journal
  Diameter .... 2.362 to 2.363 inches
  Taper limit .... 0.0003 inch
  Out-of-round limit . ... 0.0003 inch
Connecting rod journal
  Diameter .... 1.968 to 1.969 inch
  Out-of-round/taper limits .... 0.0003 inch
Main bearing oil clearance
  Standard .... 0.0004 to 0.0028 inch
  Service limit... 0.004 inch
Connecting rod bearing oil clearance
  Standard .... 0.0008 to 0.0034 inch
  Service limit .... 0.004 inch
Connecting rod endplay (side clearance) .... 0.005 to 0.013 inch

Camshaft

Endplay
  Standard .... 0.005 to 0.013 inch
  Service limit .... 0.020 inch

Cylinder head and valves

Head warpage limit .... 0.004 inch
Valve seat angle 45-degrees
Valve face angle 45-degrees
Valve margin width
  Intake
    Standard .... 1/16 inch
    Service limit .... 1/32 inch
  Exhaust
    Standard .... 1/16 inch
    Service limit... 3/64 inch
Valve stem diameter
  Intake .... 0.3124 inch
  Exhaust .... 0.3103 inch

Valve stem-to-guide clearance
    Intake .... 0.0009 to 0.0026 inch
    Exhaust . ... 0.003 to 0.0047 inch
Valve spring free length .... 2.39 inches
Valve spring installed height .... 1.65 inches

Torque specifications*   **Ft-lbs** (unless otherwise indicated)

Main bearing cap bolts .... 30 plus 1/4-turn
Connecting rod bearing cap nuts .... 40 plus 1/4-turn
Counterbalance assembly (2.5L only)
    Double-ended stud and gear cover bolts .... 105 in-lbs
    Crankshaft sprocket bolts .... 130 in-lbs
    Tensioner bolts .... 105 in-lbs
    Guide bolts .... 105 in-lbs
    Balance shaft gear bolt 21

* Note: Refer to Part A for additional torque specifications.

2.6L engine

General

Displacement .... 156 cubic inches
Cylinder compression pressure .... 130 to 150 psi at 250 rpm
Oil pressure (at 3000 rpm) .... 25 to 90 psi

Engine block

Cylinder taper limit .... 0.0008 inch
Cylinder out-of-round limit .... 0.0008 inch

Pistons and rings

Piston diameter .... 3.5866 inches
Piston ring side clearance
    Top compression ring
        Standard .... 0.0024 to 0.0039 inch
        Service limit .... 0.006 inch
    Second compression ring
        Standard .... 0.0008 to 0.0024 inch
        Service limit .... 0.0039 inch
Piston ring end gap
    Top compression ring
        Standard .... 0.010 to 0.018 inch
        Service limit . ... 0.039 inch
    Second compression ring
        Standard .... 0.010 to 0.018 inch
        Service limit .... 0.039 inch
    Oil ring
        Standard .... 0.0078 to 0.0350 inch
        Service limit .... 0.059 inch

Crankshaft and connecting rods

Endplay
    Standard .... 0.002 to 0.007 inch
Main bearing journal
    Diameter .... 2.3622 inches
    Taper limit .... 0.0004 inch
    Out-of-round limit .... 0.0004 inch
Connecting rod journal
    Diameter .... 2.086 inches
    Out-of-round/taper limits .... 0.0003 inch
Main bearing oil clearance
    Standard . ... 0.0008 to 0.0028 inch
    Service limit .... 0.004 inch
Connecting rod bearing oil clearance .... 0.0008 to 0.0028 inch
Connecting rod endplay (side clearance) .... 0.004 to 0.010 inch

Camshaft

Endplay ... . 0.004 to 0.008 inch

Silent shaft

Front bearing journal diameter .... 0.906 inch
Front bearing oil clearance .... 0.0008 to 0.0024 inch

2E

2.6L engine (continued)

Rear bearing journal diameter .... 1.693 inch
Rear bearing oil clearance... 0.0020 to 0.0035 inch

Cylinder head and valves

Head warpage limit .... 0.004 inch
Valve seat angle 45-degrees
Valve face angle 45-degrees
Valve margin width
    Intake
        Standard .... 0.047 inch
        Service limit. .... 0.028 inch
    Exhaust
        Standard .... 0.079 inch
        Service limit .... 0.039 inch
Valve stem-to-guide clearance
    Intake
        Standard .... 0.0012 to 0.0024 inch
        Service limit .... 0.004 inch
    Exhaust
        Standard .... 0.0020 to 0.0035 inch
        Service limit .... 0.006 inch
Valve spring free length
    Standard .... 1.869 inch
    Service limit .... 1.832 inch
Valve spring installed height
    Standard . ... 1.590 inch
    Service limit .... 1.629 inch
Jet valve
    Stem diameter .... 0.1693 inch
    Seat angle.. 45-degrees
    Spring free length .... 1.165 inch
    Spring pressure .... 5.5 lbs. at 0.846 in

Torque specifications*

                                          Ft-lbs (unless otherwise indicated)
Main bearing cap bolts 58
Connecting rod bearing cap nuts 34

* **Note:** *Refer to Part B for additional torque specifications.*

3.0L engine

General

Displacement .... 181 cubic inches
Cylinder compression pressure .... 178 at 250 rpm
Oil pressure .... Not available

Engine block

Cylinder diameter .... 3.586 to 3.587 inches
Cylinder taper limit .... Not available
Cylinder out-of-round limit .... Not available

Pistons and rings

Piston diameter .... 3.585 to 3.586 inches
Piston ring side clearance
    Top compression ring
        Standard .... 0.0020 to 0.0035 inch
        Service limit .... 0.004 inch
    Second compression ring
        Standard .... 0.0008 to 0.0020 inch
        Service limit .... 0.0039 inch
Piston ring end gap
    Top compression ring
        Standard .... 0.012 to 0.018 inch
        Service limit .... 0.032 inch
    Second compression ring
        Standard .... 0.010 to 0.016 inch
        Service limit .... 0.032 inch

Oil ring
  Standard .... 0.012 to 0.035 inch
  Service limit .... 0.040 inch

Crankshaft and connecting rods
Endplay (standard) .... 0.002 to 0.010 inch
Main bearing journal
  Diameter .... 2.361 to 2.362 inches
  Taper limit .... 0.0002 inch
  Out-of-round limit .... 0.001 inch
Connecting rod journal
  Diameter .... 1.968 to 1.969 inch
  Taper limit .... 0.0002 in
  Out-of-round limit .... 0.001 inch
Main bearing oil clearance .... 0.0006 to 0.0020 inch
Connecting rod bearing oil clearance .... 0.0006 to 0.0020 inch
Connecting rod endplay (side clearance)
  Standard .... 0.004 to 0.010 inch
  Service limit .... 0.016 inch

Cylinder head and valves
Head warpage limit .... 0.002 inch
Valve seat angle 45-degrees
Valve face angle 45-degrees
Valve margin width
  Intake
    Standard .... 0.047 inch
    Service limit .... 0.027 inch
  Exhaust
    Standard .... 0.079 inch
    Service limit .... 0.059 inch
Valve stem-to-guide clearance
  Intake
    Standard .... 0.001 to 0.002 inch
    Service limit .... 0.004 inch
  Exhaust
    Standard .... 0.0020 to 0.0030 inch
    Service limit .... 0.006 inch
Valve spring free length
  Standard .... 1.960 inch
  Service limit .... 1.921 inch
Valve spring installed height
  Standard .... 1.590 inch
  Service limit .... Not available
Valve stem diameter
  Intake .... 0.313 to 0.314 inch
  Exhaust .... 0.312 to 0.313 inch

Torque specifications*
Ft-lbs (unless otherwise indicated)
Main bearing cap bolts 60
Connecting rod bearing cap nuts.................................... 34

* **Note:** *Refer to Part C for additional torque specifications.*

3.3L and 3.8L engines

General
Displacement
  3.3L .... 201 cubic inches
  3.8L .... 231 cubic inches
Cylinder compression pressure .... 170 at 250 rpm
Oil pressure .... 30 to 80 psi a 3,000 rpm

Engine block
Cylinder diameter
  3.3L .... 3.660 inches
  3.8L .... 3.779 inches
Cylinder taper limit
  Standard .... 0.002 inch
  Service limit .... 0.001 inch
Cylinder out-of-round limit
  Standard .... 0.003 inch
  Service limit .... 0.001 inch

2E

3.3L and 3.8L engines (continued)

Piston and piston rings

Piston diameter	
3.3L	3.6594 to 3.6602 inches
3.8L	3.7776 to 3.7783 inches
Piston to bore clearance	0.0009 to 0.0022 inch
Piston ring side clearance	
Top compression ring	
Standard	0.0012 to 0.0033 inch
Service limit	0.004 inch
Second compression ring	
Standard	0.0012 to 0.0037 inch
Service limit	0.004 inch
Piston ring end gap	
Top compression ring	
Standard	0.012 to 0.022 inch
Service limit	0.039 inch
Second compression ring	
Standard	0.012 to 0.022 inch
Service limit	0.039 inch
Oil ring	
Standard	0.010 to 0.039 inch
Service limit	0.074 inch

Crankshaft and connecting rods

Endplay (standard)	
1984 to 1992	0.0014 to 0.0073 inch
1993 and later	0.003 to 0.009 inch
Main bearing journal	
Diameter	2.519 inches
Taper limit	0.001 inch
Out-of-round limit	0.001 inch
Connecting rod journal	
Diameter	2.283 inches
Out-of-round/taper limits	0.001 inch
Main bearing oil clearance	
Standard	0.0007 to 0.0022 inch
Service limit	0.0022 inch
Connecting rod bearing oil clearance	
Standard	0.00075 to 0.00300 inch
Service limit	0.003 inch
Connecting rod endplay (side clearance)	
Standard	0.005 to 0.015 inch
Service limit	Not available

Cylinder head and valves

Head warpage limit	0.002 inch
Valve seat angle	45-degrees
Valve face angle	44-1/2 degrees
Valve margin width	
Intake	
Standard	0.031 inch
Service limit	Not available
Exhaust	
Standard	0.047 inch
Service limit	Not available

Camshaft

Endplay	0.005 to 0.012 inch
Lobe lift	0.2678 inch
Camshaft bearing clearance	
Standard	0.001 to 0.004 inch
Service limit	0.005 inch
Camshaft journal diameter	
No. 1	1.997 to 1.999 inch
No. 2	1.980 to 1.982 inch
No. 3	1.965 to 1.967 inch
No. 4	1.949 to 1.952 inch

Camshaft bearing diameter (inside)
  No. 1 .... 2.000 to 2.001 inches
  No. 2 .... 1.984 to 1.985 inch
  No. 3 .... 1.953 to 1.954 inch
  No. 4 .... 1.950 to 1.951 inch
Valve stem-to-guide clearance
  Intake
    Standard .... 0.001 to 0.003 inch
    Service limit .... 0.010 inch
  Exhaust
    Standard .... 0.002 to 0.006 inch
    Service limit .... 0.016 inch
Valve spring free length
  Standard .... 1.909 inch
  Service limit .... Not available
Valve spring installed height (spring seat to retainer)
  Standard .... 1-17/32 to 1-19/32 inch
  Service limit .... Not available
Valve stem diameter
  Intake .... 0.312 to 0.313 inch
  Exhaust .... 0.3112 to 0.3119 inch

Torque specifications*

Ft-lbs (unless otherwise indicated)
Main bearing cap bolts .... 30 plus 1/4-turn
Camshaft thrust plate bolts .... 105 in-lbs
Camshaft sprocket bolt 40
Connecting rod bearing cap nuts .... 40 plus 1/4 -urn

* Note: *Refer to Part D for additional torque specifications.*

---

1 General information

    Included in this portion of Chapter 2 are the general overhaul proce-
dures for the cylinder head(s) and internal engine components.
    The information ranges from advice concerning preparation for an
overhaul and the purchase of replacement parts to detailed, step-by-
step procedures covering removal and installation of internal engine
components and the inspection of parts.
    The following Sections have been written based on the assumption
the engine has been removed from the vehicle. For information concerning in-vehicle engine repair, as well as removal and installation of
the external components necessary for the overhaul, see Part A (2.2L
and 2.5L engine), B (2.6L engine), C (3.0L engine) or D (3.3L and 3.8L
engines) of this Chapter.
    The Specifications included in this Part are only those necessary for
the inspection and overhaul procedures which follow. Refer to Parts A,
B, C and D for additional Specifications.

---

2 Engine overhaul - general information

Refer to illustrations 2.4a, 2.4b, 2.4c, 2.4d and 2.4e

    It's not always easy to determine when, or if, an engine should be
completely overhauled, as a number of factors must be considered.
    High mileage isn't necessarily an indication an overhaul is needed,
while low mileage doesn't preclude the need for an overhaul. Frequency of servicing is probably the most important consideration. An engine that's had regular and frequent oil and filter changes, as well as
other required maintenance, will most likely give many thousands of
miles of reliable service. Conversely, a neglected engine may require
an overhaul very early in its life.
    Excessive oil consumption is an indication that piston rings, valve
seals and/or valve guides are in need of attention. Make sure oil leaks
aren't responsible before deciding the rings and/or guides are bad.
Perform a cylinder compression check to determine the extent of the
work required (see Section 3).
    Remove the oil pressure sending unit and check the oil pressure
with a gauge installed in its place **(see illustrations)**. Compare the results to this Chapter's Specifications. As a general rule, engines
should have ten psi oil pressure for every 1,000 rpm. If the pressure is

2E

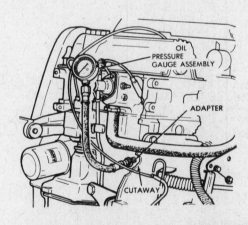

**2.4a   Remove the oil pressure sending unit (switch) and install a
pressure gauge in its place (2.5L engine shown)**

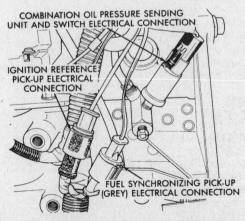

**2.4b   Location of the oil pressure switch on the
2.5L turbo engine**

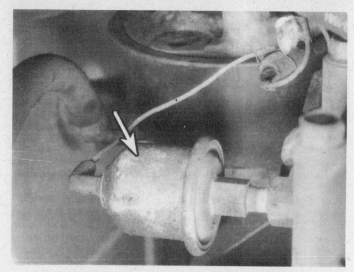

2.4c   Location of the oil pressure switch on 2.6L engines

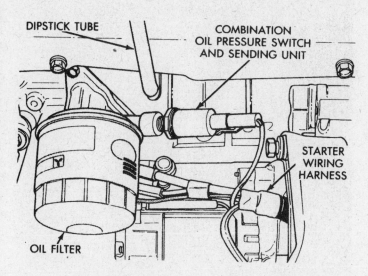

2.4d   Location of the oil pressure switch on 3.0L engines

extremely low, the bearings and/or oil pump are probably worn out.

Loss of power, rough running, knocking or metallic engine noises, excessive valve train noise and high fuel consumption rates may also point to the need for an overhaul, especially if they're all present at the same time. If a complete tune-up doesn't remedy the situation, major mechanical work is the only solution.

An engine overhaul involves restoring the internal parts to the specifications of a new engine. During an overhaul, the piston rings are replaced and the cylinder walls are reconditioned (rebored and/or honed). If a rebore is done by an automotive machine shop, new oversize pistons will also be installed. The main bearings, connecting rod bearings and camshaft bearings are generally replaced with new ones and, if necessary, the crankshaft may be reground to restore the journals. Generally, the valves are serviced as well, since they're usually in less-than-perfect condition at this point. While the engine is being overhauled, other components, such as the starter and alternator, can be rebuilt as well. The end result should be a like new engine that will give many trouble free miles. **Note:** *Critical cooling system components such as the hoses, drivebelts, thermostat and water pump MUST be replaced with new parts when an engine is overhauled. The radiator should be checked carefully to ensure it isn't clogged or leaking (see Chapter 3). Also, we don't recommend overhauling the oil pump - always install a new one when an engine is rebuilt.*

Before beginning the engine overhaul, read through the entire procedure to familiarize yourself with the scope and requirements of the job. Overhauling an engine isn't particularly difficult, if you follow all of the instructions carefully, have the necessary tools and equipment and pay close attention to all specifications; however, it can be time consuming. Plan on the vehicle being tied up for a minimum of two weeks, especially if parts must be taken to an automotive machine shop for repair or reconditioning. Check on availability of parts and make sure any necessary special tools and equipment are obtained in advance. Most work can be done with typical hand tools, although a number of precision measuring tools are required for inspecting parts to determine if they must be replaced. Often an automotive machine shop will handle the inspection of parts and offer advice concerning reconditioning and replacement. **Note:** *Always wait until the engine has been completely disassembled and all components, especially the engine block, have been inspected before deciding what service and repair operations must be performed by an automotive machine shop. Since the block's condition will be the major factor to consider when determining whether to overhaul the original engine or buy a rebuilt one, never purchase parts or have machine work done on other components until the block has been thoroughly inspected. As a general rule, time is the primary cost of an overhaul, so it doesn't pay to install worn*

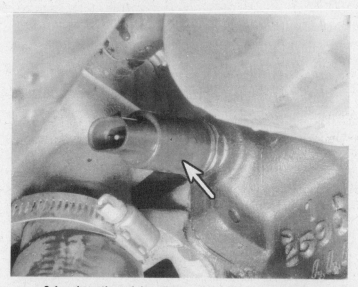

2.4e   Location of the oil pressure switch on 3.3L and 3.8L engines

or substandard parts.

As a final note, to ensure maximum life and minimum trouble from a rebuilt engine, everything must be assembled with care in a spotlessly clean environment.

3   Cylinder compression check

Refer to illustration 3.6

1   A compression check will tell you what mechanical condition the upper end (pistons, rings, valves, head gaskets) of the engine is in. Specifically, it can tell you if the compression is down due to leakage caused by worn piston rings, defective valves and seats or a blown head gasket. **Note:** *The engine must be at normal operating temperature and the battery must be fully charged for this check.*

2   Begin by cleaning the area around the spark plugs before you remove them. Compressed air should be used, if available, otherwise a small brush or even a bicycle tire pump will work. The idea is to pre-

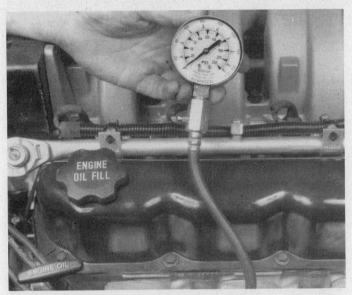

3.6   A compression gauge with a threaded fitting for the spark plug hole is preferred over the type that requires hand pressure to maintain the seal

vent dirt from getting into the cylinders as the compression check is being done.

3   Remove all of the spark plugs from the engine (see Chapter 1).

4   Block the throttle wide open.

5   Disable the fuel and ignition systems by removing the ECM fuse (see Chapter 6).

6   Install the compression gauge in the number one spark plug hole **(see illustration)**.

7   Crank the engine over at least seven compression strokes and watch the gauge. The compression should build up quickly in a healthy engine. Low compression on the first stroke, followed by gradually increasing pressure on successive strokes, indicates worn piston rings. A low compression reading on the first stroke, which doesn't build up during successive strokes, indicates leaking valves or a blown head gasket (a cracked head could also be the cause). Deposits on the undersides of the valve heads can also cause low compression. Record the highest gauge reading obtained.

8   Repeat the procedure for the remaining cylinders and compare the results to this Chapter's Specifications.

9   If the readings are below normal, add some engine oil (about three squirts from a plunger-type oil can) to each cylinder, through the spark plug hole, and repeat the test.

10   If the compression increases after the oil is added, the piston rings are definitely worn. If the compression doesn't increase significantly, the leakage is occurring at the valves or head gasket. Leakage past the valves may be caused by burned valve seats and/or faces or warped, cracked or bent valves.

11   If two adjacent cylinders have equally low compression, there's a strong possibility that the head gasket between them is blown. The appearance of coolant in the combustion chambers or the crankcase would verify this condition.

12   If one cylinder is about 20-percent lower than the others, and the engine has a slightly rough idle, a worn exhaust lobe on the camshaft could be the cause.

13   If the compression is unusually high, the combustion chambers are probably coated with carbon deposits. If that's the case, the cylinder head(s) should be removed and decarbonized.

14   If compression is way down or varies greatly between cylinders, it would be a good idea to have a leak-down test performed by an automotive repair shop. This test will pinpoint exactly where the leakage is occurring and how severe it is.

4   Engine removal - methods and precautions

If you've decided the engine must be removed for overhaul or major repair work, several preliminary steps should be taken.

Locating a suitable place to work is extremely important. Adequate work space, along with storage space for the vehicle, will be needed. If a shop or garage isn't available, at the very least a flat, level, clean work surface made of concrete or asphalt is required.

Cleaning the engine compartment and engine before beginning the removal procedure will help keep tools clean and organized.

An engine hoist or A-frame will also be necessary. Make sure the equipment is rated in excess of the combined weight of the engine and transaxle. Safety is of primary importance, considering the potential hazards involved in lifting the engine out of the vehicle.

If the engine is being removed by a novice, a helper should be available. Advice and aid from someone more experienced would also be helpful. There are many instances when one person cannot simultaneously perform all of the operations required when lifting the engine out of the vehicle.

Plan the operation ahead of time. Arrange for or obtain all of the tools and equipment you'll need prior to beginning the job. Some of the equipment necessary to perform engine removal and installation safely and with relative ease are (in addition to an engine hoist) a heavy duty floor jack, complete sets of wrenches and sockets as described in the front of this manual, wooden blocks and plenty of rags and cleaning solvent for mopping up spilled oil, coolant and gasoline. If the hoist must be rented, be sure to arrange for it in advance and perform all of the operations possible without it beforehand. This will save you money and time.

Plan for the vehicle to be out of use for quite a while. A machine shop will be required to perform some of the work which the do-it-yourselfer can't accomplish without special equipment. These shops often have a busy schedule, so it would be a good idea to consult them before removing the engine in order to accurately estimate the amount of time required to rebuild or repair components that may need work.

Always be extremely careful when removing and installing the engine. Serious injury can result from careless actions. Plan ahead, take your time and a job of this nature, although major, can be accomplished successfully.

5   Engine - removal and installation

Refer to illustrations 5.5, 5.18, 5.23 and 5.26

Warning: *Gasoline is extremely flammable, so take extra precautions when disconnecting any part of the fuel system. Don't smoke or allow open flames or bare light bulbs in or near the work area and don't work in a garage where a natural gas appliance (such as a clothes dryer or water heater) is installed. If you spill gasoline on your skin, rinse it off immediately. Have a fire extinguisher rated for gasoline fires handy and know how to use it! Also, the air conditioning system is under high pressure – have a dealer service department or service station discharge the system before disconnecting any of the hoses or fittings.*

Note: *Read through the following steps carefully and familiarize yourself with the procedure before beginning work.*

Removal

1   If the vehicle is equipped with air conditioning, have the air conditioning system discharged by a dealer service department or service station. (This isn't necessary on most 2.2L and 2.5L models).

2   Refer to Chapter 4 and relieve the fuel system pressure, then disconnect the negative cable from the battery.

3   Cover the fenders and cowl and remove the hood (see Chapter 11). Special pads are available to protect the fenders, but an old bedspread or blanket will also work.

4   Remove the air cleaner assembly (see Chapter 4).

5   Label the vacuum lines, emissions system hoses, wiring connectors, ground straps and fuel lines to ensure correct reinstallation, then

2E

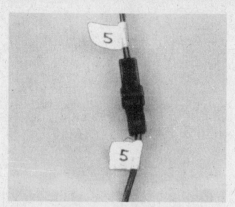

5.5. Label each wire before unplugging the connector

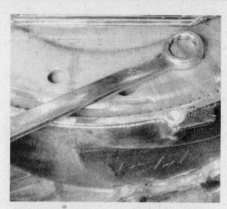

5.18   Use a box end wrench to remove the torque converter bolts

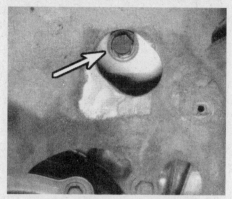

5.23   On models equipped with the 3.3L and 3.8L engines, the transaxle mount is accessed through a hole in the fenderwell (arrow)

5.26   Lift the engine off the mounts and guide it carefully around any obstacles as an assistant raises the hoist until it clears the front of the vehicle

detach them. Pieces of masking tape with numbers or letters written on them work well **(see illustration)**. If there's any possibility of confusion, make a sketch of the engine compartment and clearly label the lines, hoses and wires.

6   Raise the vehicle and support it securely on jackstands. Drain the cooling system (see Chapter 1).

7   Label and detach all coolant hoses from the engine.

8   Remove the coolant reservoir, cooling fan, shroud and radiator (see Chapter 3).

9   Remove the drivebelt(s) and idler, if equipped (see Chapter 1).

10   Disconnect the fuel lines running from the engine to the chassis (see Chapter 4). Plug or cap all open fittings/lines.

11   Disconnect the throttle linkage (and TV linkage/cruise control cable, if equipped) from the engine (see Chapters 4 and 7).

12   Unbolt the power steering pump and set it aside (see Chapter 10). Leave the lines/hoses attached and make sure the pump is kept in an upright position in the engine compartment.

13   Unbolt the air conditioning compressor (see Chapter 3) and set it aside. On 2.2 and 2.5 liter four-cylinder models, do not disconnect the hoses.

14   Drain the engine oil and remove the filter (see Chapter 1).

15   Remove the starter and the alternator (see Chapter 5).

16   Check for clearance and remove the brake master cylinder, if necessary, to allow clearance for the transaxle (see Chapter 9).

17   Disconnect the exhaust system from the engine (see Chapter 4). If the engine is equipped with a turbocharger, be sure to disconnect any lines or hoses that will hinder the removal of the engine.

18   Mark the relationship of the torque converter to the driveplate, then remove the torque converter bolts **(see illustration)**. The bolts are much easier to access at this time before the engine and transaxle

are removed. Do not remove any of the transaxle-to-engine mounting bolts.

19   Support the transaxle with a jack. Position a block of wood on the jack head to prevent damage to the transaxle.

20   Attach an engine sling or a length of chain to the lifting brackets on the engine.

21   Roll the hoist into position and connect the sling to it. Take up the slack in the sling or chain, but don't lift the engine. **Warning:** *DO NOT place any part of your body under the engine when it's supported only by a hoist or other lifting device.*

22   Remove the driveaxles (see Chapter 8).

23   Remove the transaxle-to-body mount through-bolt and pry the mount out of the frame bracket **(see illustration)**. Refer to the appropriate chapter (2A, 2B, 2C or 2D) for complete illustrations of the engine mounts.

24   Remove the engine mount-to-chassis bolts/nuts.

25   Recheck to be sure nothing is still connecting the engine to the vehicle (or transaxle, where applicable). Disconnect anything still remaining.

26   Raise the engine (or engine/transaxle assembly) slightly to disengage the mounts. Slowly raise the engine out of the vehicle **(see illustration)**. Check carefully to make sure nothing is hanging up as the hoist is raised.

27   Once the engine/transaxle assembly is out of the vehicle, lower it to the ground and support it on wood blocks. Remove the transaxle-to-engine block bolts and carefully separate the engine from the transaxle. If you're working on a vehicle with an automatic transaxle, be sure the torque converter stays in place (clamp a pair of vise-grips to the housing to keep the converter from sliding out). If you're working on a vehicle with a manual transaxle, the input shaft must be completely disengaged from the clutch.

28   Remove the clutch and flywheel or driveplate and mount the engine on an engine stand.

Installation

29   Check the engine and transaxle mounts. If they're worn or damaged, replace them.

30   If you're working on a manual transaxle equipped vehicle, install the clutch and pressure plate (see Chapter 7). Now is a good time to install a new clutch. Apply a dab of high-temperature grease to the input shaft.

31   **Caution:** *DO NOT use the transaxle-to-engine bolts to force the transaxle and engine together. If you're working on an automatic transaxle equipped vehicle, take great care when installing the torque converter, following the procedure outlined in Chapter 7.*

32   Carefully lower the engine/transaxle into the engine compartment – make sure the mounts line up. Reinstall the remaining components in the reverse order of removal. Double-check to make sure everything is hooked up right.

33   Add coolant, oil, power steering and transmission fluid as need-ed. If the brake master cylinder was removed, bleed the brakes (see Chapter 9). Recheck the fluid level and test the brakes.
34   Run the engine and check for leaks and proper operation of all accessories, then install the hood and test drive the vehicle.
35   If the air conditioning system was discharged, have it evacuated, recharged and leak tested by the shop that discharged it.

6   Engine rebuilding alternatives

The home mechanic is faced with a number of options when per-forming an engine overhaul. The decision to replace the engine block, piston/connecting rod assemblies and crankshaft depends on a num-ber of factors, with the number one consideration being the condition of the block. Other considerations are cost, access to machine shop facilities, parts availability, time required to complete the project and the extent of prior mechanical experience.

Some of the rebuilding alternatives include:
Individual parts – If the inspection procedures reveal the engine block and most engine components are in reusable condition, pur-chasing individual parts may be the most economical alternative. The block, crankshaft and piston/connecting rod assemblies should all be inspected carefully. Even if the block shows little wear, the cylinder bores should be surface honed.
Short block – A short block consists of an engine block with a crankshaft and piston/connecting rod assemblies already installed. All new bearings are incorporated and all clearances will be correct. The existing camshaft, valve train components, cylinder head(s) and exter-nal parts can be bolted to the short block with little or no machine shop work necessary.
Long block – A long block consists of a short block plus an oil pump, oil pan, cylinder head(s), rocker arm cover(s), camshaft and valve train components, timing sprockets and chain and timing chain cover. All components are installed with new bearings, seals and gaskets incor-porated throughout. The installation of manifolds and external parts is all that's necessary.

Give careful thought to which alternative is best for you and discuss the situation with local automotive machine shops, auto parts dealers and experienced rebuilders before ordering or purchasing replacement parts.

7   Engine overhaul – disassembly sequence

Refer to illustrations 7.5a, 7.5b, 7.5c, 7.5d, 7.5e, 7.5f and 7.5g
1   It's much easier to disassemble and work on the engine if it's mounted on a portable engine stand. A stand can often be rented quite cheaply from an equipment rental yard. Before it's mounted on a stand, the flywheel/driveplate should be removed from the engine.
2   If a stand isn't available, it's possible to disassemble the engine with it blocked up on the floor. Be extra careful not to tip or drop the engine when working without a stand.
3   If you're going to obtain a rebuilt engine, all external components must come off first, to be transferred to the replacement engine, just as they will if you're doing a complete engine overhaul yourself. These include:

Alternator and brackets
Emissions control components
Ignition coil/module assembly, spark plug wires and spark plugs
Thermostat and housing cover
Water pump
EFI components
Intake/exhaust manifolds
Oil filter
Engine mounts
Clutch and flywheel/driveplate

Note: *When removing the external components from the engine, pay close attention to details that may be helpful or important during instal-*

lation. Note the installed position of gaskets, seals, spacers, pins, brackets, washers, bolts and other small items.
4   If you're obtaining a short block, which consists of the engine block, crankshaft, pistons and connecting rods all assembled, then the cylinder head(s), oil pan and oil pump will have to be removed as well. See Engine rebuilding alternatives for additional information regarding the different possibilities to be considered.
5   If you're planning a complete overhaul, the engine must be disas-sembled and the internal components removed in the following gener-al order **(see illustrations):**

2.2 and 2.5 liter four-cylinder engines
Valve cover
Intake/exhaust manifolds
Rocker arm assembly
Hydraulic lash adjusters
Cylinder head
Timing belt cover
Timing belt and sprockets
Camshaft
Oil pan
Oil pump
Piston/connecting rod assemblies
Crankshaft and main bearings

2.6 liter four-cylinder engine
Valve cover
Timing chain housing
Silent shaft chain and sprockets
Timing chain and sprockets
Cylinder head and camshaft
Oil pan
Oil pump
Piston/connecting rod assemblies
Rear main oil seal housing
Crankshaft and main bearings

V6 engines
Valve covers
Exhaust manifolds
Rocker arm assemblies and camshafts (3.0L)
Rocker arms and pushrods (3.3L and 3.8L)
Intake manifold
Valve roller lifters (3.3L and 3.8L)
Cylinder heads
Timing chain/belt cover
Timing chain/belt and sprockets
Camshaft (3.0L)
Oil pan
Oil pump
Piston/connecting rod assemblies
Rear main oil seal housing
Crankshaft and main bearings

6   Before beginning the disassembly and overhaul procedures, make sure the following items are available. Also, refer to Engine over-haul – reassembly sequence for a list of tools and materials needed for engine reassembly.

Common hand tools
Small cardboard boxes or plastic bags for storing parts
Gasket scraper
Ridge reamer
Vibration damper puller
Micrometers
Telescoping gauges
Dial indicator set
Valve spring compressor
Cylinder surfacing hone
Piston ring groove cleaning tool
Electric drill motor
Tap and die set
Wire brushes
Oil gallery brushes

2E

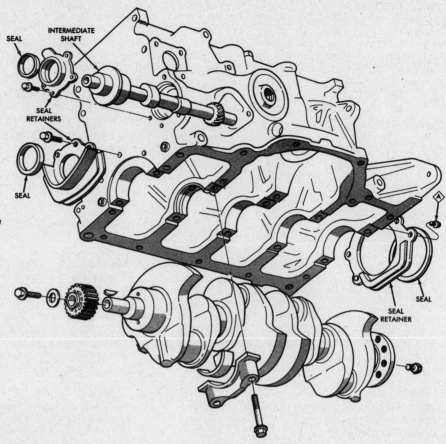

7.5a   Exploded view of the engine block and related components – 2.2L engine

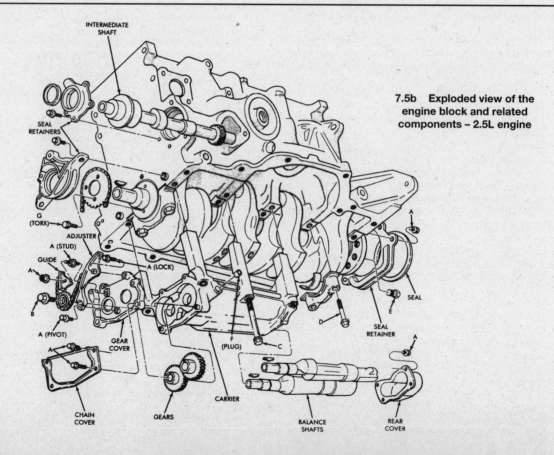

7.5b   Exploded view of the engine block and related components – 2.5L engine

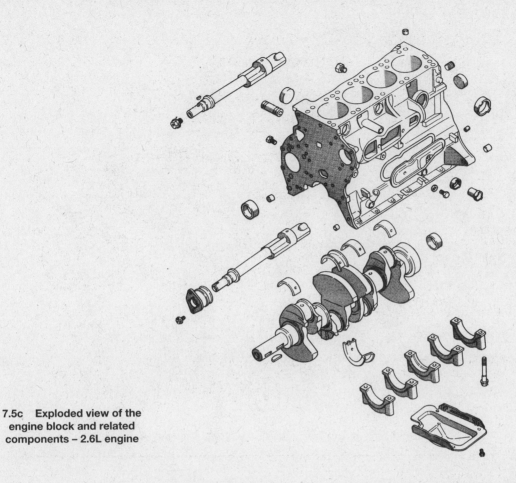

7.5c   Exploded view of the engine block and related components – 2.6L engine

2E

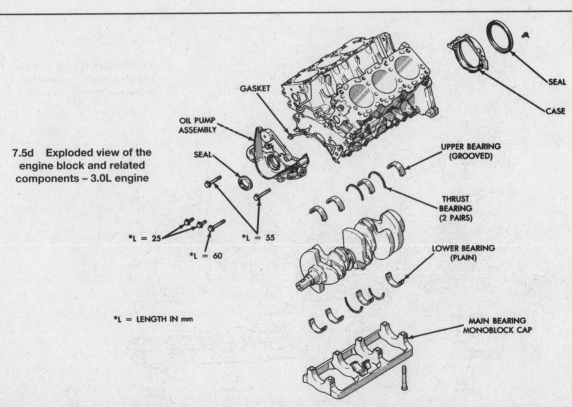

7.5d   Exploded view of the engine block and related components – 3.0L engine

GASKET

OIL PUMP ASSEMBLY

SEAL

SEAL

CASE

*L = 25

*L = 55

*L = 60

*L = LENGTH IN mm

UPPER BEARING (GROOVED)

THRUST BEARING (2 PAIRS)

LOWER BEARING (PLAIN)

MAIN BEARING MONOBLOCK CAP

7.5e   End (timing chain) view of the 3.3L and 3.8L engines

7.5f   Rear side (exhaust manifold) view of the 3.3L and 3.8L engines

7.5g   Front (intake manifold) view of the 3.3L and 3.8L engines

8.2   A small plastic bag, with an appropriate label, can be used to store the valve train components so they can be kept together and reinstalled in the original location

8.3   Use a valve spring compressor to compress the spring, then remove the keepers from the valve stem

8.4   If the valve won't pull through the guide, deburr the edge of the stem end and the area around the top of the keeper groove with a file or whetstone

8   Cylinder head – disassembly

Refer to illustrations 8.2, 8.3 and 8.4

Note: *New and rebuilt cylinder heads are commonly available for most engines at dealerships and auto parts stores. Due to the fact that some specialized tools are necessary for the disassembly and inspection procedures, and replacement parts aren't always readily available, it may be more practical and economical for the home mechanic to purchase replacement head(s) rather than taking the time to disassemble, inspect and recondition the original(s).*

1   Cylinder head disassembly involves removal of the intake and exhaust valves and related components. If you're working on a 2.2L, 2.5L, 2.6L or a 3.0L, the camshafts and housings must be removed before beginning the cylinder head disassembly procedure (see Part A, B or C of this Chapter). Label the parts or store them separately so they can be reinstalled in their original locations.

2   Before the valves are removed, arrange to label and store them, along with their related components, so they can be kept separate and reinstalled in their original locations **(see illustration)**.

3   Compress the springs on the first valve with a spring compressor and remove the keepers **(see illustration)**. Carefully release the valve spring compressor and remove the retainer, the spring and the spring seat (if used).

4   Pull the valve out of the head, then remove the oil seal from the guide. If the valve binds in the guide (won't pull through), push it back into the head and deburr the area around the keeper groove with a fine file or whetstone **(see illustration)**.

5   Repeat the procedure for the remaining valves. Remember to keep all the parts for each valve together so they can be reinstalled in the same locations.

6   Once the valves and related components have been removed and stored in an organized manner, the head should be thoroughly cleaned and inspected. If a complete engine overhaul is being done, finish the engine disassembly procedures before beginning the cylinder head cleaning and inspection process.

9   Cylinder head – cleaning and inspection

1   Thorough cleaning of the cylinder head(s) and related valve train components, followed by a detailed inspection, will enable you to decide how much valve service work must be done during the engine overhaul. **Note:** *If the engine was severely overheated, the cylinder head is probably warped.*

Cleaning

2   Scrape all traces of old gasket material and sealant off the head gasket, intake manifold and exhaust manifold mating surfaces. Be very careful not to gouge the cylinder head. Special gasket removal solvents that soften gaskets and make removal much easier are available at auto parts stores.

3   Remove all built up scale from the coolant passages.

4   Run a stiff wire brush through the various holes to remove deposits that may have formed in them.

5   Run an appropriate size tap into each of the threaded holes to remove corrosion and thread sealant that may be present. If compressed air is available, use it to clear the holes of debris produced by this operation. **Warning:** *Wear eye protection when using compressed air!*

6   Clean the rocker arm bolt threads with a wire brush.

7   Clean the cylinder head with solvent and dry it thoroughly. Compressed air will speed the drying process and ensure that all holes and recessed areas are clean. **Note:** *Decarbonizing chemicals are available and may prove very useful when cleaning cylinder heads and valve train components. They're very caustic and should be used with caution. Be sure to follow the instructions on the container.*

8   Clean the rocker arms, shafts and pushrods (3.3L and 3.8L engines only) with solvent and dry them thoroughly (don't mix them up during the cleaning process). Compressed air will speed the drying process and can be used to clean out the oil passages.

9   Clean all the valve springs, spring seats, keepers and retainers with solvent and dry them thoroughly. Do the components from one valve at a time to avoid mixing up the parts.

10   Scrape off any heavy deposits that may have formed on the valves, then use a motorized wire brush to remove deposits from the valve heads and stems. Again, make sure the valves don't get mixed up.

Inspection

Refer to illustrations 9.12, 9.14, 9.15, 9.16, 9.17 and 9.18

Note: *Be sure to perform all of the following inspection procedures before concluding machine shop work is required. Make a list of the items that need attention.*

Cylinder head

11   Inspect the head very carefully for cracks, evidence of coolant leakage and other damage. If cracks are found, check with an automotive machine shop concerning repair. If repair isn't possible, a new cylinder head should be obtained.

12   Using a straightedge and feeler gauge, check the head gasket mating surface for warpage **(see illustration)**. If the warpage exceeds the limit in this Chapter's Specifications, it can be resurfaced at an automotive machine shop. **Note:** *If the V6 engine heads are resurfaced, the intake manifold flanges will also require machining.*

13   Examine the valve seats in each of the combustion chambers. If they're pitted, cracked or burned, the head will require valve service that's beyond the scope of the home mechanic.

14   Check the valve stem-to-guide clearance by measuring the lateral movement of the valve stem with a dial indicator attached securely to the head **(see illustration)**. The valve must be in the guide and approximately 1/16-inch off the seat. The total valve stem movement indicated by the gauge needle must be divided by two to obtain the actual clearance. After this is done, if there's still some doubt regarding the condition of the valve guides, they should be checked by an automotive machine shop (the cost should be minimal).

Valves

15   Carefully inspect each valve face for uneven wear, deformation, cracks, pits and burned areas. Check the valve stem for scuffing and galling and the neck for cracks. Rotate the valve and check for any obvious indication that it's bent. Look for pits and excessive wear on the end of the stem. The presence of any of these conditions **(see illustration)** indicates the need for valve service by an automotive machine shop.

16   Measure the margin width on each valve **(see illustration)**. Any valve with a margin narrower than specified in this Chapter will have to be replaced with a new one.

Valve components

17   Check each valve spring for wear (on the ends) and pits. Measure the free length and compare it to this Chapter's Specifications **(see illustration)**. Any springs that are shorter than specified have sagged and shouldn't be reused. The tension of all springs should be checked with a special fixture before deciding they're suitable for use in a rebuilt engine (take the springs to an automotive machine shop for this check).

18   Stand each spring on a flat surface and check it for squareness **(see illustration)**. If any of the springs are distorted or sagged, replace all of them with new parts. **Note:** *Because the springs on the 3.3L engine are shaped like a beehive, have any springs that look damaged examined by a qualified machine shop.*

19   Check the spring retainers and keepers for obvious wear and cracks. Any questionable parts should be replaced with new ones, as extensive damage will occur if they fail during engine operation.

Rocker arm components (3.3L and 3.8L V6 engines only)

20   Check the rocker arm faces (the areas that contact the pushrod ends and valve stems) for pits, wear, galling, score marks and rough spots. Check the rocker arm pivot contact areas as well. Look for cracks in each rocker arm and bolt.

21   Inspect the pushrod ends for scuffing and excessive wear. Roll each pushrod on a flat surface, like a piece of plate glass, to determine if it's bent.

22   Check the rocker arm bolt mounts in the cylinder heads for damaged threads and secure installation.

23   Any damaged or excessively worn parts must be replaced with new ones.

All components

24   If the inspection process indicates the valve components are in generally poor condition and worn beyond the limits specified, which is usually the case in an engine that's being overhauled, reassemble the valves in the cylinder head and refer to Section 11 for valve servicing recommendations.

10   Valves – servicing

1   Because of the complex nature of the job and the special tools and equipment needed, servicing of the valves, the valve seats and the valve guides, commonly known as a valve job, should be done by a professional.

2   The home mechanic can remove and disassemble the head, do the initial cleaning and inspection, then reassemble and deliver it to a dealer service department or an automotive machine shop for the actual service work. Doing the inspection will enable you to see what condition the head and valvetrain components are in and will ensure that you know what work and new parts are required when dealing with an automotive machine shop.

3   The dealer service department, or automotive machine shop, will

9.12   Check the cylinder head gasket surface for warpage by trying to slip a feeler gauge under the straightedge (see this Chapter's Specifications for the maximum warpage allowed and use a feeler gauge of that thickness)

9.14   A dial indicator can be used to determine the valve stem-to-guide clearance (move the valve stem as indicated by the arrows)

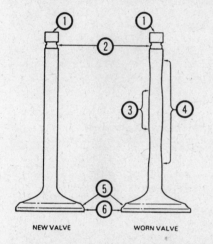

9.15 Check for valve wear at the points shown here

1   *Valve tip*
2   *Keeper groove*
3   *Stem (least worn area)*
4   *Stem (most worn area)*
5   *Valve face*
6   *Margin*

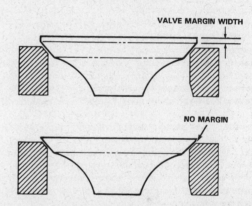

9.16   The margin width on each valve must be as specified (if no margin exists, the valve cannot be reused)

2E

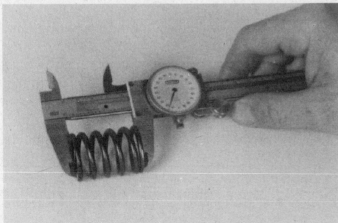

9.17   Measure the free length of each valve spring with a dial or vernier caliper

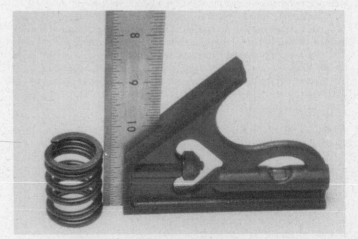

9.18   Check each valve spring for squareness

remove the valves and springs, recondition or replace the valves and valve seats, recondition the valve guides, check and replace the valve springs, rotators, spring retainers and keepers (as necessary), replace the valve seals with new ones, reassemble the valve components and make sure the installed spring height is correct. The cylinder head gasket surface will also be resurfaced if it's warped.

4   After the valve job has been performed by a professional, the head will be in like new condition. When the head is returned, be sure to clean it again before installation on the engine to remove any metal particles and abrasive grit that may still be present from the valve service or head resurfacing operations. Use compressed air, if available, to blow out all the oil holes and passages.

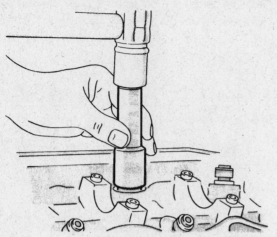

11.4   Make sure the valve stem seals are installed evenly and carefully to avoid damage

11   Cylinder head - reassembly

Refer to illustrations 11.4 and 11.6

1   Regardless of whether or not the head was sent to an automotive repair shop for valve servicing, make sure it's clean before beginning reassembly.

2   If the head was sent out for valve servicing, the valves and related components will already be in place. Begin the reassembly procedure with Step 8.

3   Install the spring seats or valve rotators (if equipped) before the valve seals.

4   Install new seals on each of the valve guides. Using a hammer and a deep socket or seal installation tool, gently tap each seal into place until it's completely seated on the guide **(see illustration)**. Don't twist or cock the seals during installation or they won't seal properly on the valve stems.

5   Beginning at one end of the head, lubricate and install the first valve. Apply moly-base grease or clean engine oil to the valve stem.

6   Position the valve springs (and shims, if used) over the valves. Compress the springs with a valve spring compressor and carefully in-stall the keepers in the groove, then slowly release the compressor and make sure the keepers seat properly. Apply a small dab of grease to each keeper to hold it in place if necessary **(see illustration)**.

7   Repeat the procedure for the remaining valves. Be sure to return the components to their original locations – don't mix them up!

8   Check the installed valve spring height with a ruler graduated in 1/32-inch increments or a dial caliper. If the head was sent out for ser-vice work, the installed height should be correct (but don't automati-cally assume it is). The measurement is taken from the top of each spring seat to the bottom of the retainer. If the height is greater than specified in this Chapter, shims can be added under the springs to correct it. **Caution:** *Do not, under any circumstances, shim the springs to the point where the installed height is less than specified.*

9   Apply moly-base grease to the rocker arm faces and the shaft, then install the rocker arm assembly on the cylinder head.

10   If you're working on an overhead camshaft engine, refer to Part A, B or C and install the camshafts, hydraulic lash adjusters and rocker arm assemblies onto the head.

12   Camshaft and bearings (3.3L and 3.8L engines only) - removal and inspection

Note: *This procedure applies to the 3.3 liter engine only. Since there isn't enough room to remove the camshaft with the engine in the vehi-cle, the engine must be out of the vehicle and mounted on a stand to perform the latter half of this procedure.*

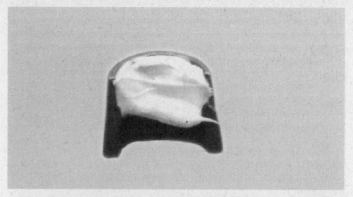

11.6   Apply a small dab of grease to each keeper as shown here before installation – it'll hold them in place on the valve stem as the spring is released

12.3   When checking the camshaft lobe lift, the dial indicator plunger must be positioned directly above and in line with the pushrod

Camshaft lobe lift check

With cylinder head installed

Refer to illustration 12.3

1   In order to determine the extent of cam lobe wear, the lobe lift should be checked prior to camshaft removal. Refer to Part D and re-move the valve cover(s).

2   Position the number one piston at TDC on the compression stroke (see Chapter 2, Part D).

3   Beginning with the number one cylinder valves, mount a dial indi-cator on the engine and position the plunger against the top surface of the first rocker arm. The plunger should be directly above and in line with the pushrod **(see illustration)**.

4   Zero the dial indicator, then very slowly turn the crankshaft in the normal direction of rotation (clockwise) until the indicator needle stops and begins to move in the opposite direction. The point at which it stops indicates maximum cam lobe lift.

5   Record this figure for future reference, then reposition the piston at TDC on the compression stroke.

6   Move the dial indicator to the other number one cylinder rocker arm and repeat the check. Be sure to record the results for each valve.

7   Repeat the check for the remaining valves. Since each piston must be at TDC on the compression stroke for this procedure, work from cylinder-to-cylinder following the firing order sequence.

8   After the check is complete, compare the results to this Chapter's Specifications. If camshaft lobe lift is less than specified, cam lobe wear has occurred and a new camshaft should be installed.

With cylinder head removed

Refer to illustration 12.9

9   If the engine has already been removed, an alternate method of

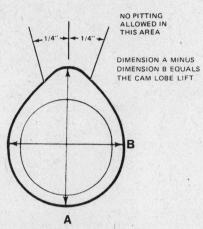

12.9   To verify camshaft lobe lift, measure the major (A) and minor (B) diameters of each lobe with a micrometer or vernier caliper – subtract each minor diameter from the major diameter to arrive at the lobe lift

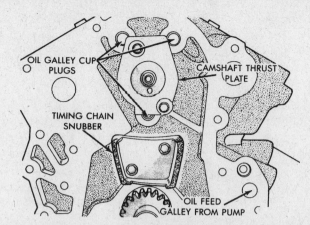

2.12   Remove the thrust plate from the front of the engine

lobe measurement can be used. Remove the camshaft as described below. Using a micrometer, measure the lobe at its highest point. Then measure the base circle perpendicular (90-degrees) to the lobe **(see illustration)**. Do this for each lobe and record the results.
10   Subtract the base circle measurement from the lobe height. The difference is the lobe lift. See Step 8 above.

Removal

Refer to illustrations 12.12

11   Refer to the appropriate Sections in Part D and remove the timing chain and sprockets, lifters and pushrods.
12   Remove the bolts and detach the camshaft thrust plate from the engine block **(see illustration)**.
13   Thread a long bolt into the camshaft sprocket bolt hole to use as a handle when removing the camshaft from the block.
14   Carefully pull the camshaft out. Support the cam near the block so the lobes don't nick or gouge the bearings as it's withdrawn.

Inspection

Refer to illustration 12.16

15   After the camshaft has been removed from the engine, cleaned with solvent and dried, inspect the bearing journals for uneven wear, pitting and evidence of seizure. If the journals are damaged, the bearing inserts in the block are probably damaged as well. Both the camshaft and bearings will have to be replaced.
16   Measure the bearing journals with a micrometer **(see illustration)** to determine if they're excessively worn or out-of-round. Refer to the Specifications in this Chapter for the correct diameter.
17   Check the camshaft lobes for heat discoloration, score marks, chipped areas, pitting and uneven wear. If the lobes and gears are in good condition and if the lobe lift measurements are as specified, the components can be reused.
18   Check the bearings in the block for wear and damage. Look for galling, pitting and discolored areas.
19   The inside diameter of each bearing can be determined with a small hole gauge and outside micrometer or an inside micrometer. Subtract the camshaft bearing journal diameter(s) from the corresponding bearing inside diameter(s) to obtain the bearing oil clearance. If it's excessive, new bearings will be required regardless of the condition of the originals. Check the Specifications listed in this Chapter.
20   Camshaft bearing replacement requires special tools and expertise that place it outside the scope of the home mechanic. Take the block to an automotive machine shop to ensure the job is done correctly.

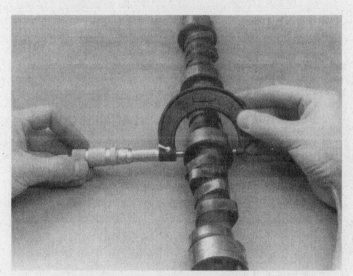

12.16   Check the diameter of each camshaft bearing journal to pinpoint excessive wear and out-of-round conditions

13   Pistons and connecting rods - removal

Refer to illustrations 13.1, 13.3 and 13.6
Note: *Prior to removing the piston/connecting rod assemblies, remove the cylinder head(s), the oil pan and the oil pump by referring to the appropriate Sections in Parts A, B, C or D of Chapter 2.*

1   Use your fingernail to feel if a ridge has formed at the upper limit of ring travel (about 1/4-inch down from the top of each cylinder). If carbon deposits or cylinder wear have produced ridges, they must be completely removed with a special tool **(see illustration)**. Follow the manufacturer's instructions provided with the tool. Failure to remove the ridges before attempting to remove the piston/connecting rod assemblies may result in piston breakage.
2   After the cylinder ridges have been removed, turn the engine upside-down so the crankshaft is facing up.
3   Before the connecting rods are removed, check the endplay with feeler gauges. Slide them between the first connecting rod and the crankshaft throw until the play is removed **(see illustration)**. The endplay is equal to the thickness of the feeler gauge(s). If the endplay exceeds the service limit, new connecting rods will be required. If new rods (or a new crankshaft) are installed, the endplay may fall under the minimum specified in this Chapter (if it does, the rods will have to be machined to restore it – consult an automotive machine shop for advice if necessary). Repeat the procedure for the remaining connecting rods.
4   Check the connecting rods and caps for identification marks. If

2E

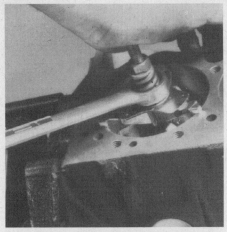

13.1   A ridge reamer is required to remove the ridge from the top of each cylinder – do this before removing the pistons!

13.3   Check the connecting rod side clearance with a feeler gauge as shown

13.6   To prevent damage to the crankshaft journals and cylinder walls, slip sections of rubber or plastic hose over the rod bolts before removing the pistons

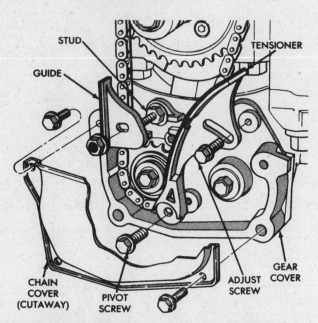

14.2   Chain cover, guide and tensioner - exploded view

they aren't plainly marked, use a small center punch to make the appropriate number of indentations on each rod and cap (1, 2, 3, etc., depending on the engine type and cylinder they're associated with).

5   Loosen each of the connecting rod cap nuts 1/2-turn at a time until they can be removed by hand. Remove the number one connecting rod cap and bearing insert. Don't drop the bearing insert out of the cap.

6   Slip a short length of plastic or rubber hose over each connecting rod cap bolt to protect the crankshaft journal and cylinder wall as the piston is removed **(see illustration)**.

7   Remove the bearing insert and push the connecting rod/piston assembly out through the top of the engine. Use a wooden or plastic hammer handle to push on the upper bearing surface in the connecting rod. If resistance is felt, double-check to make sure all of the ridge was removed from the cylinder.

8   Repeat the procedure for the remaining cylinders.

9   After removal, reassemble the connecting rod caps and bearing inserts in their respective connecting rods and install the cap nuts finger tight. Leaving the old bearing inserts in place until reassembly will help prevent the connecting rod bearing surfaces from being accidentally nicked or gouged.

10   Don't separate the pistons from the connecting rods (see Section 19 for additional information).

---

14   Counterbalance shafts (2.5L engine only) - removal, installation and chain tensioning

Note: *The counterbalance shafts can be removed only after the engine has been removed from the vehicle. It's assumed the flywheel or driveplate, timing belt, oil pan and oil pump (see Chapter 2, Part A) and piston/connecting rod assemblies have already been removed.*

Removal

Refer to illustrations 14.2, 14.3, 14.4 and 14.5

1   The balance shafts are installed in a carrier that is mounted to the lower block **(see illustration 7.5b)**. The shafts are interconnected through two gears rotating them in opposite directions. These gears are driven by a chain from the crankshaft and they are geared to rotate twice the crankshaft speed. This motion will counterbalance certain reciprocating masses within the engine.

2   Remove the chain cover, guide and tensioner from the engine block **(see illustration)**.

3   Remove the balance shaft gear and chain sprocket retaining bolts (Torx) that retain the crankshaft sprocket **(see illustration)**. Remove the chain and sprocket assembly.

4   Remove the special stud (double-ended) from the gear cover and remove the cover and balance shaft gears **(see illustration)**.

5   Remove the rear cover from the carrier and remove the balance shafts **(see illustration)**.

6   Remove the six bolts that retain the carrier to the crankcase.

Installation

Refer to illustrations 14.8 and 14.11

7   Install the balance shafts into the carrier.

8   Turn the balance shafts until both shaft keyways face up **(see illustration)**. Install the short hub drive gear on the sprocket driven shaft and the long hub gear on the gear driven shaft.

9   Install the gear cover and tighten the double-ended stud to the torque listed in this Chapter's Specifications.

10   Install the crankshaft sprocket and tighten the bolts (Torx) to the torque listed in this Chapter's Specifications.

11   Turn the crankshaft until number one is at Top Dead Center (TDC) (see Chapter 2A). The timing marks on the chain sprocket should line up with the parting line on the left side of number one main bearing

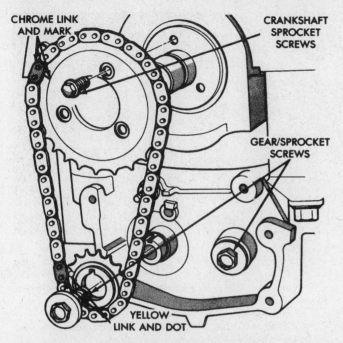

14.3   Note the location of the timing marks and the colored links before removing the assembly

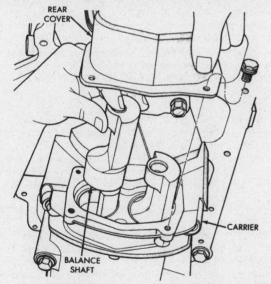

14.5   Remove the balance shafts from the carrier

cap (see illustration).

12   Place the chain over the crankshaft sprocket so that the nickel plated link of the chain is over the timing mark on the crankshaft sprocket.

13   Install the balance shaft sprocket into the chain so that the timing mark on the sprocket (yellow dot) mates with the yellow painted link on the chain.

14   With the balance shaft keyways pointing up, slide the balance shaft sprocket onto the end of the balance shaft. Note: The timing mark on the sprocket, the painted link and the arrow on the side of the gear cover should line up if the balance shafts are correctly timed.

15   Install the balance shaft bolts and tighten the bolts to the torque listed in this Chapter's Specifications. Note: Place a block of wood between the crankcase and the counterbalance crankshaft to prevent any gear rotation while tightening the bolts.

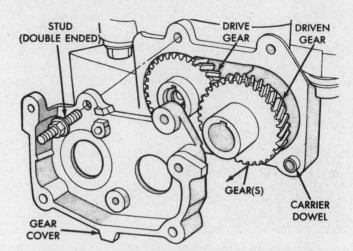

14.4   Remove the gear cover - note the different sized hubs on each balance shaft

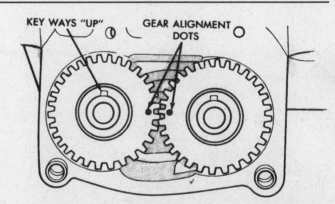

14.8   Note the position of the keyways and the alignment marks on the gears

2E

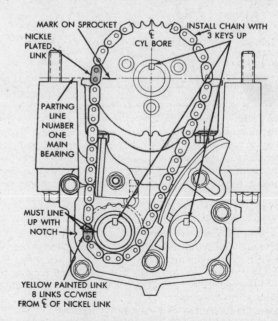

14.11   The mark on the crankshaft sprocket, the colored chain links and the mark on the counterbalance sprocket must be aligned for correct timing

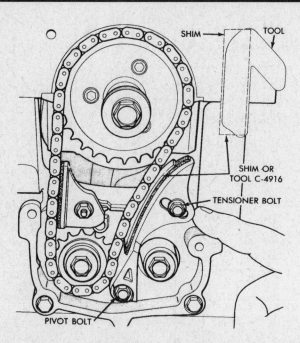

14.16   Apply tension to the chain directly behind the adjustment bolt on the tensioner

15.3   Checking the crankshaft endplay with a feeler gauge

Chain tensioning

Refer to illustration 14.16

16   Install the chain tensioner loosely. Place a shim (0.039 X 2.75 inch) between the tensioner and the chain (see illustration) or a special tool (no. C#4916) if available. Push the tensioner up against the chain. Apply firm pressure directly behind the adjustment slot to take up all the slack.

17   With the load applied, tighten the top tensioner bolt first then the bottom pivot bolt. Tighten the bolts to the torque listed in this Chapter's Specifications. Remove the shim tool.

18   Place the chain guide onto the double ended stud making sure the tab on the guide fits into the slot on the gear cover. Tighten the bolt to the torque listed in this Chapter's Specifications.

19   Install the carrier covers and tighten the bolts to the torque listed in this Chapter's Specifications.

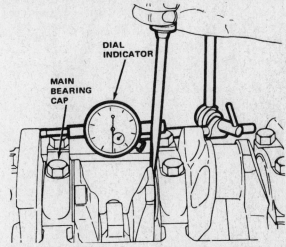

15.1   Checking crankshaft endplay with a dial indicator

15   Crankshaft - removal

Refer to illustrations 15.1, 15.3, 15.4a, 15.4b and 15.4c

Note: *The crankshaft can be removed only after the engine has been removed from the vehicle. It's assumed the flywheel or driveplate, crankshaft balancer/vibration damper, timing chain or belt, oil pan, oil pump, counterbalance shafts (if equipped) and piston/connecting rod assemblies have already been removed. The rear main oil seal housing must be unbolted and separated from the block before proceeding with crankshaft removal.*

1   Before the crankshaft is removed, check the endplay. Mount a dial indicator with the stem in line with the crankshaft, touching one of the crank throws (see illustration).

2   Push the crankshaft all the way to the rear and zero the dial indicator. Next, pry the crankshaft to the front as far as possible and check the reading on the dial indicator. The distance it moves is the endplay. If it's greater than the value listed in this Chapter's Specifications, check the crankshaft thrust surfaces for wear. If no wear is evident, new main bearings should correct the endplay.

3   If a dial indicator isn't available, feeler gauges can be used. Gently pry or push the crankshaft all the way to the front of the engine. Slip feeler gauges between the crankshaft and the front face of the thrust main bearing to determine the clearance (see illustration).

4   Check the main bearing caps to see if they're marked to indicate their locations. They should be numbered consecutively from the front of the engine to the rear. If they aren't, mark them with number stamping dies or a center-punch (see illustrations). Main bearing caps generally have a cast-in arrow, which points to the front of the engine (see illustration). Loosen the main bearing cap bolts 1/4-turn at a time each, until they can be removed by hand. Note if any stud bolts are used and make sure they're returned to their original locations when the crankshaft is reinstalled.

5   Gently tap the caps with a soft-face hammer, then separate them from the engine block. If necessary, use the bolts as levers to remove the caps. Try not to drop the bearing inserts if they come out with the caps.

6   Carefully lift the crankshaft out of the engine. It may be a good idea to have an assistant available, since the crankshaft is quite heavy. With the bearing inserts in place in the engine block and main bearing caps, return the caps to their respective locations on the engine block and tighten the bolts finger tight.

16   Engine block - cleaning

Refer to illustrations 16.4, 16.8 and 16.10

1   Remove the main bearing caps and separate the bearing inserts

15.4a   Use a center-punch or number stamping dies to mark the main bearing caps to ensure installation in their original locations on the block (make the punch marks near one of the head bolts)

15.4b   The main bearing cap numerals (arrows) are easily visible on the 3.3L and 3.8L engines

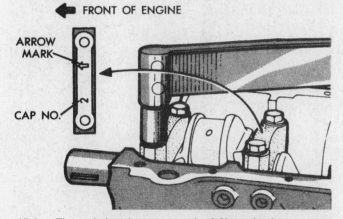

15.4c   The main bearing caps on the 2.6L engine have arrows that point to the front of the engine

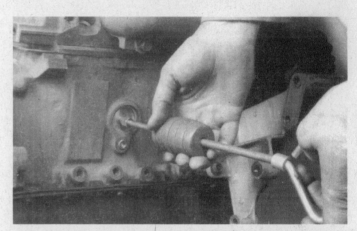

16.4   The core plugs should be removed with a puller – if they're driven into the block, they may be impossible to retrieve

2E

from the caps and the engine block. Tag the bearings, indicating which cylinder they were removed from and whether they were in the cap or the block, then set them aside.

2   Using a gasket scraper, remove all traces of gasket material from the engine block. Be very careful not to nick or gouge the gasket sealing surfaces.

3   Remove all of the covers and threaded oil gallery plugs from the block. The plugs are usually very tight   - they may have to be drilled out and the holes retapped. Use new plugs when the engine is reassembled.

4   Drill a small hole in the center of each core plug and pull them out with an auto body type dent puller **(see illustration)**. **Caution:** *The core plugs (also known as freeze or soft plugs) may be difficult or impossible to retrieve if they're driven into the block coolant passages.*

5   If the engine is extremely dirty, it should be taken to an automotive machine shop to be steam cleaned or hot tanked.

6   After the block is returned, clean all oil holes and oil galleries one more time. Brushes specifically designed for this purpose are available at most auto parts stores. Flush the passages with warm water until the water runs clear, dry the block thoroughly and wipe all machined surfaces with a light, rust preventive oil. If you have access to compressed air, use it to speed the drying process and blow out all the oil holes and galleries. **Warning:** *Wear eye protection when using compressed air!*

7   If the block isn't extremely dirty or sludged up, you can do an adequate cleaning job with hot soapy water and a stiff brush. Take plenty

16.8   All holes in the block – particularly the main bearing cap and head bolt holes – should be cleaned and restored with a tap (be sure to remove debris from the holes after this is done)

of time and do a thorough job. Regardless of the cleaning method used, be sure to clean all oil holes and galleries very thoroughly, dry the block completely and coat all machined surfaces with light oil.

8   The threaded holes in the block must be clean to ensure accurate torque readings during reassembly. Run the proper size tap into each of the holes to remove rust, corrosion, thread sealant or sludge and restore damaged threads **(see illustration)**. If possible, use compressed

16.10   A large socket on an extension can be used to drive the new core plugs into the bores

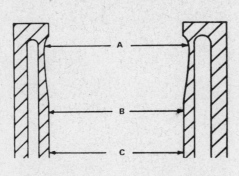

17.4a   Measure the diameter of each cylinder just under the wear ridge (A), at the center (B) and at the bottom

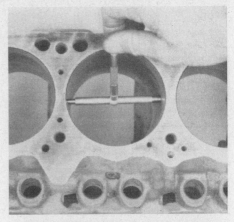

17.4b   The ability to "feel" when the telescoping gauge is at the correct point will be developed over time, so work slowly and repeat the check until you're satisfied the bore measurement is accurate

air to clear the holes of debris produced by this operation. Now is a good time to clean the threads on the head bolts and the main bearing cap bolts as well.

9   Reinstall the main bearing caps and tighten the bolts finger tight.

10   After coating the sealing surfaces of the new core plugs with Permatex no. 2 sealant, install them in the engine block **(see illustration)**. Make sure they're driven in straight and seated properly or leakage could result. Special tools are available for this purpose, but a large socket, with an outside diameter that will just slip into the core plug, a 1/2-inch drive extension and a hammer will work just as well.

11   Apply non-hardening sealant (such as Permatex no. 2 or Teflon pipe sealant) to the new oil gallery plugs and thread them into the holes in the block. Make sure they're tightened securely.

12   If the engine isn't going to be reassembled right away, cover it with a large plastic trash bag to keep it clean.

17   Engine block – inspection

Refer to illustrations 17.4a, 17.4b and 17.4c

1   Before the block is inspected, it should be cleaned as described in Section 16.

2   Visually check the block for cracks, rust and corrosion. Look for stripped threads in the threaded holes. It's also a good idea to have the block checked for hidden cracks by an automotive machine shop that has the special equipment to do this type of work. If defects are found, have the block repaired, if possible, or replaced.

3   Check the cylinder bores for scuffing and scoring.

4   Measure the diameter of each cylinder at the top (just under the ridge area), center and bottom of the cylinder bore, parallel to the crankshaft axis **(see illustrations)**. **Note:** *These measurements should not be made with the bare block mounted on an engine stand – the cylinders will be distorted and the measurements will be inaccurate.*

5   Next, measure each cylinder's diameter at the same three locations across the crankshaft axis. Compare the results to this Chapter's Specifications.

6   If the required precision measuring tools aren't available, the piston-to-cylinder clearances can be obtained, though not quite as accurately, using feeler gauge stock. Feeler gauge stock comes in 12-inch lengths and various thicknesses and is generally available at auto parts stores.

7   To check the clearance, select a feeler gauge and slip it into the cylinder along with the matching piston. The piston must be positioned exactly as it normally would be. The feeler gauge must be between the piston and cylinder on one of the thrust faces (90-degrees to the piston pin bore).

8   The piston should slip through the cylinder (with the feeler gauge in place) with moderate pressure.

9   If it falls through or slides through easily, the clearance is excessive and a new piston will be required. If the piston binds at the lower end of the cylinder and is loose toward the top, the cylinder is tapered. If tight spots are encountered as the piston/feeler gauge is rotated in the cylinder, the cylinder is out-of-round.

10   Repeat the procedure for the remaining pistons and cylinders.

11   If the cylinder walls are badly scuffed or scored, or if they're out-of-round or tapered beyond the limits given in this Chapter's Specifications, have the engine block rebored and honed at an automotive machine shop. If a rebore is done, oversize pistons and rings will be required.

12   If the cylinders are in reasonably good condition and not worn to the outside of the limits, and if the piston-to-cylinder clearances can be maintained properly, they don't have to be rebored. Honing is all that's necessary (see Section 18).

18   Cylinder honing

Refer to illustrations 18.3a and 18.3b

1   Prior to engine reassembly, the cylinder bores must be honed so the new piston rings will seat correctly and provide the best possible combustion chamber seal. **Note:** *If you don't have the tools or don't want to tackle the honing operation, most automotive machine shops will do it for a reasonable fee.*

2   Before honing the cylinders, install the main bearing caps and tighten the bolts to the torque listed in this Chapter's Specifications.

3   Two types of cylinder hones are commonly available   - the flex hone or "bottle brush" type and the more traditional surfacing hone with spring-loaded stones. Both will do the job, but for the less experienced mechanic the "bottle brush" hone will probably be easier to use. You'll also need some honing oil (kerosene will work if honing oil isn't available), rags and an electric drill motor. Proceed as follows:

   a)   Mount the hone in the drill motor, compress the stones and slip it into the first cylinder **(see illustration)**. Be sure to wear safety goggles or a face shield!

   b)   Lubricate the cylinder with plenty of honing oil, turn on the drill and move the hone up-and-down in the cylinder at a pace that will produce a fine crosshatch pattern on the cylinder walls. Ideally, the crosshatch lines should intersect at approximately a 60-degree angle **(see illustration)**. Be sure to use plenty of lubricant and don't take off any more material than is absolutely necessary to produce the desired finish. **Note:** *Piston ring manufacturers may specify a smaller crosshatch angle than the traditional 60-degrees – read and follow any*

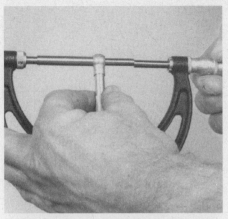

17.4c   The gauge is then measured with a micrometer to determine the bore size

18.3a   A "bottle brush" hone will produce better results if you've never honed cylinders before

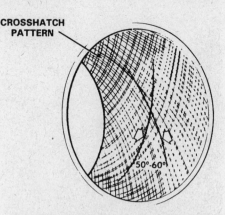

18.3b   The cylinder hone should leave a smooth, crosshatch pattern with the lines intersecting at approximately a 60-degree angle

19.4a   The piston ring grooves can be cleaned with a special tool, as shown here, . . .

19.4b   . . . or a section of a broken ring

2E

instructions included with the new rings.

   c)   Don't withdraw the hone from the cylinder while it's running. Instead, shut off the drill and continue moving the hone up-and-down in the cylinder until it comes to a complete stop, then compress the stones and withdraw the hone. If you're using a "bottle brush" type hone, stop the drill motor, then turn the chuck in the normal direction of rotation while withdrawing the hone from the cylinder.

   d)   Wipe the oil out of the cylinder and repeat the procedure for the remaining cylinders.

4   After the honing job is complete, chamfer the top edges of the cylinder bores with a small file so the rings won't catch when the pistons are installed. Be very careful not to nick the cylinder walls with the end of the file.

5   The entire engine block must be washed again very thoroughly with warm, soapy water to remove all traces of the abrasive grit produced during the honing operation. **Note:** *The bores can be considered clean when a lint-free white cloth – dampened with clean engine oil – used to wipe them out doesn't pick up any more honing residue, which will show up as gray areas on the cloth.* Be sure to run a brush through all oil holes and galleries and flush them with running water.

6   After rinsing, dry the block and apply a coat of light rust preventive oil to all machined surfaces. Wrap the block in a plastic trash bag to keep it clean and set it aside until reassembly.

---

19   Pistons and connecting rods – inspection

Refer to illustrations 19.4a, 19,4b, 19.10 and 19.11

1   Before the inspection process can be carried out, the piston/con-

necting rod assemblies must be cleaned and the original piston rings removed from the pistons. **Note:** *Always use new piston rings when the engine is reassembled.*

2   Using a piston ring installation tool, carefully remove the rings from the pistons. Be careful not to nick or gouge the pistons in the process.

3   Scrape all traces of carbon from the top of the piston. A hand held wire brush or a piece of fine emery cloth can be used once the majority of the deposits have been scraped away. Do not, under any circumstances, use a wire brush mounted in a drill motor to remove deposits from the pistons. The piston material is soft and may be eroded away by the wire brush.

4   Use a piston ring groove cleaning tool to remove carbon deposits from the ring grooves. If a tool isn't available, a piece broken off the old ring will do the job. Be very careful to remove only the carbon deposits – don't remove any metal and do not nick or scratch the sides of the ring grooves **(see illustrations)**.

5   Once the deposits have been removed, clean the piston/rod assemblies with solvent and dry them with compressed air (if available). **Warning:** *Wear eye protection. Make sure the oil return holes in the back sides of the ring grooves are clear.*

6   If the pistons and cylinder walls aren't damaged or worn excessively, and if the engine block isn't rebored, new pistons won't be necessary. Normal piston wear appears as even vertical wear on the piston thrust surfaces and slight looseness of the top ring in its groove. New piston rings, however, should always be used when an engine is rebuilt.

7   Carefully inspect each piston for cracks around the skirt, at the pin bosses and at the ring lands.

8   Look for scoring and scuffing on the thrust faces of the skirt,

19.10   Check the ring side clearance with a feeler gauge at several points around the groove

19.11   Measure the piston diameter at a 90-degree angle to the piston pin and in line with it

20.1   The oil holes should be chamfered so sharp edges don't gouge or scratch the new bearings

holes in the piston crown and burned areas at the edge of the crown. If the skirt is scored or scuffed, the engine may have been suffering from overheating and/or abnormal combustion, which caused excessively high operating temperatures. The cooling and lubrication systems should be checked thoroughly. A hole in the piston crown is an indication that abnormal combustion (preignition) was occurring. Burned areas at the edge of the piston crown are usually evidence of spark knock (detonation). If any of the above problems exist, the causes must be corrected or the damage will occur again. The causes may include intake air leaks, incorrect fuel/air mixture, low octane fuel, ignition timing and EGR system malfunctions.

9   Corrosion of the piston, in the form of small pits, indicates coolant is leaking into the combustion chamber and/or the crankcase. Again, the cause must be corrected or the problem may persist in the rebuilt engine.

10   Measure the piston ring side clearance by laying a new piston ring in each ring groove and slipping a feeler gauge in beside it **(see illustration)**. Check the clearance at three or four locations around each groove. Be sure to use the correct ring for each groove – they are different. If the side clearance is greater than specified in this Chapter, new pistons will have to be used.

11   Check the piston-to-bore clearance by measuring the bore (see Section 17) and the piston diameter. Make sure the pistons and bores are correctly matched. Measure the piston across the skirt, at a 90-degree angle to the piston pin **(see illustration)**. The measurement must be taken at a specific point, depending on the engine type, to be accurate.

   a)   The piston diameter on 2.2L four-cylinder engines is measured in line with the piston pin centerline, 1.14 inches (28.9 mm) below the top of the piston. On 2.5L engines, piston diameter is measured slightly below centerline with the piston pin.

   b)   2.6L engine pistons are measured 0.080 inches (2.0 mm) above the bottom of the piston skirt.

   c)   3.0L V6 engine pistons are measured 0.080 inches (2.0 mm) above the bottom of the piston skirt. 3.3L V6 engine pistons are measured 1.65 inches (42 mm) below the top of the piston. 3.8L V6 engine pistons are measured 1.42 inches (36 mm) below the top of the piston.

12   Subtract the piston diameter from the bore diameter to obtain the clearance. If it's greater than specified, the block will have to be rebored and new pistons and rings installed.

13   Check the piston-to-rod clearance by twisting the piston and rod in opposite directions. Any noticeable play indicates excessive wear, which must be corrected. The piston/connecting rod assemblies should be taken to an automotive machine shop to have the pistons and rods resized and new pins installed.

14   If the pistons must be removed from the connecting rods for any reason, they should be taken to an automotive machine shop. While they are there have the connecting rods checked for bend and twist,

since automotive machine shops have special equipment for this purpose. **Note:** *Unless new pistons and/or connecting rods must be installed, do not disassemble the pistons and connecting rods.*

15   Check the connecting rods for cracks and other damage. Temporarily remove the rod caps, lift out the old bearing inserts, wipe the rod and cap bearing surfaces clean and inspect them for nicks, gouges and scratches. After checking the rods, replace the old bearings, slip the caps into place and tighten the nuts finger tight. **Note:** *If the engine is being rebuilt because of a connecting rod knock, be sure to install new rods.*

20   Crankshaft - inspection

Refer to illustrations 20.1, 20.2, 20.4, 20.6 and 20.8

1   Remove all burrs from the crankshaft oil holes with a stone, file or scraper **(see illustration)**.

2   Clean the crankshaft with solvent and dry it with compressed air (if available). **Warning:** *Wear eye protection when using compressed air. Be sure to clean the oil holes with a stiff brush* **(see illustration)** *and flush them with solvent.*

3   Check the main and connecting rod bearing journals for uneven wear, scoring, pits and cracks.

4   Rub a penny across each journal several times **(see illustration)**. If a journal picks up copper from the penny, it's too rough and must be reground.

5   Check the rest of the crankshaft for cracks and other damage. It should be magnafluxed to reveal hidden cracks – an automotive machine shop will handle the procedure.

6   Using a micrometer, measure the diameter of the main and connecting rod journals and compare the results to this Chapter's Specifications **(see illustration)**. By measuring the diameter at a number of points around each journal's circumference, you'll be able to determine whether or not the journal is out-of-round. Take the measurement at each end of the journal, near the crank throws, to determine if the journal is tapered.

7   If the crankshaft journals are damaged, tapered, out-of-round or worn beyond the limits given in the Specifications, have the crankshaft reground by an automotive machine shop. Be sure to use the correct size bearing inserts if the crankshaft is reconditioned.

8   Check the oil seal journals at each end of the crankshaft for wear and damage. If the seal has worn a groove in the journal, or if it's nicked or scratched **(see illustration)**, the new seal may leak when the engine is reassembled. In some cases, an automotive machine shop may be able to repair the journal by pressing on a thin sleeve. If repair isn't feasible, a new or different crankshaft should be installed.

9   Refer to Section 21 and examine the main and rod bearing inserts.

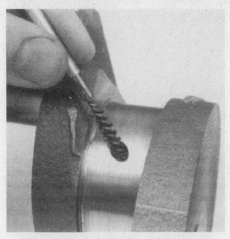

20.2   Use a wire or stiff plastic bristle brush to clean the oil passages in the crankshaft

20.4   Rubbing a penny lengthwise on each journal will reveal its condition – if copper rubs off and is embedded in the crankshaft, the journals should be reground

20.6   Measure the diameter of each crankshaft journal at several points to detect taper and out-of-round conditions

20.8   If the seals have worn grooves in the crankshaft journals, or if the seal contact surfaces are nicked or scratched, the new seals will leak

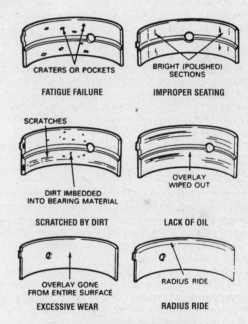

CRATERS OR POCKETS

BRIGHT (POLISHED) SECTIONS

FATIGUE FAILURE

IMPROPER SEATING

SCRATCHES

OVERLAY WIPED OUT

DIRT IMBEDDED INTO BEARING MATERIAL

SCRATCHED BY DIRT

LACK OF OIL

OVERLAY GONE FROM ENTIRE SURFACE

RADIUS RIDE

EXCESSIVE WEAR

RADIUS RIDE

21.1   Typical bearing failures

21   Main and connecting rod bearings – inspection

Refer to illustration 21.1

1   Even though the main and connecting rod bearings should be replaced with new ones during the engine overhaul, the old bearings should be retained for close examination, as they may reveal valuable information about the condition of the engine **(see illustration)**.

2   Bearing failure occurs because of lack of lubrication, the presence of dirt or other foreign particles, overloading the engine and corrosion. Regardless of the cause of bearing failure, it must be corrected before the engine is reassembled to prevent it from happening again.

3   When examining the bearings, remove them from the engine block, the main bearing caps, the connecting rods and the rod caps and lay them out on a clean surface in the same general position as their location in the engine. This will enable you to match any bearing problems with the corresponding crankshaft journal.

4   Dirt and other foreign particles get into the engine in a variety of ways. It may be left in the engine during assembly, or it may pass through filters or the PCV system. It may get into the oil, and from there into the bearings. Metal chips from machining operations and normal engine wear are often present. Abrasives are sometimes left in engine components after reconditioning, especially when parts aren't thoroughly cleaned using the proper cleaning methods. Whatever the source, these foreign objects often end up embedded in the soft bear-

ing material and are easily recognized. Large particles won't embed in the bearing and will score or gouge the bearing and journal. The best prevention for this cause of bearing failure is to clean all parts thoroughly and keep everything spotlessly clean during engine assembly. Frequent and regular engine oil and filter changes are also recommended.

5   Lack of lubrication (or lubrication breakdown) has a number of interrelated causes. Excessive heat (which thins the oil), overloading (which squeezes the oil from the bearing face) and oil leakage or throw off (from excessive bearing clearances, worn oil pump or high engine speeds) all contribute to lubrication breakdown. Blocked oil passages, which usually are the result of misaligned oil holes in a bearing shell, will also oil starve a bearing and destroy it. When lack of lubrication is the cause of bearing failure, the bearing material is wiped or extruded from the steel backing of the bearing. Temperatures may increase to the point where the steel backing turns blue from overheating.

6   Driving habits can have a definite effect on bearing life. Full throttle, low speed operation (lugging the engine) puts very high loads on bearings, which tends to squeeze out the oil film. These loads cause

2E

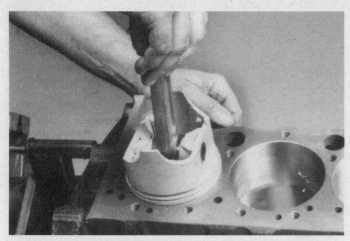

23.3   When checking piston ring end gap, the ring must be square in the cylinder bore (this is done by pushing the ring down with the top of a piston as shown)

the bearings to flex, which produces fine cracks in the bearing face (fatigue failure). Eventually the bearing material will loosen in pieces and tear away from the steel backing. Short trip driving leads to corrosion of bearings because insufficient engine heat is produced to drive off the condensed water and corrosive gases. These products collect in the engine oil, forming acid and sludge. As the oil is carried to the engine bearings, the acid attacks and corrodes the bearing material.

7   Incorrect bearing installation during engine assembly will lead to bearing failure as well. Tight fitting bearings leave insufficient oil clearance and will result in oil starvation. Dirt or foreign particles trapped behind a bearing insert result in high spots on the bearing which lead to failure.

22   Engine overhaul – reassembly sequence

1   Before beginning engine reassembly, make sure you have all the necessary new parts, gaskets and seals as well as the following items on hand:

    Common hand tools
    Torque wrench (1/2-inch drive)
    Piston ring installation tool
    Piston ring compressor
    Vibration damper installation tool
    Short lengths of rubber or plastic hose to fit over connecting
        rod bolts
    Plastigage
    Feeler gauges
    Fine-tooth file
    New engine oil
    Engine assembly lube or moly-base grease
    Gasket sealant
    Thread locking compound

2   In order to save time and avoid problems, engine reassembly must be done in the following general order:

2.2 and 2.5 liter four-cylinder engines
    Crankshaft and main bearings
    Rear main oil seal housing
    Piston/connecting rod assemblies
    Balance shafts (if equipped)
    Oil pump
    Timing belt and sprockets
    Timing belt cover
    Oil pan
    Cylinder head, camshaft, pushrods and rocker arms

    Intake/exhaust manifolds
    Valve cover
    Engine rear plate (if equipped)
    Flywheel/driveplate

2.6 liter four-cylinder engine
    Crankshaft and main bearings
    Rear main oil seal housing
    Piston/connecting rod assemblies
    Oil pump
    Oil pan
    Timing chain housing
    Timing chain and sprockets
    Silent shaft chain and sprockets
    Cylinder head and camshaft
    Intake and exhaust manifolds
    Valve cover
    Flywheel/driveplate

3.0 V6 engine
    Crankshaft and main bearings
    Rear main oil seal housing
    Piston/connecting rod assemblies
    Oil pump
    Oil pan
    Timing belt cover
    Timing belt and sprockets
    Cylinder heads and camshafts
    Intake and exhaust manifolds
    Valve covers
    Flywheel/driveplate

3.3L and 3.8L V6 engines
    Crankshaft and main bearings
    Rear main oil seal housing
    Piston/connecting rod assemblies
    Oil pump
    Camshaft
    Timing chain and sprockets
    Timing chain cover
    Oil pan
    Cylinder heads
    Valve lifters
    Rocker arms and pushrods
    Intake and exhaust manifolds
    Valve covers

23   Piston rings - installation

Refer to illustrations 23.3, 23.4, 23.5, 23.9a, 23.9b and 23.12

1   Before installing the new piston rings, the ring end gaps must be checked. It's assumed the piston ring side clearance has been checked and verified correct (see Section 19).

2   Lay out the piston/connecting rod assemblies and the new ring sets so the ring sets will be matched with the same piston and cylinder during the end gap measurement and engine assembly.

3   Insert the top (number one) ring into the first cylinder and square it up with the cylinder walls by pushing it in with the top of the piston **(see illustration)**. The ring should be near the bottom of the cylinder, at the lower limit of ring travel. **Note:** *On 3.3L and 3.8L engines, the measurement should be taken at least 0.50 inches (12.0 mm) from the bottom of the cylinder bore.*

4   To measure the end gap, slip feeler gauges between the ends of the ring until a gauge equal to the gap width is found **(see illustration)**. The feeler gauge should slide between the ring ends with a slight amount of drag. Compare the measurement to this Chapter's Specifications. If the gap is larger or smaller than specified, double-check to make sure you have the correct rings before proceeding.

5   If the gap is too small, it must be enlarged or the ring ends may come in contact with each other during engine operation, which can

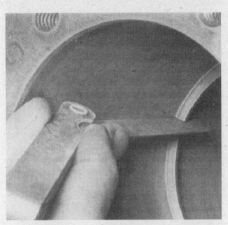

23.4 With the ring square in the cylinder, measure the end gap with a feeler gauge

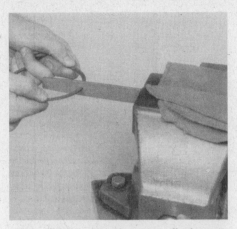

23.5 If the end gap is too small, clamp a file vise and file the ring ends (from the outside in only) to enlarge the gap slightly

23.9a Installing the spacer/expander in the oil control ring groove

23.9b DO NOT use a piston ring installation tool when installing the oil ring side rails

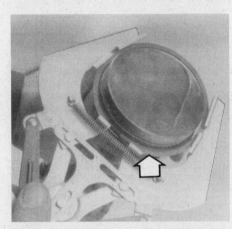

23.12 Installing the compression rings with a ring expander – the mark (arrow) must face up

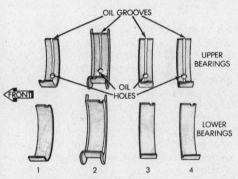

24.3a The thrust bearing is located on the number 2 journal on the 3.3L engine

cause serious engine damage. The end gap can be increased by filing the ring ends very carefully with a fine file. Mount the file in a vise equipped with soft jaws, slip the ring over the file with the ends contacting the file teeth and slowly move the ring to remove material from the ends. When performing this operation, file only from the outside in **(see illustration)**.

6   Excess end gap isn't critical unless it's greater than 0.040-inch. Again, double-check to make sure you have the correct rings for the engine.

7   Repeat the procedure for each ring that will be installed in the first cylinder and for each ring in the remaining cylinders. Remember to keep rings, pistons and cylinders matched up.

8   Once the ring end gaps have been checked/corrected, the rings can be installed on the pistons.

9   The oil control ring (lowest one on the piston) is usually installed first. It's composed of three separate components. Slip the spacer/expander into the groove **(see illustration)**. If an anti-rotation tang is used, make sure it's inserted into the drilled hole in the ring groove. Next, install the lower side rail. Don't use a piston ring installation tool on the oil ring side rails, as they may be damaged. Instead, place one end of the side rail into the groove between the spacer/expander and the ring land, hold it firmly in place and slide a finger around the piston while pushing the rail into the groove **(see illustration)**. Next, install the upper side rail in the same manner.

10   After the three oil ring components have been installed, check to make sure both the upper and lower side rails can be turned smoothly in the ring groove.

11   The number two (middle) ring is installed next. It's usually stamped with a mark, which must face up, toward the top of the piston. **Note:** *Always follow the instructions printed on the ring package or box – different manufacturers may require different approaches. Don't mix up the top and middle rings, as they have different cross sections.*

12   Use a piston ring installation tool and make sure the identification mark is facing the top of the piston, then slip the ring into the middle groove on the piston **(see illustration)**. Don't expand the ring any more than necessary to slide it over the piston.

13   Install the number one (top) ring in the same manner. Make sure the mark is facing up. Be careful not to confuse the number one and number two rings.

14   Repeat the procedure for the remaining pistons and rings.

24 Crankshaft – installation and main bearing oil clearance check

Refer to illustrations 24.3a, 24.3b, 24.11, 24.13 and 24.15

1   Crankshaft installation is the first step in engine reassembly. It's assumed at this point that the engine block and crankshaft have been cleaned, inspected and repaired or reconditioned.

2   Position the engine with the bottom facing up.

3   Remove the main bearing cap bolts and lift out the caps. Lay them out in the proper order to ensure correct installation **(see illus-**

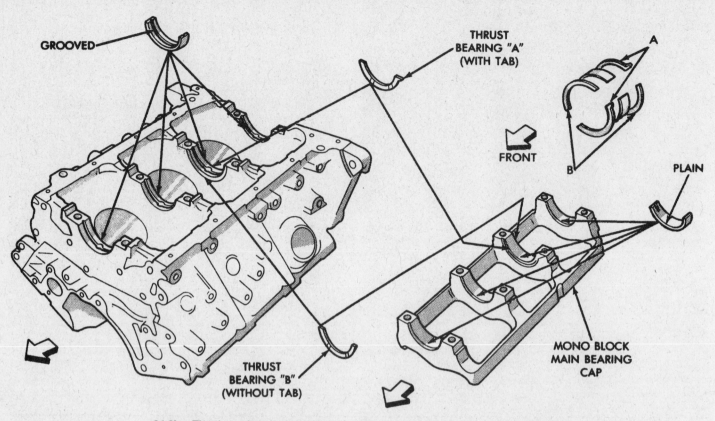

24.3b   The thrust bearings on the 3.0L engine are located on the number 3 journal

24.11   Lay the Plastigage strips (arrow) on the main bearing journals, parallel to the crankshaft centerline

tration).

4   If they're still in place, remove the original bearing inserts from the block and the main bearing caps. Wipe the bearing surfaces of the block and caps with a clean, lint-free cloth. They must be kept spotlessly clean.

Main bearing oil clearance check

Note: *Don't touch the faces of the new bearing inserts with your fingers. Oil and acids from your skin can etch the bearings.*

5   Clean the back sides of the new main bearing inserts and lay one in each main bearing saddle in the block. If one of the bearing inserts

from each set has a large groove in it, make sure the grooved insert is installed in the block. Lay the other bearing from each set in the corresponding main bearing cap. Make sure the tab on the bearing insert fits into the recess in the block or cap. **Caution:** *The oil holes in the block must line up with the oil holes in the bearing inserts. Do not hammer the bearing into place and don't nick or gouge the bearing faces. No lubrication should be used at this time.*

6   The flanged thrust bearing must be installed in the number two cap and saddle (counting from the front of the engine) on 2.6L and 3.3L and 3.8L liter engines. On the 2.2L, 2.5L and 3.0L engines, the thrust bearing must be installed in the number three (center) cap and saddle.

7   Clean the faces of the bearings in the block and the crankshaft main bearing journals with a clean, lint-free cloth.

8   Check or clean the oil holes in the crankshaft, as any dirt here can go only one way   - straight through the new bearings.

9   Once you're certain the crankshaft is clean, carefully lay it in position in the main bearings.

10   Before the crankshaft can be permanently installed, the main bearing oil clearance must be checked.

11   Cut several pieces of the appropriate size Plastigage (they should be slightly shorter than the width of the main bearings) and place one piece on each crankshaft main bearing journal, parallel with the journal axis **(see illustration)**.

12   Clean the faces of the bearings in the caps and install the caps in their original locations (don't mix them up) with the arrows pointing toward the front of the engine. Don't disturb the Plastigage.

13   Starting with the center main and working out toward the ends, tighten the main bearing cap bolts, in three steps, to the torque figure listed in this Chapter's Specifications. Don't rotate the crankshaft at any time during this operation. **Note:** *On 3.0L engines, torque the mono-block in the correct sequence* **(see illustration)**.

14   Remove the bolts and carefully lift off the main bearing caps. Keep them in order. Don't disturb the Plastigage or rotate the

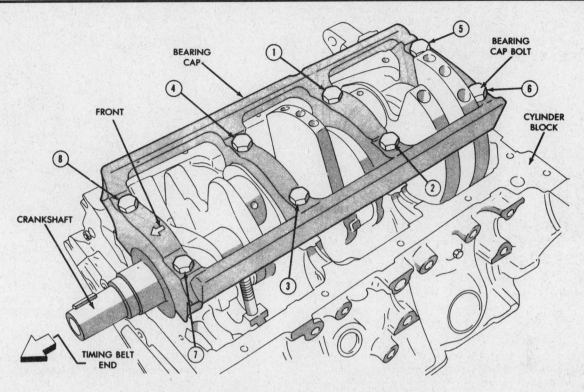

24.13   Mono-block tightening sequence on the 3.0L engine

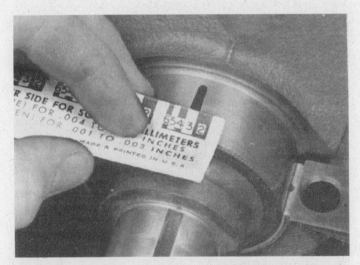

24.15   Compare the width of the crushed Plastigage to the scale on the envelope to determine the main bearing oil clearance (always take the measurement at the widest point of the Plastigage); be sure to use the correct scale – standard and metric ones are included

crankshaft. If any of the main bearing caps are difficult to remove, tap them gently from side-to-side with a soft-face hammer to loosen them.

15   Compare the width of the crushed Plastigage on each journal to the scale printed on the Plastigage envelope to obtain the main bearing oil clearance **(see illustration)**. Check the Specifications to make sure it's correct.

16   If the clearance is not as specified, the bearing inserts may be the wrong size (which means different ones will be required). Before deciding different inserts are needed, make sure no dirt or oil was between the bearing inserts and the caps or block when the clearance

was measured. If the Plastigage was wider at one end than the other, the journal may be tapered (see Section 20).

17   Carefully scrape all traces of the Plastigage material off the main bearing journals and/or the bearing faces. Use your fingernail or the edge of a credit card – don't nick or scratch the bearing faces.

Final crankshaft installation

18   Carefully lift the crankshaft out of the engine.

19   Clean the bearing faces in the block, then apply a thin, uniform layer of moly-base grease or engine assembly lube to each of the bearing surfaces. Be sure to coat the thrust faces as well as the journal face of the thrust bearing.

20   Make sure the crankshaft journals are clean, then lay the crankshaft back in place in the block.

21   Clean the faces of the bearings in the caps, then apply lubricant to them.

22   Install the caps in their original locations with the arrows pointing toward the front of the engine.

23   Install the bolts.

24   Tighten all except the thrust bearing cap bolts to the specified torque (work from the center out and approach the final torque in three steps).

25   Tighten the thrust bearing cap bolts to 10-to-12 ft-lbs.

26   Tap the ends of the crankshaft forward and backward with a lead or brass hammer to line up the main bearing and crankshaft thrust surfaces.

27   Retighten all main bearing cap bolts to the torque specified in this Chapter, starting with the center main and working out toward the ends.

28   Rotate the crankshaft a number of times by hand to check for any obvious binding.

29   The final step is to check the crankshaft endplay with feeler gauges or a dial indicator as described in Section 15. The endplay should be correct if the crankshaft thrust faces aren't worn or damaged and new bearings have been installed.

30   Refer to Section 26 and install the new rear main oil seal.

25.1   Coat the lobes and journals with cam lube

26.1   To remove the old crankshaft rear seal, support the housing on a pair of wood blocks and drive out the seal with a punch or screwdriver and hammer – make sure you don't damage the seal bore

26.2   To install the new crankshaft rear seal in the housing, simply lay the housing on a clean, flat workbench, lay a block of wood on the seal and carefully tap it into place with a hammer

25   Camshaft (3.3L and 3.8L engines only) - installation

Refer to illustration 25.1

Note: *This procedure applies to 3.3L and 3.8L V6 engines only.*

1   Lubricate the camshaft bearing journals and cam lobes with moly-base grease or engine assembly lube **(see illustration)**.
2   Slide the camshaft into the engine. Support the cam near the block and be careful not to scrape or nick the bearings.
3   Install the thrust plate and bolts. Tighten the bolts to the torque listed in this Chapter's Specifications.
4   Refer to Part D for the timing chain installation procedure.

26   Rear main oil seal - installation

Refer to illustrations 26.1, 26.2 and 26.3

Note: *The crankshaft must be installed and the main bearing caps bolted in place before the new seal and housing assembly can be bolted to the block.*

1   Remove the old seal from the housing with a hammer and punch by driving it out from the back side **(see illustration)**. Be sure to note how far it's recessed into the housing bore before removing it; the new seal will have to be recessed an equal amount. Be very careful not to scratch or otherwise damage the bore in the housing or oil leaks could develop.
2   Make sure the housing is clean, then apply a thin coat of engine oil to the outer edge of the new seal. The seal must be pressed squarely into the housing bore, so hammering it into place isn't recommended. If you don't have access to a press, sandwich the housing and seal between two smooth pieces of wood and press the seal into place with the jaws of a large vise. If you don't have a vise big enough, lay the housing on a workbench and drive the seal into place with a block of wood and hammer **(see illustration)**. The pieces of wood must be thick enough to distribute the force evenly around the entire circumference of the seal. Work slowly and make sure the seal enters the bore squarely.
3   Apply anaerobic sealant on the upper portion of the retainer **(see illustration)** before installing the housing. Lubricate the seal lips with clean engine oil or multi-purpose grease before you slip the seal/housing over the crankshaft and bolt it to the block.
4   Tighten the housing bolts a little at a time until they're all snug.

27   Pistons and connecting rods - installation and rod bearing oil clearance check

Refer to illustrations 27.4, 27.5, 27.9a, 27.9b, 27.9c, 27.9d, 27.11, 27.13 and 27.17

1   Before installing the piston/connecting rod assemblies, the cylinder walls must be perfectly clean, the top edge of each cylinder must be chamfered, and the crankshaft must be in place.
2   Remove the cap from the end of the number one connecting rod (check the marks made during removal). Remove the original bearing inserts and wipe the bearing surfaces of the connecting rod and cap with a clean, lint-free cloth. They must be kept spotlessly clean.

Connecting rod bearing oil clearance check

Note: *Don't touch the faces of the new bearing inserts with your fingers. Oil and acids from your skin can etch the bearings.*

3   Clean the back side of the new upper bearing insert, then lay it in place in the connecting rod. Make sure the tab on the bearing fits into the recess in the rod. Don't hammer the bearing insert into place and be very careful not to nick or gouge the bearing face. Don't lubricate the bearing at this time.
4   Clean the back side of the other bearing insert and install it in the rod cap. Again, make sure the tab on the bearing fits into the recess in the cap **(see illustration)**, and don't apply any lubricant. It's critically important that the mating surfaces of the bearing and connecting rod are perfectly clean and oil free when they're assembled.
5   Position the piston ring gaps at 120-degree intervals around the piston **(see illustration)**.
6   Slip a section of plastic or rubber hose over each connecting rod cap bolt.
7   Lubricate the piston and rings with clean engine oil and attach a piston ring compressor to the piston. Leave the skirt protruding about 1/4-inch to guide the piston into the cylinder. The rings must be compressed until they're flush with the piston.
8   Rotate the crankshaft until the number one connecting rod journal is at BDC (bottom dead center) and apply a coat of engine oil to the cylinder walls.
9   With the mark or notch on top of the piston **(see illustrations)** facing the front of the engine, gently insert the piston/connecting rod assembly into the number one cylinder bore and rest the bottom edge of the ring compressor on the engine block. If you're working on a 2.2L and 2.5L engines, make sure the oil hole in the lower end of the con-

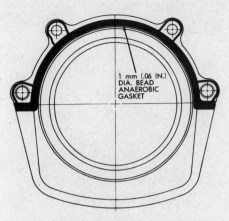

26.3   Apply anaerobic sealant onto the upper portion of the retainer

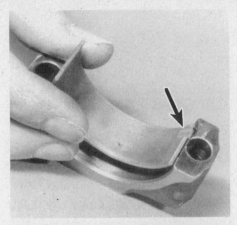

27.4   The tab on the bearing (arrow) must fit into the cap recess so the bearing will seat properly

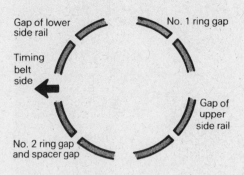

27.5   Position the ring gaps as shown here before installing the piston/connecting rod assemblies in the engine

2E

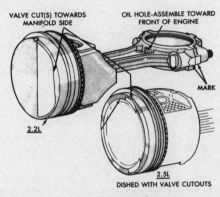

27.9a   On 2.2L and 2.5L engines, the indent on the piston and the oil hole in the rod must face the front of the engine (timing belt end) and the valve cut(s) must face the manifold side of the engine

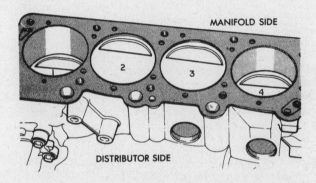

27.9b   Piston orientation after installation (2.2L engine shown, 2.5L engine similar)

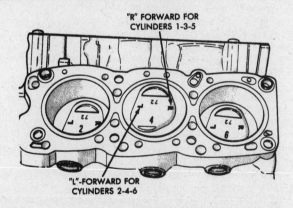

27.9c   Piston orientation after installation (3.0L engine)

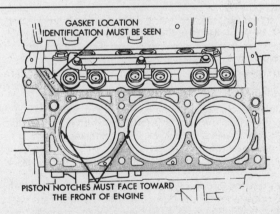

27.9d   Piston orientation after installation (3.3L and 3.8L engines)

necting rod is facing the front (timing belt) side of the engine.

10   Tap the top edge of the ring compressor to make sure it's contacting the block around its entire circumference.

11   Gently tap on the top of the piston with the end of a **wooden or plastic hammer handle (see illustration)** while guiding the end of the connecting rod into place on the crankshaft journal. The piston rings may try to pop out of the ring compressor just before entering the cylinder bore, so keep some downward pressure on the ring compressor. Work slowly, and if any resistance is felt as the piston enters the

cylinder, stop immediately. Find out what's hanging up and fix it before proceeding. Do not, for any reason, force the piston into the cylinder – you might break a ring and/or the piston.

12   Once the piston/connecting rod assembly is installed, the connecting rod bearing oil clearance must be checked before the rod cap is permanently bolted into place.

13   Cut a piece of the appropriate size Plastigage slightly shorter than the width of the connecting rod bearing and lay it in place on the number one connecting rod journal, parallel with the journal axis **(see illustration)**.

14   Clean the connecting rod cap bearing face, remove the protective

27.11 Drive the piston gently into the cylinder bore with the end of a wooden or plastic hammer handle

27.13 Lay the Plastigage strips on each rod bearing journal, parallel to the crankshaft centerline

27.17 Measuring the width of the crushed Plastigage to determine the rod bearing oil clearance (be sure to use the correct scale – standard and metric ones are included)

hoses from the connecting rod bolts and install the rod cap. Make sure the mating mark on the cap is on the same side as the mark on the connecting rod.

15   Install the nuts and tighten them to the torque listed in this Chapter's Specifications. Work up to it in three steps. **Note:** *Use a thin-wall socket to avoid erroneous torque readings that can result if the socket is wedged between the rod cap and nut. If the socket tends to wedge itself between the nut and the cap, lift up on it slightly until it no longer contacts the cap. Do not rotate the crankshaft at any time during this operation.*

16   Remove the nuts and detach the rod cap, being very careful not to disturb the Plastigage.

17   Compare the width of the crushed Plastigage to the scale printed on the Plastigage envelope to obtain the oil clearance **(see illustration)**. Compare it to this Chapter's Specifications to make sure the clearance is correct.

18   If the clearance is not as specified, the bearing inserts may be the wrong size (which means different ones will be required). Before deciding different inserts are needed, make sure no dirt or oil was between the bearing inserts and the connecting rod or cap when the clearance was measured. Also, recheck the journal diameter. If the Plastigage was wider at one end than the other, the journal may be tapered (refer to Section 20).

Final connecting rod installation

19   Carefully scrape all traces of the Plastigage material off the rod journal and/or bearing face. Be very careful not to scratch the bearing – use your fingernail or the edge of a credit card.

20   Make sure the bearing faces are perfectly clean, then apply a uniform layer of clean moly-base grease or engine assembly lube to both of them. You'll have to push the piston into the cylinder to expose the face of the bearing insert in the connecting rod – be sure to slip the protective hoses over the rod bolts first.

21   Slide the connecting rod back into place on the journal, remove the protective hoses from the rod cap bolts, install the rod cap and tighten the nuts to the torque listed in this Chapter's Specifications. Again, work up to the torque in three steps.

22   Repeat the entire procedure for the remaining pistons/connecting rods.

23   The important points to remember are . .
   a)   Keep the back sides of the bearing inserts and the insides of the connecting rods and caps perfectly clean when assembling them.
   b)   Make sure you have the correct piston/rod assembly for each cylinder.
   c)   The arrow or mark on the piston must face the front (timing chain end) of the engine.
   d)   Lubricate the cylinder walls with clean oil.

   e)   Lubricate the bearing faces when installing the rod caps after the oil clearance has been checked.

24   After all the piston/connecting rod assemblies have been properly installed, rotate the crankshaft a number of times by hand to check for any obvious binding.

25   As a final step, the connecting rod endplay must be checked. Refer to Section 13 for this procedure.

26   Compare the measured endplay to this Chapter's Specifications to make sure it's correct. If it was correct before disassembly and the original crankshaft and rods were reinstalled, it should still be right. If new rods or a new crankshaft were installed, the endplay may be inadequate. If so, the rods will have to be removed and taken to an automotive machine shop for resizing.

28   Initial start-up and break-in after overhaul

Warning: *Have a fire extinguisher handy when starting the engine for the first time.*

1   Once the engine has been installed in the vehicle, double–check the engine oil and coolant levels.

2   With the spark plugs out of the engine and the ignition system disabled (see Section 3), crank the engine until oil pressure registers on the gauge or the light goes out.

3   Install the spark plugs, hook up the plug wires and restore the ignition system functions (see Section 3).

4   Start the engine. It may take a few moments for the fuel system to build up pressure, but the engine should start without a great deal of effort. **Note:** *If backfiring occurs through the carburetor or throttle body, recheck the valve timing and ignition timing.*

5   After the engine starts, it should be allowed to warm up to normal operating temperature. While the engine is warming up, make a thorough check for fuel, oil and coolant leaks.

6   Shut the engine off and recheck the engine oil and coolant levels.

7   Drive the vehicle to an area with minimum traffic, accelerate at full throttle from 30 to 50 mph, then allow the vehicle to slow to 30 mph with the throttle closed. Repeat the procedure 10 or 12 times. This will load the piston rings and cause them to seat properly against the cylinder walls. Check again for oil and coolant leaks.

8   Drive the vehicle gently for the first 500 miles (no sustained high speeds) and keep a constant check on the oil level. It isn't unusual for an engine to use oil during the break-in period.

9   At approximately 500 to 600 miles, change the oil and filter.

10   For the next few hundred miles, drive the vehicle normally. Don't pamper it or abuse it.

11   After 2000 miles, change the oil and filter again and consider the engine broken in.

Chapter 3   Cooling, heating and air conditioning systems

Contents

Specifications

General

Radiator cap pressure rating	See Chapter 1
Thermostat rating (opening temperature)	
2.6L engine	
1984 and 1985	180-degrees F
1986 and 1987	190-degrees F
All others	195-degrees F
Cooling system capacity	See Chapter 1
Refrigerant capacity	33 to 34 ounces

Torque specifications

	Ft-lbs (unless otherwise indicated)
Thermostat housing nuts/bolts	
2.2L engine	17
2.5L engine	20
2.6L engine	15
3.0L engine	113 in-lbs
3.3L and 3.8L engines	20
Water pump pulley bolts	
1989 and earlier	120 in-lbs
1990 and later	20
Water pump mounting bolts	
2.2L and 2.5L engines	
Cover-to-housing bolts	108 in-lbs
Housing-to-block bolts	
Upper three bolts	20
Lower bolt	40
2.6L engine	
Pivot bolts and locking bolt	17
Body-to-housing bolts	80 in-lbs
3.0L engine	20
3.3L engine	105 in-lbs
Radiator mounting bolts	108 in-lbs

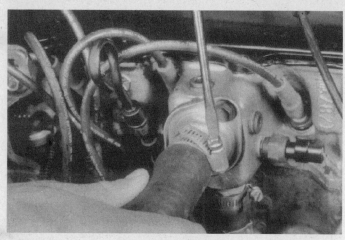

3.8   Loosen the hose clamps and remove the hose from the thermostat cover

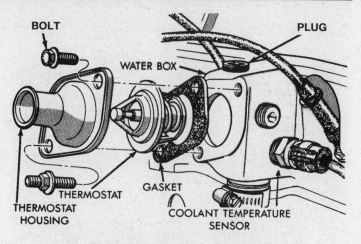

3.10a   Thermostat installation details – 2.5L four-cylinder engine (2.2L engine similar)

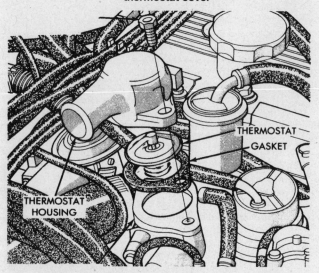

3.10b   Thermostat installation details – 2.6L four-cylinder engine

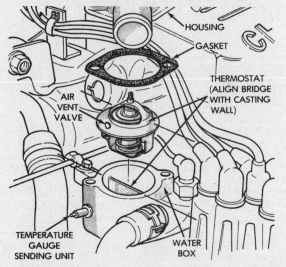

3.10c   Thermostat installation details – 3.0L V6 engine

1   General information

Engine cooling system

All vehicles covered by this manual employ a pressurized engine cooling system with thermostatically-controlled coolant circulation. An impeller type water pump mounted on the front of the block (on the rear of the block on 2.6L engines) pumps coolant through the engine. The coolant flows around the combustion chambers and toward the rear of the engine. Cast-in coolant passages direct coolant near the intake ports, exhaust ports, and spark plug areas.

A wax pellet type thermostat is located in a housing near the front of the engine. During warm-up, the closed thermostat prevents coolant from circulating through the radiator. As the engine nears normal operating temperature, the thermostat opens and allows hot coolant to travel through the radiator, where it's cooled before returning to the engine.

The cooling system is sealed by a pressure type radiator cap, which raises the boiling point of the coolant and increases the cooling efficiency of the radiator. If the system pressure exceeds the cap pressure relief value, the excess pressure in the system forces the spring-loaded valve inside the cap off its seat and allows the coolant to escape through the overflow tube into a coolant reservoir. When the system cools the excess coolant is automatically drawn from the reservoir back into the radiator.

The coolant reservoir does double duty as both the point at which

coolant is added to the cooling system to maintain the proper fluid level and as a holding tank for overheated coolant.

This type of cooling system is known as a closed design because coolant that escapes past the pressure cap is saved and reused.

Turbocharged engines have a continuous flow of coolant through the bearing water jacket. Coolant from the cylinder block (former) drain plug outlet provides a closed loop to the turbo bearing housing and back to the water box/thermostat housing.

Heating system

The heating system consists of a blower fan and heater core located in the heater box, the hoses connecting the heater core to the engine cooling system and the heater/air conditioning control head on the dashboard. Hot engine coolant is circulated through the heater core. When the heater mode is activated, a flap door opens to expose the heater box to the passenger compartment. A fan switch on the control head activates the blower motor, which forces air through the core, heating the air. Some models are equipped with an auxiliary heating/air conditioning system mounted behind the driver's seat.

Air conditioning system

The air conditioning system consists of a condenser mounted in front of the radiator, an evaporator mounted adjacent to the heater core, a compressor mounted on the engine, a filter/drier or receiver/drier (accumulator) which contains a high pressure relief valve and the plumbing connecting all of the above components.

3.10d   Remove the bolts and detach the thermostat housing from the intake manifold (3.3L and 3.8L V6 engines shown)

3.12   Carefully remove all traces of old gasket material

A blower fan forces the warmer air of the passenger compartment through the evaporator core, transferring the heat from the air to the refrigerant (sort of a "radiator in reverse"). The liquid refrigerant boils off into low pressure vapor, taking the heat with it when it leaves the evaporator.

2   Antifreeze – general information

Warning: Do not allow antifreeze to come in contact with your skin or painted surfaces of the vehicle. Rinse off spills immediately with plenty of water. Antifreeze is highly toxic if ingested. Never leave antifreeze lying around in an open container or in puddles on the floor; children and pets are attracted by it's sweet smell and may drink it. Antifreeze is also flammable, so don't store or use it near open flames. Check with local authorities about disposing of used antifreeze. Many communities have collection centers which will see that antifreeze is disposed of safely.

The cooling system should be filled with a water/ethylene glycol based antifreeze solution, which will prevent freezing down to at least -20-degrees F, or lower if local climate requires it. It also provides protection against corrosion and increases the coolant boiling point.

The cooling system should be drained, flushed and refilled at the specified intervals (see Chapter 1). Old or contaminated antifreeze solutions are likely to cause damage and encourage the formation of rust and scale in the system. Use distilled water with the antifreeze whenever possible.

Before adding antifreeze, check all hose connections, because antifreeze tends to leak through very minute openings. Engines don't normally consume coolant, so if the level goes down, find the cause and correct it.

The exact mixture of antifreeze-to-water which you should use depends on the relative weather conditions. The mixture should contain at least 50-percent antifreeze, but should never contain more than 70-percent antifreeze. Consult the mixture ratio chart on the antifreeze container before adding coolant. Hydrometers are available at most auto parts stores to test the coolant. Use antifreeze which meets the vehicle manufacturer's specifications.

3   Thermostat – check and replacement

Refer to illustrations 3.8, 3.10a, 3.10b, 3.10c, 3.10d and 3.12

Warning: Do not remove the radiator cap, drain the coolant or replace the thermostat until the engine has cooled completely.

Check

1   Before assuming the thermostat is to blame for a cooling system problem, check the coolant level, drivebelt tension (see Chapter 1) and temperature gauge operation.
2   If the engine seems to be taking a long time to warm up (based on heater output or temperature gauge operation), the thermostat is probably stuck open. Replace the thermostat with a new one.
3   If the engine runs hot, use your hand to check the temperature of the upper radiator hose. If the hose isn't hot, but the engine is, the thermostat is probably stuck closed, preventing the coolant inside the engine from escaping to the radiator. Replace the thermostat. **Caution:** *Don't drive the vehicle without a thermostat. The computer may stay in open loop and emissions and fuel economy will suffer.*
4   If the upper radiator hose is hot, it means that the coolant is flowing and the thermostat is open. Consult the Troubleshooting section at the front of this manual for cooling system diagnosis.

Replacement

5   Disconnect the negative battery cable from the battery.
6   Drain the cooling system down to the thermostat level or just below (see Chapter 1). If the coolant is relatively new or is in good condition, save and reuse it.
7   Follow the upper radiator hose to locate the thermostat housing.
8   Loosen the hose clamp, then detach the hose from the fitting **(see illustration)**. If it's stuck, grasp it near the end with a pair of adjustable pliers and twist it to break the seal, then pull it off. If the hose is old or deteriorated, cut it off and install a new one.
9   If the outer surface of the large fitting that mates with the hose is deteriorate (corroded, pitted, etc.) it may be damaged by removing the hose. If it is, the thermostat housing must be replaced.
10   Remove the bolts and detach the housing from the water box **(see illustrations)**. If the housing is stuck, tap it with a soft-face hammer, to jar it loose. Some coolant may spill as the seal is broken.
11   Note how it's installed (which end is facing the water box), then remove the thermostat.
12   Remove all traces of old gasket material and sealant from the water box and thermostat housing with a gasket scraper **(see illustration).**
13   On four-cylinder engines, apply a thin, uniform coat of RTV sealant to both sides of the new gasket, then place the new gasket on the water box. Install the thermostat over the new gasket on the water box. Make sure the spring end is directed into the water box.
14   On V6 engines, install the thermostat in the water box, spring-end first **(see illustration 3.10c)**. On 3.0L engines, align the bridge on the top of the thermostat with the casting wall in the water box. Apply a thin coat of RTV sealant to the new gasket and place the gasket over the thermostat.
15   Install the housing and bolts. Tighten the bolts to the torque listed in this Chapter's Specifications.

3

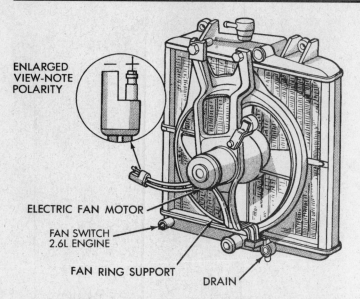

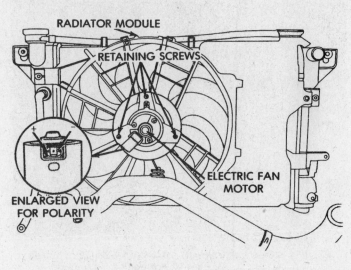

4.1a   Terminal polarity of the cooling fan electrical connector

4.1b   On some models, the electrical connector plugs into the fan motor itself

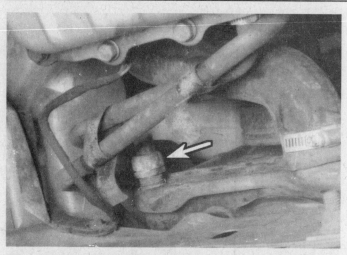

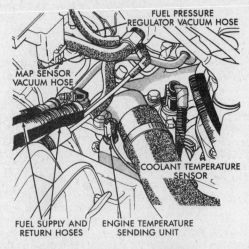

4.2a   On four-cylinder models, the fan switch is threaded into the bottom of the radiator (arrow)

4.2b   On the 3.0L V6 engine, the coolant temperature sensor is screwed into the thermostat housing (on the 3.3L and 3.8L V6 engines it's screwed into the front cylinder head)

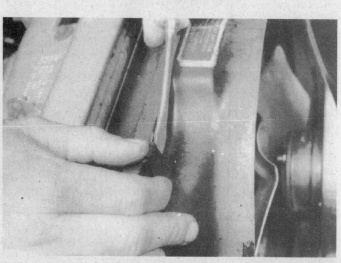

4.5a   Detach the two clips at the top of the fan shroud housing with a screwdriver . . .

16   Reattach the upper radiator hose to the housing and tighten the hose clamp securely.

17   Refill the cooling system (see Chapter 1).

18   Start the engine and allow it to reach normal operating temperature, then check for leaks and proper thermostat operation (as described in Steps 2 through 4).

---

4   Engine cooling fan and switch – check and replacement

Warning: To avoid possible injury or damage, DO NOT operate the engine with a damaged fan. Do not attempt to repair fan blades – replace a damaged fan with a new one.

Check

Refer to illustrations 4.1a, 4.1b, 4.2a, and 4.2b

1   If the engine is overheating and the cooling fan is not coming on, unplug the electrical connector at the fan motor **(see illustrations)** and use jumper wires to connect the fan directly to the battery. If the fan

4.5b   . . . then lift the assembly out of the engine compartment

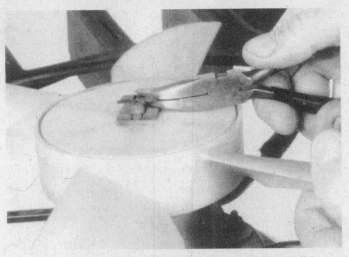

4.6   The fan retaining clip can be removed with needle-nose pliers

4.7   Removing the fan motor mounting nuts

5.4a   Loosen the clamp, slide it back and remove the hose from the radiator by working it back and forth

still doesn't work, replace the motor.

2   If the fan motor is good but still doesn't come on when the engine gets hot, the fault lies in the coolant temperature sensor or fan switch **(see illustrations)**, the engine control computer or the wiring which connects the components (on some models, fan operation is controlled by the coolant temperature sensor. On other models, a separate fan switch is employed). Unplug the electrical connector from the sensor/switch. If the fan operates, the sensor is defective. If the fan still doesn't come on, use a voltmeter or test light to check the fan circuit (wiring diagrams are included at the end of Chapter 12). Carefully check all wiring and connections. If no obvious problems are found, further diagnosis should be done by a dealer service department or repair shop.

Replacement

Fan

Refer to illustrations 4.5a, 4.5b, 4.6 and 4.7

3   Disconnect the negative battery cable.

4   Unplug the fan motor electrical connector.

5   Detach the two clips at the top of the fan shroud with a small screwdriver, then carefully lift it out of the engine compartment **(see illustrations)**.

6   To detach the fan from the motor, remove the clip from the motor shaft **(see illustration)**.

7   To detach the motor from the shroud, remove the nuts and slide the motor out of the shroud **(see illustration)**.

8   Installation is the reverse of removal.

Coolant temperature sensor/fan switch

9   Drain the cooling system.

10   Unplug the electrical connector from the sensor/switch.

11   Unscrew the sensor/switch from the thermostat housing or bottom of the radiator.

12   Wrap Teflon tape on the threads of the new sensor/switch to prevent leaks.

13   Install the sensor/switch and plug in the electrical connector.

14   Fill the cooling system (see Chapter 1).

15   Start the engine to check for leaks and for proper operation of the cooling fan.

5   Radiator/transmission oil cooler – removal and installation

Warning: Wait until the engine is cool before beginning this procedure.

Radiator

Removal

Refer to illustrations 5.4a, 5.4b, 5.5, 5.6 and 5.8

1   Disconnect the negative battery cable.

2   Drain the cooling system making sure the heater control is in the maximum heat position (see Chapter 1). If the coolant is relatively new and is in good condition, save and reuse it.

3   Remove the fan motor and shroud assembly (see Section 4).

4   Loosen the hose clamps, then detach the radiator hoses from the

3

fittings **(see illustrations)**. If they're stuck, grasp each hose near the end with a pair of adjustable pliers and twist it to break the seal, then pull it off. Be careful not to distort the radiator fittings! If the hoses are old or deteriorated, cut them off and install new ones.

5   Remove the coolant reservoir hose **(see illustration)**.

6   If the vehicle is equipped with an automatic transmission, disconnect and plug the cooler lines **(see illustration)**.

7   Unplug the electrical connector from the radiator fan switch (see Section 4).

8   Remove the radiator mounting bolts **(see illustration)**.

9   Carefully lift out the radiator. Don't spill coolant on the vehicle or scratch the paint.

10   Check the radiator for leaks and damage. If it needs repair, have a radiator shop or dealer service department perform the work, as special techniques are required.

11   Remove bugs and dirt from the radiator with compressed air and a soft brush taking care not to damage radiator cooling fins or water tubes.

Installation

12   Inspect the radiator mounts for deterioration and make sure there's no dirt or gravel in them when the radiator is installed.

13   Lower the radiator into place and push down to seat the radiator lower tabs in the mount holes provided.

14   Install the top radiator bolts and tighten them securely.

15   Lubricate all of the hose fittings lightly with white lithium grease to ease the installation.

16   Install the radiator, heater and reservoir hoses.

17   Install the transmission cooling lines, if so equipped.

18   Install the fan motor and shroud assembly, and connect the elec-

trical connector to the motor.

19   Fill the cooling system with the proper mixture of coolant and water (see Chapter 1).

20   Connect the negative battery cable.

21   Start the engine and allow it to reach normal operating temperature and check for leaks, (indicated by the upper radiator hose becoming hot). Recheck the coolant level and add more if needed.

22   If you're working on an automatic transmission equipped vehicle, check and add fluid as needed (see Chapter 1).

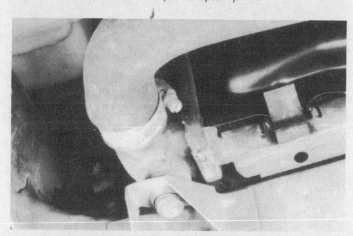

5.4b   The lower radiator hose is accessible from under the vehicle

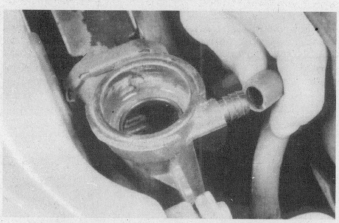

5.5   Detach the coolant reservoir hose from the fitting

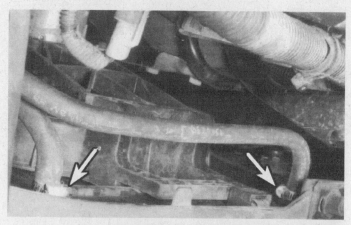

5.6   Location of the transmission cooler lines (arrows) - 3.3L and 3.8 V6 engines

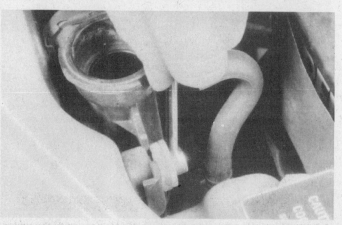

5.8   The top of the radiator is secured by two bolts (one on each side)

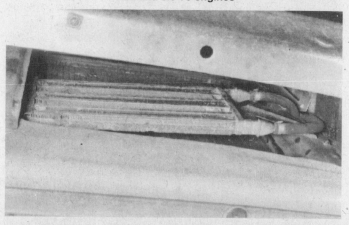

5.23a   Location of the auxiliary transmission oil cooler - 2.6L engine

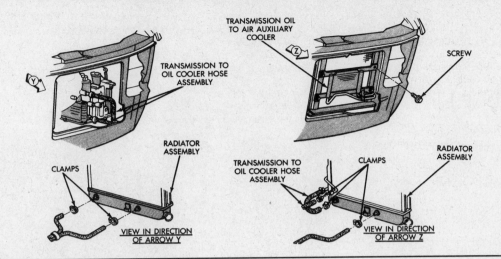

5.23b   Transmission oil cooler details

Automatic transmission oil coolers

Refer to illustrations 5.23a and 5.23b

23   There are two types of transmission oil coolers. One is internal and mounted in the radiator tank, the other is externally mounted ahead of the radiator **(see illustrations)**.

24   It is recommended that you use only approved transmission oil cooler hoses if hose replacement becomes necessary. These rubber oil hoses are molded to fit the available space. Straight hoses will kink when bent and restrict or stop the flow of transmission oil through the cooler. If the flow through the cooler is restricted or stopped the oil will not cool properly which may cause it to burn, (turning the oil from a red color to a brown color). This may also cause the transmission to fail prematurely.

6   Coolant reservoir – removal and installation

Refer to illustration 6.2

1   Detach the overflow hose at the radiator filler neck. Plug the hose so you don't spill any coolant out of the reservoir during removal.

2   Remove the mounting screws **(see illustration)** and lift the reservoir straight up. On earlier models, it will be necessary to first remove the battery.

3   Installation is the reverse of the removal.

7   Water pump – check

1   A failure in the water pump can cause serious damage due to overheating.

2   There are three ways to check the operation of the water pump while it's installed on the engine. If the pump is defective, it should be replaced with a new or rebuilt unit.

3   With the engine running at normal operating temperature, squeeze the upper radiator hose. If the water pump is working properly, a pressure surge should be felt as the hose is released. **Warning:** *Keep your hands away from the fan blades!*

4   Water pumps are equipped with weep or vent holes. If a failure occurs in the pump seal, coolant will leak from the hole. In most cases you'll need a flashlight to find the hole on the water pump from underneath to check for leaks.

5   If the water pump shaft bearings fail there may be a howling sound at the front of the engine while it's running. Shaft wear can be felt if the water pump pulley is rocked up-and-down. Don't mistake drivebelt slippage, which causes a squealing sound, for water pump bearing failure.

8   Water pump – replacement

Refer to illustration 8.3

Warning: *Wait until the engine is completely cool before beginning this procedure.*

All engines

1   Disconnect the negative battery cable from the battery.

2   Drain the cooling system (see Chapter 1). If the coolant is rela-

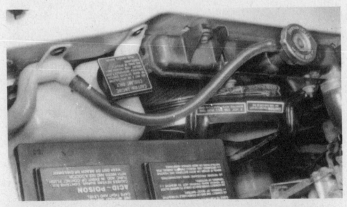

6.2   Coolant reservoir mounting details (2.6L shown, others similar)

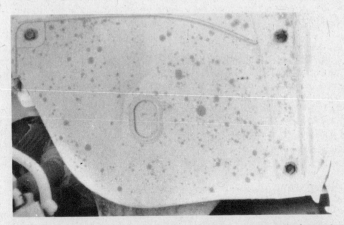

8.3   Remove the right-side splash shield for access to the water pump - it's retained by three bolts (2.6L model shown, others similar)

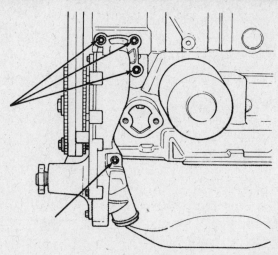

8.6   Water pump mounting bolt locations (2.2L engine shown, 2.5L engine similar)

8.7a   Remove the water pump-to-housing bolts

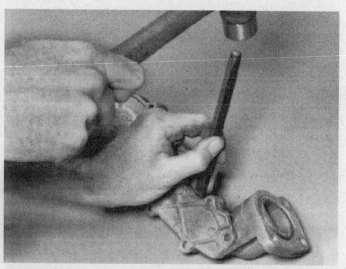

8.7b   You may have to use a hammer and chisel to separate the water pump from the housing, but be extremely careful - don't damage the mating surface of the housing

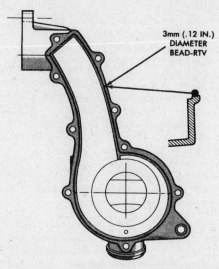

3mm (.12 IN.)
DIAMETER
BEAD-RTV

8.11   Apply a continuous bead of RTV sealant between the bolt holes and the inner edge of the housing

tively new or in good condition, save and reuse it.

3   Remove the splash shield under the right front fender for easy access to the water pump bolts **(see illustration)**. On all models except those equipped with the 2.6L engine, remove the drivebelt(s) (see Chapter 1).

4   Loosen the clamps and disconnect the hoses from the water pump. If they're stuck, grasp each hose near the end with a pair of adjustable pliers and twist it to break the seal, then pull it off. If the hoses are deteriorated, cut them off and install new ones.

2.2L and 2.5L engines

Refer to illustrations 8.4, 8.6, 8.7a, 8.7b and 8.11

5   On air-conditioned models, unbolt the compressor (see Section 15). Warning: Simply set the compressor aside – don't disconnect the lines.

6   Remove the water pump bolts **(see illustration)**, detach the drivebelt and separate the water pump and housing assembly from the engine.

7   Remove the bolts and separate the water pump from the housing **(see illustrations)**.

8   Discard the gasket and clean the mating surfaces to remove any remaining gasket material. Remove the old O-ring from the housing

and carefully clean out the groove.

9   Clean the bolt threads and the threaded holes to remove any corrosion and sealant.

10   If you're installing a new pump, compare the new pump to the old pump to make sure they're identical.

11   Apply a bead of RTV sealant to the mating surfaces of the housing **(see illustration)**. Install a new O-ring in the housing groove.

12   Attach the new pump to the housing and tighten the bolts to the torque listed in this Chapter's Specifications.

13   Clean the mating surfaces of the water pump housing and the engine block. Using a new gasket, install the pump/housing assembly on the engine and tighten the bolts to the torque listed in this Chapter's Specifications.

14   Proceed to Step 43.

2.6L engine

Refer to illustrations 8.15 and 8.17

15   Remove the cam pulley shield **(see illustration)**.

16   Remove the water pump bolts and separate the water pump/housing assembly from the engine (see illustration 8.15).

17   Remove the bolts and separate the water pump from the housing **(see illustration)**.

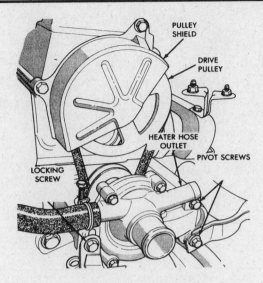

8.15 Water pump mounting details - 2.6L engine

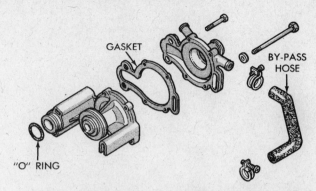

8.17 Exploded view of the water pump (2.6L engine)

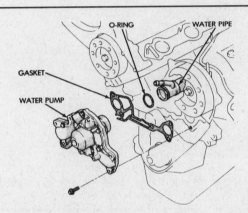

8.28 Water pump mounting details - 3.0L engine

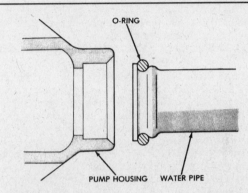

8.29 Be sure to use a new O-ring on the water pipe

8.36 The water pump on the 3.3L and 3.8L engines is retained to the housing by five bolts

18 Discard the gasket and clean the mating surfaces to remove all remaining gasket material.

19 Remove the O-ring from the housing and carefully clean out the groove.

20 Clean the bolt threads and threaded holes to remove any corrosion and sealant.

21 If you're installing a new pump, compare the new pump to the old pump to make sure they're identical.

22 Apply a thin film of RTV sealant to the gasket. Set the gasket on the housing and assemble the pump to the housing. Install the bolts and tighten them to the torque listed in this Chapter's Specifications. Install a new O-ring in the housing groove.

23 Install the water pump assembly on the engine with the bolts finger-tight.

24 Install the drivebelt and cam pulley shield, adjust the belt to the proper tension (see Chapter 1) and tighten the water pump bolts to the torque listed in this Chapter's Specifications.

25 Proceed to Step 43.

3.0L engine

Refer to illustrations 8.28 and 8.29

26 Remove the timing belt cover and timing belt (see Chapter 2, Part C).

27 Remove the air conditioning compressor (see Section 15), the alternator (see Chapter 5) and the power steering pump (see Chapter 10). Warning: Simply unbolt the compressor and set it aside – don't disconnect the hoses.

28 Remove the mounting bolts and separate the water pump from the water pipe (attached to the back of the pump) and the cylinder block (see illustration).

29 Remove all traces of old gasket material from the pump and engine mating surfaces. Remove the old O-ring from the water pipe (see illustration).

30 Clean the bolt threads and the threaded holes in the engine to remove corrosion and sealant.

31 Apply a thin film of RTV sealant to the gasket and install the gasket on the pump. Install a new O-ring on the water pipe.

32 Install the pump on the block, guiding it onto the water pipe.

33 Install the mounting bolts and tighten them to the torque listed in this Chapter's Specifications.

34 Reinstall the timing belt and cover (see Chapter 2, Part C).

35 Proceed to Step 43.

3.3L and 3.8L engines

Refer to illustration 8.36

36 Remove the bolts and detach the water pump from the front cover (see illustration).

3

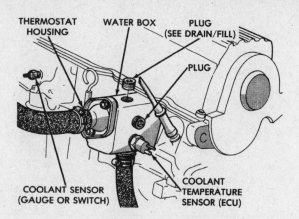

THERMOSTAT HOUSING — WATER BOX — PLUG (SEE DRAIN/FILL) — PLUG — COOLANT SENSOR (GAUGE OR SWITCH) — COOLANT TEMPERATURE SENSOR (ECU)

9.1a   Location of the coolant temperature sending unit (2.2L and 2.5L engines)

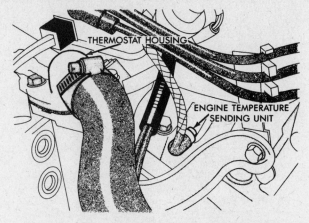

THERMOSTAT HOUSING — ENGINE TEMPERATURE SENDING UNIT

9.1b   Location of the coolant temperature sending unit (3.3L and 3.8L engines)

37   Clean the bolt threads and the threaded holes in the front cover to remove any corrosion and sealant.

38   Remove the old O-ring and clean the mating surfaces. Be careful not to gouge or scratch the mating surfaces.

39   Apply a thin bead of RTV sealant to the mating surface of the water pump and install a new O-ring in the groove.

40   Install the new pump to the front cover and tighten the bolts to the torque listed in this Chapter's Specifications.

41   Reinstall the drivebelt and check the tension (see Chapter 1).

42   Proceed to Step 43.

All engines

43   Attach the hoses to the water pump and tighten the clamps securely.

44   Reinstall any parts that were removed to gain access to the pump.

45   Install the drivebelt(s) and adjust them to the proper tension (see Chapter 1).

46   Install the splash shield.

47   Refill the cooling system with coolant (see Chapter 1).

48   Reconnect the cable to the negative terminal of the battery.

49   Start the engine and allow it to warm up, then check for leaks.

---

9   Coolant temperature sending unit – check and replacement

Refer to illustrations 9.1a and 9.1b

Check

1   The coolant temperature indicator system is composed of a light or gauge mounted in the instrument panel and a coolant temperature sending unit mounted on the thermostat housing or water box. Some of the engines covered by this manual have more than one sending unit, but only one is used for the temperature indicator system (see accompanying illustrations and illustration 3.10c).

2   If an overheating indication occurs, check the coolant level in the system. Be sure the cooling system has cooled enough to remove the radiator cap (about 30-to-45 minutes). During that time you can check the wiring between the light or gauge and the sending unit, to be sure that all wiring circuits are closed and all fuses are intact.

3   With the ignition switch turned to the start piston and the starter cranking the engine, the indicator light should be on or the gauge should give an overheat condition.

4   If the light is not on, the bulb may be burned out, the ignition switch may be faulty or the circuit may be open. To test the circuit, ground the wire to the sending unit while the ignition is on and the engine is off. If the light comes on, or the gauge moves all the way to Hot, replace the sending unit.

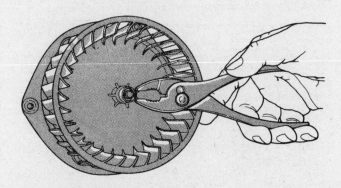

10.4   To detach the fan from the motor shaft, remove the retainer with pliers

5   As soon as the engine starts, the light should go out and remain out unless the engine overheats. Should the light stay on it may be due to a grounded wire between the light and the sending unit, a defective sending unit, or a faulty ignition switch. Check the coolant mixture to make sure it's the proper mix for your vehicle, engine type, and weather conditions.

Replacement

6   Drain the cooling system down to the level of the sensor, (make sure the cooling system is cool before work is started). Unscrew the sensor from the engine, thermostat housing, or water box, and install a new replacement. Use Teflon tape or a small amount of RTV sealant on the threads. There will be some coolant loss as the unit is removed, so be prepared to catch it. After replacement, fill the cooling system to the proper level and check for leaks.

---

10   Heater/air conditioner blower motor (front) – removal and installation

Refer to illustration 10.4

1   Disconnect the negative battery cable from the battery.

2   Working under the dash on the passenger side, disconnect the electrical connector from the blower motor.

3   Remove the five attaching screws and lower the blower motor and fan assembly from the heater/air conditioner assembly.

4   To detach the fan, remove the retainer and slide it off the motor shaft **(see illustration)**.

5   Installation is the reverse of removal.

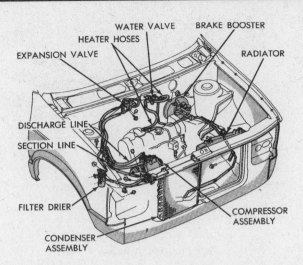

11.3   Heater and air conditioner component locations (typical)

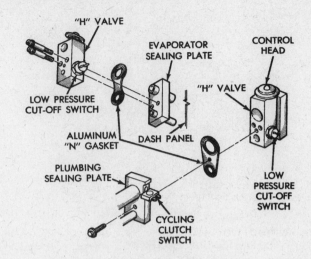

11.4   "H" valve mounting details

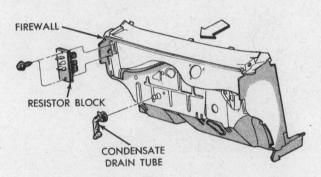

11.8   Resistor block and condensate tube locations

11   Heater core (front) – replacement

Refer to illustrations 11.3, 11.4, 11.8, 11.11, 11.18 and 11.19

1   Disconnect the negative battery cable from the battery.

2   Drain the cooling system (see Chapter 1). Have the air conditioning system discharged by a service station or other repair shop. Warning: Don't disconnect any of the air conditioning hoses until this has been done.

3   Disconnect the heater hoses from the heater core tubes at the firewall **(see illustration)** and plug the fittings to prevent coolant from spilling out during removal.

4   Remove the 8mm bolt from the center of the evaporator sealing plate **(see illustration)**.

5   Remove the two Torx bolts and carefully detach the H valve **(see illustration 11.4).**

6   Carefully move the refrigerant lines to the front of the vehicle (do not scratch the valve sealing surfaces).

7   Plug the refrigerant lines to prevent contamination to the air conditioning system.

8   Remove the condensate tube **(see illustration)**.

9   Remove the steering column-to-dash bolts and lower the column to the drivers seat.

10   Remove the lower instrument panel and the forward console (see Chapter 11).

11   Remove the four nuts that retain the assembly to the firewall **(see illustration)**.

12   Pull the right side of the instrument panel back until it reaches the passenger seat.

13   Disconnect the electrical connectors to the resistor, blower motor and the temperature control cable.

14   Disconnect the hanger strap from the heater/air conditioner

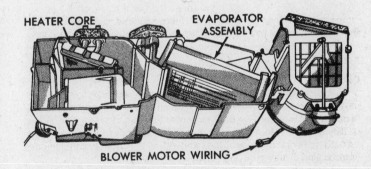

11.11   Heater/air conditioner assembly mounting screw locations (arrows) - not all screws are visible in this photo

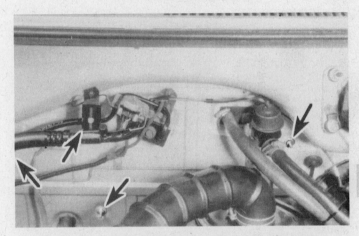

11.18   Remove the screws and lift the top off the heater/air conditioner assembly to expose the heater core (and the evaporator)

assembly and bend it out of the way.

15   Pull the heater/air conditioner assembly out from under the dash panel and remove it from the vehicle.

16   Place the heater core/air conditioner evaporator assembly on a workbench.

17   Remove the screw holding the vacuum harness and feed the harness through the hole.

18   Remove the screws and lift the cover off **(see illustration)**.

3

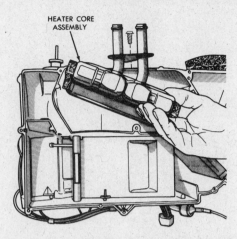

11.19   Remove the screw and lift the heater core straight up

19   Remove the screw from the heater core tube retaining bracket and lift the heater core out **(see illustration)**.
20   Installation is the reverse of removal.

12   Heater/air conditioner control assembly – removal and installation

Refer to illustrations 12.3, 12.4, 12.5, 12.5, 12.6, 12.7a, 12.7b, 12.7c and 12.8

1   Disconnect the negative battery cable.
2   Remove the control assembly cover plate (see Chapter 11).
3   Remove the two control assembly mounting screws **(see illustration)**.
4   Pull the heater/air conditioner control assembly out. Pull the bulb holder out of control assembly **(see illustration)**.
5   Disconnect the electrical connectors from the backside of the control assembly **(see illustration)**.
6   Disconnect the temperature control cable **(see illustration)**.
7   Release the locking tab with pliers and, using a screwdriver, pry the temperature control cable out of the control assembly **(see illustrations)**.
8   Disconnect the vacuum harness **(see illustration)** and remove the assembly from the dash.
9   Installation is the reverse of removal.

13   Air conditioning system – check and maintenance

Refer to illustration 13.7

Warning: *The air conditioning system is under high pressure. Do not loosen any hose fittings or remove any components until the system has been discharged by a dealer service department or service station. Always wear eye protection when disconnecting air conditioning system fittings.*

Caution: *The air conditioning system on 1993 and later models uses the non-ozone depleting refrigerant, referred to as R-134a. The R-134a refrigerant and its lubricating oil are not compatible with the R-12 system and under no circumstances should the two different types of refrigerant and lubricating oil be intermixed. If mixed, it could result in costly compressor failure due to improper lubrication.*

Check

1   The following maintenance checks should be performed on a regular basis to ensure the air conditioner continues to operate at peak efficiency.
   a)   Check the compressor drivebelt. If it's deteriorated or worn, replace it (see Chapter 1).

12.3   The heater/air conditioner control assembly is retained by two screws (arrows)

12.4   Pull the bulb holder from the back of the control assembly

12.5   Unplug the electrical connectors from the control assembly

   b)   Check the drivebelt tension and if necessary adjust it (see Chapter 1).
   c)   Check the system hoses. Look for cracks, bubbles, hard spots and deterioration. Inspect the hoses and all fittings for oil bubbles and seepage. If there's any evidence of wear, damage or leaks, replace the hose(s).
   d)   Inspect the condenser fins for leaves, bugs and other debris. Use a "fin comb" or compressed air to clean the condenser.
   e)   Make sure the system has the correct refrigerant charge.
2   It's a good idea to operate the system for about 10 minutes at least once a month, particularly during the winter. Long non-use can

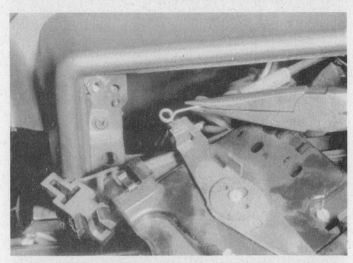

12.6   Detach the temperature control cable from the lever

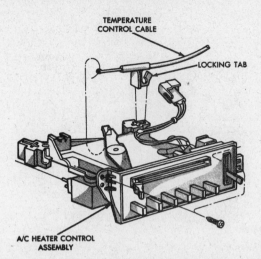

12.7a   Details of the temperature control cable

TEMPERATURE
CONTROL CABLE

LOCKING TAB

A/C HEATER CONTROL
ASSEMBLY

12.7b   Depress the locking tab with pliers . . .

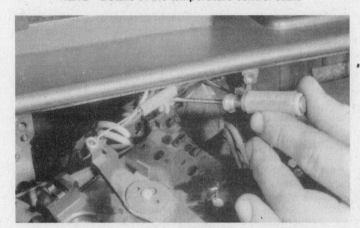

12.7c   . . . then pry the cable from the assembly

12.8   Pull the control assembly out and unplug the
vacuum harness

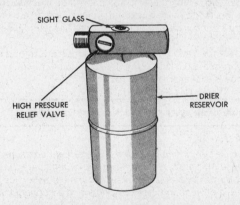

SIGHT GLASS

HIGH PRESSURE
RELIEF VALVE

DRIER
RESERVOIR

13.7   The sight glass on top of the filter-drier (or receiver-drier)
assembly enables you to view the condition of the refrigerant in
the air conditioning system while the system is operating - if the
refrigerant looks foamy, the charge is low

cause hardening and subsequent failure of the seals.

3   Because of the complexity of the air conditioning system and the special equipment necessary to service it, in-depth troubleshooting and repairs are not included in this manual (refer to the *Haynes Automotive Heating and Air Conditioning Repair Manual*). However, simple checks and component replacement procedures are provided in this Chapter.

4   The most common cause of poor cooling is simply a low system refrigerant charge. If a noticeable drop in cool air output occurs, the following quick check will help you determine if the refrigerant is low.

5   Warm the engine up to normal operating temperature.

6   Place the air conditioning temperature selector at the coldest setting. Open the doors (to make sure the air conditioning system doesn't cycle off as soon as it cools the passenger compartment).

7   With the compressor engaged – the clutch will make an audible click and the center of the clutch will rotate – inspect the sight glass, if equipped (see illustration). If the refrigerant looks foamy, it's low.

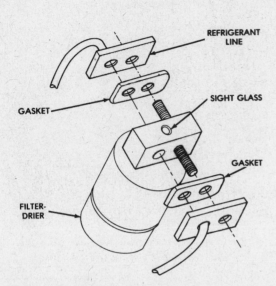

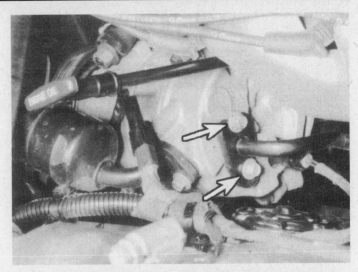

15.5   Each refrigerant line is held to the compressor with two bolts (arrows)

14.5   Typical filter-drier/receiver-drier installation details - if you plan to reinstall the same unit, be sure to plug the openings immediately after detaching the refrigerant lines

Have the system charged by a dealer service department or other qualified shop.

8   If there's no sight glass, feel the inlet and outlet pipes at the compressor. One side should be cold and one hot. If there's no perceptible difference between the two pipes, there's something wrong with the compressor or the system. It might be a low charge – it might be something else. Take the vehicle to a dealer service department or an automotive air conditioning shop.

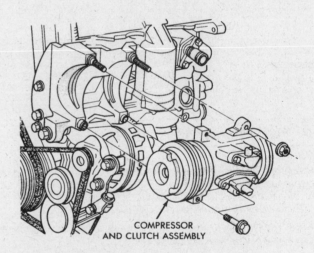

15.6   Air conditioning compressor installation details (four-cylinder model shown, others similar)

COMPRESSOR AND CLUTCH ASSEMBLY

14   Air conditioning filter-drier/receiver-drier – removal and installation

Refer to illustration 14.5

Warning: *The air conditioning system is under high pressure. DO NOT disassemble any part of the system (hoses, compressor, line fittings, etc.) until after the system has been depressurized by a dealer service department or service station.*

Caution: *Replacement filter-drier/receiver-drier units are so effective at absorbing moisture that they can quickly saturate upon exposure to the atmosphere. When installing a new unit, have all tools and supplies ready for quick reassembly to avoid having the system open any longer than necessary.*

1   The filter-drier/receiver-drier, acts as a reservoir for the system refrigerant. It's located near the radiator.
2   Have the system discharged (see Warning above).
3   Disconnect the negative battery cable from the battery.
4   Unplug any electrical connectors from the filter-drier/receiver-drier.
5   Disconnect the refrigerant lines from the filter-drier/receiver-drier **(see illustration)**.
6   Plug the open fittings to prevent entry of dirt and moisture.
7   Loosen the mounting bracket bolts and lift the filter-drier/receiver-drier out.
8   Installation is the reverse of the removal.
9   Take the vehicle back to the shop that discharged it. Have the system evacuated, recharged and leak tested.

15   Air conditioning compressor – removal and installation

Refer to illustrations 15.5 and 15.6

Warning: *The air conditioning system is under high pressure. DO NOT disassemble any part of the system (hoses, compressor, line fittings, etc.) until after the system has been depressurized by a dealer service department or service station.*

Note: *The filter-drier/receiver-drier (see Section 14) should be replaced whenever the compressor is replaced.*

1   Have the system discharged (see Warning above).
2   Disconnect the negative cable from the battery.
3   Unplug the electrical connector from the compressor clutch.
4   Remove the drivebelt (see Chapter 1).
5   Disconnect the refrigerant lines from the rear of the compressor **(see illustration)**. Plug the open fittings to prevent entry of dirt and moisture.
6   Unbolt the compressor from the mounting bracket **(see illustration)** and lift it from the vehicle.
7   If a new compressor is being installed, follow the directions with the compressor regarding the draining of excess oil prior to installation.
8   The clutch may have to be transferred from the original to the new compressor.

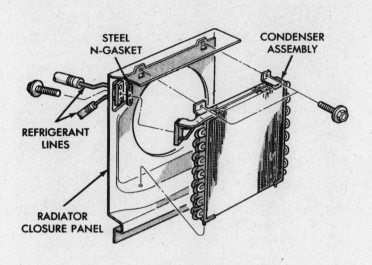

16.4   Condenser installation details

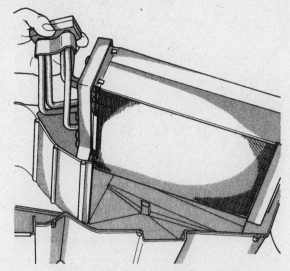

17.3   Evaporator installation details

9   Installation is the reverse of the removal. Replace all O-rings with new ones specifically made for air conditioning system use, and lubricate them with refrigerant oil.
10   Have the system evacuated, recharged and leak tested by the shop that discharged it.

16   Air conditioning condenser – removal and installation

Refer to illustration 16.4

Warning: *The air conditioning system is under high pressure. DO NOT disassemble any part of the system (hoses, compressor, line fittings, etc.) until after the system has been depressurized by a dealer service department or service station.*

Note: *The filter-drier/receiver-drier should be replaced whenever the condenser is replaced (see Section 14).*

1   Have the system discharged (see Warning above).
2   Disconnect the negative cable from the battery.
3   Remove the grille (see Chapter 11).
4   Disconnect the refrigerant lines from the condenser **(see illustration)**.
5   Plug all refrigerant lines to prevent dirt and moisture from contaminating the system.
6   Remove the two mounting bolts from the condenser **(see illustration 16.4)**.
7   Lift the condenser out of the vehicle.
8   If the original condenser will be reinstalled, store it with the line fittings on top to prevent the oil from draining out.
9   If a new condenser is being installed, pour one ounce of wax-free refrigerant oil into it prior to installation.
10   Installation is the reverse of removal. Be sure the rubber pads are in place under the condenser.
11   Have the system evacuated, recharged and leak tested by the shop that discharged it.

17   Air conditioning evaporator – removal and installation

Refer to illustration 17.3

Warning: *The air conditioning system is under high pressure. DO NOT disassemble any part of the system (hoses, compressor, line fittings, etc.) until after the system has been depressurized by a dealer service department or service station.*

1   Have the system depressurized (see Warning above).
2   Follow Steps 1 through 18 of Section 11.
3   Lift the evaporator straight up and out of the heater/air conditioner unit **(see illustration)**.
4   Installation is the reverse of removal. Have the system evacuated, recharged and leak tested by the shop that discharged it.

18   Auxiliary (rear) heater/air conditioner – general information

The rear heater-air conditioning system is located in the left rear quarter panel. The system can be operated from the front blower switch on the dashboard, regardless of the setting of the rear controls.
Air is drawn into the air intake, then enters the blower housing and is pushed through the heater core or the air conditioning evaporator. In the heat mode the air flow is directed through the outlets at the floor. In the air conditioning mode the air flow is directed through the upper air outlets.

19   Auxiliary (rear) heater/air conditioner components – removal and installation

Warning: *The air conditioning system is under under high pressure. DO NOT disassemble any part of the system (hoses, compressor, line fittings, etc.) until after the system has been depressurized by a dealer service department or service station.*

Heater/air conditioner and blower housing assembly

Refer to illustration 19.8

Warning: *Wait until the engine is completely cool before beginning this procedure.*

1   Disconnect the negative battery cable.
2   Drain the cooling system and disconnect the push-together couplings at the rear of the unit.
3   Have the air conditioning system discharged (see Warning above).
4   Use a screwdriver to carefully pry the upper and lower corners of the control panel out of the housing.
5   Carefully pull the control assembly from the housing and unplug the electrical connectors.
6   Pry the heater and air conditioner outlets from the housing.
7   Remove the left rear quarter panel trim (see Chapter 11).

3

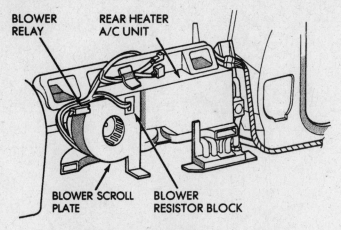

19.8 Details of the auxiliary heater/air conditioner

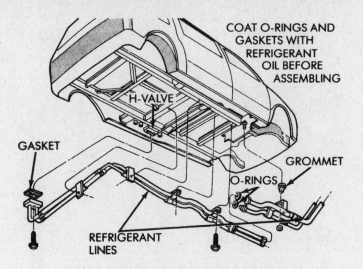

19.22 Routing details of the underbody air conditioning lines

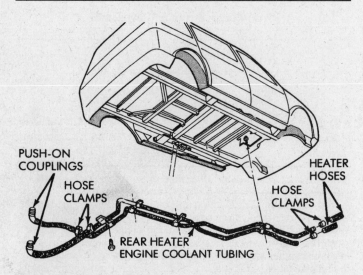

19.16 Routing details of the underbody heater plumbing

8 Disconnect the electrical connector from the resistor block and blower relay (see illustration).

9 Remove the screw on the distribution duct at the rear wheel housing.

10 Remove the three screws on the heater/air conditioner unit on the floor and the screw on the panel support. Lift the unit from the vehicle.

11 Installation is the reverse of removal.

12 Refill the cooling system (see Chapter 1). Have the system evacuated, recharged and leak tested by the shop that discharged it.

Underbody heater plumbing

Refer to illustration 19.16

Warning: *Wait until the engine is completely cool before beginning this procedure.*

13 Drain the cooling system.

14 Locate the heater hose tee fittings in the engine compartment and disconnect them.

15 Raise the vehicle and support it securely on jackstands. Disconnect the two push-together fittings at the rear heater core.

16 Remove the fasteners holding the plumbing to the underbody and lower the pipes from the vehicle (see illustration).

17 Installation is the reverse of removal.

18 Refill the cooling system.

19 Start the engine, allow it to reach normal operating temperature and check for leaks.

Underbody air conditioning plumbing

Refer to illustration 19.22

20 Have the air conditioning system discharged (see Warning above).

21 Raise the vehicle and support it securely on jackstands. Locate and disconnect the two air conditioning fittings for the underbody plumbing in the engine compartment.

22 Remove the bolt from the air conditioning plumbing block in front of the gas tank on the left side (see illustration).

23 Carefully pull lines down, remove the aluminum N-gasket and plug the line openings to prevent contamination of the system.

24 Remove the screws holding the lines to the gas tank support and support rail.

25 Remove the screws securing the lines to the underside of the vehicle.

26 Disconnect the parking brake cable connection (see Chapter 9).

27 Lower the plumbing from the vehicle.

28 If you're installing new lines don't take off the shipping caps – they will protect the ends from contamination and scratches.

29 Installation of the plumbing is the reverse of removal.

30 Have the system evacuated, recharged and leak tested by the shop that discharged it.

Chapter 4   Fuel and exhaust systems

Contents

Specifications

Fuel pressure

Carbureted models ... . 4.5 to 6 psi
Fuel injected models (engine running, vacuum hose disconnected from fuel pressure regulator)
   2.5L single point EFI engines
      1990 and earlier .... 14.5 psi
      1991 and later.. 39 psi

Specifications (continued)

Fuel injected models (engine running, vacuum hose disconnected from fuel pressure regulator) (continued)

2.5L turbo engine	39 psi
3.0L, 3.3L and 3.8L engines	48 psi

Carburetor adjustments

Curb idle speed...	See the *Emissions Control Information label* in engine compartment
Fast idle speed	See the *Emissions Control Information label* in engine compartment

2.2L engine choke vacuum kick adjustment
    Carburetor number

1984

R40069-2A	0.070 inch
R40075-2A	
R40128-2A	
R40129-2A	
R40063-2A	0.080 inch
R40070-2A	
R40072-2A	

1985

R40143A	0.095 inch
R40145A	
R40146A	
R40136A	0.075 inch
R40137A	
R40140A	
R40141A	

1986

R40229A	0.130 inch
R40230A	
R40231A	
R40232A	
R40233A	0.160 inch
R40234A	
R40240A	

2.2L engine float drop	1-7/8 inch
Dry float level	
2.2L engine	31/64 inch
2.6L engine	25/32 + 25/64 inch
2.6L engine choke breaker opening	5/64 inch or less at 50-degrees F
2.6L engine choke unloader opening	3/64 inch or more at 32-degrees F

Torque specifications

	Ft-lbs (unless otherwise indicated)
Air intake plenum mounting bolts/nuts	
3.0L engine	115 in-lbs
3.3L and 3.8L engines	250 in-lbs
Automatic idle speed (AIS) motor screws	
Single-point systems	20 in-lbs
Multi-point systems	17 in-lbs
Carburetor mounting nuts	
2.2L engine	17
2.6L engine	12.5
Fuel pressure regulator (single-point EFI)	48 in-lbs
Fuel rail mounting bolts	
Turbo engine	40
3.0L engine	115 in-lbs
3.3L and 3.8L engines	200 in-lbs
Throttle body mounting bolts/nuts	
2.5L engine	175 in-lbs
Turbo engine	175 to 225 in-lbs
3.0L engine	225 in-lbs
3.3L and 3.8L engines	175 to 225 in lbs
Turbocharger support bracket bolts	
To engine block	40
To turbocharger	20
Turbocharger-to-exhaust manifold nuts	40

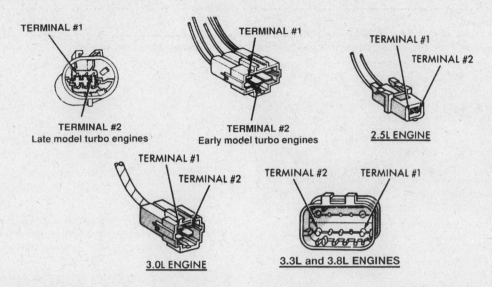

2.4   If an injector is not accessible, ground the number 1 terminal on the injector side of the harness connector and apply battery voltage to the number 2 terminal to actuate the injector and release the pressurized fuel

1   General information

Fuel system

The fuel system consists of the fuel tank, a mechanical or electric fuel pump, an air cleaner, either a carburetor or a fuel injection system and the hoses and lines which connect these components.

Earlier models are carbureted. A Holley carburetor (5220 or 6520) is used on models with the 2.2L engine. A Mikuni carburetor is used on models with the 2.6L engine. Both models have a mechanical fuel pump mounted on the engine block. The pump is driven by an eccentric cam off the intermediate shaft (2.2L) or camshaft (2.6L).

Later models are fuel-injected. Basically, two different fuel injection systems are used. A single-point (one injector) Electronic Fuel Injection (EFI) system is used on 2.5L engines. A multi-point (one injector per cylinder) EFI system is used on 2.5L turbocharged, 3.0L, 3.3L and 3.8L engines. All fuel-injected models use an in-tank electric fuel pump.

Exhaust system

The exhaust system consists of the exhaust manifold, exhaust pipes, catalytic converter and muffler. For information regarding the removal and installation of the exhaust manifold, refer to Chapter 2, Part A. For information regarding exhaust system and catalytic converter servicing, refer to the last Section in this Chapter. For further information regarding the catalytic converter, refer to Chapter 6.

2   Fuel pressure relief procedure (fuel-injected models only)

Refer to illustrations 2.4, 2.5a and 2.5b

Warning: *Gasoline is extremely flammable, so take extra precautions when you work on any part of the fuel system. Don't smoke or allow open flames or bare light bulbs near the work area, and don't work in a garage where a natural gas-type appliance (such as a water heater or clothes dryer) with a pilot light is present. If you spill any fuel on your skin, rinse it off immediately with soap and water. When you perform any kind of work on the fuel system, wear safety glasses and have a Class B type fire extinguisher on hand.*

1   The fuel system operates under pressure and may be under residual pressure even when the engine is off. Consequently any time the fuel system is worked on (such as when the fuel filter is replaced) the system must be depressurized to avoid the spraying of fuel when a

2.5a   If one of the injectors is accessible, unplug the most convenient injector connector and bleed the fuel pressure in short bursts by grounding one of the terminals and touching the other terminal (arrow) with the jumper wire clip

component is disconnected.

2   Loosen the fuel tank cap to release any pressure in the tank.

3   Unplug the electrical connector from the fuel injector. If you're working on a multi-point system disconnect the electrical connector from the injector that is the most easily accessible. If you're working on a single-point system, proceed to the next Step. If access to an injector is difficult, unplug the injector harness connector from the engine (or main) harness.

4   If the injector is accessible, ground one of the terminals with a jumper wire. If it was necessary to disconnect the main injector harness due to inadequate access to the injector(s), ground the injector terminal number 1 (on the engine side of the harness) using a jumper wire **(see illustration)**.

5   Connect a jumper wire between the other terminal (number 2 on the injector harness) and the positive (+) post of the battery, which will open the injector and depressurize the fuel system **(see illustrations)**. **Caution:** *Do not energize the injector(s) for more than five seconds. It's recommended that the pressure be bled in several spurts of one to two seconds to make sure the injector isn't damaged. The fuel pressure can be heard escaping into the throttle body or combustion chamber. When the sound is no longer heard, the system is depressurized.*

4

2.5b   On single-point EFI systems, you can easily ground an injector terminal in the connector right at the throttle body to bleed the fuel pressure – but don't activate it for more than five seconds

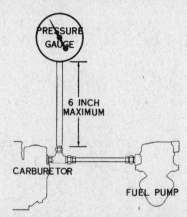

3.1   Attach the T-fitting as close to the carburetor as possible and use a six-inch (maximum) length of hose when hooking up the pressure gauge to check the fuel pump pressure

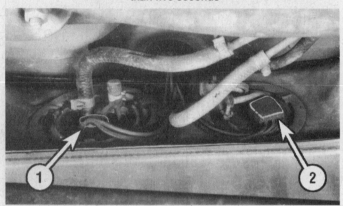

3.8   The electrical connectors for the fuel pump (1) and the fuel gauge sending unit (2) are easily accessible at the fuel tank

3.12a   Be sure the fuel gauge is connected to the inlet line (1) and not the return line (2) (single-point system)

3 Fuel pump/fuel pressure – check

Warning: Gasoline is extremely flammable, so take extra precautions when you work on any part of the fuel system. Don't smoke or allow open flames or bare light bulbs near the work area, and don't work in a garage where a natural gas-type appliance (such as a water heater or clothes dryer) with a pilot light is present. If you spill any fuel on your skin, rinse it off immediately with soap and water. When you perform any kind of work on the fuel system, wear safety glasses and have a Class B type fire extinguisher on hand.

Mechanical pump

Refer to illustration 3.1

1   Disconnect the fuel line from the carburetor and install a T-fitting **(see illustration)**. Connect a fuel pressure gauge to the T-fitting with a section of fuel hose that's no longer than six inches.

2   Disconnect the gauge from the end of the fuel hose and direct the end of the hose into an approved gasoline container. Operate the starter for a few seconds, until fuel spurts out of the hose, to vent the pump (this eliminates any air in the fuel chamber, which could affect the pressure reading). Reattach the gauge to the fuel hose.

3   Start the engine and allow it to idle. The pressure on the gauge should be about 4.5 to 6 psi, remain constant and return to zero slowly when the engine is shut off.

4   An instant pressure drop indicates a faulty outlet valve. If this occurs, or if the pressure is too high or low, replace the fuel pump with a new one. **Note:** *if the pressure is too high, check the air vent to see if it's plugged before replacing the pump.*

Electric (in-tank) pump

Voltage check

Refer to illustration 3.8

5   Remove the fuel tank cap and place your ear close to the filler neck. Have an assistant turn the ignition key to On while you listen for the sound of the in-tank pump. It should make a whirring sound. If you don't hear the pump, make the following quick checks.

6   Relieve the fuel system pressure (see Section 2).

7   Raise the rear of the vehicle and place it securely on jackstands.

8   Lower the fuel tank slightly (see Section 4) and locate the wire harness to the fuel pump **(see illustration)**.

9   Using a voltmeter, verify that there's voltage to the pump when the key is turned to On and Start.

   a)   If there is voltage to the pump, replace it.

   b)   If there is no voltage to the pump, locate the fuel pump relay or fuse, check it and replace as necessary. Trace the wires for a open or short circuit condition.

10   If the pump still doesn't work, have it checked by a dealer service department or a repair shop. Further testing requires special equipment.

Fuel pressure check

Refer to illustrations 3.12a, 3.12b, 3.14 and 3.16

11   Relieve the fuel pressure (see Section 2).

12   On single-point fuel injection systems (TBI), disconnect the 5/16-inch fuel line from the throttle body and connect a fuel pressure gauge between the fuel inlet hose and the throttle body **(see illustration)**. On multi-point fuel injection systems, remove the fitting on the fuel rail

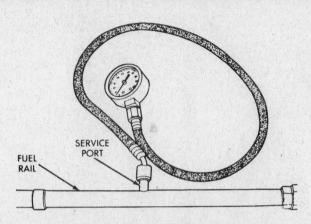

3.12b The fuel rail on multi-point systems has a service port that can be used to attach the fuel pressure gauge

3.14 Attach the fuel pressure gauge between the fuel tank and the fuel filter

3.16 Disconnect the return line and attach a length of fuel hose, directing the free end of the hose into a container - if the fuel pressure is within specifications when an assistant cranks the engine (with the ignition system disabled), check for a plugged return line

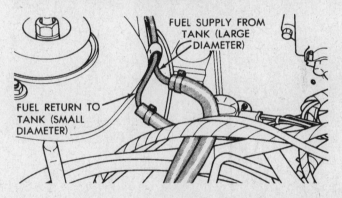

4.4 You'll see two fuel lines between the fuel tank and the carburetor or fuel injection system: A supply (larger diameter) line and a return (smaller diameter) line – drain or siphon the fuel tank through the supply hose or line

(see illustration) and install the pressure gauge. **Note:** *Late models are equipped with a quick disconnect coupler installed in the fuel line near the fuel filter. Install special tools C-4799 and adapter C-6539 as an alternative to the above method.*

13   Start the engine and disconnect the vacuum hose from the fuel pressure regulator. Record the fuel pressure, comparing your findings with the values listed in this Chapter's Specifications. When the vacuum hose is connected to the fuel pressure regulator the reading should be approximately 10 psi less than the first reading.

14   If the fuel pressure is BELOW specifications, install the pressure gauge between the fuel filter and the fuel tank **(see illustration)**.

15   If the fuel pressure increases, the fuel filter or line (between the filter and throttle body or fuel rail) is plugged or restricted. If the fuel pressure is still low, pinch the return line with a pair of pliers (wrap a rag around the hose first to prevent damage). If the pressure now goes up, replace the fuel pressure regulator. If no change in the fuel pressure is observed, check for a plugged fuel pump sock filter (screen) or a defective fuel pump.

16   If the fuel pressure is ABOVE specifications, disconnect the primary wires from the ignition coil, remove the return hose from the throttle body or fuel rail and connect a short section of hose to it. Direct the end of the hose into a suitable container and have an assistant crank the engine **(see illustration)**.

17   If the pressure is now correct, the problem is a restricted return line.

4   Fuel tank – removal and installation

Refer to illustrations 4.4 and 4.7

Warning: *Gasoline is extremely flammable, so take extra precautions when you work on any part of the fuel system. Don't smoke or allow open flames or bare light bulbs near the work area, and don't work in a garage where a natural gas-type appliance (such as a water heater or clothes dryer) with a pilot light is present. If you spill any fuel on your skin, rinse it off immediately with soap and water. When you perform any kind of work on the fuel system, wear safety glasses and have a Class B type fire extinguisher on hand.*

Removal

1   Disconnect the negative battery cable from the battery.

2   Raise the rear of the vehicle and support it securely on jackstands.

3   Remove the fuel tank filler cap.

4   Disconnect the fuel tank line (the large diameter supply line) located adjacent to the right front shock tower in the engine compartment **(see illustration)**, connect a hose and drain or siphon the tank into a metal container. **Warning:** *Do not use your mouth to start the siphoning action – use a siphoning kit, which can be purchased at most auto parts stores.*

5   Remove the screws retaining the filler tube to the body.

6   Disconnect all wires and hoses from the tank (label them first to avoid problems during installation).

4

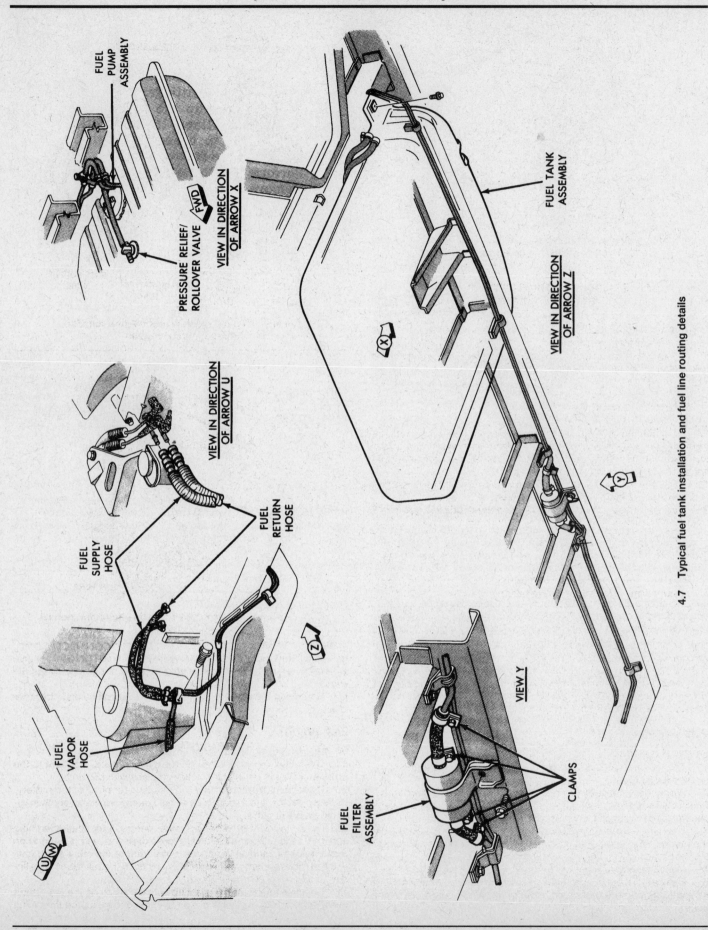

FUEL
PUMP
ASSEMBLY

PRESSURE RELIEF/
ROLLOVER VALVE

FWD

VIEW IN DIRECTION
OF ARROW X

FUEL TANK
ASSEMBLY

VIEW IN DIRECTION
OF ARROW Z

VIEW IN DIRECTION
OF ARROW U

FUEL
SUPPLY
HOSE

FUEL
RETURN
HOSE

FUEL
VAPOR
HOSE

FUEL FILTER
ASSEMBLY

CLAMPS

VIEW Y

4.7   Typical fuel tank installation and fuel line routing details

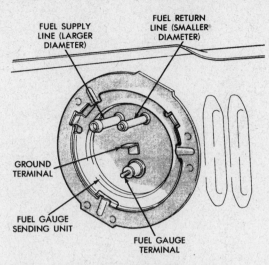

4.12a Typical fuel tank connection details (carbureted models)

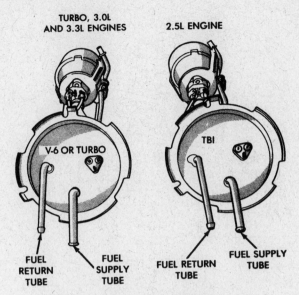

4.12b Typical fuel tank connection details (fuel-injected models)

Remove the mounting bolts or nuts **(see illustration)**, lower the tank slightly and remove the filler tube.

8 Lower the tank further and support it while disconnecting the rollover/vapor separator valve hose.

9 Remove the tank and insulator pad.

Installation

Refer to illustrations 4.12a and 4.12b

10 To install the tank, raise it into position with a jack, connect the rollover/vapor separator valve hose and place the insulator pad on the top. Connect the filler tube. **Caution:** *Be sure the vapor vent hose is not pinched between the tank and floor pan.*

11 Raise the tank with the jack, connect the retaining strap and install the retaining nuts. Tighten them securely.

12 Connect the fuel lines and wiring **(see illustrations)** and install the filler tube retaining screws.

13 Fill the fuel tank, install the cap, connect the negative battery cable and check for leaks.

---

5 Fuel pump – removal and installation

Warning: *Gasoline is extremely flammable, so take extra precautions when you work on any part of the fuel system. Don't smoke or allow open flames or bare light bulbs near the work area, and don't work in a garage where a natural gas-type appliance (such as a water heater or clothes dryer) with a pilot light is present. If you spill any fuel on your skin, rinse it off immediately with soap and water. When you perform any kind of work on the fuel system, wear safety glasses and have a Class B type fire extinguisher on hand.*

2.2L engine

Refer to illustration 5.1

1 The fuel pump is bolted to the engine block adjacent to the oil filter **(see illustration)**.

2 Disconnect the cable from the negative terminal of the battery, Place clean rags or newspaper under the fuel pump to catch any gasoline that may spill during removal.

3 Carefully unscrew the fuel line fittings and detach the lines from the pump. A flare-nut wrench should be used to prevent damage to the line fittings.

4 Unbolt and remove the fuel pump.

5 Before installation, coat both sides of the spacer block with RTV sealant, position the fuel pump and spacer in place and install the bolts.

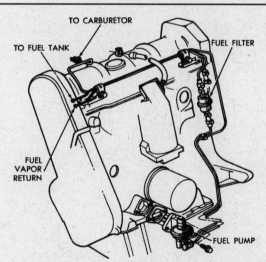

5.1 Fuel pump assembly and fuel line mounting details (2.2L engine)

6 Attach the lines to the pump and tighten the fittings securely (use a flare-nut wrench, if one is available, to prevent damage to the fittings).

7 Reconnect the cable to the battery, run the engine and check for leaks.

2.6L engine

Refer to illustrations 5.8 and 5.19

8 The fuel pump is mounted on the cylinder head, adjacent to the carburetor **(see illustration)**. It is held in place with two nuts.

9 Disconnect the cable from the negative terminal of the battery. Carefully number each spark plug to help during reinstallation, then remove the spark plugs.

10 Place your thumb over the number one cylinder spark plug hole and rotate the crankshaft in a clockwise direction (with a wrench on the large bolt attaching the pulley to the front of the crankshaft) until you can feel the compression pressure rising in the number one cylinder.

11 Continue rotating the crankshaft until the notch on the crankshaft pulley lines up with the T or zero on the timing mark tab on the timing

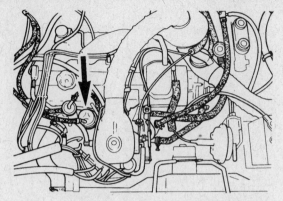

5.8   Fuel pump location (arrow) (2.6L engine)

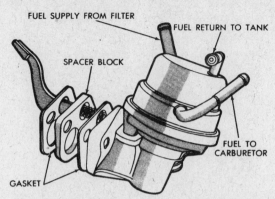

5.19   When installing the fuel pump on a 2.6L engine, be sure to place a gasket on each side of the spacer block

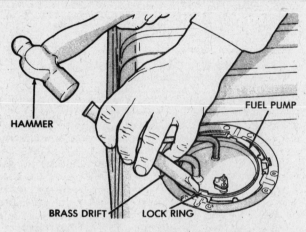

5.27a   To remove the lock ring from an electric fuel pump assembly, rotate it counterclockwise with a hammer and brass punch

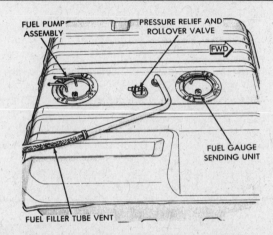

5.27b   Pre-1991 fuel injected models have separate fuel pumps and fuel gauge sending units (1991 and later models have an integral fuel pump/fuel gauge sending unit) and both units are similar in appearance – to avoid removing the wrong unit, look for two pipes (the sending unit has only one pipe)

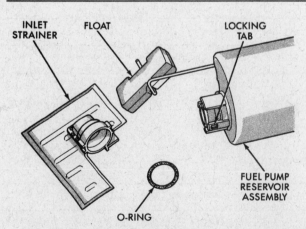

5.30   An exploded view of the inlet strainer on a 1991 and later fuel pump

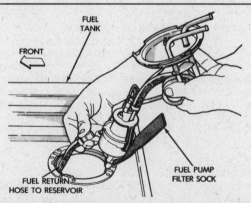

5.31   When you install an electric fuel pump, make sure you reattach the fuel return hose to the reservoir (doesn't apply to 1991 models) – this hose brings fuel from the rest of the tank into the reservoir surrounding the fuel pump when the fuel level is low

chain case. At this point, the lift of the fuel pump drive cam is reduced to a minimum, which will make the pump easier to remove (and install).
12   Install the spark plugs and hook up the wires.
13   Remove the air intake housing and carburetor-to-valve cover bracket, then remove the fuel filter mounting bolt. Loosen the hose

clamps and remove the fuel hoses from the pump fittings. Plug the ends of the hoses.
14   Remove the fuel pump mounting nuts and pull the pump off the engine. You may have to tap the pump body with a soft-faced hammer to break the gasket seal.

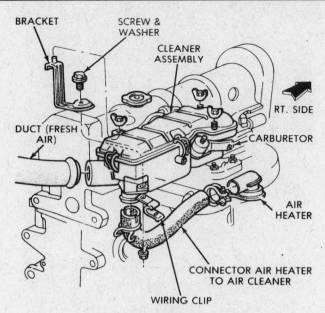

7.2a   Mounting details of the air cleaner housing –
2.2L engine

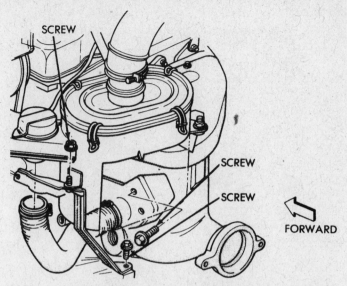

7.2b   Mounting details of the air cleaner housing – 2.6L engine

15   If the pump is difficult to remove, take off the valve cover and guide the pump rocker arm out of the head from the inside.

16   Remove the spacer block and scrape off all traces of the old gaskets and sealant.

17   Before installing the new pump, make sure that the rocker arm moves up and down without binding or sticking.

18   Coat both sides of the new gaskets with RTV-type gasket sealant before installation.

19   Slip the first gasket, the spacer block and the second gasket (in that order) onto the fuel pump mounting studs (see illustration).

20   Install the fuel pump. It may be necessary to guide the rocker arm into place from inside the head. Work slowly; there is not much clearance between the rocker arm and the valve gear.

21   Once the fuel pump is properly seated, install the mounting nuts and tighten them evenly. Do not overtighten them or the spacer block may crack.

22   Install the valve cover if it was removed.

23   Install the hoses (after inspecting them for cracks) and new hose clamps.

24   Install the filter mounting bolt, the bracket and the air intake housing.

25   Reconnect the cable to the battery, start the engine and check for fuel leaks at the hose fittings. Check for oil leaks where the fuel pump mounts on the cylinder head.

Electric in-tank pump

Refer to illustrations 5.27a, 5.27b, 5.30 and 5.31

26   Remove the fuel tank (see Section 4).

27   Use a hammer and a BRASS punch (a steel punch may cause a spark, which could be extremely dangerous when working on the fuel tank!) to remove the fuel pump lock ring. Drive it in a counterclockwise direction until it can be removed (see illustration). Fuel-injected models (except 1991 models) have separate fuel pumps and fuel gauge sending units (see illustration); 1991 and later models have an integral fuel pump/fuel gauge sending unit assembly. The lock rings for both assemblies on pre-1991 models look similar, so it's easy to confuse the two. To avoid removing the wrong assembly, make sure you remove the assembly that has two pipes – the sending unit has only one pipe.

28   Lift the fuel pump and O-ring out of the fuel tank. Discard the old O-ring.

29   Clean the sealing area of the fuel tank and install a new O-ring on

the fuel pump.

30   Inspect the fuel inlet sock filter (strainer) on the fuel pump suction tube for damage and contamination. Replace it if it's damaged. On 1991 models, bend the locking tabs on the fuel pump reservoir assembly to clear the the locking tangs on the fuel pump filter (see illustration), pull the strainer off, remove the strainer O-ring from the fuel pump reservoir body. To install the strainer on 1991 and later models, lubricate the strainer O-ring with silicone spray lube, insert the strainer O-ring into the outlet of the filter so its sits evenly on the step inside the filter outlet and push the strainer onto the inlet of the fuel pump reservoir body, making sure the locking tabs on the reservoir body lock over the locking tangs on the filter.

31   Insert the fuel pump into the tank, reattach the reservoir fuel return hose (if equipped) to the pump assembly (see illustration), place the pump in its installed position, set the lock ring in place and lock the pump into place with a hammer and a BRASS punch (drive the lock ring in a clockwise direction).

32   Install the fuel tank (see Section 4).

6   Fuel tank cleaning and repair – general information

1   All repairs to the fuel tank or filler neck should be carried out by a professional who has experience in this critical and potentially dangerous work. Even after cleaning and flushing of the fuel system, explosive fumes can remain and ignite during repair of the tank.

2   If the fuel tank is removed from the vehicle, it shouldn't be placed in an area where sparks or open flames could ignite the fumes coming out of the tank. Be especially careful inside garages where a natural gas-type appliance is located, because the pilot light could cause an explosion.

7   Air cleaner housing – removal and installation

Refer to illustrations 7.2a, 7.2b, 7.2c, 7.2d, 7.2e and 7.2f

1   Remove the air filter element (see Chapter 1).

2   Loosen the hose clamps that attach the fresh air inlet tube to the air cleaner housing (see illustrations). On carbureted (2.2L and 2.6L) engines, also loosen the hose clamp for the heated inlet air pipe at the air cleaner housing. Detach all hoses and tubes from the air cleaner housing. Label any small hoses to assure proper reassembly.

3   Remove the fastener(s) from all air cleaner mounting brackets.

4   Remove the air cleaner housing assembly.

5   While you've got the air cleaner housing removed, inspect the

4

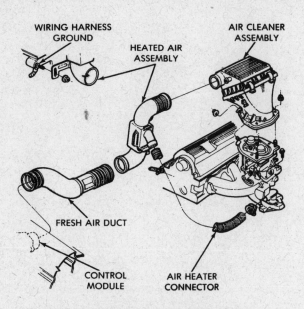

7.2c   Mounting details of the air cleaner housing – 2.5L engine

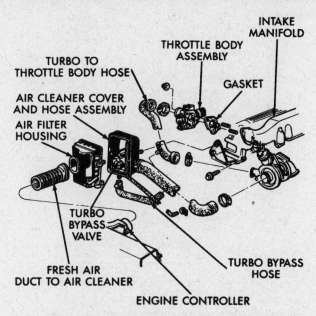

7.2d   Mounting details of the air cleaner housing – 1989 turbo engine

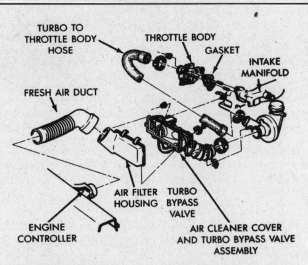

7.2e   Mounting details of the air cleaner housing – 1990 turbo engine

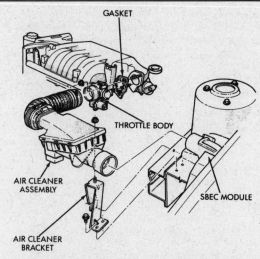

7.2f   Mounting details of the air cleaner housing – 3.3L and 3.8L engines shown, 3.0L engine similar

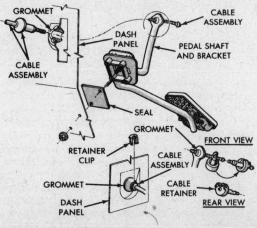

8.1   Typical accelerator pedal and cable details

fresh air inlet tube and the heated inlet air stove pipe for cracks or other damage. If either tube is damaged, replace it.

6   Installation is the reverse of removal.

---

8   Accelerator cable – removal and installation

2.2L and 2.6L engines

Refer to illustrations 8.1, 8.2a and 8.2b

1   Working inside the vehicle, remove the retaining plug and detach the cable end from the accelerator pedal shaft **(see illustration)**.

2   Working in the engine compartment, remove the clip and separate the cable from the pin or stud on the throttle lever, then detach the cable from the mounting bracket **(see illustrations)**. Compress the cable-to-bracket fitting with wide-jaw pliers.

3   Pull the cable assembly into the engine compartment and remove it from the vehicle.

4   Installation is the reverse of removal.

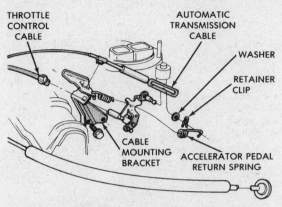

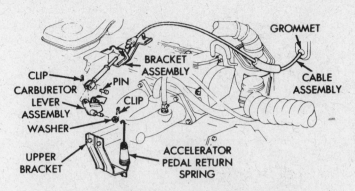

8.2a Accelerator cable details – 2.2L engine

8.2b Accelerator cable details – 2.6L engine

8.6a Use a small pair of needle-nose pliers to remove the retaining clip from the throttle lever (2.5L engine shown, other fuel-injected engines similar)

8.6b Squeeze the grommet with a pair of pliers to allow the tabs to clear the bracket (2.5L engine shown, other fuel-injected engines similar)

4

2.5L engine

Refer to illustrations 8.6a and 8.6b

5   Working inside the vehicle, remove the retainer or plug and detach the cable end from the accelerator pedal shaft **(see illustration 8.1)**. Remove the retainer clip from the cable assembly housing at the grommet and pull the cable through the firewall.

6   Working in the engine compartment, remove the retainer clip and separate the cable from the pin or stud, then detach the cable from the mounting bracket **(see illustration)**. Compress the cable-to-bracket fitting with a pair of pliers **(see illustration)**, then pull the cable through the bracket. **Note:** *If the vehicle is equipped with cruise control, mark the position of the retaining clip on the throttle lever with paint before disconnecting it.*

7   Remove the cable from the engine compartment.

8   Installation is the reverse of removal.

2.5L turbo, 3.0L, 3.3L and 3.8L engines

Refer to illustrations 8.11a, 8.11b and 8.11c

9   Working inside the vehicle, disconnect the throttle cable from the pedal shaft, then disconnect the cable from the firewall **(see illustration 8.1)**.

10   Working in the engine compartment, pull the cable housing end fitting out of the dash panel grommet, making sure the grommet remains in place.

11   Remove the throttle retainer and disconnect the throttle cable and cruise control cable (if equipped) from the throttle body **(see illustrations)**. Use a pair of pliers to compress the end fitting tabs so the cable can be separated from the mounting bracket.

12   To install the cable, insert the housing into the throttle valve on the throttle body. Insert the cable through the firewall grommet and connect it to the throttle pedal.

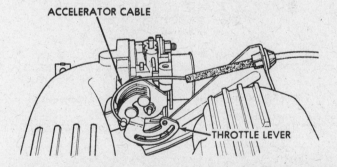

8.11a On turbo engines, rotate the throttle shaft until the cable is out of the guide groove in the bellcrank, then slide the cable end out of the bellcrank

---

9   Fuel lines and fittings – replacement

Refer to illustration 9.5a, 9.5b and 9.5c

Warning: *Gasoline is extremely flammable, so take extra precautions when you work on any part of the fuel system. Don't smoke or allow open flames or bare light bulbs near the work area, and don't work in a garage where a natural gas-type appliance (such as a water heater or clothes dryer) with a pilot light is present. If you spill any fuel on your skin, rinse it off immediately with soap and water. When you perform any kind of work on the fuel system, wear safety glasses and have a Class B type fire extinguisher on hand.*

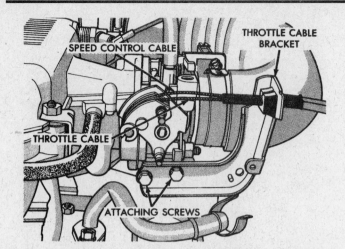

8.11b   Installation details of accelerator cable at throttle body (3.0L engine)

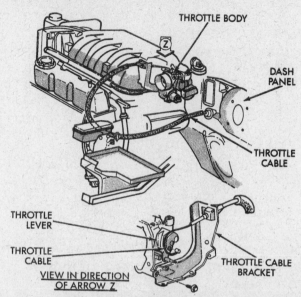

8.11c   Installation details of accelerator cable at throttle body (3.3L and 3.8L engines)

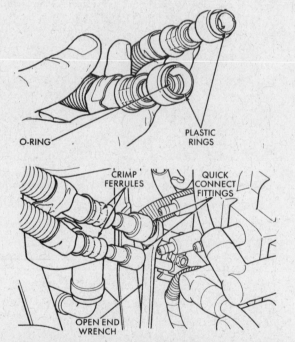

9.5a   Typical quick-connect fittings have an inner plastic lock-ring (fittings for 3.3L and 3.8L engines shown, others similar)

9.5b   To detach a quick-connect fitting from the fuel rail, depress the plastic ring . . .

9.5c   . . . and pull the line from the fuel rail - to reattach it, lubricate the end with a little bit of clean engine oil, then push on the fitting until it clicks into place and tug on it to ensure that the connection is locked into place (3.3L and 3.8L engines)

Note: *Since the EFI system is under considerable pressure, always re-place all clamps released or removed with new ones.*

1   Remove the air cleaner assembly.

2   On fuel-injected engines, relieve the fuel system pressure (see Section 2).

3   Disconnect the negative cable from the battery.

4   On carbureted engines and fuel-injected engines with conventional fuel hose clamps, loosen the hose clamps, wrap a cloth around each end of the hose to catch the residual fuel and twist and pull to remove the hose.

5   On fuel-injected engines with quick-connect fittings, push in on the plastic ring located on the end of the fitting then gently pull the fitting off the fuel rail or fuel pipe **(see illustrations)**.

6   When reconnecting quick-connect fittings, the ends of the fuel lines must be lubricated with a light coat of 30-weight engine oil. Push the fittings onto the fuel rail until they click into place, then tug on the lines to ensure the connection has been made properly.

7   When replacing hoses on fuel-injected models which use conventional hose clamps, always use hoses marked EFI/EFM and use new original equipment-type hose clamps.

8   Connect the negative battery cable, start the engine and check for leaks.

9   Install the air cleaner assembly.

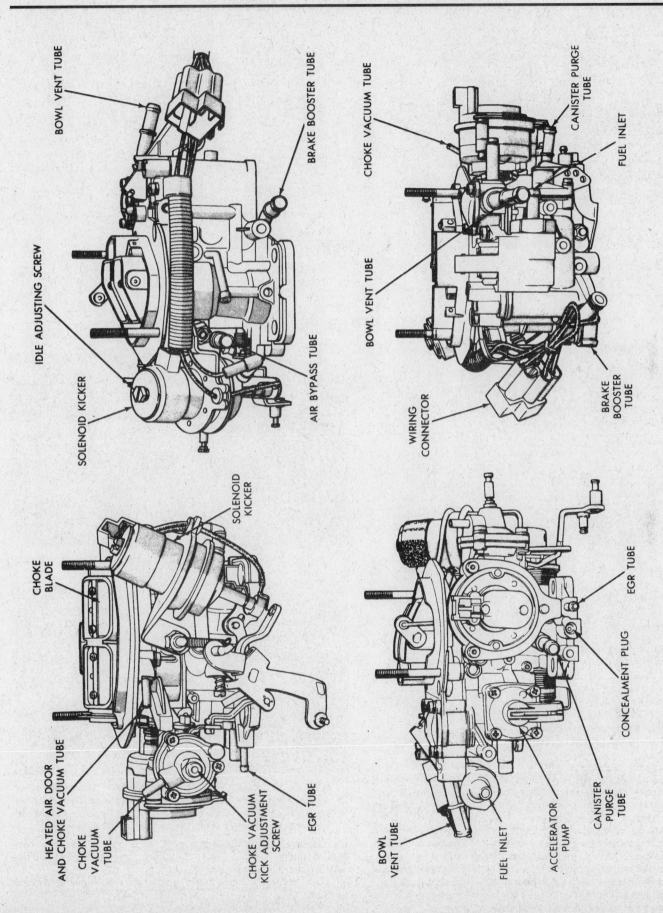

10.1a Holley Model 5220 carburetor

4

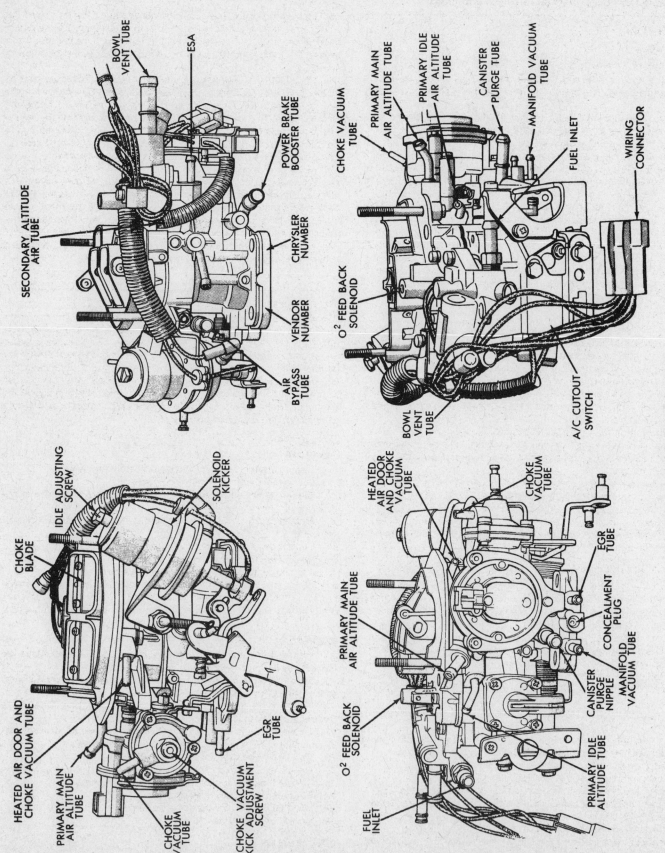

10.1b Holley Model 6520 carburetor

10 Carburetor - description and service information

Description

2.2L engine

Refer to illustrations 10.1a and 10.1b

1   Holley models 5220 and 6520 are staged dual venturi carburetors **(see illustrations)**. The primary bore is smaller than the secondary bore.

2   The secondary stage is mechanically operated by a linkage connecting the primary and secondary throttle levers.

3   The primary stage includes a curb idle and transfer system, diaphragm type accelerator pump system, main metering system and power enrichment system. On model 6520 carburetors, there's also an oxygen feedback solenoid that responds to input from the oxygen sensor.

4   The secondary stage includes a main metering system and power system. Both the primary and secondary venturi draw fuel from a common float bowl.

5   The electric automatic choke has a bimetal two-stage heating element.

6   In normal service, the idle mixture shouldn't require adjustment. The idle speed can be checked without removing the tamper resistant plug.

2.6L engine

Refer to illustrations 10.7a and 10.7b

7   The Mikuni carburetor used on these models is a downdraft two-barrel compound type carburetor **(see illustrations)**.

8   The basic components of the fuel inlet system are the fuel filter, the float needle valve and the float assembly.

9   The idle and primary metering system consists of the primary main jet, the primary pilot jet, the idle mixture adjusting screw and the primary main nozzle.

10   A fuel cut-off solenoid prevents dieseling.

11   The secondary metering system consists of the secondary main jet, secondary pilot jet, secondary main nozzle and a vacuum-controlled diaphragm.

12   The enrichment system consists of a spring-loaded, vacuum actuated diaphragm connected to an enrichment valve.

13   A mechanical accelerator pump consists of a flexible diaphragm, a diaphragm spring, a lever, a link rod and a follow-up spring.

14   A thermo-wax type automatic choke is controlled by engine coolant temperature.

Service information

15   A thorough road test and check of carburetor adjustments should be done before any major carburetor service. Specifications for some adjustments are listed on the *Vehicle Emission Control Information* label found in the engine compartment.

16   Some performance complaints directed at the carburetor are actually a result of loose, misadjusted or malfunctioning engine or electrical components. Others develop when vacuum hoses leak, are disconnected or are incorrectly routed. The proper approach to analyzing carburetor problems should include a routine check of the following areas:

17   Inspect all vacuum hoses and actuators for leaks and proper installation.

18   Tighten the intake manifold nuts and carburetor mounting nuts evenly and securely.

19   Perform a cylinder compression test.

20   Clean or replace the spark plugs as necessary.

21   Check the resistance of the spark plug wires (see Chapter 5).

22   Inspect the ignition primary wires and check the vacuum advance operation. Replace any defective parts.

23   Check the ignition timing (see Chapter 1).

24   Inspect the heat control valve in the air cleaner for proper operation (see Chapters 1 and 6).

25   Remove the carburetor air filter element and blow out any dirt

with compressed air. If the filter is extremely dirty, replace it with a new one.

26   Inspect the crankcase ventilation system (see Chapters 1 and 6).

27   Carburetor problems usually show up as flooding, hard starting, stalling, severe backfiring and poor acceleration. A carburetor that is leaking fuel and/or covered with wet-looking deposits definitely needs attention.

28   Diagnosing carburetor problems may require that the engine be started and run with the air cleaner removed. While running the engine without the air cleaner it is possible that it could backfire. A backfiring situation is likely to occur if the carburetor is malfunctioning, but removal of the air cleaner alone can lean the air/fuel mixture enough to produce an engine backfire. **Warning:** *Do not position your face directly over the carburetor opening in case of engine backfire.*

29   Once it is determined that the carburetor is indeed at fault, it should be replaced with a new or rebuilt unit, or disassembled, cleaned and reassembled using new parts where necessary. Before dismantling the carburetor, make sure you have a carburetor rebuild kit, which will include all necessary gaskets and internal parts, carburetor cleaning solvent and some means of blowing out all the internal passages of the carburetor. To do the job properly, you will also need a clean place to work and plenty of time and patience.

11 Carburetor - removal and installation

Warning: Gasoline is extremely flammable, so take extra precautions when you work on any part of the fuel system. Don't smoke or allow open flames or bare light bulbs near the work area, and don't work in a garage where a natural gas-type appliance (such as a water heater or clothes dryer) with a pilot light is present. If you spill any fuel on your skin, rinse it off immediately with soap and water. When you perform any kind of work on the fuel system, wear safety glasses and have a Class B type fire extinguisher on hand.

2.2L engine
Removal

1   Disconnect the negative battery cable from the battery.

2   Remove the air cleaner assembly.

3   Remove the fuel tank filler cap as the tank could be under some pressure.

4   Place a metal container under the fuel inlet fitting and disconnect the fitting.

5   Disconnect the wiring harness from the carburetor.

6   Disconnect the throttle linkage.

7   Tag and remove all hoses from the carburetor.

8   Remove the mounting nuts and carefully detach the carburetor from the manifold, taking care to hold it level. Do not remove the isolator mounting screws unless the isolator must be replaced with a new one.

Installation

9   Inspect the mating surfaces of the carburetor and the isolator for nicks, burrs and debris that could cause air leaks.

10   Place the carburetor in position and install the mounting nuts, taking care not to damage the fast idle lever.

11   Tighten the nuts to the torque listed in this Chapter's Specifications, following a criss-cross pattern.

12   Check all of the vacuum hoses and connections for damage, replacing them with new parts if necessary, and install them.

13   Connect the throttle linkage and the fuel line.

14   Check the operation of the throttle linkage and the choke plate.

15   Connect the wiring harness and install the air cleaner.

16   Connect the negative battery cable.

17   Start the engine and check for fuel leaks.

18   Check the engine idle speed.

2.6L engine
Removal

19   Disconnect the negative battery cable from the battery.

4

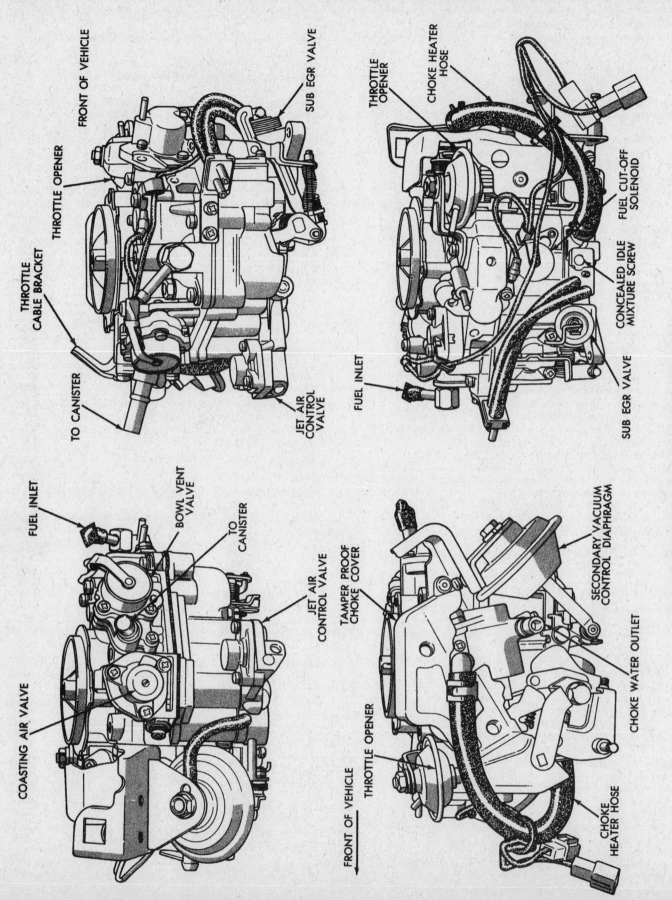

FRONT OF VEHICLE

SUB EGR VALVE

THROTTLE OPENER

THROTTLE CABLE BRACKET

TO CANISTER

JET AIR CONTROL VALVE

THROTTLE OPENER

CHOKE HEATER HOSE

FUEL CUT-OFF SOLENOID

CONCEALED IDLE MIXTURE SCREW

FUEL INLET

SUB EGR VALVE

FUEL INLET

BOWL VENT VALVE

TO CANISTER

JET AIR CONTROL VALVE

COASTING AIR VALVE

TAMPER PROOF CHOKE COVER

SECONDARY VACUUM CONTROL DIAPHRAGM

CHOKE WATER OUTLET

FRONT OF VEHICLE

THROTTLE OPENER

CHOKE HEATER HOSE

10.7a   Mikuni carburetor (California and high-altitude models)

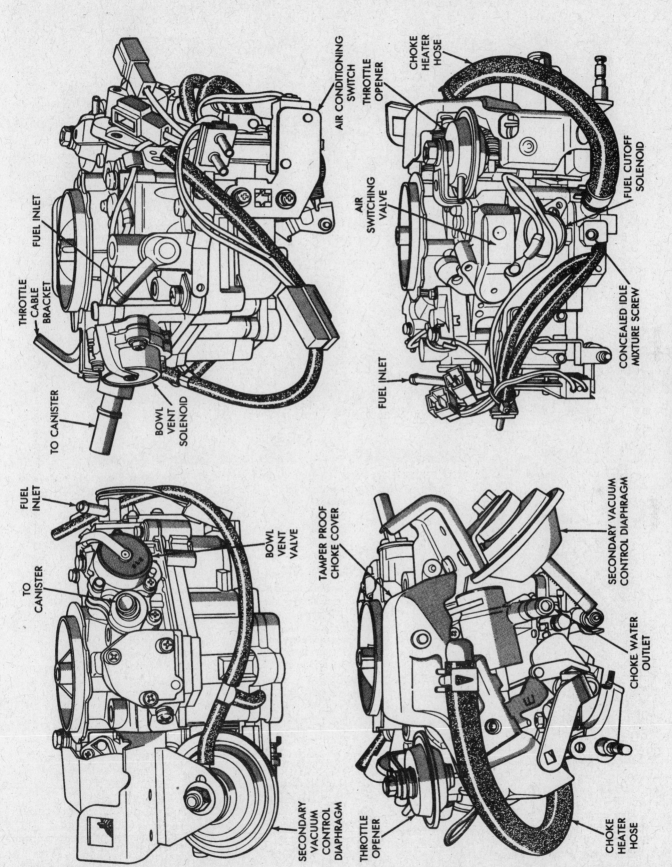

10.7b   Mikuni carburetor (Federal and Canadian models)

4

12.1a   Remove the fuel inlet fitting (2.2L engine)

12.1b   Disconnect the choke rod (2.2L engine)

12.1c   Remove the feedback solenoid mounting screws . . .

12.1d   . . . and detach the solenoid from the air horn (2.2L engine)

12.1e   Disconnect the air conditioner/idle speed solenoid anti-rattle spring (2.2L engine)

12.1f   The solenoid is held in place with two bolts (2.2L engine)

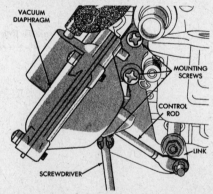

12.1g   The secondary throttle valves on 1985 and 1986 models are operated by a vacuum diaphragm which is held in place by three screws - remove the E-clip from the link post and disconnect the control rod (2.2L engine)

20   Remove the intake housing from the carburetor air horn.
21   Release any pressure which may exist in the fuel tank by removing the filler cap.
22   Drain the cooling system (see Chapter 1).
23   Remove the carburetor protector, tag the locations of the vacuum and coolant hoses and detach them from the carburetor.
24   Unplug the carburetor wiring harness connectors.
25   Place a metal container under the carburetor fuel inlet to catch any residual fuel and disconnect the fuel hose from the inlet fitting.
26   Disconnect the throttle linkage.

27   Remove the mounting bolt and nuts and carefully detach the carburetor from the manifold. Keep the carburetor level to avoid spilling fuel.

Installation
28   Check the mating surfaces of the carburetor and intake manifold for nicks, burrs and old gasket material which could cause air leaks.
29   Using a new gasket, place the carburetor in position and install the mounting nuts and bolt. Tighten them to the torque listed in this Chapter's Specifications, following a criss-cross pattern.
30   Connect the throttle linkage and the fuel hose.
31   Connect the coolant and vacuum hoses and install the carburetor protector.
32   Refill the radiator with the specified coolant (see Chapter 1).
33   Check the operation of the throttle linkage and choke plate.
34   Install the air intake housing and the fuel tank cap.
35   Connect the negative battery cable.
36   Start the engine and check for fuel leaks.
37   Check the engine idle speed (see Section 14).

12   Carburetor (2.2L engine) – overhaul

Warning: Gasoline is extremely flammable, so take extra precautions when you work on any part of the fuel system. Don't smoke or allow open flames or bare light bulbs near the work area, and don't work in a garage where a natural gas-type appliance (such as a water heater or clothes dryer) with a pilot light is present. If you spill any fuel on your skin, rinse it off immediately with soap and water. When you perform

12.1h Remove the Wide Open Throttle cut-out switch (2.2L engine)

12.1i Loosen the air horn screws in a criss-cross pattern to avoid warping it (2.2L engine)

12.1j Carefully pry up on the air horn to release it from the main body (2.2L engine)

12.1k Be careful not to bend the float as the air horn is removed (2.2L engine)

12.1l Withdraw the pivot pin and remove the float (2.2L engine)

12.1m Loosen and remove the fuel inlet needle and seat (2.2L engine)

12.1n Remove the primary and secondary main metering jets (note the numbers on them to ensure reinstallation in the correct positions) (2.2L engine)

12.1o Remove the primary and secondary air bleeds and main well tubes (note the sizes to ensure correct reinstallation) (2.2L engine)

12.1p Remove the accelerator pump discharge assembly (2.2L engine)

4

12.1q   Invert the carburetor and catch the accelerator pump discharge weight and check balls (2.2L engine)

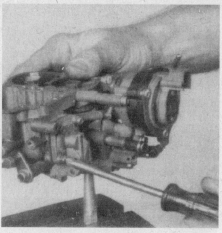

12.1r   Remove the accelerator pump cover (2.2L engine)

12.1s   Remove the pump diaphragm and spring (be careful not to damage the diaphragm) (2.2L engine)

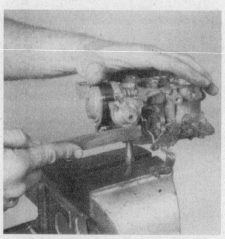

12.1t   File the head off the choke diaphragm cover rivet (if equipped) (2.2L engine)

12.1u   Remove the screws and detach the cover (2.2L engine)

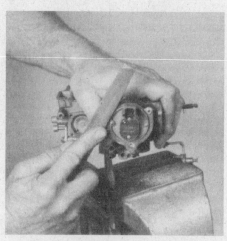

12.1v   File the heads off the choke retainer ring rivets and remove the ring (2.2L engine)

12.1w   Detach the choke housing (2.2L engine)

12.12   Rotate the choke diaphragm clockwise when installing it

12.13   Install the breakaway screw (if equipped) in the bottom hole (2.2L engine)

12.15 Insert the screws through the cover holes before installing the screw (2.2L engine)

12.16 Accelerator pump discharge passage (2.2L engine)

12.25 Measuring the distance between the bottom of the float and the air horn to determine dry float level (2.2L engine)

any kind of work on the fuel system, wear safety glasses and have a Class B type fire extinguisher on hand.

Disassembly

Refer to illustrations 12.1a through 12.1w

1   With the carburetor removed from the engine and a rebuild kit in hand, disassembly can begin. Carburetor disassembly is illustrated in a step-by-step fashion with photos. Follow the photos in the proper sequence and read the caption under each photo **(see illustrations)**.

2   Have a large, clean work area to lay out the parts as they are removed from the carburetor. Many of the parts are very small and can be lost easily if the area is cluttered.

3   Take your time during disassembly. Sketch the relationship of the various components of any assembly which appears complicated or tag the various parts to avoid confusion during reassembly. Care taken during disassembly will pay off during reassembly. Begin disassembly starting with illustration 12.1a

Cleaning and inspection

4   After disassembly, clean the carburetor components with a commercial carburetor solvent. Make sure you keep track of primary and secondary main metering jet and bleed assemblies as they must be reinstalled in their original locations.

5   The choke, vacuum diaphragms, O-rings, feedback solenoid, floats and seals should not be placed in the solvent as they could be damaged.

6   Clean the external surfaces of the carburetor with a soft brush and soak all of the parts in the solvent. If the instructions on the solvent or cleaner recommend the use of water for rinsing, hot water will produce the best results. After rinsing, all traces of water must be blown from the passages with compressed air. **Caution:** *Never clean jets with a wire, drill bit or other metal objects. The orifices could become enlarged, making the mixture too rich for proper performance.*

7   When checking parts removed from the carburetor, it is often difficult to be sure if they are serviceable. It is therefore recommended that new parts be installed, if available, when the carburetor is reassembled. The required parts should be included in the rebuild kit.

8   After the parts have been cleaned and dried, check the throttle shaft for excessive wear.

9   Check the jets for damage and restrictions. Replace them if damage is evident.

10   Check for freedom of movement of the choke mechanism in the air horn. It should move freely for proper operation.

11   Replace any worn or damaged components with new ones.

Reassembly

Refer to illustrations 12.12, 12.13, 12.15, 12.16, 12.25, 12.26, 12.27, 12.28, 12.30, 12.31, 12.36, 12.37, 12.40a, 12.40b, 12.41 and 12.42

12   Press down on the choke lever, insert the choke diaphragm and rotate it into position **(see illustration)**.

13   Position the spring and fit the cover in place. Install the two top screws snugly, followed by the breakaway screw in the bottom hole **(see illustration)**.

14   Tighten the breakaway screw until the head breaks off. Tighten the top screws evenly and securely.

15   Install the accelerator pump, spring (small end first), cover and screws **(see illustration)**.

16   Fill the float bowl with fuel to a depth of one inch and drop the check ball into the accelerator pump discharge passage **(see illustration)**.

17   Use a small brass dowel to hold the check ball in place and push the throttle lever to make sure there is resistance felt and consequently no leakage. If there is leakage, drain the fuel and stake the ball in place with one or two taps of the dowel. Remove the old ball and install the new one from the rebuild kit. Install the weight and repeat the test.

18   Install the accelerator pump discharge nozzle assembly.

19   Install the primary main well tube and high speed bleed.

20   Install the secondary main well tube and high speed bleed.

21   Install the primary main metering jet. On these carburetors the primary main metering jet will have a smaller number stamped on it than the secondary main metering jet.

22   Install the secondary main metering jet.

23   Install the fuel inlet needle and seat assembly.

24   Hook the new needle onto the float tang and lower the assembly into place. Install the float pivot pin.

25   Measure the dry float level **(see illustration)**.

26   Invert the air horn and measure the float drop **(see illustration)**.

27   Adjust the dry float level by carefully bending the inner adjustment tang until the level is within the range listed in this Chapter's Specifications **(see illustration)**.

28   Bend the outer adjustment tang to bring the float drop within the range listed in this Chapter's Specifications **(see illustration)**.

29   Install the choke seal and link and squeeze the link retainer bushing into place.

30   Position the gasket, engage the choke link and lower the air horn assembly into place **(see illustration)**.

31   Install the air horn screws and tighten them securely **(see illustration)**.

32   Install the wide open throttle cutout switch. Move the switch until the circuit is open with the throttle valve 10-degrees before the wide open position.

33   Adjust the solenoid switch by loosening the retaining screw and using a screwdriver to rotate the switch until a click is felt.

34   Tighten the bolt and screws and install the anti-rattle spring.

35   Install the idle speed solenoid.

36   Lubricate the feedback solenoid tip lightly with petroleum jelly and install a new O-ring **(see illustration)**.

37   Install a new gasket and insert the solenoid into position **(see illustration)**.

4

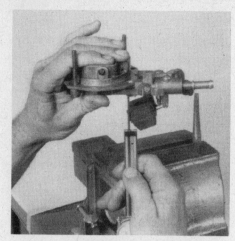

12.26   Measuring the distance from the air horn surface to the top of the float to determine float drop (2.2L engine)

12.27   Carefully bend the tang up or down to change the dry float level (2.2L engine)

12.28   Be sure to support the pivot when bending the float drop adjusting tang (2.2L engine)

12.30   Be very careful not to bend the float tangs when installing the air horn (2.2L engine)

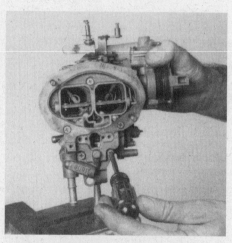

12.31   Tighten the air horn screws in a criss-cross pattern (2.2L engine)

12.36   Install a new O-ring in the solenoid groove (2.2L engine)

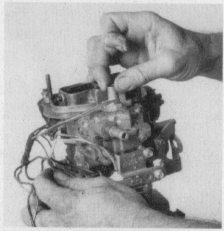

12.37   Rock the solenoid gently from side-to-side to seat the O-ring (2.2L engine)

12.40a   Installing the choke lever bushing (2.2L engine)

12.40b   Rotate the housing approximately 1/8-turn clockwise to align the rivet holes (2.2L engine)

12.41   Install pop rivets to hold the retainer ring in place (2.2L engine)

12.42   Be sure to install a new air intake housing gasket (2.2L engine)

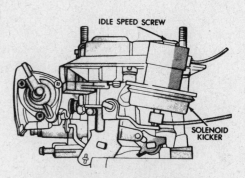

13.8   Idle speed adjusting screw location (2.2L engine)

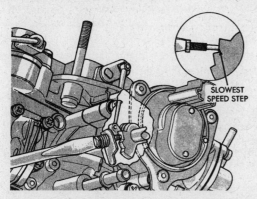

13.17   Fast idle speed adjustment details (2.2L engine)

38   Install the solenoid screws and tighten them evenly and securely.

39   Wrap a piece of Teflon tape around the threads and install the fuel inlet fitting.

40   Install the choke inner housing lever bushing, followed by the spacer and outer housing with the spring end loop over the lever **(see illustrations)**.

41   Install the choke housing rivets **(see illustration)**. The shorter rivet goes in the bottom hole.

42   Install the intake housing gasket **(see illustration)**.

13   Carburetor (2.2L engine) – adjustments

Idle speed adjustment

Refer to illustration 13.8

1   Start the engine and run it until normal operating temperature is reached.

2   Check the ignition timing and adjust as necessary (see Chapter 1), then shut off the engine.

3   On 1984 and 1985 models, disconnect and plug the vacuum connector at the CVSCC (see Chapter 6 if necessary). On 1986 models, disconnect the wires from the kicker solenoid on the left inner fender panel. On all models, disconnect the oxygen feedback system test connector located on the left inner fender panel (6520 carbureted models only).

4   Unplug the fan electrical connector and install a jumper wire so the fan will run continuously.

5   Remove the PCV valve from the vent module so the valve will draw air from the engine compartment.

6   Leave the air cleaner in place and connect a tachometer. Ground the carburetor switch with a jumper wire.

7   Start the engine.

8   Check the idle speed reading on the tachometer and compare it to the Emissions Control Information label. Turn the idle speed screw **(see illustration)** as necessary to achieve the idle speed listed in this Chapter's Specifications.

9   Shut off the engine and remove the tachometer.

10   Remove the carburetor switch jumper wire, plug in the fan connector, install the PCV valve and reinstall any vacuum hoses and wires which were disconnected.

Air conditioning idle speed adjustment

11   Air conditioned models are equipped with a system which boosts idle speed when the air conditioning compressor engages, to compensate for the greater load placed on the engine. Prior to checking the air conditioning idle speed, check the curb idle and timing (see Chapter 1) to make sure they are correct. The checks should be made with the engine at normal operating temperature.

12   When the air conditioner is engaged, the idle speed is increased by a vacuum or solenoid-type kicker.

13   Kicker operation can be checked by running the engine (at normal operating temperature), moving the temperature control to the coldest setting and then turning the air conditioning on. The kicker plunger should move in and out as the compressor clutch engages and disengages. Remove the air cleaner for better visual access to the kicker, if necessary **(see illustration 13.8)**.

14   If the idle speed doesn't change as the air conditioner cycles on and off, check the system hoses and diaphragm for leaks and make sure the vacuum solenoid (which directs vacuum to the kicker) is operating. If no defective parts are found, replace the kicker with a new one and repeat the check.

Fast idle adjustment

Refer to illustration 13.17

15   Perform Steps 1 through 6.

16   On 1986 models, disconnect the vacuum hoses from the CVSCC and plug both hoses.

17   Start the engine, open the throttle slightly and set the fast idle screw on the slowest step of the fast idle cam **(see illustration)**.

18   With the choke valve fully open, adjust the fast idle speed to the specification on the Emissions Control Information label by turning the adjustment screw.

19   Return the engine to idle, then reposition the fast idle screw on the slowest step of the fast idle cam to verify the fast idle speed. Adjust as necessary.

20   Turn off the engine, remove the tachometer and reconnect all components removed for the adjustment procedure.

Choke vacuum kick adjustment

Refer to illustration 13.25

21   Remove the air cleaner.

4

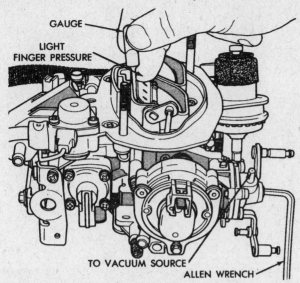

13.25   Choke vacuum kick adjustment details (2.2L engine)

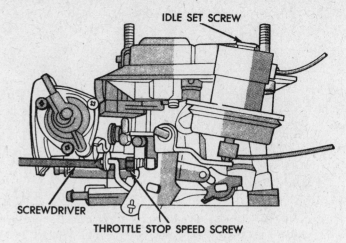

13.30   Anti-diesel adjustment details (2.2L engine)

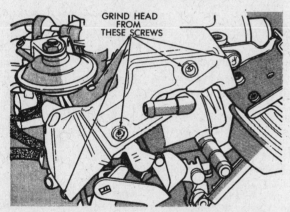

14.3a   Choke cover screw locations (2.6L engine)

22   Open the throttle, close the choke and then close the throttle so the fast idle system is trapped at the closed choke position.
23   Disconnect the carburetor vacuum hose, connect a vacuum pump and apply 15-inches of vacuum.
24   Push the choke closed so the plates are at their smallest opening (use very light pressure and do not distort the linkage). The choke system internal spring will now be compressed.
25   Insert the appropriate size drill bit or gauge between the plate and the air horn wall at the primary throttle end of the carburetor. Check the clearance against the Specifications and adjust as necessary by turning an Allen wrench inserted into the diaphragm **(see illustration)**.
26   After adjustment, replace the vacuum hose and the air cleaner assembly.

Anti-diesel adjustment

Refer to illustration 13.30

27   Warm up the engine to operating temperature, check the ignition timing (see Chapter 1), then shut it off. Connect a tachometer.
28   Remove the red wire from the 6-way connector on the carburetor side of the connector.
29   With the transaxle in Neutral, the parking brake set securely and the wheels blocked to prevent any movement, ground the carburetor idle stop switch with a jumper wire and turn the headlights off. Start the engine.
30   Adjust the throttle stop speed screw **(see illustration)** to achieve an idle speed of 700 rpm.
31   Shut off the engine, remove the tachometer, remove the jumper wire and connect the carburetor idle stop switch wire.

14   Carburetor (2.6L engine) – overhaul

Warning: *Gasoline is extremely flammable, so take extra precautions when you work on any part of the fuel system. Don't smoke or allow open flames or bare light bulbs near the work area, and don't work in a garage where a natural gas-type appliance (such as a water heater or clothes dryer) with a pilot light is present. If you spill any fuel on your skin, rinse it off immediately with soap and water. When you perform any kind of work on the fuel system, wear safety glasses and have a Class B type fire extinguisher on hand.*

Disassembly

Refer to illustrations 14.3a, 14.3b, 14.4, 14.5, 14.7 and 14.10 through 14.26

1   With the carburetor removed from the vehicle (see Section 11) and a rebuild kit on hand, disassembly can begin. Have a large, clean work area to lay out parts as they are removed. Many of the parts are very small and can be lost easily if the work area is cluttered. Take your time during disassembly and sketch the relationship of the various parts to simplify reassembly.
2   Remove the coolant hoses from the choke and throttle valve assemblies.
3   Remove the choke cover by grinding or filing off the heads of the screws **(see illustration)**. Use a small hammer and pointed punch to tap the edge of the remaining screw until it is loose **(see illustration)**. Note the relationship between the punched mark and scribed lines on the choke pinion plate. During reassembly the marks must be realigned.
4   Remove the throttle opener link E-clip, followed by the two mounting screws. Lift the opener assembly off **(see illustration)**.
5   Disconnect the ground wire, remove the mounting screw and detach the fuel cut-off solenoid **(see illustration)**.
6   Remove the throttle return spring and damper spring.
7   Remove the choke unloader clips and link, followed by the vacuum chamber (two screws) **(see illustration)**.
8   Disconnect the accelerator pump link from the throttle lever.
9   Remove the vacuum hose connector and hoses from the air horn (two screws).
10   Remove the six screws and detach the air horn from the carburetor body **(see illustration)**.
11   Slide the pivot pin out and remove the float and needle assembly **(see illustration)**. Discard the air horn gasket.

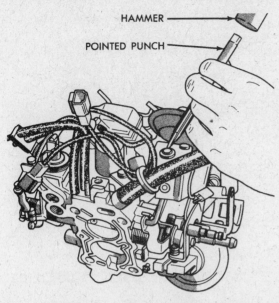

HAMMER

POINTED PUNCH

14.3b   The remaining choke cover screw must be unscrewed
with a hammer and punch (2.6L engine)

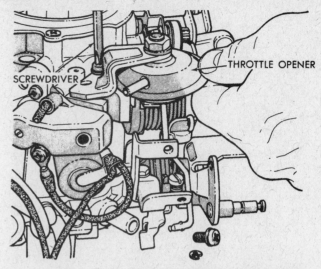

SCREWDRIVER

THROTTLE OPENER

14.4   Removing the throttle opener assembly (2.6L engine)

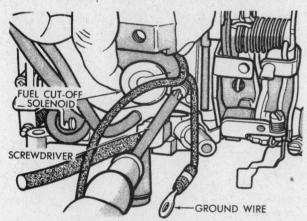

FUEL CUT-OFF
SOLENOID

SCREWDRIVER

GROUND WIRE

14.5   Removing the fuel cut-off solenoid (2.6L engine)

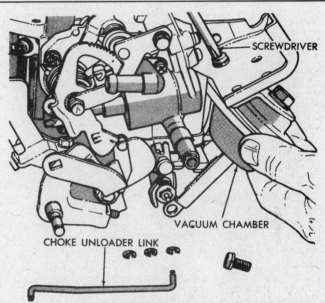

SCREWDRIVER

VACUUM CHAMBER

CHOKE UNLOADER LINK

14.7   Removing the choke link and vacuum chamber
(2.6L engine)

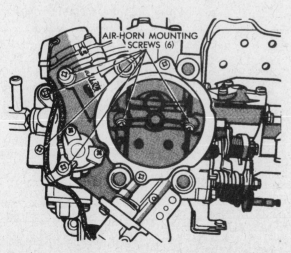

AIR-HORN MOUNTING
SCREWS (6)

14.10   Air horn mounting screw locations (2.6L engine)

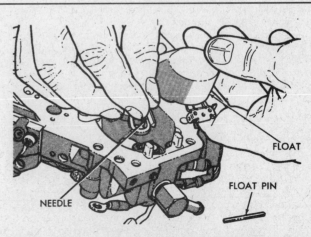

FLOAT

NEEDLE

FLOAT PIN

14.11   Removing the float and inlet needle (2.6L engine)

4

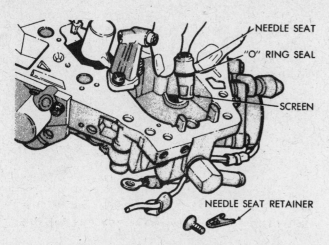

14.12   Removing the retainer and needle seat assembly (note the O-ring and filter screen) (2.6L engine)

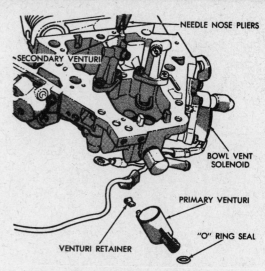

14.13   Removing the venturis (2.6L engine)

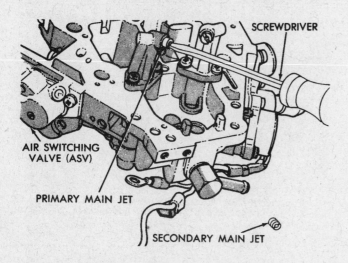

14.14   Removing the main jets (2.6L engine)

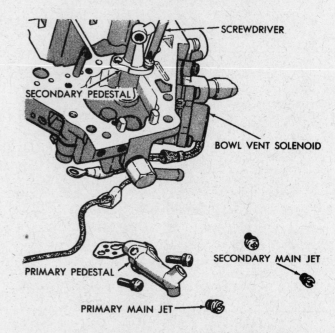

14.15   Removing the main jet pedestals (2.6L engine)

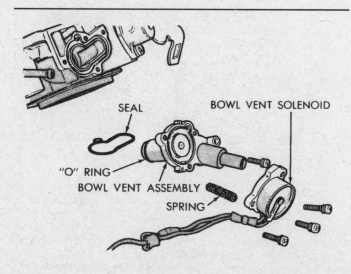

14.16   An exploded view of the bowl vent assembly components (2.6L engine)

12   Unscrew the retainer and remove the needle seat and screen assembly, taking care not to lose the shim located under the seat **(see illustration).**

13   Remove the venturis and retainers, discarding the O-rings. Mark the primary and secondary venturis so they can be reinstalled in the same positions. The primary venturis are the larger of the two **(see illustration).**

14   Unscrew the primary and secondary main jets with a screwdriver **(see illustration).** Be sure to note the numbers on the jets to simplify reassembly.

15   Remove the retaining screws and the primary and secondary jet pedestals **(see illustration).** Discard the gaskets.

16   Remove the bowl vent valve solenoid and spring (three screws), followed by the remaining screw and the bowl vent assembly **(see illustration).** Discard the O-ring.

17   Remove the Coasting Air Valve (CAV) assembly (three screws) **(see illustration).**

18   Remove the enrichment valve assembly and jet **(see illustration).**

19   Remove the Air Switching Valve (ASV) assembly **(see illustra-**

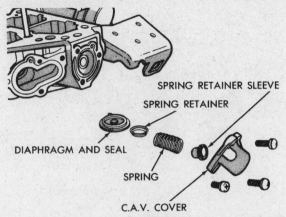

14.17 An exploded view of the CAV assembly components (2.6L engine)

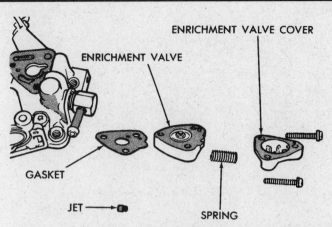

14.18 An exploded view of the enrichment valve components (2.6L engine)

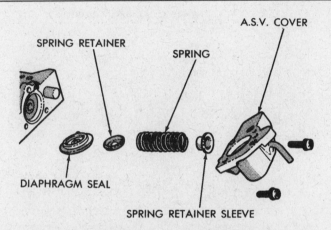

14.19 An exploded view of the Air Switching Valve (ASV) components (2.6L engine)

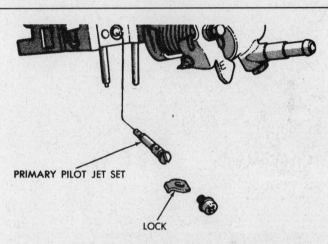

14.20 Primary pilot jet set mounting details (2.6L engine)

4

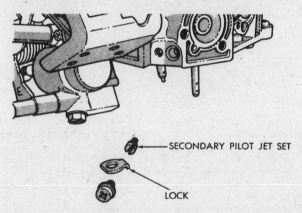

14.21 Secondary pilot jet set mounting details (2.6L engine)

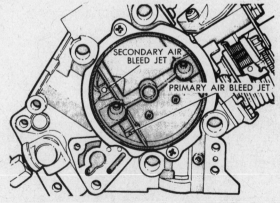

14.22 Air bleed jet locations (2.6L engine)

20 Remove the screw, lock and primary pilot jet set **(see illustration)**.

21 Remove the screw, lock and secondary pilot jet set **(see illustration)**.

22 Remove the primary and secondary air bleed jets from the top of the air horn **(see illustration)**. Be sure to note their sizes as they must be reinstalled in the same locations.

23 Turn the carburetor body over carefully and catch the weight, check ball and hex nut **(see illustration)**.

24 Remove the accelerator pump assembly **(see illustration)**.

25 Remove the Jet Air Control Valve (JACV) assembly **(see illustration)**.

26 Remove the E-clip and carefully slide the sub EGR valve pin from

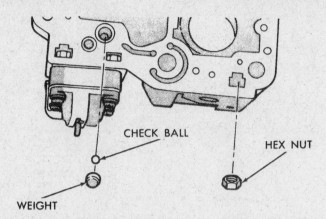

14.23   The weight, check ball and hex nut must be reinstalled in their original locations (2.6L engine)

CHECK BALL

HEX NUT

WEIGHT

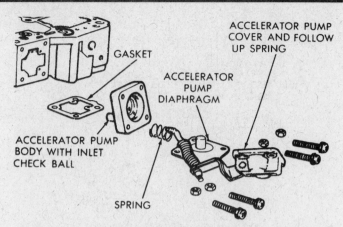

14.24   An exploded view of the accelerator pump assembly components (2.6L engine)

ACCELERATOR PUMP COVER AND FOLLOW UP SPRING

GASKET

ACCELERATOR PUMP DIAPHRAGM

ACCELERATOR PUMP BODY WITH INLET CHECK BALL

SPRING

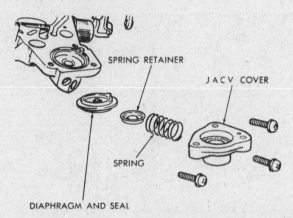

SPRING RETAINER

JACV COVER

SPRING

DIAPHRAGM AND SEAL

14.25   An exploded view of the Jet Air Control Valve (JACV) components (2.6L engine)

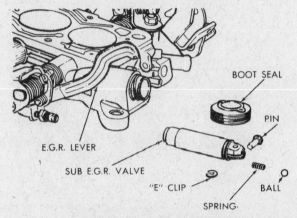

BOOT SEAL

PIN

E.G.R. LEVER

SUB E.G.R. VALVE

"E" CLIP

SPRING

BALL

14.26   An exploded view of the sub-EGR valve assembly components (2.6L engine)

the lever, taking care not to lose the steel ball and spring which maintain tension on the lever. Remove the sub EGR valve assembly **(see illustration)**.

Cleaning and inspection

27   Once the carburetor has been completely disassembled, clean the parts with a commercial carburetor solvent.
28   The choke, vacuum diaphragms, O-ring;, electric solenoids, floats and seals should not be placed in the solvent as they could be damaged.
29   Clean the external surfaces of the carburetor with a soft brush and soak all of the parts in the solvent. If the instructions on the solvent or cleaner recommend the use of water for rinsing, hot water will produce the best results. After rinsing, all traces of water must be blown from the passages with compressed air. **Caution:** *Never clean jets with a wire, drill bit or other metal objects. The orifices may be enlarged, making the mixture too rich for proper performance.*
30   When checking parts removed from the carburetor, it is often difficult to be sure if they are serviceable. It is therefore recommended that new parts be installed, if available, when the carburetor is reassembled. The required parts should be included in the carburetor rebuild kit.
31   After the parts have been cleaned and dried, check the throttle valve shaft for proper operation. If sticking or binding occurs, clean the shafts with solvent and lubricate them with engine oil.
32   Check the jets for damage and restrictions. Replace them if damage is evident.
33   Check the strainer screen for restrictions and damage.
34   Check the vacuum chamber. Push the chamber rod in, seal off

the nipple and release the rod. If the rod does not return, the vacuum chamber is most likely in good condition. If the rod returns when released, the diaphragm is defective. The vacuum chamber should be replaced with a new one if this condition exists.
35   To check the fuel cut-off solenoid, connect a jumper wire to the positive (+) terminal of a 12-volt battery and the wire from the solenoid. Connect a second jumper wire to the negative (-) terminal of the battery and the solenoid ground wire. The needle should move in (toward the solenoid) when the battery is connected and out when the battery is disconnected.

Reassembly

Refer to illustrations 14.50, 14.58a and 14.58b
36   Install the sub EGR valve components **(see illustration 14.26)**, attach the assembly to the carburetor body and secure it with the E-clip.
37   Attach the JACV components to the throttle body **(see illustration 14.25)**.
38   Install the accelerator pump assembly components **(see illustration 14.24)**.
39   Install the primary and secondary air jet bleeds in the air horn, noting that the secondary bleed has the highest number.
40   Install a new O-ring on the secondary pilot jet set, insert the assembly and install the retaining screw.
41   Install a new O-ring on the primary pilot jet set and install the assembly.
42   Attach the ASV components to the carburetor **(see illustration 14.19)**.
43   Install the jet, followed by the rest of the enrichment valve com-

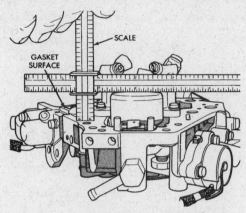

14.50   Checking the dry float level (2.6L engine)

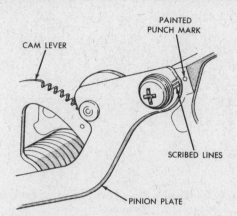

14.58a   When installing the choke, make sure the punch mark and scribed lines are correctly aligned ...

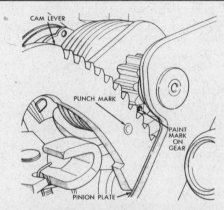

14.58b   ... and index the painted gear tooth with the punch mark on the cam lever before tightening the screws (2.6L engine)

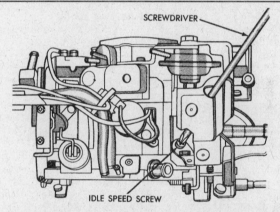

15.4   Idle speed adjusting screw location (2.6L engine)

4

ponents **(see illustration 14.18).**

44   Assemble the CAV components **(see illustration 14.17),** attach the assembly to the air horn and retain it with the three mounting screws.

45   Assemble the bowl vent valve **(see illustration 14.16),** install the valve and solenoid and tighten the mounting screws.

46   Using new gaskets, install the primary and secondary pedestals and mounting screws, followed by the main primary and secondary jets. Remember that the secondary jet has the largest number.

47   Attach new O-rings to the primary and secondary venturis and install the venturis and retainers.

48   Install a new O-ring and screen on the needle seat and install the shim in the air horn. Install the needle seat retainer and screw and tighten it securely.

49   Place the needle and float assembly in position and retain it in the air horn with the pivot pin.

50   Invert the air horn and measure the distance from the gasket surface (gasket removed) to the bottom surface of the float **(see illustration)** to determine the dry float level. Compare it to this Chapter's Specifications.

51   If the dry float level is more or less than it was during disassembly, remove the float, unscrew the inlet needle seat and add or remove shims (as necessary) to change the float height. Repeat the procedure as required until the distance is as specified.

52   Using a new gasket, attach the main body to the throttle body and install the nut, check ball and weight.

53   Attach the air horn, using a new gasket, to the main body and secure it with the six mounting screws.

54   Attach the two vacuum hoses and the wiring connector to the throttle body and engage the accelerator rod link in the throttle lever.

55   Place the vacuum chamber in position on the bracket, install the retaining screws and connect the vacuum hose and link to the secondary throttle lever. Connect the choke unloader link and retain it with the E-clips.

56   Install a new O-ring on the fuel cut-off solenoid, place the solenoid on the mixing body and install the retaining screw. Place the ground wire in position and retain it with the screw.

57   Install the throttle opener on the air horn and connect the link with the E-clip.

58   Install the choke cover, using the special breakaway screws. Make sure the punch and scribe marks and the cam lever are correctly aligned **(see illustrations).**

59   Attach the coolant hose to the carburetor and tighten the clamps.

---

15   Carburetor (2.6L engine) – idle speed adjustment

Refer to illustrations 15.4 and 15.5

1   With the transaxle in Neutral, the parking brake set and the wheels blocked to prevent any movement, turn off the lights and all accessories. Connect a tachometer to the engine, start the engine and allow it to warm up to normal operating temperature so the choke is fully open. Check the ignition timing (see Chapter 1).

2   Disconnect the cooling fan wire, then open the throttle and run the engine at 2500 rpm for 10 seconds. Return the engine to idle and wait two minutes.

3   After waiting two minutes with the curb idle stabilized, check the rpm indicated on the tachometer and make sure it is the same as specified on the Emissions Control Information label.

4   If it isn't, turn the idle speed screw to bring the rpm to the proper curb idle setting **(see illustration).**

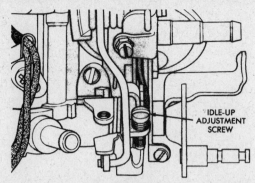

15.5   Air conditioner idle–up adjustment screw location (2.6L engine)

5   On air-conditioned models, turn on the air conditioner and, with the compressor running, adjust the idle speed to the specified rpm by turning the idle-up adjustment screw **(see illustration)**.

6   Shut off the engine, reconnect the cooling fan and remove the tachometer.

16   Fuel injection system – general information

Two types of Electronic Fuel Injection (EFI) systems are used on these models. Single-point EFI is used on the normally aspirated 2.5L four-cylinder engine; multi-point EFI is used on the turbocharged 2.5L engine and on the 3.0L, 3.3L and 3.8L V6 engines.

Both types are similar in operation. Each is an electronically controlled system which combines electronic fuel injection and electronic spark advance. The main sub-systems include the air induction, fuel delivery, fuel control, emission control and the Single Module Engine Controller (SMEC) (1987 through 1989 models), Single Board Engine Controller (SBEC) (1990 and 1991 models) or Powertrain Control Module (PCM) (1992 and later models). Each system differs slightly in the type and location of these components.

Air induction system

The air induction system includes the air cleaner, throttle body, Throttle Position Sensor (TPS), Automatic Idle Speed (AIS) motor and turbocharger (if equipped).

Fuel delivery system

The fuel delivery system provides fuel from the fuel tank into the fuel control system. It also returns any excess fuel back into the fuel tank. The system includes an in-tank electric fuel pump, fuel filter, check valves and return line. Power is supplied to the fuel pump through the power module via the Automatic Shutdown (ASD) relay. The ASD relay also controls the ignition coil, the fuel injectors and parts of the power module.

Fuel control system

On single-point EFI systems, the components of the fuel control system are the fuel pressure regulator, the fuel injector and the throttle body **(see illustrations 18.4a and 18.4b)**. On multi-point systems, they include the fuel pressure regulator, the fuel rail, the fuel injectors and the throttle body.

Fuel injectors

On both single and multi-point EFI systems, the conventional carburetor is replaced by a throttle body and injector (single-point) or throttle body, fuel rail and injectors (multi-point). On single-point EFI, the fuel is mixed with air in the throttle body and sprayed into the intake manifold, which directs it to the intake ports and cylinders. On multi-point EFI, the fuel is sprayed directly into the ports by the fuel injectors, with the intake manifold supplying only the air.

Because of the complexity of the EFI system – and the special equipment required to troubleshoot it – the home mechanic can do little diagnosis. But checking electrical and vacuum connections to make sure they're clean, tight and undamaged can often eliminate a potential or current problem. Because the SMEC/SBEC is dependent on the data provided by information sensors and transmitted through electrical and vacuum connections, a thorough visual check and repair of any damaged or loose connections, wires or vacuum hoses can save diagnostic time and unnecessary trips to the dealer or repair shop.

Besides the simple checks described in the next Section, further diagnosis is difficult, but once you've determined - with the help of your dealer - that a component is defective, we'll show you how to replace it in the following Sections.

17   Fuel injection system – check

Note: *the following procedure is based on the assumption that the fuel pressure is adequate (see Section 3).*

1   Check the ground wire connections on the intake manifold for tightness. Check all wiring harness connectors that are related to the system. Loose connectors and poor grounds can cause many problems that resemble more serious malfunctions.

2   Check to see that the battery is fully charged, as the control unit and sensors depend on an accurate supply voltage in order to properly meter the fuel.

3   Check the air filter element – a dirty or partially blocked filter will severely impede performance and economy (see Chapter 1).

4   If a blown fuse is found, replace it and see if it blows again. If it does, search for a grounded wire in the harness to the fuel pump.

5   On multi-point systems, check the air intake duct to the intake manifold for leaks, which will result in an excessively lean mixture. Also check the condition of all vacuum hoses connected to the intake manifold.

6   On multi-point systems, remove the air intake duct from the throttle body and check for dirt, carbon or other residue build-up. If it's dirty, clean it with carburetor cleaner and a toothbrush.

7   With the engine running, place a screwdriver against each injector, one at a time, and listen through the handle for a clicking sound, indicating operation.

8   The remainder of the system checks can be found in the following Sections.

18   Throttle body (single-point EFI) – removal and installation

Warning: *Gasoline is extremely flammable, so take extra precautions when you work on any part of the fuel system. Don't smoke or allow open flames or bare light bulbs near the work area, and don't work in a garage where a natural gas-type appliance (such as a water heater or clothes dryer) with a pilot light is present. If you spill any fuel on your skin, rinse it off immediately with soap and water. When you perform any kind of work on the fuel system, wear safety glasses and have a Class B type fire extinguisher on hand.*

Removal

Refer to illustration 18.4a, 18.4b and 18.8

1   Remove the air cleaner assembly (see Section 7).

2   Relieve the fuel system pressure (see Section 2).

3   Disconnect the negative cable from the battery.

4   Disconnect the vacuum hoses and electrical connectors **(see illustrations)**.

5   Disconnect the accelerator cable (see Section 8), and (if equipped) the cruise control and transaxle kickdown cable (see Chapter 7).

6   Remove the throttle return spring.

7   Place rags or newspapers under the fuel hoses to catch the residual fuel. Loosen the clamps, wrap a cloth around each fuel hose and pull them off. Remove the copper washers from the hoses, noting their locations.

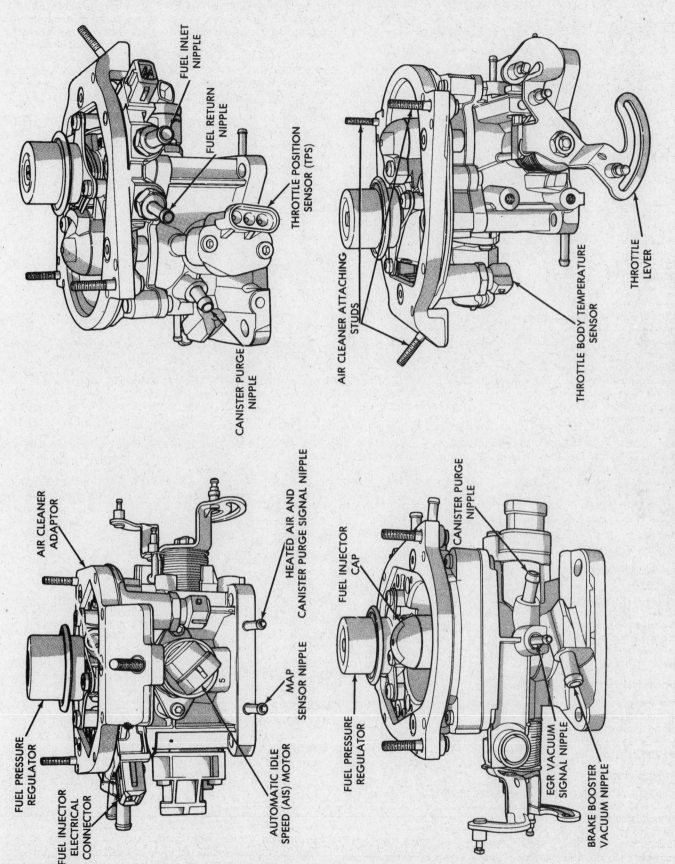

FUEL INLET NIPPLE

FUEL RETURN NIPPLE

THROTTLE POSITION SENSOR (TPS)

CANISTER PURGE NIPPLE

AIR CLEANER ATTACHING STUDS

THROTTLE BODY TEMPERATURE SENSOR

THROTTLE LEVER

AIR CLEANER ADAPTOR

HEATED AIR AND CANISTER PURGE SIGNAL NIPPLE

MAP SENSOR NIPPLE

AUTOMATIC IDLE SPEED (AIS) MOTOR

FUEL PRESSURE REGULATOR

FUEL INJECTOR ELECTRICAL CONNECTOR

FUEL INJECTOR CAP

CANISTER PURGE NIPPLE

FUEL PRESSURE REGULATOR

EGR VACUUM SIGNAL NIPPLE

BRAKE BOOSTER VACUUM NIPPLE

18.4a   Throttle body details (1987 through 1990 2.5L engines)

4

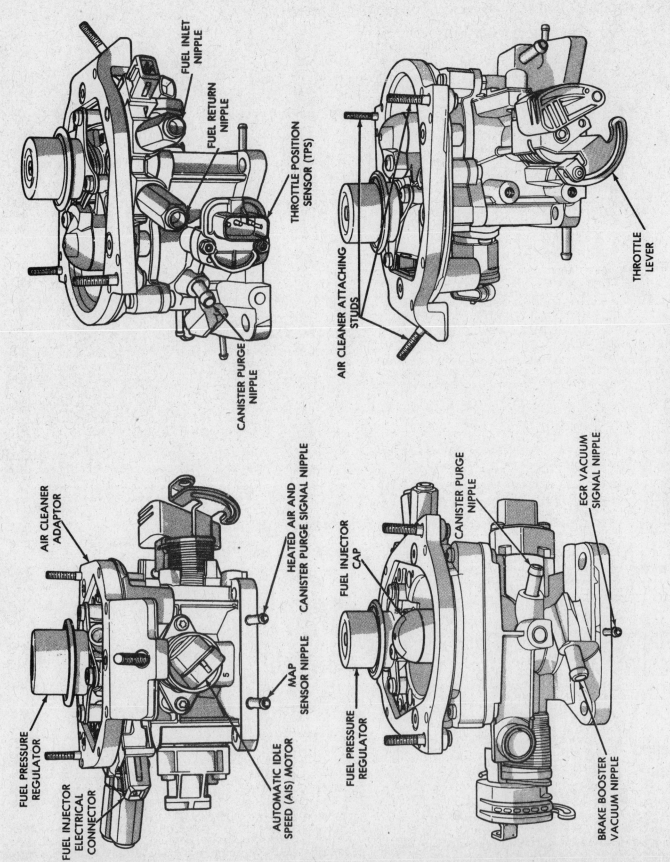

FUEL INLET NIPPLE

FUEL RETURN NIPPLE

THROTTLE POSITION SENSOR (TPS)

CANISTER PURGE NIPPLE

AIR CLEANER ATTACHING STUDS

THROTTLE LEVER

AIR CLEANER ADAPTOR

HEATED AIR AND CANISTER PURGE SIGNAL NIPPLE

MAP SENSOR NIPPLE

AUTOMATIC IDLE SPEED (AIS) MOTOR

FUEL PRESSURE REGULATOR

FUEL INJECTOR ELECTRICAL CONNECTOR

FUEL INJECTOR CAP

CANISTER PURGE NIPPLE

EGR VACUUM SIGNAL NIPPLE

FUEL PRESSURE REGULATOR

BRAKE BOOSTER VACUUM NIPPLE

18.4b   Throttle body details (1991 2.5L engine)

18.8   Remove the two long bolts (arrows) and the two short bolts (arrow) from the throttle body (the shorter rear bolt is hidden from view)

8   Remove the mounting bolts or nuts **(see illustration)** and lift the throttle body off the manifold.

Installation

9   Inspect the mating surfaces of the throttle body and the manifold for nicks, burrs and debris that could cause air leaks.
10   Using a new gasket, place the throttle body in position and install the mounting bolts or nuts.
11   Tighten the bolts or nuts to the torque listed in this Chapter's Specifications, following a criss-cross pattern. Work up to the final torque in three or four steps.
12   Check all of the vacuum hoses and electrical connectors for damage, replacing them with new parts if necessary, then connect them.
13   Connect the accelerator cable and (if equipped) cruise control and kickdown cable.
14   Connect the throttle return spring.
15   Using new clamps and washers, install the fuel hoses.
16   Check the operation of the throttle linkage.
17   Install the air cleaner assembly.
18   Connect the negative battery cable.
19   Start the engine and check for fuel leaks.

19   Fuel pressure regulator (single-point EFI) check, removal and installation

Warning: *Gasoline is extremely flammable, so take extra precautions when you work on any part of the fuel system. Don't smoke or allow open flames or bare light bulbs near the work area, and don't work in a garage where a natural gas-type appliance (such as a water heater or clothes dryer) with a pilot light is present. If you spill any fuel on your skin, rinse it off immediately with soap and water. When you perform any kind of work on the fuel system, wear safety glasses and have a Class B type fire extinguisher on hand.*

Check

1   Follow the fuel pressure checking procedure in Section 3 for diagnosis of the fuel pressure regulator.

Removal

Refer to illustrations 19.5 and 19.7
2   Remove the air cleaner assembly (see Section 7).
3   Relieve the fuel system pressure (see Section 2).
4   Disconnect the negative cable from the battery.
5   Remove the three screws (this will require a no. 25 Torx drive socket) from the regulator **(see illustration)**.
6   Wrap a cloth around the fuel inlet chamber to catch any residual

19.5   Use a Torx drive socket (no. 25) and remove the three bolts from the regulator

19.7   If the regulator is still fastened to the throttle body after the bolts have been removed, wiggle the regulator to free-up the hardened rubber seal

fuel, which is under pressure.
7   Withdraw the pressure regulator from the throttle body **(see illustration)**.
8   Carefully remove the O-ring from the pressure regulator, followed by the gasket.

Installation

9   Place a new gasket in position on the pressure regulator and carefully install a new O-ring.
10   Place the pressure regulator in position on the throttle body, press it into position and install the three mounting screws. Tighten the screws securely.
11   Connect the negative battery cable. Check carefully for any fuel leaks.
12   Install the air cleaner assembly (see Section 7).

20   Fuel injector (single-point EFI) – check, removal and installation

Warning: *Gasoline is extremely flammable, so take extra precautions when you work on any part of the fuel system. Don't smoke or allow open flames or bare light bulbs near the work area, and don't work in a garage where a natural gas-type appliance (such as a water heater or clothes dryer) with a pilot light is present. If you spill any fuel on your skin, rinse it off immediately with soap and water. When you perform any kind of work on the fuel system, wear safety glasses and have a Class B type fire extinguisher on hand.*

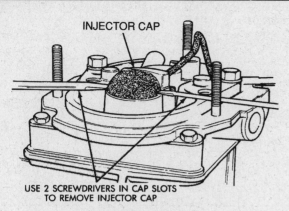

INJECTOR CAP

USE 2 SCREWDRIVERS IN CAP SLOTS
TO REMOVE INJECTOR CAP

20.7   Use two small screwdrivers to pry the injector cap off

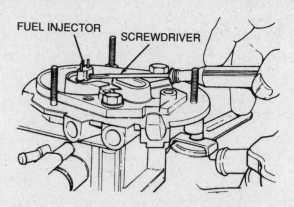

FUEL INJECTOR   SCREWDRIVER

20.8   Remove the fuel injector by inserting a small screwdriver into the slot on the injector and gently prying it up

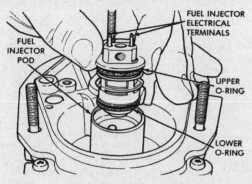

FUEL INJECTOR
ELECTRICAL
TERMINALS

FUEL
INJECTOR
POD

UPPER
O-RING

LOWER
O-RING

20.9   Fuel injector details

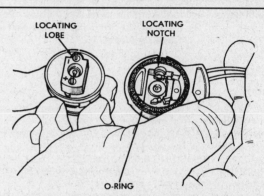

LOCATING
LOBE

LOCATING
NOTCH

O-RING

20.12a   Alignment details of the cap and injector (1987 models)

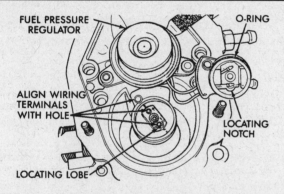

FUEL PRESSURE
REGULATOR

O-RING

ALIGN WIRING
TERMINALS
WITH HOLE

LOCATING
NOTCH

LOCATING LOBE

20.12b   Alignment details of the cap and injector (1988 through 1991 models)

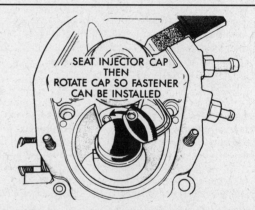

SEAT INJECTOR CAP
THEN
ROTATE CAP SO FASTENER
CAN BE INSTALLED

20.13   Rotate the cap so the screw aligns with the slot in the cap

Check

1   With the engine running, or cranking, listen to the sound from the injector with an automotive stethoscope and verify that the injector sounds as if it's operating normally. If you don't have a stethoscope, touch the area of the throttle body immediately above the fuel injector with your finger and try to determine whether the injector feels like it's operating smoothly. It should sound/feel smooth and uniform and its sound/feel should rise and fall with engine rpm. If the injector isn't operating, or sounds/feels erratic, check the injector electrical connector and the wire harness connector. If the connectors are snug, check for voltage to the injector using a special injector harness test light (available at most auto parts stores). If there's voltage to the injector and it isn't operating, or if it's operating erratically, replace it.

Removal

Refer to illustrations 20.7, 20.8 and 20.9

2   Remove the air cleaner assembly (see Section 7).
3   Relieve the fuel system pressure (see Section 2).
4   Disconnect the negative cable from the battery.
5   On 1987 models, remove the fuel pressure regulator (see Section 19).
6   Remove the Torx screw that holds the injector cap.
7   Use two small screwdrivers and carefully pry the cap off the injector using the appropriate slots **(see illustration)**.
8   Place a small screwdriver into the hole in the injector and gently pry the injector from the throttle body unit **(see illustration)**.
9   Peel the upper and lower O-rings off the fuel injector **(see illus-**

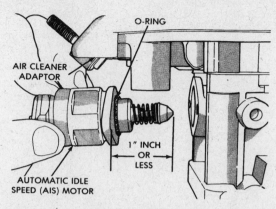

21.8   Measure the length of the pintle – if it protrudes more than 1–inch, take it to a dealer service department or other repair shop equipped with the necessary tool to have it retracted

tration). If the lower O-ring isn't on the injector, be sure to retrieve it from the throttle body.

Installation

Refer to illustrations 20.12a, 20.12b and 20.13

10   Install new O-rings on the injector and a new O-ring on the injector cap. **Note:** *New injectors come equipped with a new upper O-ring. Coat the O-rings with engine oil to help injector installation.*
11   Insert the injector into the throttle body.
12   Place the injector cap onto the injector. The injector and cap are keyed and must be aligned properly **(see illustrations)**.
13   Rotate the cap and injector to line up the attachment hole **(see illustration)**. Tighten the screws securely.
14   Connect the negative battery cable, start the engine and check for leaks.
15   Turn off the engine and install the air cleaner assembly.

21   Automatic Idle Speed (AIS) motor (single-point EFI) – check, removal and installation

Warning: Gasoline is extremely flammable, so take extra precautions when you work on any part of the fuel system. Don't smoke or allow open flames or bare light bulbs near the work area, and don't work in a garage where a natural gas-type appliance (such as a water heater or clothes dryer) with a pilot light is present. If you spill any fuel on your skin, rinse it off immediately with soap and water. When you perform any kind of work on the fuel system, wear safety glasses and have a Class B type fire extinguisher on hand.

Check

1   The Automatic Idle Speed (AIS) motor is monitored by the SMEC or the SBEC (computer). If the AIS malfunctions, a trouble code is stored in the computer's memory. To get the module to display any stored trouble codes, refer to the appropriate Section in Chapter 6. If a Code 25 is displayed, check the AIS motor circuit for problems. If necessary, replace the AIS motor.

Removal

2   Disconnect the negative cable from the battery.
3   Remove the air cleaner assembly (see Section 7).
4   Unplug the electrical connector on the AIS motor.
5   Remove the throttle body temperature sensor (see Chapter 6).
6   Remove the two retaining screws (no. 25 Torx) from the AIS motor.
7   Pull the AIS from the throttle body. Make sure the O-ring doesn't fall into the throttle body opening.

Installation

Refer to illustration 21.8

8   Prior to installation, make sure the pintle is in the retracted position. If the retracted pintle measurement is more than 1–inch, the AIS motor must be taken to a dealer service department to be retracted **(see illustration)**.
9   Install a new O-ring and insert the AIS motor into the housing, making sure the O-ring isn't dislodged.
10   Install the two retaining screws. Tighten the screws securely.
11   Plug the electrical connector.
12   Install the throttle body temperature sensor (see Chapter 6).
13   Install the air cleaner assembly and connect the negative battery cable.

22   Throttle body (multi-point EFI) – removal and installation

Warning: Gasoline is extremely flammable, so take extra precautions when you work on any part of the fuel system. Don't smoke or allow open flames or bare light bulbs near the work area, and don't work in a garage where a natural gas-type appliance (such as a water heater or clothes dryer) with a pilot light is present. If you spill any fuel on your skin, rinse it off immediately with soap and water. When you perform any kind of work on the fuel system, wear safety glasses and have a Class B type fire extinguisher on hand.

Removal

Refer to illustrations 22.5a, 22.5b and 22.5c

1   Disconnect the negative cable from the battery.
2   Remove the clamp and air cleaner hose from the throttle body (see Section 7 or 25). Remove the air cleaner assembly.
3   Remove the return spring and disconnect the accelerator cable (see Section 8) and remove the cruise control and automatic transaxle kickdown cable (if equipped) (see Chapter 7).
4   Detach the throttle cable from its bracket (see Section 8).
5   Unplug any electrical connectors from the throttle body **(see illustrations)**.
6   Mark and disconnect any vacuum hoses from the throttle body.
7   Remove the bolts and detach the throttle body from the intake manifold.

Installation

8   Place the throttle body in position and install the mounting bolts. Tighten them in a criss-cross pattern to the torque listed in this Chapter's Specifications.
9   Connect the vacuum hoses.
10   Plug in the electrical connectors.
11   Install the bracket and connect the throttle cable, return spring and (if equipped) cruise control and automatic transaxle kickdown cable.
12   Install the air cleaner hose and adapter. Tighten the clamps securely.
13   Connect the negative battery cable.

23   Automatic Idle Speed (AIS) motor (multi-point EFI) – check, removal and installation

Check

1   The Automatic Idle Speed (AIS) motor is monitored by the Logic Module, SMEC or the SBEC (computer). If the AIS motor malfunctions, a trouble code is stored in the computer's memory. To get the module to display any stored trouble codes, refer to the appropriate Section in Chapter 6. If a Code 25 is displayed, check the AIS system.

Removal

Refer to illustration 23.5

2   Disconnect the negative cable from the battery.

4

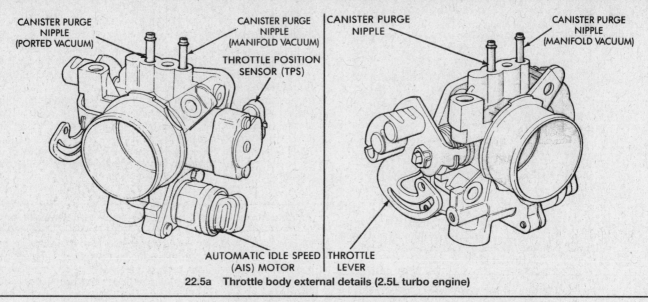

22.5a   Throttle body external details (2.5L turbo engine)

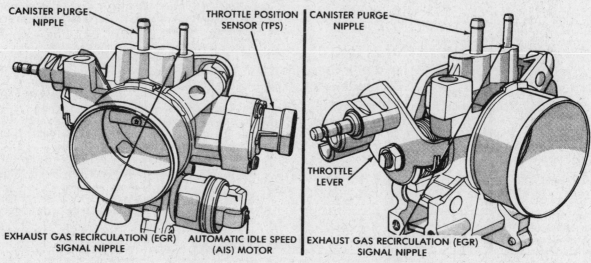

22.5b   Throttle body external details (3.0L engine)

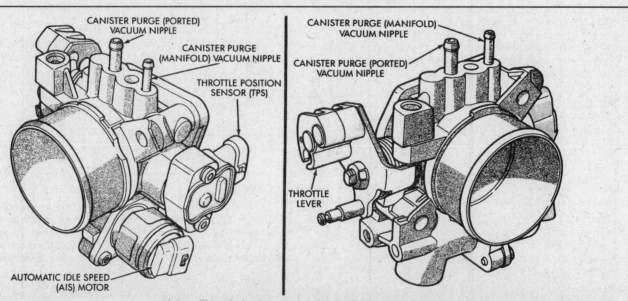

22.5c   Throttle body external details (3.3L engine)

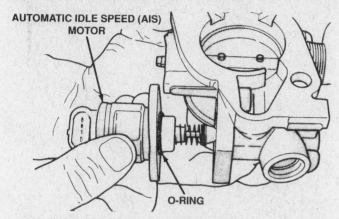

23.5   Carefully remove the AIS motor from the throttle body

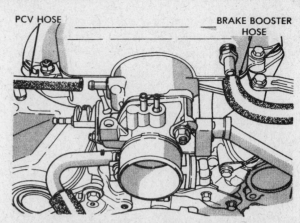

24.1   Disconnect the PCV and brake booster hoses from the air intake plenum (3.0L engine shown, 3.3L engine similar)

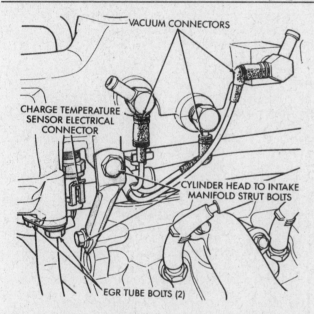

24.2   Details of the electrical and vacuum connections and the intake plenum strut (3.3L and 3.8L engines)

3   Unplug the four-way electrical connector from the AIS.
4   Remove the two AIS motor-to-throttle body screws.
5   Remove the AIS motor from the throttle body. Make sure the O-ring remains on the motor **(see illustration)**.

Installation

6   Carefully position the AIS motor (using new O-ring – new motors should be already equipped with O-rings) on the throttle body.
7   Install the screws and tighten them securely.
8   Plug in the four-way connector.
9   Connect the negative battery cable.

24   Air intake plenum (multi-point EFI) – removal and installation

Refer to illustration 24.1, 24.2, 24.6a and 24.6b

Note: The following procedure applies to 3.0L and 3.3L engines; the 2.5L turbo engine has a one-piece plenum and intake manifold. The procedure for removing and installing the turbo plenum/intake manifold is in Chapter 2, Part A.

1   Disconnect the PCV and brake booster hoses from the air intake plenum **(see illustration)**.

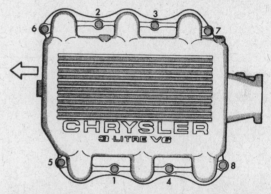

24.6a   Air intake plenum fasteners – when installing the plenum, tighten the bolts in the order shown (3.0L engine)

24.6b   Air intake plenum fasteners – when installing the plenum, tighten the bolts in the order shown (3.3L and 3.8L engines)

2   On 3.3L engines, remove the mounting bolts from the EGR tube flange, unplug the electrical connector from the charge temperature sensor, detach the vacuum harness connectors from the air intake plenum and remove the cylinder head-to-intake plenum strut **(see illustration)**.
3   On 1990 and 1991 3.0L engines, detach the ignition coil from the air intake plenum (see Chapter 5).
4   On 3.3L and 3.8L engines, detach the DIS coil pack (see Chapter 5).
5   If you're replacing the air intake plenum, remove the throttle body (see Section 22); if you're simply removing the plenum to service the lower intake manifold, the heads, etc., don't remove the throttle body from the plenum.
6   Remove the air intake plenum fasteners **(see illustrations)** from the intake manifold, remove the plenum and discard the old gaskets.

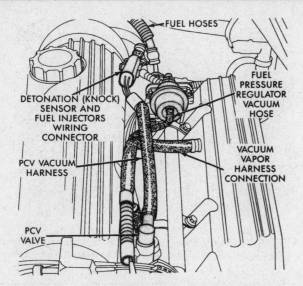

25.6   Typical fuel pressure regulator and vacuum hose layout on multi–point fuel injection systems (2.5L turbo engine)

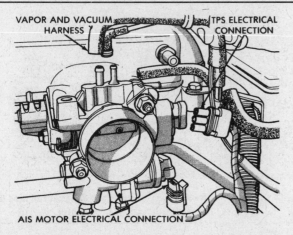

25.22   Unplug the electrical connector for the Automatic Idle Speed (AIS) motor and the Throttle Position Sensor (TPS) (3.0L engine)

Cover the intake manifold with a clean shop towel to prevent dirt and debris from entering the engine.

7   Installation is the reverse of removal. Remove the shop towel from the lower intake manifold. Make sure the gasket surface is spotless. Place the new gaskets on the lower intake manifold (on 3.0L engines, the beaded sealer faces up). Put the air intake plenum in place, install the mounting fasteners and tighten them to the torque listed in this Chapter's Specifications following the correct sequence **(see illustrations 24.6a and 24.6b)**.

---

25   Fuel rail assembly (multi-point EFI) – removal and installation

Warning: *Gasoline is extremely flammable, so take extra precautions when you work on any part of the fuel system. Don't smoke or allow open flames or bare light bulbs near the work area, and don't work in a garage where a natural gas-type appliance (such as a water heater or clothes dryer) with a pilot light is present. If you spill any fuel on your skin, rinse it off immediately with soap and water. When you perform any kind of work on the fuel system, wear safety glasses and have a Class B type fire extinguisher on hand.*

1   Relieve the fuel system pressure (see Section 2).

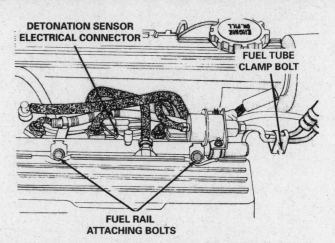

25.9   Remove the fuel rail attaching bolts (2.5L turbo engine)

2   Disconnect the negative cable from the battery.
3   Remove the air cleaner assembly (see Section 7).

2.5L turbo engine
Removal
Refer to illustrations 25.6 and 25.8

4   Remove the quick-disconnect fittings from the chassis fuel lines, or the hose clamps and hoses from the fuel rail assembly.
5   Disconnect any electrical connectors (fuel injector, detonation knock sensor, etc.) from the injector wiring harness.
6   Disconnect the vacuum hose from the fuel pressure regulator **(see illustration)** and loosen the regulator/return line nut using two wrenches. Detach the hose from the regulator.
7   Remove the PCV vacuum harness and vacuum vapor harness from the intake manifold if equipped **(see illustration 25.6)**.
8   Remove the fuel rail mounting bolts **(see illustration)**.
9   Grasp the fuel rail and injector assembly and pull the injectors straight out of their ports. Working carefully, to avoid damaging the injector O-rings, remove the rail assembly from the vehicle. The fuel injectors must not be removed until the fuel rail is detached from the vehicle.
10   Support the fuel rail and disconnect the remaining fuel hoses.

Installation
11   Prior to installation, make sure the injectors are securely seated in the fuel rail with the lock rings in place.
12   Inspect the injector holes to make sure they're clean.
13   Lubricate the injector O-rings with clean engine oil.
14   Insert the injector assemblies carefully into their ports and install the bolts and ground straps. Tighten the bolts evenly in a criss-cross pattern so the injectors are drawn evenly into place. Once the injectors are seated, tighten the bolts to the torque listed in this Chapter's Specifications.
15   Connect the injector electrical connectors to the injectors and secure the harness with the clips.
16   Install the fuel rail-to-valve cover bracket bolt.
17   Connect the fuel pressure regulator vacuum hose.
18   Reconnect the fuel supply hose. Clamp on the rail and tighten the clamp securely.
19   Check to make sure the ground straps, hoses, wiring harnesses and connectors are securely installed in their original locations.
20   Connect the negative battery cable.

3.0L engine
Removal
Refer to illustrations 25.22, 25.25, 25.26, 25.27, 25.31 and 25.32
21   Detach the accelerator cable (see Section 8) and transaxle kickdown cable (see Chapter 7).
22   Unplug the electrical connector for the Automatic Idle Speed

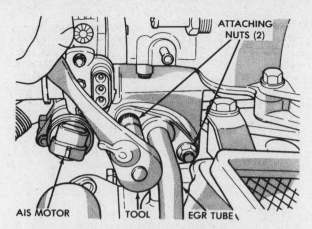

25.25 Remove these two nuts and detach the EGR tube flange from the intake plenum (3.0L engine)

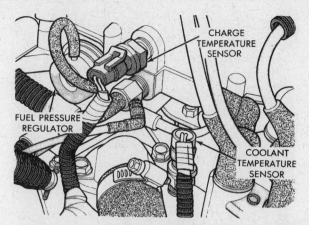

25.26 Unplug the electrical connectors from the charge temperature sensor and the coolant temperature sensor (3.0L engine)

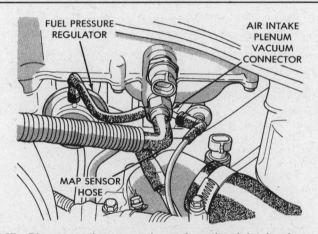

25.27 Disconnect the vacuum hoses from the air intake plenum vacuum connector (3.0L engine)

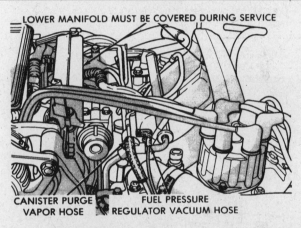

25.31 Disconnect the vacuum hoses from the fuel rail and the fuel pressure regulator (3.0L engine)

(AIS) motor and the Throttle Position Sensor (TPS) **(see illustration)**.

23   Disconnect the vacuum hose connections from the throttle body (see illustration 25.22).

24   Disconnect the PCV and brake booster hoses from the air intake plenum (see Section 24).

25   Disconnect the EGR tube flange from the intake plenum **(see illustration)**.

26   Unplug the electrical connectors from the charge temperature sensor and the coolant temperature sensor **(see illustration)**.

27   Detach the vacuum hoses from the air intake plenum vacuum connector **(see illustration)**.

28   Disconnect the fuel hoses from the fuel rail.

29   Remove the air intake plenum (see Section 24).

30   Cover the intake manifold with clean shop rags to prevent dirt and debris from entering the engine.

31   Disconnect the vacuum hoses from the fuel rail and the fuel pressure regulator **(see illustration)**.

32   Unplug the electrical connector for the fuel injector wiring harness **(see illustration)**.

33   Remove the fuel pressure regulator (see Section 27).

34   Remove the fuel rail mounting bolts and lift the fuel rail assembly from the intake manifold.

Installation

35   Make sure the injector holes are clean and all plugs have been removed.

36   Lube the injector O-rings with a drop of clean engine oil to facili-

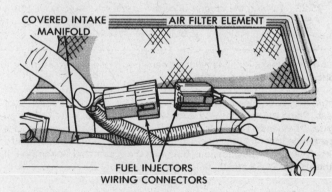

25.32 Unplug the electrical connector for the fuel injector wiring harness (3.0L engine)

tate installation.

37   Make sure all injectors are properly seated into their receiver cups with the lock ring in place (see Section 26).

38   Put the tip of each injector into its respective port. Push the assembly into place until the injectors are seated in their ports.

39   Install the fuel rail mounting bolts and tighten them to the torque listed in this Chapter's Specifications.

40   Install the fuel pressure regulator and hose assembly (see Section

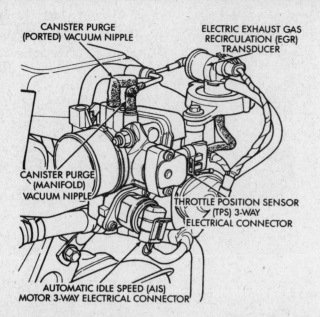

CANISTER PURGE (PORTED) VACUUM NIPPLE
ELECTRIC EXHAUST GAS RECIRCULATION (EGR) TRANSDUCER
CANISTER PURGE (MANIFOLD) VACUUM NIPPLE
THROTTLE POSITION SENSOR (TPS) 3-WAY ELECTRICAL CONNECTOR
AUTOMATIC IDLE SPEED (AIS) MOTOR 3-WAY ELECTRICAL CONNECTOR

25.55   Remove the vacuum hose harness from the throttle body (3.3L engine)

25.64   Remove the screw from the retainer bracket for the fuel tube (not visible in this photo) and remove the fuel rail retaining bolts (arrows) (3.3L engine)

tion 27). Make sure the hose clamps are snug.

41   Install the hold-down bolt for the fuel supply and return tube and the hold-down bolt for the vacuum crossover tube. Tighten both bolts securely.

42   Plug in the electrical connector for the fuel injector wiring harness.

43   Reattach the vacuum harness for the fuel pressure regulator and the fuel rail assembly.

44   Install the air intake plenum (see Section 24).

45   Connect the fuel line to the fuel rail and tighten the hose clamps securely.

46   Connect the vacuum harness to the air intake plenum.

47   Plug in the electrical connectors for the charge temperature sensor and coolant temperature sensor.

48   Reattach the EGR tube flange to the air intake plenum (see Chapter 6).

49   Reconnect the PCV and brake booster supply hoses to the intake plenum.

50   Plug in the electrical connectors for the automatic idle speed (AIS) motor and throttle position sensor (TPS).

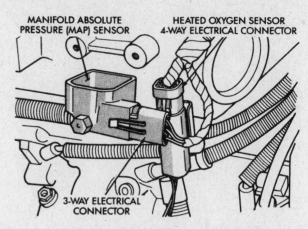

MANIFOLD ABSOLUTE PRESSURE (MAP) SENSOR
HEATED OXYGEN SENSOR 4-WAY ELECTRICAL CONNECTOR
3-WAY ELECTRICAL CONNECTOR

25.58   Unplug the electrical connectors from the MAP sensor and the oxygen sensor (3.3L engine)

51   Reconnect the vacuum vapor harness to the throttle body.

52   Reattach the accelerator cable (see Section 8) and transaxle kickdown linkage (see Chapter 7).

53   Install the air cleaner assembly.

54   Connect the negative battery cable.

3.3L and 3.8L engines

Removal

Refer to illustrations 25.55, 25.58, 25.64, 25.65 and 25.67

55   Remove the vacuum hose harness from the throttle body **(see illustration)**.

56   Remove the PCV and brake booster hoses from the air intake plenum (see Section 24).

57   Remove the mounting bolts from the EGR tube flange. Unplug the electrical connector for the charge temperature sensor. detach the vacuum harness connectors from the air intake plenum and remove the cylinder head-to-intake plenum strut (see Section 24).

58   Unplug the electrical connectors for the MAP sensor and the oxygen sensor **(see illustration)**. Remove the engine-mounted ground strap.

59   Disconnect the quick-connect fittings from the fuel rail (see Section 9).

60   Remove the DIS coil pack (see Chapter 5).

61   Remove the bolt that attaches the alternator bracket to the the intake manifold.

62   Remove the air intake plenum bolts and remove the plenum (see Section 24). Cover the intake manifold with clean shop towels to prevent dirt and debris from entering the engine.

63   Remove the vacuum harness connector from the fuel pressure regulator.

64   Remove the screw from the retainer bracket for the fuel tube and the fuel rail retaining bolts **(see illustration)**.

65   Detach the fuel rail injector clip from the alternator bracket **(see illustration)**.

66   Unplug the electrical connectors from the cam reference sensor, the coolant temperature sensor and the engine temperature sensor (see Chapter 6).

67   Remove the fuel rail **(see illustration)**. Make sure you don't damage the rubber injector O-rings as you pull the injectors from their respective ports.

Installation

68   Make sure the injector holes are clean and all plugs have been removed. Replace the O-rings if they're damaged.

69   Lubricate the injector O-rings with a drop of clean engine oil to facilitate installation.

70   Place the tip of each injector into its respective port and push the fuel rail/fuel injector assembly into place until the injectors are fully

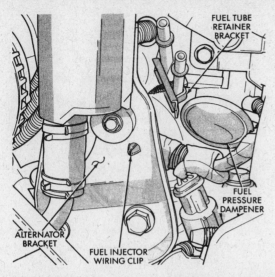

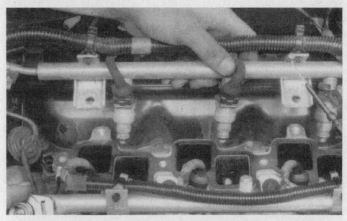

25.67   When you're removing or installing the fuel rail, you can twist either fuel rail tube independently to help wiggle the injectors loose or seat them

25.65   The fuel injector harness is clipped into the alternator bracket -   to release it, pinch the tabs together and push it through the hole

seated.

71   Install the fuel rail retaining bolts and tighten them to the torque listed in this Chapter's Specifications. Install the screw into the bracket for the fuel tube and tighten it securely.

72   Reconnect the electrical connectors for the cam reference sensor, the coolant temperature sensor and the engine temperature sensor.

73   Attach the wiring clip for the fuel injector harness to the alternator bracket.

74   Reconnect the vacuum line to the fuel pressure regulator.

75   Remove the shop towels from the lower intake manifold, clean the gasket surface, place a new gasket on the lower manifold, put the plenum (upper manifold) in position and install the bolts finger tight. Reattach the alternator bracket to the intake manifold and the cylinder head-to-intake manifold strut. Don't tighten the bolts for either bracket yet. Tighten the plenum bolts to the torque listed in this Chapter's Specifications, then tighten the alternator bracket bolt and strut bolts securely.

76   Reattach the ground strap and the electrical connectors for the MAP sensor, the oxygen sensor and the charge temperature sensor.

77   Using a new gasket, reattach the EGR tube flange to the intake manifold (see Chapter 6).

78   Reconnect the vacuum harness to the intake plenum and reconnect the PCV system.

79   Pop the wiring harness clip into the hole in the accelerator cable bracket.

80   Reconnect the electrical connectors to the AIS and the TPS.

81   Reconnect the vacuum harness to the throttle body.

82   Install the DIS ignition coil pack (see Chapter 5).

83   Reconnect the quick-connect fuel line fittings to the fuel rail (see Section 9).

84   Reattach the accelerator cable (see Section 8).

85   Install the air cleaner and hose assembly (see Section 7).

86   Connect the negative battery cable.

87   Start the engine and check for leaks.

---

26   Fuel injector(s) (multi-point EFI) – check, removal and installation

---

Refer to illustrations 26.3a, 26.3b, 26.4a, 26.4b, 26.4c, 26.5 and 26.6

Warning: Gasoline is extremely flammable, so take extra precautions when you work on any part of the fuel system. Don't smoke or allow

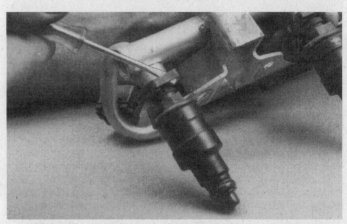

26.3a   Pry the injector lock rings off with a screwdriver

open flames or bare light bulbs near the work area, and don't work in a garage where a natural gas-type appliance (such as a water heater or clothes dryer) with a pilot light is present. If you spill any fuel on your skin, rinse it off immediately with soap and water. When you perform any kind of work on the fuel system, wear safety glasses and have a Class B type fire extinguisher on hand.

Check

1   With the engine running or cranking, listen to the sound from each injector with an automotive stethoscope and verify the injectors are all clicking the same. If you don't have a stethoscope, place the tip of a screwdriver against the injectors and press your ear against the handle of the screwdriver. Also feel the operation of each injector with your finger. It should sound/feel smooth and uniform and its sound/feel should rise and fall with engine RPM. If an injector isn't operating, or sounds/feels erratic, check the injector connector and the wire harness connector. If the connectors are snug, check for voltage to the injector using a special injector harness test light (available at most auto parts stores). If there's voltage to the injector but it isn't operating, or it sounds/feels erratic, replace the injector.

Removal

2   Remove the fuel rail assembly (see Section 25) and place the fuel rail assembly on a clean work surface so the fuel injectors are accessible.

3   Remove the injector lock ring from the fuel rail and injector by prying it off with a small screwdriver. Pull the injector straight out of the receiver cup **(see illustrations)**.

4   Inspect the injector O-rings for damage. Replace them with new ones if necessary **(see illustrations)**.

4

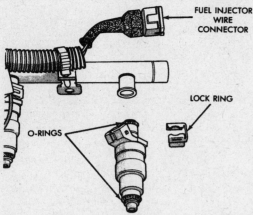

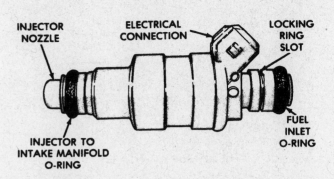

26.3b   Pull the injector straight out of the fuel rail receiver cup

26.4a   The fuel injector has two different size O-rings

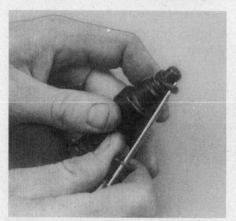

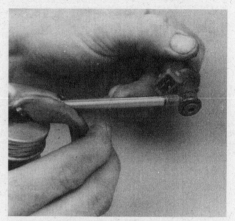

26.4b   Insert a small screwdriver under the O-ring and pry if off - be careful not to damage the injector tip

26.4c   Push the new O–ring over the tip of the injector and into the groove

26.5   A drop of clean engine oil will allow the injector to seat easily

Installation

5   Prior to installation, lubricate the O-rings with a light film of clean engine oil **(see illustration)**.

6   Push the top of the injector straight into the fuel rail receiver cup, taking care not to damage the O-ring **(see illustration)**.

7   Slide the open end of the injector clip into the top slot of the injector, onto the receiver cup ridge and into the side slots of the clip.

8   Install the fuel rail (see Section 25).

---

27   Fuel pressure regulator (multi-point EFI) – removal and installation

---

Warning: Gasoline is extremely flammable, so take extra precautions when you work on any part of the fuel system. Don't smoke or allow open flames or bare light bulbs near the work area, and don't work in a garage where a natural gas-type appliance (such as a water heater or clothes dryer) with a pilot light is present. If you spill any fuel on your skin, rinse it off immediately with soap and water. When you perform any kind of work on the fuel system, wear safety glasses and have a Class B type fire extinguisher on hand.

1   Relieve the system fuel pressure (see Section 2).

2   Disconnect the cable from the negative battery terminal.

2.5L turbo engine

Refer to illustration 27.3

3   Disconnect the vacuum hose from the fuel pressure regulator **(see illustration)**.

4   Loosen the fuel return hose clamp at the fuel pressure regulator

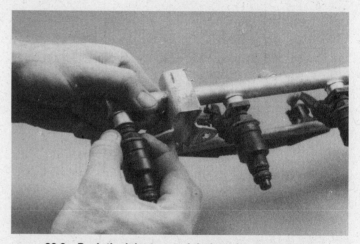

26.6   Push the injector straight into the receiver cup

tube and remove the hose.

5   Using two flare nut or open end wrenches – one on the regulator and the other on the fuel return tube nut – loosen the tube nut. Failure to use a backup wrench will cause damage.

6   Remove the fuel pressure regulator attaching nuts and remove the regulator from the fuel rail.

7   Inspect the O-ring for damage. If it's damaged, replace it.

8   Installation is the reverse of removal. Be sure to lube the O-ring with clean engine oil. And be sure to use a backup wrench when tightening the fuel return tube fitting.

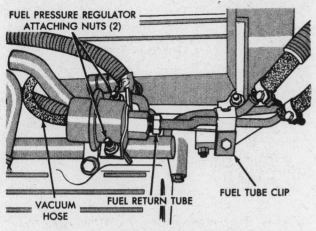

27.3   Fuel pressure regulator assembly (2.5L turbo engine)

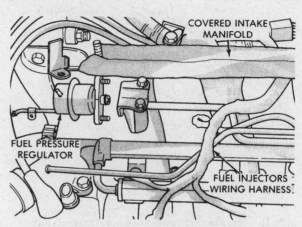

27.10   Fuel pressure regulator assembly (3.0L engine)

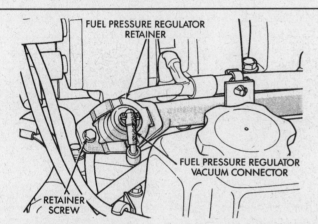

27.13   Fuel pressure regulator assembly (3.3L and 3.8L engines)

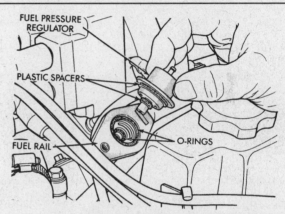

27.16   Removing the fuel pressure regulator
(3.3L and 3.8L engines)

15   Remove the fuel pressure regulator retainer.
16   Remove the fuel pressure regulator **(see illustration)**.
17   Inspect the two regulator O-rings in the fuel rail **(see illustration 27.16)**. If either O-ring is damaged, replace it.
18   Installation is the reverse of removal. Make sure the regulator has two plastic spacers and the fuel rail has two O-rings installed in the cavity.

28.4   Fuel pressure dampener assembly (2.5L turbo engine)

3.0L engine

Refer to illustration 27.10

9   Refer to Section 25 and perform Steps 21 through 32.
10   Remove the fuel pressure regulator fasteners **(see illustration)** and remove the regulator.
11   Inspect the regulator O-ring. If it's damaged, replace it.
12   Installation is the reverse of removal (see Section 25, Steps 41 through 54). Be sure to lube the regulator O-ring with clean engine oil.

3.3L and 3.8L engines

Refer to illustrations 27.13 and 27.16

13   Detach the vacuum hose from the fuel pressure regulator **(see illustration)**.
14   Remove the regulator retainer screw.

28   Fuel pressure dampener (multi-point EFI) – removal and installation

Warning: Gasoline is extremely flammable, so take extra precautions when you work on any part of the fuel system. Don't smoke or allow open flames or bare light bulbs near the work area, and don't work in a garage where a natural gas-type appliance (such as a water heater or clothes dryer) with a pilot light is present. If you spill any fuel on your skin, rinse it off immediately with soap and water. When you perform any kind of work on the fuel system, wear safety glasses and have a Class B type fire extinguisher on hand.

1   Relieve system fuel pressure (see Section 2).
2   Detach the cable from the negative battery terminal.

2.5L turbo engine

Refer to illustration 28.4

3   Disconnect the PCV system hose from the intake manifold and valve cover (see Chapter 6).
4   Place a show towel under the fuel pressure dampener to absorb fuel spillage. Using two flare nut or open end wrenches – one on the

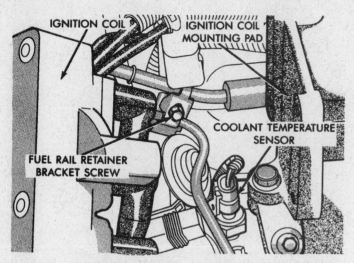

28.9   Screw for fuel rail retainer bracket and location of coolant temperature sensor (3.3L and 3.8L engines)

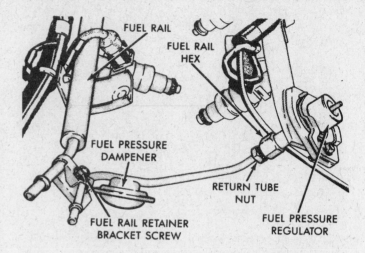

28.10   Fuel pressure dampener assembly (3.3L and 3.8L engines)

flats of the fuel rail and the other on the fuel pressure dampener - remove the fuel pressure dampener and copper sealing washer **(see illustration)**. Don't try to remove the dampener without a backup wrench or you'll damage the fuel rail.

5   Installation is the reverse of removal. Be sure to use a new copper sealing washer and tighten the dampener securely.

3.3L and 3.8L engines

Refer to illustrations 28.9 and 28.10

6   Remove the DIS coil pack fasteners and swing it out of the way to gain access to the fuel pressure dampener (see Chapter 5).

7   Disconnect the fuel hose quick-connect fitting from the fuel return tube (see Section 9).

8   Unplug the electrical connector from the coolant temperature sensor (see Chapter 6).

9   Remove the screw from the fuel rail retainer bracket **(see illustration)**.

10   Using two flare nut or open end wrenches – one on the return tube nut and the other on the fuel rail hex – loosen the return tube nut **(see illustration)**.

11   Remove the fuel pressure dampener.

12   Installation is the reverse of removal. Be sure to tighten the fuel return tube nut securely.

29   Turbocharger – general information

The turbocharger increases power by using an exhaust gas-driven turbine to pressurize the fuel/air mixture before it enters the combustion chambers. The amount of boost (intake manifold pressure) is controlled by the wastegate (exhaust bypass valve). The wastegate is operated by a spring-loaded actuator assembly which controls the maximum boost level by allowing some of the exhaust gas to bypass the turbine. The wastegate is controlled by the SMEC or SBEC.

The computerized fuel injection and emission control system is equipped with self diagnosis capabilities that can access certain turbocharging system components. Refer to Chapter 6 for information pertaining to trouble codes and diagnosis.

30   Turbocharger – check

1   While it is a relatively simple device, the turbocharger is also a precision component which can be severely damaged by an interrupted oil or coolant supply or loose or damaged ducts.

2   Due to the special techniques and equipment required, checking and diagnosis of suspected problems should be left to a dealer service department. The home mechanic can, however, check the connections and linkages for security, damage and other obvious problems.

3   Because each turbocharger has its own distinctive sound, a change in the noise level can be a sign of potential problems.

4   A high-pitched or whistling sound is a symptom of an inlet air or exhaust gas leak.

5   If an unusual sound comes from the vicinity of the turbine, the turbocharger can be removed and the turbine wheel inspected. **Caution:** *All checks must be made with the engine off and cool to the touch and the turbocharger stopped or personal injury could result. Operating the engine without all the turbocharger ducts and filters installed is also dangerous and can result in damage to the turbine wheel blades.*

6   With the engine turned off, reach inside the housing and turn the turbine wheel to make sure it spins freely. If it doesn't, it's possible the cooling oil has sludged or cooked from overheating. Push in on the turbine wheel and check for binding. The turbine should rotate freely with no binding or rubbing on the housing. If it does the turbine bearing is worn out.

7   Check the exhaust manifold for cracks and loose connections.

8   Because the turbine wheel rotates at speeds up to 140,000 rpm, severe damage can result from the interruption of coolant or contamination of the oil supply to the turbine bearings. Check for leaks in the coolant and oil inlet lines and obstructions in the oil drain back line, as this can cause severe oil loss through the turbocharger seals. Burned oil on the turbine housing is a sign of this. **Caution:** *Whenever a major engine bearing such as a main, connecting rod or camshaft bearing is replaced, the turbocharger should be flushed with clean oil.*

31   Turbocharger – removal and installation

Refer to illustrations 31.2 and 31.4

Note: *The turbocharger is removed from below the vehicle. It is not necessary to remove the cylinder head from the engine to gain access to the turbocharger and related components.*

Removal

1   Disconnect the cable from the negative terminal of the battery.

2   Drain the cooling system (see Chapter 1) and remove the air cleaner housing and ducts **(see illustration)**.

Working above the engine

3   Remove the through bolt from the front engine mount (see Chapter 2, Part A) and move the top of the engine forward (away from

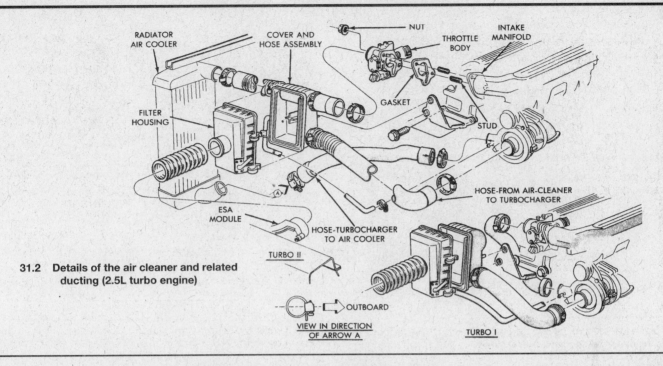

RADIATOR AIR COOLER

COVER AND HOSE ASSEMBLY

NUT

THROTTLE BODY

INTAKE MANIFOLD

FILTER HOUSING

GASKET

STUD

HOSE-FROM AIR-CLEANER TO TURBOCHARGER

ESA MODULE

HOSE-TURBOCHARGER TO AIR COOLER

TURBO II

VIEW IN DIRECTION OF ARROW A

OUTBOARD

TURBO I

31.2 Details of the air cleaner and related ducting (2.5L turbo engine)

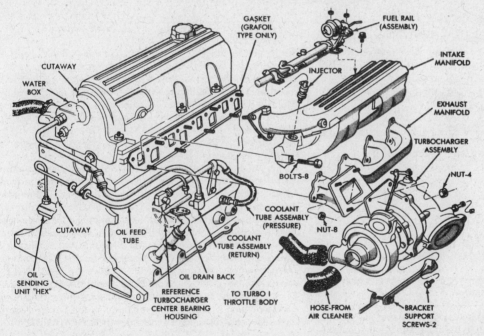

CUTAWAY

WATER BOX

GASKET (GRAFOIL TYPE ONLY)

FUEL RAIL (ASSEMBLY)

INJECTOR

INTAKE MANIFOLD

EXHAUST MANIFOLD

TURBOCHARGER ASSEMBLY

NUT-4

BOLTS-8

NUT-8

CUTAWAY

OIL FEED TUBE

COOLANT TUBE ASSEMBLY (PRESSURE)

COOLANT TUBE ASSEMBLY (RETURN)

OIL SENDING UNIT "HEX"

REFERENCE TURBOCHARGER CENTER BEARING HOUSING

TO TURBO I THROTTLE BODY

HOSE-FROM AIR CLEANER

BRACKET SUPPORT SCREWS-2

31.4 Exploded view of the turbocharger and intake and exhaust manifolds

4

the firewall).

4   Remove the coolant line from the water box and the turbocharger housing **(see illustration)**.

5   Detach the oil feed line from the turbocharger housing.

6   Remove the wastegate rod-to-gate retaining clip.

7   Remove the three (two upper and one lower) driver's side nuts retaining the turbocharger to the exhaust manifold.

8   Disconnect the oxygen sensor wire (see Chapter 6) and any vacuum lines that might be in the way.

Working below the engine

9   Loosen the right front wheel lug nuts and hub nut (see Chapter 8), raise the front of the vehicle and support it securely on jackstands.

10   Remove the right front wheel.

11   Remove the right front driveaxle (see Chapter 8).

12   Remove the bracket support from the lower portion of the turbocharger **(see illustration 31.4)**.

13   Separate the oil drain-back tube fitting from the turbocharger housing and remove the fitting and the hose.

14   Remove the last remaining turbocharger-to-exhaust manifold nut.

15   Disconnect the exhaust pipe joint from the turbocharger housing.

16   Remove the lower coolant line and turbocharger inlet fitting.

17   Lift the turbocharger off its mounting studs and lower the assembly down and out of the vehicle.

Installation

18   Carefully clean the mating surfaces of the turbocharger and exhaust manifold.

19   Place the turbocharger in position on the manifold studs.

20   Apply anti-seize compound to the studs and install the nuts.

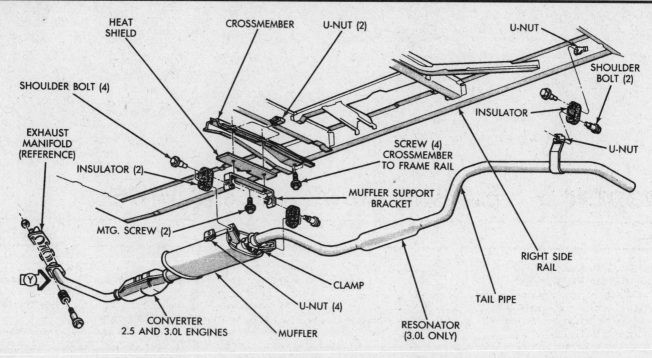

32.1   Exhaust system details - typical

Tighten the nuts to the torque listed in this Chapter's Specifications.

21   Apply thread sealant into the lower inlet coolant line fitting and install the fitting into the turbocharger housing.

22   Install the lower coolant line.

23   Install the oil drain-back tube and fitting along with a new gasket, to the turbocharger housing.

24   Install the turbocharger-to-block support bracket and bolts and make them finger tight to prevent binding. Tighten the bolts to the torque listed in this Chapter's Specifications.

25   Reposition the exhaust pipe and tighten the bolts securely.

26   Install the driveaxle (see Chapter 8) and the right front wheel.

27   Reconnect the oxygen sensor electrical connector and any vacuum lines that were disconnected.

28   Install the wastegate rod-to-gate retaining clip.

29   Attach the oil feed line to the turbocharger bearing housing. Tighten the fitting securely.

30   Apply sealant to the water box and turbocharger return coolant line end fittings and install the lines. Tighten them securely.

31   Align the engine mount within the crossmember bracket and tighten the bolts to the torque listed in the Chapter 2A Specifications.

32   Check the coolant level and add some, if necessary (see Chapter 1).

33   Change the engine oil (see Chapter 1).

32   Exhaust system servicing – general information

Refer to illustration 32.1

Warning: *Inspection and repair of exhaust system components should be done only with the engine and exhaust components completely cool. Also, when working under the vehicle, make sure it's securely supported on jackstands.*

1   The exhaust system **(see illustration)** consists of the exhaust manifold(s), the catalytic converter, the muffler, the tailpipe and all connecting pipes, brackets, hangers and clamps. The exhaust system is attached to the body with mounting brackets and rubber hangers. If any of the parts are improperly installed, excessive noise and vibration will be transmitted to the body.

2   Conduct regular inspections of the exhaust system to keep it safe and quiet. Look for any damaged or bent parts, open seams, holes, loose connections, excessive corrosion or other defects which could allow exhaust fumes to enter the vehicle. Deteriorated exhaust system components shouldn't be repaired; they should be replaced with new parts.

3   If the exhaust system components are extremely corroded or rusted together, welding equipment will probably be required to remove them. The convenient way to accomplish this is to have a muffler repair shop remove the corroded sections with a cutting torch. If, however, you want to save money by doing it yourself (and you don't have a welding outfit with a cutting torch), simply cut off the old components with a hacksaw. If you have compressed air, special pneumatic cutting chisels can also be used. If you do decide to tackle the job at home, be sure to wear safety goggles to protect your eyes from metal chips and work gloves to protect your hands.

4   Here are some simple guidelines to follow when repairing the exhaust system:

a) Work from the back to the front when removing exhaust system components.

b) Apply penetrating oil to the component fasteners to make them easier to remove.

c) Use new gaskets, hangers and clamps when installing exhaust system components.

d) Apply anti-seize compound to the threads of all exhaust system fasteners during reassembly.

e) Be sure to allow sufficient clearance between newly installed parts and all points on the underbody to avoid overheating the floor pan and possibly damaging the interior carpet and insulation. Pay particularly close attention to the catalytic converter and heat shields.

Chapter 5 Engine electrical systems

Contents

Specifications

Ignition coil resistance (by coil manufacturer)

Diamond
    1988 and 1989
        Primary .... 1.34 to 1.55 ohms
        Secondary .... 15 to 19 k-ohms
    1990 through 1993
        3.3L
            Primary .... 0.52 to 0.63 ohms
            Secondary .... 11.6 to 15.8 k-ohms
        All others
            Epoxy
                Primary.. 0.97 to 1.18 ohms
                Secondary .... 11 to 15.3 k-ohms
            Oil-filled (1990 only)
                Primary.. 1.34 to 1.55 ohms
                Secondary .... 15 to 19 k-ohms
    1994 and later models
        3.3L and 3.8L
            Primary .... 0.45 to 0.65 ohms
            Secondary .... 7 to 15.8 K-ohms
Echlin or Essex
    1984 through 1987
        Primary .... 1.41 to 1.62 ohms
        Secondary .... 9 to 12.2 k-ohms
    1988 through 1990
        Primary .... 1.34 to 1.55 ohms
        Secondary .... 9 to 12.2 k-ohms
Marshall (1990 3.3L)
    Primary .... 0.53 to 0.65 ohms
    Secondary.. 7 to 9 k-ohms

5

Mitsubishi (1984 through 1987)
   Primary .... 0.7 to 0.85 ohms
   Secondary.. 9 to 11 k-ohms
Prestolite
   1984 through 1987
      Primary .... 1.60 to 1.79 ohms
      Secondary .... 9.4 to 11.7 k-ohms
   1988 through 1990
      Primary .... 1.34 to 1.55 ohms
      Secondary .... 9.4 to 11.7 k-ohms
Toyodenso
   Four-cylinder
      Primary .... 0.95 to 1.20 ohms
      Secondary .... 11.3 13.3 k-ohms
   3.3L
      1990 through 1993
         Primary .... 0.51 to 0.61 ohms
         Secondary .... 11.5 to 13.5 K-ohms
   3.3L and 3.8L
      1994 and later
         Primary .... 0.45 to 0.65 ohms
         Secondary .... 7 to 15.8 K-ohms

1   General information

The engine electrical systems include all ignition, charging and starting components. Because of their engine-related functions, these components are discussed separately from chassis electrical devices such as the lights, the instruments, etc. (which are included in Chapter 12). Always observe the following precautions when working on the electrical systems:

  a) Be extremely careful when servicing engine electrical components. They are easily damaged if checked, connected or handled improperly.
  b) Never leave the ignition switch on for long periods of time with the engine off.
  c) Don't disconnect the battery cables while the engine is running.
  d) Maintain correct polarity when connecting a battery cable from another vehicle during jump starting.
  e) Always disconnect the negative cable first and hook it up last or the battery may be shorted by the tool being used to loosen the cable clamps. It's also a good idea to review the safety-related information regarding the engine electrical systems located in the Safety First section near the front of this manual before beginning any operation included in this Chapter.

2   Battery – emergency jump starting

Refer to the Booster battery (jump) starting procedure at the front of this manual.

3   Battery – removal and installation

Refer to illustration 3.2

1 **Caution:** *Always disconnect the negative cable first and hook it up last or the battery may be shorted by the tool being used to loosen the cable clamps.* Disconnect both cables from the battery terminals.
2 Remove the battery hold-down clamp **(see illustration)**.
3 Lift out the battery. Be careful - it's heavy.
4 While the battery is out, inspect the carrier (tray) for corrosion (see Chapter 1).
5 If you're replacing the battery, make sure you purchase one that's identical, with the same dimensions, amperage rating, cold cranking rating, etc.
6 Installation is the reverse of removal.

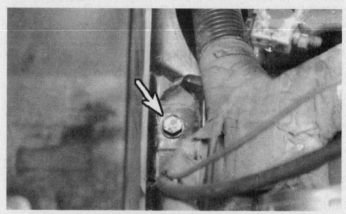

3.2   To remove the battery, unscrew the hold-down bolt (arrow) and remove the hold-down clamp

4   Battery cables – check and replacement

1 Periodically inspect the entire length of each battery cable for damage, cracked or burned insulation and corrosion. Poor battery cable connections can cause starting problems and decreased engine performance.
2 Check the cable-to-terminal connections at the ends of the cables for cracks, loose wire strands and corrosion. The presence of white, fluffy deposits under the insulation at the cable terminal connection is a sign that the cable is corroded and should be replaced. Check the terminals for distortion, missing mounting bolts and corrosion.
3 When removing the cables, always disconnect the negative cable first and hook it up last or the battery may be shorted by the tool used to loosen the cable clamps. Even if only the positive cable is being replaced, be sure to disconnect the negative cable from the battery first (see Chapter 1 for further information regarding battery cable removal).
4 Disconnect the old cables from the battery, then trace each of them to their opposite ends and detach them from the starter solenoid and ground terminals. Note the routing of each cable to ensure correct installation.
5 If you're replacing either or both of the old cables, take them with you when buying new cables. It's very important to replace the cables with identical parts. Cables have characteristics that make them easy to identify: Positive cables are usually red, larger in cross-section and

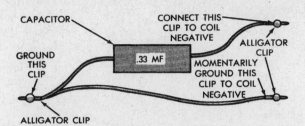

6.2a   When checking the SCC (2.2L engine), a special test tool can be fabricated from a 0.33 mfd capacitor and some wire and alligator clips

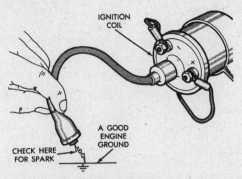

6.2b   The spark at the coil wire must be bright blue and well-defined

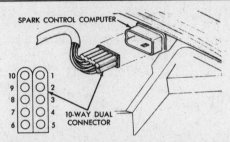

6.4   Disconnecting the ten-wire harness connector from the SCC (2.2L engine)

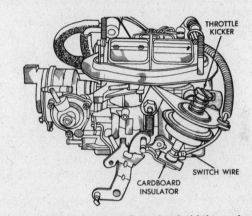

6.8   Use a thin piece of cardboard to hold the carburetor switch open and measure the voltage at the switch wire terminal (2.2L engine)

have a larger diameter battery post clamp; ground cables are usually black, smaller in cross-section and have a slightly smaller diameter clamp for the negative post.

6   Clean the threads of the solenoid or ground connection with a wire brush to remove rust and corrosion. Apply a light coat of battery terminal corrosion inhibitor, or petroleum jelly, to the threads to prevent future corrosion.

7   Attach the cable to the solenoid or ground connection and tighten the mounting nut/bolt securely.

8   Before connecting a new cable to the battery, make sure it reaches the battery post without having to be stretched.

9   Connect the positive cable first, followed by the negative cable.

5   Ignition system – general information

The ignition system includes the ignition switch, the battery, the coil, the primary (low voltage) and secondary (high voltage) wiring circuits, the distributor (except 3.3L and 3.8L models) and the spark plugs. Models with the 3.3L and 3.8L V6 engine don't have a distributor – they're equipped with a Direct Ignition System (DIS) instead. DIS is a distributorless system. Its three main components are the coil pack, the crankshaft timing sensor and the camshaft reference sensor. The crankshaft and camshaft sensors are both Hall Effect timing devices (for more information on the crankshaft and camshaft sensors, refer to Chapter 6).

On 1984 through 1987 models, the ignition system is controlled by the Spark Control Computer (SCC). On 1988 and 1989 models, it's controlled by a computer known as the Single Module Engine Controller (SMEC). The SMEC monitors coolant temperature, engine rpm and available intake manifold vacuum to ensure a perfectly timed spark under all driving conditions. Later versions of the ignition computer are referred to by Chrysler as the Single-Board Engine Controller (SBEC), but they're functionally similar to the SMEC. For more information regarding the SMEC or the SBEC, refer to Chapter 6.

6   Ignition system – check

Warning: The secondary ignition system voltage is very high (over 30,000 volts). Use extreme care when performing the following checks so you don't get shocked.

2.2L engine

Refer to illustrations 6.2a, 6.2b, 6.4, 6.8, 6.11, 6.13, 6.14, 6.16, 6.17, 6.18, 6.19, 6.21 and 6.22

1   Prior to testing the spark control computer (SCC), check the coil and battery to make sure they are in good operating condition. Inspect the electrical harness and wires for shorts, cracked and worn insulation and all connectors for security. Check the vacuum hose for kinks, damage and secure connection.

2   Connect the special test tool **(see illustration)** to the negative terminal of the coil and ground the other end. Pull the coil wire from the distributor and place it 1/4-inch from a good ground **(see illustration)**. With the ignition switch on, momentarily touch the remaining test lead to the negative coil terminal. A spark should jump from the coil wire to ground.

3   If there is a spark, proceed to Step 8.

4   If there is no spark, turn off the ignition switch, disconnect the ten wire harness connector at the SCC **(see illustration)** and repeat the test. If a spark is now produced, the computer output is shorted and the spark control computer must be replaced with a new one.

5   If there was no spark, check the voltage at the coil positive terminal to make sure it is within one volt of battery voltage.

6   If there was no voltage reading, check the wiring between the battery and the positive terminal of the coil.

7   If there was a proper voltage reading, check the voltage at the coil negative terminal. This reading should also be within one volt of the battery voltage. If there is no voltage or there is voltage but no spark was produced when performing the test in Step 2, replace the coil with a new one.

8   If there is a voltage reading but the engine will not start, use a thin piece of cardboard to hold the carburetor switch open **(see illustration)** and measure the voltage at the switch. The reading should be at

5

6.11   Checking the voltage at the ten-wire connector cavity (2.2L engine)

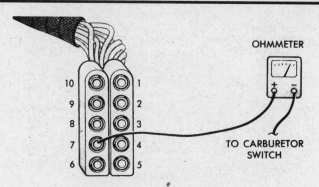

6.13   Checking for continuity between cavity 7 and the carburetor switch (2.2L engine)

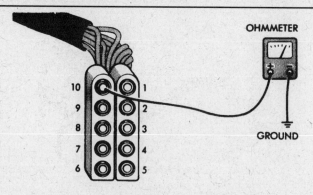

6.14   Checking for continuity between cavity 10 and a good ground (2.2L engine)

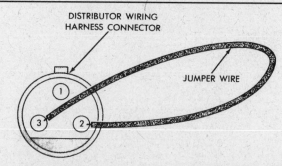

6.16   The jumper wire must be connected between cavities 2 and 3 in the distributor wiring harness connector (2.2L engine)

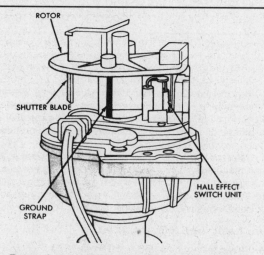

6.17   Rotor shutter blade and ground strap locations (2.2L engine)

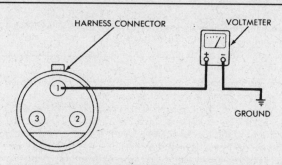

6.18   Checking for voltage between the distributor harness connector cavity 1 and a good ground (2.2L engine)

least five volts.

9   If the voltage reading is correct, go on to Step 16.

10   If there is no voltage, turn off the ignition switch and unplug the SCC ten wire connector.

11   Turn the switch on and check the voltage at cavity 2 of the connector **(see illustration)**. It should be within one volt of battery voltage.

12   If there is no voltage reading, check for continuity between cavity 2 and the battery. Repair the circuit and repeat the test in Step 11.

13   If there is voltage present, turn off the ignition switch and check for continuity between cavity 7 and the carburetor switch **(see illustration)**. If no continuity is present, check for an open wire between cav-

ity 7 and the carburetor switch and repair the circuit.

14   If there is continuity present, check for continuity between cavity 10 and a good ground **(see illustration)**. If there is continuity, it will be necessary to replace the computer with a new one as power is going into it but not out. Repeat the test in Step 8.

15   If continuity is not present, check for an open wire.

16   If the wiring is alright and the engine will not start, plug the ten wire connector into the computer and unplug the distributor wire harness connector. Connect a jumper wire between cavities 2 and 3 of the connector **(see illustration)**. Hold the coil wire near a good ground, turn the ignition switch on and break the circuit at cavity 2 or 3 several times. A bright blue spark should occur at the coil wire.

17   If sparks are produced but the engine still does not start, replace the distributor pick-up assembly (also called a Hall effect switch) (see Section 10), making sure the shutter blades are grounded **(see illustration)**. With the ignition switched off, check for a good ground on the distributor shaft with an ohmmeter. It may be necessary to seat the rotor securely on the shaft to obtain a good ground. Connect one lead of the ohmmeter to the shutter blade and the other to a good ground and make sure there is continuity. If there is none, push the rotor down on the shaft until continuity is indicated.

18   Repeat the test in Step 16 and if there is no spark present, mea-

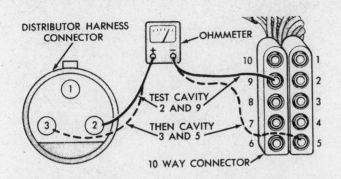

6.19   Checking for continuity between the distributor and the SCC connector cavities (2.2L engine)

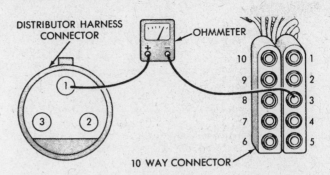

6.21   Checking for continuity between the distributor harness connector cavity 1 and the SCC connector cavity 3 (2.2L engine)

6.22   Checking for voltage between SCC connector cavities 10 and 2 (2.2L engine)

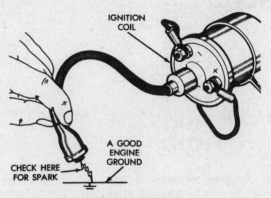

6.28   Checking the coil for spark (2.5L engine)

sure the voltage at cavity 1 of the distributor connector **(see illustration)**. It should be within one volt of battery voltage.

19   If the voltage is correct, turn off the ignition, unplug the ten wire connector from the computer and check for continuity between cavity 2 of the distributor harness and cavity 9 of the computer connector. Follow this by checking between cavity 3 of the distributor harness and cavity 5 of the computer connector **(see illustration)**. If there is no continuity, find and repair the fault in the harness. If there is continuity, replace the computer with a new one as power is going into it but not coming out.

20   Repeat the test in Step 16.

21   If no voltage is present when making the check in Step 18, turn off the ignition, unplug the computer ten wire connector and check for continuity between cavity 1 of the distributor harness connector and cavity 3 of the computer connector **(see illustration)**. If there is no continuity, repair the wire and repeat the test in Step 16.

22   If there is continuity, turn on the ignition switch and check for voltage between cavities 2 and 10 of the computer connector **(see illustration)**. If there is voltage, the computer is faulty and must be replaced with a new one. Repeat the test in Step 16. If there is no voltage, check and repair the ground wire, as the computer is not grounded. Repeat the Step 16 test.

2.6L engine

23   Remove the high voltage coil wire from the distributor cap and hold the end about 1/4-inch from a good engine ground. Operate the starter and look for a series of bright blue sparks at the coil wire.

24   If sparks occur, and they are bright blue and well defined, continue to operate the starter while slowly moving the coil wire away from the ground. As this is done, look for arcing and sparking at the coil tower. If it occurs, replace the coil with a new one. If arcing does not occur at the coil tower, the ignition system is producing the necessary

high secondary voltage. However, make sure the voltage is getting to the spark plugs by checking the rotor, distributor cap, spark plug wires and spark plugs as described in Chapter 1. If the results are positive, the ignition system is not the reason the engine will not start.

25   If no sparks occurred, or if they were weak or intermittent, measure the voltage at the ignition coil negative terminal with the ignition switch on. It should be the same as battery voltage. If it is three volts or less, the igniter is defective. If no voltage was present, check the coil and wires for an open circuit.

26   Refer to Step 2 and perform the check described there.

27   If no spark was produced, check for voltage at the positive coil terminal with the ignition switch on. Battery voltage should be indicated. If it is, the coil is defective. If no voltage is present, check the associated wires and connections.

2.5L, turbo and 3.0L engines

Refer to illustrations 6.28, 6.33a, 6.33b and 6.35

28   Remove the coil secondary cable from the distributor cap. Hold the end of the cable about 1/4-inch from a good engine ground and crank the engine. Check for a consistent spark as the engine is cranked **(see illustration)**.

29   If the spark is not constant or there is no spark, connect a voltmeter to the coil positive terminal and crank the engine for five seconds. If the voltage is near zero during this test refer to the Trouble codes in Chapter 6.

30   If the voltage is at near battery voltage (approximately 12.4 volts) at the start of the test but drops to zero after one to two seconds of cranking, refer to the Trouble codes in Chapter 6.

31   If the voltage remains at near battery voltage for the five seconds, turn off the ignition key, remove the 14-way (or 60-way on later models) connector from the SMEC/SBEC and check for any spread terminals.

5

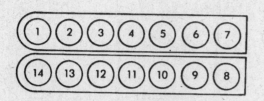

6.33a   Terminal guide for SMEC 14-way electrical connector (1987 through 1989 2.5L engine)

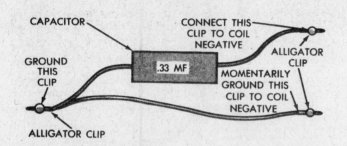

6.35   You'll need to fabricate a special jumper wire to ground the negative terminal of the coil on a 2.5L engine

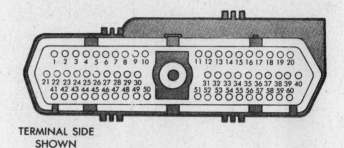

TERMINAL SIDE SHOWN

6.33b   Terminal guide for SBEC 60-way electrical connector – when jumpering to a terminal, be extremely careful not to touch any other terminals or you may damage the SBEC (1990 and later 2.5L engine)

6.39   To use a calibrated ignition tester (available at most auto parts stores), simply disconnect a spark plug wire, attach the wire to the tester and clip the tester to a good ground – if there is enough power to fire the plug, sparks will be clearly visible between the electrode tip and the tester body as the engine is turned over

32   Remove the coil positive terminal lead and connect a jumper wire between the battery positive terminal and the coil positive terminal.
33   On SMEC-equipped engines (1987 through 1989 models), momentarily ground terminal No. 12 of the 14-way connector **(see illustration)** with a jumper wire. On SBEC-equipped engines (1990 and later models), ground terminal No. 19 of the 60-way connector **(see illustration)**.
34   If a spark is generated, replace the SMEC/SBEC.
35   If no spark is generated, connect a special jumper wire **(see illustration)** to ground the coil negative terminal.
36   If a spark is now produced, check the wiring harness for an open condition.
37   If no spark is produced, replace the coil.

Quick test for any engine

Refer to illustration 6.39
38   If the engine turns over but won't start, disconnect the spark plug wire from any spark plug and attach it to a calibrated ignition tester (available at most auto parts stores).
39   Connect the clip on the tester to a bolt or metal bracket on the engine **(see illustration)**. If you're unable to obtain a calibrated ignition tester, remove the wire from one of the spark plugs and, using an insulated tool, hold the end of the wire about 1/4-inch from a good ground. **Caution:** *If the spark plug is moved more than 1/4-inch away from the engine ground on a DIS-type coil (3.3L engines), it could damage the spark plug wire.*
40   Crank the engine and watch the end of the tester or spark plug wire to see if bright blue, well-defined sparks occur. If you're not using a calibrated tester, have an assistant crank the engine for you. **Warning:** *Keep clear of drivebelts and other moving engine components that could injure you.*
41   If sparks occur, sufficient voltage is reaching the plug to fire it (repeat the check at the remaining plug wires to verify the wires and coils [3.3L models] or wires, distributor cap and rotor [all others] are OK). However, the plugs themselves may be fouled, so remove them and check them as described in Chapter 1.
42   If no sparks, or intermittent sparks occur on a DIS-type system, proceed to Section 7 and check the coil pack. On a conventional ignition system, if no sparks or intermittent sparks occur, remove the dis-

tributor cap and check the cap and rotor as described in Chapter 1. If moisture is present, dry out the cap and rotor, then reinstall the cap.
43   If there's still no spark, detach the coil secondary wire from the distributor cap and hook it up to the tester (reattach the plug wire to the spark plug), then repeat the spark check. Again, if you don't have a tester, hold the end of the wire about 1/4-inch from a good ground. If sparks occur now, the distributor cap, rotor or plug wire(s) may be defective.
44   If no sparks occur, check the wire connections at the coil to make sure they're clean and tight. Check for voltage to the coil. Make any necessary repairs, then repeat the check again.
45   If there's still no spark, the coil-to-cap wire may be bad (check the resistance with an ohmmeter – it should be 7000 ohms per foot or less). If a known good wire doesn't make any difference in the test results, check the coil (see Section 7). If it's OK, the pick-up assembly (see Section 10) or ignition module may be defective.

---

7   Ignition coil – check and replacement

Conventional coil

Refer to illustrations 7.2a, 7.2b, 7.4a, 7.4b, 7.5a and 7.5b
1   Detach the cable from the negative battery terminal.

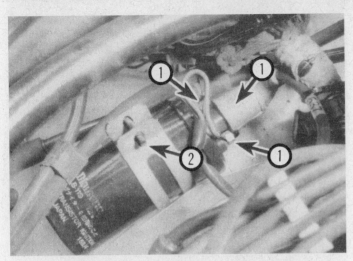

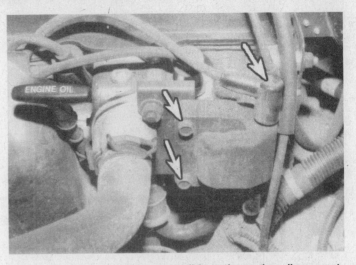

7.2a   To remove the earlier type coil from the right inner fenderwell, disconnect the primary wires and the high-tension cable (1), then remove the mounting bracket bolt – if the coil is bad, loosen the clamp pinch screw (2) and transfer the clamp/mounting bracket to the new coil

7.2b   To remove the later type coil from the engine, disconnect the primary wire connector and the high-tension cable (arrow), then remove the mounting bolts (arrows)

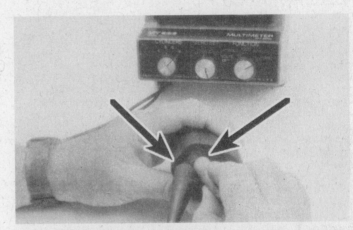

7.4a   To check the coil primary resistance on an earlier type coil, touch the leads of an ohmmeter to the positive and negative primary terminals (arrows) and compare your reading with the coil primary resistance listed in this Chapter's Specifications

7.4b   To check the coil primary resistance on a later type coil, touch the leads of an ohmmeter to the positive and negative primary terminals (arrows) and compare your reading with the coil primary resistance listed in this Chapter's Specifications

2   Mark the wires and terminals with pieces of numbered tape, then remove the primary wires and the high-tension lead from the coil **(see illustrations)**. Disconnect the coil mounting bracket, remove the coil/bracket assembly, clean the outer case and check it for cracks and other damage.

3   Clean the coil primary terminals and check the coil tower terminal for corrosion. Clean it with a wire brush if any corrosion is found.

4   Check the coil primary resistance by attaching the leads of an ohmmeter to the positive and negative terminals **(see illustrations)**. Compare your readings to the primary resistance listed in this Chapter's Specifications.

5   Check the coil secondary resistance by hooking one of the ohmmeter leads to one of the primary terminals and the other ohmmeter lead to the large center terminal **(see illustrations)**. Compare your readings to the secondary resistance listed in this Chapter's Specifications.

6   If the measured resistances are not as specified, the coil is probably defective and should be replaced with a new one.

7   For proper ignition system operation, all coil terminals and wire leads must be kept clean and dry.

8   Install the coil in the vehicle and hook up the wires.

9   Attach the cable to the negative battery terminal.

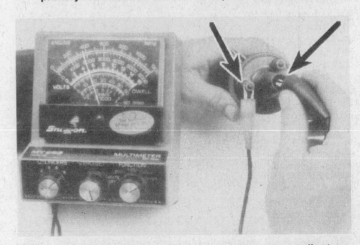

7.5a   To check the coil secondary resistance on an earlier type coil, touch one lead of the ohmmeter to one of the primary terminals and the other lead to the high-tension terminal (arrows), then compare your reading to the coil secondary resistance listed in this Chapter's Specifications

5

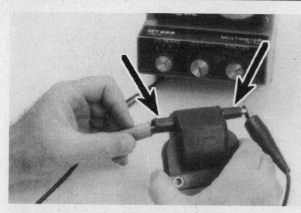

7.5b   To check the coil secondary resistance on a later type coil, touch one lead of the ohmmeter to one of the primary terminals and the other lead to the high-tension terminal (arrows), then compare your reading to the coil secondary resistance listed in this Chapter's Specifications

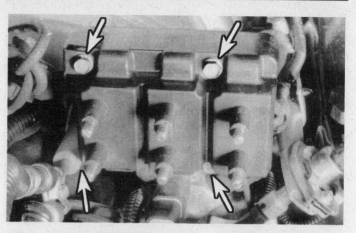

7.11   To detach the coil pack from an engine equipped with the Direct Ignition System (DIS), remove these four bolts (arrows)

7.12   The electrical connector for the DIS coil pack is easier to unplug if you remove the coil pack mounting bolts first and lift the pack up slightly

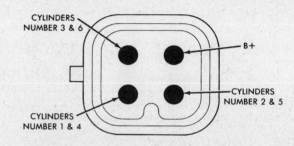

7.13a   Terminal guide for measuring the primary resistance of the coil pack at the electrical connector (coil-pack-side of the connector shown) – check between the B+ terminal and each of the other terminals in the connector

7.13b   When measuring the primary resistance at the coil-pack-side of the electrical connector for the coil pack, make sure the test lead probes are making a good contact with the terminals – which are small and very close together – or you'll get an incorrect resistance reading

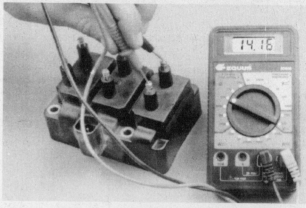

7.14   To measure the secondary resistance of each coil in the DIS coil pack, touch the test lead probes to the twin terminals of the paired high-tension towers

10   Clearly label the six spark plug cables, then detach them from the coil pack. Measure the resistance of each cable. It should be 3 to 12 k-ohms per foot of cable. Replace any cable not within tolerance.

11   Remove the four coil pack mounting bolts **(see illustration)**.

12   Lift up the coil pack and unplug the electrical connector **(see illustration)**.

13   Measure the resistance on the primary side of each coil with a digital ohmmeter **(see illustrations)** and compare your readings to the primary resistance listed in this Chapter's Specifications for the brand of coil pack (Diamond or Toyodenso) used on your engine.

14   Measure the secondary resistance of the coil between the paired high tension towers of each group of cylinders **(see illustration)** and compare your readings to the secondary resistance listed in this

Direct Ignition System (DIS) coil pack (3.3L and 3.8L models)

Refer to illustrations 7.11, 7.12, 7.13a, 7.13b and 7.14

Note: *The DIS coil pack doesn't have to be removed from the engine for testing – we've done so only for the sake of clarity.*

8.3a Before you remove the distributor from a 2.2L, 2.5L or turbo engine, trace the electrical lead for the Hall Effect pick-up from the distributor to its connector (arrow) at the engine wire harness and unplug it (2.2L shown, 2.5L and turbo similar)

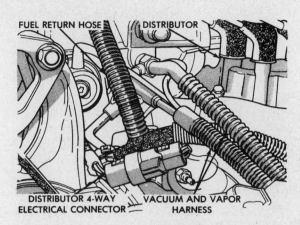

8.3b Before you remove the distributor from a 3.0L engine, trace the electrical lead for the photo-optic sensing unit from the distributor housing to its connector harness and unplug it

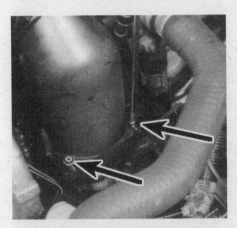

8.4 On 2.2L, 2.5L and turbo engines, remove these two screws (arrows) and remove the distributor splash shield (2.2L engine shown, other two similar)

8.7 Mark the position of the rotor tip on the distributor base and mark the relationship of the base to the block (arrow) (2.5L engine shown)

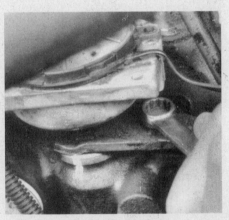

8.8 Remove the hold–down bolt and clamp, then pull the distributor straight up (2.5L engine shown)

5

Chapter's Specifications for the brand of coil pack used on your engine.

15 If any coil in the coil pack fails either of the above tests, replace the coil pack.

16 Installation is the reverse of removal.

---

8   Distributor – removal and installation

Removal

Refer to illustrations 8.3a, 8.3b, 8.4, 8.7 and 8.8

1   Disconnect the cable from the negative terminal of the battery.
2   Detach the primary lead from the coil.
3   Unplug the electrical connector for the Hall Effect pick-up (2.2L, 2.5L and turbo engines) **(see illustration)**, the pick-up coil (2.6L engine) or the photo-optic sensing unit (3.0L engine) **(see illustration)**. Follow the wires as they exit the distributor to find the connector.
4   On 2.2L, 2.5L and turbo engines, remove the distributor splash shield **(see illustration)**.
5   Look for a raised "1" on the distributor cap. This marks the location for the number one cylinder spark plug wire terminal. If the cap doesn't have a mark for the number one terminal, locate the number

one spark plug and trace the wire back to the terminal on the cap.
6   Remove the distributor cap (see Chapter 1) and turn the engine over until the rotor is pointing toward the number one spark plug wire terminal (see the locating TDC procedure in Chapter 2, if necessary).
7   Make a mark on the edge of the distributor base directly below the rotor tip and in line with it. Also, mark the distributor base and the engine block to ensure that the distributor will be reinstalled correctly **(see illustration)**.
8   Remove the distributor hold down-bolt and clamp **(see illustration)**, then pull the distributor straight up to remove it. **Caution:** *DO NOT turn the crankshaft while the distributor is out of the engine, or the alignment marks will be useless.*

Installation

Refer to illustrations 8.10a and 8.10b

Note: *If the crankshaft has been moved while the distributor is out, the number one piston must be repositioned at TDC. This can be done by feeling for compression pressure at the number one plug hole as the crankshaft is turned. Once compression is felt, align the ignition timing zero mark with the pointer.*

9   Insert the distributor into the engine in exactly the same relationship to the block that it was when removed.
10   On 2.2L, 2.5L and turbo engines, make sure the lugs on the lower end of the distributor shaft fit into the slot in the upper end of the oil

8.10a When you install the distributor on a 2.2L, 2.5L or turbo engine, be sure to align the tangs (arrows) on the end of the distributor shaft . . .

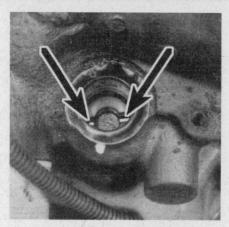

8.10b . . . with the slots (arrows) in the top of the oil pump driveshaft

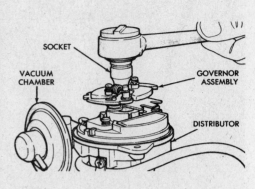

9.5 Use a socket or box wrench to remove the governor assembly retaining bolt (2.6L engine)

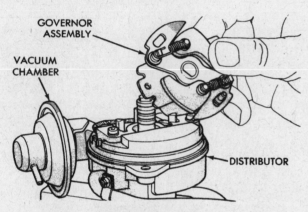

9.6 Remove the governor assembly (2.6L engine)

10.4 To replace the Hall Effect pick-up assembly on the distributor used on 2.2L, 2.5L and turbo engines, simply remove the rotor and lift the pick-up unit off the distributor housing (distributor assembly removed for clarity)

pump shaft **(see illustrations)**. If they don't, the distributor won't seat completely. On all distributors, recheck the alignment marks between the distributor base and block to verify the distributor is in the same position it was before removal. Also check the rotor to see if it's aligned with the mark you made on the edge of the distributor base.

11   Place the hold-down clamp (if equipped) in position and loosely install the hold-down bolt.

12   Install the distributor cap.

13   Plug in the electrical connector for the Hall Effect pick-up (2.2L, 2.5L and turbo engines), the pick-up coil (2.6L engine) or the photo optical sensing unit (3.0L engine).

14   Reattach the spark plug wires to the plugs (if removed).

15   Connect the cable to the negative terminal of the battery.

16   Check the ignition timing (see Chapter 1) and tighten the distributor hold-down bolt securely.

---

9   Governor (centrifugal advance) unit (2.6L engine) – check and replacement

---

Check

1   Connect a timing light to the engine in accordance with the manufacturer's instructions (see the ignition timing procedure in Chapter 1). Start the engine and allow it to warm up. With the engine idling, detach the vacuum line (the one without stripes) from the vacuum chamber. Slowly accelerate the engine and note whether ignition tim-

ing advances evenly, proportionate to engine speed.

2   If the advance is excessive, the governor spring is weakened; if the advance is abrupt, the spring is broken. If the advance is insufficient, a governor weight or a cam is defective. In either case, replace the governor assembly.

Replacement

Refer to illustrations 9.5 and 9.6

3   Remove the distributor (see Section 8). **Note:** *The governor unit can be removed with the distributor installed on the engine, but it's easier with the distributor removed.*

4   Remove the rotor (see Chapter 1).

5   Remove the governor assembly retaining bolt **(see illustration)**. **Note:** *This bolt is torqued very tightly – use a box wrench or socket – not an open end wrench – to loosen it.*

6   Remove the governor assembly **(see illustration)**. **Note:** *We recommend replacing the entire governor assembly as a single unit. But the individual springs and weights are also available separately. If you decide to replace an individual spring or weight, make sure you note which spring is attached to each weight prior to disassembly. The tension of each spring is calibrated to match its respective weight, so it must be reinstalled in its original position. The easiest way to identify a spring is to note the number of its coils: The stronger spring has more coils, the weaker spring, less.*

10.9   Before removing the pick-up assembly from the distributor used on the 2.6L engine, remove this screw (arrow) to detach the clamp that secures the electrical lead to the distributor housing

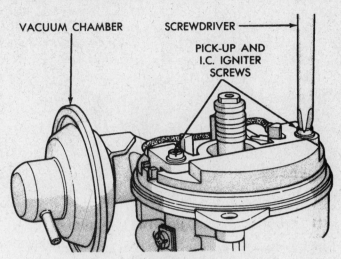

10.10a   Remove these two screws from the pick-up coil/IC igniter unit (2.6L engine)

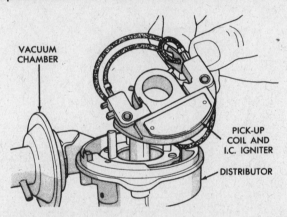

10.10b   Remove the pick-up coil/IC igniter unit from the distributor housing (2.6L engine)

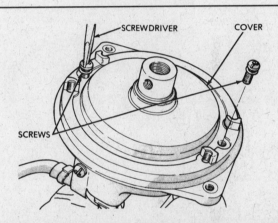

10.15   To get at the photo-optic sensing unit on a 3.0L distributor, remove these two screws (arrows) and this protective cover

7   Reassembly is the reverse of disassembly.
8   Install the rotor (see Chapter 1) and the distributor, if removed (see Section 8).

10   Pick-up assembly – replacement

1   Disconnect the cable from the negative terminal of the battery.

Hall effect pick-up assembly (2.2L, 2.5L and turbo engines)

Refer to illustration 10.4

Note: *The Hall Effect pick-up assembly inside the distributor supplies the basic ignition timing signal to the computer. On 2.2L engines, the check for the Hall Effect pick-up is part of the ignition system check in Section 6. On 2.5L and turbo engines, the check for the Hall Effect pick-up is part of a larger diagnostic procedure for the entire electronic spark advance system, and is beyond the scope of the home mechanic. But the replacement procedure itself is easy once you've verified that the Hall Effect unit is bad.*

2   Remove the distributor splash shield and cap and disconnect the Hall Effect electrical connector (see Section 8).
3   Remove the distributor cap and rotor (see Chapter 1).
4   Lift the pick-up assembly off the distributor shaft **(see illustration).**

5   Installation is the reverse of removal. On 2.2L models, check that the shutter blades are grounded (see Section 6, Step 17).

Pick-up coil/IC igniter assembly (2.6L engine)

Refer to illustrations 10.9, 10.10a and 10.10b

6   Remove the distributor (see Section 8). **Note:** *The pick-up coil/IC igniter assembly can be removed with the distributor installed on the engine, but it's easier with the distributor removed.*
7   Remove the rotor (see Chapter 1).
8   Remove the governor assembly (see Section 9).
9   Remove the screw from the clamp which secures the lead for the pick-up coil to the distributor housing **(see illustration).**
10   Remove the two retaining screws from the pick-up coil/IC igniter assembly **(see illustration)** and remove the assembly **(see illustration)**
11   Reassembly is the reverse of disassembly.
12   Install the governor assembly (see Section 9), the distributor, if removed (see Section 8), and the rotor and cap (see Chapter 1).

Photo-optical sensing unit (3.0L engine)

Refer to illustrations 10.15, 10.16, 10.17a, 10.17b and 10.19

13   Remove the distributor (see Section 8).
14   Remove the rotor (see Chapter 1).
15   Remove the protective cover from the distributor housing **(see illustration).**

5

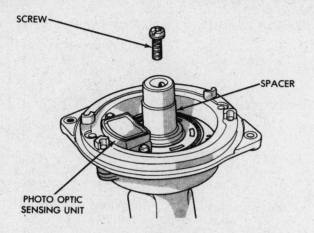

10.16   Remove the screw (arrow) from the spacer and remove the spacer (3.0L engine)

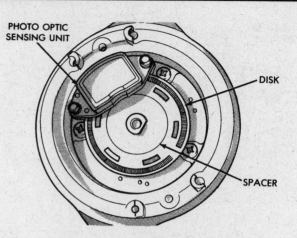

10.17a   Carefully remove the upper disk spacer, the disk and the lower disk spacer (underneath the disk, not visible in this illustration)

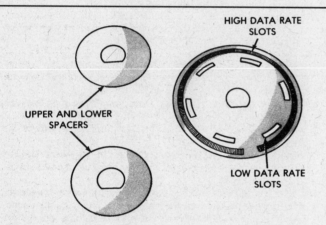

10.17b   Note how the upper and lower disk spacers and the disk itself are keyed to prevent incorrect reassembly

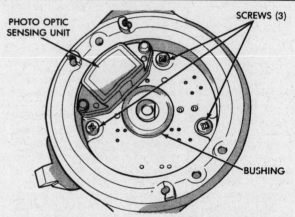

10.19   Remove the bushing (arrow) from the photo-optic sensing unit, remove these three screws (arrows) and remove the photo-optic sensing unit

16   Remove the screw from the spacer **(see illustration)** and remove the spacer.

17   Carefully remove the upper disk spacer, the disk and the lower disk spacer **(see illustration)**. **Note:** *The disk and spacers are keyed to ensure proper reassembly* **(see illustration)**.

18   Check the disk for warpage, cracks or damaged slots. If any damage is evident, replace the disk.

19   Remove the bushing from the photo-optic sensing unit, remove the three screws from the sensing unit **(see illustration)** and remove the sensing unit.

20   Reassembly is the reverse of disassembly.

21   Install the distributor (see Section 8) and install the rotor and cap (see Chapter 1).

11   Vacuum advance unit (2.6L engine) – check and replacement

Note: The vacuum advance unit is also referred to as a vacuum chamber and a vacuum governor assembly.

Check

1   Here's a little test for quickly checking the vacuum advance unit: Start the engine and warm it up, hook up a tachometer in accordance with the manufacturer's instructions, bring the engine speed up to 2500 rpm and note whether the engine speed is affected as you dis-connect, then reconnect, the vacuum line. If there's no change in engine speed, the vacuum advance unit is faulty.

2   Here's a more precise way to check the vacuum advance unit: Disconnect the vacuum line from the distributor and connect a vac-uum pump in its place. Hook up a timing light in accordance with the manufacturer's instructions (see the ignition timing procedure in Chap-ter 1). Run the engine at idle and slowly apply vacuum – the timing should advance evenly, proportionate to the amount of vacuum applied.

3   If the advance is excessive, the vacuum controller spring is worn or sagging; if the advance is abrupt, the spring is broken. If the advance is insufficient – or there's no advance at all – the breaker plate is faulty or the diaphragm is broken. In either case, replace the vacuum advance unit.

Replacement

Refer to illustrations 11.8 and 11.9

4   Remove the distributor (see Section 8). **Note:** *The vacuum advance unit can be removed with the distributor installed on the engine, but it's much easier to replace with the distributor removed.*

5   Remove the rotor (see Chapter 1).

6   Remove the governor assembly (see Section 9).

7   Remove the pick-up coil and IC igniter assembly (see Sec-tion 10).

8   Remove the two retaining screws from the vacuum governor assembly **(see illustration)**.

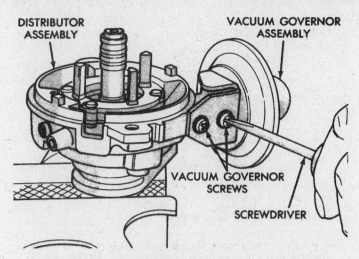

11.8   Remove the two vacuum governor screws (arrows) (2.6L engine)

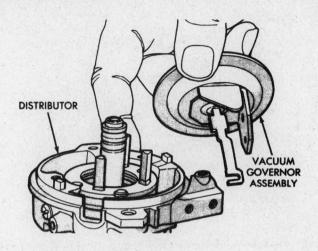

11.9   Remove the vacuum governor assembly (2.6L engine)

9   Remove the vacuum governor assembly **(see illustration)**.
10   Reassembly is the reverse of disassembly.
11   Install the distributor (see Section 8).

12   Charging system – general information and precautions

The charging system includes the alternator, an internal or external voltage regulator or a regulator within the logic module (computer), a charge indicator, the battery, a fusible link and the wiring between all the components. The charging system supplies electrical power for the ignition system, the lights, the radio, etc. The alternator is driven by a drivebelt at the front of the engine.

The purpose of the voltage regulator is to limit the alternator's voltage to a preset value. This prevents power surges, circuit overloads, etc., during peak voltage output.

The fusible link is a short length of insulated wire integral with the engine compartment wiring harness. The link is four wire gauges smaller in diameter than the circuit it protects. Production fusible links and their identification flags are identified by the flag color. See Chapter 12 for additional information regarding fusible links.

The charging system doesn't ordinarily require periodic maintenance. However, the drivebelt, battery and wires and connections should be inspected at the intervals outlined in Chapter 1.

The dashboard warning light should come on when the ignition key is turned to Start, then go off immediately. If it remains on, there is a malfunction in the charging system (see Section 13). Some vehicles are also equipped with a voltmeter. If the voltmeter indicates abnormally high or low voltage, check the charging system (see Section 13). Be very careful when making electrical circuit connections to a vehicle equipped with an alternator and note the following:

a) When reconnecting wires to the alternator from the battery, be sure to note the polarity.
b) Before using arc welding equipment to repair any part of the vehicle, disconnect the wires from the alternator and the battery terminals.
c) Never start the engine with a battery charger connected.
d) Always disconnect both battery leads before using a battery charger.
e) The alternator is turned by an engine drivebelt which could cause serious injury if your hands, hair or clothes become entangled in it with the engine running.
f) Because the alternator is connected directly to the battery, it could arc or cause a fire if overloaded or shorted out.
g) Wrap a plastic bag over the alternator and secure it with rubber bands before steam cleaning the engine.

13   Charging system – check

1   If a malfunction occurs in the charging circuit, don't automatically assume the alternator is causing the problem. First check the following items:

a) Check the drivebelt tension and condition (Chapter 1). Replace it if it's worn or deteriorated.
b) Make sure the alternator mounting and adjustment bolts are tight.
c) Inspect the alternator wiring harness and the connectors at the alternator and voltage regulator. They must be in good condition and tight.
d) Check the fusible link (if equipped) located between the starter solenoid and the alternator. If it's burned, determine the cause, repair the circuit and replace the link (the vehicle won't start and/or the accessories won't work if the fusible link blows). Sometimes a fusible link may look good, but still be bad. If in doubt, remove it and check it for continuity.
e) Start the engine and check the alternator for abnormal noises (a shrieking or squealing sound indicates a bad bearing).
f) Check the specific gravity of the battery electrolyte. If it's low, charge the battery (doesn't apply to maintenance free batteries).
g) Make sure the battery is fully charged (one bad cell in a battery can cause overcharging by the alternator).
h) Disconnect the battery cables (negative first, then positive). Inspect the battery posts and the cable clamps for corrosion. Clean them thoroughly if necessary (see Chapter 1). Reconnect the cable to the positive terminal.
i) With the key off, connect a test light between the negative battery post and the disconnected negative cable clamp.
1) If the test light does not come on, reattach the clamp and proceed to the next Step.
2) If the test light comes on, there is a short (drain) in the electrical system of the vehicle. The short must be repaired before the charging system can be checked.
3) Disconnect the alternator wiring harness.
(a) If the light goes out, the alternator is bad.
(b) If the light stays on, pull each fuse until the light goes out (this will tell you which component is shorted).

2   Using a voltmeter, check the battery voltage with the engine off. It should be approximately 12-volts.
3   Start the engine and check the battery voltage again. It should now be approximately 14 to 15 volts.
4   Turn on the headlights. The voltage should drop, and then come back up, if the charging system is working properly.

5

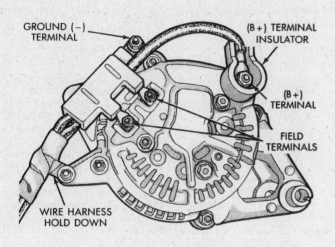

14.2   **Typical alternator electrical connections**

5   If the voltage reading is more than the specified charging voltage, replace the voltage regulator. On later models, the regulator is inside the computer and can't be replaced; on these vehicles, you'll have to replace the computer (see Chapter 6).

6   If the voltage reading is less than the specified voltage, the alternator diode(s), stator or rectifier may be bad or the voltage regulator may be malfunctioning.

14   Alternator – removal and installation

Refer to illustrations 14.2, 14.3a, 14.3b, 14.3c, 14.3d, 14.3e and 14.3f

1   Detach the cable from the negative terminal of the battery.

2   Detach the electrical connector(s) from the alternator **(see illustration)**. **Note:** *On most vehicles, the alternator is located in front of the engine block. But on 3.3L and 3.8L models, it's located behind the engine, so it's impossible to get at the alternator connectors from above. If you've got a 3.3L or 3.8L model, raise the front of the vehicle and place it securely on jackstands, then access the electrical connectors from below.*

3   Loosen the alternator adjustment and pivot bolts and detach the

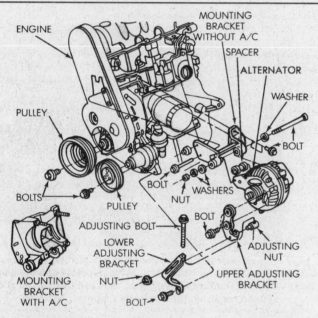

14.3a   **An exploded view of the mounting hardware for a typical earlier Chrysler alternator installation (four-cylinder engines)**

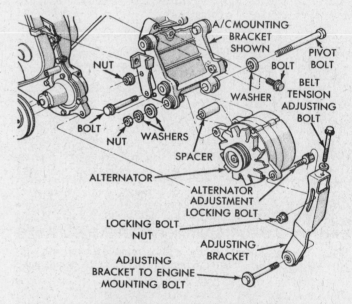

14.3b   **An exploded view of a typical later Chrysler alternator installation (four-cylinder engines)**

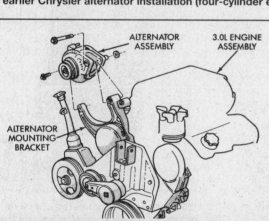

14.3c   **An exploded view of the mounting hardware for the alternator on a 3.0L engine**

14.3d   **To remove the alternator from a 3.3L engine, remove this upper mounting bolt (arrow), . . .**

drivebelt **(see illustrations)**.

4   Remove the adjustment and pivot bolts and separate the alternator from the engine.

5   If you're replacing the alternator, take the old one with you when purchasing a replacement unit. Make sure the new/rebuilt unit looks identical to the old alternator. Look at the terminals – they should be the same in number, size and location as the terminals on the old alternator. Finally, look at the identification numbers – they will be stamped into the housing or printed on a tag attached to the housing. Make sure the numbers are the same on both alternators.

6   Many new/rebuilt alternators DO NOT have a pulley installed, so you may have to switch the pulley from the old unit to the new/rebuilt one. When buying an alternator, find out the shop's policy regarding pulleys – some shops will perform this service free of charge.

7   Installation is the reverse of removal.

8   After the alternator is installed, adjust the drivebelt tension (see Chapter 1).

9   Check the charging voltage to verify proper operation of the alternator (see Section 13).

---

15   Alternator brushes – replacement

Note: If the brushes on alternators used on 1990 and later models are worn, the alternator must be exchanged for a rebuilt unit.

14.3e   . . . from underneath the vehicle, remove the nut and bolt (arrows) and remove this reinforcement between the engine and the timing belt cover, . . .

1   Disconnect the negative cable at the battery. Label the wires and detach them from the alternator terminals.

Bosch alternator

Refer to illustrations 15.2, 15.3 and 15.5

2   Loosen the brush holder mounting screws a little at a time to prevent distortion of the holder, then remove them **(see illustration)**.

3   Remove the brush holder from the alternator **(see illustration)**.

4   If the brushes appear to be significantly worn, or if they don't move smoothly in the brush holder, replace the brush holder assembly.

5   Before installing the brush holder assembly, check for continuity between each brush and the appropriate field terminal **(see illustration)**.

6   Install the brush holder. Make sure the brushes seat correctly.

7   Hold the brush holder securely in place and install the screws. Tighten them evenly, a little at a time, so the holder isn't distorted. Once the screws are snug, tighten them securely.

8   Reconnect the negative battery cable.

Chrysler 60, 65 and 78-amp alternators

Refer to illustration 15.11

9   Remove the alternator (see Section 14).

10   The brushes are mounted in plastic holders which locate them in

14.3f   . . . remove this lower mounting bolt (arrow) and remove the alternator by taking it out through the gap between the engine and the firewall from underneath (you can't remove it from above without removing the alternator mounting bracket)

5

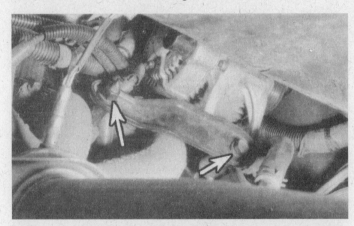

15.2   On Bosch alternators, loosen the brush holder mounting screws (arrows) in small increments, moving from screw to screw, so the holder won't be warped . . .

15.3   . . . and remove the brush holder assembly

15.5   Using an ohmmeter, check for continuity between each brush and the appropriate field terminal (if there's no continuity, switch one of the leads to the other field terminal or brush)

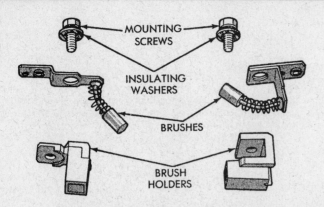

15.11   On Chrysler 60, 65 and 78-amp alternators, the brushes
are held in the holders with screws – when installing the brushes,
the insulating washers must be in place

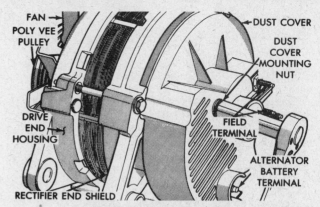

15.16   On Chrysler 40 and 90-amp alternators, remove the nut
and detach the dust cover

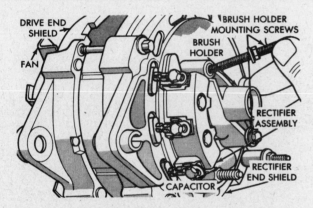

15.17a   To replace the brushes on Chrysler 40 and 90-amp
alternators, remove the brush holder mounting screws . . .

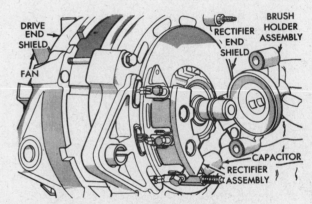

15.17b   . . . and detach the brush holder

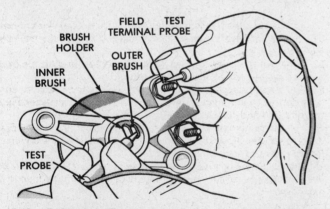

15.18   Before installing the brush holder assembly on 40 and
90-amp Chrysler alternators, use an ohmmeter to verify
continuity between each brush and the appropriate field
terminal (if there's no continuity, switch one of the leads to the
other field terminal or brush)

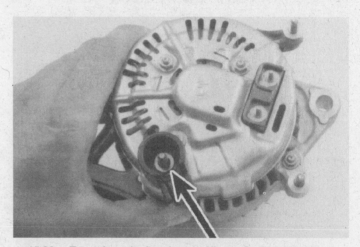

15.20   To replace the brushes on Nippondenso alternators,
remove the B+ terminal insulator nut, washer and insulator

the proper position.

11   Remove the brush mounting screws and insulating washers and
separate the brush assemblies from the rectifier end shield **(see illustration)**.

12   If the brushes appear to be significantly worn or are oil soaked or
damaged, replace them with new ones.

13   Make sure the brushes move smoothly in the holders.

14   Insert the brush assemblies into the rectifier end shield and install

the screws and washers. Tighten the screws securely. Make sure the
brushes aren't grounded.

15   Install the alternator.

Chrysler 40 and 90-amp alternators

Refer to illustrations 15.16, 15.17a, 15.17b and 15.18

16   Remove the nut and detach the dust cover from the rear of the
alternator **(see illustration)**.

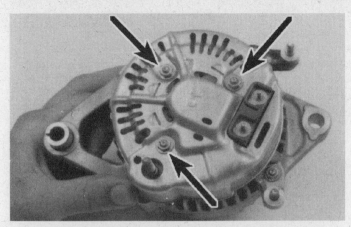

15.21   Remove the rear cover attaching nuts (arrows) and remove the rear cover (Nippondenso alternators)

15.22a   Remove the brush holder attaching screws (arrows) ...

15.22b   ... and remove the brush holder assembly (Nippondenso alternators)

15.24   Depress the brushes with your index finger as you slide the brush holder into place

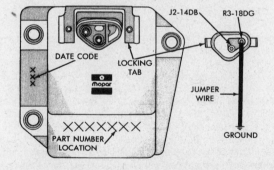

16.2   A typical Chrysler external electronic voltage regulator

17   Remove the brush holder mounting screws and separate the brush holder from the end shield **(see illustrations)**.

18   Before installing the new brush holder assembly, check for continuity between each brush and the appropriate field terminal **(see illustration)**.

19   Installation is the reverse of removal. Be careful when sliding the brushes over the slip rings and don't overtighten the brush holder screws.

Nippondenso alternators

Refer to illustrations 15.20, 15.21, 15.22a, 15.22b and 15.24

20   With the alternator removed from the vehicle (see the previous Section), remove the B+ insulator nut and insulator **(see illustration)**.

21   Remove the rear cover attaching nuts and remove the rear cover **(see illustration)**.

22   Remove the brush holder attaching screws and lift the brush holder from the alternator **(see illustrations)**.

23   Before installing the new brush holder assembly, check for continuity between each brush and the appropriate field terminal **(see illustrations 15.5 and 15.18)**.

24   To install the brush holder assembly, use your finger to depress the brushes **(see illustration)**, then slide the holder over the commutator slip rings and screw it into place.

25   Installation is otherwise the reverse of removal. When installing the B+ insulator, be sure to align the guide tang with the hole in the rear cover.

16   Voltage regulator – description

Refer to illustration 16.2

1   The voltage regulator is a device that regulates vehicle electrical system voltage by limiting output voltage generated by the alternator. It accomplishes this task by limiting the amount of current passing through the alternator field windings. The regulators used on some models covered by this manual are electronic – there are no moving parts and they're not adjustable like older mechanical regulators.

2   On pre-1987 models, the voltage regulator used with Chrysler alternators is an external solid-state device **(see illustration)** located in the engine compartment. If this type of regulator goes bad, replacement is straight-forward. The regulator used with Mitsubishi alternators (2.6L engines) is an internal component located inside the alterna-

5

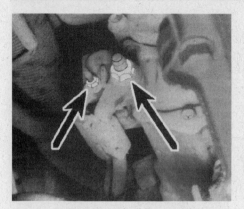

19.3   Label the wires (arrows) before disconnecting them from the starter assembly

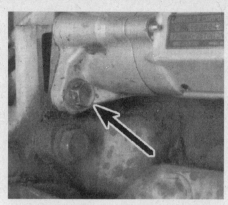

19.4a   On 2.2L, 2.5L and turbo engines, remove this starter motor mounting bolt (arrow) from underneath the vehicle and, . . .

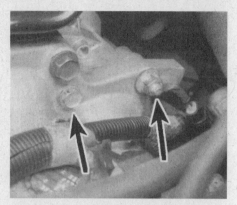

19.4b   . . . remove the other mounting bolt and the nut (arrows) from above, then remove the starter

tor. If a Mitsubishi regulator is bad, exchange the alternator for a rebuilt unit; replacement of the voltage regulator – which involves considerable disassembly of the alternator and some soldering – is impractical.

3   On some 1987 and all later models, the voltage regulator is integrated into the logic module, the single-module engine controller (SMEC) or the single-board engine controller (SBEC) of the fuel injection system. Special diagnostic tools are needed to check the regulator. Only a dealer service department and some repair shops have these tools. If the regulator is faulty, the computer must be replaced. Computer replacement is covered by a Federally-mandated extended warranty (see your owner's manual or consult your dealer for details). If the computer is out of warranty and you want to replace it yourself, see Chapter 6.

17   Starting system – general information and precautions

The sole function of the starting system is to turn over the engine quickly enough to allow it to start.

The starting system consists of the battery, the starter motor, the starter solenoid, the switch and the wires connecting them. The solenoid is mounted directly on the starter motor.

The solenoid/starter motor assembly is installed on the lower part of the engine, next to the transaxle bellhousing.

When the ignition key is turned to the Start position, the starter solenoid is actuated through the starter control circuit. The starter solenoid then connects the battery to the starter. The battery supplies the electrical energy to the starter motor, which does the actual work of cranking the engine.

The the starter on a vehicle equipped with an automatic transmission can only be operated when the transmission selector lever is in Park or Neutral.

Always observe the following precautions when working on the starting system:
  a) Excessive cranking of the starter motor can overheat it and cause serious damage. Never operate the starter motor for more than 30 seconds at a time without pausing to allow it to cool for at least two minutes.
  b) The starter is connected directly to the battery and could arc or cause a fire if mishandled, overloaded or shorted out.
  c) Always detach the cable from the negative terminal of the battery before working on the starting system.

18   Starter motor – in-vehicle check

Note: Before diagnosing starter problems, make sure the battery is fully charged.

1   If the starter motor doesn't turn at all when the switch is operated, make sure the shift lever is in Neutral or Park (automatic transmission).

2   Make sure the battery is charged and all cables, both at the battery and starter solenoid terminals, are clean and secure.

3   If the starter motor spins but the engine isn't cranking, the overrunning clutch in the starter motor is slipping and the starter motor must be replaced.

4   If, when the switch is actuated, the starter motor doesn't operate at all but the solenoid clicks, then the problem lies with either the battery, the main solenoid contacts or the starter motor itself (or the engine is seized).

5   If the solenoid plunger can't be heard when the switch is actuated, the battery is bad, the fusible link is burned (the circuit is open) or the solenoid itself is defective.

6   To check the solenoid, connect a jumper lead between the battery (+) and the ignition switch wire terminal (the small terminal) on the solenoid. If the starter motor now operates, the solenoid is OK and the problem is in the ignition switch, neutral start switch or the wiring.

7   If the starter motor still doesn't operate, remove the starter/solenoid assembly for disassembly, testing and repair.

8   If the starter motor cranks the engine at an abnormally slow speed, first make sure the battery is fully charged and all terminal connections are tight. If the engine is partially seized, or has the wrong viscosity oil in it, it will crank slowly.

9   Run the engine until normal operating temperature is reached, then disconnect the coil wire from the distributor cap and ground it on the engine.

10   Connect a voltmeter positive lead to the positive battery post and connect the negative lead to the negative post.

11   Crank the engine and take the voltmeter readings as soon as a steady figure is indicated. Don't allow the starter motor to turn for more than 30 seconds at a time. A reading of 9 volts or more, with the starter motor turning at normal cranking speed, is normal. If the reading is 9 volts or more but the cranking speed is slow, the motor is faulty. If the reading is less than 9 volts and the cranking speed is slow, the solenoid contacts are probably burned, the starter motor is bad, the battery is discharged or there's a bad connection.

19   Starter motor assembly – removal and installation

Refer to illustrations 19.3, 19.4a, 19.4b, 19.4c and 19.4d

1   Detach the cable from the negative terminal of the battery.

2   Raise the vehicle and support it securely on jackstands.

3   Clearly label, then disconnect the wires from the terminals on the starter motor and solenoid **(see illustration)**.

4   Remove the mounting bolts **(see illustrations)** and detach the starter.

5   Installation is the reverse of removal.

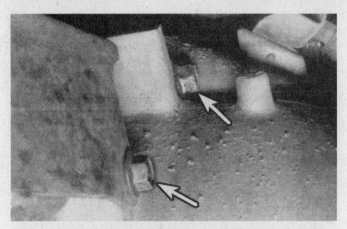

19.4c   On 2.6L engines, remove these two starter mounting bolts (arrows) and remove the starter

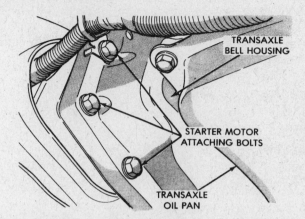

19.4d   On 3.0L engines, remove these three starter mounting bolts (arrows) and remove the starter (three starter mounting bolts on 3.3L engine similar)

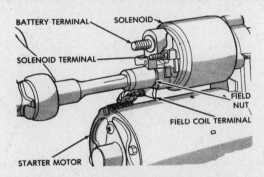

20.3a   Before disconnecting the solenoid from a Bosch starter motor, remove the field terminal nut, . . .

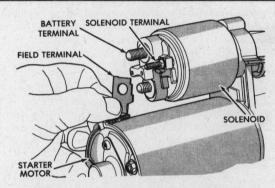

20.3b   . . . disconnect the field terminal, . . .

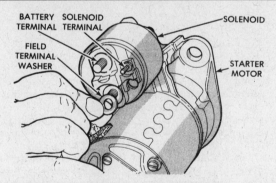

20.3c   . . . and remove the washer

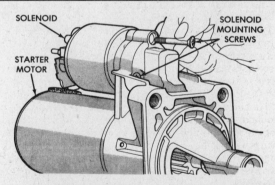

20.4   To detach the solenoid from a Bosch starter motor, remove these three screws (arrows)

20   Starter motor/solenoid/gear reduction assembly – replacement

1   Disconnect the cable from the negative terminal of the battery.
2   Remove the starter motor (see Section 19).

Bosch

Refer to illustrations 20.3a, 20.3b, 20.3c, 20.4 and 20.5

3   Remove the field terminal nut, disconnect the field terminal and remove the washer **(see illustrations)**.
4   Remove the three solenoid mounting screws **(see illustration)**.
5   Work the solenoid off the shift fork and detach it from the drive end housing **(see illustration)**.
6   Installation is the reverse of removal.

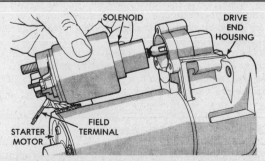

20.5   On a Bosch starter motor, work the solenoid off the shift fork and detach it from the drive end housing

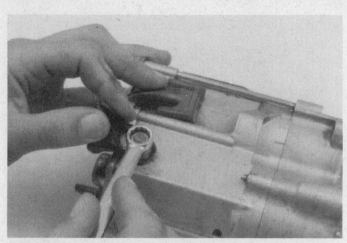

20.7   If you're replacing the starter motor or solenoid on a Nippondenso starter motor, disconnect the field coil strap from the solenoid terminal (if you're replacing the gear reduction assembly, you can leave the solenoid and starter wired together and simply disconnect both of them as a single unit from the gear reduction housing)

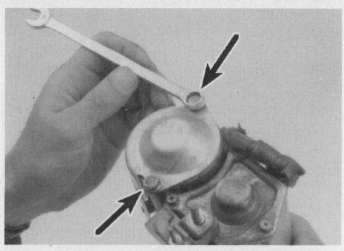

20.8a   To detach a Nippondenso starter motor from the gear reduction assembly, remove these two long through-bolts (arrows) . . .

20.8b   . . . and separate the starter motor from the gear reduction housing

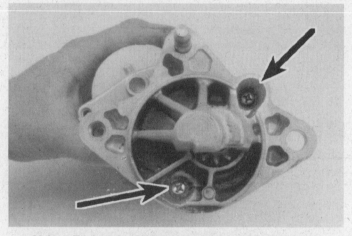

20.9a   To detach a Nippondenso solenoid from the gear reduction assembly, remove the starter, remove these two Phillips screws (arrows) . . .

Nippondenso

Refer to illustrations 20.7, 20.8a, 20.8b, 20.9a and 20.9b

7   If you're replacing the starter motor or solenoid, disconnect the field coil strap from the solenoid terminal **(see illustration)**; if you're replacing the gear reduction assembly, skip this step and proceed to the next step.

8   To detach the starter motor from the gear reduction assembly, simply remove the two long through-bolts and pull off the starter **(see illustrations)**.

9   To detach the solenoid from the gear reduction assembly, remove the starter, then remove the two Phillips screws from the gear reduction assembly and pull off the solenoid **(see illustrations)**.

10   Installation is the reverse of removal.

20.9b   . . . and separate the solenoid from the gear reduction housing

Chapter 6   Emissions control systems

Contents

6

Specifications

General (2.2L engine only)

Charcoal canister delay valve test vacuum	10 in Hg
EGR valve test vacuum	10 in Hg
EGR valve travel	1/8 inch

Torque specifications

	Ft-lbs (unless otherwise indicated)
Camshaft reference sensor retaining bolt (3.3L and 3.8L)	105 in-lbs
Crankshaft reference sensor retaining bolt (3.3L and 3.8L).	105 in-lbs
EGR valve (all engines)	
EGR valve mounting bolts	200 in-lbs
EGR tube bolts	200 in-lbs
EGR tube-to-valve screws	95 in-lbs

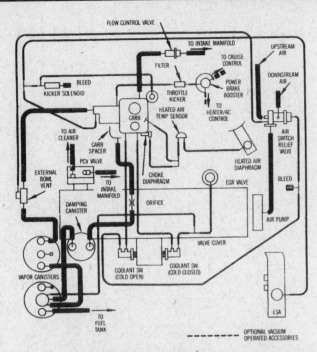

1.10a   Vacuum hose routing for 1984 2.2L California models (Federal and Canadian models similar)

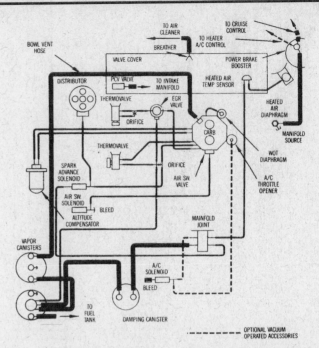

1.10b   Vacuum hose routing for 1984 2.6L California models

1   General information

Refer to illustrations 1.10a through 1.10j and 1.13

To prevent pollution of the atmosphere from incompletely burned and evaporating gases, and to maintain good driveability and fuel economy, a number of emission control systems are incorporated. The principal systems are . . .

Air aspirator system (2.6L Federal and Canadian models)
Air injection system (2.2L engine)
Automatic choke system (2.2L and 2.6L engines)
Catalytic converter (all engines)
Electronic feedback carburetor system (2.2L engine)
Evaporative emissions control system (all engines)
Exhaust Gas Recirculation (EGR) system (all engines)
Heated inlet air system (2.2L and 2.5L engines)
High altitude compensation system (2.6L engine)
Jet Air Control Valve (JACV) (2.6L engine)
Oxygen sensor (all engines)
Mikuni carburetor system (2.6L engine)
Positive Crankcase Ventilation (PCV) system (all engines)
Pulse Air Feeder (PAF) system (2.6L engine)
Single Module Engine Controller (SMEC)/Single Board Engine Controller (SBEC), information sensors and self-diagnosis system (2.5L, 3.0L, 3.3L and 3.8L engines)
Throttle opener (idle-up) system (2.6L engine)

Since these vehicles are equipped with either a 2.2L, 2.5L, 2.6L, 3.0L or 3.3L engine, many emission control devices are used. Some of these devices or systems are exclusive to a particular engine, while others are applicable to all models. All systems will be described in this Chapter so that all models will be covered.

All engines are equipped with a Fuel Evaporative Emissions Control (EVAP) system, an Exhaust Gas Recirculation (EGR) system, a Positive Crankcase Ventilation (PCV) system and a catalytic converter. The 2.2L, 2.5L and 2.6L engines also use a heated inlet air system. The 2.2L and 2.6L engines also use an automatic choke and various other emissions systems to improve cold starting and/or enhance driveability while the engine is still cold or is being driven at high altitude.

The 2.2L engine has an air injection system and an electronic feedback carburetor system. The electronic feedback carburetor works in conjunction with an oxygen sensor located in the exhaust system and a spark control computer. The three work together to constantly monitor exhaust gas oxygen content and vary the spark timing and fuel mixture so that emissions are always within limits.

The 2.6L engine features a Pulse Air Feeder (PAF) air injection system which injects air into the exhaust system between the front and rear catalytic converter to reduce emissions. Also, a Jet Air Control Valve (JACV) system is used to inject a very lean fuel mixture into the combustion chamber and improve efficiency and thus emissions.

The 2.5L engine is equipped with a computer-controlled, "single-point" (one injector in the throttle body) electronic fuel injection (EFI) system; the 2.5L turbo, 3.0L, 3.3L and 3.8L engines are equipped with "multi-point" (injector in each intake port) EFI systems. EFI systems deliver a precise air/fuel mixture ratio under all driving conditions. At their heart is a computer known as a Single Module Engine Controller (SMEC) (1987 through 1989 models) or a Single Board Engine Controller (SBEC) (1990 and 1991 models).

The SMEC/SBEC regulates ignition timing, the air/fuel ratio, various emission control devices, the cooling fan, the charging system, the idle speed and (on the 3.0L, 3.3L and 3.8L engines) speed control. The SMEC/SBEC can even update and revise its own programming in response to changing operating conditions. Various sensors provide the necessary inputs for the SMEC to regulate the flow of fuel to the injector. These include the Manifold Absolute Pressure (MAP) sensor, the Throttle Position Sensor (TPS), the oxygen sensor, the coolant temperature sensor and the throttle body temperature sensor (all engines); the vehicle distance sensor (2.5L engines); the charge temperature and vehicle speed sensors (3.0L, 3.3L and 3.8L engines); and the camshaft, crankshaft and knock sensors (3.3L and 3.8L engines).

Besides these sensors, various switches and relays also provide information to the SMEC/SBEC. These include the neutral safety switch and air conditioning clutch switch (or cut-out relay) (all engines); the auto shutdown relay (2.5L engines); and the brake switch and speed control switch (3.0L, 3.3L and 3.8L engines). All inputs to the SMEC/SBEC are converted into digital signals which are "read" by the SMEC and converted into changes in either the fuel flow, the ignition timing, or both. The SMEC constantly monitors many of its own input and output circuits. If a fault is found in a system, the information is

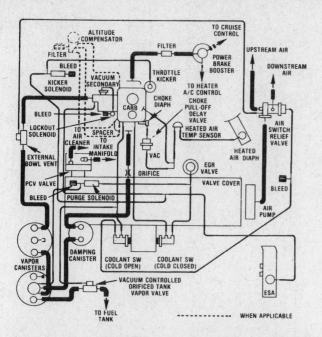

1.10c   Vacuum hose routing for 1985, 1986 and 1987 2.2L California models (Federal and Canadian models similar)

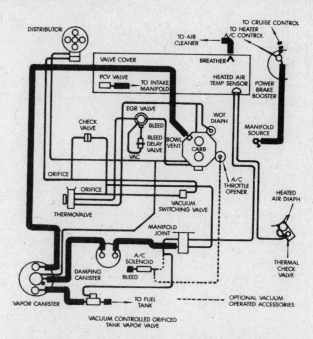

1.10d   Vacuum hose routing for 1986 2.6L Federal models

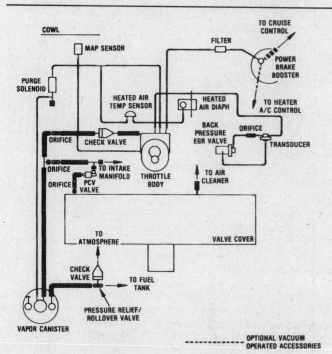

1.10e   Vacuum hose routing for 1987 2.5L models

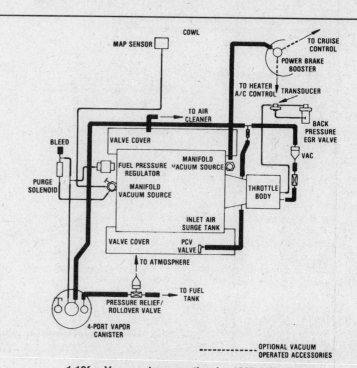

1.10f   Vacuum hose routing for 1987 3.0L models (1988 models similar)

6

stored in the SMEC's memory. You can output this information and display it on the check engine light on the dash.

The Sections in this Chapter include general descriptions, checking procedures within the scope of the home mechanic and component replacement procedures (when possible) for each of the systems listed above.

Before assuming an emissions control system is malfunctioning, check the fuel and ignition systems carefully. The diagnosis of some emission control devices requires specialized tools, equipment and training. If checking and servicing become too difficult or if a procedure is beyond your ability, consult a dealer service department. Remember, the most frequent cause of emissions problems is simply a loose or broken vacuum hose or wire, so always check the hose and wiring connections first **(see illustrations)**.

This doesn't mean, however, that emission control systems are particularly difficult to maintain and repair. You can quickly and easily perform many checks and do most of the regular maintenance at home with common tune-up and hand tools. **Note:** *Because of a Federally*

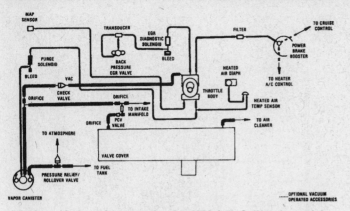

1.10g   Vacuum hose routing for 1988 2.5L California models (others similar)

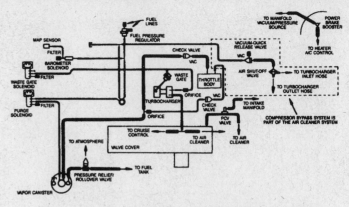

1.10h   Vacuum hose routing for 1989 2.5L turbo Federal, California and Canadian models

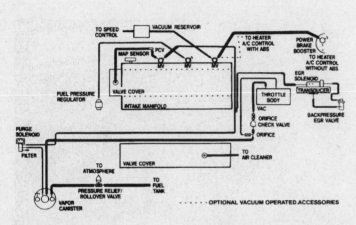

1.10i   Vacuum hose routing for 1990 3.3L California models (Federal, Canadian and 1991through 1993 models similar)

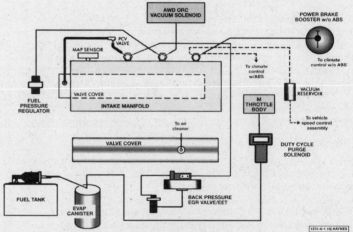

1.10j   Vacuum hose routing for 1994 and later 3.0L and 3.8L engines

mandated extended warranty which covers the emission control system components, check with your dealer about warranty coverage before working on any emissions-related systems. Once the warranty has expired, you may wish to perform some of the component checks and/or replacement procedures in this Chapter to save money.

Pay close attention to any special precautions outlined in this Chapter. It should be noted that the illustrations of the various systems may not exactly match the system installed on your vehicle because of changes made by the manufacturer during production or from year-to-year.

A Vehicle Emissions Control Information (VECI) label (earlier models) or an Emissions, Adjustment and Routing (EAR) label is located in the engine compartment **(see accompanying illustration and illustrations 1.10a through 1.10j)**. This label contains important emissions specifications and adjustment information. When servicing the engine

or emissions systems, the VECI label in your particular vehicle should always be checked for up-to-date information.

2   Electronic feedback carburetor system

Note: *This Section applies only to earlier models with the 2.2L engine.*

General description

1   The electronic feedback carburetor emission system relies on an electronic signal, which is generated by an exhaust gas sensor, to control a variety of devices and keep emissions within limits. The system works in conjunction with a three-way catalyst to control the levels of carbon monoxide, hydrocarbons and oxides of nitrogen.
2   The system operates in two modes: open loop and closed loop.

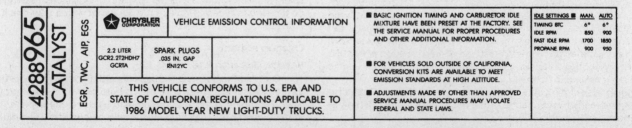

1.13   Typical Vehicle Emission Control Information (VECI) label

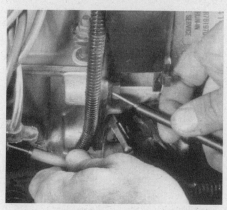

2.7 Checking the vacuum switch for continuity (2.2L engine)

2.11 Grounding pin 15 of the six-pin connector (2.2L engine)

2.14 Grounding the oxygen sensor wire to the negative battery post (2.2L engine)

When the engine is cold, the air/fuel mixture is controlled by the computer in accordance with a program designed in at the time of production. The air/fuel mixture during this time will be richer to allow for proper engine warm-up. When the engine is at operating temperature, the system operates at closed loop and the air/fuel mixture is varied depending on the information supplied by the exhaust gas sensor.

3   The system consists of the carburetor, computer, air switching valve, coolant control engine vacuum switch, catalytic converters and oxygen sensor.

Checking

4   Prior to checking the system, check the computer for proper operation. Also, make sure that all vacuum hoses and electrical wires are properly routed and securely connected.

5   Apply 16 in Hg of vacuum to the computer with a vacuum pump. Disconnect the hose from the air switching valve and connect a vacuum gauge to the hose (see Step 6 below). Start the engine and allow it to warm up to operating temperature. Run the engine at approximately 2000 rpm for two minutes and make sure the carburetor switch is not grounded.

Air switching system

Refer to illustration 2.7

6   Right after starting the engine, there should be a vacuum reading which will slowly drop to zero as the engine warms up.

7   If there is no vacuum, check the Coolant Controlled Engine Vacuum Switch (CCEVS) for continuity. If there is no continuity, correct the fault or replace the switch **(see illustration)**.

8   With the engine at operating temperature, shut it off, remove the vacuum hose from the valve and then connect a hand vacuum pump to the valve. Start the engine and make sure air blows out of the side port. Apply vacuum to the valve. Air should now blow out of the bottom port of the valve.

9   Before proceeding, check the engine temperature sensor.

Carburetor regulator

Refer to illustration 2.11

10   Remove the computer vacuum hose and plug it. Connect a vacuum pump to the carburetor and apply 14 in Hg of vacuum. With the engine at 2000 rpm, disconnect the regulator solenoid connector at the solenoid. On non-air conditioned models, only the green wire should be disconnected. The engine speed should increase at least 50 rpm. Reconnect the solenoid wire(s) and make sure that the engine speed slowly returns to normal.

11   Unplug the six pin connector from the combustion control computer and momentarily connect a ground to connector pin 15 **(see illustration)**.

12   Engine speed should decrease at least 50 rpm. If it does not, check the carburetor for air leaks.

2.16 Holding the choke closed while testing the oxygen sensor (2.2L engine)

Electronic fuel control computer

Refer to illustration 2.14

13   With the engine at normal operating temperature and the carburetor switch not grounded, connect a tachometer.

14   Start the engine and maintain an idle of 2000 rpm. Connect a voltmeter to the green solenoid output wire which leads to the carburetor. Disconnect the electrical harness at the oxygen sensor and connect a jumper wire between the harness connector and the negative battery terminal **(see illustration)**.

15   The engine speed should increase at least 50 rpm and the voltmeter should read at least nine volts. With the wire held in one hand, touch the battery positive terminal with your other hand. The engine speed should drop by a least 50 rpm and the voltmeter reading should be three volts or less. Replace the computer with a new one if it fails both tests.

Oxygen sensor

Refer to illustration 2.16

16   Connect the voltmeter to the solenoid output wire, reconnect the oxygen sensor and make sure the carburetor switch is not grounded. Start the engine, run it at 2000 rpm and hold the choke plates closed **(see illustration)**. This simulates a full rich condition and within ten seconds the voltage should drop to three volts or less. If it does not, disconnect the PCV hose. This simulates a full lean condition and the voltage should increase to nine volts or more. Do not take more than

6

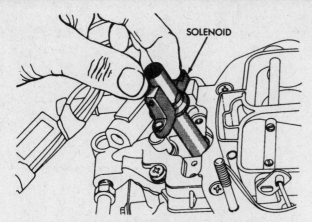

2.20   The carburetor solenoid is attached to the top of the carburetor with two screws (2.2L engine)

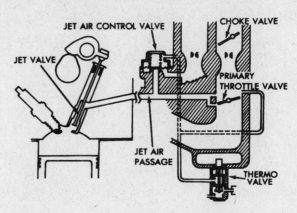

3.5   Jet Air Control Valve (JACV) system (2.6L engine)

90 seconds to complete these tests. If the sensor fails both tests, replace it with a new one.

Component replacement

Refer to illustration 2.20

17   To replace the Spark Control Computer, remove the battery, disconnect the vacuum hose and electrical connectors, remove the three retaining screws and lift the assembly from the engine compartment.

18   Mark the hose locations on the air switching valve, remove the hoses and disconnect the valve.

19   The CCEVS is replaced by removing the vacuum hoses and unscrewing the valve. Coat the threads of the new valve with gasket sealant prior to installation.

20   To replace the carburetor solenoid, unplug the electrical connector and remove the two retaining screws. Detach the solenoid from the carburetor **(see illustration)**.

21   Disconnect the oxygen sensor wire and use a wrench to unscrew the sensor. Use a tap to clean the threads in the exhaust manifold. If the sensor is to be reinstalled, apply anti-seize compound to the threads. New sensors already have the anti-seize compound on their threads.

3   Mikuni carburetor system

Note: *This Section applies only to models with the 2.6L engine.*

General description

Refer to illustration 3.5

1   The Mikuni carburetor on 2.6L engines is equipped with a variety of devices which reduce emissions while maintaining driveability.

2   The system consists of a Coasting Air Valve (CAV), Air Switching Valve (ASV), Deceleration Spark Advance System (DSAS), High Altitude Compensation (HAC) (on some models), Jet Air Control Valve (JACV) and a throttle opener.

3   The CAV, ASV and DSAS reduce hydrocarbon emissions while maintaining driveability and fuel economy by shutting off fuel flow and advancing the spark during deceleration.

4   The HAC maintains the proper fuel/air mixture during high altitude driving by means of an atmospheric pressure sensitive bellows.

5   The JACV helps decrease HC and CO emissions, while the choke is operating, by opening to allow additional jet air flow and eliminating an over rich condition **(see illustration)**.

6   The throttle opener controls the engine idle speed during operation of the air conditioner.

Checking

ASV and CAV

Refer to illustrations 3.7a and 3.7b

7   With the engine at idle, unplug the solenoid valve electrical connector. If the idle speed drops or the engine stalls, the ASV and CAV are operating properly. With the engine again at idle, check the solenoid connector with a voltmeter. If no voltage is present, the wiring or speed sensor is faulty. Check the solenoid connector with the engine at 2500 rpm to make sure there is voltage. If there is no voltage, there is a fault in the speed sensor and it must be replaced with a new one **(see illustrations)**.

DSAS

Refer to illustration 3.8

8   Connect a timing light and allow the engine to run at idle. With the timing light on the timing marks, disconnect the electrical connector

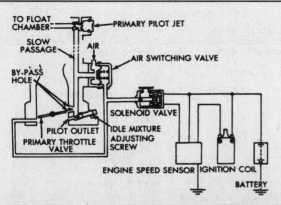

3.7a   Air Switching Valve (ASV) system (2.6L engine)

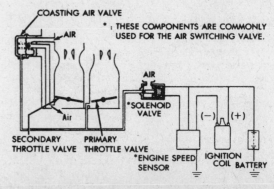

3.7b   Coasting Air Valve (CAV) system (2.6L engine)

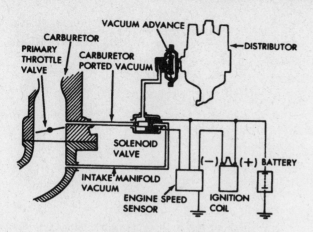

3.8   Deceleration Spark Advance System (DSAS) (2.6L engine)

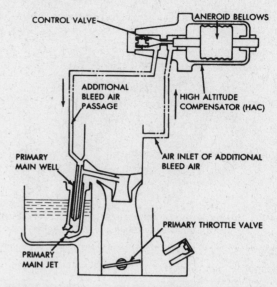

3.9   High Altitude Compensation (HAC) system (2.6L engine)

from the solenoid valve. If the timing does not advance, the solenoid valve and/or advance mechanism are faulty **(see illustration).**

HAC

Refer to illustration 3.9

9   Since special equipment is required to test the HAC, checking is confined to making sure associated hoses and connections are secure **(see illustration).**

Throttle opener

10   With the engine idling, turn on the air conditioner. If the idle speed does not increase, there is a fault in the solenoid kicker, engine speed sensor or wiring.

Component replacement

11   Locate the solenoid valve or speed sensor by tracing the wires or hoses from the component which they control. Disconnect the wires and/or hoses and install a new unit.

---

4   Automatic choke system

Note: *This Section applies only to earlier models with the 2.2L or 2.6L engine.*

General description

Refer to illustrations 4.3 and 4.4

1   The automatic choke system temporarily supplies a rich fuel/air

mixture to the engine by closing the choke plate(s) during cold engine starting.

2   On 2.2L engines, the choke is electrically operated, while 2.6L engines use sealed wax pellet-type choke systems.

3   On 2.2L engines, an electric signal from the oil pressure switch operates the choke control switch and activates the choke heater so that it slowly opens the choke plates as the engine warms up **(see illustration)**. This progressively leans out the mixture until the engine is warmed up.

4   On 2.6L engines, the wax pellet thermo sensing unit opens the choke as the coolant temperature increases. When started from cold, the choke valve is partially opened by a vacuum kicker actuated by manifold vacuum. This prevents an overly rich air/fuel mixture and the resultant increased emissions. The fast idle cam on the choke set lever controls the rate of throttle valve opening. If the vehicle is driven with a wide open throttle setting when cold, the choke is opened by the choke unloader so the mixture will not be overly rich **(see illustration)**.

Checking

5   Refer to Chapter 1 for the automatic choke checking procedure.

Component replacement

6   Choke component replacement is covered in Chapter 4.

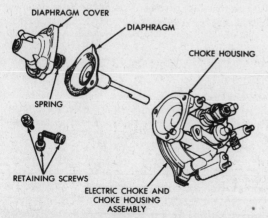

4.3   An exploded view of the electric choke components on a 2.2L engine

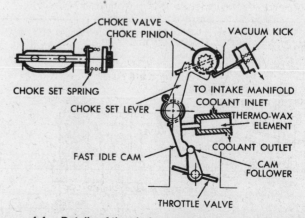

4.4   Details of the choke components on a 2.6L engine

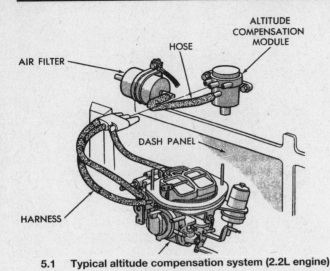

5.1   Typical altitude compensation system (2.2L engine)

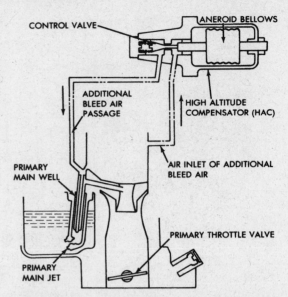

5.2   Typical altitude compensation system (2.6L engine)

5   High altitude compensation system

Refer to illustrations 5.1 and 5.2

Note: *This Section applies only to models with a 2.2L or 2.6L engine.*

1   Some 2.2L models are equipped with an altitude compensation system **(see illustration)** which compensates for thinner air by using various air bleeds which act in parallel with the normal fixed air bleeds in the carburetor idle, primary and secondary circuits at higher altitudes. These air bleeds consist of tapered needles which are moved in orifices by an aneroid bellows housed inside an altitude compensation module mounted in the engine compartment. Outside air passes through an air filter, through the compensation module and into the carburetor. The system is designed so no air can flow through until atmospheric pressure is below a predetermined level. Air flow gradually increases as atmospheric pressure increases.

2   Some 2.6L models are also equipped with an altitude compensation system **(see illustration)**. A small cylindrical bellows chamber, located in the engine compartment, is connected to the carburetor via a pair of air bleed hoses. The bellows is vented to the atmosphere at the top of the carburetor. Atmospheric pressure expands or contracts the bellows. When the vehicle is operated at a higher altitude, i.e. thinner air, the bellows begins to expand. A small brass tapered-seat valve is raised off its seat by the bellows, allowing extra air to enter the main air bleeds. How much the calibrated bellows opens is proportional to the altitude. When the vehicle leaves the higher altitude, i.e. the air gets thicker, the bellows gradually contracts and the extra air bleeds are closed off.

3   Neither of these systems is likely to malfunction. If the engine starts running too rich (mileage goes down suddenly, engine is hard to start, plugs fouled, etc.), check all the hoses in the system. Make sure all connections are tight and there are no tears in the hoses. If the problem persists, take the vehicle to a dealer service department or other repair shop and have the system checked.

6   Throttle opener (idle-up) system

Note: *This Section applies only to models with a 2.6L engine.*

The throttle opener (or idle-up) system raises the engine idle speed when the air conditioning compressor is operating. The system consists of the throttle opener assembly, a solenoid valve, an engine speed sensor and a compressor switch for the air conditioning unit. When the switch is turned on – and the engine speed sensor detects the engine speed at or below the specified value – the solenoid valve opens, transmitting intake manifold vacuum to the throttle opener. The

throttle opener opens the throttle valve slightly via the throttle opener lever, increasing engine idle speed to compensate for the extra load imposed by the compressor. When the compressor switch is turned off, the throttle opener system stops working and the engine returns to its normal idle speed. The engine speed sensor in the air switching valve system is used to monitor the engine speed. When engine speed is at or below the specified value, the air switching valve system doesn't operate; when engine speed is above this value, the switching valve system works as designed.

If the throttle opener system fails to operate as described above when the air conditioning system is operating, check the wiring. Make sure all connections are clean and tight. If the throttle opener still doesn't work properly, take the vehicle to a dealer and have it checked.

7   Jet Air Control Valve (JACV) system

Note: *This Section applies only to models with the 2.6L engine.*

1   The jet air system utilizes an additional intake valve (jet valve) which provides for air, or a super lean mixture, to be drawn from the air intake into the cylinder. The jet valve is operated by the same cam as the intake valve. They use a common rocker arm so the jet valve and the intake valve open and close simultaneously.

2   On the intake stroke of the engine, fuel/air mixture flows through the intake ports into the combustion chamber. At the same time, jet air is forced into the combustion chamber because of the pressure difference between the jet intake in the throttle bore and the jet valve in the cylinder as the piston moves down. At small throttle openings, there is a large pressure difference, giving the jet air a high velocity. This scavenges the residual gases around the spark plug and creates good ignition conditions. It also produces a strong swirl in the combustion chamber, which lasts throughout the compression stroke and improves flame propagation after ignition, assuring high combustion efficiency and lowering exhaust emissions. As the throttle opening is increased, less jet air is forced in and jet swirl diminishes, but the increased flow through the intake valve ensures satisfactory combustion.

3   A thermo valve which works in conjunction with the EGR system controls the air flow to the jet valve.

4   Maintenance consists of adjusting the jet valve clearances at the same time the intake and exhaust valves are adjusted, as described in Chapter 1.

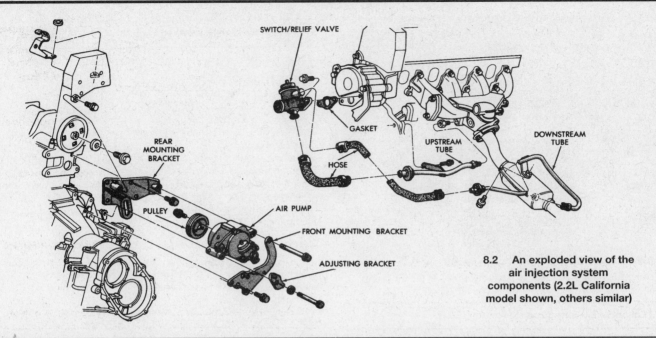

8.2   An exploded view of the air injection system components (2.2L California model shown, others similar)

8   Air Injection (AI) system

Note: *This Section applies only to models with the 2.2L engine.*

General description

Refer to illustration 8.2

1   This system supplies air under pressure to the exhaust ports to promote the combustion of unburned hydrocarbons and carbon monoxide before they are allowed to exit the exhaust.

2   The AI system consists of an air pump driven by a belt from the rear of the camshaft, a relief valve and associated hoses and check valves, which protect the system from hot exhaust gases **(see illustration)**.

Checking

General

3   Visually check the hoses, tubes and connections for cracks, loose fittings and separated parts. Use soapy water to isolate a suspected leak.

4   Check the drivebelt condition and tension.

Air pump

5   The air pump can only be checked using special equipment. Noise from the pump can be due to improper drivebelt tension, faulty relief or check valves, loose mounting bolts and leaking hoses or connections. If these conditions have been corrected and the pump still makes excessive noise, there is a good chance that it is faulty.

Relief valve

6   If air can be heard escaping from the relief valve with the engine at idle, the valve is faulty and must be replaced with a new one.

Check valve

7   Remove the hose from the inlet tube. If exhaust gas escapes past the inlet tube, the check valve is faulty and must be replaced.

Component replacement

Air pump

Refer to illustrations 8.9, 8.10 and 8.16

8   Remove the air hoses from the air pump and the relief valve.

9   Remove the air pump drivebelt pulley shield **(see illustration)**.

10   Loosen the pump pivot and adjustment bolts and remove the drivebelt **(see illustration)**.

8.9   Removing the air pump drivebelt shield mounting bolts

8.10   Loosening the air pump pivot bolt

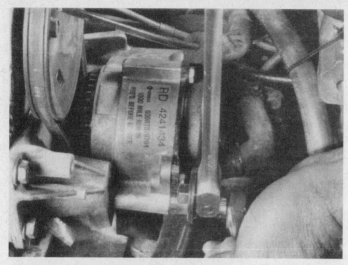

8.16   Use a breaker bar to apply leverage to the air pump bracket as the bolts are tightened

11   Remove the bolts and detach the pump from the engine.

12   Remove the relief valve from the pump and clean all gasket material from the valve mating surface.

13   Attach the relief valve to the new air pump, using a new gasket. Transfer the pulley from the old pump to the new one.

14   With the drivebelt over the air pump pulley, place the pump in position and loosely install the bolts.

15   Loosen the rear air pump bracket-to-transaxle housing bolts.

16   Place the drivebelt on the camshaft pulley, use a breaker bar to exert pressure on the bracket (not the pump housing) and adjust the belt until the tension is correct (see Chapter 1). Tighten the locking bolt, followed by the pivot bolt **(see illustration)**.

17   Tighten the air pump bracket bolt securely, install the pulley shield and reconnect the hoses to the pump and relief valve.

Relief valve

18   Disconnect the hoses from the relief valve, remove the two bolts and detach the valve from the pump. Carefully remove any gasket material from the valve and pump mating surfaces.

19   Place a new gasket in position and install the valve, tightening the bolts securely. Reconnect the hoses.

Check valve

20   Disconnect the hose from the valve inlet and remove the nut securing the tube to the exhaust manifold or converter. Loosen the starter motor bolt and remove the check valve from the engine.

21   Attach the new valve to the exhaust manifold or converter, tighten the starter motor bolt and connect the air hose.

9   Pulse Air Feeder (PAF) system

Note: *This Section applies only to models with a 2.6L engine.*

General description
Refer to illustration 9.2

1   The PAF system injects air into the exhaust system between the front and rear catalytic converters, using the engine power pulsations. This injected air increases the efficiency of the rear converter and reduces emissions.

2   The system consists of a main reed valve, sub reed valve and associated hoses. Air is drawn from the air cleaner into the main reed valve which is actuated by the pressure pulsations from within the crankcase. The air passes to the sub reed valve, which is actuated by the exhaust system pulsations, to the exhaust system and then the rear converter **(see illustration)**.

Checking

3   Disconnect the hose from the air cleaner and, with the engine running, place your hand over the end. If no vacuum is felt, check the hoses for leaks. If the hoses are alright, replace the PAF assembly with a new one.

Component replacement

4   Remove the air deflector duct from the right side of the radiator. Remove the carburetor shield, the oil dipstick and the dipstick tube. Remove the PAF mounting bolts.

5   Raise the vehicle and support it securely.

6   Disconnect the hoses and remove the PAF assembly from the vehicle.

7   Place the new pulse air feeder assembly in position and connect the hoses.

8   Lower the vehicle and install the mounting bolts. Check the dipstick O-ring to make sure it is in good condition and install the dipstick and tube. Install the carburetor shield and radiator air deflector.

10   Air aspirator system

Note: *This Section applies only to models with the 2.6L engine.*

General description

1   The aspirator system uses exhaust pulsations to draw fresh air from the air cleaner into the exhaust system. This reduces carbon monoxide (CO) and, to a lesser degree, hydrocarbon (HC) emissions.

2   The system is composed of aspirator valves and tubes, a Y connector and various hoses.

3   The aspirator valves work most efficiently at idle and slightly off idle, where the negative exhaust pulses are strongest. The valves remain closed at higher engine speeds.

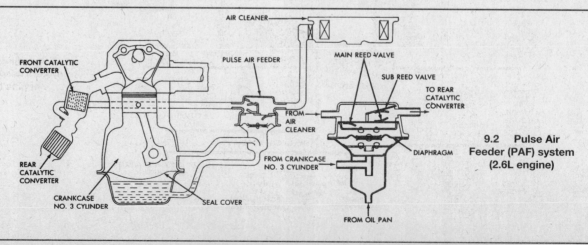

9.2   Pulse Air Feeder (PAF) system (2.6L engine)

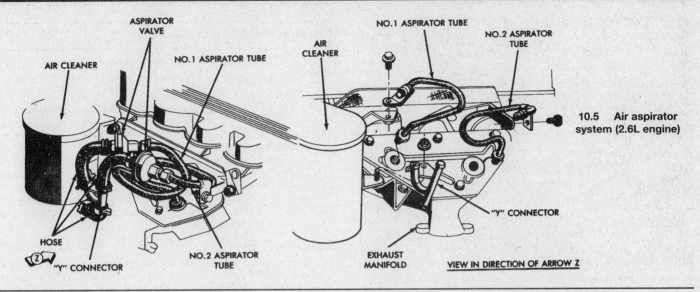

10.5   Air aspirator system (2.6L engine)

VIEW IN DIRECTION OF ARROW Z

Checking

Refer to illustration 10.5

4   Aspirator valve failure results in excessive exhaust system noise from under the hood and hardening of the rubber hose from the valve to the air cleaner.

5   If exhaust noise is excessive, check the valve-to-exhaust manifold joint and the valve and air cleaner hose connections for leaks **(see illustration)**. If the manifold joint is leaking, retighten the tube fitting securely. If the hose connections are leaking, install new hose clamps (if the hose has not hardened).

6   To determine if the valve has failed, disconnect the hose from the inlet. With the engine idling (transmission in Neutral), the exhaust pulses should be felt at the inlet. If a steady stream of exhaust gases is escaping from the inlet, the valve is defective and should be replaced with a new one.

Component replacement

7   The valves can be replaced by removing the hose clamp, detaching the hose and unscrewing the tube fitting.

8   The aspirator tubes can be replaced by unscrewing the fittings at the valve and manifold and removing the bracket bolt.

11   Single Module Engine Controller (SMEC)/Single Board Engine Controller (SBEC) and information sensors – description

Note: *This Section applies only to 1987 and later models with EFI systems.*

SMEC/SBEC

Refer to illustrations 11.2a, 11.2b, 11.2c and 11.2d

1   The electronic fuel injection (EFI) system provides the correct air-fuel ratio under all driving conditions. The 2.5L engine is equipped with a computer-controlled, "single-point" (one injector in the throttle body) electronic fuel injection (EFI) system. The 2.5L turbo, 3.0L and 3.3L engines are equipped with similar "multi-point" (injector in each intake port) EFI systems.

2   The "brain" of all EFI systems is a computer known as a Single Module Engine Controller (SMEC) (1987 through 1989 models) or a Single Board Engine Controller (SBEC) (1990 and 1991 models) **(see illustrations)**. The SMEC/SBEC is located at the front left corner of the engine compartment, between the battery and the left inner fender panel.

3   The SMEC/SBEC receives variable voltage inputs from a variety

6

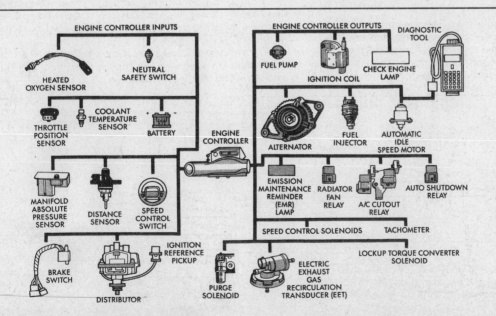

11.2a   Single-point EFI system used on the 2.5L engine (typical)

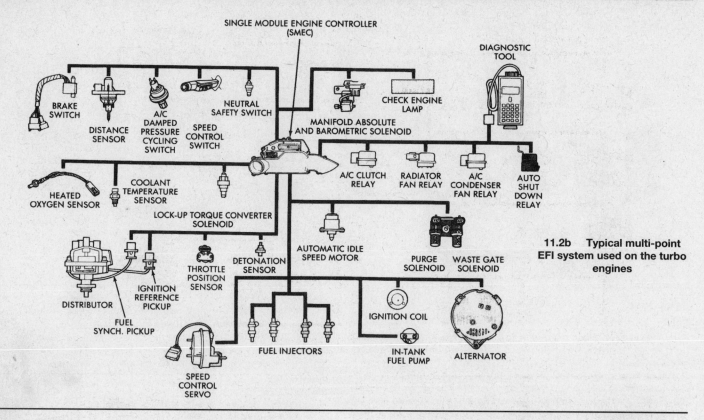

11.2b   Typical multi-point EFI system used on the turbo engines

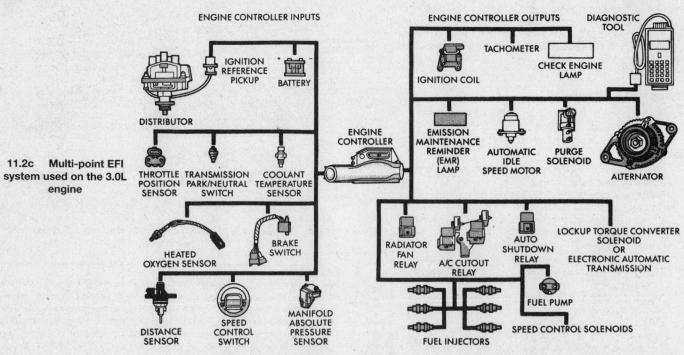

11.2c   Multi-point EFI system used on the 3.0L engine

of sensors, switches and relays. All inputs are converted into digital signals which are "read" by the SMEC/SBEC, which constantly fine-tunes such variables as ignition timing, spark advance, ignition coil dwell, fuel injector pulse width and idle speed to minimize exhaust emissions and enhance driveability. It also controls the operation of the radiator cooling fan, the alternator charging rate and such emissions-related components as the EGR solenoids and the purge solenoid for the EVAP canister. The SMEC/SBEC even updates and revises its own programming in response to changing operating conditions.

4   The SMEC/SBEC also constantly monitors many of its own input and output circuits. If a fault is found in the EFI system, the information is stored in the SMEC/SBEC memory. You really can't check or test the components of the EFI system without an expensive factory tool, the Diagnostic Readout Box DRB II (number C-4805) or its equivalent, but you can often determine where a problem is coming from, or at

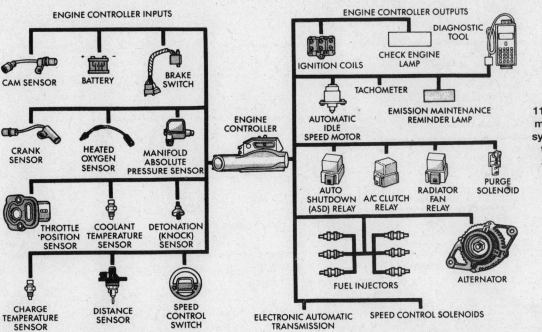

11.2d Typical multi-point EFI system used on the 3.3L and 3.8L engines

least which circuit it's in. This process always begins with reading any stored fault codes to identify the general location of a problem, followed by a thorough visual inspection of the system components to ensure that everything is properly connected and/or plugged in. The most common cause of a problem in any EFI system is a loose or corroded electrical connector or a loose vacuum line. To learn how to output this information and display it on the Check Engine light on the dash, refer to Section 12.

Information sensors

Refer to illustrations 11.6, 11.8, 11.9, 11.11, 11.12, 11.14a, 11.14b, 11.14c, 11.14d, 11.14e, 11.16 and 11.18

5   Various components provide basic information to the SMEC; they include:

   Air conditioning cut-out relay (2.5L, turbo and 3.0L engines)
   Auto shutdown relay (all engines)
   Brake switch (turbo, 3.0L, 3.3L and 3.8L engines)
   Camshaft reference sensor (3.3L and 3.8L engines)
   Charge temperature sensor (3.0L and 1991 and earlier
      3.3L engines)
   Coolant temperature sensor (all engines)
   Crankshaft reference sensor (3.3L and 3.8L engines)
   Detonation (knock) sensor (turbo and 1991 and earlier
      3.3L engines)
   Manifold Absolute Pressure (MAP) sensor (all engines)
   Neutral safety switch (all engines)
   Oxygen sensor (all engines)
   Speed control switch (all engines)
   Throttle body temperature sensor (1987 and later 2.5L engines)
   Throttle Position Sensor (TPS) (all engines)
   Transmission neutral-safety switch (turbo and 3.0L engine)
   Vehicle distance sensor (2.5L and turbo engines)
   Vehicle speed sensor (3.0L, 3.3L and 3.8L engines)

Air conditioning cut-out relay (2.5L, turbo and 3.0L engines)

Refer to illustration 11.6

6   The air conditioning cut-out relay **(see illustration)** is connected in series electrically with the air conditioner damped pressure switch,

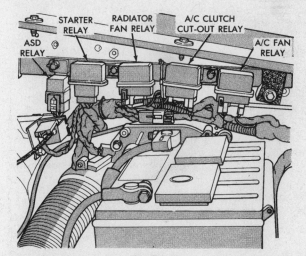

11.6   Typical array of engine compartment relays, located next to battery

the air conditioner switch and (on 2.5L engines) the radiator/condenser fan relay. The cut-out relay is energized (in its closed position) when the engine is operating. When the SMEC/SBEC senses a low idle speed, or the throttle position sensor indicates a wide open throttle condition, the cut-out relay is de-energized, its contacts open and the air conditioner clutch is prevented from engaging. The cut-out relay is located on the left inner fender panel, next to the battery and right above the SMEC/SBEC.

Auto shutdown relay (all engines)

7   If there's no ignition (distributor) signal (2.5L, turbo and 3.0L engines), or cam or crank reference sensor signal (3.3L engine), present when the ignition key is turned to the Run position, the auto shutdown relay interrupts power to the electric fuel pump, the fuel injectors, the ignition coil and (on 1988 and later models) the heated oxygen sensor. The cut-out relay is located on the left inner fender panel, next to the battery and right above the SMEC/SBEC.

11.8   The camshaft reference sensor (arrow) is located in the top of the timing chain cover on 3.3L and 3.8L engines

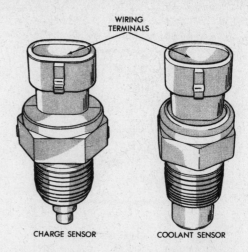

11.9   Typical charge temperature sensor (3.0L engine) and coolant temperature sensor (all engines)

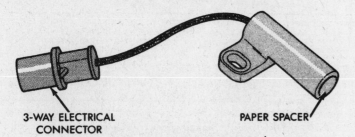

3-WAY ELECTRICAL CONNECTOR   PAPER SPACER

11.11   The crankshaft reference sensor used on 3.3L and 3.8L engines

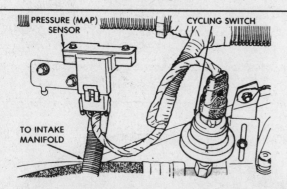

PRESSURE (MAP) SENSOR   CYCLING SWITCH

TO INTAKE MANIFOLD

11.14a   Manifold Absolute Pressure (MAP) sensor used on 1987 through 1989 2.5L engines and 1987 and 1988 3.0L engines

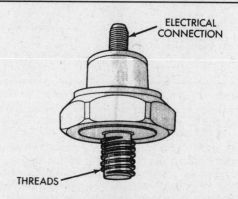

11.12   The detonation (knock) sensor used on turbo and 1991 and earlier 3.3L engines

Camshaft reference sensor (3.3L and 3.8L engines)
Refer to illustration 11.8

8   The cam reference sensor **(see illustration)** is mounted on top of the engine timing chain cover. The sensor reads camshaft position by sensing slots on the cam sprocket. The sensor then sends a coded signal to the SBEC, which uses this information to determine whether the fuel injectors and ignition coils are correctly synchronized.

Charge temperature sensor (3.0L and 1991 and earlier 3.3L engines)
Refer to illustration 11.9

9   The charge temperature sensor **(see illustration)**, which is mounted in the underside of the intake manifold, measures the temperature of the incoming air and sends this information to the SMEC/SBEC. This data is used by the SMEC/SBEC to modify the ratio of fuel to air.

Coolant temperature sensor (all engines)

10   The coolant temperature sensor (see illustration 11.9), which is threaded into the thermostat housing, monitors coolant temperature and sends this information to the SMEC/SBEC. This data, along with the information from the charge temperature sensor, is used by the SMEC/SBEC to determine the correct air/fuel mixture and idle speed while the engine is warming up. The sensor is also used to turn on the radiator fan.

Crankshaft reference sensor (3.3L and 3.8L engines)
Refer to illustration 11.11

11   The crank timing sensor **(see illustration)** is mounted on the transaxle bellhousing. This sensor sends information to the SBEC regarding engine crankshaft position. The sensor "reads" slots (sets of four per cylinder) on the torque converter driveplate.

Detonation (knock) sensor (turbo and 1991 and earlier 3.3L engines)
Refer to illustration 11.12

12   The detonation (knock) sensor **(see illustration)** generates a signal when spark knock occurs in the combustion chambers. It's mounted on the intake manifold (turbo) or block (3.3L engine) where detonation in each cylinder can be detected. The sensor provides information used by the SMEC/SBEC to modify spark advance and eliminate detonation.

Distributor pick-up (1991 2.5L and 3.0L engines)

13   On 1991 2.5L and 3.0L engines, engine speed input is supplied to

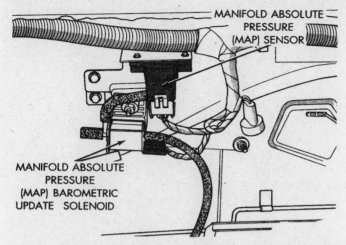

11.14b   Manifold Absolute Pressure (MAP) sensor used on the 1989 turbo engine

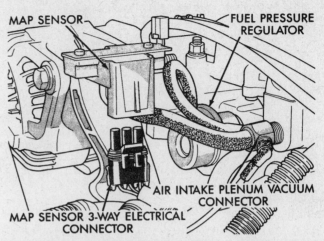

11.14c   Manifold Absolute Pressure (MAP) sensor used on 1989 and 1990 3.0L engines

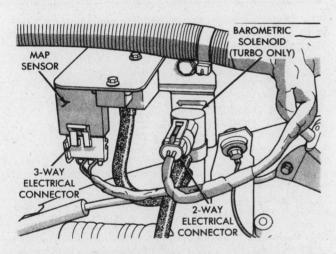

11.14d   Manifold Absolute Pressure (MAP) sensor used on 1990 2.5L and turbo engines

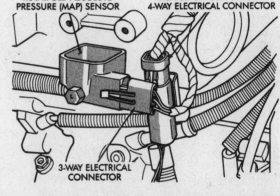

11.14e   Manifold Absolute Pressure (MAP) sensor used on 1989 and 1990 3.3L engines

the SMEC/SBEC by the distributor Hall effect pick-up (2.5L engines) or the optical system pick-up (3.0L engines). The distributor uses an internal shutter and Hall effect sensor (2.5L engines) or an internal metal disc and optical sensor (3.0L engines) to create a pulsing signal that is sent to the SMEC/SBEC. These electronic pulses are converted to engine rpm information.

Manifold Absolute Pressure (MAP) sensor (all engines)

Refer to illustrations 11.14a, 11.14b, 11.14c, 11.14d and 11.14e

14   The MAP sensor **(see illustrations)** is located on the firewall. It monitors intake manifold vacuum through a vacuum line to the throttle body. The MAP sensor transmits this data, along with data on barometric pressure, in the form of a variable voltage output to the SMEC/SBEC. When combined with data from other sensors, this information help the SMEC/SBEC determine the correct air-fuel mixture ratio.

Miscellaneous switches (all engines)

15   Various switches (such as the transmission neutral safety switch, the air conditioning switch, the speed control switch and the brake light switch) provide information to the SMEC/SBEC, which adjusts engine operation in accordance with what switch states are present at these inputs. The state of these switch inputs (high/low) is difficult to determine without the DRB II diagnostic meter.

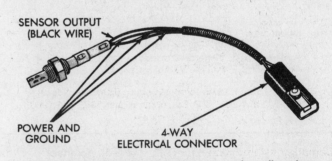

11.16   Typical heated oxygen sensor used on all engines

Oxygen sensor (all engines)

Refer to illustration 11.16

16   The oxygen sensor **(see illustration)**, which is mounted in the exhaust manifold (the rear manifold on the 3.0L and 3.3L engines), produces a voltage signal when exposed to the oxygen present in the exhaust gases. The sensor is electrically heated internally for faster switching when the engine is running. When there's a lot of oxygen present (lean mixture), the sensor produces a low voltage signal; when there's little oxygen present (rich mixture), it produces a signal of higher voltage. By monitoring the oxygen content and converting it to electrical voltage, the sensor acts as a lean-rich switch. The voltage signal to the SMEC/SBEC alters the pulse width of the injector(s).

6

Throttle body temperature sensor (2.5L engine)

17   The throttle body temperature sensor, which is mounted in the throttle body, monitors the temperature of the throttle body (fuel temperature). When transmitted to the SMEC/SBEC, this data helps determine the correct air/fuel mixture during a hot restart condition.

Throttle Position Sensor (TPS) (all engines)

Refer to illustration 11.18

18   The TPS **(see illustration)**, which is located on the throttle body, monitors the angle of the throttle plate. The voltage produced increases or decreases in accordance with the opening angle of the throttle plate. This data, when relayed to the SMEC/SBEC, along with data from several other sensors, enables the computer to adjust the air/fuel ratio in accordance with the operating conditions, such as acceleration, deceleration, idle and wide open throttle.

Vehicle distance (speed) sensor (2.5L, turbo, 3.3L and 3.8L engines)

19   The vehicle distance (speed) sensor, which is located in the transaxle extension housing, senses vehicle motion. It generates eight pulses for every revolution of the driveaxle and transmits them as voltage signals to the SMEC/SBEC. These signals are compared by the SMEC/SBEC with a closed throttle signal from the throttle position sensor so it can distinguish between a closed throttle deceleration and a normal idle (vehicle stopped) condition. Under decel conditions, the SMEC/SBEC controls the AIS motor to maintain the desired MAP value; under idle conditions, the SMEC/SBEC adjusts the AIS motor to maintain the desired engine speed.

12   Self-diagnosis system – description and code access

Note 1: *Before outputting the trouble codes, thoroughly inspect ALL electrical connectors and hoses. Make sure all electrical connections are tight, clean and free of corrosion; make sure all hoses are properly connected, fit tightly and are in good condition (no cracks or tears).*

Note 2: *On the models covered by this manual, the CHECK ENGINE light, located in the instrument panel, flashes on for three seconds as a bulb test when the engine is started. The light comes on and stays on when there's a problem in the EFI system and can also be used to diagnose problems in the EFI system.*

1   The self-diagnosis information contained in the SBEC/SMEC can be accessed either by the ignition key or by using a special tool called the Diagnostic Readout Box (DRB II). This tool is attached to the diagnostic connector in the engine compartment and reads the codes and parameters on the digital display screen. The tool is expensive and most home mechanics prefer to use the alternate method. The drawback with the ignition key method is that it does not access all the available codes for display. If you're still unable to determine the cause of a problem after extracting any stored codes, have the vehicle's self-diagnosis information analyzed by a dealer service department or other properly-equipped repair shop.

2   To obtain the codes using the ignition key method, first set the parking brake and put the transaxle in Park (automatic) or Neutral (manual). Raise the engine speed to approximately 2500 rpm and slowly let the speed down to idle. Also cycle the air conditioning system (on briefly, then off). Next, if the vehicle is equipped with an auto-

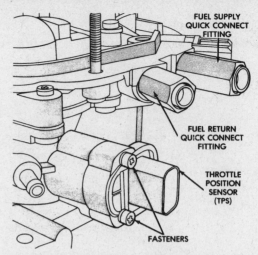

11.18   Throttle Position Sensor (TPS) on the throttle body of a 2.5L engine with single-point EFI

matic transmission, with your foot on the brake, select each position on the transmission (Reverse, Drive, Low etc) and bring the shifter back to Park. This will allow the computer to obtain any fault codes that might be linked to any of the sensors controlled by the transmission, engine speed or air conditioning system.

3   To display the codes on the dashboard (CHECK ENGINE light), turn the ignition key ON, OFF, ON, OFF and finally ON. The codes will begin to flash. The light will blink the number of the first digit then pause and blink the number of the second digit. For example: Code 23, throttle body temperature sensor circuit, would be indicated by two flashes, then a pause followed by three flashes.

4   Certain criteria must be met for a fault code to be entered into the engine controller memory. The criteria may be a specific range of engine rpm, engine temperature or input voltage to the engine controller. It is possible that a fault code for a particular monitored circuit may not be entered into the memory despite a malfunction. This may happen because one of the fault code criteria has not been met. For example, the engine must be operating between 750 and 2000 rpm in order to monitor the Map sensor circuit correctly. If the engine speed is raised above 2400 rpm, the MAP sensor output circuit shorts to ground and will not allow a fault code to be entered into the memory. Then again, the exact opposite could occur: A code is entered into the memory that suggests a malfunction within another component that is not monitored by the computer. For example, a fuel pressure problem cannot register a fault directly but will instead cause a rich/lean fuel mixture problem. Consequently, this will cause an oxygen sensor malfunction, resulting in a stored code in the computer for the oxygen sensor. In other words, the sensors and circuits are highly interrelated with each other and with the fuel injection system.

5   The following table is a list of the trouble codes, the circuit or system which is causing the code and a brief description of the nature of the problem. From the descriptions provided, you should be able to troubleshoot the faulty circuit or component. If you can't, take the vehicle to a dealer service department or other qualified repair shop.

Fault code	Circuit	Description of fault condition
Code 88	N/A	Start of test (pre-1989 models)
Code 11	No ignition reference signal	No distributor reference signal detected during engine cranking
Code 12	Number of key-ons since last fault or since faults were erased	Direct battery input to controller disconnected within last 50 to 100 ignition key-ons.
Code 13* **	Slow change in MAP idle signal or No change in MAP from Start to Run	No variation in MAP sensor signal is detected. No difference is recognized between the engine MAP reading and the stored barometric pressure reading.

Fault code	Circuit	Description of fault condition
Code 14* **	MAP voltage too low	MAP sensor input below minimum acceptable voltage.
	or	
	MAP voltage too high	MAP sensor input above maximum acceptable level.
Code 15**	No vehicle speed signal	No distance sensor signal detected during road load conditions.
Code 16* **	Battery input sense	Battery voltage sense input not detected during engine running.
Code 17	Engine runs cold too long	Engine coolant temperature remains below normal operating temperatures during vehicle travel (thermostat problem).
Code 21**	Oxygen sensor signal stays at center	Neither rich nor lean signal is detected from oxygen sensor input.
	or	
	Oxygen sensor shorted to voltage	Oxygen sensor input voltage maintained above normal range (1990 and later models).
Code 22* **	Coolant sensor voltage too low	Coolant temperature sensor input below minimum acceptable voltage.
	or	
	Coolant sensor voltage too high	Coolant temperature sensor input above maximum acceptable voltage.
Code 23	Throttle body temperature voltage low	Throttle body temperature sensor input below minimum acceptable voltage (single-point EFI systems only).
	or	
	Throttle body temperature voltage high	Throttle body temperature sensor input above maximum acceptable voltage (single-point EFI systems only).
	or	
	Charge temperature voltage low	Charge temperature sensor input below the minimum acceptable voltage (1990 3.3L engine)
	or	
	Charge temperature voltage high	Charge temperature sensor input above the maximum acceptable voltage (1990 3.3L engine)
Code 24* **	Throttle Position Sensor voltage low	Throttle position sensor input below minimum acceptable voltage.
	or	
	Throttle Position Sensor voltage high	Throttle position sensor input above maximum acceptable voltage.
Code 25**	Automatic Idle Speed motor circuits	Shorted condition detected in one or more of AIS control circuits.
Code 26* **	Injector 1 peak current (pre-1990 single-point systems).	High resistance condition detected in injector output circuit.
	or	
	INJ 1 peak current not reached	High resistance condition detected in the INJ 1 injector bank circuit (1989 turbo and all multi-point systems).
	or	
	INJ 2 peak current not reached	High resistance condition detected in the INJ 2 injector bank circuit (1989 turbo and all multi-point systems).
	or	
	INJ 3 peak current not reached	High resistance condition detected in the INJ 3 injector bank circuit (all multi-point systems, except turbos).
Code 27* **	Injector 1 control circuit	Injector output driver doesn't respond properly to the control signal (single-point systems).
	or	
	INJ 1 control circuit	Injector number one output driver doesn't respond properly to the control signal (turbo and multi-point systems).
	or	
	INJ 2 control circuit	Injector number two output driver doesn't respond properly to the control signal (turbo and multi-point systems).
	or	
	INJ 3 control circuit	Injector number three output driver doesn't respond properly to the control signal (1990 turbo and all multi-point systems).
	or	
	INJ 4 control circuit	Injector number four output driver doesn't respond properly to the control signal (1990 turbo systems).
Code 31**	Purge solenoid circuit	An open or shorted condition detected in purge solenoid circuit.
Code 32**	EGR solenoid circuit	An open or shorted condition detected in the EGR solenoid circuit (some California models).
	or	
	EGR system failure	Required change in air/fuel ratio not detected during diagnostic test (some California models).
Code 33	Air conditioning clutch relay circuit	An open or shorted condition detected in the air conditioning clutch relay circuit.
Code 34	Speed control solenoid circuits	An open or shorted condition detected in the speed control vacuum or vent solenoid circuits.
Code 35	Radiator fan relay circuit	An open or shorted condition detected in the radiator fan relay circuit.
Code 36* **	Wastegate solenoid	An open or shorted condition detected in the turbocharger wastegate control solenoid circuit (turbos only).

6

Fault code	Circuit	Description of fault condition
Code 37	Part throttle unlock solenoid circuit	An open or shorted condition detected in the torque converter part throttle unlock solenoid circuit (automatic transaxles only).
Code 41* **	Alternator field not switching properly	An open or shorted condition detected in the alternator field control circuit.
Code 42	Auto shutdown relay control circuit	An open or shorted condition detected in the auto shutdown relay circuit.
	or	
	Z1 voltage sense	No Z1 voltage sensed when auto shutdown relay is energized (turbo systems only).
	or	
	No ASD relay voltage sense at controller	No ASD relay voltage sensed when ASD relay is energized (1991 multi-point systems).
Code 43	Ignition control circuit	Output driver stage for ignition coil doesn't respond properly to the dwell control signal (1989 turbos).
	or	
	Ignition coil number one circuit	Peak primary circuit current not achieved with maximum dwell time (1990 3.3L engine).
	or	
	Ignition coil number two circuit	Peak primary circuit current not achieved with maximum dwell time (1990 3.3L engine).
	or	
	Ignition coil number three circuit	Peak primary circuit current not achieved with maximum dwell time (1990 3.3L engine).
Code 44	FJ2 voltage sense	No FJ2 voltage present at logic board during controller operation (1987 through 1989 single-point systems; 1987 and 1988 multi-point systems; turbo models).
Code 45	Boost limit exceeded	MAP reading above overboost limit detected during engine operation (turbo systems only).
Code 46* **	Charging system voltage too high	Battery voltage sense input above target charging voltage during engine operation.
Code 47* **	Charging system voltage too low	Battery voltage sense input below target charging voltage during engine operation, and no significant change in voltage detected during active test of alternator output.
Code 51**	Oxygen sensor signal stays below center	Oxygen sensor signal input indicates lean fuel/air ratio condition during engine operation.
Code 52**	Oxygen sensor signal stays above center	Oxygen sensor signal input indicates rich fuel/air ratio condition during engine operation.
	or	
	Excessive leaning	Adaptive fuel value leaned excessively due to a sustained rich condition.
Code 53	Internal controller failure	Internal engine controller fault condition detected.
Code 54* **	No sync pick-up signal	No fuel sync signal detected during engine rotation. Completion of fault code display on the Check Engine light (turbos only).
Code 55	N/A	Completion of fault code display on the Check Engine light.
Code 61*	BARO read solenoid	An open or shorted condition detected in the BARO read solenoid circuit (turbo models only).
Code 62	Controller failure (EMR miles not stored)	Unsuccessful attempt to update EMR mileage in the controller EPROM.
Code 63	Controller failure (EEPROM write denied)	Unsuccessful attempt to write to an EEPROM location by the controller.

*   These codes light up the Check Engine light on the instrument panel
**   These codes light up the Check Engine light on the instrument panel on vehicles with special California emissions controls

---

13   Information sensors – replacement

Camshaft reference sensor (3.3L and 3.8L engines)

1   Unplug the cam reference sensor lead at the electrical connector **(see illustration 11.8)**.
2   Loosen the cam reference sensor retaining bolt enough to allow the slot in the sensor bracket to slide past the bolt.
3   Remove the sensor from the timing chain cover. An O-ring seal on the sensor will make the sensor difficult to pull out of the cover, but it'll come if you persist. **Caution:** Don't pull on the sensor wire or you'll damage it.
4   If you're reinstalling the same sensor, remove the old spacer, clean off the sensor face and install a new spacer on the face. Inspect the O-ring too. Replace it if it's damaged.
5   If you installing a new sensor, make sure a new paper spacer is already installed on the face and the O-ring is properly positioned in its groove.
6   Apply a couple of drops of oil to the O-ring prior to installation. When you install the sensor, push it down until it contacts the cam timing gear. Hold it in this position while you tighten the retaining bolt to the torque listed in this Chapter's Specifications.
7   After you plug in the sensor lead, make sure the lead is routed away from the accessory drivebelt.

Charge temperature sensor (3.0L, and 1991 and earlier 3.3L engines)

Refer to illustrations 13.8a and 13.8b
8   Locate the charge temperature sensor on the right (passenger side) end of the air intake plenum **(see illustrations)**.
9   Unplug the electrical connector from the sensor.
10   Unscrew the sensor.

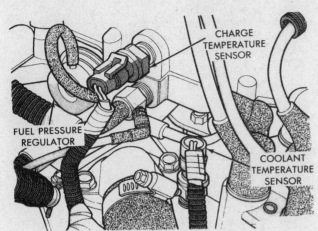

13.8a   Charge temperature and coolant temperature sensors (3.0L engine)

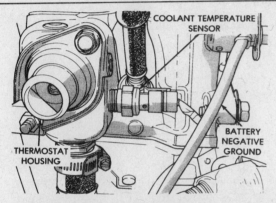

13.13a   Coolant temperature sensor (2.5L engine shown, turbo model similar)

11   Coat the threads of the new sensor (or the old one, if you're reinstalling it) with teflon tape, screw it in and tighten securely.
12   Reattach the electrical connector.

Coolant temperature sensor

Refer to illustrations 13.13a and 13.13b

Warning: *Wait until the engine is completely cool before replacing the coolant temperature sensor.*

13   The coolant temperature sensor is mounted in the thermostat

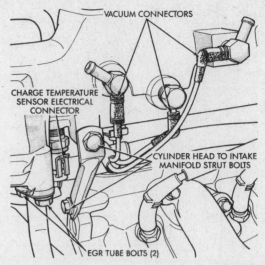

13.8b   Charge temperature sensor (arrow) (3.3L engine)

housing (**see illustrations; for 3.0L engine, see illustration 13.8a**).
14   Open the radiator cap to release any residual pressure. Squeeze the upper radiator hose and reinstall the cap (this will create a slight vacuum in the cooling system, which will minimize coolant loss).
15   Unplug the electrical connector from the coolant temperature sensor, unscrew the sensor and remove it.
16   Coat the threads of the new sensor (or the old one, if you're reinstalling it) with teflon tape, or a non-hardening thread sealant, screw it in, tighten securely and reattach the electrical lead.
17   Check the coolant level and add coolant if necessary.

Crankshaft reference sensor (3.3L and 3.8L engines)

Refer to illustration 13.18

18   Unplug the electrical connector from the crankshaft reference sensor (**see illustration**).
19   Loosen the crank reference sensor retaining bolt.
20   Remove the sensor from the transaxle housing.
21   If you're reinstalling the same sensor, remove the old spacer, clean off the sensor face and install a new spacer on the face.
22   If you installing a new sensor, make sure a new paper spacer is already installed on the face.
23   When you install the sensor, push it down until it contacts the driveplate. Hold it in this position while you tighten the retaining bolt to the torque listed in this Chapter's Specifications.
24   Plug in the sensor electrical connector.

6

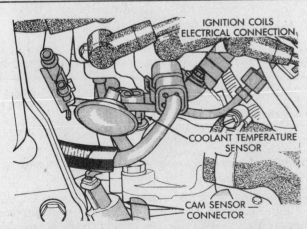

13.13b   Coolant temperature sensor (3.3L and 3.8L engines)

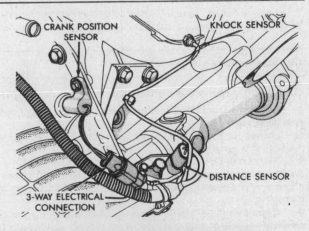

13.18   Crankshaft reference and distance sensors (3.3L and 3.8L engines)

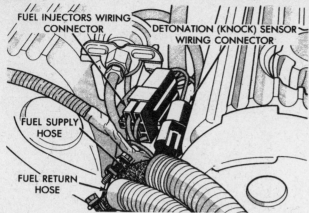

13.25a   Electrical connector for detonation (knock) sensor (turbo engine)

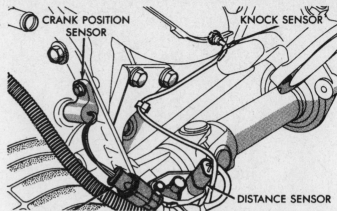

13.25b   Electrical connector for detonation (knock) sensor (3.3L engine)

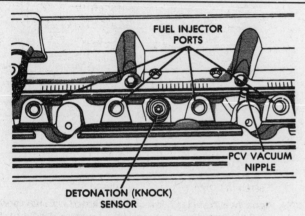

13.26a   Detonation (knock) sensor (turbo engine)

13.26b   Detonation (knock) sensor (3.3L engine)

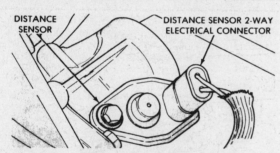

13.28   Typical distance (speed) sensor

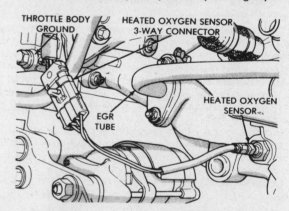

13.36a   Electrical connector for oxygen sensor (2.5L engine)

Detonation (knock) sensor (turbo and 1991 and earlier 3.3L engines)

Refer to illustrations 13.25a, 13.25b, 13.26a and 13.26b

25   Unplug the electrical connector to the detonation (knock) sensor **(see illustrations)**.
26   Unscrew the sensor **(see illustrations)**.
27   Installation is the reverse of removal.

Distance (speed) sensor

Refer to illustration 13.28

28   The distance (speed) sensor is located in the transaxle extension housing **(see illustration)**.
29   Unplug the electrical connector.
30   Remove the retaining bolt and lift the sensor from the transaxle.
31   Installation is the reverse of removal.

Manifold Absolute Pressure (MAP) sensor

32   Detach the vacuum hose from the sensor **(see illustrations 11.14a through 11.14e)**.
33   Unplug the electrical connector from the sensor.
34   Remove the sensor mounting bolts and remove the sensor.
35   Installation is the reverse of removal.

Oxygen sensor

Refer to illustrations 13.36a, 13.36b, 13.36c and 13.36d

36   Unplug the oxygen sensor electrical connector **(see illustrations)**.

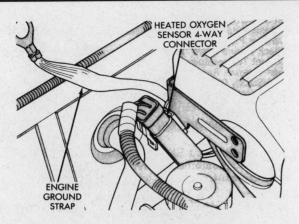

13.36b   Electrical connector for oxygen sensor (turbo engine)

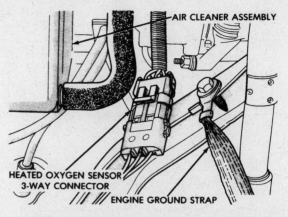

13.36c   Electrical connector for oxygen sensor (3.0L engine)

13.36d   Electrical connector for the oxygen sensor (3.3L and 3.8L engines)

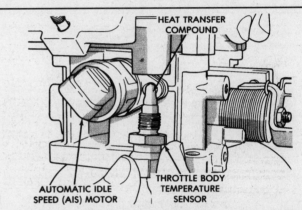

13.47   Apply heat transfer compound (included with new sensor) to the tip of the throttle body temperature sensor (1987 through 1990 2.5L engine)

37   The sensor is threaded into the exhaust manifold. To locate it, simply trace the electrical lead. On some models it may be easier to remove if you raise the front of the vehicle (support it securely on jackstands) for access to the underside of the engine compartment.

38   Unscrew the sensor. Chrysler recommends using special tool C-4907 for heated sensors (more important if, for example, you're simply removing a good sensor from a bad manifold and planning to reinstall it in another manifold).

39   Use a tap to clean the threads in the exhaust manifold.

40   If you're reinstalling the same sensor, apply a film of anti-seize compound to the threads. A new sensor should already have the anti-seize compound on the threads; if it doesn't, put some on.

41   Install the sensor, tighten it securely and plug in the electrical connector.

Throttle body temperature sensor
(1987 through 1990 2.5L engine)

Refer to illustration 13.47

42   Remove the air cleaner (see Chapter 4).

43   Disconnect the throttle cables from the throttle lever (see Chapter 4).

44   Remove the screws from the throttle cable bracket and remove the bracket.

45   Pulling downward, unplug the electrical connector from the sensor.

46   Remove the sensor.

47   Apply heat transfer compound (included with sensor) to the sensor tip **(see illustration)**.

48   Install the sensor and tighten it securely.

49   The remainder of installation is the reverse of removal.

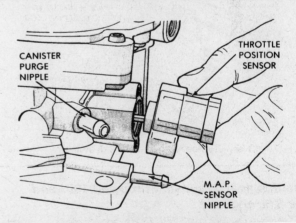

13.52a   Removing the Throttle Position Sensor (TPS) from the throttle body of a 2.5L engine

Throttle Position Sensor (TPS)

Refer to illustrations 13.52a, 13.52b and 13.52c

50   On 2.5L engines, remove the air cleaner assembly (see Chapter 4).

51   Unplug the electrical connector from the TPS (three-wire connector).

52   Remove the two screws retaining the TPS to the throttle body, pull the TPS off the throttle shaft and remove the TPS **(see illustrations)**.

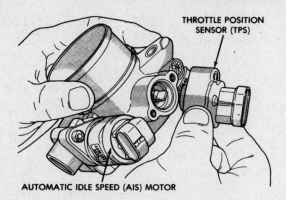

13.52b   Removing the Throttle Position Sensor (TPS) from the throttle body of a turbo or 3.0L engine

53   Installation is the reverse of removal. Make sure the flat tip of the throttle shaft seats properly into the slot in the TPS. Tighten the retaining screws securely.

14   Positive Crankcase Ventilation (PCV) system

General description

Refer to illustrations 14.1a, 14.1b, 14.1c, 14.1d, 14.1e and 14.1f

13.52c   Location of the Throttle Position Sensor (TPS) (3.3L and 3.8L engines)

1   The Positive Crankcase Ventilation (PCV) system **(see illustrations)** is designed to reduce hydrocarbon emissions (HC) by routing blow-by gases (fuel/air mixture that escapes from the combustion chamber past the piston rings into the crankcase) from the crankcase to the intake manifold and combustion chambers, where they are burned during engine operation.
2   The system is very simple and consists of rubber hoses and a small, replaceable metering valve (PCV valve).

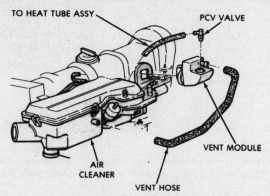

14.1a   Positive Crankcase Ventilation (PCV) system (2.2L engine)

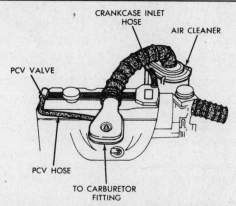

14.1b   Positive Crankcase Ventilation (PCV) system (2.6L engine)

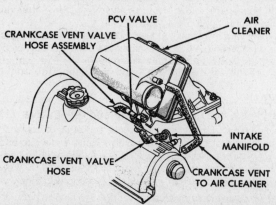

14.1c   Positive Crankcase Ventilation (PCV) system (2.5L engine)

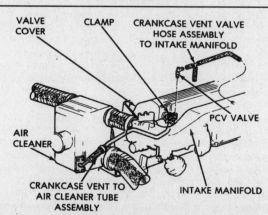

14.1d   Positive Crankcase Ventilation (PCV) system (2.5L turbo engine)

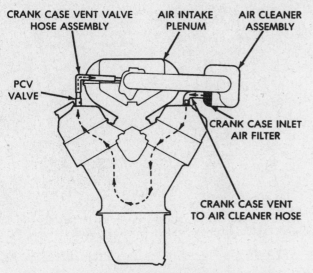

CRANK CASE VENT VALVE
HOSE ASSEMBLY   AIR INTAKE   AIR CLEANER
                    PLENUM   ASSEMBLY

PCV
VALVE

CRANK CASE INLET
AIR FILTER

CRANK CASE VENT
TO AIR CLEANER HOSE

14.1e   Positive Crankcase Ventilation (PCV) system
(3.0L engine)

14.1f   Positive Crankcase Ventilation (PCV) system
(3.3L and 3.8L engines)

Checking and component replacement

Refer to illustration 14.3

3   With the engine running at idle, pull the PCV valve out of the mount and place your finger over the valve inlet **(see illustration)**. A strong vacuum will be felt and a hissing noise will be heard if the valve is operating properly. Replace the valve with a new one, as described in Chapter 1, if it is not functioning as described. Do not attempt to clean the old valve.

---

15   Evaporative emissions control (EVAP) system

General description

1   This system is designed to trap and store fuel that evaporates from the carburetor and fuel tank and would normally enter the atmosphere in the form of hydrocarbon (HC) emissions.
2   The system used on carbureted (2.2L and 2.6L) engines consists of a charcoal-filled canister, a damping canister, a combination rollover/separator valve, a bowl vent valve and connecting lines and hoses. Later carbureted models also have a Vacuum-Controlled Orificed Tank Vapor Valve (VCOTVV). The system used on fuel-injected (2.5L, turbo, 3.0L, 3.3L and 3.8L) engines is similar.
3   When the engine is off and a high pressure begins to build up in the fuel tank (caused by fuel evaporation), the charcoal in the canister absorbs the fuel vapor. On some models, vapor from the carburetor float bowl also enters the canister. When the engine is started (cold), the charcoal continues to absorb and store fuel vapor. As the engine warms up, the stored fuel vapors are routed to the intake manifold or air cleaner and combustion chambers where they are burned during normal engine operation.
4   The canister is purged using air from the air injection pump delay or purge valve.
5   On 2.6L engines a damping canister serves as a purge control device. The fuel vapors released from the main canister pass through the damping canister and are momentarily held before passing to the intake manifold. When the engine is shut off, a bowl vent valve opens so that the carburetor is vented directly to the main canister.
6   Fuel-injected (2.5L, turbo, 3.0L, 3.3L and 3.8L) engines have a device known as a purge solenoid which prevents canister purging during engine warm-up, for a certain time period after hot starts and during certain idle conditions. Under these conditions, the SMEC/SBEC grounds the SMEC/SBEC, which energizes it, preventing

14.3   To check the PCV valve, detach it with the engine running – you should hear a hissing sound coming from the valve and you should feel a strong vacuum when you place your finger over the end of the valve

6

vacuum from reaching the canister valve. When the engine reaches a specified operating temperature and the specified time delay interval has elapsed, the solenoid is ungrounded, and de-energized. Vacuum can again flow to the canister purge valve and purge fuel vapors through the throttle body.
7   The relief valve, which is mounted in the fuel tank filler cap, is calibrated to open when the fuel tank vacuum or pressure reaches a certain level. This vents the fuel tank and relieves the high vacuum or pressure.

Checking

Canister, lines, hoses, fuel filler cap end relief valve

8   Check the canister and lines for cracks and other damage.
9   To check the filler cap and relief valve, remove the cap and detach the valve by unscrewing it. Look for a damaged or deformed gasket and make sure the relief valve is not stuck open. If the valve or gasket is not in good condition, replace the filler cap with a new one.

Canister vacuum delay valve

Refer to illustration 15.10

10   A symptom of a failed delay valve is difficulty in starting the en-

15.10   To check the canister delay valve, apply vacuum with a hand pump

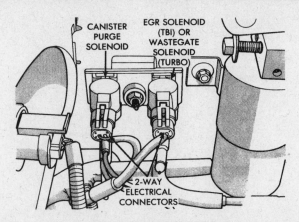

15.16a   Typical canister purge solenoid installation, on right inner fender well, right behind right headlight (turbo engine shown, 2.5L engine similar)

gine when it is hot. Disconnect the top vacuum hose **(see illustration)** and connect a vacuum pump to it. If the valve cannot hold the amount of vacuum listed in this Chapter's Specifications, replace the canister with a new one.

Canister purge solenoid

11   The canister purge solenoid is controlled by the SMEC/SBEC. A Code 31 on the Check Engine light indicates a malfunction somewhere in the circuit for this device, but determining whether the circuit or the solenoid is the problem is part of a larger diagnostic test that – unless you've got a DRB II (Miller C-4805 or equivalent) – can only be conducted by a dealer service department or other repair shop equipped with this tool.

Component replacement
Canister

12   The canister is located in the corner of the engine compartment, below the headlight.
13   Disconnect the vacuum hoses.
14   Remove the mounting bolts and lower the canister, removing it from beneath the vehicle.
15   Installation is the reverse of removal.

Canister purge solenoid

Refer to illustrations 15.16a and 15.16b
16   The canister purge solenoid is located on the right inner fender

well, right behind the headlight **(see illustrations)**. To replace it, unplug the electrical connector, remove the bracket mounting bolt and detach the solenoid from the bracket. Installation is the reverse of removal.

---

16   Heated inlet air system

General description

Refer to illustrations 16.2, 16.3, 16.4 and 16.6
1   The heated inlet air system is designed to improve driveability, reduce emissions and prevent carburetor icing in cold weather by directing hot air from around the exhaust manifold to the air cleaner intake.
2   On 2.2L engines the system is made up of two circuits **(see illustration)**. When the outside air temperature is below 10-degrees F., the carburetor intake air flows through the flexible connector, up through the air cleaner and into the carburetor. When the air temperature is above 15-degrees F., air enters the air cleaner through the outside air duct.
3   On 2.6L engines, the door in the air cleaner assembly is controlled by a vacuum motor which is actuated by a bi-metal temperature sensor **(see illustration)**. The sensor reacts to both intake manifold vacuum and the air temperature inside the air cleaner itself. When the air temperature inside the air horn is 85-degrees F. or below, the air bleed valve in the sensor remains closed and intake manifold vacu-

15.16b   Typical canister purge solenoid installation (3.3L engine)

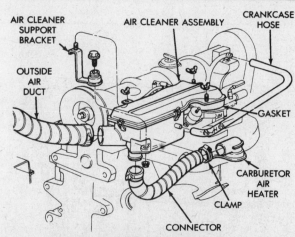

16.2   Heated inlet air system (2.2L engine)

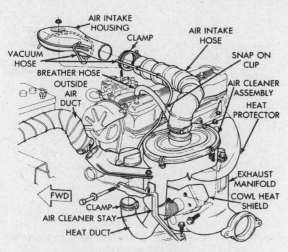

16.3   Heated inlet air system (2.6L engine)

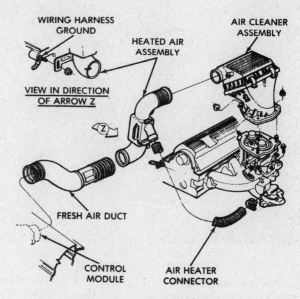

16.4   Heated inlet air system (2.5L engine)

um opens the air control door to direct heated air to the carburetor. When the air temperature inside the air cleaner is 113-degrees F. or above, the sensor air bleed valve opens the air duct door, allowing outside air directly into the carburetor. At temperatures between the two extremes, the sensor provides a blend of outside and heated air to the carburetor.

4   On 2.5L engines, the temperature of the incoming air is controlled by intake manifold vacuum, a temperature sensor and a vacuum diaphragm which operates the heat control door in the snorkel **(see illustration)**.

5   When ambient air temperature is 15 or more degrees F. above the control temperature, incoming air flows through the snorkel (the outside air inlet).

6   When the ambient air temperature is below the control temperature during start-up, air flows through both the snorkel and the stove (the inlet heated by the exhaust manifold). The colder the ambient air, the greater the flow of air through the stove; the warmer the air, the greater the flow of air through the snorkel. The amount of air flowing through each inlet is regulated by a heat control door in the snorkel to maintain a predetermined temperature at the temperature sensor mounted inside the air cleaner housing **(see illustration)**.

Checking

General

7   Refer to Chapter 1 for the general checking procedure. If the system is not operating properly, check the individual components as fol-

lows.

8   Check all vacuum hoses for cracks, kinks, proper routing and broken sections. Make sure the shrouds and ducts are in good condition as well.

2.2L engine

Refer to illustration 16.11

9   Remove the air cleaner assembly from the engine and allow it to cool to 65-degrees F. Apply 20 in Hg of vacuum to the sensor, using a hand vacuum pump.

10   The duct door should be in the up (heat on) position with the vacuum applied. If it is not, check the vacuum diaphragm.

11   To check the diaphragm, slowly apply vacuum with the hand pump while observing the door **(see illustration)**.

12   The duct door should not begin to open at less than 2 in Hg and should be fully open at 4 in Hg or less. With 20 in Hg applied, the diaphragm should not bleed down more than 10 in Hg in five minutes.

13   Replace the sensor and/or vacuum diaphragm with new units if they fail any of the tests. Test the new unit(s) as described before reinstalling the air cleaner assembly.

2.6L engine

14   With the engine cold and the air temperature less than 85 degrees F., see if the air control valve is in the up (heat on) position.

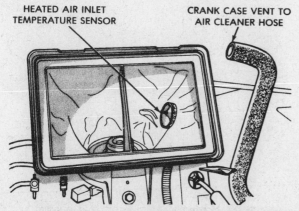

16.6   Temperature sensor for heated inlet air system (2.5L engine)

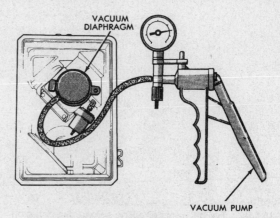

16.11   Checking the vacuum diaphragm with a vacuum pump (2.2L engine)

6

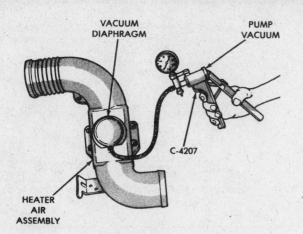

16.23   Checking the vacuum diaphragm with a vacuum pump (2.5L engine)

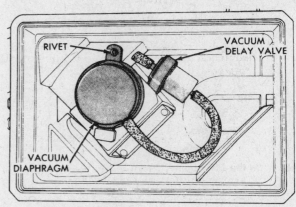

16.26   Remove the rivet to replace the vacuum diaphragm on a 2.2L engine

15   Warm up the engine to operating temperature. With the air temperature at the entrance to the snorkel at 113-degrees F., the door should be in the down (heat off) position.

16   Remove the air cleaner assembly from the engine and allow it to cool to 85-degrees F. Connect a hand vacuum pump to the sensor.

17   Apply 15 in Hg of vacuum to the sensor and see if the door is now in the up (heat on) position. If it is not, check the vacuum motor.

18   Apply 10 in Hg vacuum to the motor with the vacuum pump and see if the valve is in the up position. If it is not, replace the motor with a new one. On these vehicles the vacuum motor is an integral part of the air cleaner body and the entire assembly must be replaced.

2.5L engine

Refer to illustration 16.23

19   Make sure all vacuum hoses and the flexible connector tube between the stove and the air cleaner are properly connected and free of tears.

20   With a cold engine and ambient temperature below 115-degrees F., the heat control door in the snorkel should be in the up (heat on) position.

21   With the engine warmed up and running, check the air temperature entering the snorkel or at the sensor. When the air temperature entering the outer end of the snorkel is 140 or more degrees F., the door should be in the down or (heat off) position.

22   Remove the air cleaner from the engine and allow it to cool down to 115-degrees F. Apply 20 in Hg of vacuum to the temperature sensor – the door should be in the up (heat on) position. If the door doesn't rise to the heat on position, check the vacuum diaphragm for proper operation.

23   To test the diaphragm, apply 20 in Hg of vacuum with a vacuum pump **(see illustration)**. The diaphragm shouldn't bleed down more than 10 in Hg of vacuum in five minutes. And the door shouldn't lift off the bottom of the snorkel at less than 2 in Hg of vacuum, but it should be in the full up position with no more than 4 in Hg of vacuum.

24   If the vacuum diaphragm doesn't perform as described above, replace the heated air assembly.

25   If the vacuum diaphragm does perform satisfactorily – but the temperature being maintained is still incorrect – replace the temperature sensor and repeat Steps 20 and 21.

Component replacement

2.2L engine

Vacuum diaphragm

Refer to illustration 16.26

26   With the air cleaner removed, disconnect the vacuum hose and drill out the retaining rivet **(see illustration)**.

27   Disengage the diaphragm by tipping it forward slightly while turning it slightly counterclockwise. Once disengaged, the unit can be removed by moving it to one side, disconnecting the rod from the control door and detaching it from the air cleaner assembly.

28   Check the control door for free travel by raising it to the full up position and allowing it to fall closed. If it does not close easily, free it up. Check the hinge pin for free movement also, using compressed air or spray cleaner to remove any foreign matter.

29   To install the diaphragm, insert the rod end into the control door and position the diaphragm tangs in the slot, turning the diaphragm clockwise until it engages. Rivet the tab in place.

30   Connect the vacuum hose.

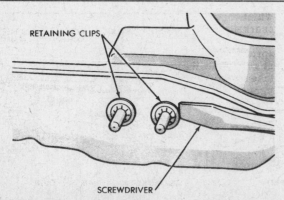

16.31   Pry off the temperature sensor retaining clips with a screwdriver

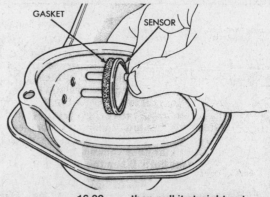

16.32   ... then pull it straight out

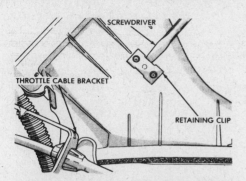

16.37   On the 2.5L engine, pry off the temperature sensor retaining clip(s) with a screwdriver

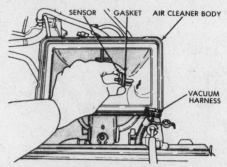

16.39   Installing the temperature sensor and gasket into the air cleaner on a 2.5L engine

Sensor

Refer to illustrations 16.31 and 16.32

31   Disconnect the vacuum hoses and use a screwdriver to pry off the retaining clips **(see illustration)**.

32   Detach the sensor from the housing **(see illustration)**.

33   Place the gasket on the new sensor, insert the sensor into the housing, hold it in place so the gasket is compressed to form a good seal and install the new retainer clips.

34   Connect the vacuum hoses.

2.5L engine

Sensor

Refer to illustrations 16.37 and 16.39

35   Remove the air cleaner housing (see Chapter 4).

36   Detach the vacuum hoses from the sensor.

37   Remove the retainer clip(s) with a screwdriver **(see illustration)**. Discard the old clip(s). New clips are supplied with the new sensor.

38   Remove the sensor and gasket. Discard the old gasket. A new one is included with the new sensor.

39   Put the new gasket on the new sensor and install them **(see illustration)**. Pressing against the outer diameter of the sensor to compress the gasket and form an airtight seal, install the retaining clip(s).

40   Reattach the vacuum hoses and install the air cleaner housing.

---

17   Exhaust Gas Recirculation (EGR) system

General description

1   The Exhaust Gas Recirculation (EGR) system reduces oxides of nitrogen (NOx) in the exhaust emissions and helps prevent spark knock by recirculating some of the exhaust gases back through the intake to dilute the air/fuel mixture, which in turn reduce the peak flame

temperature during combustion (a high combustion temperature is the primary cause of NOx). The main component in all EGR systems is the EGR valve.

Carbureted engines

2   On 2.2L engines, the EGR valve operates in conjunction with the Coolant Vacuum Switch Cold Closed (CVSCC) valve. This coolant valve and the EGR valve remain shut at low engine temperatures. At higher temperatures, the coolant valve opens, allowing vacuum to be applied to the EGR valve, and exhaust gas to recirculate. On 2.6L engines, a sub-EGR valve is operated directly by the throttle linkage, while a dual EGR valve is controlled by carburetor vacuum. The primary valve of the dual EGR valve operates during small openings of the throttle and the secondary valve takes over when the opening is larger. The vacuum which operates the dual EGR valve is supplied by a coolant temperature actuated thermo valve so that EGR function doesn't affect driveability.

Fuel-injected engines

Refer to illustrations 17.3a, 17.3b and 17.4

3   On 2.5L, 3.0L, 3.3L and 3.8L engines, a backpressure type EGR valve is ported to the throttle body. On 2.5L and 3.0L engines, a backpressure transducer measures the amount of exhaust gas backpressure on the exhaust side of the EGR valve and varies the strength of the vacuum signal applied to the EGR valve **(see illustrations)**. The transducer uses this backpressure signal to provide the correct amount of recirculated gases under any condition. All California models with this system have on-board diagnostic capabilities.

4   On 3.3L and 3.8L engines, an electric EGR transducer (EET) serves as a backpressure transducer and an electric vacuum solenoid combined into a single unit **(see illustration)**. The vacuum solenoid part of the EET receives an electrical signal from the SMEC/SBEC and, using this signal, regulates the vacuum flowing through to the transducer part of the EET. The backpressure transducer measures the

6

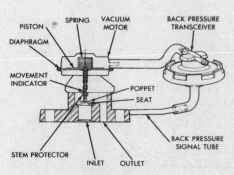

17.3a   EGR and backpressure transducer assembly (2.5L engine)

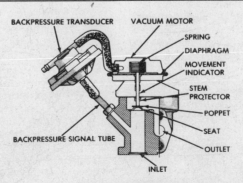

17.3b   EGR and backpressure transducer assembly (3.0L engine)

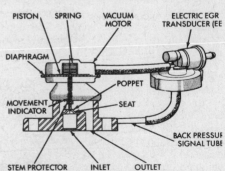

17.4   EGR and electric EGR transducer assembly (3.3L and 3.8L engines)

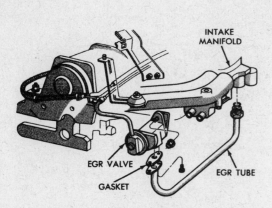

17.5   An exploded view of the EGR system components (2.2L engine)

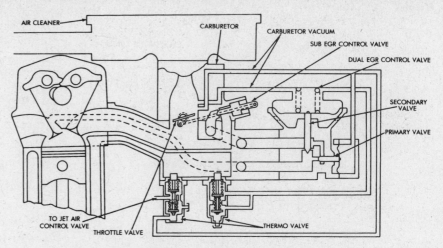

17.12   Schematic of the EGR system (2.6L engine)

amount of exhaust gas backpressure on the exhaust side of the EGR valve and varies the strength of the vacuum signal applied to the EGR valve. The transducer uses this backpressure signal to provide the correct amount of exhaust gas recirculation under all conditions. On California models, the SMEC/SBEC monitors this system for malfunctions and stores a trouble code when a fault is detected in the system.

Checking

2.2L engine

Refer to illustration 17.5

5   Check all hoses for cracks, kinks, broken sections and proper connection (see illustration). Inspect all connections for damage, cracks and leaks.

6   To check the EGR valve operation, bring the engine up to operating temperature and, with the transmission in Neutral (tires blocked to prevent movement), allow it to idle for 70 seconds. Open the throttle abruptly so that the engine speed is between 2000 and 3000 rpm and then allow it to close. The EGR valve stem should move if the control system is working properly. The test should be repeated several times. Movement of the stem indicates that the control system is functioning correctly.

7   If the EGR valve stem does not move, check all of the hose connections to make sure they are not leaking or clogged. Disconnect the vacuum hose and apply the amount of vacuum listed in this Chapter's Specifications with a hand pump. If the stem still does not move, replace the EGR valve with a new one. If the valve does open, measure the valve travel to make sure it is within the specified limit.

8   Apply vacuum with the pump and then clamp the hose shut. The valve should stay open for 30 seconds or longer. If it does not, the diaphragm is leaking and the valve should be replaced with a new one.

9   To check the coolant valve (CVSCC) located in the thermostat housing, bypass it with a length of 3/16-inch tubing. If the EGR valve did not operate under the conditions described in Step 6, but does operate properly with the CVSCC bypassed, the CVSCC is defective and should be replaced.

10   If the EGR valve does not operate with the CVSCC bypassed, the carburetor must be removed to check and clean the slot-type port in the throttle bore and the vacuum passages and orifices in the throttle body. Use solvent to remove deposits and check for flow with light air pressure.

11   Remove the EGR valve and inspect the poppet and seat area for deposits. If the deposits are more than a thin film of carbon, the valve should be cleaned. To clean the valve, apply solvent and allow it to penetrate and soften the deposits, making sure that none gets on the valve diaphragm, as it could be damaged. Use a vacuum pump to hold the valve open and carefully scrape the deposits from the seat and

poppet area with a tool. Inspect the poppet and stem for wear and replace the valve with a new one if wear is found.

2.6L engine

Refer to illustration 17.12

12   Check all hoses and connections for cracks, kinks, damage and correct installation (see illustration).

13   With the engine cold, start and run it at idle. Block the tires to prevent any movement of the vehicle during testing.

14   Increase the speed to 2500 rpm and check the secondary EGR valve to make sure that it does not operate when the engine is cold. If it does, the thermo valve is faulty and must be replaced with a new one.

15   Allow the engine to warm up and observe the secondary EGR valve to see that it opens as the temperature rises and the idle speed increases. If it does not open, the secondary EGR valve itself or the thermo valve is faulty.

16   To check the secondary EGR valve and the thermo valve, disconnect the green striped vacuum hose from the carburetor and connect a vacuum pump to the hose. Apply six inches of vacuum with the pump as you open the sub EGR valve.

17   If the engine idle becomes unstable, the secondary valve of the dual EGR is operating properly. If the idle speed is unchanged, the secondary valve or the thermo valve is faulty and must be replaced with a new one.

18   Reconnect the green striped hose and disconnect the yellow striped hose at the carburetor.

19   Connect the hand vacuum pump to the hose and, while opening the sub EGR valve, apply six inches of vacuum.

20   If the idle becomes unstable, the EGR primary valve is operating properly. If the idle is unchanged, the EGR primary valve or the thermo valve is not operating and should be replaced with a new one.

2.5L, 3.0L, 3.3L and 3.8L engines

21   Inspect all hoses between the throttle body, intake manifold and EGR control valve for leaks. Make sure all hoses are snug and in good condition. Replace any hoses that are hardened, cracked or melted, any replace any faulty connectors.

22   Warm up the engine, allow it to idle for 70 seconds with the throttle closed, then abruptly accelerate the engine to about 2000 (but not over 3000) rpm. The EGR valve stem should visible move during this procedure. You can tell if the stem moves by noting any change in the relative position of the groove in the stem (see illustrations 17.3a and 17.3b). Repeat this operation several times to verify the stem is really moving. Stem movement indicates that the control system is operating correctly. If the stem isn't moving, go to Step 24.

23   To determine whether EGR gas is flowing through the system, hook up a hand-operated vacuum pump to the EGR valve vacuum

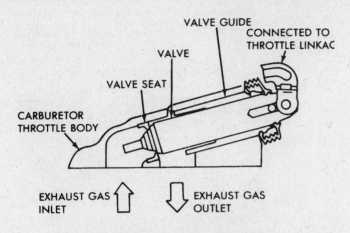

17.41   Sub-EGR valve layout (2.6L engine)

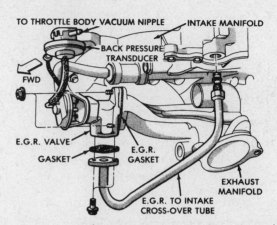

17.44a   EGR mounting details (1987 2.5L engine)

motor. With the engine running at idle speed, slowly apply vacuum. Engine speed should begin to drop when the applied vacuum reaches 2 to 3.5 in Hg. Engine speed should drop quickly, and the engine may even stall. This indicates EGR gas is flowing through the system.

24   The most likely cause of a non-operable EGR valve stem is the hoses. Verify that all hose connections are good. Make sure there are no leaks anywhere in the system and all hoses are open. Replace any defective hoses.

25   Disconnect the hose harness from the EGR vacuum transducer and hook up an auxiliary vacuum supply. Raise the engine rpm to 2000 rpm and apply 10 in Hg of vacuum while observing valve stem movement.

26   If the stem still doesn't move, replace the valve/transducer assembly.

27   If the valve stem now moves (about 1/8-inch of travel), hold the vacuum supply to check for a leaking diaphragm. The valve should remain open for 30 seconds or longer.

28   If the diaphragm is leaking, replace the valve/transducer assembly.

29   If the EGR valve stem and diaphragm are operating satisfactorily when an external vacuum source is applied (but didn't work correctly when the system was tested) the control system is probably defective, a passage is plugged or – on California models with EET and on-board diagnostics – a solenoid or the solenoid control circuit in the control system is bad. Go to the next Step.

30   Remove the throttle body (see Chapter 4) and inspect the port in the throttle bore and the associated passages in the throttle body. Remove any deposits with a suitable solvent and check for air flow through these passages with light air pressure. Install the throttle body and re-check the EGR system. Cleaning these passages usually restores normal operation of the EGR system.

31   To verify a defective solenoid or solenoid control circuit on a California model with EET and on-board diagnostics, output any stored trouble codes (see Section 12). The Check Engine light should display a Code 32. Any further diagnosis of this problem should be referred to a dealer service department.

32   What if the engine won't idle, dies when returning to idle or has a very rough or slow idle? Either the EGR valve is leaking in its closed position, or the EGR tube to the intake manifold is leaking.

33   To determine whether the EGR valve is leaking in its closed position, detach the vacuum hose from the EGR valve with the engine idling. The idle should pick up immediately and smooth out.

34   If it doesn't, turn off the engine and remove the air cleaner to expose the throttle body inlet (on turbo engines, remove the compressor-out hose at the throttle body). Disconnect the backpressure hose from the EGR valve. Using a nozzle with a rubber tip, force compressed air (about 50 to 60 psi) through the steel backpressure tube on the EGR valve while opening and closing the throttle plate. If the sound from the compressed air changes distinctly, the poppet is leaking and air is entering the intake manifold. Replace the EGR valve.

35   To determine whether the EGR tube to the intake manifold is leaking on a 2.5L, a 3.3L or a 3.8L engine, loosen the tube and retighten it to the torque listed in this Chapter's Specifications, then recheck the system for leaks.

36   To determine whether the EGR tube to the intake manifold is leaking on a 3.0L engine, remove the tube and inspect the tube seal on the gasket. The tube end should be uniformly indented on the gasket with no evidence of exhaust gas leakage. If you see any sign of leakage, replace the gaskets and tighten the flange nuts to the torque listed in this Chapter's Specifications, then recheck the system for leaks.

37   If an EGR leak persists, replace the EGR tube and gaskets.

Component replacement

2.2L engine

38   The CVSCC can be replaced by removing the vacuum hoses and unscrewing the valve.

39   To replace the EGR valve, remove the air cleaner, air injection pump and shield. Disconnect the metal tube and vacuum hose, remove the two retaining nuts and detach the valve.

2.6L engine

Refer to illustration 17.41

40   The dual EGR valve is located on the lower part of the intake manifold. It is replaced by removing the vacuum hoses and unbolting it. It may be necessary to tap the valve gently with a soft-faced hammer to break the gasket seal so it can be removed. Use a new gasket when installing the valve and check the vacuum hoses for proper routing.

41   The sub EGR valve is located on the base of the carburetor and is connected by a linkage **(see illustration)**. Pry off the spring clip and remove the pin attaching the plunger to the linkage. Hold the end of the linkage up and remove the spring and the steel ball from the end of the plunger.

42   Slip the rubber boot off and slide the plunger out of the carburetor throttle body. Before installing the plunger, lubricate it with a small amount of light oil. Install the steel ball and spring, hold the linkage in place and insert the pin. Carefully slide the spring clip into place, then check for smooth operation of the valve plunger.

43   The thermal valves are threaded into the intake manifold. Drain some coolant (see Chapter 1), then pull off the vacuum hose and unscrew the valve from the housing.

2.5L engine

Refer to illustrations 17.44a and 17.44b

44   To remove the EGR valve, disconnect the vacuum line from the EGR valve (inspect and replace it if damaged), remove the mounting bolts from the valve **(see illustrations)** and remove the valve. Discard the old gasket.

45   Clean the gasket surface and inspect it for any signs of exhaust gas leaks and cracks.

6

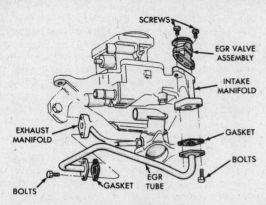

17.44b　EGR mounting details (1988 and later 2.5L engines)

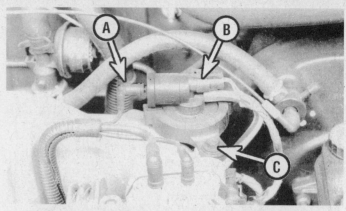

17.54　EGR valve mounting details (3.3L and 3.8L engines)
A　Vacuum line
B　Electrical connector　　　C　Mounting bolt

46　Installation is the reverse of removal. Use a new gasket and tighten the EGR valve to the torque listed in this Chapter's Specifications.
47　To remove the EGR tube, remove the four attaching bolts **(see illustration 17.44a or 17.44b)**, remove the tube and discard the gaskets.
48　Clean the gasket mounting surfaces of the the intake and exhaust manifold and the EGR tube flanges. Look for evidence of exhaust gas leaks and cracks.
49　Installation is the reverse of removal. Using new gaskets, loosely tighten all four bolts, then tighten them to the torque listed in this Chapter's Specifications.

3.0L engine

50　Remove the EGR valve mounting nuts from the exhaust manifold and the EGR flange bolts from the valve itself.
51　Remove the EGR valve tube flange nuts from the intake manifold. Remove the valve and tube assembly and discard the old gaskets.
52　Clean all gasket mating surfaces and inspect them for evidence of exhaust gas leaks and cracks.
53　Installation is the reverse of removal. Using a new gasket, loosely install the EGR tube to the EGR valve. Then install new gaskets on both the intake and exhaust manifolds, position the EGR valve and tube loosely on the engine and tighten the EGR tube flange nuts, EGR tube-to-valve screws and EGR valve-to-exhaust manifold nuts to the torque listed in this Chapter's Specifications.

3.3L and 3.8L engines

Refer to illustration 17.54
54　Disconnect the vacuum line **(see illustration)** from the Electric EGR Transducer (EET). Inspect it for damage.
55　Unplug the electrical connector from the EET **(see illustration 17.54).**
56　Remove the EGR valve bolts **(see illustration 17.54)** from the intake manifold.
57　Open the EGR transducer clip and remove the electric EGR transducer.
58　Remove the EGR valve from the intake manifold. Discard the old gasket.
59　Clean the gasket mating surfaces. Look for any signs of exhaust gas leaks and cracks.
60　Installation is the reverse of removal. Install the EGR valve with a new gasket onto the intake manifold, install the attaching bolts and tighten them to the torque listed in this Chapter's Specifications. Clip the EET in place with the orientation tab in the slot and the snap closed. Plug in the electrical connector and reattach the vacuum hose.
61　To remove the EGR tube, remove the attaching bolts from the intake and exhaust manifolds, remove the tube, discard the old gaskets, clean the gasket surfaces and inspect them for exhaust gas leaks and cracks. Using new gaskets, loosely install the EGR tube on the intake and exhaust manifolds and tighten the attaching bolts to the torque listed in this Chapter's Specifications.

18　Catalytic converter

General description

1　The catalytic converter is designed to reduce hydrocarbon (HC) and carbon monoxide (CO) pollutants in the exhaust gases. The converter oxidizes these components and converts them to water and carbon dioxide.
2　The system on these vehicles consists of a mini-oxidizer converter and a main under floor converter. The mini-oxidizer converter begins the exhaust gas oxidization, which is then completed by the main converter.
3　If large amounts of unburned gasoline enter the catalyst, it may overheat and cause a fire. Always observe the following precautions:

　Use only unleaded gasoline
　Avoid prolonged idling
　Do not run the engine with a nearly empty fuel tank
　Do not prolong engine compression checks
　Avoid coasting with the ignition turned Off
　Do not dispose of a used catalytic converter along with oily or gasoline soaked parts

Checking

4　The catalytic converter requires little if any maintenance and servicing at regular intervals. However, the system should be inspected whenever the vehicle is raised on a lift or if the exhaust system is checked or serviced.
5　Check all connections in the exhaust pipe assembly for looseness and damage. Also check all the clamps for damage, cracks and missing fasteners. Check the rubber hangers for cracks.
6　The converter itself should be checked for damage and dents (maximum 3/4-inch deep) which could affect its performance and/or be hazardous to your health. At the same time the converter is inspected, check the heat shields under it, as well as the heat insulator above it, for damage and loose fasteners.

Component replacement

7　Do not attempt to remove the catalytic converter until the complete exhaust system is cool. Raise the vehicle and support it securely on jackstands. Apply some penetrating oil to the clamp bolts and allow it to soak in. Disconnect the oxygen sensor (if equipped) from the converter.
8　Remove the bolts and the rubber hangers, then separate the converter from the exhaust pipe. Remove the old gaskets if they are stuck to the pipes.
9　Installation of the converter is the reverse of removal. Use new exhaust pipe gaskets and tighten the clamp nuts to the specified torque. Replace the oxygen sensor wires (if equipped), start the engine and check carefully for exhaust leaks.

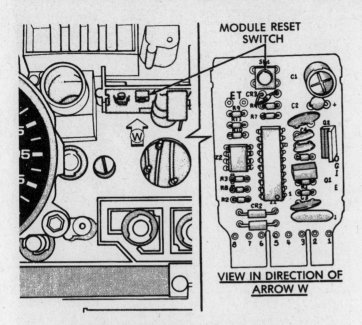

19.3   The module reset switch on the back of the instrument cluster (1987 through 1988 models)

19   Emissions Maintenance (MAINT REQD) Reminder Light

General information and reset procedures

The Emissions Maintenance Reminder light is designed to be a reminder to service the vehicle emissions control systems. It is not a warning, only a reminder to perform emissions servicing. The EMR Module will illuminate the MAINT REQD light at a predetermined time or mileage, depending on model. The light will stay on until the emission service is performed and the light is reset. The components that require servicing are the EGR system, PCV system, EVAP system and the oxygen sensor. Refer to the Maintenance Schedule and the appropriate sections of this chapter for details on checking and replacing the components if necessary. Procedures for resetting the reminder light are as follows:

1984 through 1986 models

Locate a green, red, tan or white plastic case behind the instrument panel in the lower left cluster area, back of the instrument panel or top right of the glove box. Slide the case from the bracket and open the cover. Remove the 9 volt battery and insert a small screwdriver into hole in the switch, closing the contacts. Replace the battery with a new 9 volt alkaline type battery. Close the case and slide the switch back into the bracket. Note: Don't disconnect the vehicle battery during the reset procedure. The battery must be connected to prevent power loss to the computer.

1987 and 1988 models

Refer to illustration 19.3

A reset switch is located in the Emissions Maintenance Reminder (EMR) Module. To access the EMR module, remove the instrument cluster bezel (see Chapter 11), the instrument cluster lens and the fuel gauge or tachometer. Insert a small screwdriver into the hole in the module and reset the switch (see illustration). Don't disconnect the battery before resetting the EMR Module. Replace the fuel gauge, instrument cluster lens and bezel.

1989 and later models

A special DRB-II "scan" tool is required to reset the EMR module on 1989 and later models. Take the vehicle to a dealer service department or independent mechanic that has the correct tool.

6

Notes

Chapter 7 Part A   Manual transaxle

Contents

Specifications

General

Transaxle type
1984 through 1986	
A-460	Four-speed
A-465	Five-speed
A-525	Five-speed
1987 through 1988	
A-520	Five-speed
1989	
A-520	Five-speed
A-555 (Turbo)	Five-speed
1990	
A-523	Five-speed
A-568 (Turbo)	Five-speed
1991 and later	
A-523	Five-speed
Fluid type and capacity	See Chapter 1

Torque specifications

	Ft-lbs (unless otherwise indicated)
Selector shaft lock pin	105 in-lbs
Gearshift housing-to-case bolts	21
Gearshift lever nut (1984 through 1989 only)	21
Anti-rotation link bracket-to-stud nut	17
Strut-to-block or case bolts	70
Fill plug	
A-568 (turbo	Press-in rubber plug
All others	24
Clutch housing (transaxle-to-engine) bolts	70
Mount-to-block and case bolts	70
Shift linkage adjusting screw (1987 through 1989 models)	20 in-lbs
Speedometer drive assembly bolt	60 in-lbs
End cover bolts	21
Selector/crossover cable adjusting screw	
1984 through 1987	55 in-lbs
1988 on	70 in-lbs

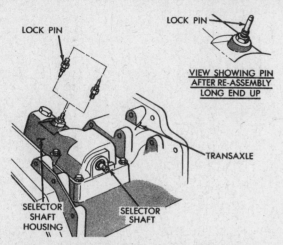

2.2 Remove the selector shaft lock pin, flip it over, then reinstall it in the same hole - move the selector shaft until the lock pin drops into the hole in the selector shaft, then tighten the lock pin

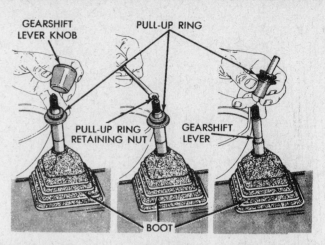

2.3a Gearshift knob and pull–up ring removal (1984 through 1989 models)

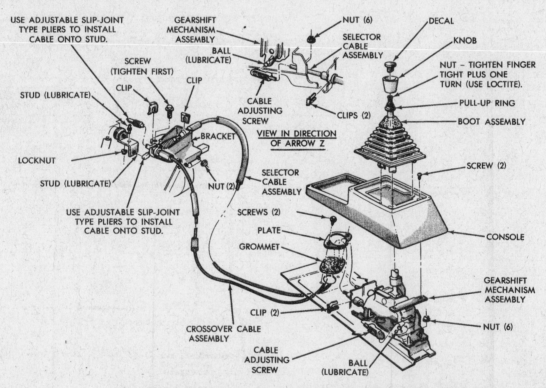

2.3b   Shift linkage components - exploded view (1984 through 1989 models)

1   General information

The vehicles covered by this manual are equipped with a four- or five-speed manual transaxle, a three-speed automatic transaxle or a four-speed Ultradrive electronic automatic transaxle. The information on manual transaxles is in this Part of Chapter 7. Service procedures for the automatic transaxles are contained in Chapter 7, Part B.

Each manual transaxle is a compact, two-piece, lightweight aluminum alloy housing containing both the transmission and the differential assemblies.

Because of the complexity, unavailablity of replacement parts and specal tools required, internal repair of the manual transaxle by the home mechanic is not recommended. The bulk of information in this Chapter is devoted to removal and installation procedures.

2   Gearshift linkage – adjustment

Refer to illustrations 2.2, 2.3a, 2.3b, 2.4a, 2.4b, 2.6, 2.7, 2.8, 2.13, 2.14, 2.15, 2.19, 2.20 and 2.23

1   Raise the hood and place a pad or a fender cover on the fender to protect it.

2   Remove the lock pin from the transaxle selector shaft housing **(see illustration)**. Reverse the lock pin so the longer end is down and

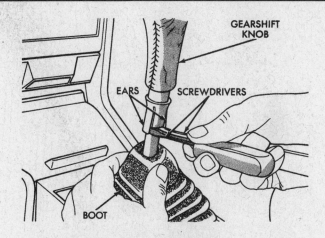

2.4a Gearshift knob removal (1990 and 1991 models)

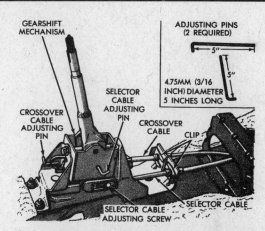

2.6 Fabricate the cable adjusting pins and install them as shown here (1984 through 1986 models)

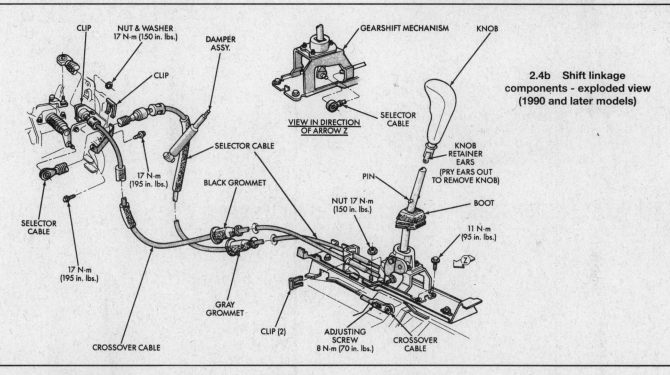

2.4b Shift linkage components - exploded view (1990 and later models)

reinstall it into its hole while moving the selector shaft in. When the lock pin aligns with the hole in the selector shaft, thread it into place so the shaft is locked in the first/second (1984 through 1986) or third/fourth (1987 and later) neutral position.

3   On 1984 through 1989 models, pull off the gearshift knob, remove the pull-up ring retaining nut and lift off the pull-up ring (see illustrations). Remove the shifter boot and console (see Chapter 11).

4   On 1990 and later models, pry the tabs out with two screwdrivers, one on each side, then lift the shifter knob off (see illustrations). Remove the shifter boot and console (see Chapter 11).

1984 through 1986 models

5   Fabricate two five-inch long adjusting pins from 5/32-inch wire. Bend one end of each wire at a right angle so the pins are easy to grasp.

6   Insert one adjusting pin into the crossover cable hole of the shaft mechanism and the other into the selector cable hole (see illustration).

7   Loosen the selector cable adjusting screw, then use an in-lb torque wrench to tighten it to the torque listed in this Chapter's Specifications (see illustration).

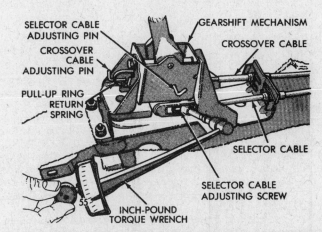

2.7 Adjusting the selector cable with a torque wrench (1984 through 1986 models)

7A

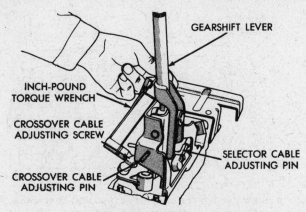

2.8   Adjusting the crossover cable with a torque wrench (1984 through 1986 models)

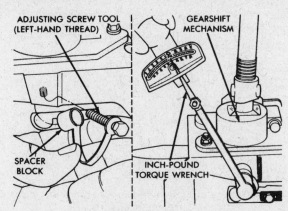

2.13   Install the adjusting screw and spacer block as shown (1987 through 1989 models)

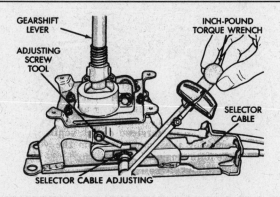

2.14   Tightening the selector cable adjusting screw (1987 through 1989 models)

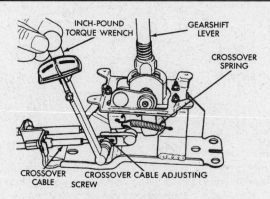

2.15   Tightening the crossover cable adjusting screw (1987 through 1989 models)

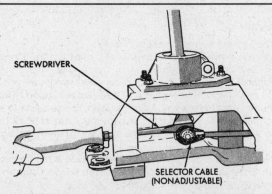

2.19   Use a screwdriver to pry the end of each cable off its ballstud - the crossover cable is located on the other side of the shifter assembly (1990 and later models)

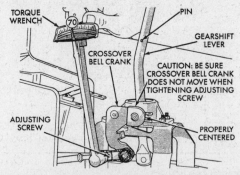

2.20   Be sure the crossover bellcrank is properly centered, then tighten the adjusting screw (1990 and later models)

8   Loosen the crossover cable adjusting screw, then use an in-lb torque wrench to tighten it to the torque listed in this Chapter's Specifications **(see illustration)**.

9   Remove the adjusting pins from the shift mechanism.

10   Install the console, shift boot, pull-up ring and nut and shift knob.

11   Unscrew the lock pin from the selector housing, reinstall it with the longer end up and tighten it to the torque listed in this Chapter's Specifications.

12   Check the shifter operation in First and Reverse and make sure the Reverse lock out mechanism works properly.

1987 through 1989 models

13   Remove the adjusting screw tool from the shifter and install it as shown **(see illustration)**. Tighten the adjusting screw to to torque listed in this Chapter's Specifications.

14   Loosen the selector cable adjusting screw, then tighten it to the torque listed in this Chapter's Specifications **(see illustration)**.

15   Loosen the crossover cable adjusting screw, then tighten in to the torque listed in this Chapter's Specifications **(see illustration)**.

16   Remove the adjusting screw tool and re-install it in its original location on the shifter.

17   Unscrew the lock pin from the selector housing, reinstall it with the longer end up and tighten it to the torque listed in this Chapter's Specifications.

18   Check the gearshift cables for proper connection at the transaxle. Check the shifter operation in First and Reverse and make sure the Reverse lock out mechanism works properly. Install the console, shift boot and shift knob.

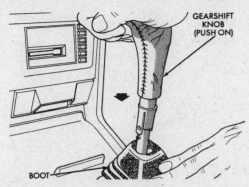

2.23   On 1990 and later models, install the shift knob by pushing straight down

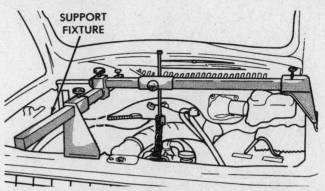

3.3   A support fixture that supports the engine from above, like the one shown here, is preferred

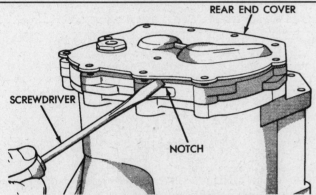

3.6   After removing the screws, carefully pry off the rear end cover with a screwdriver inserted in the notch

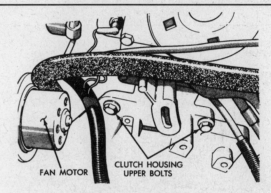

3.8   Upper clutch housing bolt locations

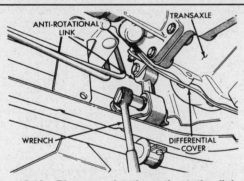

3.10   Disconnecting the anti–rotation link

1990 and later models

19   Use a screwdriver to pry the selector cable and crossover cable off the shifter mechanism **(see illustration)**.

20   Install the crossover cable by pressing it onto the ballstud. Loosen the crossover cable adjusting screw, properly center the crossover bellcrank, then tighten the adjusting screw to the torque listed in this Chapter's Specifications **(see illustration)**. Be sure the crossover bellcrank does not move when tightening the adjusting screw.

21   Install the selector cable by pressing it into place on the ballstud.

22   Check both shift cables to be sure they are connected properly at the transaxle.

23   Reinstall the shifter console, boot, and the gearshift knob **(see illustration)**.

24   Unscrew the lock pin from the selector housing, reinstall it with the longer end up and tighten it to the torque listed in this Chapter's Specifications.

25   Check the shifter operation in First and Reverse and make sure the Reverse lock out mechanism functions properly.

3   Manual transaxle – removal and installation

Refer to illustrations. 3.3, 3.6, 3.8, 3.10, 3.12 and 3.20

Removal

1   Disconnect the negative battery cable.

2   Remove the hood (see Chapter 11), raise the front end of the vechicle and support it securely.

3   Attach a "lifting eye" to the number four cylinder exhaust manifold bolt and support the engine with the special support fixture **(see illustration)**. An alternative is, if care is taken, to use a jack to support the engine from below, under the oil pan. Use a wood block between the pan and jack head to spread the load and prevent damaging the pan.

4   Disconnect the gearshift linkage and bracket at the transaxle (see Section 2). Also disconnect the clutch cable (see Chapter 8) and speedometer drive gear (see Section 5).

5   Remove the wheels and the left splash shield. Disconnect any exhaust components that would interfere with transaxle removal (see Chapter 4).

6   Place a large drain pan (at least three quarts capacity) under the transaxle and drain the fluid by removing the rear end cover **(see illustration)**.

7   Place a jack under the transaxle to support it. Preferably, this should be a specially designed transaxle jack with safety chains.

8   Remove the clutch housing (transaxle-to-engine) bolts **(see illustration)**.

9   Remove the left engine mount.

10   Unbolt the anti-rotation link **(see illustration)**.

11   Remove the driveaxles as described in Chapter 8.

12   Carefully pull the transaxle away from the engine and lower it to the floor **(see illustration)**.

13   With the transaxle removed, the clutch components are now accessible and can be inspected. In most cases, new clutch components should be routinely installed when the transaxle is removed (see Chapter 8).

7A

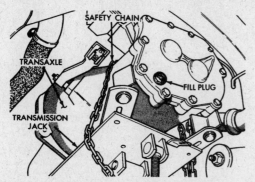

3.12   Support the transaxle with a jack when removing it (note the safety chain)

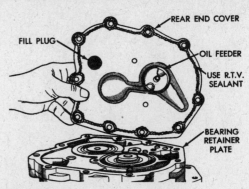

3.20   Apply RTV sealant as shown (be sure to go around the bolt holes) when installing the rear end cover

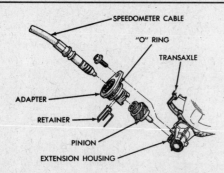

5.2   Speedometer drive assembly - exploded view

Installation

Note: *Before installing the transaxle, fabricate two locating pins. Cut the heads off two proper-size bolts with a hacksaw and remove any burrs from the ends with a file or a grinder. Then use the hacksaw to cut slots in the ends of the locating pins so they can be unscrewed with a screwdriver and replaced with bolts.*

14   If removed, install the clutch components (see Chapter 8).

15   Install the two locating pins in place of the top two clutch housing bolts.

16   With the transaxle secured to the jack with a chain, raise it into position behind the engine, then carefully slide it forward, engaging the input shaft with the clutch plate hub splines. Do not use excessive force to install the transaxle – if the input shaft does not slide into place, reajust the angle of the transaxle so it is level and/or turn the input shaft so the splines engage properly with the clutch plate hub.

17   Install the clutch housing bolts. Tighten the bolts securely (don't forget to remove the locating pins and replace them with bolts).

18   Install the anti-rotation link and tighten the nut to the torque listed in this Chapter's Specifications.

19   Install the left engine mount and tighten it securely.

20   If the transaxle rear cover has not been installed prior to this point, clean the cover and mating surfaces thoroughly. Apply a 1/8-inch bead of RTV sealant to the cover **(see illustration)** and install the cover and bolts.

21   Fill the transaxle to the bottom of the fill plug hole with the specified lubricant (see Chapter 1).

22   Install the various items removed previously, refering to Chapter 8 for the driveaxles and Chapter 4 for information regarding the exhaust system.

23   Remove the jack(s) (and fixture, if used) supporting the engine and transaxle.

24   Make a final check that all wires, hoses, gearshift linkages (see Section 2), and the speedometer cable (see Section 5) have been connected.

25   Lower the front of the vehicle.

26   Connect the negative battery cable. Road test the vechicle for proper operation and check for leaks.

4   Manual transaxle overhaul – general information

Overhauling a manual transaxle is a difficult job for the do-it-yourselfer. It involves the disassembly and reassembly of many small parts. Numerous clearances must be precisely measured and, if necessary, changed with select-fit spacers and snap-rings. As a result, if transaxle problems arise, it can be removed and installed by a competent do-it-yourselfer, but overhaul be left to a transmission repair shop. Rebuilt transaxles may be available – check with your dealer parts department and suto parts stores. At any rate, the time and money involved in an overhaul is almost sure to exceed the cost of a rebuilt unit.

Nevertheless, it's not impossible for an inexperienced mechanic to rebuild a transaxle if the special tools are available and the job is done in a deliberate step-by-step manner and nothing is overlooked.

The tools necessary for an overhaul include internal and external snap-ring pliers, a bearing puller, a slide hammer, a set of pin punches, a dial indicator and possibly a hydraulic press. In addition, a large, sturdy workbench and a vise or transaxle stand will be required.

During disassembly of the transaxle, make careful notes of how each piece comes off, where it fits in relation to other pieces and what holds it in place.

Before taking the transaxle apart for repair, it will help if you have some idea what area of the transaxle is malfunctioning. Certain problems can be closely tied to specific areas in the transaxle, which can make component examination and replacment easier. Refer to the Troubleshooting Section at the front of this manual for information regarding possible sources of trouble.

5   Speedometer drive pinion – removal and installation

Refer to illustration 5.2

Removal

1   The speedometer drive pinion assembly is located in the differential extension housing.

2   Remove the retaining bolt and carefully work the assembly up and out of the extension housing **(see illustration)**.

3   Remove the retainer and separate the pinion from the adapter.

4   Check the speedometer cable to make sure that transaxle fluid has not leaked into it. If there is fluid in the cable, remove the adapter and replace the O-ring with a new one. Reconnect the cable to the adapter.

5   Install a new O-ring to the outside of the retainer. Connect the adapter to the pinion gear, making sure the retainer is securely seated.

Installation

6   Make sure the mating surfaces of the adapter and the extension housing are clean, as any debris could cause misalignment of the pinion.

7   Attach the assembly to the transaxle, install the retaining bolt and tighten it securely.

Chapter 7 Part B   Automatic transaxle

Contents

7B

Specifications

Fluid type and capacity .... See Chapter 1

Band adjustment .... See Chapter 1

Torque specifications   **Ft-lbs** (unless otherwise indicated)

Driveplate-to-torque converter bolts

1984 and 1985	40
1986 on.	55
Neutral start switch	25
Throttle cable-to-transaxle bolt	105 in-lbs

A-604 Ultradrive

Output speed sensor	20
PRNDL switch	25

1   General information

All vehicles covered in this manual come equipped with a four or five-speed manual transaxle, a three-speed automatic, or a four-speed Ultradrive electronic automatic transaxle. All information on the automatic transaxles is included in this Part of Chapter 7. Information on the manual transaxle can be found in Part A of this Chapter.

The transaxle combines into a compact front-wheel-drive system a torque converter, attached to the crankshaft through a driveplate, an automatic transmission, and a differential.

The A-604 or 41TE Ultradrive electronic four-speed transaxle is conventional in that it uses hydraulic clutches to shift a planetary geartrain. What is unique to the A-604 or 41TE Ultradrive is the use of fully-adaptive controls. These adaptive controls are based on real-time feedback sensor information similar to electronic antilock braking system.

Due to the complexity of the automatic transaxles and the need for special equipment and expertise to perform most service operations, this Chapter contains only general diagnosis, seal replacement, adjustments and removal and installation procedures.

If the transaxle requires major work, it should be left to a dealer service department or an automatic transmission repair shop.

2   Diagnosis – general

Note: Automatic transaxle malfunctions may be caused by five general conditions: Poor engine performance, improper adjustments, hydraulic-mechanical, or electronic malfunctions. Diagnosis of these problems should always begin with a check of the easily repaired items: fluid level and condition (see Chapter 1), shift linkage adjustment and throttle cable adjustment (see Sections 5 and 6). Next, perform a road test to determine if the problem has been corrected or if more diagnosis is necessary. If the problem persists after the preliminary tests and corrections are completed, additional diagnosis should be done by a dealer service department or transmission repair shop. Refer to the Troubleshooting Section at the front of this manual for transaxle problem diagnosis.

Preliminary checks

1   Drive the vehicle to warm the transaxle to normal operating temperature.

2   Check the fluid level as described in Chapter 1:
   a) If the fluid level is unusually low, add enough to bring the level within the designated area on the dipstick, then check for external leaks.
   b) If the fluid level is abnormally high, drain off the excess, then check the drained fluid for contamination by coolant. The presence of engine coolant in the automatic transmission fluid indicates that a failure has occurred in the internal radiator walls that separate the coolant from the transmission fluid (see Chapter 3).
   c) If the fluid is foaming, drain it and refill the transaxle, then check for coolant in the fluid or a high fluid level.

3   Check the engine idle speed. **Note:** *If the engine is malfunctioning, don't proceed with the preliminary checks until it has been repaired and runs normally.*

4   Check the throttle valve cable for freedom of movement. Adjust it if necessary (see Section 6). **Note:** *The throttle valve cable may function properly when the engine is off and cold, but may malfunction once the engine is hot. Check it cold and at normal engine operating temperature.*

5   Inspect the shift linkage (see Section 5). Make sure it's properly adjusted and operates smoothly.

Fluid leak diagnosis

6   Most fluid leaks are easy to locate visually. Repair usually consist of replacing a seal or gasket. If a leak is difficult to find, the following procedure may help.

7   Identify the fluid. Make sure it's transmission fluid and not engine oil or brake fluid (automatic transmission fluid is a deep red color).

8   Try to pinpoint the source of the leak. Drive the vehicle several miles, then park it over a large sheet of cardboard. After a minute or two you should be able to locate the leak by determining the source of the fluid dripping onto the cardboard.

9   Make a careful visual inspection of the suspected component and the areas immediately around it. Pay particular attention to gasket mating surfaces. A mirror is often helpful for finding leaks in areas that are hard to see.

10   If the leak still can't be found, clean the suspected area thoroughly with a degreaser or solvent, then dry it.

11   Drive the vehicle for several miles at normal operating temperature and varying speeds. After driving the vehicle, visually inspect the suspected component again.

12   Once the leak has been located, the cause must be determined before it can be properly repaired. If a gasket is replaced but the sealing flange is bent, the new gasket won't stop the leak. The bent flange must be straightened.

13   Before attempting to repair a leak, check to make sure the following conditions are corrected or they may cause another leak. **Note:** *Some of the following conditions can't be fixed without highly specialized tools and expertise. Such problems must be referred to a transmission shop or a dealer service department.*

Gasket leaks

14   Check the pan periodically. Make sure the bolts are all in place (and none are missing) and tight, the gasket is good condition and the pan is flat (dents in the pan may indicate damage to the valve body inside).

15   If the pan gasket is leaking, the fluid level or the fluid pressure may be too high, the vent may be plugged, the pan bolts may be too tight, the pan sealing flange may be warped, the sealing surface of the transaxle housing may be damaged, the gasket may be damaged or the transaxle casting may be cracked or porous. If sealant is used in place of a gasket, it may be the wrong sealant.

Seal leaks

16   If a transaxle seal is leaking, the fluid level or pressure may be too high, the vent may be plugged (these models are vented through the hollow dipstick), the seal bore may be damaged, the seal itself may be damaged or improperly installed, the surface of the shaft protruding through the seal may be damaged or a loose bearing may be causing excessive shaft movement. Check for a leak at the oil pump seal by removing the torque converter inspection plate and looking for trails of fluid or a puddle of fluid in the torque converter housing.

17   Make sure the dipstick tube seal is in good condition and the tube is properly seated. Periodically check the area around the speedometer gear or sensor for leakage. If transmission fluid is evident, check the O-ring for damage. Also inspect the side gear shaft oil seals for leakage.

Case leaks

18   If the case itself appears to be leaking, the casting is porous and will have to be repaired or replaced.

19   Make sure the oil cooler hose fittings are tight and in good condition.

Fluid comes out of the filler opening

20   If this condition occurs, the transaxle is overfilled, there is coolant in the fluid, the case is porous, the dipstick is incorrect, the vent is plugged or the drain back holes are plugged.

3   Oil seal – replacement

Refer to illustrations 3.3, 3.4, 3.8 and 3.9

1   **Note:** *If your vehicle has been sitting for any length of time (six months or longer), the transaxle oil pump seal may leak. First add transmission oil sealer. Old or dry transaxle seals shrink and cause*

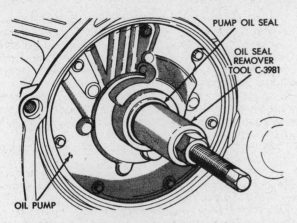

3.3   Transaxle oil pump seal removal using tool C-3981

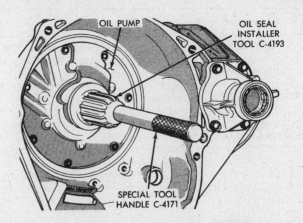

3.4   Transaxle oil pump seal installation using tools
C-4171 and C-4193

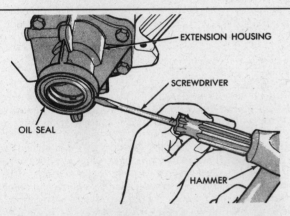

3.8   Extension housing seal removal using a screwdriver

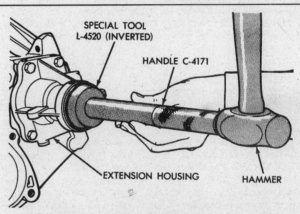

3.9   Extension housing seal installation using tools
L-4520 and C-4171

leaks. Adding an oil sealer will swell the seal and sometimes stop it from leaking. If this does not restore the old seal and stop the leaking at the seals, the leaking seal(s) will have to be replaced.

Oil pump seal

Note: The transaxle oil pump (front) seal can be replaced without removing the oil pump.

2   To replace the transaxle oil pump seal, the transaxle and torque converter will have to be removed. Refer to Section 8 for transaxle removal.

3   If available, use the factory seal removal tool (number C-3981). Screw the seal remover into the seal, then tighten the screw to draw the seal out **(see illustration)**. If the factory tool is not available, use a hook-type seal removal tool (available from automotive tool suppliers). If a hook-type tool is not available, try using a screwdriver or other prying tool to pry the seal up, moving around the seal. Be careful not to scratch the input shaft or the seal bore.

4   If available, use the factory tools (numbers C-4193 [the installer] and C-4171 [the handle]) to install the new seal. Place the seal in the opening (lip side facing in), then drive the seal in until it bottoms in the seal bore **(see illustration)**. If the factory tools are not available, use a small block of wood and a hammer to carefully tap the seal into place, tapping all the way around the seal until it bottoms in the seal bore.

Extension housing (right side driveaxle) seal

Note: Replacing the left side driveaxle oil seal requires removing the differential bearing retainer (a special tool is needed) and pressing the new seal into the retainer with an arbor press. This procedure is beyond the scope of the home mechanic.

5   The extension housing seal is located in the extension housing,

which is bolted to the right side of the transaxle.

6   Raise the vehicle and support it securely on jackstands.

7   Remove the right driveaxle (see Chapter 8).

8   Using a srewdriver or other prying tool, pry the seal out of the extension housing **(see illustration)**.

9   Coat the lip and outside diameter of the new seal with transmission fluid. Place the new seal over the opening (lip side facing in). Use a socket the same size as the outside diameter of the seal or a wood block and carefully tap the socket or wood with a hammer, driving the seal into place. If available, you should use the factory tool (numbers L-4520 and C-4171 handle). With these tools drive the new seal into the extension housing **(see illustration)**.

---

4   Transaxle mount – check and replacement

This procedure is covered with the *Engine mounts – check and replacement* procedures in Chapter 2.

---

5   Shift cable – check and adjustment

Check

1   Check the operation of the transaxle in each shift lever position (try to start the engine in each position – the starter should operate in the Park and Neutral positions only). If operation is not as described, try adjusting the shift cable, as described below. If operation still is not correct, check the neutral start switch (see Section 7).

7B

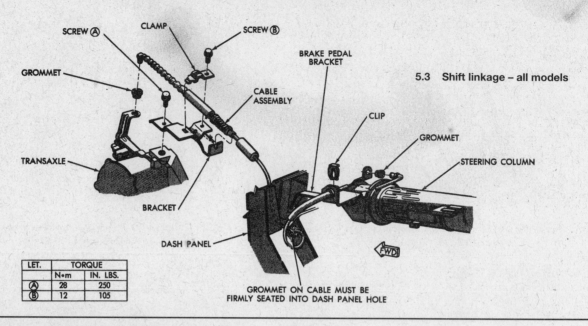

5.3   Shift linkage – all models

LET.	TORQUE	
	N•m	IN. LBS.
Ⓐ	28	250
Ⓑ	12	105

GROMMET ON CABLE MUST BE FIRMLY SEATED INTO DASH PANEL HOLE

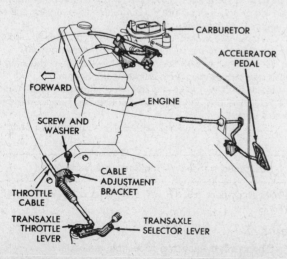

5.5   Tightening the shift cable bolt – note one hand keeping pressure on the shift lever (arrow) as the bolt is tightened

Adjustment

Refer to illustrations 5.3 and 5.5

2   Place the shift lever in park.

3   Working in the engine compartment, loosen the shift cable clamp bolt on the transaxle bracket **(see illustration)**.

4   Pull the shift lever all the way to the detent (Park position) by hand.

5   Keeping pressure on the shift lever, tighten the cable clamp bolt **(see illustration)**.

6   Check the shift lever and try to start the engine in all the shift stops. The engine should start only when the lever is in the Park or Neutral position.

6   Throttle cable – check and adjustment (except A-604 and 41TE Ultradrive)

Note: *The A-604 and 41TE Ultradrive transmission does not have a transmission throttle cable.*

Refer to illustrations 6.4 and 6.7.

Check

1   The throttle pressure cable adjustment is important to the proper operation of the transaxle. If the adjustment is long, the transaxle will

6.4   Throttle cable layout – 1984 and 1985 models

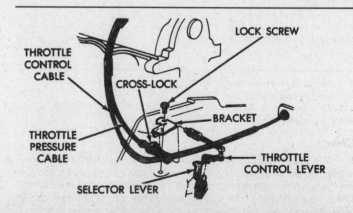

6.7   Throttle cable layout – 1986 and later models

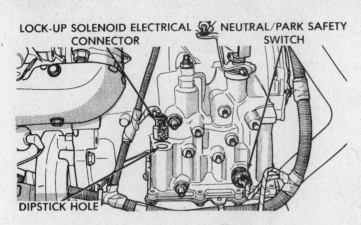

7.1a   Neutral start (safety) switch location – three-speed automatic transaxle

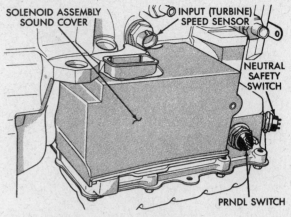

7.1b   Neutral start (safety) switch location – four-speed automatic transaxle (A-604 Ultradrive)

shift early. If the adjustment is too short, the transaxle will shift late.

2   The throttle cable controls a valve in the transaxle which governs the shift quality and speed. If shifting is harsh or erratic, the throttle cable should be adjusted.

Adjustment

1984 and 1985 models

3   The adjustment must be made with the engine at normal operating temperature.

4   Loosen the adjustment bracket lock screw **(see illustration)**

5   To ensure proper adjustment, the bracket must be free to slide back-and-forth. If necessary, remove it and clean the slot and sliding surfaces as well as the screw.

6   Slide the bracket to the left (toward the engine) to the limit of its travel. Release the bracket and move the throttle lever all the way to the right, against the internal stop, then tighten the adjustment bracket lock screw to 105 in-lb.

1986 and later models

7   Loosen the cable mounting bracket lock screw and position the bracket so the alignment tabs are in contact with the transaxle casting. Tighten the lock screw to 105 in-lb **(see illustration)**

8   Release the cross-lock on the cable assembly by pulling up on it. To ensure proper adjustment, the cable must be free to slide all the way toward the engine, against the stop, after the cross-lock is released.

9   Move the transaxle throttle control lever clockwise as far as possible (against the internal stop) and press the cross-lock down into the locked position.

10   Do not lubricate any of the linkage components on later models.

All models

11   Check the cable action (connect the choke if disconnected). Move the transaxle throttle cable all the way forward, release it slowly and make sure that it returns completely.

---

7   Neutral start and back-up light switch – check and replacement

Refer to illustrations 7.1a, 7.1b and 7.7

Check

1   The neutral start switch and back-up switch is located at the lower front edge of the transaxle **(see illustrations)** . The switch controls the back-up light and the starting of the engine in Park and Neutral. The center terminal of the switch grounds the starter solenoid circuit when the transaxle is in Park or Neutral, allowing the engine to start.

2   Prior to checking the switch, make sure the gearshift linkage is

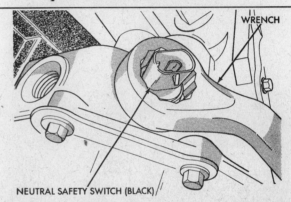

7.7   Neutral start (safety) switch removal (A-604 Ultradrive)

properly adjusted (see Section 5).

3   Unplug the connector and use an ohmmeter to check for continuity between the center terminal and the case. Continuity should exist only when the transaxle is in Park or Neutral.

4   Check for continuity between the two outer terminals. Continuity should exist only when the transaxle is in Reverse. No continuity should exist between either outer terminal and the case.

5   If the switch fails any of the tests, replace it with a new one.

Replacement

6   Position a drain pan under the switch to catch the fluid released when the switch is removed. If not already done, unplug the electrical connector from the switch.

7   Unscrew the switch from the transaxle, using a box-end wrench to avoid damage to the switch housing **(see illustration)**

8   Move the shift lever from Park to Neutral while checking that the switch operating fingers are centered in the opening.

9   Install the new switch, tighten it to the torque listed in this Chapter's Specifications and plug in the connector. Repeat the checks on the new switch.

10   Check the fluid level and add fluid as required (see Chapter 1).

---

8   Automatic transaxle – removal and installation

Refer to illustrations 8.5, 8.6, 8.7, 8.10, 8.12, 8.16a, 8.16b, 8.17, 8.20 and 8.24

Removal

1   Disconnect the negative cable from the battery.

2   On 2.2L and 2.5L engines, remove the air injection pump (see

7B

8.5   The weight of the engine must be supported with the special fixture or a jack as the transaxle is removed

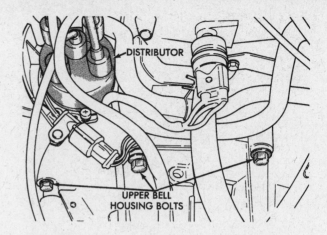

8.6   Locations of the upper bellhousing bolts

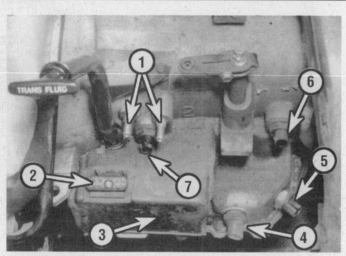

8.7   Transaxle left side – A-604 and 41TE Ultradrive

1 Transaxle cooler lines	*5 Neutral start switch*
2 Eight-pin connector	*6 Output speed sensor*
3 Solenoid assembly cover	*7 Input turbine speed sensor*
4 PRNDL switch	

Chapter 6).

3   Remove the air cleaner and the air injection pump support bracket.

4   Disconnect the transaxle shift and throttle position cables and fasten them out of the way.

5   Support the engine from above with the special fixture **(see illustration)**, or from below with a jack (place a block of wood between the jack and the engine oil pan to prevent damage).

6   Remove the upper bellhousing bolts **(see illustration)**.

7   Remove the speedometer drive gear (see Chapter 7a, Section 5) and unplug all electrical connectors **(see illustration)**.

8   Raise the vehicle and support it securely on jackstands.

9   Drain the transaxle fluid (see Chapter 1).

10   Remove the under-vehicle and left splash shields **(see illustration)**.

11   Remove the torque converter cover.

12   Mark the torque converter and driveplate so they can be reinstalled in the same position **(see illustration)**.

13   Remove the torque converter-to-driveplate bolts. Turn the crankshaft with a large wrench on the crankshaft pulley bolt to gain access to each of the driveplate bolts.

14   Remove the starter motor (see Chapter 5).

15   Remove the driveaxles (see Chapter 8).

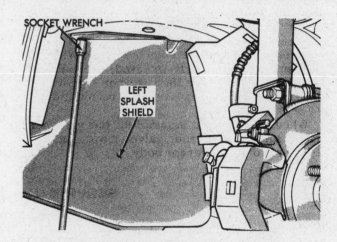

8.10   Left side splash shield removal

16   Disconnect the fluid cooler hoses at the transaxle and plug them **(see illustrations)**.

17   Loosen the sway bar bushing bolts, then unbolt the ends from the lower control arms and pull the sway bar down out of the way **(see illustration)**.

18   On models so equipped, disconnect the vacuum hose(s).

19   Remove any exhaust components that will interfere with the transaxle removal (see Chapter 4).

20   Support the transaxle with a jack – preferably a special jack made for this purpose. Safety chains will help steady the transaxle on the jack **(see illustration)**.

21   Remove any other chassis or suspension components that will interfere with the transaxle removal.

22   Remove the front and left engine mounts and the engine mount bracket on the front crossmember (see Chapter 2).

23   Remove the remaining bolts securing the transaxle to the engine.

24   Move the transaxle back to disengage it from the engine block dowel pins. You may have to use a prybar or a large screwdriver to pry the transaxle from the engine **(see illustration)**. **Note:** *Secure the torque converter to the transaxle with wire from two bolt holes 180-degrees apart so it won't fall out during removal.*

25   Lower the transaxle from the vehicle.

Installation

26   Prior to installation, make sure the torque converter hub is securely engaged in the pump.

27   With the transaxle secured to the jack and the torque converter

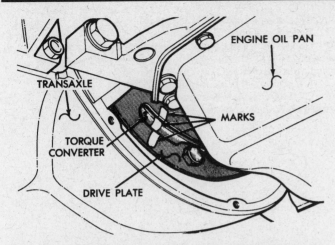

8.12 Be sure to mark the torque converter and driveplate so they can be reattached in the same position

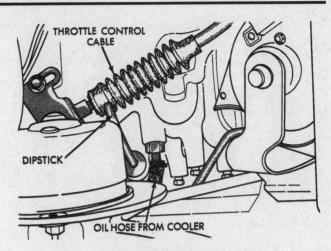

8.16a Location of one of the cooler hoses (three-speed automatic)

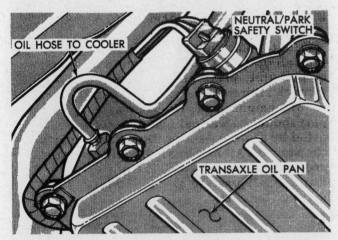

8.16b Locations of a cooler hose and the neutral start switch (A-604 Ultradrive)

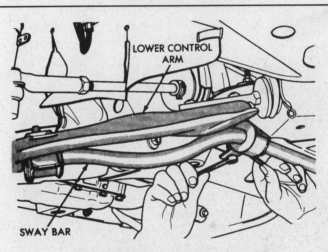

8.17 Removing the sway bar mount bolts

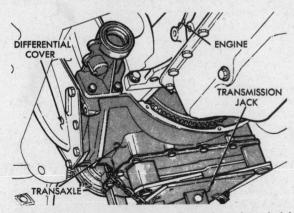

8.20 Transaxle jack positioning (note the safety chain)

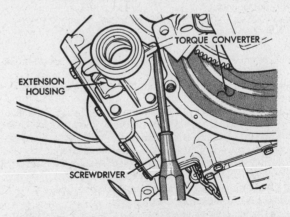

8.24 Use a large screwdriver to pry the transaxle away from the engine

secured to the transaxle, raise it into position.

28 Turn the torque converter to line up with the holes in the driveplate. Line up the marks you made on the torque converter and driveplate.

29 Move the transaxle forward carefully until the dowel pins and transaxle housing are engaged.

30 Install the transaxle housing-to-engine bolts. Tighten them securely.

31 Install the torque converter-to-driveplate bolts. Tighten the bolts to the torque listed in this Chapter's Specifications.

32 Install the engine mounts and bracket.

33 Install the suspension and chassis components that were re-

7B

moved. Tighten the bolts and nuts to the torque listed in this Chapter's Specifications.

34   Remove the jack supporting the transaxle.
35   Install the starter motor (see Chapter 5).
36   Connect the vacuum hose(s) (if equipped).
37   Connect the shift and throttle valve linkages.
38   Attach all the electrical connectors.
39   Install the torque converter cover and splash shields.
40   Install the driveaxles (see Chapter 8).
41   Connect the speedometer cable.
42   Connect any exhaust components that were removed or disconnected.
43   Lower the vehicle.
44   Adjust the shift cable (see Section 5).
45   Fill the transaxle with transmission fluid (see Chapter 1), run the vehicle and check for leaks.

Chapter 8   Clutch and driveaxles

Contents

Specifications

Clutch disc lining thickness (minimum) 1/32-inch

Driveaxle dimensions

	Inch	mm
1984		
G.K.N.		
Right	21.3 to 21.6	542 to 549
Left	10.6 to 11.2	270 to 285
A.C.I		
Right	20.5 to 20.9	520 to 532
Left	10.0 to 10.6	255 to 270
1985		
G.K.N.		
Right	21.3 to 21.6	542 to 449
Left	10.6 to 11.9	270 to 285
A.C.I.		
Right	20.5 to 20.9	520 to 532
Left	10.0 to 10.6	255 to 270
1986		
G.K.N.		
Right	21.3 to 21.6	542 to 549
Left	10.6 to 11.2	270 to 285
Citroen		
Right	20.5 to 20.9	520 to 532
Left	10.0 to 10.6	255 to 270
1987		
2.2L and 2.6L		
G.K.N.		
Right	21.3 to 21.6	542 to 549
Left	9.4 to 10.0	238 to 253
Citroen		
Right	20.5 to 20.9	520 to 532
Left	8.8 to 9.4	223 to 238
2.5L and 3.0L	Not available	
1988 (G.K.N.)		
Right	20.9 to 21.2	530 to 538
Left	9.6 to 9.9	243 to 251
1989		
2.5L non-turbo and 3.0L (G.K.N.)		
Right	20.9 to 21.2	530 to 538
Left	9.6 to 9.9	243 to 251
2.5L turbo (G.K.N.) (right and left)	9.6 to 9.9	243 to 251
1990		
3.0L, 2.5L non-turbo and 2.5L turbo with automatic transaxle (G.K.N.)		
Right	20.9 to 21.2	530 to 538
Left	9.6 to 9.9	243 to 251
3.3L and 2.5L turbo with manual transaxle (G.K.N.)		
Right	9.6 to 9.9	243 to 251
Left	9.6 to 9.9	243 to 251
1991		
Right	20.5 to 20.9	520 to 530
Left	9.0 to 9.4	228 to 238

Driveaxle dimensions (continued)

	Inch	mm
1992		
3.0L and 3.3L		
Right	18.7 to 19.1	476 to 486
Left	7.2 to 7.6	184 to 194
2.5L with manual transaxle		
Right	18.7 to 19.1	476 to 486
Left	8.4 to 8.8	213 to 223
2.5L with automatic transaxle		
Right	18.9 to 19.3	480 to 490
Left...	7.3 to 7.7	185 to 195
1993		
3.0L and 3.3L		
Right	18.7 to 19.1	476 to 486
Left	7.2 to 7.6	184 to 194
2.5L with manual transaxle		
Right	18.7 to 19.1	476 to 486
Left	8.2 to 8.6	209 to 220
2.5L with automatic transaxle		
Right	18.7 to 19.1	476 to 486
Left...	7.3 to 7.7	185 to 195
1994 and later		
3.0L, 3.3L and 3.8L		
Right	18.7 to 19.1	476 to 486
Left	7.2 to 7.6	184 to 194
2.5L with manual transaxle		
Right	18.7 to 19.1	476 to 486
Left...	7.2 to 7.6	184 to 194
2.5L with automatic transaxle		
Right	18.7 to 19.1	476 to 486
Left...	7.3 to 7.7	185 to 195

Torque specifications

	Ft-lbs
Clutch pressure plate-to-flywheel bolts	21
Intermediate shaft bearing-to-bracket screws	21
Intermediate shaft bracket-to-engine block screws	40
Driveaxle nut..	180

1   General information

The information in this Chapter deals with the components from the rear of the engine to the front (drive) wheels (except for the transaxle, which is covered in the previous Chapter). In this Chapter, the components are grouped into two categories: Clutch and driveaxles. Separate Sections within this Chapter offer general information, checks and repair procedures for components in each of the two groups.

Warning: *Since nearly all the procedures included in this Chapter involve working under the vehicle, make sure it's securely supported on sturdy jackstands or on a hoist where it can be easily raised and lowered.*

2   Clutch – description and check

1   All vehicles with a manual transaxle have a single dry plate, diaphragm spring-type clutch. The clutch disc has a splined hub which allows it to slide along the splines of the transaxle input shaft or mainshaft. The clutch disc is held in place against the flywheel by the pressure plate springs. During disengagement (when shifting gears for example), the clutch pedal is depressed, which operates a cable, actuating the release lever so the release bearing or plate pushes on the pressure plate springs, disengaging the clutch.

2   The release mechanism incorporates a self-adjusting device which compensates for clutch disc wear **(see illustration 3.2)**. A spring in the clutch pedal arm maintains tension on the cable and the adjuster pivot grabs the positioner adjuster when the pedal is depressed and the clutch is released. Consequently, the slack is always taken up in the cable, making adjustment unnecessary.

3   When pressure is applied to the pedal to release the clutch, the cable pulls against the end of the release lever, which turns a shaft connected to the clutch release fork. As the fork pivots, the release bearing pushes against the fingers of the diaphragm springs in the pressure plate assembly, which in turn disengages the clutch plate.

4   Terminology can be a problem when discussing the clutch components because common names are in some cases different from those used by the manufacturer. For example, the clutch disc is also called the clutch plate or driven plate, the clutch release bearing is sometimes called a throwout bearing and the release fork is sometimes called the release lever.

5   Other than to replace components with obvious damage, some preliminary checks should be performed to diagnose clutch problems.

a)   The first check should be of the clutch cable adjustment (if applicable). If there's too much slack in the cable, the clutch won't release completely, making gear engagement difficult or impossible.

b)   To check clutch "spin-down time," run the engine at normal idle speed with the transaxle in Neutral (clutch pedal up – engaged). Disengage the clutch (pedal down), wait several seconds and shift the transaxle into Reverse. No grinding noise should be heard. A grinding noise would most likely indicate a problem in the pressure plate or the clutch disc.

c)   To check for complete clutch release, run the engine (with the parking brake applied to prevent vehicle movement) and hold the clutch pedal approximately 1/2-inch from the floor. Shift the transaxle between First and Reverse gear several times. If the shift is rough, component failure is indicated, or as stated above, the cable is out of adjustment.

d)   Visually inspect the pivot bushing at the top of the clutch pedal

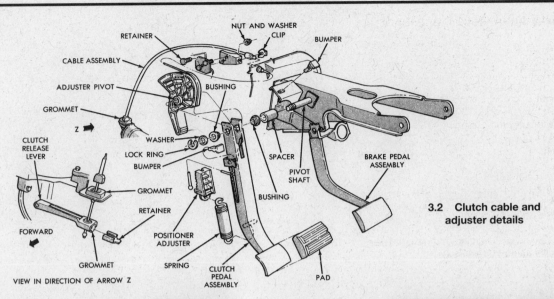

VIEW IN DIRECTION OF ARROW Z

3.2 Clutch cable and adjuster details

4.2 Before you remove the release bearing, note how it's retained by the spring clip, then slide it off the input shaft

4.4a To remove the release shaft and fork, pry off this E-clip, . . .

to make sure there's no binding or excessive play.

e) A clutch pedal that's difficult to operate is most likely caused by a faulty clutch cable. Check the cable where it enters the housing for frayed wires, rust and other signs of corrosion. If it looks good, lubricate the cable with penetrating oil. If pedal operation improves, the cable is worn out and should be replaced.

3 Clutch cable – removal and installation

Refer to illustration 3.2

1 Raise the front of the vehicle and support it securely on jackstands. Apply the parking brake and block the rear wheels so the vehicle can't roll off the stands.

2 Remove the clip and disengage the cable housing from the retainer bracket **(see illustration)**.

3 Remove the clutch cable retainer and disengage the cable end from the clutch release lever on the transmission **(see illustration 3.2)**.

4 Pull the lower end of the cable out of the grommet in the transmission mount.

5 Working inside the vehicle, disengage the cable end from the clutch pedal.

6 Pull the cable through the firewall to remove it.

7 When installing the new cable, hook the ends to the pedal and transmission lever first, then pull on the housing and engage the cable in the retainer bracket. Don't forget to install the clip.

8 Operate the pedal several times to allow the self-adjuster mechanism to take up slack in the cable.

4 Clutch release bearing and release fork – removal and installation

Refer to illustrations 4.2, 4.4a, 4.4b and 4.4c

Warning: *Dust produced by clutch wear and deposited on clutch components may contain asbestos, which is a health hazard. DO NOT blow it out with compressed air or inhale any of it. DO NOT use gasoline or petroleum–based solvents to clean off the dust. Brake system cleaner should be used to flush the dust into a drain pan. After the clutch components are wiped clean with rags, dispose of the contaminated rags and cleaner in a sealed, marked container.*

1 Remove the transaxle (see Chapter 7, Part A).

2 Disengage the ends of the spring clip and detach the release bearing from the fork **(see illustration)**.

3 Hold the center of the bearing and turn the outer portion while applying pressure. If it doesn't turn smoothly or if it's noisy, install a new one. It's a good idea to replace it anyway, when you consider the time and effort spent on removing the transaxle. However, if you elect to reinstall the old bearing, wipe it off with a clean rag. Don't immerse the bearing in solvent – it's sealed for life and would be ruined by the solvent.

4 Check the release fork ends for excessive wear. If the fork must be replaced, remove the E-clip from the clutch release shaft, slide the

8

4.4b . . . slide the shaft out far enough to pull off the bushing, . . .

4.4c . . . slide off the fork and remove the shaft

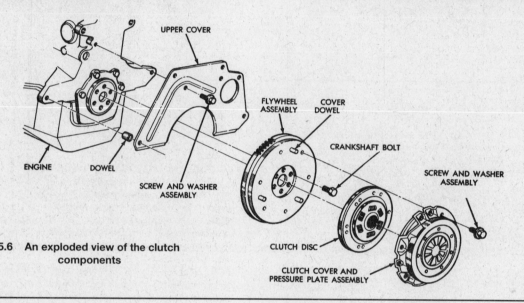

5.6 An exploded view of the clutch components

UPPER COVER

ENGINE

DOWEL

SCREW AND WASHER ASSEMBLY

FLYWHEEL ASSEMBLY

COVER DOWEL

CRANKSHAFT BOLT

SCREW AND WASHER ASSEMBLY

CLUTCH DISC

CLUTCH COVER AND PRESSURE PLATE ASSEMBLY

shaft out of the clutch housing and remove the fork **(see illustrations)**.
5   If the shaft bushings are worn, replace them.
6   Lubricate the release shaft bushings with high-temperature grease, slide the shaft part way into the housing and hold the fork in position. Continue to slide the shaft into place, through the fork, until it seats in the inner bushing.
7   Install the E-clip in the shaft groove. Make sure it's seated correctly.
8   Lubricate the release fork ends with a small amount of high-temperature grease (don't overdo it). Lubricate the release bearing bore with the same grease.
9   Install the release bearing on the fork. Make sure the wire retainer is properly engaged.
10   Install the transaxle.

---

5   Clutch components – removal, inspection and installation

Warning: Dust produced by clutch wear and deposited on clutch components may contain asbestos, which is a health hazard. DO NOT blow it out with compressed air or inhale any of it. DO NOT use gasoline or petroleum-based solvents to clean off the dust. Brake system cleaner should be used to flush the dust into a drain pan. After the clutch components are wiped clean with rags, dispose of the contaminated rags and cleaner in a sealed, marked container.

Removal
Refer to illustration 5.6
1   Access to the clutch components is normally accomplished by removing the transaxle, leaving the engine in the vehicle. Of course, if the engine is being removed for major overhaul, then check the clutch for wear and replace worn components as necessary. However, the relatively low cost of the clutch components, compared to the time and trouble spent gaining access to them, warrants their replacement anytime the engine or transaxle is removed (unless they're new or in near perfect condition). The following procedures are based on the assumption the engine will stay in place.
2   Referring to Chapter 7, Part A, remove the transaxle from the vehicle. Support the engine while the transaxle is out. Preferably, an engine hoist should be used to support it from above. However, if a jack is used underneath the engine, make sure a piece of wood is positioned between the jack and oil pan to spread the load. **Caution:** *The pick-up for the oil pump is very close to the bottom of the oil pan. If the pan is bent or distorted in any way, engine oil starvation could occur.*
3   The clutch release fork and release bearing can remain attached to the transaxle housing (see Section 4 for the procedures to follow when checking and replacing the release bearing and related components).
4   To support the clutch disc during removal, install a clutch alignment tool through the clutch disc hub.
5   Carefully inspect the flywheel and pressure plate for indexing marks. The marks are usually an X, an O or a white letter. If they can't

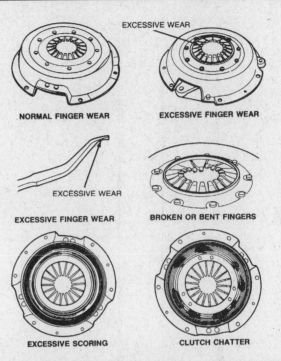

5.9   The clutch disc

1   **Lining** – *will wear down in use*
2   **Rivets** – *secure the lining and will damage the
        pressure plate or flywheel surface if allowed to contact it*
3   **Marks** – *"flywheel side" or something similar*

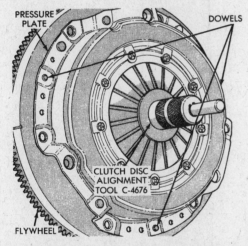

**5.13   Use an alignment tool to center the clutch disc, then
tighten the pressure plate bolts**

**5.11   Replace the pressure plate if excessive wear or
damage is noted**

be found, scribe marks yourself so the pressure plate and flywheel will be in the same alignment during installation.

6   Loosen the pressure plate-to-flywheel bolts a little at a time, following a criss-cross pattern, until all spring pressure is relieved. Hold the pressure plate in place and remove the bolts, then detach the pressure plate and clutch disc **(see illustration)**.

Inspection

Refer to illustrations 5.9 and 5.11

7   Ordinarily, when a problem occurs in the clutch, it can be attributed to wear of the clutch disc. However, all components should be inspected at this time. **Note:** *If the clutch components are contaminated with oil, there will be shiny, black, glazed spots on the clutch disc lining, which will cause the clutch to slip. Replacing clutch components won't completely solve the problem – be sure to check the crankshaft rear oil seal and the transaxle input shaft/mainshaft seal for leaks. If it looks like a seal is leaking, be sure to install a new one to avoid the same problem with a new clutch.*

8   Inspect the flywheel for cracks, heat checking, grooves and other obvious defects. If the imperfections are slight, a machine shop can machine the surface flat and smooth, which is highly recommended regardless of the surface appearance. Refer to Chapter 2 for the fly-

wheel removal and installation procedure.

9   Inspect the lining on the clutch disc. There should be at least 1/16-inch of lining above the rivet heads. Check for loose rivets, distortion, cracks, broken springs and other obvious damage **(see illustration)**. As mentioned above, ordinarily the clutch disc is routinely replaced, so if in doubt about its condition, replace it with a new one.

10   The release bearing should also be replaced along with the clutch disc (see Section 4).

11   Check the machined surfaces and the diaphragm spring fingers of the pressure plate **(see illustration)**. If the surface is scored or otherwise damaged, replace the pressure plate. Also check for obvious damage, distortion, cracks, etc. Light glazing can be removed with emery cloth. If the pressure plate must be replaced, new and factory-rebuilt units are available.

Installation

Refer to illustration 5.13

12   Before installation, clean the flywheel and pressure plate machined surfaces with lacquer thinner, acetone or brake system cleaner. It's important to keep these surfaces, and the clutch disc lining, clean and free of oil or grease. Handle the parts only with clean hands.

13   Position the clutch disc and pressure plate against the flywheel with the clutch held in place with an alignment tool **(see illustration)**. Make sure it's installed properly (most replacement clutch plates will be marked "flywheel side" or something similar – if it's not marked, install the clutch disc with the damper springs toward the transaxle).

14   Tighten the pressure plate-to-flywheel bolts only finger tight, working around the pressure plate.

15   Center the clutch disc by ensuring the alignment tool extends through the splined hub and into the pocket in the crankshaft. Wiggle the tool up, down or side-to-side as needed to center the disc. Tighten the pressure plate-to-flywheel bolts a little at a time, working in a criss-cross pattern to prevent cover distortion. After all the bolts are snug, tighten them to the torque listed in this Chapter's Specifications. Remove the alignment tool.

16   Using high-temperature grease, lubricate the release bearing (refer to Section 4). Also apply a light coat of grease on the release lever contact areas and the transaxle input shaft.

8

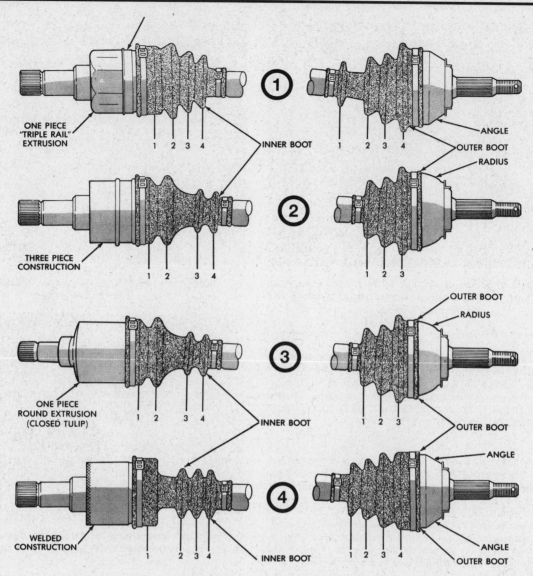

ONE PIECE
"TRIPLE RAIL"
EXTRUSION

INNER BOOT

ANGLE
OUTER BOOT
RADIUS

THREE PIECE
CONSTRUCTION

ONE PIECE
ROUND EXTRUSION
(CLOSED TULIP)

OUTER BOOT
RADIUS

INNER BOOT

OUTER BOOT

WELDED
CONSTRUCTION

INNER BOOT

ANGLE

ANGLE
OUTER BOOT

6.4   Use this chart to identify the brand of driveaxles used on your vehicle:

| 1 | ACI | 3 | GKN ("closed tulip" – one-piece round extrusion) |
| 2 | GKN ("open tulip" – three-piece construction) | 4 | Citroen |

17   Install the clutch release bearing as described in Section 4.
18   Install the transaxle and all components removed previously.
Tighten all fasteners to the proper torque specifications.

6   Driveaxles – general information and inspection

General information

Refer to illustration 6.4

Power from the engine passes through the clutch and transaxle to the front wheels via two driveaxles. Most models have unequal length driveaxles; turbocharged and 3.3L models use equal-length driveaxles. On these models, the inner end of the right driveaxle is connected to an intermediate shaft; the point at which the two are connected is supported by a bearing and bracket. The inner end of the intermediate shaft is connected to the differential side gear via a Cardan type joint.

Each driveaxle assembly consists of three parts: A "tripod" type inner CV joint, a "Rzeppa" type outer CV joint and an axle shaft which connects the two. Outer CV joint housings on both equal and unequal

length driveaxles have a splined stub axle which engages with the front hub and is retained by a large nut. Inner CV joint housings have a short, splined stub axle which engages with the differential side gear (the CV joint housing for the right driveaxle on equal length systems engages with the intermediate shaft. On some driveaxles, a circlip in a groove near the tip of the stub axle expands into a groove in the bore of the side gear or intermediate shaft when the stub axle is properly seated, locking the inner end of the tripod CV joint to the side gear or intermediate shaft. On other driveaxles, the inner splined end of the CV joint housing is held in place by a spring inside the CV joint housing which pushes the housing toward the transaxle, keeping the stub axle fully seated in the differential side gears.

As the driveaxles move through their range of travel, ball bearings inside the CV joint housings allow them to operate at various lengths and angles.   These bearings must be lubricated with special grease and protected by rubber boots. You should periodically inspect these boots for tears and/or grease leaking out. Torn boots allow dirt and moisture to enter the CV joints; if not fixed, a simple tear accelerates bearing wear and eventually causes premature failure. The inner CV joint can be rebuilt if necessary; the outer CV cannot – if it fails, you'll

7.2   If there's no assistant handy to apply the brakes while you unscrew the hub nut, use a large screwdriver or prybar to immobilize the hub

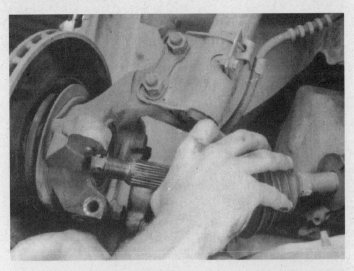

7.7   Swing the steering knuckle away from the transaxle and pull out the driveaxle

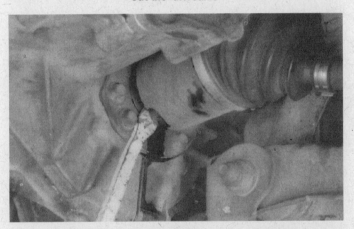

7.8   Pry the inner end of the the CV joint out of the differential side gears with a large screwdriver or prybar

have to replace it.

The vehicles covered by this manual can be equipped with driveaxles manufactured by ACI, GKN or Citroen **(see illustration)**. If, after referring to the illustration, you're still unable to determine the manufacturer, take the driveaxle assembly with you when buying boots or CV joint parts. Don't try to substitute one brand of driveaxle for another or swap parts from one brand to another.

Inspection

Periodically, inspect the boots for leaks, damage and deterioration (see Chapter 1). Replace damaged CV joint boots immediately or the CV joints may be damaged. You must remove the driveaxle (see Section 7) to replace the boots. Some auto parts stores carry a convenient alternative: "Split-type" replacement boots can be installed without removing the driveaxle from the vehicle. This design is handy for emergency repairs when you're traveling, but it's not a substitute for one-piece boots. When a boot is torn, you must remove the driveaxle and disassemble, clean and inspect the CV joint to make sure no moisture and dirt – which greatly accelerate bearing wear – have already caused damage.

The most common symptom of worn or damaged CV joints, besides lubricant leaks, is a clicking noise in turns, a clunk when accelerating from a coasting condition or vibration at highway speeds.

To check for wear in the CV joints and driveaxle shafts, grasp each axle (one at a time) and rotate it in both directions while holding the CV joint housings. Watch for movement, indicating worn splines or sloppy CV joints. Also, check the driveaxle shafts for cracks and distortion.

7   Driveaxles – removal and installation

Removal

Refer to illustrations 7.2, 7.7 and 7.8

1   Remove the wheel cover (or hub cover). Remove the front hub nut cotter pin, nut lock and wave washer, if equipped. With the weight of the vehicle on the wheels, loosen the hub nut.
2   Loosen the wheel lug nuts, raise the front of the vehicle and support it securely on jackstands (apply the parking brake and block the rear wheels). Remove the lug nuts, the front wheel, the hub nut and the big washer **(see illustration)**.
3   If you're removing the right driveaxle from a vehicle with unequal length driveaxles, remove the speedometer drive gear (see Chapter 7) prior to removing the right axle.

4   Remove the steering knuckle-to-balljoint clamp bolt (see Chapter 10).
5   Disconnect the stabilizer bar from the suspension arm to allow enough movement to separate the balljoint (see Chapter 10).
6   Pry the lower balljoint stud out of the steering knuckle (see Chapter 10).
7   Grasp the outer CV joint and the steering knuckle and pull the steering knuckle out to separate the driveaxle from the hub **(see illustration)**. Be careful not to damage the CV joint boot. **Caution:** *Don't pry on or damage the wear sleeve on the CV joint when separating it from the hub.*
8   Pry the inner end of the CV joint out of the differential (or intermediate shaft) with a large screwdriver or prybar **(see illustration)**.
9   The driveaxles, when in place, secure the hub bearing assemblies. If the vehicle must be supported or moved on the front wheels while the driveaxles are out, install bolts through the hubs and thread nuts onto them to keep the bearings from loosening.

Installation

10   Prior to installation, clean the wear sleeve on the driveaxle outer CV joint and the seal in the hub. Lubricate the entire circumference of the seal lip and fill the seal cavity with grease. Apply a 1/4-inch bead of grease to the wear sleeve seal contact area as well.
11   On driveaxles equipped with circlips, install new circlips in the inner CV joint shaft grooves.
12   Apply a small amount of multi-purpose grease to the splines at

8

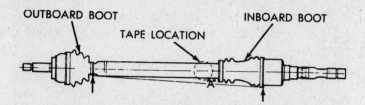

7.22   Measure the distance between the arrows to verify that the driveaxle is the correct length when installed

each end of the driveaxle. Place the driveaxle in position and carefully insert the inner end of the shaft into the transaxle.

13   Push the steering knuckle out and insert the outer splined shaft of the CV joint into the hub.

14   Insert the balljoint stud into the steering knuckle, install the clamp bolt and tighten it to the torque listed in the Chapter 10 Specifications.

15   Reattach the stabilizer bar (see Chapter 10).

16   Install the speedometer drive gear (see Chapter 7).

17   Install the wheels and hand tighten the wheel lug nuts. Install the spacer washer and hub nut and tighten the nut securely (don't try to tighten it to the specified torque yet).

18   Lower the vehicle and tighten the wheel lug nuts to the torque listed in the Chapter 1 Specifications.

19   Tighten the driveaxle hub nut to the torque listed in this Chapter's Specifications, then install the wave washer, nut lock and a new cotter pin.

Driveaxle position check

Refer to illustration 7.22

20   Later model vehicles have engine mounts with slotted holes that allow for side-to-side positioning of the engine. If the vertical bolts on the right or left upper engine mounts have been loosened for any reason, or if the vehicle has been damaged structurally at the front end, driveaxle length must be checked/corrected. A driveaxle that's shorter than required will result in objectionable noise, while a driveaxle that's longer than necessary may result in damage.

21   The vehicle must be completely assembled, the front wheels must be properly aligned and pointing straight ahead and the weight of the vehicle must be on all four wheels.

22   Using a tape measure, check the distance from the inner edge of the outboard boot to the inner edge of the inboard boot on both

driveaxles. Take the measurement at the lower edge of the driveaxles (six o'clock position) **(see illustration)**. Compare the measurement with the length listed in this Chapter's Specifications. Note that the required dimension varies with transaxle type and driveaxle manufacturer (see illustration 6.4 to identify the driveaxle type).

23   If the dimensions aren't as specified, the mount bolts can be loosened and the engine repositioned to obtain the specified driveaxle lengths. If the engine can't be moved enough within the range of the slotted engine mounts, check for damaged or distorted support brackets and side rails.

24   If the engine is moved, see Chapter 7 and adjust the shift linkage.

---

8   Intermediate shaft – removal and installation

Removal

Refer to illustration 8.3

1   Remove the right driveaxle (see Section 7).

2   Remove the speedometer drive gear from the transaxle extension housing (see Chapter 7).

3   Remove the bearing bracket mounting screws **(see illustration)**.

4   Place a drain pan underneath the right side of the transaxle to catch any fluid/lubricant that leaks out during removal of the intermediate shaft. Grasp the intermediate shaft securely with both hands and pull it out of the transaxle.

Installation

5   Place the intermediate shaft and bearing assembly in position and carefully insert the splined stub axle into the transaxle.

6   Place the bearing bracket in position, install the bracket mounting screws and tighten them to the torque listed in this Chapter's Specifications.

7   Lubricate the splines inside the pilot bore of the intermediate shaft with a liberal amount of multi-purpose grease.

8   Install the right driveaxle (see Section 7).

9   Check and, if necessary, add the recommended type of transaxle fluid/lubricant to bring it up to the proper level (see Chapter 1).

---

9   Constant velocity (CV) joints – disassembly, inspection and reassembly

1   Obtain a CV joint rebuild or replacement kit.

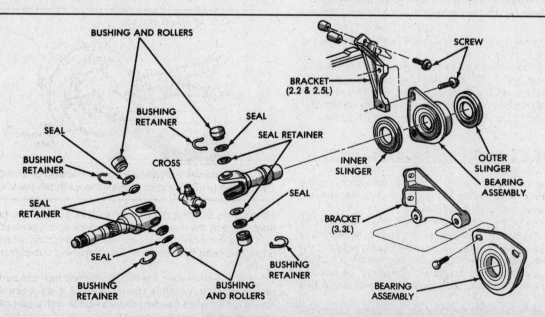

8.3   Exploded view of the intermediate shaft assembly

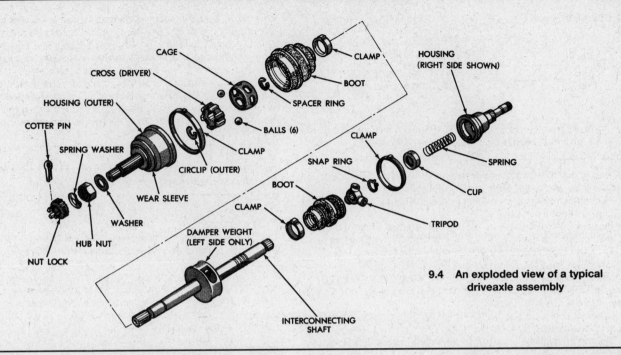

9.4   An exploded view of a typical driveaxle assembly

9.5   To separate the tripod from the housing of a Citroen inner CV joint, carefully pry up on the retainer at each bearing roller

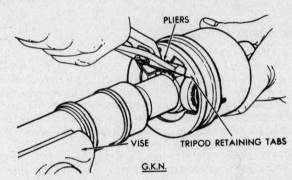

9.6   To separate the tripod from the housing of a GKN inner CV joint, bend up the retaining tabs with a pair of pliers

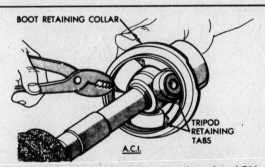

9.7   To separate the tripod from the housing of an ACI inner CV joint, compress the spring and bend each tab back with pliers

2   Remove the driveaxles (see Section 7) and identify which types of CV joints are installed (see Section 6).
3   Place one of the driveaxles in a vise, using wood blocks to protect it from the vise jaws. If the CV joint has been operating properly with no noise or vibration, replace the boot as described in Section 10. If the CV joint is badly worn or has run for some time with no lubricant due to a damaged boot, it should be disassembled and inspected.

Inner CV joint

Refer to illustrations 9.4, 9.5, 9.6, 9.7, 9.9a, 9.9b, 9.13, 9.15, 9.20, 9.22a, 9.22b, 9.22c and 9.23

4   Remove the clamps and slide the boot back to gain access to the tripod **(see illustration)**. Depending on the type of CV joint involved, separate the tripod from the housing as follows.
5   Citroen driveaxles utilize a tripod retainer ring which is rolled into a groove in the housing. Deform the retainer ring slightly at each roller with a screwdriver **(see illustration)**. The retention spring will push the housing off the tripod. The retainer ring can also be carefully cut off the housing. New rings are included in the rebuild kit and can be installed by rolling the edge into the machined groove in the housing with a hammer and punch.
6   On GKN driveaxles, the retaining tabs are an integral part of the housing cover. Hold the housing and lightly compress the retention spring while bending the tabs up with a pair of pliers **(see illustration)**. Support the housing as the retention spring pushes it off the tripod. This will prevent the housing from reaching an unacceptable angle and keep the tripod rollers from being pulled from the tripod studs.
7   On ACI driveaxles, the tripod retaining tabs are part of the boot retaining collar, which is staked in place. Compress the retaining spring lightly while bending the tabs back with a pair of pliers **(see illustration)**. Be sure to support the housing as the spring pushes it off the tripod.

8

9.9a   The tripod is held on the axleshaft by a snap-ring - remove it with a pair of snap-ring pliers

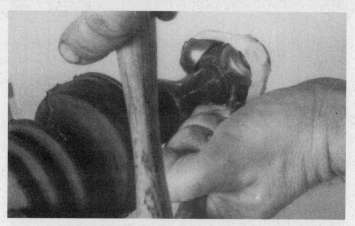

9.9b   Secure the bearings with tape and drive the tripod off the shaft with a brass punch and a hammer

9.13   On Citroen driveaxles, use adjustable pliers to detach the CV joint retainer ring

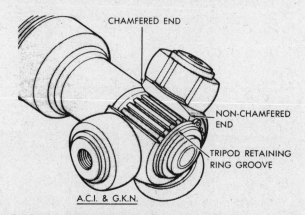

9.15   On GKN and ACI CV joints, the non-chamfered end of the tripod must face out when installed on the driveaxle splines

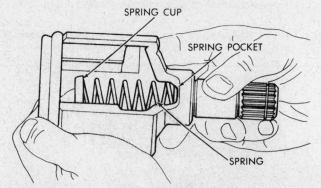

9.20   When assembling the inner CV joint, make sure the spring is seated securely in the spring pocket and the spring cup is installed on the outer end

9.22a   On Citroen driveaxles, make sure the bearing grooves in the housing have been greased, slide the housing over the tripod

8   When removing the housing from the tripod, hold the rollers in place on the studs to prevent the rollers and needle bearings from falling. After the tripod is out of the housing, secure the rollers in place with tape.

9   Remove the snap-ring **(see illustration)** and use a brass punch to drive the bearing and tripod assembly off the splined shaft **(see illustration)**.

10   Clean the grease from the tripod assembly. Check for score marks, wear, corrosion and excessive play. Replace any damaged or worn components.

11   Inspect the inner splined area of the bearing tripod for wear and damage. Replace parts as necessary.

12   Remove all old grease from the housing. Inspect the housing splines, ball races, spring, spring cup and the spherical end of the shaft for wear, damage, nicks and corrosion. Replace parts as necessary.

13   Place the housing in a vise and remove the retainer ring with a pair of pliers **(see illustration)**.

14   Install the new boot on the axle.

15   On GKN and ACI driveaxles, slide the tripod onto the shaft with the non-chamfered end facing out (next to the snap-ring groove) **(see illustration)**.

9.22b . . . then stake the new retainer ring in place with a hammer and punch

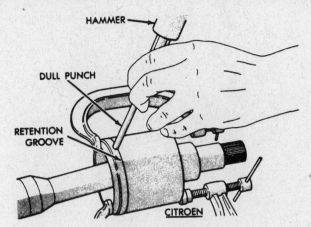

9.22c If the retainer ring slips while you're staking it, use a pair of C-clamps to hold it in place

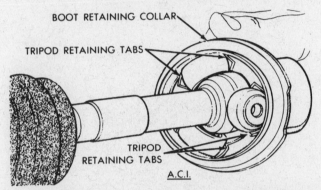

9.23 On ACI driveaxles, press the housing onto the tripod – but don't try to bend the retaining tabs back to their original positions

9.27a Give the outer CV joint housing a sharp tap with a soft-face hammer to disengage it from the internal circlip installed in a groove on the outer end of the axleshaft . . .

9.27b . . . and remove the outer CV joint housing

16   Citroen driveaxles are equipped with tripods that can be installed with either end out (both ends are the same). Be sure to install the wire ring tripod retainer on the interconnecting shaft before sliding the tripod onto the shaft.

17   If necessary, use a section of pipe or a socket and hammer to carefully tap the tripod onto the shaft until it just clears the snap-ring groove.

18   Install a new snap-ring and make sure it's seated in the groove.

19   On GKN driveaxles, distribute two of the three or four packets of grease supplied with the kit in the boot and the remaining packet(s) in the housing. On ACI driveaxles, distribute one of the two supplied packets of grease in the boot and the remaining packet in the housing. On Citroen driveaxles, distribute two-thirds of the grease in the packet in the boot and the remaining amount in the housing. Make sure the grease is applied to the bearing grooves in the housing.

20   Position the spring in the housing spring pocket with the cup attached to the exposed end of the spring **(see illustration)**. Apply a small amount of grease to the concave surface of the spring cup.

21   On GKN driveaxles, slip the tripod into the housing and bend the retaining ring tabs down to their original positions. Make sure the tabs retain the tripod in the housing.

22   On Citroen driveaxles, slide the housing over the tripod until it bottoms **(see illustration)**. Install a new retainer ring by rolling the edge into the machined groove in the housing with a hammer and punch **(see illustration)**. If the retainer ring won't stay in place during this operation, hold it with two C-clamps **(see illustration)**. Make sure the retainer ring secures the tripod in the housing.

23   On ACI driveaxles, slip the tripod into the housing but don't bend the retaining tabs **(see illustration)** back to their original positions. Reattach the boot instead, which will hold the housing on the shaft. When the driveaxle is reinstalled on the vehicle, make sure the tripod is re-engaged in the housing.

24   Make sure the retention spring is centered in the housing spring pocket when the tripod is installed and seated in the spring cup.

25   Install the boot and retaining clamp (see Section 10).

Outer CV joint

Refer to illustrations 9.27a, 9.27b, 9.31, 9.32, 9.33, 9.34, 9.37, 9.41 and 9.45

26   Remove the boot clamps and push the boot back.

27   Wipe the grease out of the joint. Use a soft-face hammer to drive the housing off the axle **(see illustrations)**. Support the CV joint as this is done and rap the housing sharply on the outer edge to dislodge it from the internal circlip installed on the shaft.

8

9.31   After removing the grease, mark the bearing cage, cross and housing to ensure that they're reinstalled in the same relationship to one another

9.32   With the cage and cross tilted like this, remove the ball bearings one at a time

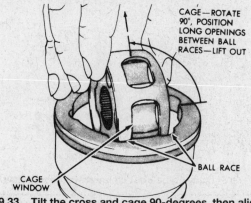

9.33   Tilt the cross and cage 90-degrees, then align the windows in the cage with the lands and rotate the cross up and out of the outer race

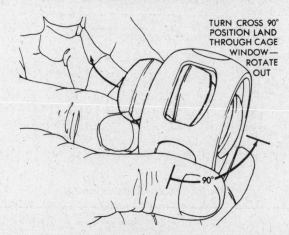

9.34   Turn the cross 90-degrees, align the race lands with the cage windows and rotate the race out of the cage

28   Slide the boot off the driveaxle. If the CV joint was operating properly and the grease doesn't appear to be contaminated, just replace the boot (see Section 10). Bypass the following disassembly procedure. If the CV joint was noisy or the grease was contaminated, proceed with the disassembly procedure to determine if it should be replaced with a new one.

29   Remove the circlip from the driveaxle groove and discard it (the rebuild kit will include a new circlip). GKN and ACI driveaxles are equipped with a large spacer ring, which must not be removed unless the driveaxle is being replaced with a new one.

30   Clean the axle spline area and check the splines for wear, damage and corrosion.

31   Clean the outer CV joint bearing assembly with a clean cloth to remove excess grease. Mark the relative position of the bearing cage, cross and housing **(see illustration)**.

32   Grip the housing shaft securely in the wood blocks in the vise. Push down one side of the cage and remove the ball bearing from the opposite side. Repeat the procedure in a criss-cross pattern until all of the balls are removed **(see illustration)**. If the joint is tight, tap on the cross (not the cage) with a hammer and brass punch.

33   Remove the bearing cage assembly from the housing by tilting it vertically and aligning two opposing elongated cage windows in the area between the ball grooves **(see illustration)**.

34   Turn the cross 90-degrees to the cage and align one of the spherical lands with an elongated cage window. Raise the land into the window and swivel the cross out of the cage **(see illustration)**.

35   Clean all of the parts with solvent and dry them with compressed air (if available).

36   Inspect the housing, splines, balls and races for damage, corro-

9.37   If the wear sleeve (on models so equipped) requires replacement, pry it off the housing with a large screwdriver

sion, wear and cracks. Check the cross for wear and scoring in the races. If any of the components are not serviceable, the entire CV joint assembly must be replaced with a new one.

37   Check the outer housing wear sleeve for damage and distortion. If it's damaged or worn, pry the sleeve off the housing **(see illustration)** and replace it with a new one. A special tool is available for installing the new sleeve, but a large section of pipe slightly smaller in diameter than the outer edge of the sleeve will work if care is exercised (don't nick or gouge the seal mating surface).

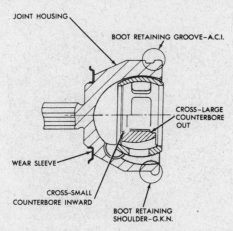

9.41   On GKN and ACI CV joints, make sure the large counterbore faces out when the joint is reassembled

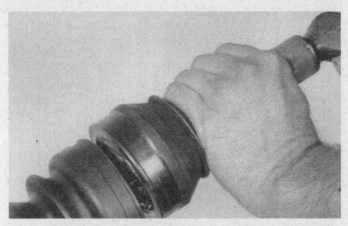

9.45   Strike the end of the housing shaft with a soft-face hammer to engage it with the shaft circlip

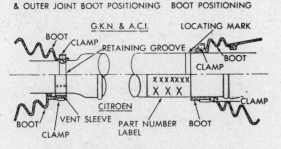

10.9   CV joint boot installation details

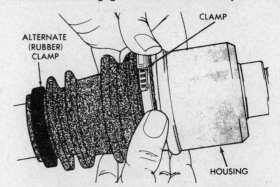

10.11   GKN ladder-type boot clamp installation details

38   Apply a thin coat of oil to all CV joint components before beginning reassembly.

39   Align the marks and install the cross in the cage so one of the lands fits into the elongated window.

40   Rotate the cross into position in the cage and install the assembly in the CV joint housing, again using the elongated window for clearance.

41   Rotate the cage into position in the housing. On GKN and ACI driveaxles, the large counterbore of the cross must face out **(see illustration)**. On Citroen driveaxles, the cage and cross chamfers must face out. On all driveaxles, make sure the marks made during disassembly face out and are aligned.

42   Pack the lubricant from the kit into the ball races and grooves.

43   Install the balls into the elongated holes, one at a time, until they're all in position.

44   Place the driveaxle in the vise and slide the boot over it. Install a new circlip in the axle groove, taking care not to twist it.

45   Place the CV joint housing in position on the axle, align the splines and rap it sharply with a soft-face hammer **(see illustration)**. Make sure it's seated on the circlip by attempting to pull it off the shaft.

46   Install the boot (see Section 10).

47   Install the driveaxle (see Section 7).

10   Constant velocity (CV) joint boots – replacement

Note: If the instructions supplied with the replacement boot kit differ from the instructions here, follow the ones with the new boots. A special tool is required to install the factory-supplied boot clamps, so it may be a good idea to leave the entire procedure to a dealer service department. Do-it-yourself kits which offer greatly simplified installation may be available for your vehicle. Consult an auto parts store or dealer parts department for more information on these kits.

1   If the boot is cut, torn or leaking, it must be replaced and the CV joint inspected as soon as possible. Even a small amount of dirt in the joint can cause premature wear and failure. Obtain a replacement boot kit before beginning this procedure.

2   Remove the driveaxle (see Section 7).

3   Disassemble the CV joint and remove the boot as described in Section 9.

4   Inspect the CV joint to determine if its been damaged by contamination or running with too little lubricant. If you have any doubts about the condition of the joint components, perform the inspection procedures described in Section 9.

5   Clean the old grease out of the CV joint and repack it with the grease supplied with the kit.

6   Pack the interior of the new boot with the remaining grease.

7   Install the boot and clamps as follows.

GKN and ACI driveaxles

Refer to illustrations 10.9, 10.11, 10.12, 10.17, 10.18 and 10.19

8   GKN units generally are equipped with metal ladder-type clamps. However, two alternative clamps are also used. They include a small rubber clamp at the shaft end of the inner CV joint and a large spring-type clamp on the housing. 1991 and later model outer CV joint boots use a different type of clamp (see Step 16).

9   If so equipped, slide the small rubber clamp over the shaft. Slide the small end of the boot over the shaft and position it as follows: On right inner joints, the small end of the boot lip must be aligned with the mark on the shaft. On left inner and all outer joints, position the small end of the boot in the groove in the shaft **(see illustration)**.

10   Place the rubber clamp in the boot groove (if so equipped) or install the metal clamp.

11   Make sure the boot is properly located on the shaft, then locate the metal clamp tangs in the slots, making the clamp as tight as possible by hand **(see illustration)**.

8

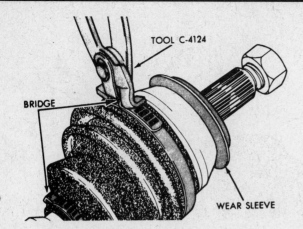

10.12   Use this special crimping tool to pinch the clamp bridge

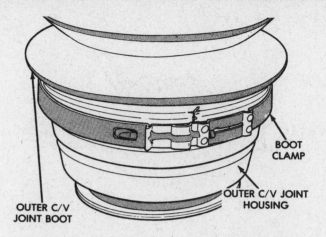

10.17   On 1991 and later models, make sure the outer CV joint boot clamp is installed squarely in the boot groove

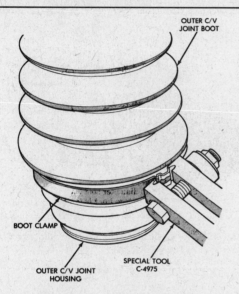

10.18   Open the tool jaws so they fit over the boot clamp tabs

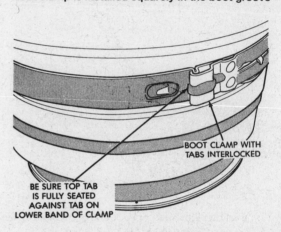

10.19   Tighten the tool until the boot clamp tabs interlock

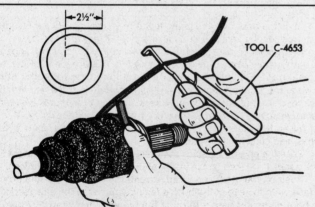

10.23   Wrap the clamp around the boot twice, leaving about 2-1/2 inches of extra material, then cut off the excess

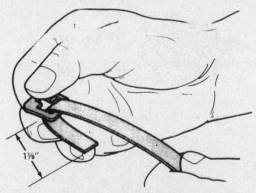

10.24   Pass the strap around the buckle and fold it back about 1-1/8 inch on the inside of the buckle

12   Squeeze the clamp bridge with tool number C-4124 (or equivalent) to complete the tightening procedure (on later models, use tool C-4653 or equivalent) **(see illustration)**. Don't cut through the clamp bridge or damage the rubber boot.

13   Reassemble the CV joints and driveaxle components (see Section 9).

14   Locate the large end of the boot over the shoulder or in the groove in the housing (make sure the boot isn't twisted).

15   Install the spring-type clamp or ladder-type clamp. If a ladder-type clamp is used, repeat the tightening procedure described in Steps 11 and 12.

1991 and later outer CV joint boot

16   Before installing the boot on the shaft, slide the small boot clamp onto the shaft. Slide the boot onto the shaft and seat it securely in the boot groove **(see illustration 10.9)**.

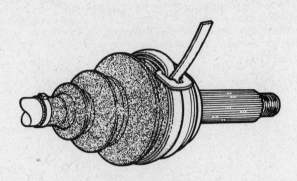

10.26a   Install the strap on the boot and bend it back so it can't unwind

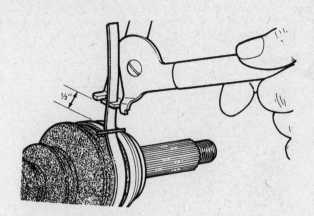

10.26b   Attach the tool about 1/2-inch from the buckle . . .

10.27   . . . then push the tool forward and up to engage the tool hook in the buckle eye

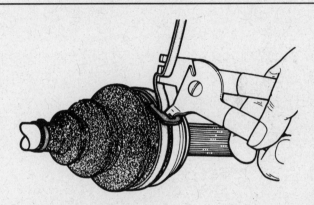

10.28a   Close the tool handles slowly to tighten the clamp strap, . . .

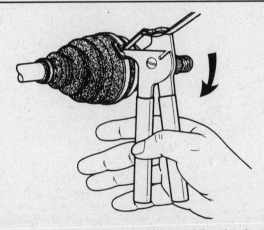

10.28b   . . . then rotate the tool down while releasing the pressure on the handles (allow the handles to open)

17   Place the clamp squarely in the groove **(see illustration)**.
18   Open the jaws of special tool number C-4975 until the clamp tabs are between the jaws **(see illustration)**.
19   Tighten the bolt on the tool until the boot clamp tabs interlock with each other **(see illustration)**.
20   Reassemble the CV joints and driveaxle components (see Section 9). Following the same procedure, install the boot clamp on the large end of the CV joint.

Citroen driveaxles

Refer to illustrations 10.23, 10.24, 10.26a, 10.26b, 10.27, 10.28a and 10.28b

21   Slide the boot over the shaft. If you're installing an outer CV joint boot, position the vent sleeve under the boot clamp groove.
22   On right inner joints, align the boot lip face with the inner edge of the part number label. If the label is missing, use the mark left by the original boot. On left inner and all outer joints, position the boot between the locating shoulders and align the edge of the lip with the mark made by the original boot. **Note:** *Clamping procedures are identical for attaching the boot to the shaft and the CV joint housing.*
23   Wrap the clamping strap around the boot twice, plus 2-1/2 inches, and cut it off **(see illustration)**.
24   Pass the end of the strap through the buckle opening and fold it back about 1-1/8 inch on the inside of the buckle **(see illustration)**.
25   Position the clamping strap around the boot, on the clamping surface, with the eye of the buckle facing you. Wrap the strap around the boot once and pass it through the buckle, then wrap it around a second time and pass it through the buckle again.
26   Fold the strap back slightly to prevent it from unwinding itself **(see illustration)**, then open the special tool (C-4653) and place the strap in the narrow slot, about 1/2-inch from the buckle **(see illustration)**.
27   Hold the strap with one hand and push the tool forward and up slightly, then fit the tool hook into the buckle eye **(see illustration)**.
28   Tighten the strap by closing the tool handles **(see illustration)**, then rotate the tool down slowly while releasing the pressure on the handles **(see illustration)**. Allow the handles to open progressively,

8

then open the tool all the way and slide it sideways off the strap. **Caution:** *Never fold the strap back or rotate the tool down while squeezing the handles together (if this is done, the strap will break).*

29 If the strap isn't tight enough, repeat the procedure. Always engage the tool about 1/2-inch from the buckle. Make sure the strap moves smoothly as tightening force is applied and don't allow the buckle to fold over as the strap passes through it.

30 When the strap is tight, cut it off 1/8-inch above the buckle and fold it back neatly. It must not overlap the edge of the buckle.

31 Repeat the procedure for the remaining boot clamps.

Chapter 9 Brakes

Contents

Specifications

Brake fluid type.. See Chapter 1

Disc brakes

Brake pad wear limit	See Chapter 1
Minimum disc thickness..	See specs cast into disc
Disc runout (maximum)	0.005 inch
Disc thickness (parallelism) variation limit............................	0.0005 inch

Drum brakes

Brake shoe wear limit...	See Chapter 1
Drum	
Maximum diameter	See specs cast into drum
Out-of-round (maximum)	0.002 inch

Torque specifications

	Ft-lbs (unless otherwise indicated)
Master cylinder-to-booster nuts...	17 to 25
Power brake booster-to-firewall nuts..	17 to 25
Caliper guide pin(s)	
ATE	18 to 26
Kelsey-Hayes...	25 to 35
Caliper mounting bracket-to-steering	
knuckle bolts..	130 to 190
Brake hose-to-caliper inlet fitting bolt..	19 to 29
Wheel cylinder-to-brake backing plate bolts	75 in-lbs
Brake backing plate-to-rear axle bolts	
1986 and earlier	35 to 55
1987 and later	65 to 94
Hydraulic assembly mounting nuts (ABS-equipped models)............	21

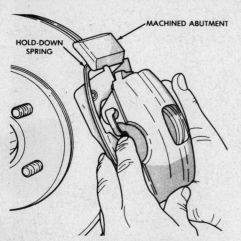

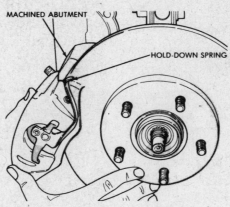

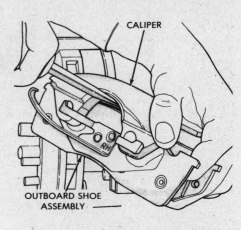

2.3a To remove an ATE caliper, unscrew the guide pins and lift the caliper off the caliper mounting bracket, then detach the hold-down spring which hooks into the abutment (right side) . . .

2.3b . . . or inserts under it (left side)

2.5 Use a screwdriver to pry the outer ATE pad out of the caliper

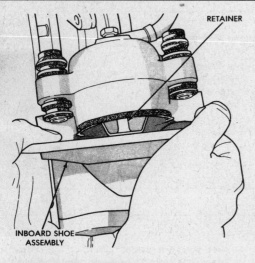

2.6 Grasp the inner pad with both hands and pull it straight out until the retainer is detached from the piston

2.7 Hang the caliper out of the way on a piece of wire – DO NOT let it hang by the brake hose!

1 General information

All models are equipped with hydraulically-operated front disc and rear drum brakes.

The front brakes use a single-piston, floating-caliper design. Disc brake calipers from two different manufacturers – ATE and Kelsey-Hayes – are used on the vehicles covered in this manual. They differ in design, so parts are not interchangeable. ATE calipers have two guide pins; some Kelsey-Hayes calipers have two guide pins and some have only one guide pin. 1989 through 1991 two-pin Kelsey-Hayes calipers are similar to ATE calipers.

The rear drum brakes are a leading/trailing design with automatic adjustment.

Front-wheel drive vehicles tend to wear the front brake pads at a faster rate than rear-drive vehicles. Consequently, it's very important to inspect the brake pads frequently to make sure they haven't worn to the point where the disc itself is scored or damaged. Note that the pad thickness limit on these models includes the metal portion of the brake pad, not just the lining material (see Chapter 1).

The hydraulic system consists of two separate circuits. The master cylinder has a separate section in the reservoir for each circuit – in the event of a leak or failure in one hydraulic circuit, the other circuit will remain operative.

Some later models have an Anti-lock Braking system (ABS) that aids vehicle stability during heavy braking or on wet or uneven road surfaces. All non-ABS models have a load sensing dual proportioning valve which modulates the rear brake pressure depending on vehicle load.

All models are equipped with a cable-actuated parking brake, which operates the rear brakes.

2 Disc brake pads – replacement

Warning: *Disc brake pads must be replaced on both front wheels at the same time – never replace the pads on only one wheel. Also, the dust created by the brake system may contain asbestos, which is harmful to your health. Never blow it out with compressed air and don't inhale any of it. An approved filtering mask should be worn when working on the brakes. Do not, under any circumstances, use petroleum-based solvents to clean brake parts. Use brake system cleaner or clean brake fluid only!*

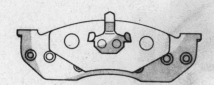

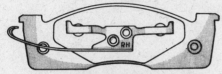

INBOARD SHOE ASSEMBLY
(RIGHT AND LEFT COMMON)

OUTBOARD SHOE ASSEMBLY
(RIGHT SIDE SHOWN)

**2.10   Outer right and left ATE pads are different – be sure to
check the markings before installing them**

Note: *When servicing the disc brakes, use high-quality, nationally recognized, name-brand parts.*

1   Raise the front of the vehicle and support it securely on jackstands. Block the rear wheels and apply the parking brake, then remove the front wheels. **Note:** *The pad replacement procedure varies,
depending on whether you have ATE or Kelsey-Hayes calipers. Check
a caliper. If the caliper mounts on machined abutments on the steering
knuckle and has a hold-down spring like the one shown in illustrations
2.3a and 2.3b, it's an ATE caliper; if not, it's a Kelsey-Hayes caliper.*

ATE caliper

Refer to illustrations 2.3a, 2.3b, 2.5, 2.6, 2.7 and 2.10

2   On pre-1989 models, loosen the caliper guide pins enough to allow the caliper to be removed; the pins should be removed only if the
bushings are being replaced (see Section 3). On 1989 and later models, the bushings are of a different design and the pins can be removed if necessary.
3   Grasp the caliper securely and pull the bottom out and off the
lower machined abutment while detaching the hold-down spring from
the upper abutment **(see illustrations)**.
4   Move the caliper forward and off the brake disc. The pads will remain with the caliper.
5   Use a screwdriver to pry the outer pad out of the caliper **(see illustration)**.
6   Remove the inner pad by pulling it away from the piston **(see illustration)**.
7   Support the caliper out of the way with a wire hanger **(see illustration)**. **Warning:** *Don't allow the caliper to hang by the brake hose!*
8   Inspect the caliper and adapter for wear, damage, rust and evidence of brake fluid leaks. If the caliper-to-adapter mating surfaces
are rusty, clean them thoroughly with a wire brush (the caliper must
be free to move as the brakes are applied). Also inspect the brake disc
(see Section 4).
9   Apply a thin film of Mopar Lubricant (No. 2932524) or high-temperature brake grease to the caliper-to-adapter mating surfaces. Remove the protective paper from the noise suppression gasket on both
pads.
10   Siphon out a small amount of brake fluid from the master cylinder
reservoir, then use a piece of wood to carefully push the piston into
the caliper bore to provide clearance for the new pads. If you don't
want to siphon fluid from the reservoir, remove the reservoir cap(s) and
place rags or newspapers underneath the reservoir to catch the overflow that will occur when the piston is pushed back to make room for
the new pads. Before installation, note that the outer pads are marked
"L" and "R" to denote left and right **(see illustration)**.
11   Install the inner brake pad by pressing the retainer into the piston
recess. **Caution:** *Don't get any grease on the pad lining material, gasket surface or brake disc.*

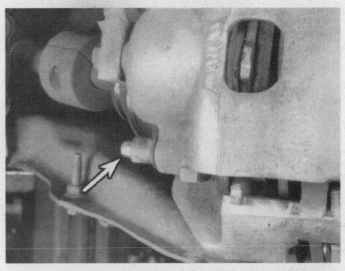

**2.18a   To get at the pads, remove the guide pin (arrow) (single-
pin caliper shown; some calipers have two), . . .**

**2.18b   . . . and pivot the caliper up and off the caliper mounting
bracket (a typical single-pin caliper shown)**

12   Connect the hold-down spring to the caliper and press the outer
pad into position.
13   Connect the hold-down spring to the upper machined abutment
and rotate the caliper into position over the brake disc **(see illustrations 2.3a and 2.3b)**.
14   Install the guide pins by hand – don't cross-thread them. Tighten
the guide pins to the torque listed in this Chapter's Specifications.
15   Install the wheel, hand tighten the wheel lug nuts and lower the
vehicle. Tighten the lug nuts to the torque listed in the Chapter 1 Specifications.
16   Repeat Steps 2 through 15 for the other caliper.
17   Pump the brake pedal several times to bring the pads into contact with the disc. Check the brake fluid level (see Chapter 1). Drive the
vehicle in an isolated area and make several stops to wear off any foreign material on the pads and seat them on the disc.

Kelsey-Hayes caliper

Refer to illustrations 2.18a, 2.18b, 2.20a, 2.20b, 2.20c, 2.21 and 2.26

18   Remove the caliper guide pin(s) **(see illustration)**, swing up the
lower end of the caliper and pull it off the caliper mounting bracket
(see illustration). **Note:** *It may be necessary to wedge a screwdriver
between the caliper and mounting bracket and pry slightly to break the*

9

2.20a   To remove the outer pad from a single-pin type, simply pull it straight off – then remove the anti-rattle spring clip (arrow) and transfer it to the new outer pad

2.20b   To remove the outer pad from a double-pin type, remove the pad shim . . .

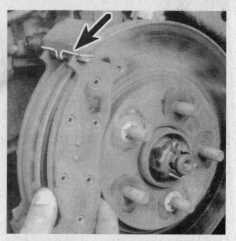

2.20c   . . . disengage the upper end of the brake pad backing plate from the anti-rattle spring and remove the pad – after you remove the inner pad, the anti-rattle spring (arrow) will fall out of the caliper mounting bracket, so note how it's installed BEFORE you remove the inner pad

2.21   After removing the inner pad from a single-pin type, remove the anti-rattle spring clip (arrow) and transfer it to the new inner pad

2.26   Apply anti-squeal compound to the shims (if equipped) when replacing the brake pads

gasket adhesive seals.

19   Support the caliper out of the way with a wire hanger (see illustration 2.7). **Warning:** *Don't allow the caliper to hang by the brake hose!*

20   Detach the outer brake pad and shim (if equipped) from the caliper mounting bracket **(see illustrations)**. If you're replacing the pads on a single-pin caliper, remove the anti-rattle spring and install it on the new outer pad.

21   Detach the inner brake pad and shim, if equipped **(see illustration)**. If you're replacing the pads on a single-pin caliper, remove the anti-rattle spring and install it on the new inner pad. If you're replacing the pads on a double-pin caliper, note how the anti-rattle spring clip is installed on the caliper mounting bracket, in case it falls off before you install the new pads.

22   Inspect the caliper and caliper mounting bracket for wear, damage, rust and evidence of fluid leaks. If the caliper-to-bracket mating surfaces are rusty, clean them thoroughly with a wire brush (the caliper must be able to move freely when the brakes are applied). Also inspect the brake disc (see Section 4)

23   Siphon some brake fluid from the master cylinder reservoir, or place rags or newspapers underneath the reservoir to catch the overflow that will occur when the piston is pushed back to make room for the new pads. Then use a piece of wood to carefully push the piston

into the caliper bore far enough to provide clearance for the new pads.

24   Apply a thin film of Mopar Lubricant (no. 2932524) or high-temperature brake grease to the adapter-to-brake pad and caliper mating surfaces. Remove the protective paper from the noise suppression gasket on both pads.

25   Install the inner brake pad, making sure the anti-rattle spring is secure. **Caution:** *Don't get any grease on the pad lining material, gasket surface or brake disc.*

26   Apply anti-squeal compound (available at auto parts stores) to the shim, if equipped, and install the shim **(see illustration)**.

27   Place the outer pad in position in the caliper mounting bracket.

28   Slide the caliper into position over the pad and disc assembly.

29   Install the guide pin(s) and tighten it/them to the torque listed in this Chapter's Specifications. Don't cross-thread the guide pin(s) during installation.

30   Repeat Steps 18 through 29 for the other caliper.

31   Install the wheel, hand tighten the wheel lug nuts and lower the vehicle. Tighten the lug nuts to the torque listed in the Chapter 1 Specifications.

32   Pump the brake pedal several times to bring the pads into contact with the disc. Check the brake fluid level (see Chapter 1). Drive the vehicle in an isolated area and make several stops to wear off any foreign material on the pads and seat them on the disc.

3.2 Place some shop rags or newspapers under the brake hose inlet fitting before – and plug it to prevent contamination right after – you disconnect it

3.6 Place a piece of wood between the caliper and the piston, then force the piston out of the caliper bore with compressed air – be sure to keep your hands and fingers out of the way during this procedure

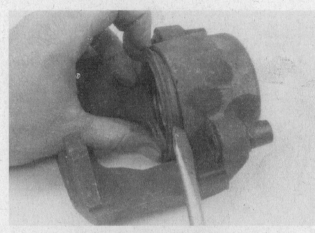

3.7 Use a screwdriver to pry the dust boot out of the caliper bore

3.8 Remove the piston seal with a wood pencil or a plastic eating utensil so you don't damage the bore and seal groove

3 Disc brake caliper – removal, overhaul and installation

Warning 1: *Dust created by the brake system may contain asbestos, which is harmful to your health. Never blow it out with compressed air and don't inhale any of it. An approved filtering mask should be worn when working on the brakes. Do not, under any circumstances, use petroleum-based solvents to clean brake parts. Use brake cleaner or clean brake fluid only!*

Warning 2: *On ABS-equipped models, de-pressurize the accumulator before disconnecting any brake lines or hoses or personal injury or damage to the vehicle's painted surfaces may result (see Section 7, Step 14).*

Note: *If an overhaul is indicated (usually because of fluid leakage), explore all options before beginning the job. New and factory rebuilt calipers are available on an exchange basis, which makes this job quite easy. If it's decided to rebuild the calipers, make sure a rebuild kit is available before proceeding. Always rebuild the calipers in pairs – never rebuild just one of them.*

Removal

Refer to illustration 3.2

1 Loosen the wheel lug nuts, raise the front of the vehicle and support it securely on jackstands. Remove the front wheels.

2 **Note:** *Don't remove the brake hose from the caliper if you're only*

removing the caliper to gain access to other components. If you're removing the caliper for overhaul, remove the brake hose inlet fitting bolt and detach the hose **(see illustration)**. *Have a rag handy to catch spilled fluid and wrap a plastic bag tightly around the end of the hose to prevent fluid loss and contamination.*

3 Remove the caliper guide pin(s) and detach the caliper from the vehicle (see Section 2).

Overhaul

Refer to illustrations 3.6, 3.7, 3.8, 3.9a, 3.9b, 3.9c, 3.9d, 3.14 and 3.15

4 Remove the brake pads (see Section 2).

5 Clean the exterior of the caliper with brake cleaner or new brake fluid. Never use gasoline, kerosene or petroleum-based cleaning solvents. Place the caliper on a clean workbench.

6 Position a wooden block or several shop rags in the caliper as a cushion, then use compressed air to remove the piston from the caliper **(see illustration)**. Use only enough air pressure to ease the piston out of the bore. If the piston is blown out, even with the cushion in place, it may be damaged. **Warning:** *Never place your fingers in front of the piston in an attempt to catch or protect it when applying compressed air – serious injury could result!*

7 Carefully pry the dust boot out of the caliper bore **(see illustration)**.

8 Using a wood or plastic tool, remove the piston seal from the groove in the caliper bore **(see illustration)**. Metal tools may damage the bore.

9

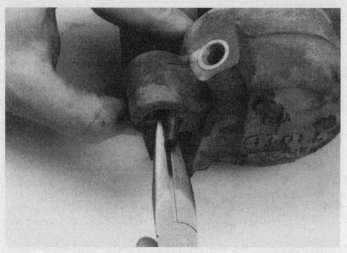

3.9a   Grab the ends of the mounting pin bushings with needle-nose pliers and push them through the caliper ears with a twisting motion

9   Remove the caliper bleeder screw, then remove and discard the caliper (guide) pin bushing(s) from the caliper ears. Discard all rubber parts **(see illustrations)**.

10   Clean the remaining parts with brake system cleaner or new brake fluid then blow them dry with compressed air.

11   Carefully examine the piston for nicks, burrs and excessive wear. If surface defects are present, the parts must be replaced.

12   Check the caliper bore in a similar way. Light polishing with crocus cloth is permissible to remove light corrosion and stains, but rust or pitting will require caliper replacement.

13   When reassembling the caliper, lubricate the bore and seal with clean brake fluid. Position the seal in the caliper bore groove – make sure it isn't twisted.

14   Lubricate the piston with clean brake fluid, install it squarely in the bore and apply pressure to bottom it in the caliper **(see illustration)**.

15   Stretch the dust boot over the groove in the piston, then carefully seat it in the caliper bore **(see illustration)**.

16   Install the bleeder screw.

17   Install new caliper pin bushings (and sleeves, if equipped).

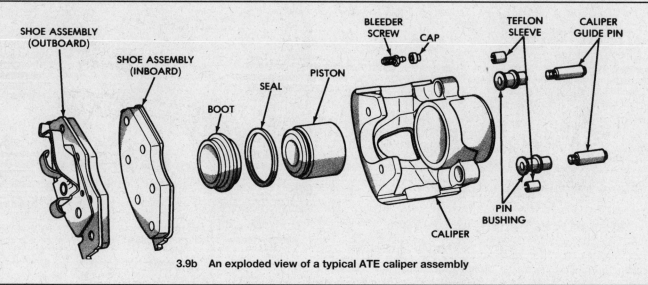

3.9b   An exploded view of a typical ATE caliper assembly

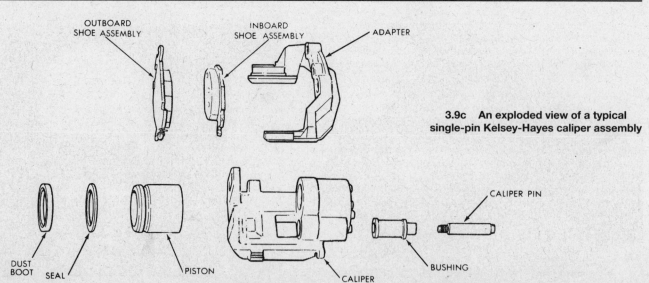

3.9c   An exploded view of a typical single-pin Kelsey-Hayes caliper assembly

Installation

18   Inspect the caliper guide pin(s) for excessive corrosion. Replace them if necessary.

19   Clean the caliper and caliper mounting bracket contact surfaces with a wire brush, then apply a thin film of high-temperature brake grease to them.

20   Install the brake pads and caliper (see Section 2).

21   Install the brake hose and inlet fitting bolt, using new copper washers, then tighten the bolt to the torque listed in this Chapter's Specifications.

22   If the line was disconnected, be sure to bleed the brakes (see Section 9).

23   Install the wheels and lower the vehicle. Tighten the lug nuts to the torque listed in the Chapter 1 Specifications.

24   After the job has been completed, firmly depress the brake pedal a few times to bring the pads into contact with the disc.

25   Check brake operation before driving the vehicle in traffic.

4   Brake disc – inspection, removal and installation

1   Loosen the wheel lug nuts, raise the vehicle and support it securely on jackstands. Remove the wheel and reinstall the lug nuts to hold the disc in place.

2   Remove the brake caliper (see Section 3). It's not necessary to disconnect the brake hose. After removing the caliper guide pin(s), suspend the caliper out of the way with a piece of wire. Don't let the caliper hang by the hose and don't stretch or twist the hose.

Inspection

Refer to illustrations 4.4a, 4.4b, 4.5a and 4.5b

3   Visually inspect the disc surface for scoring and other damage. Light scratches and shallow grooves are normal after use and may not affect brake operation, but deep score marks – over 0.015-inch (0.38 mm) – require disc removal and refinishing by an automotive machine shop. Be sure to check both sides of the disc. If pulsating has been

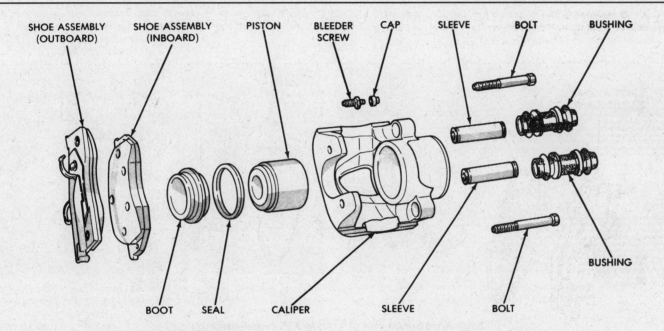

3.9d   An exploded view of a typical double-pin Kelsey-Hayes caliper assembly

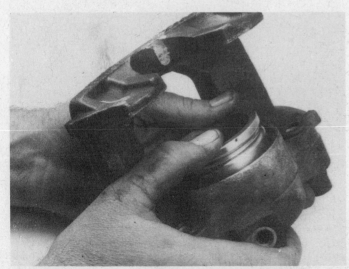

3.14   When you install the piston, make sure it doesn't become cocked as you push it into its bore in the caliper

3.15   If the correct seal driver tool isn't available, use a drift punch to tap around the edge until the dust boot is seated

9

4.4a   Make sure the lug nuts are in place and evenly tightened, then measure the disc runout with a dial indicator

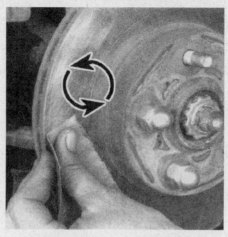

4.4b   Using a swirling motion, remove the glaze from the disc surface with sandpaper or emery cloth

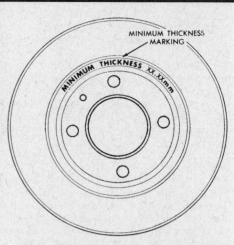

4.5a   The disc can be resurfaced by an automotive machine shop, provided the machining operation doesn't result in a disc thickness less than the minimum stamped on it

4.5b   Measure the disc thickness with a micrometer at several points around its circumference

4.6a   If the discs on your vehicle use retaining washers like this, pull them off with a pair of needle-nose pliers and discard them

noticed during application of the brakes, suspect disc runout.

4　To check disc runout, mount a dial indicator with the stem resting about 1/2-inch from the outer edge of the disc **(see illustration)**. Set the indicator to zero and turn the disc. The indicator reading should not exceed the maximum allowable runout listed in this Chapter's Specifications. If it does, the disc should be refinished by an automotive machine shop. **Note:** *Professionals recommend resurfacing of brake discs regardless of the dial indicator reading (to produce a smooth, flat surface that will eliminate brake pedal pulsations and other undesirable symptoms related to questionable discs). At the very least, if you elect not to have the discs resurfaced, deglaze them with sandpaper or emery cloth (use a swirling motion to ensure a non-directional finish)* **(see illustration)**.

5　The disc must not be machined to a thickness less than the minimum cast into the inside of the disc **(see illustration)**. The disc thickness can be checked with a micrometer **(see illustration)**.

Removal

Refer to illustrations 4.6a and 4.6b

6　Remove the lug nuts you installed to hold the disc in place during inspection. The discs on some models are equipped with retaining washers to prevent them from slipping off while the caliper is removed; if the discs on your vehicle are so equipped, remove the washer with needle-nose pliers **(see illustration)** and discard it. Slide the disc off the threaded studs **(see illustration)**.

4.6b   When you remove the disc, make sure you don't damage the threads on the wheel studs

Installation

7　Place the disc in position over the threaded studs.

8　Install the caliper and brake pads (see Section 3). Tighten the caliper guide pin(s) to the torque listed in this Chapter's Specifications.

9　Install the wheel and lug nuts, then lower the vehicle to the ground. Tighten the lug nuts to the torque listed in the Chapter 1 Specifications.

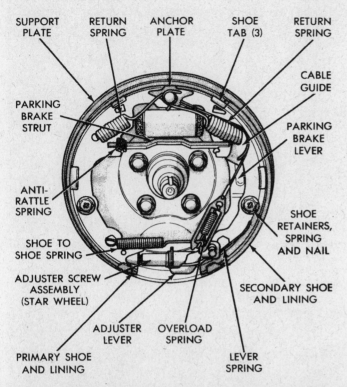

SUPPORT PLATE · RETURN SPRING · ANCHOR PLATE · SHOE TAB (3) · RETURN SPRING · CABLE GUIDE · PARKING BRAKE STRUT · PARKING BRAKE LEVER · ANTI-RATTLE SPRING · SHOE RETAINERS, SPRING AND NAIL · SHOE TO SHOE SPRING · SECONDARY SHOE AND LINING · ADJUSTER SCREW ASSEMBLY (STAR WHEEL) · ADJUSTER LEVER · OVERLOAD SPRING · LEVER SPRING · PRIMARY SHOE AND LINING

5.3   A typical rear drum brake assembly (left side shown)

5.4   A special brake spring tool, like the one shown here, is necessary to remove the return springs – tools like this are available inexpensively at auto parts stores

5.5a   Lift the adjuster cable off anchor pin . . .

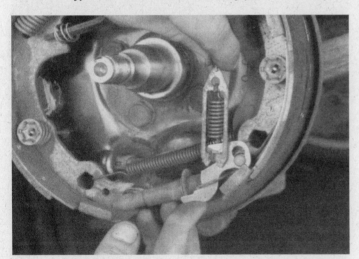

5.5b   . . . disconnect the overload spring at the other end and . . .

10   Depress the brake pedal a few times to bring the brake pads into contact with the disc. Bleeding of the system isn't necessary unless the brake hose was disconnected from the caliper. Check the operation of the brakes carefully before driving the vehicle in traffic.

---

5   Brake shoes – replacement

Refer to illustrations 5.3, 5.4, 5.5a, 5.5b, 5.5c, 5.5d, 5.7a, 5.7b, 5.8, 5.9, 5.10, 5.13, 5.15, 5.18, 5.20, 5.22, 5.25 and 5.33

Warning: *Drum brake shoes must be replaced on both rear wheels at the same time – never replace the shoes on only one wheel. Also, the dust created by the brake system may contain asbestos, which is harmful to your health. Never blow it out with compressed air and don't inhale any of it. An approved filtering mask should be worn when working on the brakes. Do not, under any circumstances, use petroleum-*

based solvents to clean brake parts. Use brake system cleaner or clean brake fluid only! **Note:** *When servicing the drum brakes, use high-quality, nationally-recognized, name-brand parts.*

Removal

1   Raise the rear of the vehicle, support it securely on jackstands and block the front wheels. Remove the rear wheels. Begin working on the left wheel brake assembly first. Work on only one brake assembly at a time so you can use the other side for reference.

2   Remove the hub/brake drum assembly (see Chapter 1). If the drum won't slide off, you'll have to back off the automatic adjuster screw, as follows. Remove the rubber plug from the rear of the brake backing plate, then insert a thin screwdriver through the hole and use it to push the adjuster lever off the adjuster screw **(see illustration 5.3).** Insert another screwdriver or brake adjusting tool and use it to turn the star wheel on the adjuster screw (push down on the tool) until the drum will pull off.

3   Use brake system cleaner to remove dust and brake fluid from the shoe assembly components **(see illustration). Warning:** *Brake dust may contain asbestos, which is harmful to your health. Do not blow it out of the brake shoe assembly with compressed air and do not inhale any of it.*

4   Hold the adjuster lever off the adjuster screw and back off the adjuster screw completely. Remove the brake shoe return springs, noting that the secondary spring overlaps the primary spring **(see illustration).**

5   Slide the eye of the automatic adjuster cable off the anchor plate, detach it from the adjuster lever, then remove the cable guide and an-

9

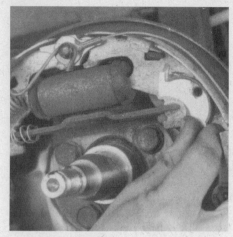

5.5c . . . remove the cable guide

5.5d   Lift the anchor plate off the pin

5.7a   Use needle-nose pliers to unhook the shoe-to-shoe spring

5.7b   With the spring removed, detach the adjuster screw (star wheel) assembly

5.8   Remove the parking brake strut and anti-rattle spring

5.9   Use a brake hold-down spring tool or pliers to depress the hold-down spring and turn the retainer

chor plate **(see illustrations)**.

6   Disconnect the adjuster lever from the spring by rotating it until the large hole in the lever is aligned with the pin, then pulling out on the lever until the lever is disengaged from the pin. Work the lever out from under the spring, then remove the spring from the pin.

7   Remove the shoe-to-shoe spring with pliers, then detach the adjuster screw assembly **(see illustrations)**.

8   Remove the parking brake strut **(see illustration)**.

9   Remove the hold-down springs by depressing the retainer with a pair of pliers or a special tool and turning the retainer until its slot aligns with the flattened end of the pin (nail); release pressure and the spring and retainer should come off **(see illustration)**. Lift the shoes off the backing plate.

10   Disconnect the parking brake lever from the parking brake cable. Place the assembly on a work surface and remove the parking brake lever by rotating it until it slips out of the slot, then transfer the lever to the new shoe **(see illustration)**.

11   It may be necessary to transfer the adjuster lever pins from the old shoes to the new ones. This can usually be done with a punch (to remove them), a small socket (to install them) and a hammer.

Inspection

12   Check the shoe linings to make sure they indicate full contact with the drum. Shoes with uneven wear must be replaced.

13   Check the drum for cracks, score marks and signs of overheating. Measure the inside diameter of the drum and compare it to the size stamped on the drum **(see illustration)**. Minor imperfections in the drum surface can be removed with fine emery paper. Deeper score marks can be removed by having the drum resurfaced by an automotive machine shop (as long as the maximum diameter is not exceeded). **Note:** *Professionals recommend resurfacing the drums whenever the shoes are replaced. Replace the brake drum with a new one if it is not usable.*

14   Check the brake springs for signs of discolored paint, indicating overheating, and distorted end coils. Replace them with new ones if necessary. **Note:** *Since the continuous heating/cooling cycles the brake assembly is subjected to cause springs to fatigue (wear out) quickly, we recommend replacing the return, hold-down and shoe-to-shoe springs whenever the shoes are replaced.*

15   Check the adjuster screw assembly and threads for bent, corroded and damaged components. Replace the assembly if the screw threads are damaged or rusted. Clean the threads and lubricate them, along with the contact areas on the button and washer, with white lithium-based grease **(see illustration)**.

16   Carefully peel back the wheel cylinder boots and check for damage and signs of leakage.

17   Rebuild or replace the wheel cylinder if there is any sign of leakage around the boots (see Section 6).

18   Check for rough or rusted shoe contact areas on the backing plate (sand them lightly, if necessary), then lubricate the contact points with high-temperature grease **(see illustration)**. Also lubricate the contact points on the anchor pin.

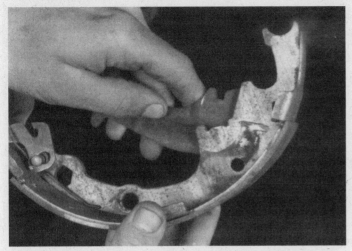

5.10   Rotate the parking brake lever and slip it out of the shoe

5.13   The maximum allowable inside diameter of the drum is stamped on it

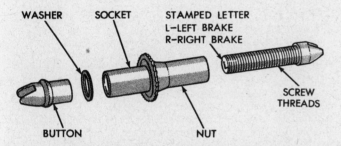

WASHER   SOCKET   STAMPED LETTER
L–LEFT BRAKE
R–RIGHT BRAKE

SCREW THREADS

BUTTON   NUT

5.15   Adjuster components – exploded view

5.18   The area on the backing plate where the brake shoes contact it must be smooth and lubricated with high-temperature grease

5.20   Push down on the spring and turn it until the retainer locks in place

Installation

19   Slide the primary shoe into position on the backing plate and engage the upper end against the anchor pin and piston.

20   Insert the pin through the backing plate from the rear and hold it in place while installing the hold-down spring and retainer **(see illustration)**.

21   Install the anchor plate, hook the free end of the adjuster cable over the anchor pin and connect the primary shoe return spring.

22   Install the anti-rattle spring on the parking brake strut and install the parking brake strut **(see illustration)**.

23   Attach the parking brake lever to the cable and install the parking brake lever into the rectangular hole in the secondary brake shoe. To attach the lever to the cable, slide the cable spring back along the ca-

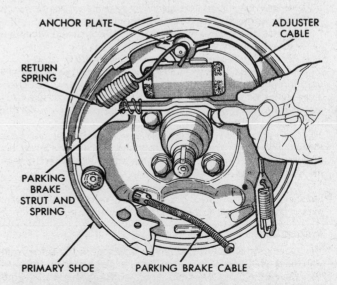

ANCHOR PLATE   ADJUSTER CABLE

RETURN SPRING

PARKING BRAKE STRUT AND SPRING

PRIMARY SHOE   PARKING BRAKE CABLE

5.22   Seat the parking brake strut into the slot in the shoe

9

5.25 Here's the cable guide and return spring correctly installed – note how the adjuster cable is routed around the cable guide

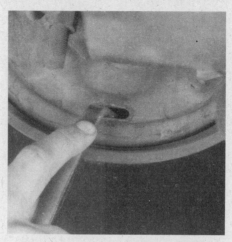

5.33 Insert the screwdriver or brake adjusting tool (shown here) into the hole and turn the star wheel

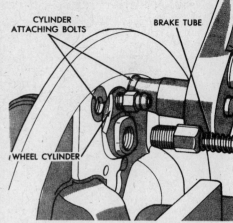

6.4 To detach the wheel cylinder from the brake backing plate, disconnect the brake tube fitting and remove the two attaching bolts

ble and hold it in place with needle-nose pliers while you slide the lever onto the cable.

24   Place the secondary shoe in position, engaging it with the wheel cylinder piston and the free end of the strut. Insert the pin through the backing plate from the rear and hold it in place while installing the hold-down spring and retainer.

25   Install the cable guide by inserting the rim into the secondary shoe web and connect the return spring **(see illustration)**.

26   Secure the ends of the return springs around the anchor by squeezing them with pliers until they are parallel.

27   Install the adjuster with the star wheel next to the secondary shoe.

28   Install the shoe-to-shoe spring.

29   Install the adjuster lever spring over the shoe pivot pin, then insert the adjuster under the spring and over the pin.

30   Route the adjuster cable around the guide (make sure it's pulled tight) and connect it to the adjuster lever. Put a small amount of high-temperature grease along the cable, where it contacts the cable guide.

31   Check the operation of the adjuster by pulling the cable to the rear. The star wheel should rotate up.

32   Install the hub/drum assembly and the wheel. Repeat the procedure on the right wheel.

33   After the shoes and drums are in place on both wheels, install the wheels and adjust each brake assembly, as follows:

   a)   Remove the rubber plug from the hole in the backing plate.

   b)   Insert a narrow screwdriver or brake adjusting tool through the hole in the backing plate and turn the star wheel until the brake drags slightly as the tire is turned **(see illustration)**.

   c)   Back off the star wheel until the tire turns freely (it will be necessary to use another screwdriver to hold the adjuster lever off the star wheel – see Step 2).

   d)   Repeat the adjustment on the opposite wheel.

   e)   Install the plugs in the backing plate access holes.

34   Adjust the parking brake (see Section 10).

35   Lower the vehicle and check the brake operation very carefully before placing the vehicle into normal service.

6   Wheel cylinder – removal, overhaul and installation

Warning: *On ABS-equipped models, de-pressurize the accumulator before beginning this procedure or personal injury or damage to the vehicle's painted surfaces may result (see Section 7, Step 14).*

Note: *Before deciding to rebuild a wheel cylinder, make sure parts are available. It's sometimes more practical to simply replace the old wheel cylinder with a new or rebuilt unit instead of rebuilding it.*

Removal

Refer to illustration 6.4

1   Raise the rear of the vehicle and support it securely on jackstands, then block the front wheels. Remove the rear wheels.

2   Remove the rear hub/drum (see Chapter 1) and the brake shoes (see Section 5).

3   Disconnect the brake line (tube) from the back of the wheel cylinder and plug it. Use a flare-nut wrench, if available.

4   Unbolt the wheel cylinder and remove it from the backing plate **(see illustration)**. Clean the backing plate and wheel cylinder mating surfaces.

Overhaul

Refer to illustration 6.5

Note: *You'll need a clean place to work, clean rags, some newspapers, a wheel cylinder rebuild kit, a container of brake fluid and some denatured alcohol to perform a wheel cylinder overhaul.*

5   Remove the bleeder screw **(see illustration)** and check to make sure it is not obstructed.

6   Carefully pry the boots from the wheel cylinder and remove them.

7   Push in on one piston and force out the opposite piston, cups and spring from the bore.

8   Clean the wheel cylinder, pistons and spring with clean brake fluid, denatured alcohol or brake system solvent and dry them with compressed air. **Warning:** *Do not, under any circumstances, use petroleum-based solvents or gasoline to clean brake parts.*

9   Check the cylinder bore and pistons for score marks and corrosion (pitting). Slight imperfections in the bore can be removed with fine crocus cloth (use a circular motion). Black stains on the cylinder walls are caused by the cups and will not impair brake operation. If the pistons or wheel cylinder bore are badly scored or pitted, replace the wheel cylinder.

10   Lubricate the components with clean brake fluid or brake assembly lubricant prior to installation.

11   With the cylinder bore coated with clean brake fluid or brake assembly lube, install the spring and clip expanders. Install the cups in each end of the cylinder. Make sure the open ends of the cups are facing each other.

12   Engage the boot on the piston and slide the assembly into the bore. Carefully press the boot over the cylinder end until it is seated. Repeat the procedure for the remaining boot and piston.

13   Install the bleeder screw.

Installation

14   Apply RTV-type sealant to the wheel cylinder mating surface of the backing plate.

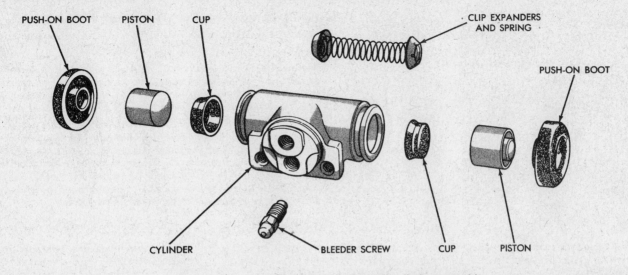

6.5   An exploded view of a typical wheel cylinder assembly

15   To install the wheel cylinder, hold it in position, install the mounting bolts and tighten them to the specified torque.

16   Unplug the brake line, insert it into the wheel cylinder fitting and carefully thread the flare nut into place. Once the nut is properly started, tighten it securely with a wrench (use a flare nut wrench if available). **Caution:** *Be extra careful when attaching the flare-nut, since it is easy to cross-thread it.*

17   Install the brake shoes (see Section 5) and the hub/drum (see Chapter 1).

18   Bleed the brakes (see Section 9).

19   Install the wheels and lower the vehicle. Check the brake operation very carefully before placing the vehicle into normal service.

7   Master cylinder/hydraulic assembly – removal and installation

Master cylinder (models not equipped with ABS)

Refer to illustration 7.2

Note: *The master cylinder installed on these vehicles cannot be rebuilt. If problems are encountered, replace it with a new unit.*

1   Place a container and several layers of newspaper under the master cylinder to catch spilled brake fluid.

2   Unscrew the steel line flare-nuts **(see illustration)**, remove the lines and cap them. Use a flare-nut wrench, if available, to unscrew the nuts. Allow the fluid in the master cylinder to drain into the container.

3   Remove the mounting nuts and detach the master cylinder from the booster. If you are installing a new master cylinder, it may be necessary to transfer the plastic fluid reservoir to the new master cylinder. To do so, first drain the reservoir, then place the aluminum portion of the master cylinder in a vise and use your hand (no tools) to gently pull the reservoir off while gently rocking it back and forth. Replace the two rubber grommets with new ones, put them in place in the master cylinder, lubricate them with clean brake fluid and press the reservoir back into place, using a rocking motion. Make sure the bottom of the reservoir touches the top of each grommet.

4   Every time the master cylinder is removed, the complete hydraulic system must be bled. The time required to bleed the system can be reduced if the master cylinder is filled with fluid and bench bled before the master cylinder is installed on the vehicle.

5   Insert threaded plugs of the correct size into the cylinder outlet holes and fill both reservoirs with brake fluid. The master cylinder should be supported in a level manner so that brake fluid will not spill during the bench bleeding procedure.

7.2   To remove the master cylinder, disconnect the two brake line fittings (1) with a flare-nut wrench and remove the two mounting nuts (2)

6   Loosen one plug at a time and push the piston assembly into the bore (use a Phillips screwdriver) to force air from the master cylinder. To prevent air from being drawn back into the cylinder, the plug must be tightened before allowing the piston to return to its original position.

7   Since high pressure is not involved in the bench bleeding procedure, an alternative to the removal and replacement of the plug with each stroke of the piston assembly is available. Before pushing in on the piston assembly, remove the plug, then depress the piston as described above. Before releasing the piston, however, instead of replacing the plug, simply put your finger tightly over the hole to keep air from being drawn back into the master cylinder. Wait several seconds for brake fluid to be drawn from the reservoir into the piston bore, then depress the piston again, removing your finger as the brake fluid is expelled. Be sure to put your finger back over the hole each time before releasing the piston. When the bleeding procedure is complete for that port, replace the plug and tighten it snugly before going on to the other port to repeat the procedure.

8   Stroke the piston three or four times for each outlet to ensure that all air has been expelled.

9   Refill the master cylinder reservoirs and install the caps. **Note:** *The reservoirs should only be filled to the top of the reservoir divider to prevent overflowing when the caps are installed.*

9

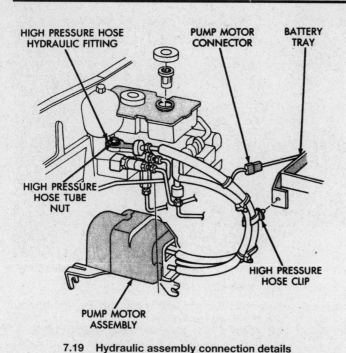

HIGH PRESSURE HOSE
HYDRAULIC FITTING

PUMP MOTOR
CONNECTOR

BATTERY
TRAY

HIGH PRESSURE
HOSE TUBE
NUT

HIGH PRESSURE
HOSE CLIP

PUMP MOTOR
ASSEMBLY

7.19 Hydraulic assembly connection details

10   To install the master cylinder, hold it in position, align the pushrod and master cylinder piston and install the mounting nuts finger tight.

11   Install the lines and carefully start the flare-nuts, taking care not to cross-thread them. Since the master cylinder is still loose, you can move it as necessary to help the flare-nuts thread correctly. After they have been started by hand, tighten them securely with a flare-nut wrench.

12   Tighten the master cylinder mounting nuts to the torque listed in this Chapter's Specifications.

13   Fill the master cylinder reservoir and bleed the brakes (see Section 9).

Hydraulic assembly (1991 through 1993 models equipped with ABS)

Refer to illustrations 7.19 and 7.22

Warning: *Before you perform this procedure, you must depressurize the accumulator as described in Step 14. Otherwise, personal injury and/or damage to the painted surfaces of the vehicle may result. Also, never attempt to disassemble the hydraulic assembly or personal injury or component damage may result.*

Note: *On ABS-equipped models, the brake master cylinder is part of an integrated hydraulic assembly and the master cylinder should not be separated from this assembly. Testing the hydraulic assembly is beyond the scope of the home mechanic. However, if the unit has been diagnosed defective by a dealer service department or other qualified shop, you can remove and install the assembly yourself.*

Removal

14   De-pressurize the hydraulic accumulator by pressing the brake pedal a minimum of 40 times with the ignition switch Off. Use about 50 pounds of force when pressing the pedal. When the accumulator is depressurized, you will notice the pedal is harder to press; press the pedal a few additional times after you feel this. **Warning:** *Leave the ignition switch Off during the entire time brake lines are disconnected or the accumulator will once again pressurize. It's a good idea to disconnect the cable from the negative terminal of the battery.*

15   Remove the air cleaner and fresh air intake duct (see Chapter 4).

16   Remove the windshield washer fluid reservoir.

17   Disconnect all electrical connectors from the hydraulic assembly

18   Siphon off as much fluid as possible from the brake fluid reservoir.

19   Disconnect the pump high-pressure hose from the hydraulic assembly **(see illustration)**.

20   Disconnect the pump return hose from the steel tube. Cap the end of the steel tube.

21   Disconnect all brake lines from the hydraulic assembly.

22   Working under the instrument panel, position a small screwdriver between the center tang on the retainer clip and the pin in the brake pedal. Rotate the screwdriver enough to allow the retainer clip center tang to pass over the end of the brake pedal pin **(see illustration)**. Re-

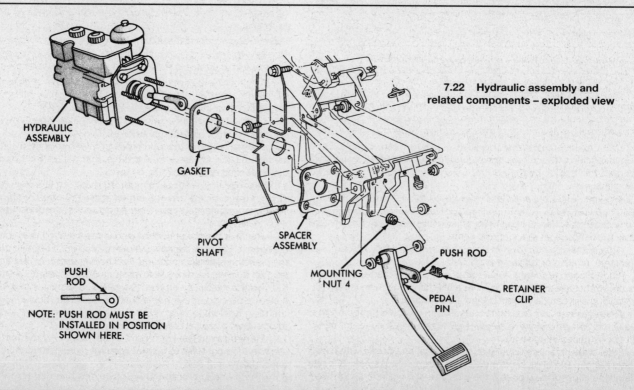

HYDRAULIC
ASSEMBLY

GASKET

PIVOT
SHAFT

SPACER
ASSEMBLY

MOUNTING
NUT 4

PUSH ROD

RETAINER
CLIP

PEDAL
PIN

PUSH
ROD

NOTE: PUSH ROD MUST BE
INSTALLED IN POSITION
SHOWN HERE.

**7.22 Hydraulic assembly and
related components – exploded view**

8.4a   To detach a metal brake line from the flexible hose, loosen the fitting with a flare-nut wrench . . .

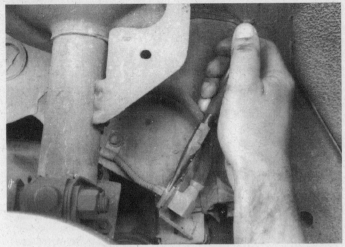

8.4b   . . . then pull off the retaining clip with needle-nose pliers

move and discard the retainer clip. Pull the pushrod off the pedal pin
23   While an assistant supports the hydraulic assembly, remove the four hydraulic assembly nuts from under the instrument panel. Remove the hydraulic assembly

Installation

24   Have an assistant hold the hydraulic assembly in position on the firewall while you install the hydraulic assembly mounting nuts. Tighten them to the torque listed in this Chapter's Specifications.
25   Coat the bearing surface of the pedal pin with multi-purpose grease.
26   Connect the pushrod to the pedal pin and install a new retainer clip. The pushrod must be assembled to the pedal pin as shown in **illustration 7.22.**
27   The remainder of installation is the reverse of removal. Be sure to tighten all brake line/hose connections securely.
28   Refill the fluid reservoir and bleed the brakes (see Section 9).
29   Check for leaks and carefully check the operation of the brakes before driving the vehicle in traffic.

8   Brake hoses and lines – inspection and replacement

Refer to illustrations 8.4a and 8.4b

Warning: *On ABS-equipped models, depressurize the accumulator before disconnecting any hoses or lines or personal injury or damage to the vehicle's painted surfaces may result (see Section 7, Step 14).*

1   About every six months, the flexible hoses which connect the steel brake lines with the rear brakes and the front calipers should be inspected for cracks, chafing of the outer cover, leaks, blisters and other damage.
2   Replacement steel and flexible brake lines are commonly available from dealer parts departments and auto parts stores. Do not, under any circumstances, use anything other than steel lines or approved flexible brake hoses as replacement items.
3   When installing the brake line, leave at least 3/4-inch between the line and any moving or vibrating parts.
4   When disconnecting a hose and a line, loosen the fitting with a flare-nut wrench **(see illustration)**. Once the fitting has been loosened, the retaining clip can be removed **(see illustration)**.
5   When connecting two hoses, use open-end wrenches on the hose ends. When connecting two hoses, make sure they're not bent, twisted or strained in any way.
6   Steel brake lines are usually retained at several points with clips. Always remove the clips before detaching a steel brake line. Always reinstall the clips (or new ones if the old ones are damaged) when re-

placing a brake line – they provide support and keep the lines from vibrating, which can eventually break them.
7   After installing a line or hose, bleed the brakes (see Section 9).

9   Brake hydraulic system – bleeding

Refer to illustration 9.8

Warning 1: *Wear eye protection when bleeding the brake system. If the fluid comes in contact with your eyes, immediately rinse them with water and seek medical attention.*

Warning 2: *On 1991 through 1993 ABS-equipped models, de-pressurize the accumulator as described in Section 7, Step 14 or personal injury or damage to the vehicle's painted surfaces may result.*

Warning 3: *1994 and later ABS-equipped vehicles require the use of a special electronic tool (DRB-II scan tool or equivalent) to bleed the ABS modulator assembly. For this reason, any repairs to, or bleeding of, the system should be left to an authorized dealership service department.*

Note: *Bleeding the hydraulic system is necessary to remove air that manages to find its way into the system when it's been opened during removal and installation of a hose, line, caliper or master cylinder.*

1   It'll probably be necessary to bleed the system at all four brakes if air has entered the system due to low fluid level, or if the brake lines have been disconnected at the master cylinder.
2   If a brake line was disconnected only at a wheel, then only that caliper or wheel cylinder must be bled.
3   If a brake line is disconnected at a fitting located between the master cylinder and any of the brakes, that part of the system served by the disconnected line must be bled.
4   Remove any residual vacuum from the brake power booster by applying the brake several times with the engine off. On ABS-equipped models, depressurize the accumulator, as described in Section 7, Step 14.
5   Remove the brake fluid reservoir caps and fill the reservoir with brake fluid. Reinstall the cover. **Note:** *Check the fluid level often during the bleeding operation and add fluid as necessary to prevent the fluid level from falling low enough to allow air into the master cylinder.*
6   Have an assistant on hand, as well as a supply of new brake fluid, a clear plastic container partially filled with clean brake fluid, a length of tubing (preferably clear) to fit over the bleeder screw and a wrench to open and close the bleeder screw.
7   Beginning at the right rear wheel, loosen the bleeder screw slightly, then tighten it to a point where it's snug but can still be loosened quickly and easily.
8   Place one end of the tubing over the bleeder screw and sub-

9

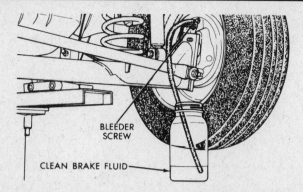

9.8 When bleeding the brakes, push one end of a clear plastic tube onto the bleeder screw at the caliper or wheel cylinder and submerge the other end in a container of brake fluid; build up pressure in the lines with the brake pedal and open the bleeder screw – air expelled from the lines is visible as bubbles; when the bubbles disappear, you've bled the line to that caliper or wheel cylinder

merge the other end in brake fluid in the container **(see illustration)**.

9   Have your assistant pump the brakes slowly a few times to get pressure in the system, then hold the pedal down firmly.

10   While the pedal is held down, open the bleeder screw. Watch for air bubbles to exit the submerged end of the tube. When the fluid flow slows, tighten the screw and have your assistant release the pedal.

11   Repeat Steps 9 and 10 until no more air is seen leaving the tube, then tighten the bleeder screw and proceed to the left rear wheel, the right front wheel and the left front wheel, in that order, and perform the same procedure. Be sure to check the fluid in the master cylinder reservoir frequently.

12   Never use old brake fluid. It contains moisture which will deteriorate the brake system components and boil when the fluid gets hot.

13   Refill the reservoir with fluid at the end of the operation.

14   Check the operation of the brakes. The pedal should feel solid when depressed, with no sponginess. If necessary, repeat the entire process. **Warning:** *Don't operate the vehicle if you're in doubt about the condition of the brake system.*

10   Parking brake – adjustment

1   The rear drum brakes must be in proper working order before adjusting the parking brake (see Section 5).

2   Block the front wheels to prevent vehicle movement, raise the rear of the vehicle and support it securely on jackstands. Release the parking brake.

1989 and earlier models

Refer to illustration 10.4

3   Clean the cable adjuster threads with a wire brush and lubricate them with multi-purpose grease.

4   Loosen the adjusting nut **(see illustration)** until there's slack in the cable.

5   Have an assistant rotate the rear wheels to make sure they turn easily.

6   Tighten the adjusting nut until a slight drag can be felt when the rear wheels are turned. You may have to keep the adjuster rod from turning by holding it with a wrench or pair of pliers.

7   Loosen the nut until the rear wheels turn freely, then back it off an additional two full turns.

1990 and later models

Refer to illustrations 10.8, 10.10 and 10.12

8   Detach the cover from the adjuster housing **(see illustration)**.

9   Clean and lubricate the adjuster threads.

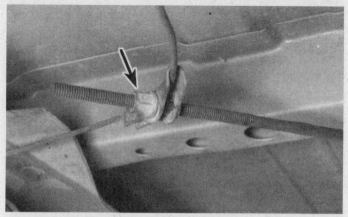

10.4   Turn this nut to adjust the parking brake (1989 and earlier models)

10.8   Push in on the tabs (arrows) with a small screwdriver while pulling the cover straight down

10   Make sure the parking brake is released and back off the adjusting nut until the cable is slack **(see illustration)**.

11   Apply the parking brake all the way to the floor.

12   Mark the bent nail portion of the adjuster with white paint approximately 1/4-inch (6 mm) from the bracket **(see illustration)**.

13   Tighten the adjusting nut until the alignment mark is even with the edge of the bracket. If the bent nail end hook extends all the way into the bracket, replace it with a new one.

14   Install the cover.

All models

15   Apply and release the parking brake several times to make sure it operates properly. It must lock the rear wheels when applied and the wheels must turn easily, without dragging, when it's released.

16   Lower the vehicle.

11   Parking brake cables – removal and installation

1   Raise the rear of the vehicle and support it securely on jackstands.

1989 and earlier models

Front cable

Refer to illustration 11.8

2   Working under the vehicle, loosen the adjusting nut until there's slack in the cable **(see illustration 10.4)**.

3   Disengage the front cable from the connector.

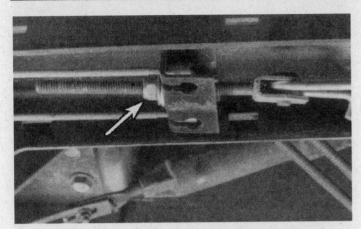

10.10   1990 and later model adjusting nut (arrow)

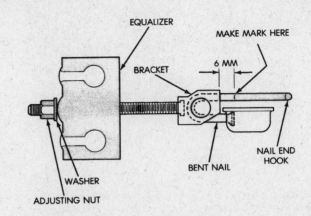

10.12   With the cable slack and the parking brake applied, mark the adjuster at the point shown (1990 and later models)

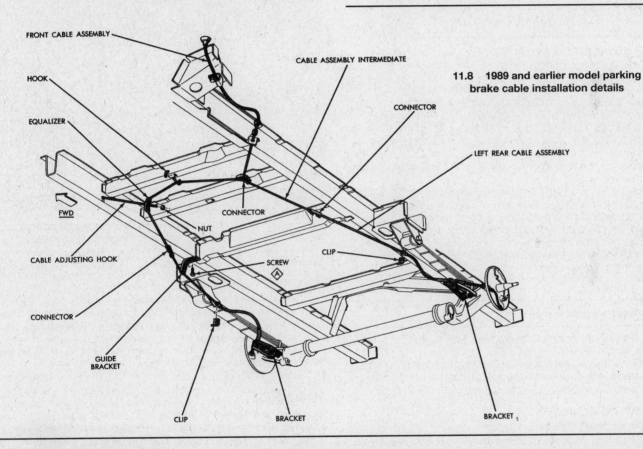

11.8   1989 and earlier model parking brake cable installation details

4   Loosen the cable housing retainers from the frame rail bracket and the parking brake pedal assembly.

5   From inside the vehicle, lift up the driver's side floor mat and detach the rubber seal from the hole.

6   Pull up on the forward end of the front cable to disconnect it.

7   Pull the cable assembly through the hole in the floor.

8   Installation is the reverse of removal **(see illustration)**.

9   Adjust the parking brake (see Section 10).

Rear cable

10   Remove the rear wheel and the hub/drum assembly on the side of the vehicle the cable to be replaced is located (see Chapter 1).

11   Back off the adjusting nut **(see illustration 10.4)** until the cable is slack and detach the cable from the connector.

12   Disconnect the clip from the brake cable bracket.

13   Disconnect the cable from the parking brake lever on the brake shoe.

14   Locate the retainer at the end of the rear cable, where it enters the brake shoe backing plate. Pinch this retainer with pliers (or use a hose clamp) and pull the retainer through the backing plate.

15   After pulling the cable through the backing plate, detach it from the bracket located under the spring.

16   The above procedure also applies to the other rear cable.

17   Installation is the reverse of removal **(see illustration 11.8)**.

18   Adjust the parking brake (see Section 10).

1990 and later models

Front cable

Refer to illustration 11.21

19   Working under the vehicle, loosen the adjusting nut until there's slack in the cable **(see illustration 10.10)**.

9

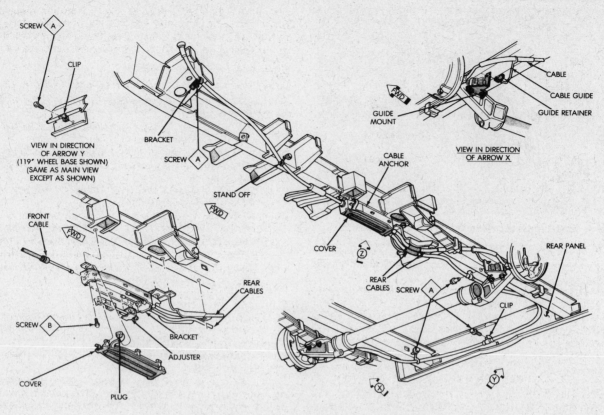

11.21 1990 and later model parking brake cable

20   Detach the front cable from the adjuster and cable housing from the anchor bracket by sliding a 14 mm box wrench over the cable housing retainer end to compress the three fingers, then pulling the cable housing out.

21   Detach the cable guide brackets from the frame rail and loosen the cable housing at the pedal assembly **(see illustration)**.

22   From inside the vehicle, lift up the driver's side floor mat and detach the rubber seal from the hole.

23   Pull cable end forward, then disconnect the button from the clevis. Tap the end of the cable housing out of the pedal assembly bracket.

24   Pull the cable assembly through the hole in the floor.

25   Installation is the reverse of removal.

26   Adjust the parking brake (see Section 10).

Rear cable

27   Remove the rear wheel and the hub/drum assembly on the side of the vehicle the cable to be replaced is located (see Chapter 1).

28   Back off the adjusting nut **(see illustration 10.10)** until the cable is slack and detach the cable from the equalizer **(see illustration 10.12)**.

29   Disconnect the cable from the anchor bracket by sliding a 14 mm box wrench over the retainer end to compress the three fingers, then pulling the cable out.

30   Remove any cable wrap-around clips.

31   Detach the cable guide wires **(see illustration 11.21)**.

32   Disconnect the cable from the brake shoe lever.

33   Locate the retainer at the end of the rear cable, where it enters the brake shoe backing plate. Pinch this retainer with pliers (or use a hose clamp) and pull the cable through the backing plate and detach it from the bracket under the spring.

34   The above procedure also applies to the other rear cable.

35   Installation is the reverse of removal.

36   Adjust the parking brake (see Section 10).

12   Power brake booster – check, removal and installation

Note: *This procedure does not apply to ABS-equipped models.*

Operating check

1   Depress the brake pedal several times with the engine off and make sure there's no change in the pedal reserve distance.

2   Depress the pedal and start the engine. If the pedal goes down slightly, operation is normal.

Airtightness check

3   Start the engine and turn it off after one or two minutes. Slowly depress the brake pedal several times. If the pedal goes down farther the first time but gradually rises after the second or third depression, the booster is airtight.

4   Depress the brake pedal while the engine is running, then stop the engine with the pedal depressed. If there's no change in the pedal reserve travel (distance between the pedal and the floor) after holding the pedal for 30 seconds, the booster is airtight.

Removal and installation

5   Power brake booster units should not be disassembled. They require special tools not normally found in most service stations or shops. They're fairly complex and because of their critical relationship to brake performance it's best to replace a defective booster unit with a new or rebuilt one.

6   To remove the booster, first remove the brake master cylinder (see Section 7).

7   Disconnect the hose between the engine and the booster. Make sure you don't damage this hose when removing it from the booster fitting.

8   On vehicles with a manual transaxle, remove the clutch cable mounting bracket. Also push aside the wiring harness on the shock

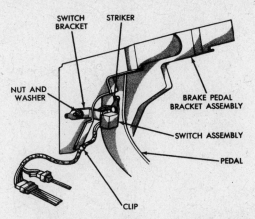

13.1   Installation details of the brake light switch

tower. If you need more room, unplug the harness at the bulkhead multi-connector.

9   Working under the dash, position a small screwdriver between the center tang on the retainer clip and the pin in the brake pedal, then rotate the screwdriver enough to allow the retainer clip center tang to pass over the end of the brake pedal pin and pull it from the pin. Disconnect the pushrod from the pedal pin. Discard the retainer clip and use a new one on reassembly.

10   Remove the nuts and washers holding the brake booster to the firewall. You may need a light to see them – they're up under the dash.

11   Slide the booster straight out until the studs clear the holes and lift it (along with any installed gaskets) out of the engine compartment.

12   Lubricate the bearing surfaces of the brake pedal pin and the tip of the pushrod with multi-purpose grease.

13   Install the booster, along with any previously installed gaskets. Connect the pushrod to the pedal pin and install a new retainer clip.

14   The remainder of installation is the reverse of the removal procedure. Tighten the booster mounting nuts to the torque listed in this Chapter's Specifications.

15   Adjust the brake light switch (see Section 13).

13   Brake light switch – check and replacement

Refer to illustration 13.1

1   The brake light switch **(see illustration)** is located under the

dash, at the upper end of the brake pedal assembly. A plunger on the switch is in constant contact with a striker at the top of the pedal assembly. When the pedal is depressed, the striker moves forward, releasing the plunger, which closes the circuit to the brake lights.

Check

Note: *Refer to the Wiring Diagrams at the end of Chapter 12.*

2   Use a test light to verify that there's voltage in the wire between the battery and the switch.
   a) If there isn't, find the short or open and fix it (see Chapter 12).
   b) If there is, proceed to the next Step.

3   Now use the test light to verify that there's no voltage in the wire between the switch and the brake lights when the brake pedal is not depressed.
   a) If there is, the switch is shorted – replace it (see below).
   b) If there isn't, proceed to the next Step.

4   Now depress the brake pedal and use the test light to verify that there's voltage in the wire between the switch and the brake lights.
   a) If there is, the switch itself is functioning normally – the problem is somewhere between the switch and the brake lights.
   b) If there isn't, the switch is has an open – replace it (see below).

Replacement

5   Unplug the electrical connector.

6   Grasp the switch securely and unplug it from the switch bracket.

7   To install the new switch, insert it into the switch bracket and plug in the electrical connector.

8   Push the switch forward as far as it will go. The brake pedal will move forward slightly.

9   Gently pull back on the brake pedal (very little movement is needed). This brings the plunger toward the switch until the brake pedal can't go any further. The switch then ratchets backward to the correct position. No further adjustment is necessary.

14   Anti-lock Brake System (ABS) – general information

Refer to illustrations 14.1a and 14.1b

Description

Some 1991 and later models have an Anti-Lock Brake System (ABS) designed to maintain vehicle maneuverability, directional stability and optimum deceleration under severe braking conditions on most road surfaces. It does so by monitoring the rotational speed of the wheels and controlling the brake line pressure to the wheels during braking. This prevents the wheels from locking up prematurely during hard braking.

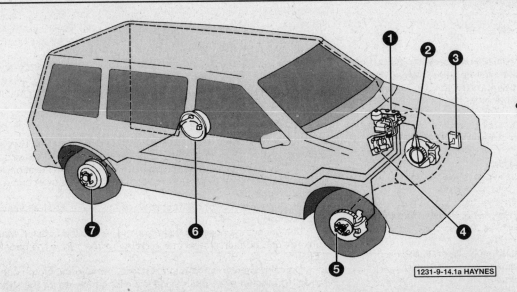

14.1a Anti-lock Brake System components (1991 through 1993)

1   *Integrated actuator, modulator asssembly*
2   *Wheel speed sensor*
3   *Electronic control unit*
4   *Motor pump assembly*
5   *Disc brakes*
6   *Wheel speed sensor*
7   *Drum brakes*

1231-9-14.1a HAYNES

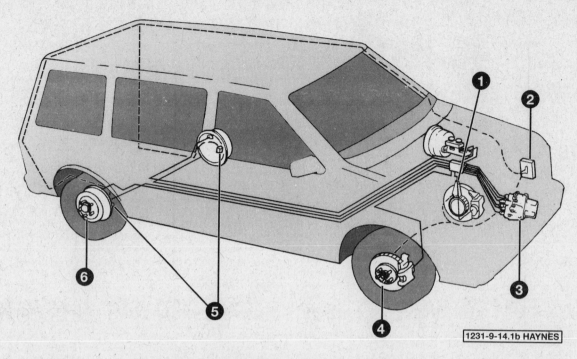

14.1b Anti-lock Brake System components (1994 and later)

1 Wheel speed sensor	3 Modulator assembly	5 Wheel speed sensor
2 Electronic control unit	4 Disc brakes	6 Drum brakes

Components
Pump

The pump, which is driven by an electric motor, provides high-pressure brake fluid to the hydraulic assembly, where it is stored in the hydraulic bladder accumulator.

Hydraulic assembly (1991 through 1993)

The integral hydraulic assembly includes a booster/master cylinder, modulator, hydraulic bladder accumulator and fluid reservoir. Basically, the assembly regulates hydraulic pressure (stored in the accumulator) to meet the demands of the braking system. The hydraulic assembly is located on the firewall on the driver's side of the vehicle **(see illustrations)**.

Modulator assembly (1994 and later)

The 1994 and later system uses a standard master cylinder and vacuum booster. The modulator assembly contains the electronic valves used for brake pressure modulation, the hydraulic brake fluid accumulators and the pump/motor assembly. The modulator assembly is located along the left front frame rail, underneath the battery.

Electronic control unit

The electronic control unit is mounted in the left front corner of the engine compartment and is the "brain" for the system. The function of the control unit is to accept and process information received from the wheel speed sensors to control the hydraulic line pressure, avoiding wheel lock up. The control unit also constantly monitors the system, even under normal driving conditions, to find faults with the system.

If a problem develops within the system, the Brake Warning light will glow on the dashboard. A diagnostic code will also be stored, which, when retrieved by a service technician, will indicate the problem area or component.

Wheel speed sensors

A speed sensor is mounted at each wheel. The speed sensors send signals to the electronic control unit indicating wheel rotational speed.

Diagnosis and repair

If the Brake Warning light on the dashboard comes on and stays on, make sure the parking brake is not applied and there's no problem with the brake hydraulic system. If neither of these is the cause the ABS system is probably malfunctioning. Although a special electronic tester is necessary to properly diagnose the system, the home mechanic can perform a few preliminary checks before taking the vehicle to a dealer service department which is equipped with this tester.

a) Make sure the brakes, calipers and wheel cylinders are in good condition.

b) Check the electrical connectors at the electronic control unit.

c) Check the fuses.

d   Follow the wiring harness to the speed sensors and brake light switch and make sure all connections are secure and the wiring isn't damaged.

If the above preliminary checks don't rectify the problem, the vehicle should be diagnosed by a dealer service department.

Chapter 10 Suspension and steering systems

Contents

Specifications

Torque specifications	Ft-lbs
Front suspension	
Balljoint clamp bolt/nut	
1990 and earlier	70
1991 and later	105
Driveaxle hub nut	See Chapter 8
Bolt-on hub unit bolt	45
Control arm	
Pivot bolt nut(s)	
1990 and earlier	105
1991 and later	125
Stub strut nut	70
Stabilizer bar bolts	
1990 and earlier	25
1991 and later	50
Strut assembly	
Strut-to-steering knuckle nuts	75
Upper mounting nuts	20

10

Rear suspension

Leaf spring
Rear shackle nuts	35
U-bolt nuts	60
Front pivot bolt nut	100
Front hanger-to-frame bolts.	45

Shock absorber mounting bolts
Upper	
1984	50
1985 and later	85
Lower	
1984	50
1985 and later	80

Sway bar
Bushing retainer-to-axle bracket bolts	45
Link arm-to-frame rail bracket bolt/nut	45
Link arm-to-bar bolt/nut	45
Link arm bracket-to-frame rail bolts	25
Spindle/brake assembly mounting bolts	80

Steering

Crossmember mounting bolts	90
Tie-rod end jam nut	55
Steering gear mounting bolts/nuts	
1988 and earlier	21
1989 and later	50
Steering wheel retaining nut	45
Tie-rod end-to-steering knuckle nut	35 to 38
Wheel lug nuts	See Chapter 1

1   General information

Refer to illustrations 1.1 and 1.2

Front suspension is by MacPherson struts. The steering knuckle is located by a control arm and both front control arms are connected by a stabilizer bar **(see illustration)**.

The rear suspension features a tubular axle with leaf springs **(see illustration)**. Damping is handled by vertically-mounted shock absorbers located between the axle and the chassis. Some later models are equipped with a rear stabilizer bar.

The rack-and-pinion steering gear is located behind the engine and actuates the steering arms which are integral with the steering knuckles. Power assist is optional and the steering column is designed to collapse in the event of an accident.

Note: These vehicles use a combination of standard and metric fasteners on the various suspension and steering components, so it would be a good idea to have both types of tools available when beginning work.

Frequently, when working on the suspension or steering system components, you may come across fasteners which seem impossible to loosen. These fasteners on the underside of the vehicle are continually subjected to water, road grime, mud, etc., and can become rusted or frozen, making them extremely difficult to remove. In order to unscrew these stubborn fasteners without damaging them (or other components), be sure to use lots of penetrating oil and allow it to soak in for a while. Using a wire brush to clean exposed threads will also ease removal of the nut or bolt and prevent damage to the threads. Sometimes a sharp blow with a hammer and punch will break the bond between a nut and bolt threads, but care must be taken to prevent the punch from slipping off the fastener and ruining the threads. Heating the stuck fastener and surrounding area with a torch sometimes helps too, but isn't recommended because of the obvious dangers associated with fire. Long breaker bars and extension, or "cheater", pipes will increase leverage, but never use an extension pipe on a ratchet – the ratcheting mechanism could be damaged. Sometimes tightening the nut or bolt first will help to break it loose. Fasteners that require drastic measures to remove should always be replaced with new ones.

Since most of the procedures dealt with in this Chapter involve jacking up the vehicle and working underneath it, a good pair of jackstands will be needed. A hydraulic floor jack is the preferred type of jack to lift the vehicle, and it can also be used to support certain components during various operations. **Warning:** *Never, under any circumstances, rely on a jack to support the vehicle while working on it. Whenever any of the suspension or steering fasteners are loosened or removed they must be inspected and, if necessary, replaced with new ones of the same part number or of original equipment quality and design. Torque specifications must be followed for proper reassembly and component retention. Never attempt to heat or straighten any suspension or steering components. Instead, replace any bent or damaged part with a new one.*

2   Strut assembly – removal and installation

Refer to illustrations 2.3, 2.5, 2.6

1   Loosen the front wheel lug nuts.

2   Raise the vehicle and support it securely on jackstands. Remove the front wheels.

3   Mark the relationship of the cam bolt to the steering knuckle **(see illustration)**.

4   Remove the strut-to-steering knuckle nuts, bolts and washer plate.

5   Disconnect the brake hose bracket from the strut **(see illustration)**.

6   Remove the upper mounting nuts **(see illustration)**, disengage the strut from the steering knuckle and detach it from the vehicle.

7   Inspect the strut and coil spring assembly for leaking fluid, dents, damage and corrosion. If the strut is leaking or damaged, see Section 3.

8   To install the strut, place it in position with the studs extending up through the shock tower. Install the nuts and tighten them to the torque listed in this Chapter's Specifications.

9   Attach the strut to the steering knuckle, then insert the strut-to-steering knuckle bolts and washer plate.

10   Align the marks you made on the knuckle and strut. Install the

1.1 Front suspension components

1 Steering arm
2 Strut assembly
3 Stabilizer bar
4 Power steering lines
5 Steering gear
6 Control arm

10

1.2 Rear suspension components

1   Leaf spring   2   Shock absorber   3   Axle

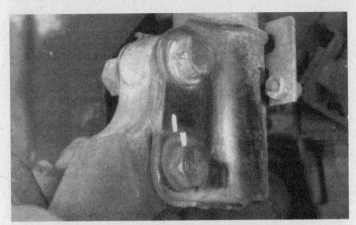

2.3   Paint or scribe an alignment mark across the cam bolt and the knuckle itself to ensure proper realignment of the strut and knuckle on reassembly

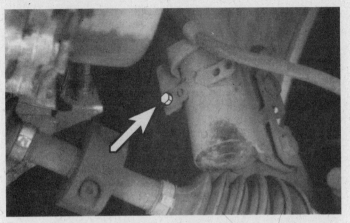

2.5   Remove this bolt (arrow) and detach the brake hose bracket from the strut

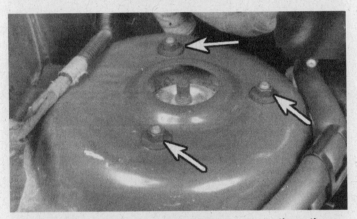

2.6   Working in the engine compartment, remove these three upper mounting nuts (arrows)

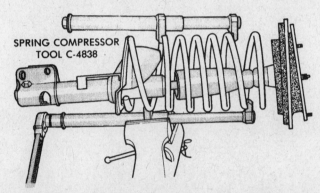

3.4   Install the spring compressor in accordance with the tool manufacturer's instructions and compress the spring until all pressure is relieved from the upper spring seat

nuts on the strut-to-steering knuckle bolts and tighten them to the torque listed in this Chapter's Specifications.

11   Attach the brake hose bracket to the strut.

12   Install the wheels and lower the vehicle. It would be a good idea to have the front wheel alignment checked by an alignment shop.

3   Strut – replacement

Refer to illustrations 3.4, 3.5 and 3.6

Note: *You'll need a spring compressor for this procedure. Spring compressors are available on a daily rental basis at most auto parts stores or equipment yards.*

1   If the struts or coil springs exhibit the telltale signs of wear (leaking fluid, loss of damping capability, chipped, sagging or cracked coil springs) explore all options before beginning any work. The strut insert assemblies are not serviceable and must be replaced if a problem develops. However, strut assemblies complete with springs may be available on an exchange basis, which eliminates much time and work. Whichever route you choose to take, check on the cost and availability of parts before disassembling your vehicle. **Warning:** *Disassembling a strut assembly is a potentially dangerous undertaking and utmost attention must be directed to the job at hand, or serious bodily injury may result. Use only a high-quality spring compressor and carefully follow the manufacturer's instructions furnished with the tool. After removing the coil spring from the strut assembly, set it aside in a safe, isolated area (a steel cabinet is preferred).*

2   Remove the strut and spring assembly (see Section 2).

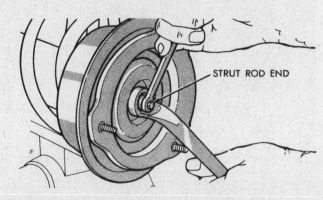

3.5   To remove the damper shaft nut, hold the shaft in place with a box wrench and loosen the nut with another box wrench

3   Mount the strut assembly in a vise. Line the vise jaws with wood or rags to prevent damage to the unit and don't tighten the vise excessively.

4   Install the spring compressor in accordance with the manufacturer's instructions **(see illustration)**. Compress the spring until you can wiggle the mount assembly and spring seat.

5   To loosen the damper shaft nut, hold the shaft with a box-end wrench while loosening the shaft nut with another box-end wrench **(see illustration)**.

10

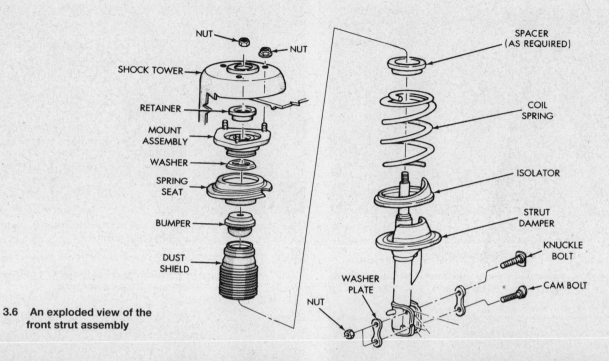

**3.6   An exploded view of the
front strut assembly**

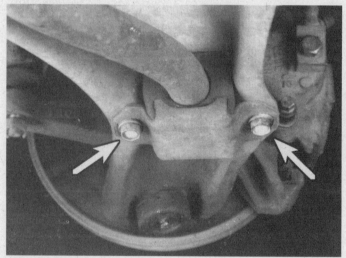

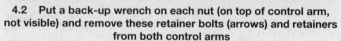

**4.2   Put a back-up wrench on each nut (on top of control arm,
not visible) and remove these retainer bolts (arrows) and retainers
from both control arms**

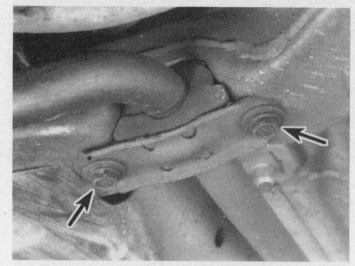

**4.3   Remove these clamp bolts (arrows) and both clamps from
the crossmember**

6   Disassemble the strut assembly and lay out the parts in exactly the same order as shown **(see illustration)**. **Warning:** *When removing the compressed spring, lift it off very carefully and set it in a safe place, such as a steel cabinet. Keep the ends of the spring away from your body.*

7   Inspect all rubber parts for damage, cracking and hardness and replace as necessary.

8   Reassembly is the reverse of disassembly. Be careful not to damage the damper shaft or the strut will leak. When installing the spring, be sure the spring ends mesh with the spring anti-rotation stops provided by the spring upper and lower seats.

4   Front stabilizer bar – removal and installation

Refer to illustrations 4.2 and 4.3

1   Loosen the front wheel lug nuts, raise the front of the vehicle, support it securely on jackstands and remove the front wheels.

2   Remove the stabilizer bar retainer bolts, nuts and retainers from the control arms **(see illustration)**.

3   Support the stabilizer bar and remove the stabilizer bar clamp bolts and clamps from the crossmember **(see illustration)**. Remove the stabilizer bar from the vehicle.

4   Check the bar for damage, corrosion and signs of twisting.

5   Check the clamps, bushings and retainers for distortion, damage and wear. Replace the inner bushings by prying them open at the split and removing them. Install the new bushings with the curved surface up and the split facing toward the front of the vehicle. The outer bushings can be removed by cutting them off or hammering them from the bar. Force the new bushings onto the end of the bar until 1/2-inch of the bar is protruding. Silicone spray lubricant will ease this process.

6   Attach the bar to the crossmember, then install the clamps, bolts and nuts, but don't tighten them completely yet.

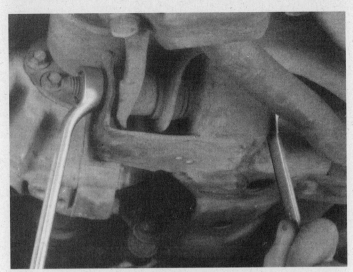

5.3 Use a back-up wrench to remove the pivot bolt and nut from the front of the control arm

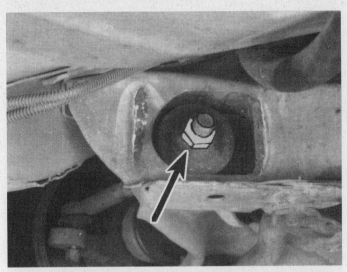

5.4a On earlier models, remove this nut (arrow) from the stub strut at the rear of the control arm

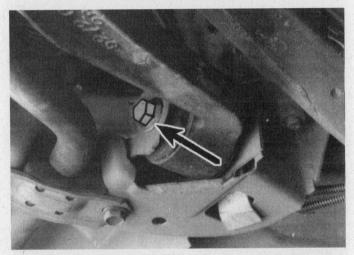

5.4b On later models, remove this through bolt from the rear of the control arm

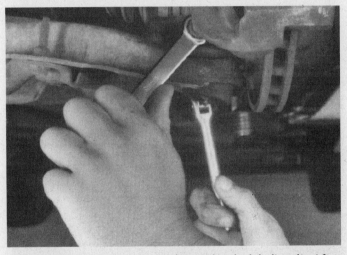

5.5 Using a back-up wrench, remove the pinch bolt and nut for the balljoint stud clamp at the bottom of the steering knuckle, then pull the control arm down to separate the stud from the knuckle

7   Install the bushing retainers and bolts on the control arms, but don't tighten the bolts completely yet.
8   Raise the control arms to normal ride height and tighten the bolts to the torque listed in this Chapter's Specifications.
9   Install the wheels and lower the vehicle.

5   Control arm – removal, inspection and installation

Refer to illustrations 5.3, 5.4a, 5.4b, 5.5, 5.9a and 5.9b

1   Raise the front of the vehicle, support it securely on jackstands and remove the front wheels.
2   Disconnect the stabilizer bar from the control arms (see Section 4) and rotate the bar down, out of the way.
3   Remove the front pivot bolt and nut from the control arm **(see illustration)**.
4   On earlier models, remove the rear stub strut nut, retainer and bushing **(see illustration)** from the control arm; on later models, remove the rear pivot bolt and nut **(see illustration)** from the control arm.

5   Remove the balljoint pinch bolt and nut from the steering knuckle **(see illustration)**.
6   Pull the balljoint stud from the steering knuckle. **Caution:** *Do not move the steering knuckle/strut assembly out or you may separate the inner CV joint.*
7   Remove the control arm by pulling it down and forward (earlier models) or straight down (later models).
8   Inspect the control arm for distortion and the bushings for wear, damage and deterioration. If the control arm is damaged or bent, replace it. If an inner pivot bushing or a balljoint are worn, have them replaced by a dealer service department or repair shop with the special tools necessary to do the job. **Note:** *Some bushings are not serviceable and the entire control arm must be replaced if the bushings are worn.* You can replace damaged or worn stub strut bushings yourself. Simply slide them off the strut and slide on the replacements.
9   Installation is the reverse of removal **(see illustrations)**. Don't tighten the pivot bolt(s) and stub strut nut until the vehicle is at normal ride height.
10   After you've installed the wheels and lowered the vehicle so that its weight is on the suspension, tighten the pivot bolt and stub strut nuts to the torque listed in this Chapter's Specifications.

10

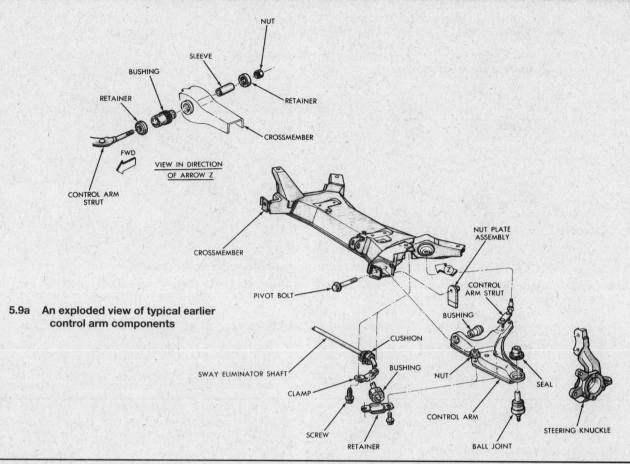

5.9a   An exploded view of typical earlier control arm components

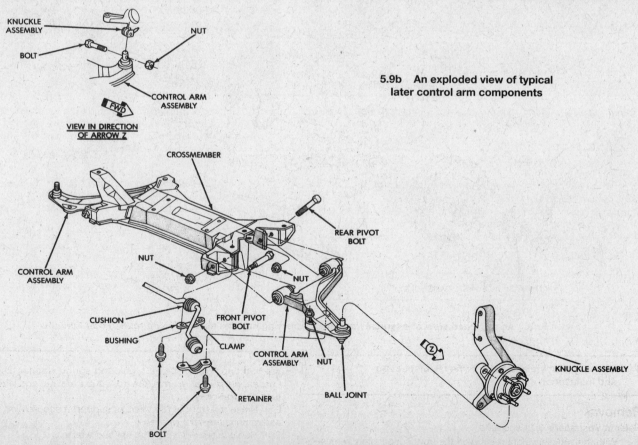

5.9b   An exploded view of typical later control arm components

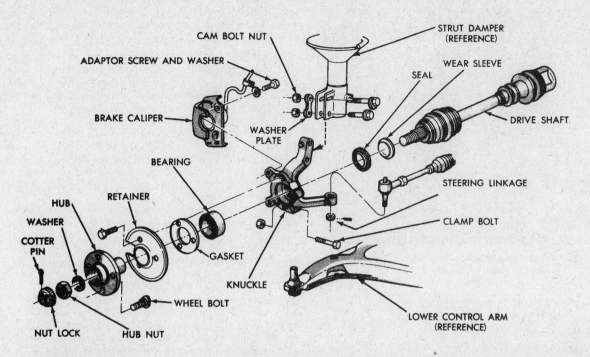

6.1a   An exploded view of a typical earlier model steering knuckle assembly and related components

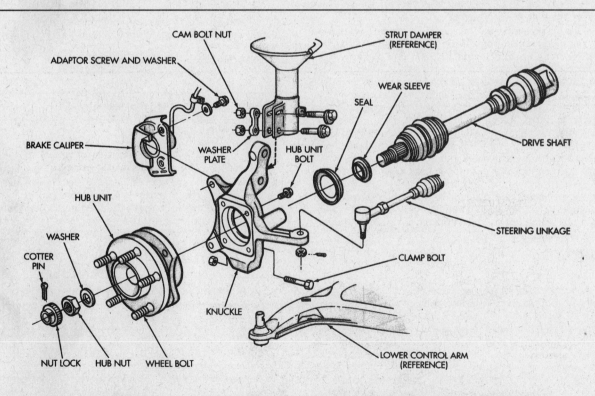

6.1b   An exploded view of a typical later model steering knuckle assembly and related components

---

6   Steering knuckle and hub – removal, inspection and installation

Removal

Refer to illustrations 6.1a and 6.1b

1   With the vehicle weight resting on the front suspension, remove the hub cap, cotter pin, nut lock and spring washer (if equipped). Loosen, but do not remove, the front hub (axle) nut and wheel lug nuts **(see illustrations)**.

2   Raise the front of the vehicle, support it securely on jackstands and remove the front wheels.

3   Remove the driveaxle hub nut and washer.

7.2   Try to lever the steering knuckle from side to side with a prybar or large screwdriver

4   Push the driveaxle in until it is free of the hub. It may be necessary to tap on the axle end with a brass drift punch and hammer to dislodge the driveaxle from the hub.

5   Remove the cotter pin and loosen the nut and use a puller to disconnect the tie-rod end from the steering knuckle (see Section 14).

6   Move the tie-rod out of the way and secure it with a piece of wire.

7   Disconnect the brake hose bracket from the strut by removing the bolt and retainer **(see illustration 2.5)**

8   Remove the caliper and brake pads (see Chapter 9), then remove the caliper mounting bracket from the steering knuckle. Taking care not to twist the brake hose, hang the caliper out of the way in the wheel well with a piece of wire.

9   Detach the stabilizer bar retainer bolts from the control arms (see Section 4) and pull the stabilizer bar down and out of the way.

10   Remove the retainer washer (if equipped) from the wheel stud and pull off the brake disc.

11   Mark the strut-to-steering knuckle relationship (see Section 2).

12   Remove the balljoint pinch bolt and nut and disengage the balljoint from the hub (see Section 5).

13   Remove the steering knuckle-to-strut bolts and nuts (see Section 5).

14   With the knuckle and hub assembly in the straight-ahead position, grasp it securely and pull it directly out and off the driveaxle splines. **Caution:** *Be careful not to pull the driveaxle out or you may disengage the inner CV joint.*

Inspection

Pressed-in bearing

15   Place the assembly on a clean work surface and wipe it off with a lint-free cloth. Inspect the knuckle for rust, damage and cracks. Check the bearings by rotating them to make sure they move freely. The bearings should be packed with an adequate supply of clean grease. If there is too little grease, or if the grease is contaminated with dirt, clean the bearings and inspect them for wear, scoring and looseness. Repack the bearings with the specified lubricant. Inspect the grease seals to make sure they are not torn or leaking. Further disassembly will have to be left to your dealer service department or a repair shop because of the special tools required.

Bolt-on bearing unit

16   Some later model long-wheelbase models use a sealed bolt-in front hub unit. Check the hub unit by rotating it to make sure it moves freely. If the hub is damaged, corroded, or doesn't turn easily, remove the four bolts and lift the hub unit off the knuckle. Make sure the recess in the knuckle is clean and free of nicks, corrosion and other damage. Place the new hub and bearing unit in position and install the bolts. Tighten the bolts in a criss-cross pattern to the torque listed in

this Chapter's Specifications. The manufacturer recommends that a new seal be installed on the back side of the knuckle whenever the hub unit is replaced.

Installation

17   Prior to installation, clean the CV joint seal and the hub grease seal with solvent (don't get any solvent on the CV joint boot). Lubricate the entire circumference of the CV joint wear sleeve and seal contact surface with multi-purpose grease (see Chapter 8).

18   Carefully place the knuckle and hub assembly in position. Align the splines of the axle and the hub and slide the hub into place.

19   Install the knuckle-to-strut bolts and nuts, followed by the balljoint pinch bolt and nut. Adjust the knuckle so that the marks you made between the strut and the knuckle are aligned. Install the washer plate and nuts and tighten the nuts to the torque listed in this Chapter's Specifications.

20   Reattach the tie-rod end to the steering knuckle, tighten the nut and install a new cotter pin (see Section 14).

21   Install the brake disc, pads and caliper/adapter assembly (see Chapter 9).

22   Reattach the brake hose bracket to the strut.

23   Attach the ends of the stabilizer bar to the control arms and tighten the retainer fasteners to the torque listed in this Chapter's Specifications.

24   Push the CV joint completely into the hub to make sure it is seated and install the washer and hub nut finger tight.

25   Install the wheels, hand tighten the lug nuts, lower the vehicle and tighten the wheel lug nuts to the torque specified in Chapter 1.

26   With an assistant applying the brakes, tighten the hub nut to the torque specified in Chapter 8. Install the spring washer, nut lock and a new cotter pin.

27   With the weight of the vehicle on the suspension, check the steering knuckle and balljoint nuts to make sure they are tightened properly.

28   Have the vehicle front end alignment checked.

---

7   Balljoints – check and replacement

Refer to illustration 7.2

1   The suspension balljoints are designed to operate without freeplay.

2   To check for wear, place a prybar or large screwdriver between the control arm and the underside of the steering knuckle and try to lever the knuckle from side to side **(see illustration)**.

3   If there is any movement, the balljoint is worn and must be replaced with a new one. Remove the control arm (see Section 5) and take it to a dealer service department or automotive machine shop to have the old balljoint pressed out and a new one pressed in.

---

8   Rear shock absorbers – removal and installation

Refer to illustrations 8.2, 8.3a and 8.3b

Removal

1   Loosen the wheel lug nuts, raise the rear of the vehicle and support it securely on jackstands.

2   Support the axle with jack and remove the rear wheels **(see illustration)**.

3   Remove the lower and upper shock mounting bolts **(see illustrations)** and detach the shock absorber.

Installation

4   Hold the new shock absorber in position and install the bolts. Tighten the upper bolt to the torque listed in this Chapter's Specifications and the lower bolt snugly. Remove the jack, lower the vehicle and tighten the lower bolt to the torque listed in this Chapter's Specifications.

8.2   When removing the shock absorbers, the axle must be raised slightly to remove tension from the shocks – this is easily done with a jack

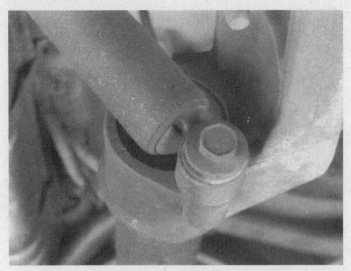

8.3a   Remove the lower shock absorber bolt . . .

8.3b   . . . followed by the upper bolt

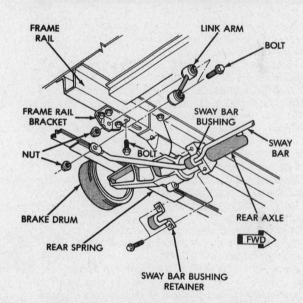

11.2   To remove the sway bar, remove the lower bolt from each link arm, loosen the two bolts on each bushing retainer, support the sway bar and remove the retainer bolts

---

9   Rear hub/drum assembly – removal and installation

This procedure is covered in Chapter 1 as a part of the *Rear wheel bearing check, repack and adjustment* procedure.

---

10   Rear spindle – inspection, removal and installation

Removal

1   Remove the rear hub/drum (see Section 9).
2   Clean the axle and inspect the bearing contact surfaces for wear and damage.
3   The spindle should be replaced with a new one if it is bent, damaged or worn.
4   Disconnect the parking brake cable from the brake assembly (see Chapter 9).
5   Disconnect and plug the rear brake line at the wheel cylinder (see Chapter 9).
6   Remove the four backing plate mounting bolts and detach the brake assembly and spindle. The bolts may have Torx-type heads, which require a special tool for removal. Be sure to mark the location of any spindle shims.

Installation

7   Place the shim(s) (if equipped), spindle and brake assembly in position, install the bolts and tighten them to the torque listed in this Chapter's Specifications, following a criss-cross pattern.
8   Connect the brake line and parking brake cable.
9   Install the hub/drum (see Section 9), bleed the brakes and adjust the parking brake (see Chapter 9).

---

11   Rear sway bar (1991 and later models) – removal and installation

Refer to illustration 11.2

Removal

1   Raise the rear of the vehicle and support it securely on jack-stands.
2   Remove the two lower sway bar link arm bolts **(see illustration)**.
3   Loosen the four sway bar bushing retainer bolts.

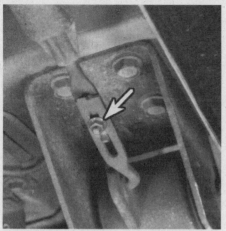

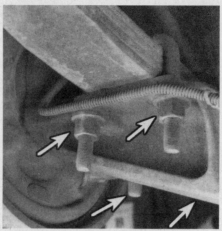

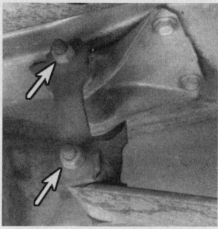

12.3   Mark the nut location (arrow), remove the nut and bolt, then disconnect the proportioning valve link

12.5   Remove the U-bolt nuts (arrows)

12.7   Remove the spring shackle nuts (arrows)

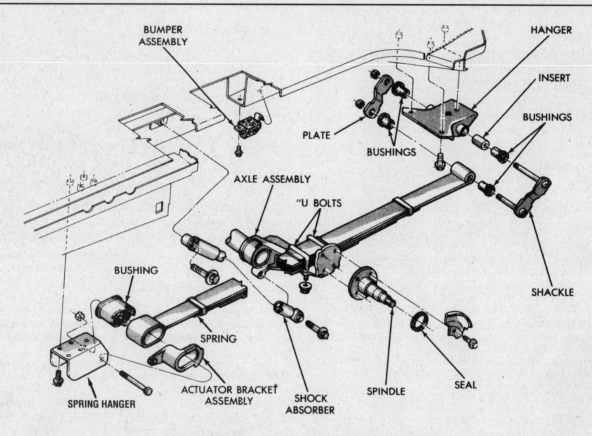

12.8   Rear spring and axle assembly installation details

4   Hold the sway bar in place, remove the bushing retainer bolts, then lower the sway bar from the vehicle.

Installation

5   Connect the link arms with the bolts finger tight.
6   Place the sway bar in position on the axle with the slits in the bushings facing up and install the bolts finger tight.
7   Lower the vehicle weight onto the suspension and tighten the bolts to the torque listed in the Specifications Section at the beginning of this Chapter.

12   Rear leaf springs and axle – removal and installation

Refer to illustrations 12.3, 12.5, 12.7 and 12.8

Removal

1   Loosen the rear wheel lug nuts, raise the rear of the vehicle and support it securely on jackstands. Remove the rear wheels.
2   Jack up the rear axle slightly, just until the weight is off the rear springs, then support the axle at this height with jackstands.

13.3   Turn the center pad over and unplug the horn wires (arrows)

13.4   After you've removed the steering wheel nut, mark the relationship of the steering wheel hub to the shaft to ensure proper alignment at reassembly

13.5   Use a bolt-type puller like this one to remove the steering wheel

3   If the springs are being removed, disconnect the brake proportioning valve link from the left side spring (see illustration). If you're removing the rear axle, disconnect the parking brake cables and brake hoses from the axle (see Chapter 9).
4   Remove the bolts from the lower ends of the shock absorbers.
5   Remove the nuts and detach the U-bolts (see illustration).
6   Lower the rear axle, allowing the springs to hang free.
7   Remove the nuts and detach the spring shackles (see illustration).
8   Remove the front spring hanger bolts and lower the springs from the vehicle (see illustration).

Installation

9   Raise the front ends of the springs into position and install the spring hanger bolts. Tighten the bolts to the torque listed in this Chapter's Specifications. Connect the brake proportioning valve link to the marked position.
10   Raise the rear end of the spring into place and connect the shackles, with the nuts finger tight.
11   Raise the axle with the jack until it is centered under the center bolt, install the U-bolts, plate and nuts. Tighten the nuts to the torque listed in this Chapter's Specifications.
12   Connect the lower ends of the shock absorbers and install the bolts finger tight. Connect the brake hoses and cables, if disconnected. Install the wheels.
13   Lower the vehicle weight onto the suspension and tighten the front pivot bolt (if loosened), shock absorber bolts and shackle nuts to the torques listed in this Chapter's Specifications.
14   If the brake hoses were disconnected, bleed the brakes (see Chapter 9).

13   Steering wheel – removal and installation

Warning: 1991 and later models are equipped with an air bag. To avoid possible damage to this system, on these models the following procedure should be left to a dealer service department because of the special tools and techniques required.

Refer to illustrations 13.3, 13.4 and 13.5

1   Disconnect the negative cable at the battery. Place the cable out of the way so it cannot accidentally come in contact with the negative terminal of the battery, as this would once again allow power into the electrical system of the vehicle.
2   Disconnect the center pad assembly by unscrewing the two screws at the back of the steering wheel.

14.2a   To disconnect the tie-rod end from the steering knuckle, remove the cotter pin and loosen the castellated nut, . . .

3   Disconnect the horn wires and remove the center pad assembly (see illustration).
4   Remove the steering wheel retaining nut and mark the relationship of the steering shaft and hub to simplify installation (see illustration).
5   Use a bolt-type puller to remove the steering wheel (see illustration). **Caution:** *Do not hammer on the shaft to remove the steering wheel.*
6   To install the wheel, align the mark on the steering wheel hub with the mark made on the shaft during removal and slip the wheel onto the shaft. Install the hub nut (and damper if removed) and tighten it to the torque listed in this Chapter's Specifications.
7   Install the center pad assembly.
8   Connect the negative battery cable.

14   Tie-rod ends – removal and installation

Refer to illustrations 14.2a, 14.2b, 14.3a and 14.3b

1   Raise the front of the vehicle, support it securely on jackstands, block the rear wheels and set the parking brake. Remove the front wheels.
2   Remove the tie-rod-to-steering knuckle cotter pin, loosen the nut, then disconnect the tie-rod from the steering knuckle with a puller (see illustrations).

10

14.2b . . . install a puller and separate the tie-rod end from the knuckle; note how the nut is still in place, loosened a few turns – this will prevent the components from separating violently

14.3a Using a back-up wrench on the tie-rod end, loosen the jam nut with another wrench . . .

14.3b . . . then paint an alignment mark on the threads of the tie-rod to mark the position of the tie-rod end

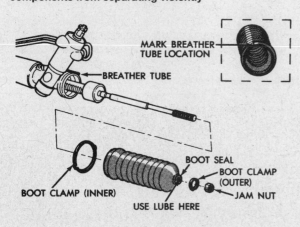

MARK BREATHER TUBE LOCATION

BREATHER TUBE

BOOT SEAL

BOOT CLAMP (OUTER)

BOOT CLAMP (INNER)

USE LUBE HERE

JAM NUT

15.4 Steering gear boot replacement details

3   Loosen the jam nut (**see illustration**), mark the position of the tie-rod end on the tie-rod (**see illustration**), unscrew the tie-rod end and remove it.
4   To install the tie-rod end, thread it onto the rod to the marked position and tighten the jam nut securely.
5   Connect the tie-rod end to the steering knuckle, install the nut and tighten it to the torque listed in this Chapter's Specifications. Install a new cotter pin.
6   Have the front end alignment checked by a dealer service department or an alignment shop.

---

15   Steering gear boots – replacement

Refer to illustration 15.4
1   Raise the vehicle and support it securely on jackstands.
2   Remove the tie-rod end (see Section 14).
3   Remove the boot clamp(s).
4   Mark the location of the breather tube on the boot (if the same boot will be reinstalled), use a small screwdriver to lift the boot out of the groove in the steering gear and remove the boot (**see illustration**).
5   Prior to installation, lubricate the boot groove for the steering tie-rod with silicone-type grease.
6   Slide the new boot into position on the steering gear until it seats in the groove and install a new inner clamp. Make sure the breather tube fits securely in the boot.

7   Install the clamp(s).
8   Install the tie-rod end.
9   Lower the vehicle.
10   Have the front end alignment checked by a dealer service department or an alignment shop.

---

16   Steering gear – removal and installation

Warning: On air bag-equipped models, always disconnect the negative battery cable when working in the vicinity of the instrument panel or steering column to avoid the possibility of accidental deployment of the airbag, which could cause personal injury.

Removal

Refer to illustrations 16.3, 16.7 and 16.8
1   Loosen the wheel lug nuts, raise the vehicle, support it securely on jackstands and remove the front wheels.
2   Disconnect the tie-rod ends from the steering knuckles (see Section 14).
3   Support the front crossmember with a jack (**see illustration**). Disconnect the engine damper strut from the crossmember (if so equipped).
4   Remove the four bolts holding the crossmember to the body.
5   Lower the jack and crossmember far enough to gain access to the U-joint between the steering input shaft and the intermediate shaft of the steering column.
6   Remove the boot that protects the U-joint. Mark the relationship of the U-joint to the intermediate shaft so it can be re-connected the same way. Remove the pinch bolt from the U-joint. Lower the crossmember a little farther to separate the U-joint from the intermediate shaft (the U-joint stays with the steering gear).
7   On power-steering-equipped models, disconnect the lines (**see illustration**) and drain the fluid into a container.
8   Remove the steering gear mounting bolts (**see illustration**) and separate it from the crossmember by withdrawing it to the left side of the vehicle.

Installation

9   Position the steering gear on the crossmember, install the steering gear mounting bolts and tighten them securely.
10   Raise the crossmember and steering gear into position with the jack.
11   On power steering equipped models, reconnect the lines. Use new O-rings on the fittings.

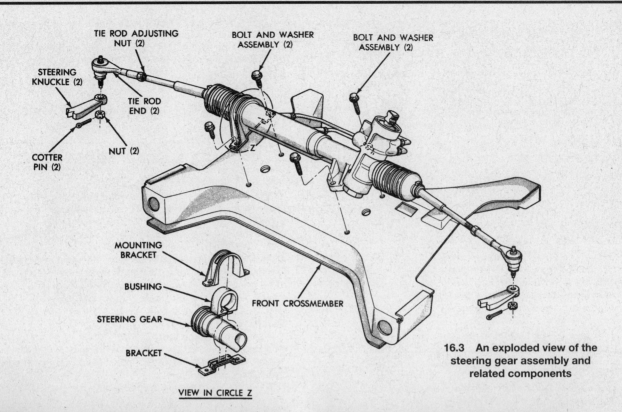

TIE ROD ADJUSTING NUT (2)

STEERING KNUCKLE (2)

TIE ROD END (2)

COTTER PIN (2)

NUT (2)

BOLT AND WASHER ASSEMBLY (2)

BOLT AND WASHER ASSEMBLY (2)

MOUNTING BRACKET

BUSHING

STEERING GEAR

BRACKET

FRONT CROSSMEMBER

VIEW IN CIRCLE Z

16.3   An exploded view of the steering gear assembly and related components

16.7   On models with power steering, disconnect these two line fittings (arrows) – the lower arrow points at one of the two driver's side mounting bolts for the steering gear (the other one, not visible in this photo, is right behind it, on the back side of the steering gear assembly)

16.8   The two passenger's side steering gear mounting bolts (arrows)

12   Connect the U-joint to the intermediate shaft, aligning the marks made on disassembly.
13   Install the U-joint pinch bolt.
14   Install the U-joint boot.
15   Install the four crossmember bolts – starting with the right rear bolt, which is the pilot bolt – and tighten them securely. Connect the engine damper strut (if so equipped).
16   Attach the tie-rod ends to the steering knuckles (see Section 14).
17   Install the front wheels and lower the vehicle.
18   On power steering equipped models, start the engine and bleed the steering system (see Section 18). While the engine is running, check for leaks at the hose connections.
19   Have the front end alignment checked by a dealer service department or an alignment shop.

17   Power steering pump – removal and installation

Note: *Metric fasteners are used on the power steering pump.*

Models with 2.6L engine

1   Open the hood and place a container under the pump for fluid to drain into. Disconnect and plug the power steering pump hoses at the pump. Plug the pump ports.
2   Loosen the pump pivot and adjustment bolts and detach the drivebelt (see Chapter 1).
3   Remove the bolts from the pump mounting bracket and lift the pump and bracket from the engine compartment
4   Installation is the reverse of removal. Use new O-rings at the hose connections.

10

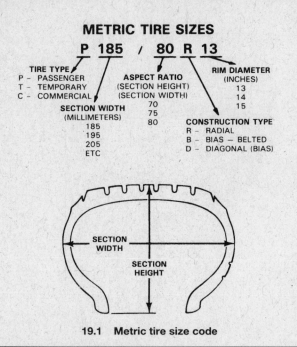

METRIC TIRE SIZES

P 185 / 80 R 13

TIRE TYPE
P – PASSENGER
T – TEMPORARY
C – COMMERCIAL

ASPECT RATIO
(SECTION HEIGHT)
(SECTION WIDTH)
70
75
80

SECTION WIDTH
(MILLIMETERS)
185
195
205
ETC

RIM DIAMETER
(INCHES)
13
14
15

CONSTRUCTION TYPE
R – RADIAL
B – BIAS – BELTED
D – DIAGONAL (BIAS)

SECTION WIDTH

SECTION HEIGHT

19.1   Metric tire size code

All other models

5   Open the hood and disconnect the two wires from the air conditioner clutch cycling switch (if equipped).
6   On models so equipped, loosen and remove the drivebelt adjusting lock screw from the front of the pump.
7   Raise the vehicle and support it securely on jackstands.
8   Disconnect the pump return hose and drain the fluid from the pump into a container.
9   While the pump is draining, remove the right side splash shield that protects the drivebelts.
10   Disconnect both hoses from the pump. Cap all open hose ends to prevent contamination.
11   Loosen the two lower pump mounting fasteners – a bolt and a stud nut, disconnect the drivebelt, then remove the fasteners.
12   To remove the pump, move it rearward to clear the mounting bracket, then remove the bracket. Then rotate the pump clockwise until the pump pulley faces toward the rear of the vehicle and pull the pump up and out.
13   Installation is the reverse of removal. Make sure the tab on the mounting bracket is in the lower left front mounting hole. Be sure to use new O-rings when you attach the hoses to the pump. Don't tighten the fasteners until you've adjusted the belt tension.

All models

14   Adjust the belt to the proper tension (see Chapter l) and tighten the fasteners.
15   Fill the pump with the specified fluid (see Chapter 1).
16   Start the engine, bleed the air from the system (see Section 18) and check the fluid level.

18   Power steering system – bleeding

1   Following any operation where the power steering fluid lines have been disconnected, the power steering system must be bled to remove all air and obtain proper steering performance.
2   With the front wheels in the straight-ahead position, check the power steering fluid level (see Chapter 1). If it's low, add fluid.
3   Start the engine and allow it to run at fast idle. Recheck the fluid level and add more, if necessary.
4   Bleed the system by turning the wheels from side-to-side, without hitting the stops. This will work the air out of the system. Keep the reservoir full of fluid as this is done.
5   When the air is worked out of the system, return the wheels to the straight-ahead position and leave the vehicle running for several more minutes before shutting it off.
6   Road test the vehicle to make sure the steering system is functioning normally and noise free.
7   Recheck the fluid level to make sure it's correct (see Chapter 1).

19   Wheels and tires – general information

Refer to illustration 19.1

All vehicles covered by this manual are equipped with metric-size fiberglass or steel-belted radial tires **(see illustration)**. The installation of different size or other type tires may affect the ride and handling of the vehicle. Don't mix different types of tires, such as radials and bias belted, on the same vehicle; handling may be seriously affected. Always try to replace tires in pairs on the same axle. However, if only one tire is being replaced, be sure it's the same size, structure and tread design as the other. Because tire pressure has a substantial effect on handling and wear, the pressure in all tires should be checked at least once a month or before any extended trips (see Chapter 1).

Wheels must be replaced if they're bent, dented, leak air, have elongated bolt holes, are heavily rusted, out of vertical symmetry or if the lug nuts won't stay tight. Wheel repairs by welding or peening aren't recommended.

Tire and wheel balance is important to the overall handling, braking and performance of the vehicle. Unbalanced wheels can adversely affect handling and ride characteristics as well as tire life. Whenever a tire is installed on a wheel, the tire and wheel should be balanced by a shop with the proper equipment.

20   Front end alignment – general information

A front end alignment refers to the adjustments made to the front wheels so they're in proper angular relationship to the suspension and the ground. Front wheels that are out of proper alignment not only affect steering control, but also increase tire wear. The front end adjustments normally required are camber and toe-in.

Getting the proper front wheel alignment is a very exacting process in which complicated and expensive machines are necessary to perform the job properly. Because of this, you should have a technician with the proper equipment perform these tasks. We will, however, use this space to give you a basic idea of what's involved with front end alignment so you can better understand the process and deal intelligently with the shop that does the work.

Toe-in is the turning in of the front wheels. The purpose of a toe specification is to ensure parallel rolling of the front wheels. In a vehicle with zero toe-in, the distance between the front edges of the wheels will be the same as the distance between the rear edges of the wheels. The actual amount of toe-in is normally only a fraction of an inch. Toe-in adjustment is controlled by the positions of the tie-rod ends on the tie-rods. Incorrect toe-in will cause the tires to wear improperly by making them scrub against the road surface.

Camber is the tilting of the front wheels from vertical when viewed from the front of the vehicle. When the wheels tilt out at the top, the camber is said to be positive (+). When the wheels tilt in at the top the camber is negative (-). The amount of tilt is measured in degrees from vertical – this measurement is called the camber angle. This angle affects the amount of tire tread contacting the road and compensates for changes in the suspension geometry when the vehicle is cornering or travelling over an undulating surface. Camber is adjusted with a cam bolt at each strut-to-steering knuckle joint.

Caster is the tilting of the top of the front steering axis from vertical. A tilt toward the rear is positive caster and a tilt toward the front is negative caster. Caster isn't adjustable on these vehicles.

Chapter 11   Body

Contents

1   General information

These models feature a "unibody" layout, using a floor pan with front and rear frame side rails which support the body components, front and rear suspension systems and other mechanical components. Certain components are particularly vulnerable to accident damage and can be unbolted and repaired or replaced. Among these parts are the body moldings, bumpers, the hood and trunk lids and all glass. Only general body maintenance practices and body panel repair procedures within the scope of the do-it-yourselfer are included in this Chapter.

2   Body – maintenance

1   The condition of your vehicle's body is very important, because the resale value depends a great deal on it. It's much more difficult to repair a neglected or damaged body than it is to repair mechanical components. The hidden areas of the body, such as the wheel wells, the frame and the engine compartment, are equally important, although they don't require as frequent attention as the rest of the body.
2   Once a year, or every 12,000 miles, it's a good idea to have the underside of the body steam cleaned. All traces of dirt and oil will be removed and the area can then be inspected carefully for rust, damaged brake lines, frayed electrical wires, damaged cables and other problems. The front suspension components should be greased after completion of this job.

3   At the same time, clean the engine and the engine compartment with a steam cleaner or water-soluble degreaser.
4   The wheel wells should be given close attention, since undercoating can peel away and stones and dirt thrown up by the tires can cause the paint to chip and flake, allowing rust to set in. If rust is found, clean down to the bare metal and apply an anti-rust paint.
5   The body should be washed about once a week. Wet the vehicle thoroughly to soften the dirt, then wash it down with a soft sponge and plenty of clean soapy water. If the surplus dirt is not washed off very carefully, it can wear down the paint.
6   Spots of tar or asphalt thrown up from the road should be removed with a cloth soaked in solvent.
7   Once every six months, wax the body and chrome trim. If a chrome cleaner is used to remove rust from any of the vehicle's plated parts, remember that the cleaner also removes part of the chrome, so use it sparingly.

3   Vinyl trim – maintenance

Don't clean vinyl trim with detergents, caustic soap or petroleum-based cleaners. Plain soap and water works just fine, with a soft brush to clean dirt that may be ingrained. Wash the vinyl as frequently as the rest of the vehicle. After cleaning, application of a high-quality rubber and vinyl protectant will help prevent oxidation and cracks. The protectant can also be applied to weatherstripping, vacuum lines and rubber hoses, which often fail as a result of chemical degradation, and to the tires.

4   Upholstery and carpets – maintenance

1   Every three months remove the carpets or mats and clean the interior of the vehicle (more frequently if necessary). Vacuum the upholstery and carpets to remove loose dirt and dust.

2   Leather upholstery requires special care. Stains should be removed with warm water and a very mild soap solution. Use a clean, damp cloth to remove the soap, then wipe again with a dry cloth. Never use alcohol, gasoline, nail polish remover or thinner to clean leather upholstery.

3   After cleaning, regularly treat leather upholstery with a leather wax. Never use car wax on leather upholstery.

4   In areas where the interior of the vehicle is subject to bright sunlight, cover leather seats with a sheet if the vehicle is to be left out for any length of time.

5   Body repair – minor damage

Repair of scratches

1   If the scratch is superficial and does not penetrate to the metal of the body, repair is very simple. Lightly rub the scratched area with a fine rubbing compound to remove loose paint and built up wax. Rinse the area with clean water.

2   Apply touch-up paint to the scratch, using a small brush. Continue to apply thin layers of paint until the surface of the paint in the scratch is level with the surrounding paint. Allow the new paint at least two weeks to harden, then blend it into the surrounding paint by rubbing with a very fine rubbing compound. Finally, apply a coat of wax to the scratch area.

3   If the scratch has penetrated the paint and exposed the metal of the body, causing the metal to rust, a different repair technique is required. Remove all loose rust from the bottom of the scratch with a pocket knife, then apply rust inhibiting paint to prevent the formation of rust in the future. Using a rubber or nylon applicator, coat the scratched area with glaze-type filler. If required, the filler can be mixed with thinner to provide a very thin paste, which is ideal for filling narrow scratches. Before the glaze filler in the scratch hardens, wrap a piece of smooth cotton cloth around the tip of a finger. Dip the cloth in thinner and then quickly wipe it along the surface of the scratch. This will ensure that the surface of the filler is slightly hollow. The scratch can now be painted over as described earlier in this section.

Repair of dents

See photo sequence

4   When repairing dents, the first job is to pull the dent out until the affected area is as close as possible to its original shape. There is no point in trying to restore the original shape completely as the metal in the damaged area will have stretched on impact and cannot be restored to its original contours. It is better to bring the level of the dent up to a point which is about 1/8-inch below the level of the surrounding metal. In cases where the dent is very shallow, it is not worth trying to pull it out at all.

5   If the back side of the dent is accessible, it can be hammered out gently from behind using a soft-face hammer. While doing this, hold a block of wood firmly against the opposite side of the metal to absorb the hammer blows and prevent the metal from being stretched.

6   If the dent is in a section of the body which has double layers, or some other factor makes it inaccessible from behind, a different technique is required. Drill several small holes through the metal inside the damaged area, particularly in the deeper sections. Screw long, self tapping screws into the holes just enough for them to get a good grip in the metal. Now the dent can be pulled out by pulling on the protruding heads of the screws with locking pliers.

7   The next stage of repair is the removal of paint from the damaged area and from an inch or so of the surrounding metal. This is easily done with a wire brush or sanding disk in a drill motor, although it can be done just as effectively by hand with sandpaper. To complete the preparation for filling, score the surface of the bare metal with a screwdriver or the tang of a file or drill small holes in the affected area. This will provide a good grip for the filler material. To complete the repair, see the Section on filling and painting.

Repair of rust holes or gashes

8   Remove all paint from the affected area and from an inch or so of the surrounding metal using a sanding disk or wire brush mounted in a drill motor. If these are not available, a few sheets of sandpaper will do the job just as effectively.

9   With the paint removed, you will be able to determine the severity of the corrosion and decide whether to replace the whole panel, if possible, or repair the affected area. New body panels are not as expensive as most people think and it is often quicker to install a new panel than to repair large areas of rust.

10   Remove all trim pieces from the affected area except those which will act as a guide to the original shape of the damaged body, such as headlight shells, etc. Using metal snips or a hacksaw blade, remove all loose metal and any other metal that is badly affected by rust. Hammer the edges of the hole inward to create a slight depression for the filler material.

11   Wire brush the affected area to remove the powdery rust from the surface of the metal. If the back of the rusted area is accessible, treat it with rust inhibiting paint.

12   Before filling is done, block the hole in some way. This can be done with sheet metal riveted or screwed into place, or by stuffing the hole with wire mesh.

13   Once the hole is blocked off, the affected area can be filled and painted. See the following subsection on filling and painting.

Filling and painting

14   Many types of body fillers are available, but generally speaking, body repair kits which contain filler paste and a tube of resin hardener are best for this type of repair work. A wide, flexible plastic or nylon applicator will be necessary for imparting a smooth and contoured finish to the surface of the filler material. Mix up a small amount of filler on a clean piece of wood or cardboard (use the hardener sparingly). Follow the manufacturer's instructions on the package, otherwise the filler will set incorrectly.

15   Using the applicator, apply the filler paste to the prepared area. Draw the applicator across the surface of the filler to achieve the desired contour and to level the filler surface. As soon as a contour that approximates the original one is achieved, stop working the paste. If you continue, the paste will begin to stick to the applicator. Continue to add thin layers of paste at 20-minute intervals until the level of the filler is just above the surrounding metal.

16   Once the filler has hardened, the excess can be removed with a body file. From then on, progressively finer grades of sandpaper should be used, starting with a 180-grit paper and finishing with 600-grit wet-or-dry paper. Always wrap the sandpaper around a flat rubber or wooden block, otherwise the surface of the filler will not be completely flat. During the sanding of the filler surface, the wet-or-dry paper should be periodically rinsed in water. This will ensure that a very smooth finish is produced in the final stage.

17   At this point, the repair area should be surrounded by a ring of bare metal, which in turn should be encircled by the finely feathered edge of good paint. Rinse the repair area with clean water until all of the dust produced by the sanding operation is gone.

18   Spray the entire area with a light coat of primer. This will reveal any imperfections in the surface of the filler. Repair the imperfections with fresh filler paste or glaze filler and once more smooth the surface with sandpaper. Repeat this spray-and-repair procedure until you are satisfied that the surface of the filler and the feathered edge of the paint are perfect. Rinse the area with clean water and allow it to dry completely.

19   The repair area is now ready for painting. Spray painting must be carried out in a warm, dry, windless and dust free atmosphere. These conditions can be created if you have access to a large indoor work area, but if you are forced to work in the open, you will have to pick the day very carefully. If you are working indoors, dousing the floor in the

work area with water will help settle the dust which would otherwise be in the air. If the repair area is confined to one body panel, mask off the surrounding panels. This will help minimize the effects of a slight mismatch in paint color. Trim pieces such as chrome strips, door handles, etc., will also need to be masked off or removed. Use masking tape and several thicknesses of newspaper for the masking operations.

20   Before spraying, shake the paint can thoroughly, then spray a test area until the spray painting technique is mastered. Cover the repair area with a thick coat of primer. The thickness should be built up using several thin layers of primer rather than one thick one. Using 600-grit wet-or-dry sandpaper, rub down the surface of the primer until it is very smooth. While doing this, the work area should be thoroughly rinsed with water and the wet-or-dry sandpaper periodically rinsed as well. Allow the primer to dry before spraying additional coats.

21   Spray on the top coat, again building up the thickness by using several thin layers of paint. Begin spraying in the center of the repair area and then, using a circular motion, work out until the whole repair area and about two inches of the surrounding original paint is covered. Remove all masking material 10 to 15 minutes after spraying on the final coat of paint. Allow the new paint at least two weeks to harden, then use a very fine rubbing compound to blend the edges of the new paint into the existing paint. Finally, apply a coat of wax.

6   Body repair – major damage

1   Major damage must be repaired by an auto body shop specifically equipped to perform unibody repairs. These shops have the specialized equipment required to do the job properly.

2   If the damage is extensive, the body must be checked for proper alignment or the vehicle's handling characteristics may be adversely affected and other components may wear at an accelerated rate.

3   Due to the fact that all of the major body components (hood, fenders, etc.) are separate and replaceable units, any seriously damaged components should be replaced rather than repaired. Sometimes the components can be found in a wrecking yard that specializes in used vehicle components, often at considerable savings over the cost of new parts.

7   Hinges and locks – maintenance

Once every 3000 miles, or every three months, the hinges and latch assemblies on the doors, hood and trunk should be given a few drops of light oil or lock lubricant. The door latch strikers should also be lubricated with a thin coat of grease to reduce wear and ensure free movement. Lubricate the door and trunk locks with spray-on graphite lubricant.

8   Fixed glass – replacement

Replacement of the windshield and fixed glass requires the use of special fast-setting adhesive/caulk materials and some specialized tools and techniques. These operations should be left to a dealer service department or a shop specializing in glass work.

9   Hood – removal, installation and adjustment

Refer to illustrations 9.2, 9.10, 9.11 and 9.12

Note: *The hood is heavy and somewhat awkward to remove and install – at least two people should perform this procedure.*

Removal and installation

1   Use blankets or pads to cover the cowl area of the body and the fenders. This will protect the body and paint as the hood is lifted off.

2   Scribe alignment marks around the bolt heads to insure proper alignment during installation (a permanent-type felt-tip marker also will work for this) **(see illustration).**

3   Disconnect any cables or wire harnesses which will interfere with removal.

4   Have an assistant support the weight of the hood. Remove the hinge-to-hood nuts or bolts.

5   Lift off the hood.

6   Installation is the reverse of removal.

Adjustment

7   Fore-and-aft and side-to-side adjustment of the hood is done by moving the hood in relation to the hinge plate after loosening the bolts or nuts.

8   Scribe or trace a line around the entire hinge plate so you can judge the amount of movement.

9   Loosen the bolts or nuts and move the hood into correct alignment. Move it only a little at a time. Tighten the hinge bolts or nuts and carefully lower the hood to check the alignment.

10   Adjust the hood bumpers on the radiator support so the hood is flush with the fenders when closed **(see illustration).**

11   The safety catch assembly on the hood itself can also be adjusted fore-and-aft after loosening the bolts **(see illustration).**

9.2   **Use a marking pen to outline the hinge plate and bolt heads**

9.10   **Adjust the hood vertically by screwing the hood bumpers in or out**

9.11   **Loosen the bolts (arrows) to adjust the safety catch assembly, then adjust it fore or aft (arrow)**

These photos illustrate a method of repairing simple dents. They are intended to supplement *Body repair - minor damage* in this Chapter and should not be used as the sole instructions for body repair on these vehicles.

1   If you can't access the backside of the body panel to hammer out the dent, pull it out with a slide-hammer-type dent puller. In the deepest portion of the dent or along the crease line, drill or punch hole(s) at least one inch apart . . .

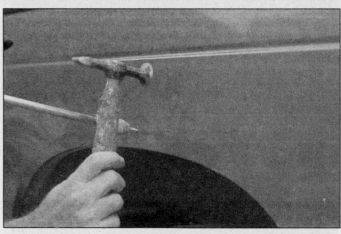

2   . . . then screw the slide-hammer into the hole and operate it. Tap with a hammer near the edge of the dent to help 'pop' the metal back to its original shape. When you're finished, the dent area should be close to its original contour and about 1/8-inch below the surface of the surrounding metal

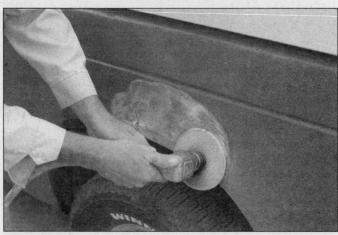

3   Using coarse-grit sandpaper, remove the paint down to the bare metal. Hand sanding works fine, but the disc sander shown here makes the job faster. Use finer (about 320-grit) sandpaper to feather-edge the paint at least one inch around the dent area

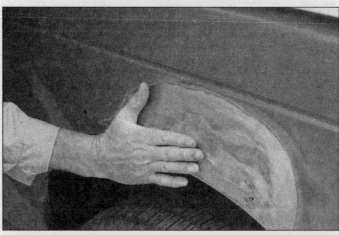

4   When the paint is removed, touch will probably be more helpful than sight for telling if the metal is straight. Hammer down the high spots or raise the low spots as necessary. Clean the repair area with wax/silicone remover

5   Following label instructions, mix up a batch of plastic filler and hardener. The ratio of filler to hardener is critical, and, if you mix it incorrectly, it will either not cure properly or cure too quickly (you won't have time to file and sand it into shape)

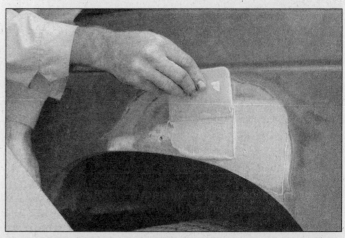

6   Working quickly so the filler doesn't harden, use a plastic applicator to press the body filler firmly into the metal, assuring it bonds completely. Work the filler until it matches the original contour and is slightly above the surrounding metal

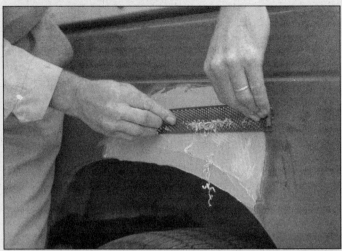

7   Let the filler harden until you can just dent it with your fingernail. Use a body file or Surform tool (shown here) to rough-shape the filler

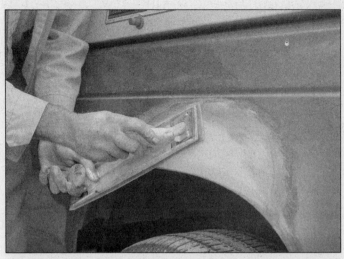

8   Use coarse-grit sandpaper and a sanding board or block to work the filler down until it's smooth and even. Work down to finer grits of sandpaper - always using a board or block - ending up with 360 or 400 grit

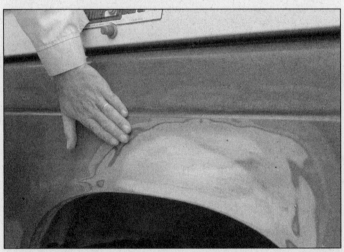

9   You shouldn't be able to feel any ridge at the transition from the filler to the bare metal or from the bare metal to the old paint. As soon as the repair is flat and uniform, remove the dust and mask off the adjacent panels or trim pieces

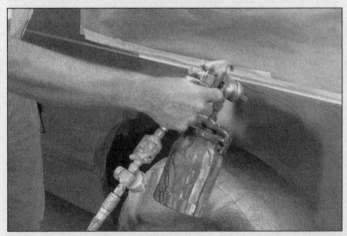

10   Apply several layers of primer to the area. Don't spray the primer on too heavy, so it sags or runs, and make sure each coat is dry before you spray on the next one. A professional-type spray gun is being used here, but aerosol spray primer is available inexpensively from auto parts stores

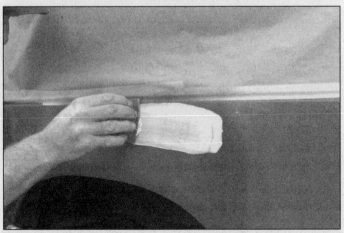

11   The primer will help reveal imperfections or scratches. Fill these with glazing compound. Follow the label instructions and sand it with 360 or 400-grit sandpaper until it's smooth. Repeat the glazing, sanding and respraying until the primer reveals a perfectly smooth surface

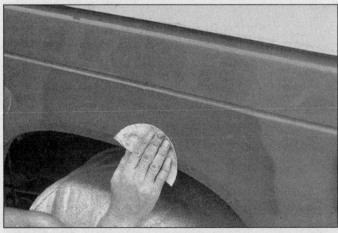

12   Finish sand the primer with very fine sandpaper (400 or 600-grit) to remove the primer overspray. Clean the area with water and allow it to dry. Use a tack rag to remove any dust, then apply the finish coat. Don't attempt to rub out or wax the repair area until the paint has dried completely (at least two weeks)

12   The hood latch assembly on the body can also be adjusted side-to-side after loosening the bolts **(see illustration)**.

13   The hood latch assembly, as well as the hinges, should be periodically lubricated with white lithium-base grease to prevent sticking and wear.

---

10   Bumpers – removal and installation

Refer to illustrations 10.1, 10.5a and 10.5b

Warning: *On air bag-equipped models, always disconnect the negative battery cable when working in the vicinity of the impact sensors (behind the front bumper) to avoid the possibility of accidental deployment of the airbag, which could cause personal injury.*

1   Remove the end cap-to-bumper bolts and the two end cap-to-fender bolts **(see illustration)**.

2   Remove the end cap-to-bumper nut and separate the end cap from the bumper. Repeat this procedure for the other side.

3   Disconnect any wiring or other components that would interfere with bumper removal.

4   Support the bumper with a block of wood and a jack or jackstand or have an assistant support the bumper as the bolts are removed.

5   Remove the mounting bolts and detach the bumper **(see illustrations)**.

6   Installation is the reverse of removal.

7   Tighten the mounting bolts securely.

8   Install the rub strip and any other components that were removed.

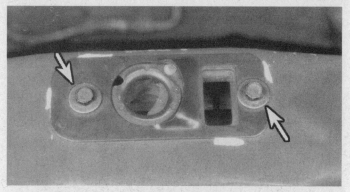

9.12   Loosen the bolts (arrows) to adjust the hood latch assembly

---

11   Door trim panel – removal and installation

Front door

Refer to illustrations 11.2a, 11.2b, 11.2c, 11.2d and 11.4

1   Disconnect the negative cable from the battery.

2   Remove all door trim panel retaining screws and door pull/armrest assemblies **(see illustrations)**.

3   On manual window models, remove the window crank. On power window models, remove the screw, pry out the control switch assembly and unplug it.

4   Insert a putty knife between the trim panel and the door **(see illustration)** and disengage the retaining clips. Work around the outer

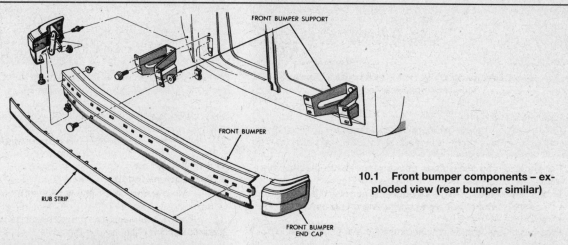

10.1   Front bumper components – exploded view (rear bumper similar)

FRONT BUMPER SUPPORT

FRONT BUMPER

FRONT BUMPER END CAP

RUB STRIP

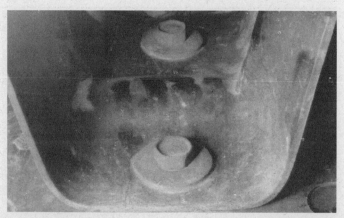

10.5a   Remove the front bumper support bolts

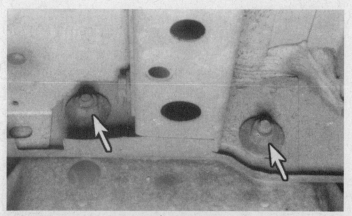

10.5b   Remove the nuts (arrows) from the rear bumper mounts

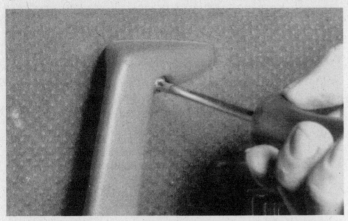

11.2a   Remove the mounting screw from the upper section of the armrest

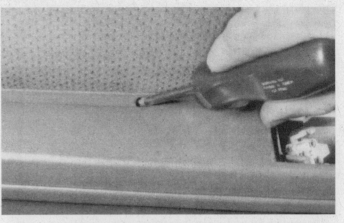

11.2b   The other armrest mounting screw is tucked inside the formed indentation (pocket)

11.2c   Use a flat bladed screwdriver and pry the cover off the power window switch

11.2d   Use a flat bladed screwdriver to remove the inside door handle cover

edge until the panel is free.

5   Once all of the clips are disengaged, detach the trim panel, un-plug any wire harness connectors and remove the trim panel from the vehicle.

6   For access to the inner door, carefully peel back the plastic watershield.

7   Prior to installation of the door panel, be sure to reinstall any clips in the panel which may have come out during the removal procedure and remain in the door itself.

8   Plug in the wire harness connectors and place the panel in posi-tion in the door. Press the trim panel into place until the clips are seated.

9   Install the armrest/door pulls and the window switch or crank.

Sliding door

Refer to illustration 11.11

10   Close the door and remove the latch remote control trim pan-el/bezel.

11   Remove the plugs and the screws on the upper arm trim cover **(see illustration)** and remove the cover.

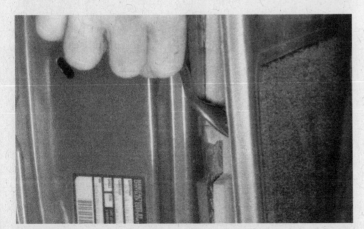

11.4   Use a special upholstery tool or a putty knife and carefully pry the panel off the door

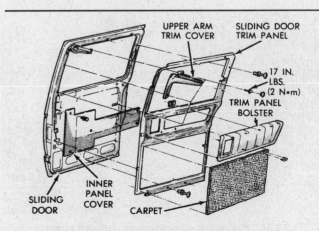

11.11   Sliding door trim panel details

11

12.2a Remove the mounting screws (arrows) from the inside door latch and carefully pull the assembly out to gain access to the link rods

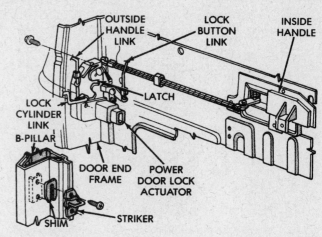

12.2b Door latch and rod linkage details on 1991 and later models

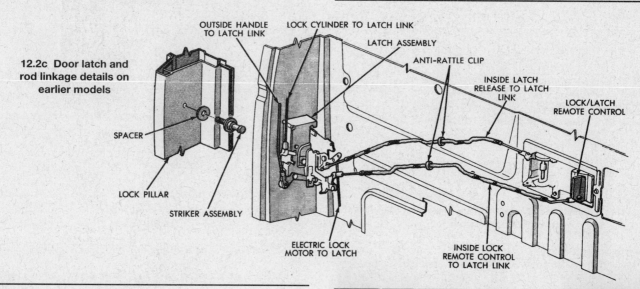

12.2c Door latch and rod linkage details on earlier models

12 Remove the plastic trim panel bolster fasteners.
13 Remove the frogleg fasteners from the door trim panel and remove the panel.
14 Installation is the reverse of removal.

12 Door latch, lock cylinder and outside handle – removal and installation

Door latch
Front door

Refer to illustrations 12.2a, 12.2b, 12.2c and 12.3

1 Close the window completely and remove the door trim panel and watershield (see Section 11).
2 Disconnect the link rods from the latch **(see illustrations)**.
3 Remove the three Torx-head mounting screws **(see illustration)** on the exterior door jamb. It may be necessary to use an impact-type screwdriver to loosen them.
4 Pull the two halves of the latch out of the door.
5 Place the latch in position and install the screws. Tighten the screws securely.
6 Connect the link rods to the latch.
7 Check the door to make sure it closes properly. Readjust the latch (by loosening the screws and moving it) as necessary until the door closes smoothly (with the door handle flush with the door).

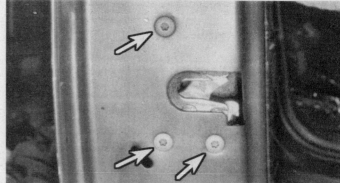

12.3 Remove the Torx drive bolts (arrows) from the outside of the door

Sliding door
Removal and installation

Refer to illustrations 12.9

8 The sliding door latch and handle assembly consolidates the door locks, latch and handles in one easy to service unit.
9 Refer to Section 11 and remove the trim panel, then remove the eight latch and handle control assembly-to-door bolts **(see illustration)**.

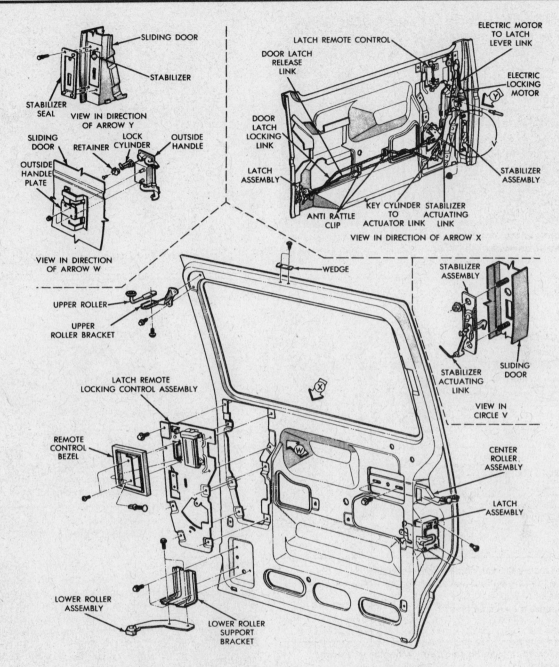

12.9   Sliding door latch, lock and handle components – exploded view

10   Disconnect the linkage and wiring harness.
11   Detach the control assembly.
12   Installation is the reverse of removal.

Latch adjustment
Refer to illustrations 12.14, 12.15, 12.16 and 12.17

13   The latch and handle assembly can be adjusted at several points when it fails to operate properly. They include the lock knob, inside handle, outside handle and the front hook.
14   Perform the lock knob adjustment with the door open. Loosen the lower Allen head screw on the control assembly, then lock the latch by pulling the locking link forward and tighten the Allen head screw to 25 in-lbs **(see illustration)**.
15   Adjust the inside handle by loosening the upper Allen head screw on the left side of the assembly. Insert a screwdriver through the square hole in the assembly and pull the latch link up far enough to re-

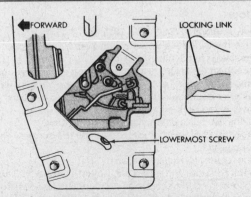

12.14   Sliding door lock knob adjustments

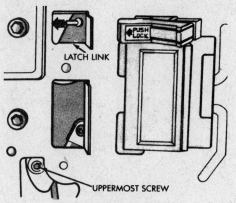

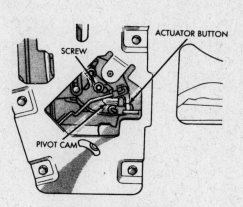

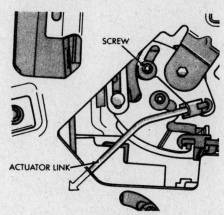

12.15   Sliding door inside handle adjustments

12.16   Sliding door outside handle adjustments

12.17   Sliding door front hook adjustments

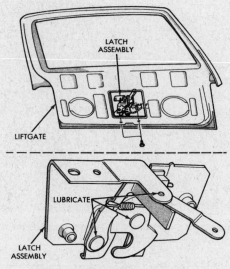

12.19   Liftgate latch assembly

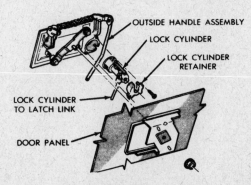

12.22   Door outside handle assembly and lock cylinder components – exploded view

use a screwdriver to push the key lock cylinder retainer off and withdraw the lock cylinder **(see illustration)** from the door.
23   Installation is the reverse of removal.

Sliding door
24   Refer to Section 11 and remove the trim panel.
25   Remove the latch and handle assembly (see previous procedure).
26   Remove the two handle retaining nuts from inside the door and detach the outside handle assembly **(see illustration 12.9)**.
27   Remove the screws and detach the lock cylinder from the outside handle assembly.
28   Installation is the reverse of removal.

Liftgate
29   Remove the liftgate latch assembly (see previous procedure).
30   Remove the nut that retains the lock cylinder to the latch assembly.
31   Installation is the reverse of removal.

Outside handle
Front door
32   Remove the front door trim panel (see Section 11).
33   Disconnect the outside handle (remote control) link from the latch, remove the mounting nuts and detach the handle from the door **(see illustration 12.22)**.
34   Place the handle in position, attach the link and install the nuts. Tighten the nuts securely.

Sliding door and liftgate
35   Follow the previous procedures for latch and cylinder lock removal and detach the outside handle from the lock assembly.

move all free play. Tighten the screw to 25 in-lbs **(see illustration)**.
16   The outside handle can be adjusted by loosening the lower Allen head screw in the central pivot. Hold the central pivot cam against the outside handle actuator button and tighten the screw to 25 in-lbs **(see illustration)**.
17   The front hook adjustment must be done with the door closed. Loosen the upper Allen head screw in the central pivot. Push the front hook actuator link forward until it bottoms on the hook and tighten the screw to 25 in-lbs **(see illustration)**.

Liftgate
Refer to illustration 12.19
18   Remove the trim panel and the water shield from the inside of the liftgate (see Section 11).
19   Remove the screws that mount the latch assembly to the bottom of the liftgate **(see illustration)**.
20   Remove any cables or link rods attached to the assembly.
21   Installation is the reverse of removal.

Lock cylinder
Front door
Refer to illustration 12.22
22   Remove the outside door handle (see below). Disconnect the link,

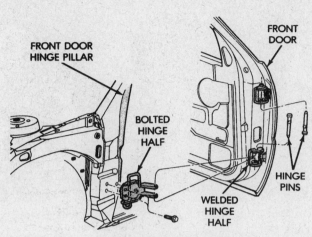

13.4   Door hinge details

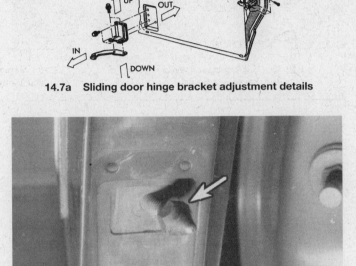

14.7a   Sliding door hinge bracket adjustment details

14.7b   Be sure to mark the latch bolts with paint before removing them from the sliding door

14.7c   Adjust the door stop to increase or decrease the distance to the panel

13   Front door – removal and installation

Refer to illustration 13.4

1   Remove the door trim panel (see Section 11). Disconnect any wire harness connectors and push them through the door opening so they won't interfere with door removal.

2   Remove the front fender (see Section 26) to gain access to the hinge bolts. **Note:** *It is possible to remove the front door without removing the fender by using a sharp punch and tapping the hinge pins from the assembly.*

3   Place a jack or jackstand under the door or have an assistant on hand to support it when the hinge bolts are removed. **Note:** *If a jack or jackstand is used, place a rag between it and the door to protect the door's painted surfaces.*

4   Remove the hinge-to-door bolts or drive out the pins and carefully lift off the door **(see illustration)**.

5   Installation is the reverse of removal.

6   Following installation of the door, check the alignment and adjust it if necessary as follows:

 a) Up-and-down and forward-and-backward adjustments are made by carefully bending the hinges slightly, using a special tool.

 b) The door lock striker can also be adjusted both up-and-down and sideways to provide positive engagement with the lock mechanism. This is done by loosening the mounting bolts and moving the striker as necessary.

14   Sliding door – removal, installation and adjustment

Removal and installation

1   Remove the upper and lower roller covers **(see illustration 12.9)**.

2   Use paint and mark the position of the roller bracket at both the door and the roller arm assembly.

3   Support the door with a block of wood and a floor jack.

4   Remove the bolt from the upper roller bracket to the upper roller. Do the same for the lower roller.

5   Remove the roller bracket from the door.

6   Installation is the reverse of removal.

Adjustment

Refer to illustrations 14.7a, 14.7b and 14.7c

7   If the character line location, gap sizes and operation of the hinges and other door systems is not satisfactory, the door can be adjusted by loosening the roller assembly mounting bolts and repositioning the brackets **(see illustrations)**.

8   The following sequence is recommended to ensure correct adjustment.

9   Adjust the front door-to-pillar and front fender relationship.

 a) The gap between the right pillar and the right front door must be 1/4-inch.

 b) The gap between the right fender and right front door must be 1/4-inch.

 c) The fender and door character lines must match up.

11

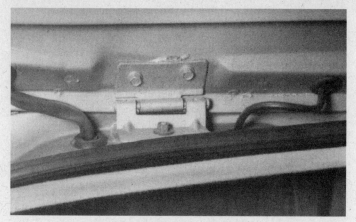

15.5   Remove the liftgate-to-hinge bolts, not the hinge-to-body bolts

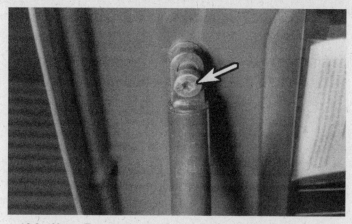

16.2   Use a Torx socket and remove the upper liftgate mount

10   Adjust the sliding door-to-front door and quarter panel relationship.

   a) The gap between the back of a properly adjusted front door and the front edge of the sliding door must be 5/16-inch at the top and bottom.

   b) The gap between the right quarter panel and the sliding door must be 1/4-inch at both the top and bottom.

   c) The character lines of the right fender, right front door, sliding door and quarter panel must match up.

15   Liftgate – removal, installation and adjustment

Refer to illustration 15.5

1   Have an assistant support the liftgate in its fully open position.

2   Disconnect all cables and wire harness connectors that would interfere with removal of the liftgate.

3   Mark or scribe around the hinge flanges.

4   While an assistant supports the liftgate, detach the support struts (see Section 16).

5   Remove the hinge bolts **(see illustration)** and detach the liftgate from the vehicle.

6   Installation is the reverse of removal.

7   After installation, close the liftgate and make sure it's in proper alignment with the surrounding body panels. Adjustments are made by changing the position of the hinge bolts in the slots. To adjust it, loosen the hinge bolts and reposition the hinges either side-to-side or fore-and-aft the desired amount and retighten the bolts.

8   The engagement of the liftgate can be adjusted by loosening the lock striker bolts, repositioning the striker and retightening the bolts.

16   Liftgate strut replacement

Refer to illustrations 16.2 and 16.3

1   Have an assistant support the liftgate in its fully open position.

2   Use a Torx drive socket and remove the upper mount where it attaches to the liftgate **(see illustration)**.

3   Remove the trim panel mounting screws in the vicinity of the strut (see Section 22) and carefully peal back the panels to gain access to the body strut mount **(see illustration)**.

4   Remove the mounting bolt where the strut attaches to the body **(see illustration 16.3)**.

5   Carefully lower the liftgate back down to a closed position.

6   Installation is the reverse of removal.

17   Front door window glass – removal and installation

Refer to illustration 17.3

1   Remove the door trim panel and watershield (see Section 11).

2   Reinstall the crank and raise (or lower) the glass partially until the window regulator assembly is visible through the access hole **(see illustration 12.9)**.

3   Remove the two nuts that secure the glass to the regulator **(see illustration)**.

4   Pull the door glass up and out of the door.

5   Installation is the reverse of removal.

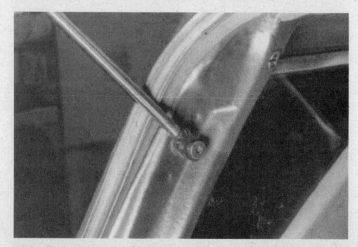

16.3   Carefully fold back the interior trim panel to access the other strut mount

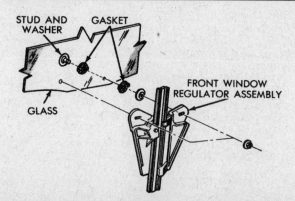

STUD AND WASHER   GASKET

FRONT WINDOW REGULATOR ASSEMBLY

GLASS

17.3   The door glass is attached to the regulator flange with two nuts

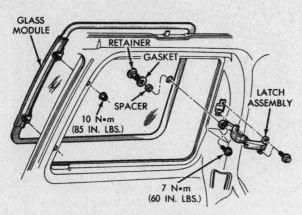

18.2   Interior door glass details

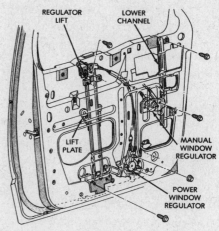

19.5a   The inner door components on 1991 and later models

18   Hinged glass – removal and installation

Refer to illustration 18.2

1   Remove the interior trim panels that surround the window that is to be replaced (see Section 22).
2   Remove the glass-to-latch mounting screws **(see illustration)**.
3   Remove the nuts that hold the hinge to the door or the aperture panel.
4   Remove the glass assembly. If you are replacing it with a new window, transfer the latch attaching components to the new glass assembly.
5   Installation is the reverse of removal.

19   Window regulator – removal and installation

Refer to illustrations 19.5a, 19.5b and 19.5c

1   Remove the door trim panel and the water shield (see Section 11).
2   Remove the bolts that hold the door glass to the window lift plate (see Section 17) and slowly lower the glass and allow it to sit on the bottom of the door.

3   Disconnect the cable from the negative post on the battery.
4   If the vehicle is equipped with a power regulator, disconnect the power regulator electrical connector from the door trim panel.
5   Remove the bolts that hold the regulator to the door inner panel **(see illustrations). Note:** *Some models use rivets to fasten the regulators to the inner door panel. Use an electric drill and a appropriate size drill bit to drill out the regulator mounting rivet heads.*
6   Push-in the fasteners that hold the regulator cables to disengage them from the inner door panel.
7   Carefully remove the regulator from the door panel.
8   Installation is the reverse of removal.

20   Console – removal and installation

Center console (1991 and later models only)

Refer to illustrations 20.2

1   Remove the center instrument cluster bezel (see Section 23).

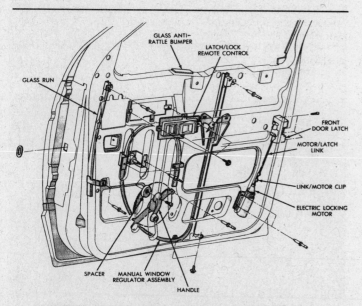

19.5b   The inner door components on 1990 and earlier models

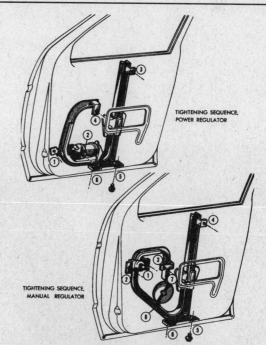

19.5c   Install new bolts after the rivets have been drilled out and torque them to 90 in-lbs in the sequence shown

11

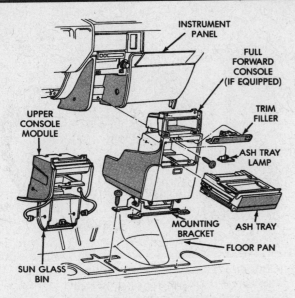

20.2   Front center console mounting details on the 1991 and later models

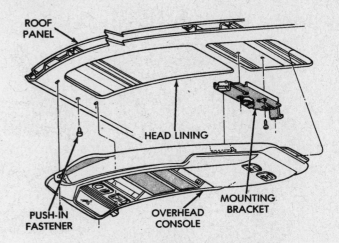

20.10a   Overhead console details on the 1991 and later models

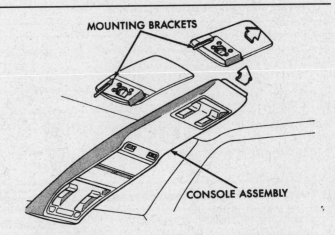

20.10b   Overhead console details on the early models

2   Remove the screws that hold the top of the console to the instrument panel **(see illustration)**.
3   Remove the ashtray and remove the screws that hold the console to the instrument panel.
4   Separate the upper console module from the instrument panel, if equipped.
5   Disconnect the ashtray lamp wire connector.
6   Remove the screws holding the bottom of the console to the floor bracket.
7   Separate the console from the vehicle.
8   Installation is the reverse of removal.

Overhead console

Refer to illustrations 20.10a and 20.10b
9   Disengage the sunvisor ends from the overhead console.
10   Remove the screws holding the overhead console to the roof located at the front of the console **(see illustrations)**.
11   Slide the overhead console forward to disengage the clips holding the rear of the console to the roof.
12   Disconnect the wire connectors from the back of the console and separate the console from the vehicle.
13   Installation is the reverse of removal. **Note:** *While pressing the console upwards, slide the console forward until the console snaps onto the mounting bracket.*

21   Lower dashboard panels – removal and installation

Refer to illustration 21.1
1   Locate the lower dashboard trim panel below the steering column. Remove the mounting screws **(see illustration)** from the panel.
2   Lower the panel and remove it from the vehicle.
3   Installation is the reverse of removal.

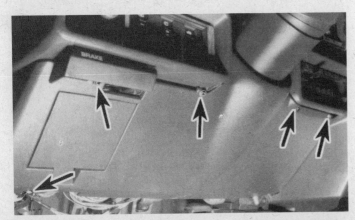

21.1   Remove the screws that mount the lower dashboard panel to the upper panel

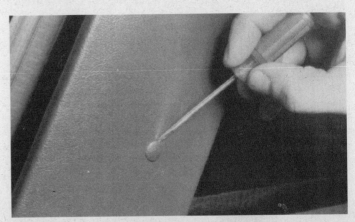

22.1   Carefully pry the plastic plug from the trim panel with a small, flat bladed screwdriver.

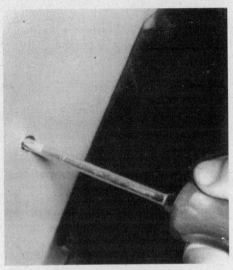

22.3   Remove the mounting screw with a Phillips screwdriver

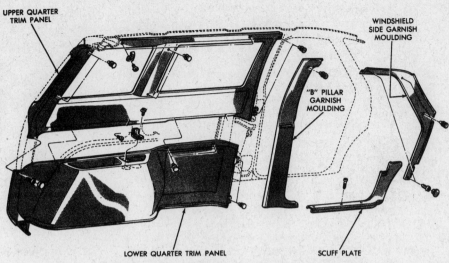

22.4a   Typical interior trim panels on the left side

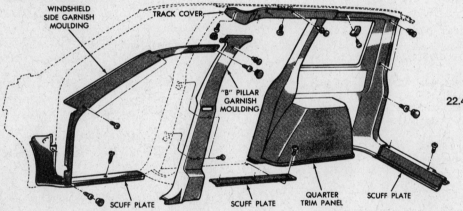

22.4b   Typical interior trim panels on the right side

22   Interior trim panels – removal and installation

Refer to illustrations 22.1, 22.3, 22.4a and 22.4b

1   Remove the plastic plugs from the trim panel that is being removed. Use a dull, flat bladed screwdriver **(see illustration)**.
2   Remove any moulding pieces or scuff plates that border the trim panel.
3   Remove the mounting screws with a Phillips head screwdriver **(see illustration)**.
4   Separate the trim panel from the body **(see illustrations)**.
5   Installation is the reverse of removal.

23   Instrument cluster bezel – removal and installation

Refer to illustration 23.1 and 23.7

Warning: *On air bag-equipped models, always disconnect the negative battery cable when working in the vicinity of the instrument panel or steering column to avoid the possibility of accidental deployment of the airbag, which could cause personal injury.*

1990 and earlier

1   Remove the screws from the bezel **(see illustration)**.
2   Pull the bezel toward the bottom, detach it from the dashboard and remove it.
3   Installation is the reverse of removal.

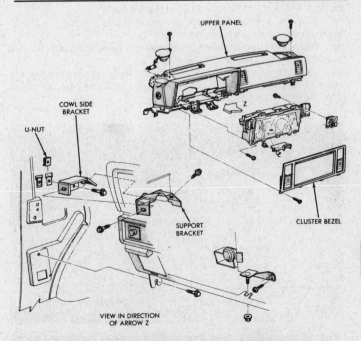

23.1   Instrument cluster bezel details (1990 and earlier)

11

1991 through 1993

4   Remove the warning indicator grille by carefully prying up with a flat blade tool.

5   Remove the screws from the warning indicator module, disconnect the electrical connector and remove the module.

6   Remove the lower steering column cover, set the parking brake and shift the gear selector into low (if equipped).

7   Remove the bezel screws **(see illustration)**, disconnect the switch electrical connectors and remove the bezel.

8   Installation is the reverse of removal.

1994 and later

9   Remove the top cover **(see illustration 24.1b).** Use a flat blade tool to carefully pry up on each end, then continue prying across the full length of the cover until free.

10   Remove the cluster bezel grille. Use a hook tool, inserted into the openings, to pull up on the grille.

11   Remove the message center assembly screws, pry up on either end and remove the module. Disconnect the electrical connectors.

12   Remove the center bezel by pulling on each corner to disconnect the attaching clips. Disconnect any electrical connectors.

13   Remove the instrument cluster bezel screws, pull up and rearward on the top edge of the bezel and remove the bezel. Disconnect any electrical connectors.

14   Installation is the reverse of removal.

24   Dashboard panels – removal and installation

Refer to illustrations 24.1a, 24.1b and 24.1c

1   Remove the screws, if equipped, from the panel/bezel that will be removed **(see illustrations)**.

2   Pry the panel/bezel out carefully without damaging the material. Be sure all the necessary knobs or screws have been removed. Detach it from the dashboard.

3   Installation is the reverse of removal.

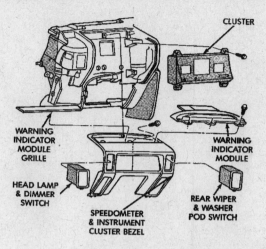

23.7   Instrument cluster bezel details (1991 through 1993)

25   Radiator grille – removal and installation

Refer to illustration 25.2

Warning: *On air bag-equipped models, always disconnect the negative battery cable when working in the vicinity of the impact sensors (behind the front bumper) to avoid the possibility of accidental deployment of the airbag, which could cause personal injury.*

1   Open the hood for access to the upper retaining bolt(s).

2   Remove the screws **(see illustration)** and lift the grille from the body.

3   To install, place the grille in position and install the bolts and screws.

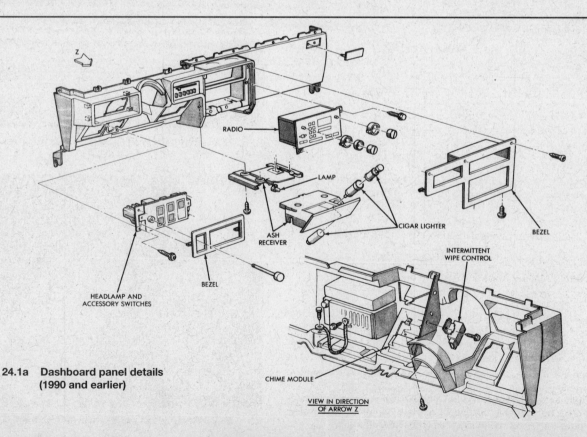

24.1a   Dashboard panel details (1990 and earlier)

24.1b Dashboard panel details (1994 and later)

1   Left pod switch
2   Right pod switch
3   Cluster bezel
4   Hood and message center assembly
5   Cluster bezel grille
6   Top cover
7   Speaker
8   Remote keyless entry module
9   Passenger airbag module
10   Speaker
11   Instrument panel
12   Cigar lighter shell, clamp and lamp
13   A/C heater control
14   Cigar lighter assembly
15   Ash receiver assembly
16   Center bezel
17   Radio
18   Cluster assembly
19   Nameplate

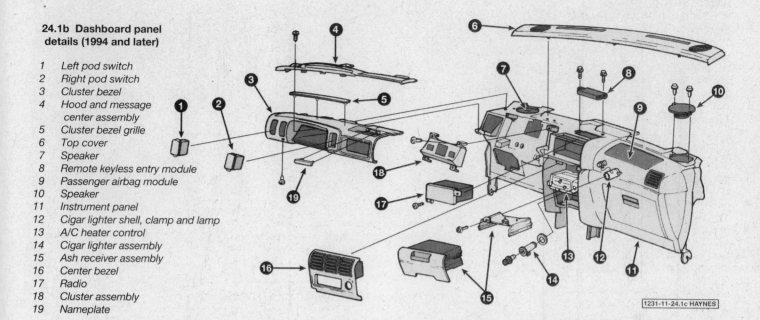

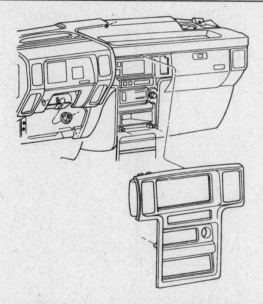

24.1c   Center console panel on the 1991 models

26   Front fender – removal and installation

Refer to illustration 26.3

Warning: *On air bag-equipped models, always disconnect the negative battery cable when working in the vicinity of the impact sensors (behind the front bumper) to avoid the possibility of accidental deployment of the airbag, which could cause personal injury.*

1   Raise the vehicle, support it securely on jackstands and remove the front wheel.
2   Disconnect the antenna and all light bulb wiring harness connectors and other components that would interfere with fender removal.
3   Remove the fender mounting bolts **(see illustration)**.

25.2   Remove the Phillips head screws (arrows) from the grille

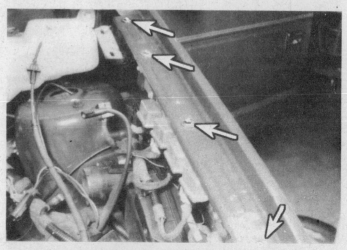

26.3   Remove the bolts (arrows) from the front fender

11

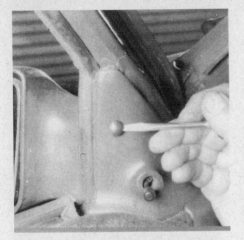

27.2   Remove the plastic plug from the mirror trim panel

27.3   Remove the upper retaining screw from the trim panel

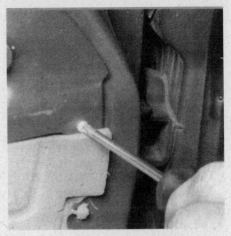

27.4   Remove the lower retaining screw from the trim panel

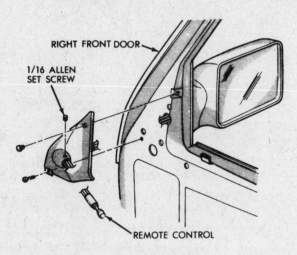

RIGHT FRONT DOOR

1/16 ALLEN SET SCREW

REMOTE CONTROL

27.5a   Typical remote control mirror mounting details (van models)

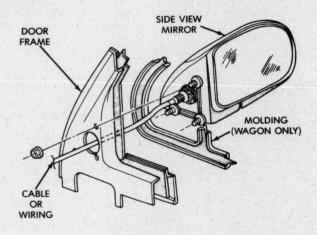

DOOR FRAME

SIDE VIEW MIRROR

MOLDING (WAGON ONLY)

CABLE OR WIRING

27.5b   Typical remote control mirror mounting details (wagon models)

4   Detach the fender. It's a good idea to have an assistant support the fender while it's being moved away from the vehicle to prevent damage to the surrounding body panels.
5   Installation is the reverse of removal.
6   Tighten all nuts, bolts and screws securely.

27   Mirrors – removal and installation

Refer to illustrations 27.2, 27.3, 27.4, 27.5a and 27.5b
1   Remove the door trim panel (Section 11).
2   Use a flat bladed screwdriver **(see illustration)** and remove the plastic plug from the inside trim panel.
3   Remove the panel screw with a Phillips head screwdriver **(see illustration)**.
4   Remove the lower panel screw **(see illustration)**. **Note:** *The inside door trim panel must be removed first.*
5   On remote control systems, use an Allen head socket and remove the retaining bolt adjacent to the remote control **(see illustrations)**.
6   Remove the nuts/screws and detach the mirror. On power mirrors, unplug the electrical connector.
7   Installation is the reverse of removal.

28   Engine splash shields – removal and installation

Refer to illustrations 28.2a and 28.2b
1   Loosen the wheel lug nuts, raise the front of the vehicle and support it securely on jackstands. Remove the wheel(s).
2   The wheelhouse splash shield is retained by screws and plastic (tree-type) fasteners, which generally aren't reusable after removal. Carefully pry the fasteners out with pliers or wire cutters **(see illustration)**. The transaxle and engine drivebelt splash shields are held in place by bolts **(see illustration)**
3   After all the screws and fasteners have been removed, detach the splash shield.
4   To install a splash shield, hold it in position and install the screws and new plastic fasteners.

29   Seats – removal and installation

Refer to illustrations 29.2, 29.10a and 29.10b

Front seats
1   Raise the front of the vehicle and support it securely on jackstands.

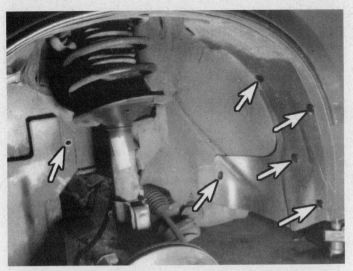

28.2a Locations of the wheelhouse splash shield retaining bolts and fasteners (arrows) – note that the shields are assembled in sections.

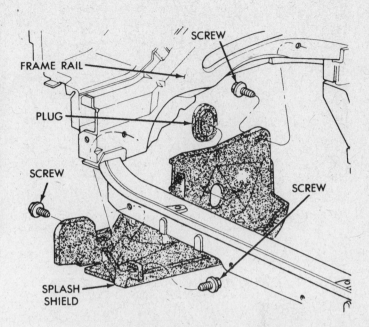

28.2b Engine drivebelt splash shield details

Left front seat

2 Tilt the seat backwards, reach under the seat and pull the latch connector wire toward the drivers door until it is released from the lever assembly **(see illustration).**
3 Turn the cable end 90 degrees to separate it from the lever assembly.
4 Remove the nuts/washers that fasten the seat riser to the floor pan.
5 Disconnect the electrical connectors and remove the seat.
6 Installation is the reverse of removal.

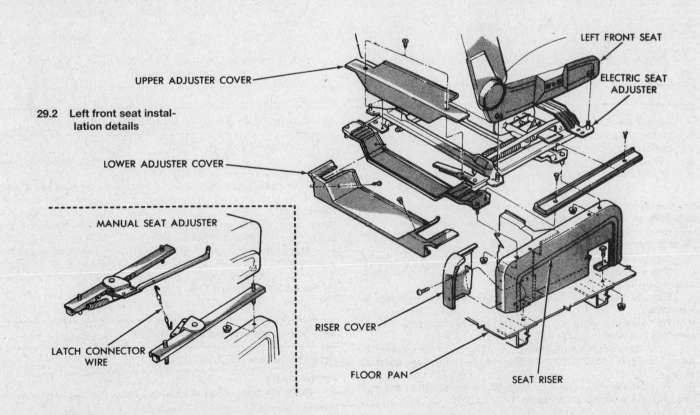

29.2 Left front seat installation details

11

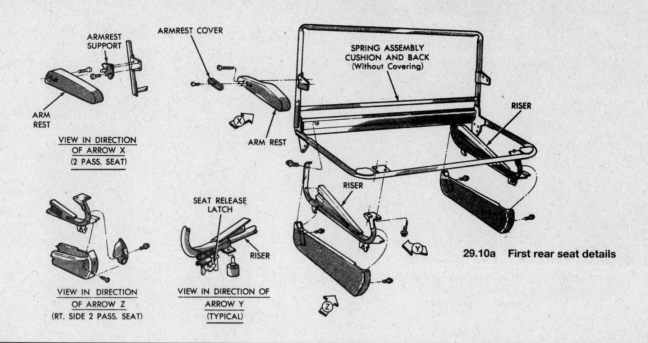

VIEW IN DIRECTION
OF ARROW X
(2 PASS. SEAT)

VIEW IN DIRECTION
OF ARROW Z
(RT. SIDE 2 PASS. SEAT)

VIEW IN DIRECTION OF
ARROW Y
(TYPICAL)

29.10a   First rear seat details

Right front seat

7   Remove the nuts/washers that fasten the seat riser to the floor pan.
8   Lift the seat from the vehicle.
9   Installation is the reverse of removal.

Rear seats

10   Lift the release latch handle on both sides until the front of the seat assembly is separated from the floor pan strikers (see illustrations).
11   Tilt the seat toward the rear of the vehicle.
12   Remove the rear seat from the vehicle.
13   Installation is the reverse of removal.

30   Seat belt check

1   Check the seat belts, buckles, latch plates and guide loops for obvious damage and signs of wear.
2   See if the seat belt reminder light comes on when the key is turned to the Run or Start positions. A chime should also sound.
3   The seat belts are designed to lock up during a sudden stop or impact, yet allow free movement during normal driving. Make sure the retractors return the belt against your chest while driving and rewind the belt fully when the buckle is unlatched.
4   If any of the above checks reveal problems with the seat belt system, replace parts as

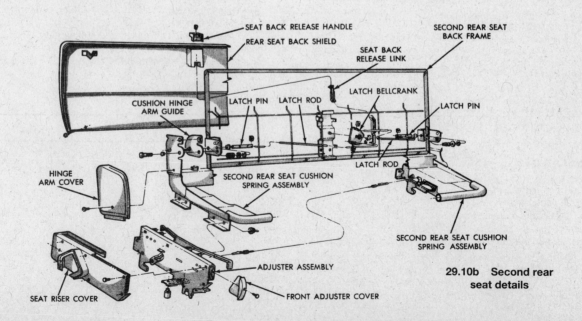

29.10b   Second rear
seat details

Chapter 12   Chassis electrical system

Contents

Specifications

Light bulb types
Headlight
    Sealed beam type PH4606
    Quartz-halogen type 6052
Park/turn signal light 2057NA
Side marker light 168
Speedometer and instrument cluster... 194
Dome light 211-2
License plate light 158
Back-up light 1156
Brake/tail light 1156
High-mounted brake light 912
Turn signal light 1156
Side marker light 168

1   General information

The electrical system is a 12-volt, negative ground type. Power for the lights and all electrical accessories is supplied by a lead/acid-type battery which is charged by the alternator.

This Chapter covers repair and service procedures for the various electrical components not associated with the engine. Information on the battery, alternator, distributor and starter motor can be found in Chapter 5. **Caution:** *When working on the electrical system, disconnect the negative battery cable from the battery to prevent electrical shorts and/or fires.*

2   Electrical troubleshooting – general information

A typical electrical circuit consists of an electrical component, any switches, relays, motors, fuses, fusible links or circuit breakers related to the component and the wiring and connectors that link the component to both the battery and the chassis. To help pinpoint an electrical circuit problem, wiring diagrams are included at the end of this Chapter.

Before tackling any troublesome electrical circuit, first study the appropriate wiring diagrams to get a complete understanding of what makes up that individual circuit. Trouble spots, for instance, can often be narrowed down by noting if other components related to the circuit are operating properly. If several components or circuits fail at one time, chances are the problem is in a fuse or ground connection, because several circuits are often routed through the same fuse and ground connections.

Electrical problems usually stem from simple causes, such as loose or corroded connections, a blown fuse, a melted fusible link or a bad relay. Visually inspect the condition of all fuses, wires and connections in a problem circuit before troubleshooting it.

If testing instruments are going to be utilized, use the diagrams to plan ahead of time where to make the necessary connections to accurately pinpoint the trouble spot.

The basic tools needed for electrical troubleshooting include a circuit tester or voltmeter (a 12-volt bulb with a set of test leads can also be used), a continuity tester (which includes a bulb, battery and set of test leads) and a jumper wire, preferably with a circuit breaker incorporated, which can be used to bypass electrical components. Before attempting to locate a problem with test instruments, use the wiring diagram(s) to decide where to make the connections.

Voltage checks

Voltage checks should be performed if a circuit isn't functioning properly. Connect one lead of a circuit tester to either the negative battery terminal or a known good ground. Connect the other lead to a connector in the circuit being tested, preferably nearest to the battery or fuse. If the bulb of the tester lights, voltage is present, which means the part of the circuit between the connector and the battery is problem free. Continue checking the rest of the circuit in the same fashion. When you reach a point where no voltage is present, the problem lies between that point and the last test point with voltage. Most of the time the problem can be traced to a loose connection. **Note:** *Keep in mind that some circuits receive voltage only when the ignition key is in the Accessory or Run position.*

Finding a short

One method of finding a short in a circuit is to remove the fuse and connect a test light or voltmeter in its place to the fuse terminals. There should be no voltage present in the circuit. Move the wiring harness from side-to-side while watching the test light. If the bulb lights, there's a short to ground somewhere in that area, probably where the insulation has rubbed through. The same test can be performed on each component in the circuit, even a switch.

Ground check

Perform a ground test to check whether a component is properly

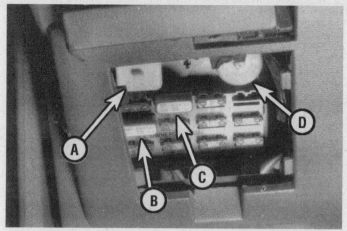

3.1a   Pull off the cover from the lower left (driver's side) of the dashboard to access the fuse block (3.3L V6 model shown, other models similar)

A   Horn relay
B   Circuit breaker for power door locks, seats and mirrors
C   Circuit breaker for power window motors, sunroof and power vent widows
D   Turn signal flasher

grounded. Disconnect the battery and connect one lead of a self-powered test light, known as a continuity tester, to a known good ground. Connect the other lead to the wire or ground connection being tested. If the bulb lights, the ground is good. If the bulb doesn't light, the ground is no good.

Continuity check

A continuity check is done to determine if there are breaks in a circuit – if it's capable of passing electricity properly. With the circuit off (no power in the circuit), a self-powered continuity tester can be used to check it. Connect the test leads to both ends of the circuit (or to the "power" end and a good ground) – if the test light comes on the circuit is passing current properly. If the light doesn't come on, there's a break (open) somewhere in the circuit. The same procedure can be used to test a switch by connecting the continuity tester to the switch terminals. With the switch on, the test light should come on.

Finding an open circuit

When diagnosing for possible open circuits, it's often difficult to locate them by sight because oxidation or terminal misalignment are hidden by the connectors. Merely wiggling a connector on a sensor or in the wiring harness may correct the open circuit condition. Remember this when an open is indicated when troubleshooting a circuit. Intermittent problems may also be caused by oxidized or loose connections. Electrical troubleshooting is simple if you keep in mind that all electrical circuits are basically electricity running from the battery, through the wires, switches, relays, fuses and fusible links to each electrical component (light bulb, motor, etc.) and to ground, where it's passed back to the battery. Any electrical problem is an interruption in the flow of electricity to and from the battery.

3   Fuses – general information

Refer to illustrations 3.1a, 3.1b and 3.3

The electrical circuits of the vehicle are protected by a combination of fuses, fusible links (see Section 4) and circuit breakers (see Section 5). Most of the fuses, and some of the circuit breakers, are located on the fuse block, which is located under the instrument panel on the left side of the dashboard **(see illustrations)**.

Each fuse is designed to protect a specific circuit, which is imprinted on the fuse panel itself. We've included a terminal guide to a typical

CAVITY	FUSE/ COLOR	ITEMS FUSED
1	20 AMP YL	HAZARD FLASHER
2	20 AMP YL	BACK-UP LAMPS, A/C FAN AND CLUTCH RELAY, HEATED REAR WINDOW SWITCH, REAR SEAT HEATER AND A/C AND OVERHEAD CONSOLE
3	30 AMP C/BRKR SILVER CAN	POWER WINDOW MOTORS AND SUNROOF, POWER VENT WINDOWS
4	30 AMP LG	A/C, OR HEATER BLOWER MOTOR
5	20 AMP YL	PARK, TAIL, SIDE MARKER AND LICENSE LAMPS; CLOCK, RADIO AND OVERHEAD CONSOLE DISPLAY INTENSITY
6	20 AMP YL	STOPLAMPS AND CHIMES
7	25 AMP NAT	HORNS, CIGAR LIGHTER AND NAME BRAND SPEAKER AMP FEED
8	30 AMP C/BRKR SILVER CAN	POWER DOOR LOCKS, SEATS AND MIRRORS
9	10 AMP RD	RADIO AND CLOCK DISPLAY
10	20 AMP YL	TURN SIGNAL LAMPS AND VAN CONVERSION RELAY
11	20 AMP YL	WINDSHIELD WIPER AND WASHERS
12	4 AMP PK	CLUSTER, A/C AND HEATER CONTROL, SWITCH TITLE, ASH RECEIVER, RADIO, CIGAR LIGHTER, OVERHEAD CONSOLE LAMPS, REAR SEAT HEATER, AND A/C SWITCH LAMPS

CAVITY	FUSE/ COLOR	ITEMS FUSED
13	5 AMP TN	FUEL, VOLTAGE, OIL AND TEMPERATURE GAUGES, BRAKE WARNING LIFTGATE OPEN, SEAT BELT WARNING MODULE, UPSHIFT, AND CHECK ENGINE WARNING AND EMISSION MAINTENANCE REMINDER, SPEED CONTROL
14	20 AMP YL	REAR WASH WIPE AND LIFTGATE RELEASE, LIFTGATE INTERLOCK ELECTRONIC MODULE (MANUAL TRANSMISSION)
15	10 AMP RD	UNDERSEAT STORAGE, LOWER CONSOLE, DOME, CARGO IGNITION SWITCH, HEADLAMP, COURTESY AND VANITY MIRROR, READING, COURTESY, CONSOLE LAMPS AND RADIO MEMORY
16	25 AMP NAT	POWER VENT WINDOWS

AMPS	FUSE	COLOR CODE
3	VT	VIOLET
4	PK	PINK
5	TN	TAN
10	RD	RED
20	YL	YELLOW
25	NAT	NATURAL
30	LG	LIGHT GREEN

FUSE BLOCK

CIRCUIT BREAKER

TURN SIGNAL FLASHER

IGNITION LAMP THERMAL TIME DELAY RELAY

HORN RELAY

3.1b   Terminal guide for a typical fuse, relay, circuit breaker block (1990 model shown, other models similar – refer to your owner's manual for a guide to the panel on your vehicle)

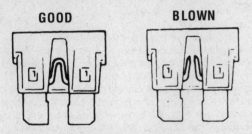

GOOD   BLOWN

3.3   The fuses used on these models can be checked visually to determine if they are blown

Be sure to replace blown fuses with the correct type. Fuses of different ratings are physically interchangeable, but only fuses of the proper rating should be used. Replacing a fuse with one of a higher or lower value than specified is not recommended. Each electrical circuit needs a specific amount of protection. The amperage value of each fuse is molded into the fuse body.

If the replacement fuse immediately fails, don't replace it again until the cause of the problem is isolated and corrected. In most cases, the cause will be a short circuit in the wiring caused by a broken or deteriorated wire.

4   Fusible links – general information

Refer to illustration 4.3

Some circuits are protected by fusible links. The links are used in circuits which are not ordinarily fused, such as the ignition circuit.

Although the fusible links appear to be a heavier gauge than the wires they're protecting, the appearance is due to the thick insulation. All fusible links are four wire gauges smaller than the wire they're designed to protect. fusible links can't be repaired, but a new link of the same size wire can be installed. The procedure is as follows:

a) Disconnect the negative cable from the battery.
b) Disconnect the fusible link from the wiring harness.
c) Cut the damaged fusible link out of the wire just behind the connector.

fuse block, though not all earlier vehicles use this many fuses. The location of most fuses is virtually identical on all models. If you're unable to determine the circuit protected by a fuse's abbreviated identification imprinted on the fuse block, refer to the fuse block guide in your owner's manual.

Miniaturized fuses are employed in the fuse block. These compact fuses, with blade terminal design, allow fingertip removal and replacement. If an electrical component fails, always check the fuse first. The fuses can be quickly checked by probing the exposed blades at the top of each fuse with a test light. If the fuse has power at one blade but not the other, it's blown. This can be verified by pulling the fuse and inspecting it visually **(see illustration)**.

12

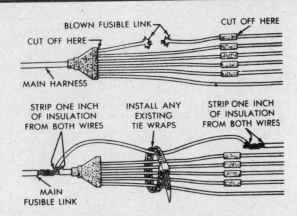

4.3   Fusible link repair details

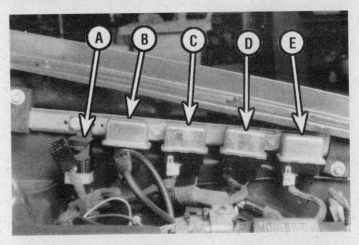

6.1   Several relays are located in the engine compartment, adjacent to the battery (3.3L V6 shown; 3.0 V6 and 2.5L four-cylinder (including turbo) engines have identical layout)

A *Auto shutdown relay*
B *Starter relay*
C *Radiator fan relay*
D *Air conditioning clutch cutout relay*
E *Air conditioning condenser relay*

7.7   Location of the hazard flasher unit (arrow)

d) Strip the insulation back approximately 1-inch **(see illustration)**.
e) Position the connector on the new fusible link and crimp it into place.
f) Use rosin core solder at each end of the new link to obtain a good connection.
g) Use plenty of electrical tape around the soldered joint. No wires should be exposed.
h) Connect the negative battery cable. Test the circuit for proper operation.

5   Circuit breakers – general information

Circuit breakers protect components such as power door locks, power mirror motors, power seat motors, power vent windows, power window motors, sunroofs and headlights. Most circuit breakers are located on the fuse block **(see illustrations 3.1a and 3.1b)**. On some models the circuit breaker resets itself automatically, so an electrical overload in the circuit will cause it to open momentarily, then come back on. If the circuit doesn't come back on, check it immediately. Once the condition is corrected, the circuit breaker will resume its normal function. Some circuit breakers have a button on top and must be reset manually.

6   Relays – general information

Refer to illustration 6.1

A relay is an electric switch that allows a small current to control a much larger current. Relays are often used to transmit current to remote components such as radiator fans, starter motors and clutch cutouts on air conditioning compressors. Most relays are located right

7.9   To replace the hazard flasher unit, simply pull it forward until it detaches from its mounting bracket and unplug the electrical connector

in the engine compartment **(see illustration)**; others, like horn relays, are located on the fuse block under the dash **(see illustrations 3.1a and 3.1b)**. If a relay is defective, the component won't operate properly.

If a faulty relay is suspected, it can be removed and tested by a dealer service department or a repair shop. Defective relays must be replaced as a unit.

7   Turn signal and hazard flashers – check and replacement

Warning: *On 1991 and later models, which are equipped with airbags, always disconnect the negative battery cable when working in the vicinity of the instrument panel or steering column to avoid the possibility of accidental deployment of the airbag, which could cause personal injury.*

Note: *1992 and later models; the turn signal and hazard flashers are incorporated into one unit, known as the combination flasher, and is located at the left lower corner of the relay bank, adjacent to the fuse box.*

Turn-signal flasher

1   The turn-signal flasher, a small canister-shaped unit located on the fuse panel (see Section 3) flashes the turn signals **(see illustra-**

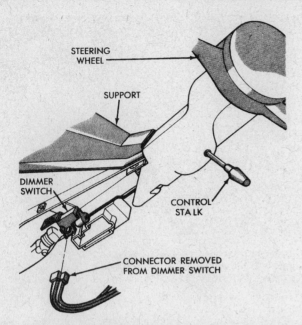

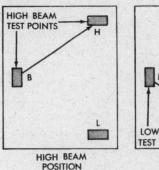

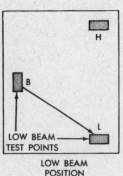

8.2   Unplug the electrical connector from the dimmer switch

8.3   Terminal continuity guide for the electrical connector of the headlight dimmer switch

tions 3.1a and 3.1b).

2   When the flasher unit is functioning properly, an audible click can be heard during its operation. If the turn signals fail on one side or the other and the flasher unit doesn't make its characteristic clicking sound, a faulty turn signal bulb is indicated.

3   If both turn signals fail to blink, the problem may be due to a blown fuse, a faulty flasher unit, a broken switch or a loose or open connection. If a quick check of the fuse box indicates the turn signal fuse has blown, check the wiring for a short before installing a new fuse.

4   To replace the flasher, simply pull it straight out of the fuse panel.

5   Make sure the replacement is identical to the original. Compare the old one to the new one before installing it.

6   Installation is the reverse of removal.

Hazard flasher

Refer to illustrations 7.7 and 7.9

7   The hazard flasher, a small canister located below the fuse block, just forward of the lower edge of the dashboard **(see illustration)**, flashes all four turn signals simultaneously when activated.

8   The hazard flasher is checked just like the turn signal flasher (see Steps 2 and 3).

9   To replace the hazard flasher, pull it forward to disengage it from its mounting bracket, then unplug the electrical connector **(see illustration)**.

10   Make sure the replacement is identical to the original. Compare the old one to the new one before installing it.

11   Installation is the reverse of removal.

8   Headlight dimmer switch – check, replacement and adjustment (1990 and earlier)

Warning: *On 1991 and later models, the headlight dimmer switch is part of the multi-function switch located in the steering column. Since 1991 and later models are equipped with an airbag system, to avoid possible damage to this system, or accidental deployment of the airbag, it is recommended that any work involving airbag system components be left to a dealer service department or other qualified repair shop.*

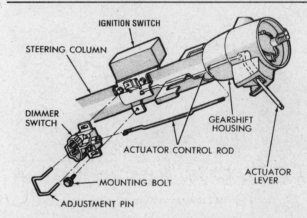

8.7   An exploded view of one type of dimmer switch assembly – you can fabricate your own adjustment pin using a piece of coat hanger or a paper clip, or just use two drill bits

Check

Refer to illustrations 8.2 and 8.3

1   The headlight dimmer switch is located on the left side of the steering column.

2   Unplug the electrical connector from the dimmer switch **(see illustration)**.

3   Using an ohmmeter, check for continuity between the terminals of the switch **(see illustration)**. There should be continuity between terminals B and H on the high beam position and between terminals B and L on the low beam position.

4   If the indicated continuity isn't as specified, replace the switch.

Replacement

Refer to illustration 8.7

5   Remove the steering column cover **(see illustration 9.8)**.

6   Tape the dimmer switch rod to the steering column to prevent the rod from falling out of the notch in the actuator lever.

7   Remove the screws attaching the switch to the column **(see illustration)**.

8   Unplug the electrical connector and remove the switch.

9   To install the new switch, attach the electrical connector first, then position the switch and install the switch mounting screws, but don't tighten them.

Adjustment

Refer to illustrations 8.11a and 8.11b

10   If the dimmer switch on your vehicle looks like the unit in illustration 8.7, fabricate a U-shaped adjustment pin similar to the one shown

12

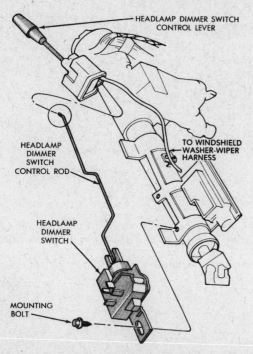

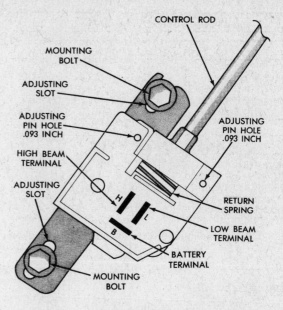

8.11b   ... and adjustment details for this type

8.11a   An exploded view of a second type of dimmer switch assembly used on some models covered in this manual, ...

in that illustration and insert it into the switch hole in the adjustment position. Remove the tape holding the rod, adjust the switch by gently pushing up on the switch to take up the slack in the rod and tighten the mounting screws. Remove the pin.

11   If the switch on your vehicle looks like this **(see illustration)**, fabricate a pair of adjustment pins or drill bits with a diameter of 0.093-inch, insert them into the two pin holes **(see illustration)**, push the switch body up the column to remove any freeplay between the rod and the switch and tighten the mounting screws securely. Remove the pins or drills.

12   Check the switch for proper operation.

13   The remainder of installation is the reverse of removal.

9   Turn signal/hazard warning switch – check and replacement (1990 and earlier)

Warning: *On 1991 and later models, the turn signal switch is part of the multi-function switch located in the steering column. Since 1991 and later models are equipped with an airbag system, to avoid possible damage to this system, or accidental deployment of the airbag, it is recommended that any work involving airbag system components be left to a dealer service department or other qualified repair shop.*

1   The turn signal switch is located at the top end of the steering column and is operated by the multi-function control stalk. The hazard warning switch is mounted under the turn signal switch, next to the ignition key light.

Check

Refer to illustrations 9.4 and 9.5

2   Disconnect the negative cable from the battery.

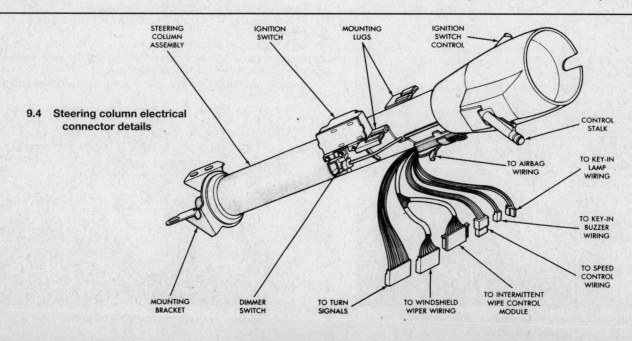

9.4   Steering column electrical connector details

SWITCH CONTINUITY CHART			
Turn Signal Switch			
Switch Position:	Left	Neutral	Right
Continuity Between:	7 and 4	10 and 9	7 and 5
Continuity Between:	7 and 8	10 and 8	7 and 9
Continuity Between:	10 and 9		10 and 8
Hazard Warning Switch			
Switch Position:	Off	On	
Continuity Between:	10 and 9	6 and 4	
Continuity Between:	10 and 8	6 and 5	
Continuity Between:		6 and 8	
Continuity Between:		6 and 9	

9.5   Turn signal and hazard switch continuity check details

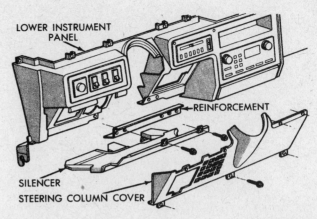

9.8   Exploded view of the steering column cover, the silencer and the reinforcement (floor-shift model shown, column shift similar)

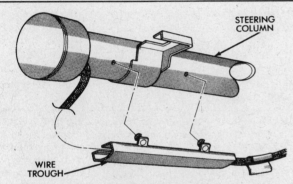

9.9   Trough for turn signal switch wire harness

3   Remove the steering column cover.
4   Unplug the turn signal switch electrical connector **(see illustration)**.
5   Use an ohmmeter or self-powered test light to check for continuity between the indicated switch connector terminals **(see illustration)**.
6   Replace the turn signal or hazard switch if the continuity is not as specified.

Replacement
Refer to illustrations 9.8, 9.9, 9.10a, 9.10b, 9.10c, 9.11, 9.12, 9.14a and 9.14b

7   Disconnect the negative battery cable, then remove the steering

9.10a   Install a lock plate removal tool to depress the lock plate . . .

wheel (see Chapter 10).
8   On floor-shift models, remove the lower steering column cover, the silencer and the reinforcement **(see illustration)**.
9   Detach the wiring harness trough **(see illustration)** from the steering column.
10   On tilt-columns, install a lock plate removal tool **(see illustration)**, depress the lock plate, remove the retaining ring **(see illustration)** and remove the lock plate **(see illustration)**.
11   Remove the horn contact plate/cancelling cam **(see illustration)**.

9.10b   . . . remove the retaining ring from the steering shaft . . .

9.10c   . . . and remove the lock plate

12

9.11   Remove the horn contact plate/cancelling cam (arrow points to upper bearing spring, which you don't need to remove for this procedure, but you do need to remove if you're replacing the wiper/washer switch assembly)

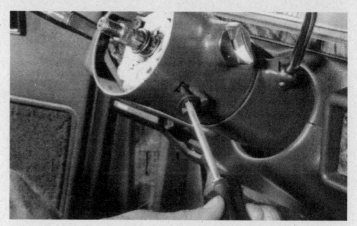

9.12   Remove the hazard flasher button

9.14a   Remove the three switch retaining screws, ...

9.14b   ... gently pull up on the switch assembly and carefully pull the switch and harness up and out of the steering column assembly

WIPER SWITCH CONTINUITY CHART Two Speed Motor (With Non-Concealed Wipers)		
Off	**Low**	**High**
B to P₁	B to P₁	B to P₁
A to P₂	B to A	B to H
H—Open	P₂—Open	P₂—Open
	H—Open	A—Open
B to W	B to W	B to W
(In Wash)	(In Wash)	(In Wash)

10.5a   Two-speed wiper switch continuity check chart (non-concealed wipers) – continuity should be as specified in the three switch positions (1984 models)

WIPER SWITCH CONTINUITY CHART Two Speed Switch		
Off	**Low**	**High**
B+ to P₁	B+ to P₁	B+ to P₁
L to P₂	B+ to L	B+ to H
H—Open	P₂—Open	P₂—Open
	H—Open	L—Open
B+ to W	B+ to W	B+ to W
(In Wash)	(In Wash)	(In Wash)

10.5b   Two-speed wiper switch continuity check chart (concealed wipers) – continuity should be as specified in the three switch positions (1985 through 1987 models)

12   Remove the hazard flasher button **(see illustration)**.
13   Remove the screw which connects the wiper-washer switch to the turn signal switch pivot. Don't remove or disturb the wiper-washer switch assembly.
14   Remove the three switch retaining screws **(see illustration)**, gently pull up on the switch assembly and carefully thread the switch wires up through and out the top of the steering column **(see illustra-**

tion). **Note:** *It may be helpful to wrap electrical tape around the lower end of the wiring harness and the electrical connector, to reduce the possibility of the connector becoming stuck inside the column.*
15   Installation is the reverse of removal. Don't forget to lubricate the steering shaft contact surfaces with multi-purpose grease, and make sure the dimmer switch rod is positioned securely in the pocket of the control stalk.

**INTERMITTENT WIPE SWITCH CONTINUITY CHART
NON-TILT**

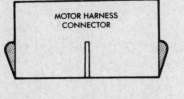
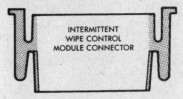

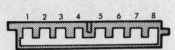
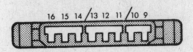

VIEW FROM TERMINAL SIDE

SWITCH POSITION	CONTINUITY BETWEEN
OFF	PIN 1-13, PIN 3-10, PIN 4-11, PIN 5-12
DELAY	PIN 1-13, PIN 3-10, PIN 4-16, PIN 4-11, PIN 4-9, PIN 5-12, PIN 8-15, PIN 9-16, PIN 11-16, PIN 9-11
LOW	PIN 1-13, PIN 3-10, PIN 4-7, PIN 4-11, PIN 5-12, PIN 7-11
HIGH	PIN 1-13, PIN 3-10, PIN 4-6, PIN 4-11, PIN 5-12, PIN 6-11

10.5c   Intermittent wiper switch continuity check chart – continuity should be as specified in the four switch positions (1990 models)

INTERMITTENT WIPE SWITCH CONTINUITY CHART	
SWITCH POSITION	CONTINUITY BETWEEN
OFF	L and P_2
DELAY	P_1 and I_1 R and I_1* I_2 and G
LOW	P_1 and L
HIGH	P_1 and H

*Resistance at maximum delay position should be between 270,000 ohms and 330,000 ohms.
*Resistance at minimum delay position should be zero with ohmmeter set on the high ohm scale.

10.5d   Intermittent wiper switch continuity check chart – continuity should be as specified in the four switch positions (1988 and 1989 models)

10   Wiper/washer switch – check and replacement (1990 and earlier)

Warning: *On 1991 and later models, the windshield wiper/washer switch is part of the multi-function switch located in the steering column. Since 1991 and later models are equipped with an airbag system, to avoid possible damage to this system, or accidental deployment of the airbag, it is recommended that any work involving airbag system components be left to a dealer service department or other qualified repair shop.*

Check

Refer to illustrations 10.5a, 10.5b, 10.5c and 10.5d
1   All models are equipped with a multi-function lever, located on the left side of the steering column, which controls the wiper/washer, the turn signals and the dimmer switches. The wipers on earlier models are simply two speeds (low and high); later models also have a delay mode; 1991 and later models have low, high and two delay modes (maximum delay and minimum delay). But the procedure for checking all switches is the same – only the terminal designations differ.
2   Disconnect the negative cable from the battery.

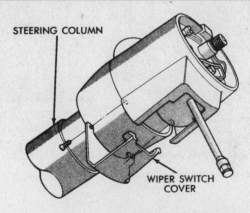

10.10   Details of the wiper/washer switch cover (standard column)

3   Remove the steering column lower cover (see Chapter 11).
4   Unplug the electrical connector **(see illustration 9.4)**.
5   Use an ohmmeter or self-powered test light to check for continuity between the switch terminals at the electrical connector **(see illustrations)**.
6   Replace the wiper/washer switch if the continuity is not as specified.

Replacement

Refer to illustrations 10.10, 10.14, 10.15, 10.17, 10.19, 10.20, 10.21, 10.22a, 10.22b and 10.24
7   On tilt-column models, remove the steering wheel (see Chapter 10).
8   Remove the lower steering column cover, the silencer and the lower reinforcement **(see illustration 9.8)**.
9   Detach the wiring harness trough from the steering column **(see illustration 9.9)**.
10   On standard-column models, remove the washer/wiper switch cover **(see illustration)**. Rotate the cover upward.
11   On tilt-column models, remove the lock plate, canceling cam and upper bearing spring **(see illustrations 9.10a, 9.10b, 9.10c)**.
12   On tilt-column models, remove the switch stalk actuator screw

12

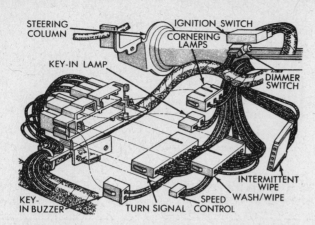

10.14   The steering column electrical connectors (typical)

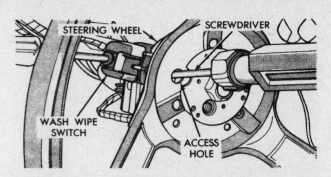

10.15   On standard-column models, rotate the ignition key to the Off position and turn the steering wheel so the access hole in the hub area is at the 9 o'clock position; then, using a flat-bladed screwdriver, loosen the turn signal lever screw through this access hole

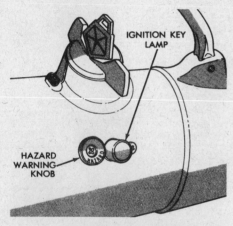

10.17   On tilt-column models, remove the ignition key lamp

10.19   Remove the three housing cover screws (arrows) and lift the housing from the column

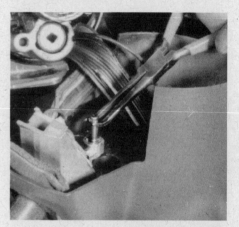

10.20   Remove the washer/wiper switch pivot pin with a pair of needle-nose pliers – if you can't pull it out with pliers, drive it out with a small drift

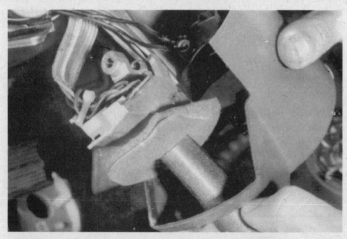

10.21   Remove the washer/wiper switch assembly (tilt-column model shown, standard column similar)

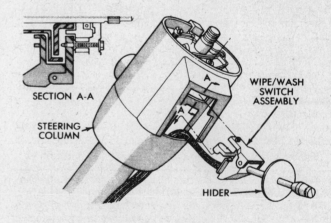

10.22a   Pull the hider up the control stalk . . .

and arm.

13   On tilt-column models, remove the hazard switch knob (see illustration 9.12).

14   Unplug the electrical connector down at the bottom of the steering column (see illustration).

15   On standard-column models, rotate the ignition key to the Off position and turn the steering wheel so the access hole in the hub area is

at the 9 o'clock position. Using a flat-bladed screwdriver, loosen the turn signal lever screw through this access hole (see illustration).

16   On tilt-column models, remove the three turn signal switch retaining screws (see illustration 9.14a) and remove the turn signal switch.

17   On tilt-column models, remove the ignition key lamp (see illustration).

18   On tilt-column models, remove the ignition key lock cylinder (see

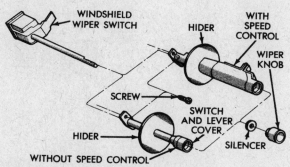

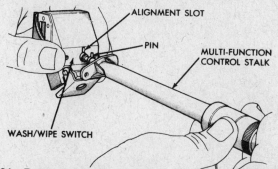

10.22b ... and remove the two screws that attach the control stalk sleeve to the washer/wiper switch

10.24 Rotate the control stalk shaft to its full clockwise position and remove the shaft from the switch by pulling it straight out

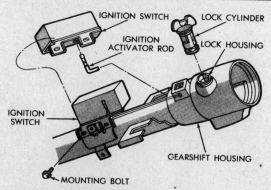

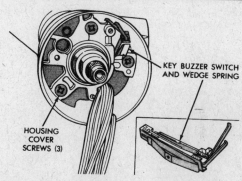

11.14 An exploded view of the ignition switch assembly

12.3a This is what the key buzzer switch and wedge spring looks like ...

Section 12).

19   On tilt-column models, remove the three housing cover screws **(see illustration)** and remove the housing. This will require the use of a Torx bit.

20   On tilt-column models, remove the washer/wiper switch pivot pin **(see illustration)**.

21   Remove the washer/wiper switch assembly **(see illustration)**.

22   Pull the hider up the control stalk and remove the two screws that attach the control stalk sleeve to the washer/wiper switch **(see illustrations)**. Use tape to hold the dimmer switch rod in place.

23   Remove the washer/wiper switch control knob from the end of the multifunction control stalk **(see illustration 10.22b)**.

24   Rotate the control stalk shaft to its full clockwise position and remove the shaft from the switch by pulling straight out of the switch **(see illustration)**.

25   Installation is the reverse of removal.

11   Ignition switch – check and replacement (1990 and earlier)

Warning: *1991 and later models are equipped with an airbag system. To avoid possible damage to this system or accidental deployment of the airbag it is recommended that any work involving airbag system components be left to a dealer service department or other qualified repair shop.*

Check

1   The ignition switch is located on top of the steering column and is actuated by a rod attached to the key lock cylinder.

2   Remove the switch (see Steps 5 through 14).

3   Referring to the Wiring Diagrams at the end of this Chapter, turn the ignition key to each position and, using an ohmmeter or self-powered test light, verify that there's continuity between the ignition switch terminals for each key position.

4   If the switch does not have correct continuity, replace it.

Replacement

Refer to illustration 11.14

5   Disconnect the negative cable from the battery.

6   Remove the steering column cover **(see illustration 9.8)**

7   On models equipped with an automatic transaxle, place the gear selector lever in the Drive position and unplug the indicator electrical lead.

8   Remove the lower panel reinforcement **(see illustration 9.8)**.

9   Remove the five nuts which attach the steering column to the support bracket.

10   Lower the column for access to the ignition switch.

11   Unplug the electrical connector from the ignition switch.

12   Insert the key into the lock cylinder and turn it to the Lock position.

13   Tape the ignition switch rod to the steering column to prevent the rod from falling out of the lock cylinder assembly.

14   Remove the two mounting bolts from the ignition switch and remove the switch **(see illustration)**.

15   Installation is the reverse of removal. As the switch is engaged to the actuator rod, push up on the switch to remove any slack from the rod before fully tightening the bolts.

12   Ignition key lock cylinder – replacement (1990 and earlier)

Warning: *1991 and later models are equipped with an airbag system. To avoid possible damage to this system or accidental deployment of the airbag it is recommended that any work involving airbag system components be left to a dealer service department or other qualified repair shop.*

Refer to illustration 12.3a, 12.3b and 12.4

1   Remove the steering wheel (see Chapter 10).

2   Detach the turn signal/hazard warning switch assembly and let it hang out of the way (see Section 9).

3   Turn the ignition key to the On position and extract the key

12

12.3b   . . . to get it out, grasp it with a pair of needle-nose pliers and pull – make a note of how the switch/spring assembly is installed to ensure that you put it back in the same way (or it won't work)

12.4   To remove the ignition key lock cylinder, insert a small screwdriver into the slot next to the boss for the switch mounting screw (the right-hand slot), depress the spring latch at the bottom of the slot and pull out the lock

13.4   Carefully pry the trim bezel loose from the dashboard with a small screwdriver, then pull it off

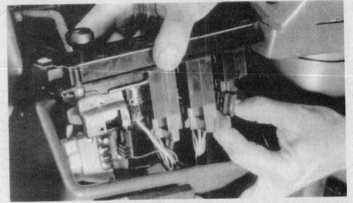

13.5   To remove the switch plate, remove the four retaining screws (arrows)

13.6   Pull the switch assembly out of the dash and unplug the electrical connectors

buzzer switch and wedge spring (see illustrations).
4   Turn the ignition key to the Lock position, insert a small screwdriver into the slot next to the boss for the switch mounting screw (the right-hand slot), depress the spring latch at the bottom of the slot and pull out the lock (see illustration).
5   Installation is the reverse of removal.

---

13   Headlight switch – check and replacement

Check

1   The headlight switch assembly is the far left switch on the switch plate at the lower left corner of the dashboard. To check the switch, you'll need to pull the switch plate assembly out of the dash (see Steps 4 and 5) so you can check continuity at the terminals on the backside of the switch.
2   Referring to the Wiring Diagrams at the end of this Chapter, use an ohmmeter to verify that there's no continuity across the terminals – when the switch is at the Off position and that there is continuity when the switch is at the On position.
3   If the switch doesn't perform as described, replace it.

Replacement

1990 and earlier

Refer to illustrations 13.4, 13.5, 13.6 and 13.7
4   Pry off the trim bezel (see illustration).

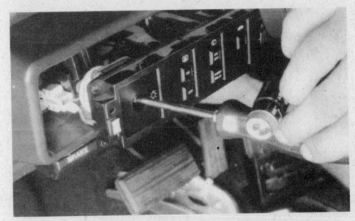

13.7   To remove the headlight switch from the switch plate, unscrew the retainer with a nut driver

5   Remove the four switch plate retaining screws (see illustration) and pull it out.
6   Pull the switch assembly out of the dash and unplug the electrical connectors (see illustration).
7   Pull off the headlight knob and unscrew the retainer (see illustration).
8   Remove the headlight switch.
9   Installation is the reverse of removal.

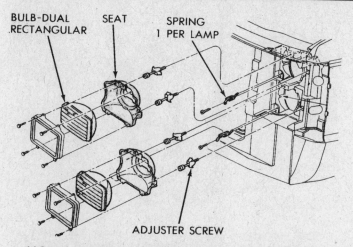

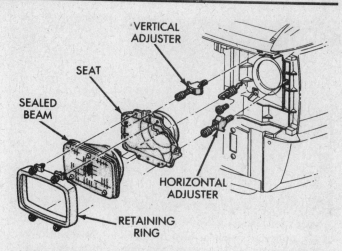

14.3a   An exploded view of a dual sealed beam assembly

14.3b   An exploded view of a single sealed beam assembly

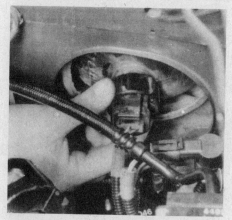

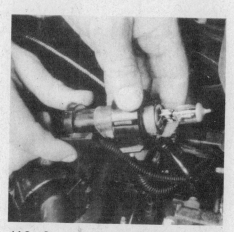

14.8a   To replace a halogen headlight bulb, unscrew the retaining ring . . .

14.8b   . . . and pull the holder out of the headlight lens assembly

14.9   Grasp the halogen bulb holder and unplug the electrical connector

1991 and later

10   Remove the instrument cluster bezel (see Chapter 11).
11   Disconnect the electrical connector to the switch. Depress the locking tabs on the switch and push it out of the bezel.
12   Installation is the reverse of removal.

14   Headlights – removal and installation

1   Disconnect the negative cable from the battery.

Sealed-beam headlights

Refer to illustrations 14.3a and 14.3b

2   Remove the screws from the headlight bezel and remove the bezel.
3   Remove the headlight retainer screws and remove the retainer – don't disturb the adjustment screws **(see illustrations)**.
4   Pull out the sealed beam unit and unplug the electrical connector by pulling it straight off.
5   Installation is the reverse of removal.
6   Adjust the headlights when you're done (see Section 15).

Halogen headlights

Refer to illustration 14.8a, 14.8b and 14.9

Warning: *Halogen bulbs are gas-filled and under pressure and may shatter if the surface is scratched or the bulb is dropped. Wear eye protection and handle the bulbs carefully, grasping only the base whenever possible. Don't touch the surface of the bulb with your fin-*

gers because the oil from your skin could cause it to overheat and fail prematurely. If you do touch the bulb surface, clean it with rubbing alcohol.

7   Open the hood. On left side (driver's side) headlights, it many be necessary to detach the engine coolant reservoir and move it out of the way (see Chapter 3).
8   Reach behind the headlight assembly, unscrew the bulb retaining ring and pull the holder assembly out for access to the bulb **(see illustrations)**.
9   Unplug the electrical connector from the bulb holder **(see illustration)**.
10   Grasp the bulb holder and pull the bulb straight out.
11   Installation is the reverse of removal.

15   Headlights – adjustment

Refer to illustrations 15.1a and 15.1b

Note: *The headlights must be aimed correctly. If adjusted incorrectly, they could temporarily blind the driver of an oncoming vehicle and cause an accident or seriously reduce your ability to see the road. The headlights should be checked for proper aim every 12 months and any time a new headlight is installed or front end body work is performed. The following procedure is only an interim step to provide temporary adjustment until the headlights can be adjusted by a properly equipped shop.*

1   Headlights have two spring loaded adjusting screws, one for horizontal (left-and-right) movement and one for vertical (up-and-down)

12

15.1a   On some halogen-type headlights, the upper adjustment screw (arrow) is for horizontal adjustment, the lower screw (arrow) is for vertical adjustment

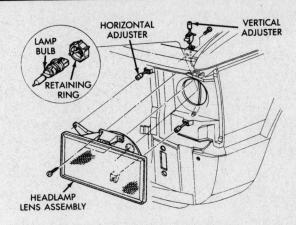

15.1b   On some halogen-type headlights, the upper front screw is for horizontal adjustment, the upper rear screw is for vertical adjustment

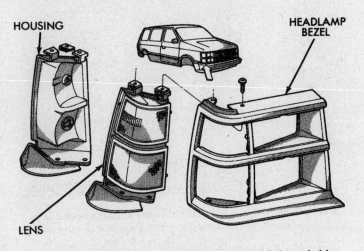

16.1a   Typical front parking light, turn signal light and side marker light bezel and lenses (dual sealed-beam type headlights)

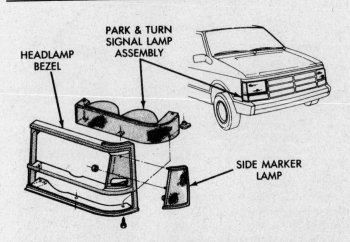

16.1b   Typical front parking light, turn signal light and side marker light bezel and lenses (single sealed-beam type headlights)

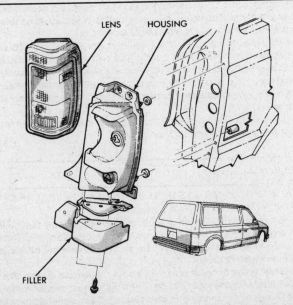

16.1c   Typical tail light, turn signal light, back-up light and side marker light lens and housing

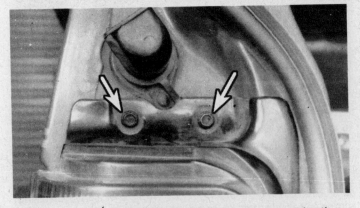

16.1d   To get at the light bulbs inside the rear lens, raise the liftgate, remove these two screws (arrows), . . .

movement. On vehicles with earlier dual sealed-beam type headlight assemblies, the horizontal adjusting screw for each headlight is at the top and the vertical adjusting screw is either also on the top (upper headlight) or on the side (lower headlight). On later single sealed-beam type headlights, the vertical adjusting screw is on the top and the horizontal adjusting screw is on the side. On models with aero-type halogen headlights, the horizontal adjusting screw is on the top and the

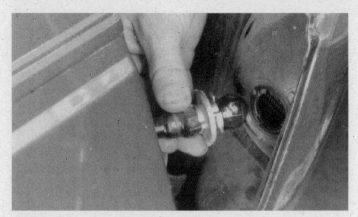

16.1e . . . turn the bulb holder counterclockwise, pull it out of the housing . . .

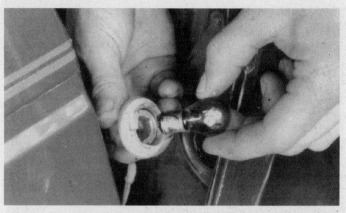

16.1f . . . then turn the bulb counterclockwise and pull it out of the holder

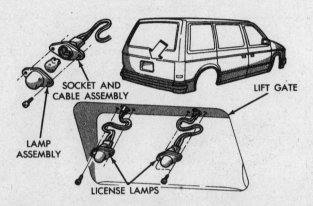

16.1g Exploded view of typical license plate lights

SOCKET AND CABLE ASSEMBLY

LIFT GATE

LAMP ASSEMBLY

LICENSE LAMPS

16.2a To remove a bulb holder from the instrument cluster, simply turn it counterclockwise and pull straight out – the bulb can then be pulled from the holder

6   Starting with the low beam adjustment, position the high intensity zone so it's two inches below the horizontal line and two inches to the right of the headlight vertical line. Adjustment is made by turning the top adjusting screw clockwise to raise the beam and counterclockwise to lower the beam. The adjusting screw on the side should be used in the same manner to move the beam left or right.

7   With the high beams on, the high intensity zone should be vertically centered with the exact center just below the horizontal line. **Note:** *It may not be possible to position the headlight aim exactly for both high and low beams. If a compromise must be made, keep in mind that the low beams are the most used and have the greatest effect on driver safety.*

8   Have the headlights adjusted by a dealer service department or service station at the earliest opportunity.

16.2b To replace a bulb in the headlight switch panel, simply pull it straight out

vertical adjusting screw is either on the bottom or on the upper back side of the headlight assembly **(see illustrations)**. Refer to the illustrations accompanying the previous Section for the location of adjusting screws on typical sealed-beam type headlight assemblies.

2   This procedure requires a blank wall 25 feet in front of the vehicle and a level floor.

3   Position masking tape vertically on the wall in reference to the vehicle centerline and the centerlines of both headlights.

4   Position a horizontal tape line in reference to the centerline of all the headlights. **Note:** *It may be easier to position the tape on the wall with the vehicle parked only a few inches away.*

5   Adjustment should be made with the vehicle sitting level, the gas tank half-full and no unusually heavy load in the vehicle.

16 Bulb replacement

Refer to illustrations 16.1a, 16.1b, 16.1c, 16.1d, 16.1e, 16.1f, 16.1g, 16.2a, 16.2b, 16.3a, 16.3b and 16.3c

1   The lenses of most exterior lights are held in place by trim bezels, which are secured to the vehicle with a combination of clips and screws. To replace burned out bulbs, simply remove the bezels and lenses **(see illustrations)**.

2   Several types of bulbs are used inside the vehicle. Some, like instrument cluster bulbs (see Section 19 for instrument cluster removal), can be removed by pushing in and turning them counterclockwise **(see illustration)**. Others, such as the headlight switch illumination bulb, can be removed by simply pulling them straight out of the socket **(see illustration)**.

12

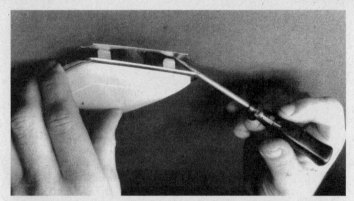

16.3a   To replace a dome light, pry the assembly from the headliner with a small screwdriver . . .

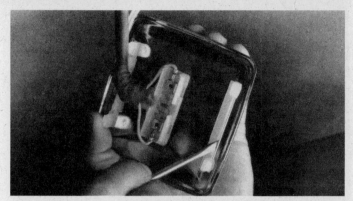

16.3b   . . . separate the lens from the housing, . . .

16.3c   . . . then grasp the bulb and pull it out of the clips

17.3   The radio bezel is held in place by five screws (arrows) (To get at the two screws underneath – not visible in this photo – remove the ashtray)

17.4a   To remove the radio, remove these two screws (arrows) . . .

17.4b   . . . and pull the radio out far enough to get at the wires on the back

3   To replace a dome light bulb, pry the lamp assembly out of the headliner with a small screwdriver, separate the lens from the base and pull the bulb out of its mounting clips (see illustrations).

17   Radio – removal and installation

Refer to illustrations 17.3, 17.4a, 17.4b and 17.5

1   Disconnect the negative battery cable from the battery.
2   Remove the ashtray.
3   Remove the screws and detach the bezel from the dash (see illustrations). **Note:** *On 1991 and later models, see Chapter 11 for in-*

strument panel bezel details.
4   Remove the radio mounting screws (see illustration) and pull the radio out of the dash panel (see illustration).
5   Unplug the antenna lead and disconnect the electrical connectors (see illustration).
6   Installation is the reverse of removal.

18   Antenna – removal and installation

Refer to illustration 18.1

1   To remove the antenna, simply unscrew it from its base (see il-

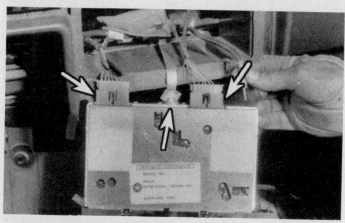

17.5   Disconnect the antenna lead, the ground lead and the electrical connectors and remove the radio

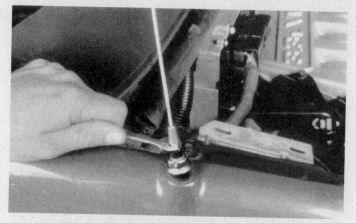

18.1   Unscrew the antenna with a small wrench

19.3a   Instrument cluster mounting screws (arrows) (typical)

19.3b   Pull the instrument cluster as far out as it'll go, then reach behind it and disconnect the speedometer cable clip and the electrical connectors (typical)

lustration).
2   Installation is the reverse of removal. be sure the threads of the base free of corrosion to ensure a good connection.
3   If it's necessary to remove the base, a special socket is required. This tool can be purchased at most auto parts stores.

19   Instrument cluster – removal and installation

Refer to illustrations 19.3a and 19.3b
1   Disconnect the negative cable from the battery.
2   Remove the cluster bezel (see Chapter 11).
3   Remove the cluster mounting screws **(see illustration)**. Pull the assembly out **(see illustration)**, reach behind the cluster and depress the speedometer cable clip. Detach the cable from the speedometer, unplug the electrical connectors and remove the cluster from the dash.

20   Windshield wiper motor – check and replacement

Check

1   If the wiper motor does not run at all, first check the fuse block for a blown fuse (see Section 3).
2   Check the wiper switch (see Section 10).
3   Turn the ignition switch and wiper switch on.
4   Connect a jumper wire between the wiper motor and ground, then retest. If the motor works now, repair the ground connection.
5   If the wipers still don't work, turn on the wipers and check for voltage at the motor connector. If there's voltage, remove the motor

20.8   Flip up the hinged cover on the shaft end of the wiper arm and remove the nut (arrow)

and check it off the vehicle with fused jumper wires from the battery. If the motor now works, check for binding linkage. If the motor still doesn't work, replace it.
6   If there's no voltage at the motor, the problem is in the switch or wiring.

Replacement

Refer to illustrations 20.8, 20.9, 20.10, 20.11, 20.12 and 20.13
7   Disconnect the negative cable from the battery.

12

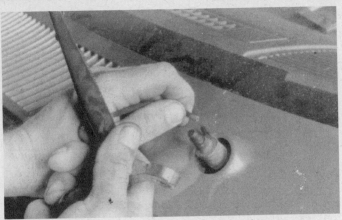

20.9   Detach the washer hose and remove the wiper arm

20.10   Remove the six retaining screws from the plastic cowl, flip up the cowl and detach the washer hoses (arrows)

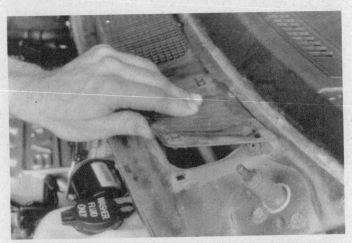

20.11   Remove the leaf screen to get at the wiper linkage

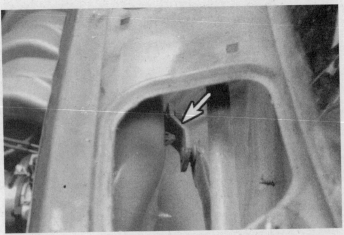

20.12   Remove this nut (arrow) and detach the crank arm from the wiper motor

8   Flip up the hinged cover on the shaft end of the wiper arms and remove the nuts **(see illustration)**.
9   Detach the washer hoses and remove the wiper arms **(see illustration)**.
10   Remove the six cowl retaining screws (three in the grille and three along the front edge), lift up the cowl, detach the washer hose **(see illustration)** and remove the cowl.
11   Remove the screen **(see illustration)**.
12   Remove the nut that attaches the crank arm to the motor and detach the crank **(see illustration)**.
13   Unplug the wiper motor electrical connector and remove the mounting nuts **(see illustration)**.
14   Installation is the reverse of removal.

21   Power window system – description and check

The power window system operates the electric motors mounted in the doors which lower and raise the windows. The system consists of the control switches, the motors, glass mechanisms (regulators) and the associated wiring.
Because of the complexity of the power window system and the special tools and techniques required for diagnosis, repair should be left to a dealer service department or a repair shop. However, it is possible for the home mechanic to make simple checks of the wiring connections and motors for minor faults which can be easily repaired. These include:

a) Inspect the power window actuating switches for broken wires and loose connections.
b) Check the power window fuse/and or circuit breaker.
c) Remove the door panel(s) and check the power window motor wires to see if they're loose or damaged. Inspect the glass mechanisms for damage which could cause binding.

22   Power door lock system – description and check

The power door lock system operates the door lock actuators mounted in each door. The system consists of the switches, actuators and associated wiring. Since special tools and techniques are required to diagnose the system, it should be left to a dealer service department or a repair shop. However, it is possible for the home mechanic to make simple checks of the wiring connections and actuators for minor faults which can be easily repaired. These include:

a) Check the system fuse and/or circuit breaker.
b) Check the switch wires for damage and loose connections. Check the switches for continuity.
c) Remove the door panel(s) and check the actuator wiring connections to see if they're loose or damaged. Inspect the actuator rods (if equipped) to make sure they aren't bent or damaged. Inspect the actuator wiring for damaged or loose connections. The actuator can be checked by applying battery power momentarily. A discernible click indicates that the solenoid is operating properly.

20.13 Unplug the electrical connector (arrow), remove the three mounting nuts (arrows) and remove the wiper motor

23   Cruise control system – description and check

The cruise control system maintains vehicle speed with a vacuum-actuated servo motor located in the engine compartment, which is connected to the throttle linkage by a cable. The system consists of the servo motor, clutch switch, brake switch, control switches, a relay and associated vacuum hoses.

Because of the complexity of the cruise control system and the special tools and techniques required for diagnosis, repair should be left to a dealer service department or other repair shop. However, it's possible for the home mechanic to make simple checks of the wiring and vacuum connections for minor faults which can be easily repaired. These include:

a) Inspect the cruise control actuating switches for broken wires and loose connections.
b) Check the cruise control fuse.
c) The cruise control system is operated by vacuum so it's critical that all vacuum switches, hoses and connections are secure. Check the hoses in the engine compartment for tight connections, cracks and obvious vacuum leaks.

24   Remote keyless entry system

The remote keyless entry system allows the vehicle owner to unlock and lock the vehicles doors and unlatch the liftgate from a dis-

WIRE COLOR CODE CHART					
COLOR CODE	COLOR	STANDARD TRACER COLOR	COLOR CODE	COLOR	STANDARD TRACER CODE
BK	BLACK	WT	PK	PINK	BK OR WH
BR	BROWN	WT	RD	RED	WT
DB	DARK BLUE	WT	TN	TAN	WT
DG	DARK GREEN	WT	VT	VIOLET	WT
GY	GRAY	BK	WT	WHITE	BK
LB	LIGHT BLUE	BK	YL	YELLOW	BK
LG	LIGHT GREEN	BK	*	WITH TRACER	
OR	ORANGE	BK			

25.2 Wire color code chart

tance of approximately 23 feet. This system consists of switches, actuators and associated wiring. Since special tools and techniques are required to diagnose the system, it should be left to a dealer service department or a repair shop.

25   Wiring diagrams general information

Refer to illustration 25.2

Since it isn't possible to include all wiring diagrams for every year covered by this manual, the following diagrams are typical and most commonly needed. Prior to troubleshooting any circuits, check the fuse and circuit breakers (if equipped) to make sure they're in good condition. Make sure the battery is properly charged and check the cable connections (see Chapter 1). When checking a circuit, make sure all connectors are clean, with no broken or loose terminals. When unplugging a connector, don't pull on the wires. Pull only on the connector housings.

Refer to the accompanying table for the wire color codes applicable to the diagrams in this manual **(see illustration)**.

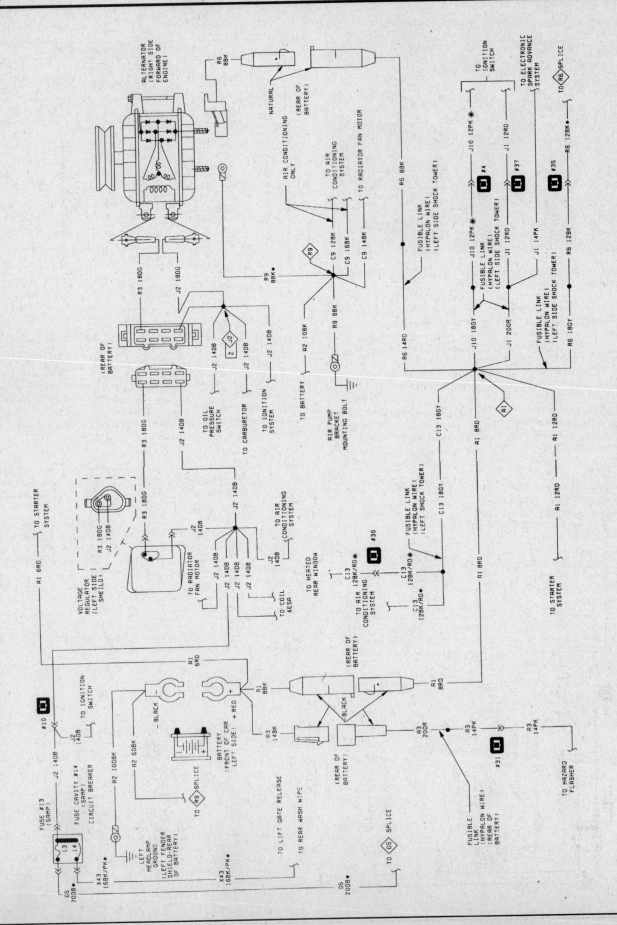

Typical charging system circuit (2.2L engine)

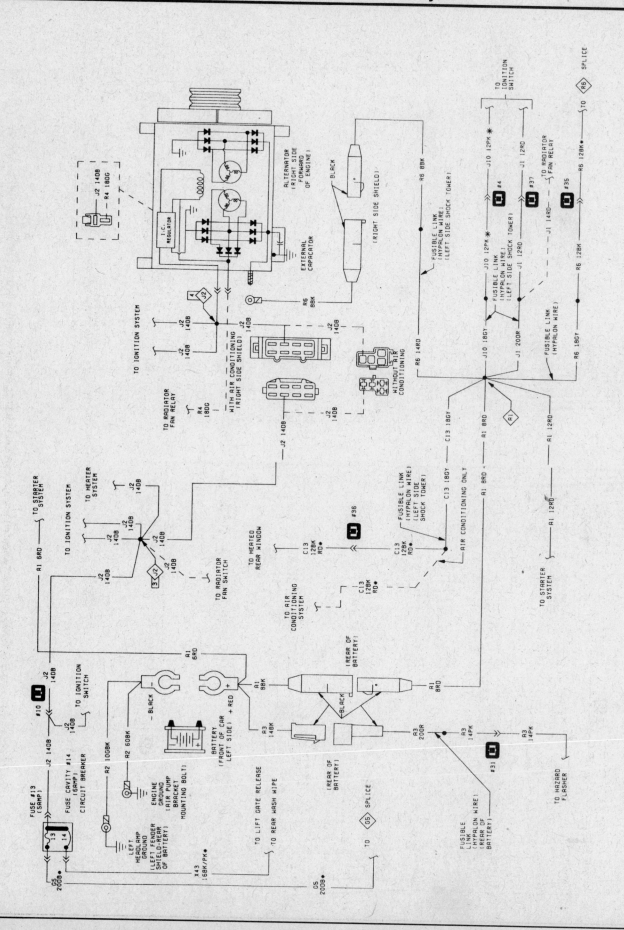

Typical charging system circuit (2.6L engine)

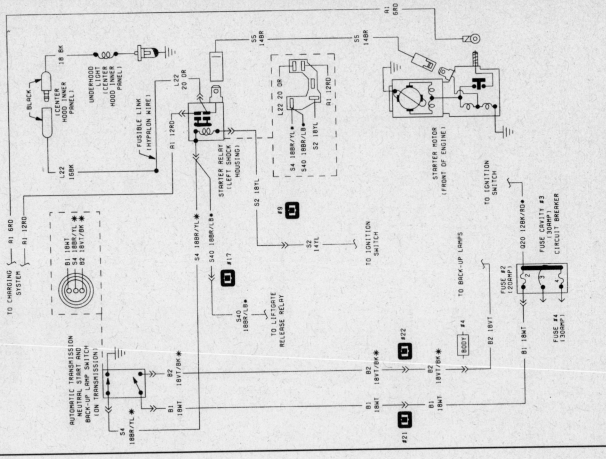

Typical starting system circuit (2.6L engine)

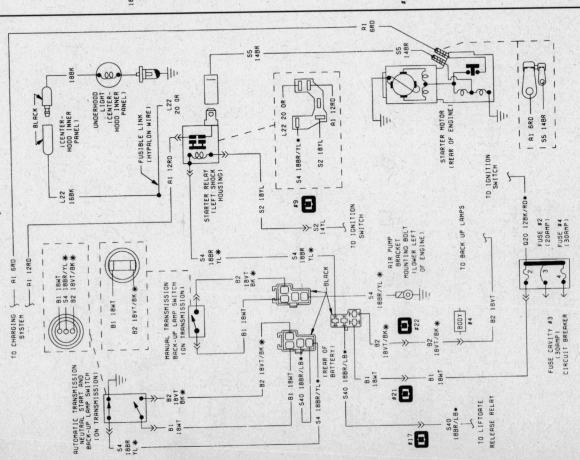

Typical starting system circuit (2.2L engine)

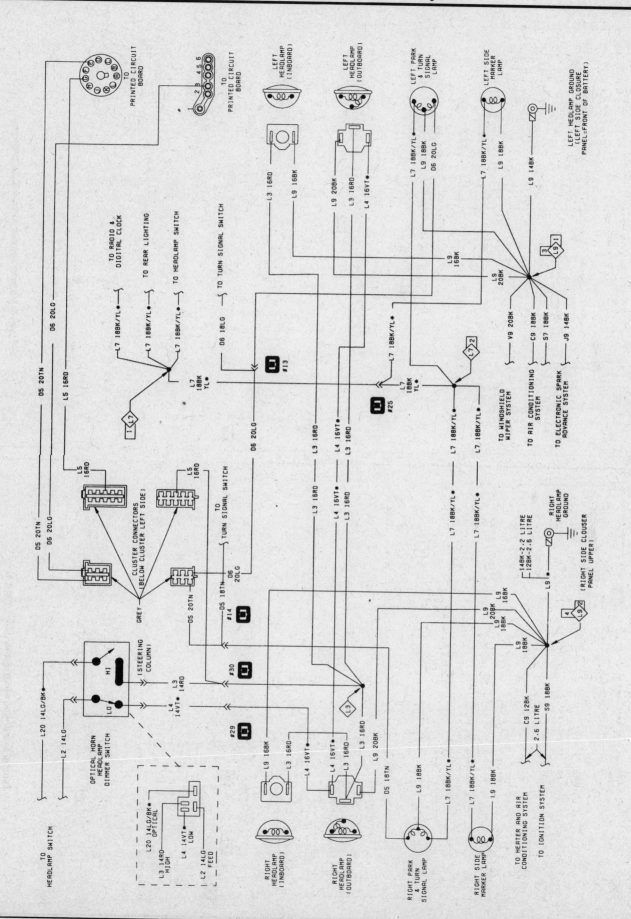

Typical early model front lighting system circuit

Fuel injection and ignition systems (3.0L engine) (1 of 6)

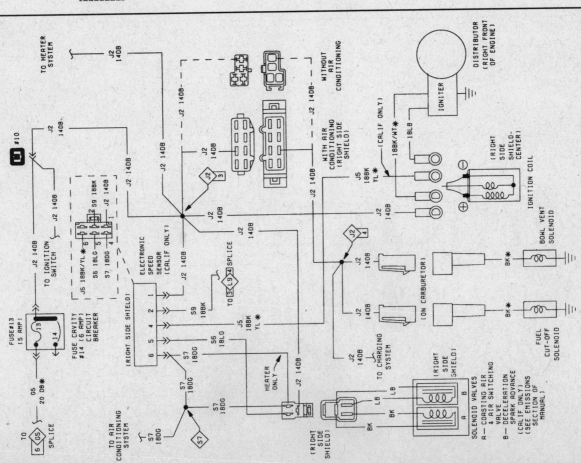

Typical electronic ignition system circuit (2.6L engine)

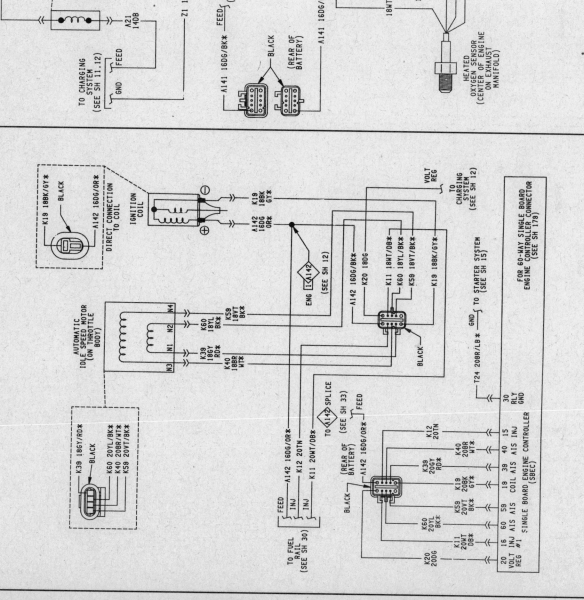
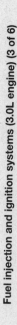

Fuel injection and ignition systems (3.0L engine) (3 of 6)

Fuel injection and ignition systems (3.0L engine) (2 of 6)

12

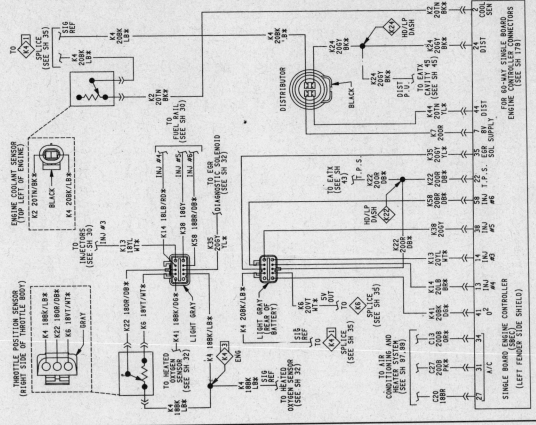

Fuel injection and ignition systems (3.0L engine) (5 of 6)

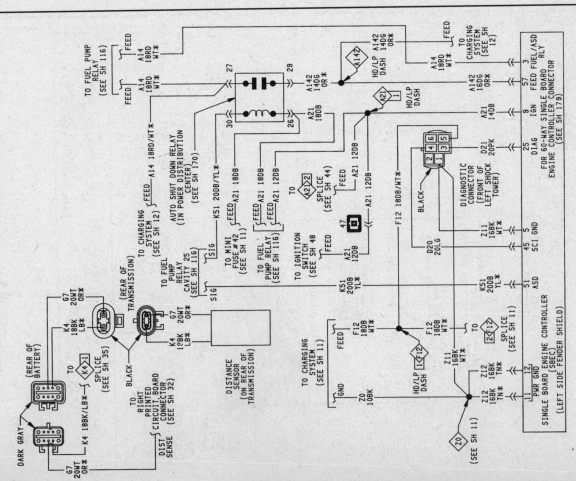

Fuel injection and ignition systems (3.0L engine) (4 of 6)

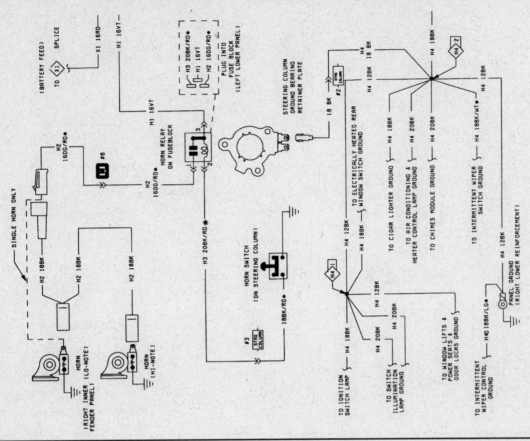

Typical horn circuit

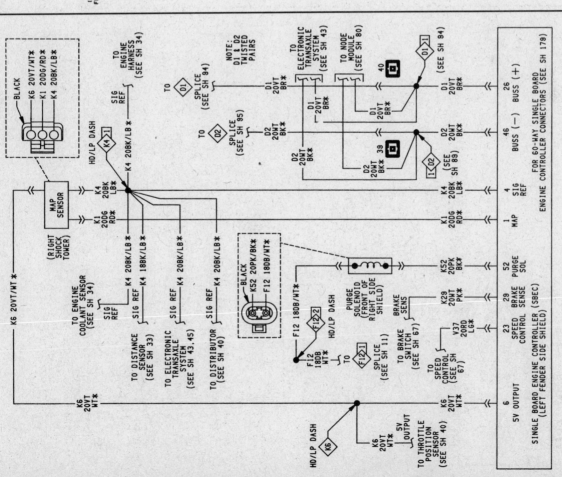

Fuel injection and ignition systems (3.0L engine) (6 of 6)

12

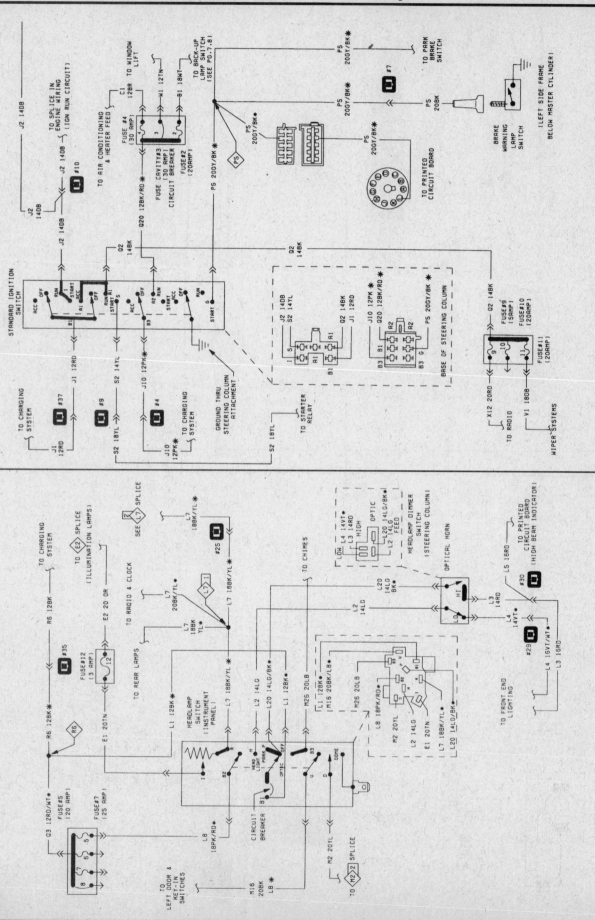

Typical early model ignition switch circuit

Typical early model headlight switch circuit

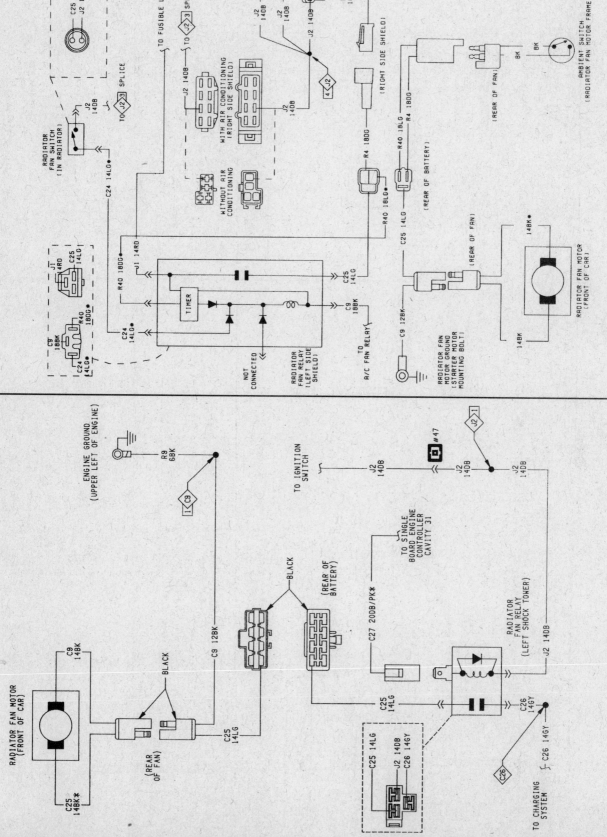

Radiator fan motor circuit (2.6L California model)

Radiator fan motor circuit (2.5L, 3.0L and 3.3L engines)

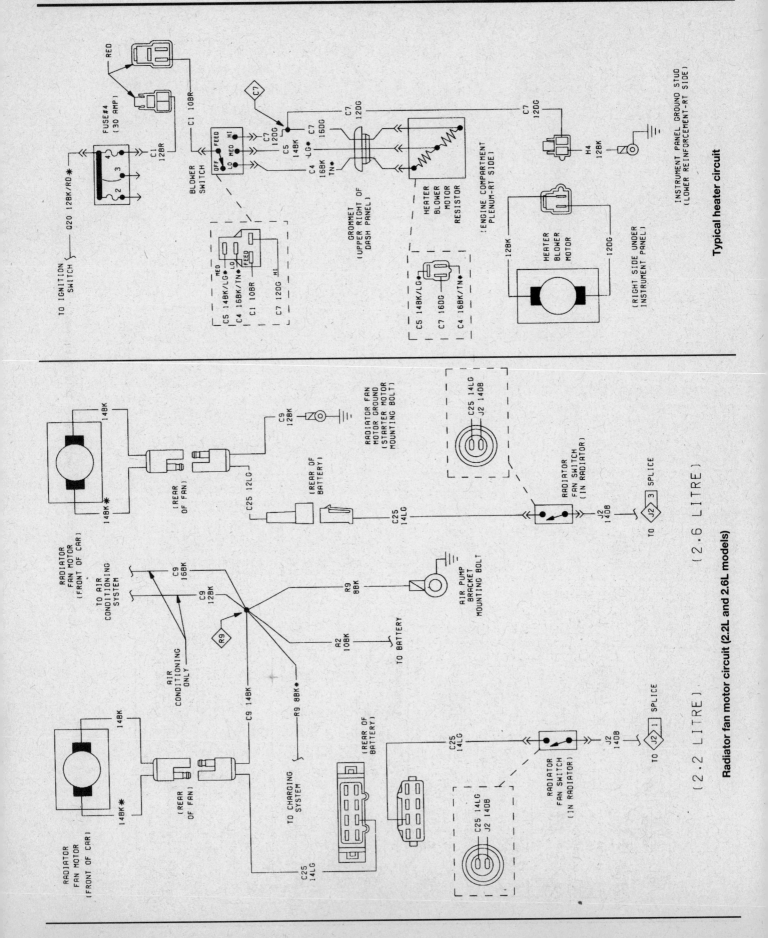

Typical heater circuit

Radiator fan motor circuit (2.2L and 2.6L models)

(2.6 LITRE)

(2.2 LITRE)

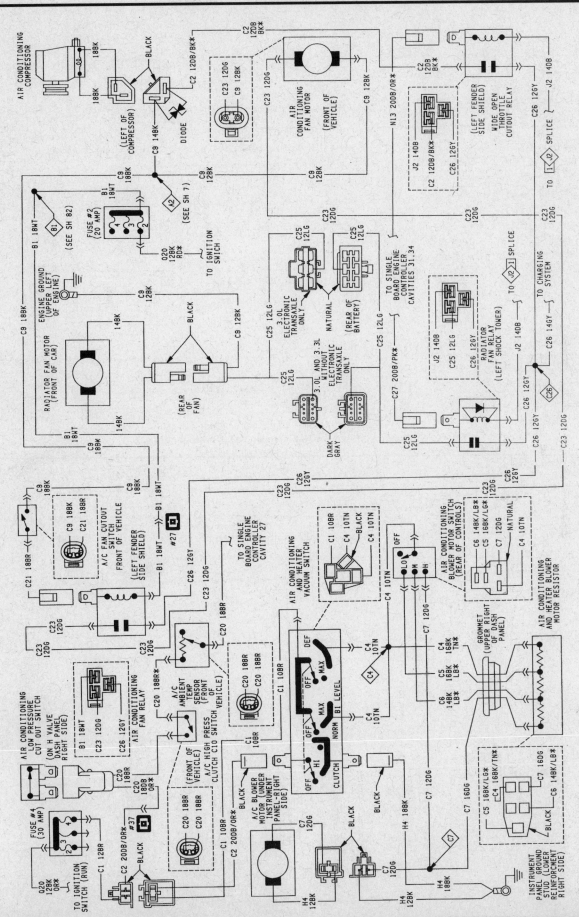

Air conditioning system wiring diagram (3.0L and 3.3L engines)

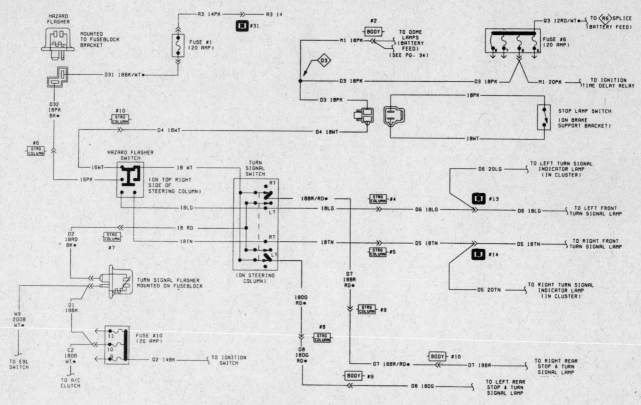

Typical early model stop, turn and hazard flasher system circuit

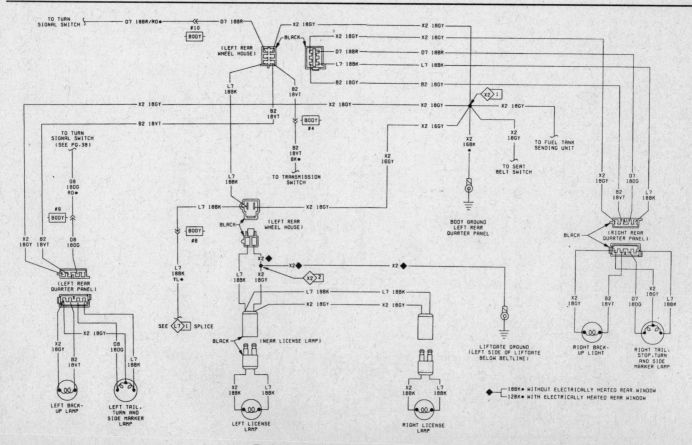

Typical early model rear lighting circuit

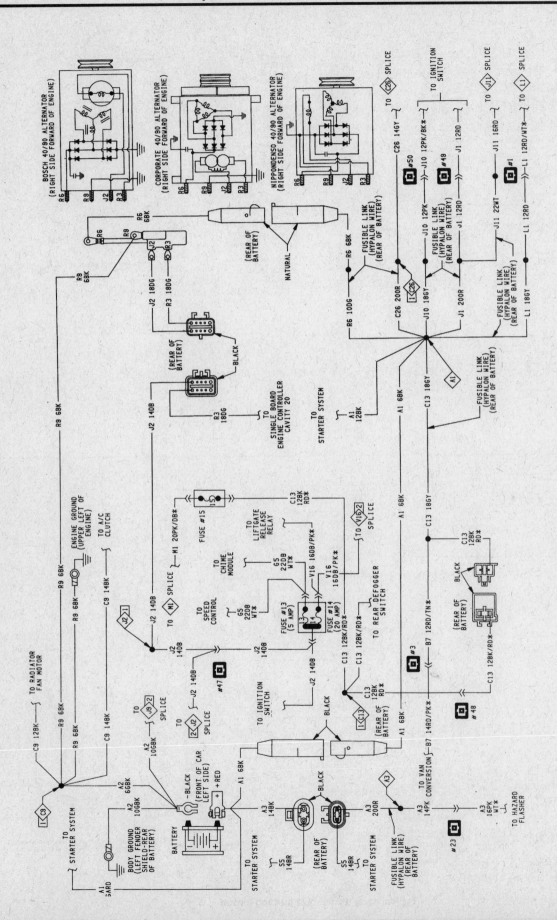

Typical charging system circuit (2.5L engine)

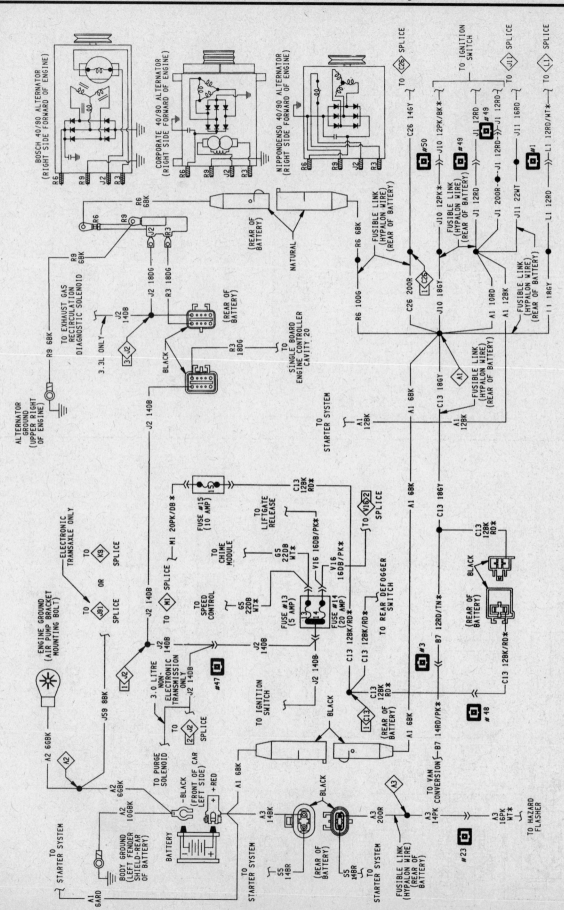

Typical charging system circuit (3.0L and 3.3L engines)

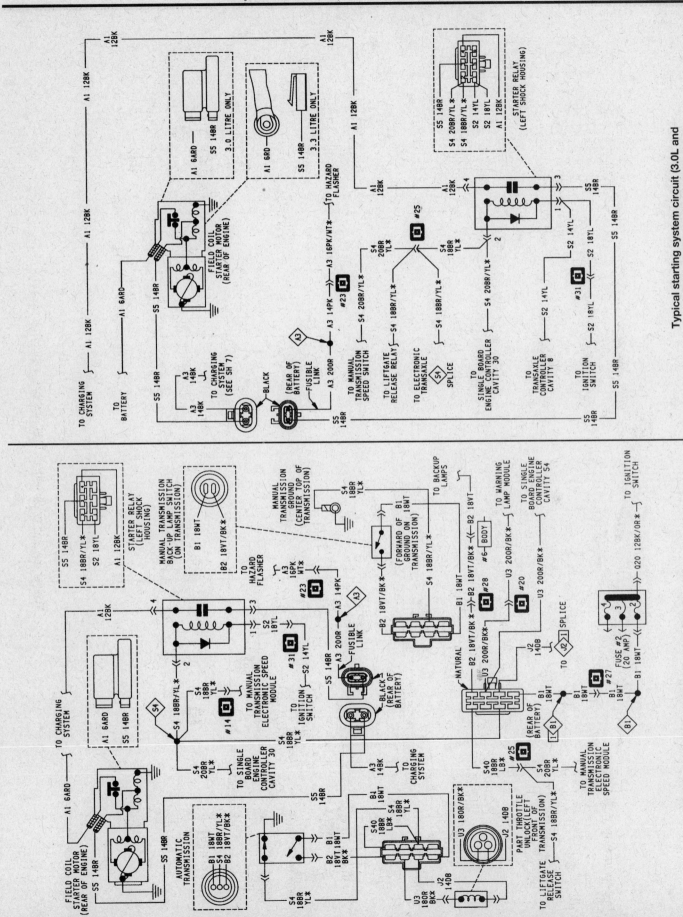

Typical starting system circuit (3.0L and 3.3L engine with electronic transaxle)

Typical starting system circuit (2.5L TBI engine)

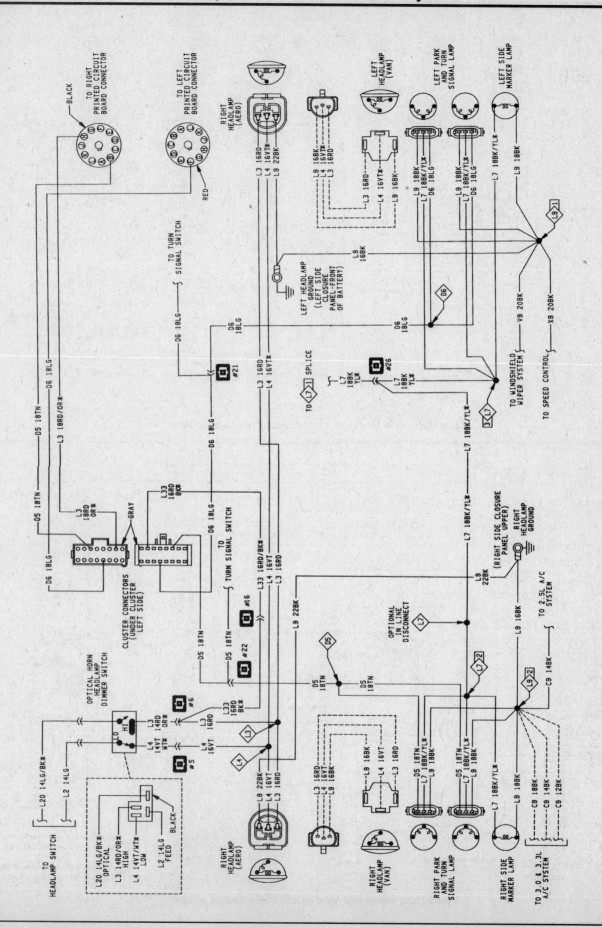

Typical later model front end lighting system circuit

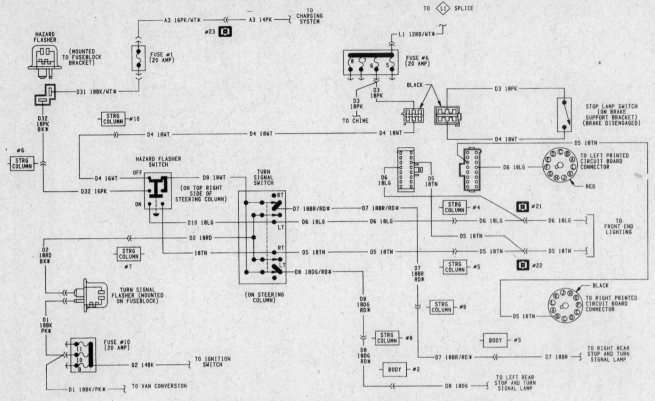

Typical late model stop, turn and hazard flasher system circuit

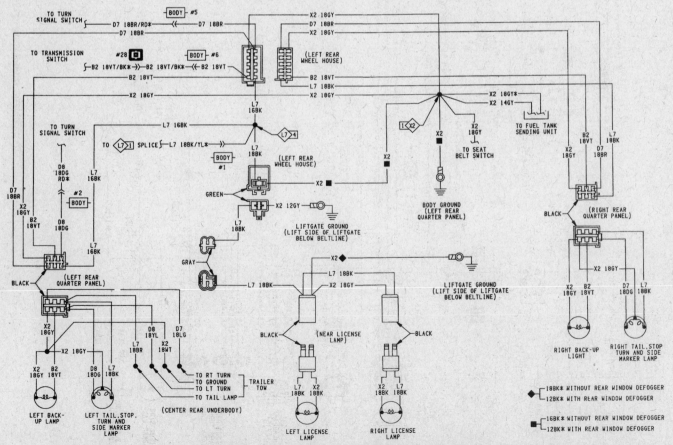

Typical late model rear lighting and trailer towing circuit

12

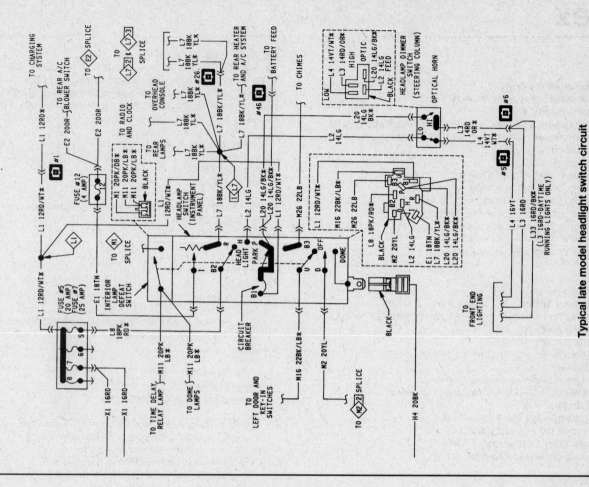

Typical late model headlight switch circuit

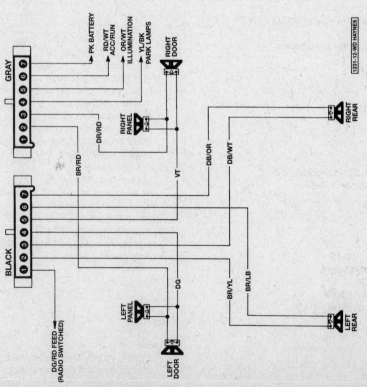

Typical radio connectors circuit

1231-12-WD HAYNES

Index

Index

Index